Politics & Society in the Contemporary MIDDLE EAST

THIRD EDITION

Politics & Society in the Contemporary MIDDLE EAST

edited by
Michele Penner Angrist

BOULDER
LONDON

Published in the United States of America in 2019 by
Lynne Rienner Publishers, Inc.
1800 30th Street, Boulder, Colorado 80301
www.rienner.com

and in the United Kingdom by
Lynne Rienner Publishers, Inc.
Gray's Inn House, 127 Clerkenwell Road, London EC1 5DB
www.eurospanbookstore.com/rienner

Library of Congress Cataloging-in-Publication Data
Names: Angrist, Michele Penner, 1970– editor.
Title: Politics & society in the contemporary Middle East / edited by Michele Penner Angrist.
Other titles: Politics and society in the contemporary Middle East
Description: Third edition. | Boulder, Colorado : Lynne Rienner Publishers, Inc., 2019. | Includes bibliographical references and index.
Identifiers: LCCN 2019001771 | ISBN 9781626378056 (pbk. : alk. paper)
Subjects: LCSH: Middle East—Politics and government—1979– | Middle East—Politics and government—1979– —Case studies.
Classification: LCC JQ1758.A58 P655 2019 | DDC 320.956—dc23
LC record available at https://lccn.loc.gov/2019001771

British Cataloguing in Publication Data
A Cataloguing in Publication record for this book is available from the British Library.

Printed and bound in the United States of America

The paper used in this publication meets the requirements of the American National Standard for Permanence of Paper for Printed Library Materials Z39.48-1992.

5 4 3 2

Contents

Tables and Figures

Tables

Figures

1

The Making of Middle East Politics

Michele Penner Angrist

As we approach the third decade of the twenty-first century, headlines from the Middle East are dramatic and worrisome, and often characterized by upheaval and change. There has been the years-long civil war in Syria that has caused domestic disaster and sparked massive movements of internally displaced persons and refugees. There have been famine and desperation in Yemen in the face of a complex military conflict stemming from internal divisions and exacerbated by external intervention. A Saudi Arabian journalist was murdered and dismembered inside the walls of his own embassy. Turkey—once a model for the possibility of democratic politics in the region—has veered toward dictatorship. There is a steady drumbeat of reporting on human rights abuses in Bahrain, alongside restrictions and crackdowns on peaceful oppositional actors in Egypt. How should such headlines be understood? What conclusions can we draw about the peoples and politics of this important region of the world? In this book, we seek to provide key historical knowledge and a set of analytical anchors to ground readers as they track, assess, and make sense of future developments.

Politics in the Middle East has not always been so turbulent. In fact, its contemporary political history has alternated between stability and heady change. Imperial control by European powers gave way to an epoch of transformations in the middle of the twentieth century as the states of the Middle East became sovereign entities. After the dust from this upheaval settled, for decades, citizens of the region were governed for the most part by authoritarian regimes that appeared stable despite the failure of those regimes to deliver security, prosperity, and dignity to their peoples. Appearances were deceiving, however, and, beginning in December 2010 and throughout 2011, demonstrators confronted dictators across the region, demanding more accountable, more participatory, and less corrupt governance. After decades in office, leaders fell from power in Tunisia, then Egypt, then Libya and Yemen, while another plunged Syria into civil war in an effort to cling to power. Political turbulence also struck the region's monarchies, as citizens in Bahrain, Morocco, and Jordan called for thoroughgoing changes to the rules of the political game.

The early days of the Arab Spring raised the hopes of many that freer, more participatory political systems would be built in its wake. Near the ten-year anniversary of the start of those uprisings, however, the balance sheet is sobering. One can be reasonably optimistic about the prospects for more competitive, freer politics in just one country: Tunisia. After a brief, dramatic experiment with free elections that elevated a member of the Muslim Brotherhood to the presidency, Egypt reverted to a military-led authoritarian regime when armed forces commander Abdel Fattah al-Sisi felled the government of Mohammad Morsi and obliterated the Muslim Brotherhood. Syria, Yemen, and Libya sank into conflict as a result of domestic divides and the interventions of outside actors. Anarchy in these places generated humanitarian catastrophe and enormous refugee flows while widening opportunities for extremist nonstate actors such as al-Qaeda and the Islamic State in Iraq and Syria (ISIS) to operate. Authoritarian leaders who survived the Arab Spring scrambled to buttress their rule, with several destabilizing effects—including heightened regional sectarianism.

Contributors to this text introduce readers to the contemporary comparative politics of the Middle East. Scholars of comparative politics study the internal political dynamics of countries. In this volume, we will explore how Middle Eastern governments are structured, who opposes those governments and why, and how oppositions work to bring about change. Some comparativists tackle this task by deeply mastering the internal politics of one country. Others study a country's domestic politics while comparing and contrasting what they find with what is happening in other national contexts. Comparativists typically ask themselves what political trends are similar across countries—but also what differences exist, and why? Why did several authoritarian regimes buckle in the face of Arab Spring uprisings, while many more survived? Some buckled relatively peacefully, while significant blood was shed elsewhere—why? Why did the Arab Spring thus far lead to more democratic politics only in Tunisia? What historical, social, and economic factors explain the similarities and the differences that we observe? This is the stuff of comparative politics. We learn about broader political science processes by studying a collection of countries' politics individually as well as in relation to one another. This text allows the reader to do both.

Let us now turn to defining the Middle East. This turns out to be a complex task. The moniker *Middle East* was not attached to the area by its residents. Rather, beginning in the nineteenth century, political elites in Europe and the United States coined the terms *Near East* and *Middle East* to refer to (various delineations of) territories that lay between Western Europe and the Far East (China, Japan, etc.). Because the term *Middle East* was bestowed on the region by outside powers according to their own political, strategic, and geographic perspectives, it has been criticized as West- or Euro-centric. Still, it is in wide use today and typically refers to the geographic region bounded to the north by Turkey, to the east by Iran, to the west by Egypt, and to the south by the Arabian Peninsula (see Figure 1.1). In addition to Egypt, Turkey, and Iran, the Middle East includes Saudi Arabia, Yemen, Oman, the United Arab Emirates (UAE), Qatar, Bahrain, Kuwait, Israel, Palestine, Jordan, Iraq, Syria, and Lebanon.

The material in this book also encompasses North Africa, referring to the northernmost tier of African countries that border the Mediterranean Sea: Morocco, Algeria, Tunisia, and Libya. These countries share a great deal in common with the political dynamics of the countries of the Middle East. MENA is a commonly used acronym referring to the Middle East and North Africa thus delineated, and readers will encounter it in this text. When used in this volume, the term *Middle East* refers to the countries of the Middle East and North Africa (those highlighted in Figure 1.1).

An Overview of States in the Region Today

The Middle East encompasses twenty countries that are home to approximately 500 million people. Most of these countries are Arab, meaning that their citizens speak the Arabic language and perceive that they have a shared historical, cultural, and social experience as Arabs. Three of the twenty countries are not Arab, however. The national language of Israel is Hebrew, and while many Israelis speak Arabic, the historical, cultural, and social bond for the majority of Israelis emerges from their identity as Jews. Turkey and Iran also are not Arab countries. Turks are a different ethnic group and speak Turkish, a language that linguistically is unrelated to Arabic. The dominant language in Iran is Farsi, which—although written in Arabic script—also is unrelated to Arabic.

Many unwittingly think that the "Middle East" and the "Muslim world" are one and the same. Certainly, the majority of people living in

Figure 1.1 Map of the Middle East and North Africa

all Middle East countries save Israel are Muslim. At the same time, religious minorities—especially Jews and Christians—are to be found in most of them. For example, Christians of a variety of denominations (Maronite Catholic, Greek Orthodox, and others) make up perhaps as much as 40 percent of the Lebanese population, while nearly 10 percent of Egyptians are Coptic Christians. Meanwhile, the Muslim world extends well beyond the Middle East. Muslim-majority countries are found in sub-Saharan Africa, Central Asia, and South and Southeast Asia. Thus the Middle East is just a small slice of the Muslim world in terms of both geography and population. Indeed, a majority of the world's Muslims live outside of the Middle East.

Table 1.1 provides key statistical information about the countries of the Middle East. In terms of sheer size, Algeria, Saudi Arabia, Libya, and Iran are the largest Middle East countries; Bahrain and Palestine, by contrast, occupy tiny pieces of territory. In terms of population, Egypt, Turkey, and Iran are the region's powerhouses, with populations upward of 80 million, while tiny Bahrain has a population of less than 2 million. More than 90 percent of Israelis, Kuwaitis, and Qataris live in urban areas, compared to only 35 percent of Yemenis and only 43 percent of Egyptians. Populations are growing most rapidly in Iraq, Palestine, and Yemen, where the average number of births per woman is above 4; by contrast, seven Middle East countries have fertility rates at or below the replacement rate of 2.1 births per woman. On a per capita basis, the economies of Qatar, Kuwait, the United Arab Emirates, and Israel produce the most. Yemen is the region's poorest country measured in terms of economic output, followed by Palestine and Egypt. Finally, the proportion of adult females who are literate ranges from just 38 percent in Iraq, to 68 percent in Algeria, to 98 percent in Qatar. There is thus considerable variation in the region when it comes to land area, population, and indicators of development.

A central focus of the discipline of comparative politics is the type of governmental system a country has. Often referred to with the term *regime,* a governmental system refers not to the particular group of individuals filling key offices at a given point in time—this is simply a government—but rather more broadly to the processes by which leaders are selected (election? dynastic succession? military coup?) and how those leaders in turn exercise power (in consultation with others according to the rule of law? individually and arbitrarily? somewhere in between?). For decades and until the Arab uprisings of 2010–2011, systems of government in the Middle East were, almost without exception, authoritarian. Indeed for the last quarter of the twentieth century and the first decade of the twenty-first, the region was a global outlier.

Table 1.1 Statistical Snapshot of Middle East Countries

Country	Land Area (sq. km)	Population 2016	Urban Population (% of total) 2016	Fertility Rate, Total (births per woman) 2015	GDP per Capita (constant 2010 US$) 2016	Literacy Rate, Adult Female (% of females ages 15 and above) 2005–2015
Algeria	2,381,741	40,606,052	71	2.8	4,828	68
Bahrain	771	1,425,171	89	2.1	22,436	92
Egypt	995,450	95,688,681	43	3.3	2,724	67
Iran	1,628,760	80,277,428	74	1.7	6,734	80
Iraq	434,320	37,202,572	70	4.4	5,696	38
Israel	21,640	8,547,100	92	3.1	33,673	n.a.
Jordan	88,780	9,455,802	84	3.4	3,258	97
Kuwait	17,820	4,052,584	98	2.0	35,251	95
Lebanon	10,230	6,006,668	88	1.7	7,144	88
Libya	1,759,540	6,293,253	79	2.3	4,579	82
Morocco	446,300	35,276,786	61	2.5	3,196	59
Oman	309,500	4,424,762	78	2.7	17,071	86
Palestine	6,020	4,551,566	75	4.1	2,571	95
Qatar	11,610	2,569,804	99	1.9	66,411	98
Saudi Arabia	2,149,690	32,275,687	83	2.6	21,395	91
Syria	183,630	18,430,453	58	3.0	n.a.	74
Tunisia	155,360	11,403,248	67	2.2	4,265	72
Turkey	769,630	79,512,426	74	2.1	14,117	93
United Arab Emirates	83,600	9,269,612	86	1.8	40,864	92
Yemen	527,970	27,584,213	35	4.1	680	45

Source: World Bank, *World Development Indicators,* various years (Washington, DC).
Notes: For GDP/capita, the Libya figure is from 2011; the Bahrain and Oman figures are from 2015.
n.a. indicates data are not available.

While every other area of the world saw (at least some) dictatorships fall and democracies erected in their stead, dictatorships in the Middle East stood firm. The prevalence and endurance of authoritarian rule in the region prior to 2011 are a crucial context for understanding contemporary politics in the Middle East.

What, generally, does authoritarian rule look like? Leaders are not selected through free and fair elections, and a relatively narrow group of people control the state apparatus and are not held accountable for their decisions by the broader public. Although there is variation from case to case, political rights and civil liberties are generally quite limited. *Political rights* refer to norms such as free and fair elections for the chief executive and the legislature; the ability of citizens to organize in multiple political parties and compete in elections free from interference by the military or other powerful groups; the absence of discrimination against cultural, ethnic, religious, or other minority groups; and transparent, accountable, noncorrupt government. *Civil liberties* refer to freedom of expression and belief, freedom of association and organization, the rule of law, and individual rights.[1] Table 1.2 lists the rankings given to Middle East countries for political rights and civil liberties in 2010 and 2017 by Freedom House, a prominent nongovernmental organization that gauges such rights globally.

Table 1.2 demonstrates that in 2017 only two countries—Israel and Tunisia—scored between 1 and 3 on the political rights scale and could be considered relatively free. Meanwhile, eighteen of twenty countries scored a 5, 6, or 7—on the "not free" end of the scale. While many countries have slightly better civil liberties scores, the overall civil liberties picture is very similar to that for political rights. The table also gives us a sketch of the medium-term impact of the Arab Spring on the region: eleven countries' political rights scores remained identical from 2010 to 2017; scores worsened in seven countries (Bahrain, Kuwait, Lebanon, Turkey, Yemen, the UAE, and Palestine); and scores improved in only two countries (Jordan and Tunisia).

While most Middle Eastern regimes thus remain authoritarian, they are not homogeneously so. Dictatorship takes more than one form in the area. The two main variants are monarchies and republics. The monarchies are led by kings whose reigns are not conferred by elections; instead, when incumbents die or become incapacitated, leadership is passed down hereditarily through ruling families. In monarchies, power rests in and emanates from the ruling family and those elites that are allied to it. The region's monarchies are Saudi Arabia, Qatar, the UAE, Morocco, Kuwait, Bahrain, Jordan, and Oman.

Table 1.2 Political Rights and Civil Liberties in the Middle East According to Freedom House

	Political Rights		Civil Liberties	
Country	2010	2017	2010	2017
Algeria	6	6	5	5
Bahrain	6	7	5	6
Egypt	6	6	5	6
Iran	6	6	6	6
Iraq	5	5	6	6
Israel	1	1	2	3
Jordan	6	5	5	5
Kuwait	4	5	5	5
Lebanon	5	6	3	4
Libya	7	7	7	6
Morocco	5	5	4	5
Oman	6	6	5	5
Palestine[a]	6/6	7/7	5/6	5/6
Qatar	6	6	5	5
Saudi Arabia	7	7	6	7
Syria	7	7	6	7
Tunisia	7	2	5	3
Turkey	3	5	3	6
United Arab Emirates	6	7	5	6
Yemen	6	7	5	6

Source: Freedom House, http://www.freedomhouse.org.
Notes: Scale is 1–7, with 1 denoting "most free" and 7 denoting "least free."
a. First value is for the West Bank; second value is for the Gaza Strip.

The region's authoritarian republics are led by presidents, whose terms in office are conferred by elections. Elections are not free or fair, but they are held, usually at regular intervals, both for the chief executive position and for national parliaments. In these republics, political power typically emanates from powerful presidents who command the loyalty of preponderant political parties, are backed by the military, and have access to large amounts of state revenue that can be used to cultivate clients and co-opt opponents. Historically, Algeria, Egypt, Iraq, Syria, Tunisia, and Yemen were the region's authoritarian republics. US and coalition forces dismantled Saddam Hussein's Baath Party regime in Iraq after 2003 and replaced it with a more competitive electoral regime. The Arab Spring brought significant change to several other authoritarian republics, with Yemen and Syria sinking into violent conflict and Tunisia managing a remarkable—if fragile—transition to democracy.

In Algeria, Egypt, and the monarchies of the Middle East, the position of president or king is formidable. Opposition parties and movements have no realistic chance of forcing turnover at the level of chief executive. This is not the case everywhere in the Middle East, however. Israel holds free and fair multiparty elections for seats in its parliament, and the prime ministerial position has changed hands regularly over the past many decades. In Turkey, with a handful of exceptions, multiparty elections have determined which parties sit in parliament and make up the cabinet. In addition, the offices of the prime minister and president have rotated among several political parties on the left and the right of the political spectrum. Lebanon and Iraq also hold multiparty elections to determine the composition of parliaments and cabinets, which then set policy in those countries. The Freedom House scores for Lebanon, Turkey, and Iraq are substantially below those for Israel, however, because politics in these countries is characterized by corruption, discriminatory practices, and/or the presence of armed militias, depending on the case. Still, on the basic matter of whether or not incumbent chief executives are able to be replaced through elections, these countries have been host to a politics that is freer than in the monarchies and authoritarian republics. At the same time, as Chapters 2 and 19 will show, it is not clear that Turkey will remain in this category given the increasingly authoritarian tendencies of its president, Recep Tayyip Erdoğan.

Iran's political system constitutes a category of its own, one that features both democratic and authoritarian elements. In the Islamic Republic of Iran, citizens go to the polls regularly to elect a president and parliament. Historically, such polls have been fair and have featured competition among several political factions. The presidency too has rotated among these factions over the course of the past generation. Yet, a body called the Council of Guardians constrains these elected institutions by vetting all would-be candidates for office. The council also can veto legislation passed by these elected bodies. Ultimate power lies in the hands of Iran's (indirectly elected) Supreme Leader, who controls that country's armed and security forces, judiciary, and media. Iran's 2017 Freedom House political rights score was a 6, indicating that the authoritarian elements of Iran's political system overpower and marginalize its democratic elements.

This is an introductory taste of contemporary political dynamics in the Middle East. The proceeding chapters go into much more detail, both by theme and by country. As a foundation for what is to come, the remainder of this chapter explores a set of crucial historical legacies that bear on Middle East politics and society today.

Essential Historical Background

Islamization and Arabization

How did the Middle East come to be predominantly Muslim in terms of faith and predominantly Arab in terms of language and ethnicity? The establishment and spread of Islam began in the seventh century C.E., and it was this process that also Arabized large portions of the region. Prior to the rise of Islam, two empires dominated the Middle East. The Sasanids ruled what is today Iraq and Iran, while the Byzantines ruled the Anatolian Peninsula (modern Turkey), northern Syria, and parts of North Africa, Egypt, and those territories that lie immediately east of the Mediterranean Sea (modern-day Lebanon, Israel, and Palestine). In 610 C.E., a young caravan trader named Muhammad began receiving revelations. He would become the Prophet of Islam, a new faith that was born in Mecca and Medina (cities in what is today Saudi Arabia).

Islam was strictly monotheistic, which stood in contrast to the pagan beliefs of the majority of the tribes that inhabited the Arabian Peninsula at the time. It exhorted members of those tribes—which often were at war with one another—to see themselves as brothers instead, and to submit to the one true god, Allah. Islam also preached the importance of justice and of caring for the weak in society (the poor, the sick, orphans, and the like). Although Muhammad encountered considerable resistance from those to whom his prophecy represented a threat, by the end of his lifetime he had built a new Muslim community, commanding the loyalty of most tribes in the Arabian Peninsula. Upon his death, the realm of Islam exploded geographically. Arabian tribesmen, with zeal inspired by their new faith and by the prospect of power and wealth, carried the banner of Islam northward into the Fertile Crescent (today's Lebanon, Syria, Iraq, Jordan, Israel, and Palestine), then eastward to Iran and westward across North Africa and even into Spain. These expansions destroyed part of the Byzantine and all of the Sasanid empires and paved the way for the creation of two successive Islamic empires: the Umayyad Empire (661–750 C.E.), with its capital at Damascus, and the Abbasid Empire (750–945 C.E.), with its capital at Baghdad.

Prior to Islam's emergence, Arabic-speaking tribes lived primarily in the Arabian Peninsula. With the Arab-Muslim conquests into the broader Middle East and subsequent building of empires, the pace of Arab peoples moving into the region picked up. Arabic, the language of the conquering empires, became the language of written communication with regard to administrative, religious, and cultural affairs. Non-Arabs gradually adopted the tongue as a result. Over an even longer period of time than Arabization consumed, a majority of people in the lands conquered by Muslim armies became converts to the new faith. These were not forced conversions, however. These Islamic empires allowed Jews, Christians, and Zoroastrians to practice their religions unimpeded as long as they paid special taxes. Conversions occurred slowly, out of political expediency (to be of the same faith as the ruling elite had its rewards), due to commercial interest (Islamic law and networks facilitated trade), as well as out of an acquired shared cultural and social experience.

The Ottoman Empire

The last great Islamic empire was the Ottoman Empire, founded by Turkic tribes beginning in the thirteenth century and centered on the imperial capital Istanbul. At their peak in the mid-sixteenth century C.E., the Ottomans controlled a breathtaking swath of territory, extending from deep into southeastern Europe, eastward to the Iranian border, southward through the Levant and parts of the Arabian Peninsula, and across North Africa to the Moroccan border. The Ottoman sultan controlled a professional army and sat atop a substantial bureaucracy that administrated imperial affairs. He was also the caliph of the Islamic umma (community or nation) and used Islam to legitimate his rule. Sharia (Islamic law) constituted a core element of Ottoman law, and the ulama (clerics) staffed the empire's court and educational systems. While this was an Islamic empire, other religious communities were allowed considerable leeway in terms of freedom of worship and control over local community affairs such as education and social services.

Two things are crucial to understand about the Ottoman Empire. First, it represented the last era in world history when the Middle East constituted a politically, economically, and militarily more powerful entity than "the West" (meaning, for that time period, Europe and Russia). During the 1500s the Ottomans challenged Venice, Italy, and Spain for supremacy in the Mediterranean. The Ottoman Empire also laid siege to the Habsburg capital of Vienna twice—once in 1529 and again in 1683. While it was victorious neither time, it did implant a pronounced sense of threat among Europeans.

The second critical point is that the tables began to turn in the seventeenth century as European states became increasingly powerful while the Ottoman Empire weakened. European powers successfully challenged the Ottomans for control over lucrative trade routes and penetrated the Ottoman Empire with European-controlled operations that imported European products and exported raw materials. These developments harmed the Ottomans economically, reducing revenues accruing to Ottoman coffers. Politically, modern nation-states emerged in Europe, as did nationalism, defined by James Gelvin as the "belief that because a given population shares (or can be made to share) certain identifiable characteristics—religion, language, shared history, and so on—it merits an independent existence" (2008: 56). Nationalist ideals undermined the multiethnic Ottoman Empire by inspiring many of its subject peoples to attempt to secede. Finally, by the turn of the nineteenth century, European armies had become more professional and deadly, utilizing new technologies, tactics, and organizational strategies. Meanwhile, internal to the empire, the quality of sultans was declining and the central government was weakening relative to provincial power-holders. Military morale and discipline too were waning, in part because the inflation that struck Eurasia at this time devalued troops' pay.

Ottoman elites were painfully aware of this turn of events. In the late 1600s the Ottomans lost territories to Russia, the Habsburgs, Venice, and Poland. In 1656 the Venetians destroyed the Ottoman naval fleet. In the late 1700s the Russians repeatedly and successfully advanced on the Ottomans. European culture increasingly influenced Ottoman elites, who imported architectural and painting styles, furniture—even tulips. By the 1800s, nationalist movements had arisen in Serbia, Greece, Romania, and Bulgaria, and these successfully seceded from the Ottoman Empire.

Ottoman elites were alarmed, of course, and as early as the 1600s began to ponder how they could reform the empire in order to better compete with their European rivals. As the Ottoman community engaged in deep debates, one camp concluded that if the Ottomans were to become a match for the Europeans, they would need to adopt European innovations in military affairs (training and tactics) and politics (parliaments). A second camp reached a quite different diagnosis of the problem, however, concluding that Ottoman weakness was a reflection of declining faith. The answer, then, was a return to a reinvigorated and purified Islam, not the mimicking of European ways.

The former camp won out, for a time anyway. During the late eighteenth century and through much of the nineteenth, Ottoman sultans attempted to radically restructure the empire's operations to defend against further European encroachment. They changed how their subjects were taxed, both to increase loyalty and to increase revenues flowing to the empire's coffers. They created an Ottoman parliament, modeled after the British and French institutions—in the hope that more inclusive, consultative governance would make for improved subject loyalty and better policy. They brought in European advisers to train new army units in modern warfare techniques, and they overhauled their educational, legal, and bureaucratic systems.

It would be too little, too late. The reforms implemented during the nineteenth century faced significant internal resistance, and thus their effectiveness was limited. What's more, the Ottomans could not stem the tide of nationalism and the desire of many Ottoman subject peoples to have their own state. When World War I ended, the Ottomans were on the losing side and would soon be extinguished as an empire.

European Imperialism in the Middle East

The Ottomans' painful experience of decline vis-à-vis an increasingly powerful set of European countries was only the first of a series of conflicts between the Middle East and Europe. The second was an era of direct rule by Britain, France, and Italy over much of the territory of the Middle East. Table 1.3 illustrates which European power controlled what Middle East territory (identified by contemporary country names). Sometimes geostrategic affairs motivated the colonizers. Britain's footprint in the Middle East turned on two main concerns: securing access to regional oil supplies and protecting key access routes to India, the "jewel" of the British Crown. Depending on the case, France generally was motivated by its relations with Christian communities and by commercial interests. Intra-European rivalry and the prestige that was attached to overseas colonies also motivated these powers.

Table 1.3 European Imperialism in the Middle East

Country	European Power	Type of Authority	Years
Algeria	France	Colonial	1830–1962
Bahrain	Britain	Treaty	1880–1971
Egypt	Britain	Colonial	1882–1936
Iran	n.a.	n.a.	n.a.
Iraq	Britain	Mandate	1920–1932
Israel	Britain	Mandate	1920–1948
Jordan	Britain	Mandate	1920–1946
Kuwait	Britain	Treaty	1899–1961
Lebanon	France	Mandate	1920–1943
Libya	Italy	Colonial	1911–1951
Morocco	France	Colonial	1912–1956
Oman	n.a.	n.a.	n.a.
Palestine	Britain	Mandate	1920–1948
Qatar	Britain	Treaty	1916–1971
Saudi Arabia	n.a.	n.a.	n.a.
Syria	France	Mandate	1920–1946
Tunisia	France	Colonial	1881–1956
Turkey	n.a.	n.a.	n.a.
United Arab Emirates	Britain	Treaty	1892–1971
Yemen, South	Britain	Colonial	1839–1967
Yemen, North	n.a.	n.a.	n.a.

Note: n.a. indicates not applicable; territory was never controlled by a European power.

The degree to which European powers took over the reins of power in their respective holdings varied substantially. In part this depended on the type of intervention. Generally, holdings acquired prior to World War I were colonies, territories that European powers conquered unapologetically and exploited for their own purposes in the context of global great-power competition. Holdings acquired after World War I were awarded by the League of Nations under the mandate system in the context of new international norms regarding European control over distant lands. Where they acted as mandatory powers, Europeans ostensibly had an obligation to protect natives' welfare and prepare them for independence. In the Persian Gulf, British imperialism took the form of treaty relationships negotiated with the ruling families of the small states that lined the coast.

In what ways did European power impact the region during this era? On one end of the spectrum, in Kuwait and the UAE, for example, Britain controlled foreign policy and port operations while leaving domestic political arrangements largely alone. In Morocco, the French took over domestic affairs—but did so by penetrating and harnessing existing indigenous institutions (like the monarchy), leaving them intact. By contrast, in Algeria, France uprooted and resettled tribes, destroyed domestic religious institutions, confiscated land, settled more than 150,000 Europeans, and ultimately annexed the entire country (as three separate French provinces). Even more dramatically, at the end of World War I, France and Britain literally drew the modern-day boundaries of Lebanon, Syria, Iraq, Jordan, and Israel/Palestine; engineered their respective political systems; and—in Iraq and Jordan—selected which kings would be placed on their respective thrones.

European rule had substantial socioeconomic impacts as well. France and Britain used their colonies as export markets for cheap European manufactured goods that competed with locally made products, hurting domestic artisan and craftsman classes. European powers also relied on their imperial holdings as a source of raw materials (cotton, wheat, etc.). These dynamics integrated the Middle East into global markets in a dependent manner as exporters of agricultural or primary (raw material) products, a fact that was an obstacle to future development and prosperity. While European control shaped the economic trajectories of Middle East states in key ways, the European powers' disposition toward their Middle East subjects was one of superiority and contempt. France and Britain legitimized their holdings in part with the idea that they had a "civilizing" mission in the region. They looked down on Islam and facilitated the entrance of Christian missionaries into Middle East societies. Another key impact of the colonial period was a domestic divide that emerged in Middle Eastern countries between urban elites who often adopted European ideas and culture, on the one hand, and the rural masses who remained more oriented toward Arab-Islamic culture, on the other.

Several countries in the region escaped the yoke of direct European rule. Turkey was the successor state to the Ottoman Empire in its core Anatolian Peninsula territory. While European powers had clear designs on that land in the wake of World War I, an Ottoman army officer named Mustafa Kemal organized Turks into a national movement and fought an independence war to establish the borders of what today is Turkey. In Iran, the Qajar dynasty ruled from the late 1700s through the early twentieth century, when power shifted into the hands of Reza Khan and subsequently to his son, Mohammad Reza Shah Pahlavi. Saudi Arabia is the product of the statebuilding efforts of the Al Saud tribe, which beginning in the early 1700s sought to expand and consolidate its power in the Arabian Peninsula. The campaign had its ups and downs, but by 1932, Saudi Arabia was a nation-state and has been independent ever since. Prior to its unification in 1990, Yemen had existed as two separate countries for over a century and a half: Britain ruled South Yemen as a colony, while North Yemen escaped European control. The Gulf state of Oman did as well.

Creation of the State of Israel

If Europe was the source of imperialist policies that left a strong imprint on the borders, politics, economies, and cultures of the Middle East, so too was it the birthplace of the modern story of the emergence of Israel. In the late nineteenth century, in the face of various forms of discrimination against Jews—including violent pogroms against Jewish communities in Russia and Eastern Europe—a man named Theodor Herzl began to advance the Zionist case that Jews constituted a nation, one that needed its own state in order to ensure that Jews could live in security and dignity in a land where they constituted a majority. He and like-minded Jewish leaders worked to make this vision a reality. They built institutions to raise awareness about and funds for the project, and they sought diplomatic support. Zionist diplomatic overtures ultimately found success in Britain, which, in the 1917 Balfour Declaration, lent its support to the creation of a Jewish national "home" in Palestine.

That support took concrete form at the close of World War I when the League of Nations portioned out the lands east of the Mediterranean Sea to France and Britain as mandates. The legal document establishing the Palestine Mandate included the language of the Balfour Declaration. The pace of Jewish migration from Europe to Palestine, which had already begun in the late 1800s, began to pick up, with major waves of migration occurring after World War I and in the 1930s. Tens of thousands of European Jews purchased land, settled, and began building new lives, new communities, and new institutions (including collective farms, a labor federation, schools, hospitals, and social services) in Palestine. At that time, the vast majority of the inhabitants of Palestine (90 percent in 1917) were Arab. They saw Zionism and the influx of Jewish immigrants as threatening to Arab political, economic, and cultural interests.

From 1920 to 1947, Britain attempted to manage what would prove to be an intractable conflict. The number of Jews in Palestine grew, as did the amount of land owned and worked by Jews. A rise in Arab landlessness and poverty followed, as the Arabs who had worked the lands purchased by Jews were forced to find employment elsewhere. Frustration and despair grew within the Arab community. Violence between Jews and Arabs broke out in the late 1920s and again in the mid-1930s. The economic strains of the Great Depression, and then Adolph Hitler's execution of millions of Jews during World War II, sharpened the conflict. In 1947, Britain, exhausted by the war and unable to reconcile Jews and Arabs, took its leave of Palestine and turned the problem over to the newly created United Nations.

The United Nations proposed that the territory of the Palestine Mandate be partitioned into two states, with Jerusalem—a city dear to Jews but also to Arab Christians and Muslims—as an international protectorate. The proposed Jewish state would have enclosed 55 percent of the land at a time when Jews represented approximately 32 percent of the population and owned 6 percent of the land. While the Jewish community accepted the UN proposal, Palestinian Arabs saw it as unjust—and rejected it. This impasse would mean war. With the international community unable to effect a solution, those on the ground prepared to fight. During the mandate years the Jewish community in Palestine had built a military organization, the Haganah, which now went into action seeking to secure the territories the partition plan had designated for the Jewish state. On May 14, 1948, Zionist leaders proclaimed the State of Israel. Almost immediately, the surrounding Arab countries invaded. Israel would be victorious in this war, extending the lands under its control beyond what would have been its borders according to the UN partition. The conflict between the newly created Jewish state and its Arab neighbors continues to the present.

Pathways from Colonialism

Israel was becoming a reality in the Middle East at about the same time that Middle Eastern populations were preparing to throw off the yoke of European domination. Egypt and Iraq achieved independence relatively early, in the 1930s (see Table 1.3). A wave of independence achievements then came during and after World War II, with Lebanon, Jordan, Syria, Libya, Morocco, and Tunisia becoming independent—in that order—between 1943 and 1956. Kuwait, Algeria, and (South) Yemen became independent in the 1960s, and Bahrain, Qatar, and the UAE followed in 1971.

Forcing the French and the British to take their leave was a task that varied in difficulty depending on the setting. Kuwait and the UAE had it relatively easy, as British domestic political discontent with the costs of imperialism prompted a more or less unilateral withdrawal. More often, independence was the product of nationalist movements that arose across the region, called on France and Britain to depart, and put pressure on them to do so. These movements tended to take the form of political parties—for example, the Wafd in Egypt, the Neo-Destour in Tunisia, and Istiqlal in Morocco. In Jordan, Iraq, Syria, and Egypt, nationalist movements used a variety of approaches to get their point across. These ranged from simple entreaties and signature-gathering campaigns, on the one hand, to demonstrations, protests, strikes, boycotts, and sometimes even riots, on the other. The goal was to show France and Britain that attempting to retain control over their Middle East holdings was going to be an increasingly difficult endeavor—and that the costs of staying outweighed the benefits. In all of these cases, the approaches seemed to work. France and Britain came to the negotiating table and granted independence to these countries—all with little to no violence.

Nationalist movements in Tunisia and South Yemen faced comparatively stiffer resistance from France and Britain, respectively. In these cases, nationalist contests dragged on longer and involved more violent methods, including bombings and assassinations. By far the most bitter independence battle, however, took place in Algeria. France was willing to let go of Syria—a League of Nations mandate that it was officially obliged to prepare for independence—without too much of a fight after having been the mandatory power there for approximately a generation. But Algeria was a colony, not a mandate, and France had been in control there for well over a century. Algeria had been politically integrated into France, and tens of thousands of French citizens had settled there. When in the 1950s a nationalist party called the National Liberation Front (FLN) took shape, it met strong French resistance. Algerian independence came in 1962, but only after a bloody, eight-year war that took some 700,000 lives.

In the wake of the physical departure of the imperial powers, however, the extent to which Middle Eastern countries were independent was debatable. Often, nominally independent states maintained political, economic, and military ties to their former masters. While this may seem counterintuitive—after all, there was a great deal of ill will and anger toward the Europeans—newly independent Middle East countries were often too weak to do otherwise. In some instances, they were simply unable to force Europeans to leave completely. For example, while Egypt technically became independent in 1936—becoming a member of the League of Nations that year—Britain still controlled Egyptian foreign policy and the Suez Canal. In other instances, leaders maintained those ties more voluntarily, understanding that they could benefit from ongoing political-military support from and trade relations with their former masters. The postindependence Iraqi regime, for example, received significant British military aid, equipment, and assistance, and allowed Britain to retain basing rights in the country. In Jordan, a British officer, Sir John Bagot Glubb, remained commander of the Jordanian army until 1957.

In many cases, these postindependence ties to European powers either endure to the present day or have been redrawn to the United States, which, with France and Britain exhausted at the end of World War II, rose to become the preeminent Western power and a pivotal external player in Middle East politics. Morocco, Tunisia, and Algeria maintained close political, economic, and cultural ties with France, for example. Jordan maintained close ties to Britain, but also cultivated increasingly strong links with the United States over time. Mohammad Reza Shah Pahlavi made Iran a key US political and military ally in the region. And in the Gulf, Saudi Arabia and the smaller Gulf states came to depend on the United States for security in the wake of the British departure.

In Syria, Egypt, and Iraq, however, lingering ties to European powers after independence did not survive the powerful domestic dissent they generated. In those societies a power struggle emerged that pitted conservative, established elites who had served France or Britain and presided over enduring ties to their former masters against a younger, "challenger" generation (often civil servants, workers, students, and peasants) that disagreed with conservative elites on a variety of issues. While conservative elites were content with the economic status quo, challenger forces—often organized into socialist and communist parties—pushed for land reforms, the nationalization of industry, and other redistributive policies designed to address the skewed distribution of wealth they saw in their societies. Challenger forces also strongly objected to conservative elites' enduring ties to Europe. For challengers, European imperialism was a humiliating chapter in the history of their nations, one they could not close the book on until those ties were broken. Such ties were especially difficult to stomach in the wake of

British support for Zionism. When in 1948 Arab armies were humiliated by Israel, tensions reached a breaking point. Challenger forces blamed conservative elites for failing to shepherd national economic, political, and military development in ways that would have allowed Arab states to stand truly independent and militarily victorious in the region.

What followed in Syria, Egypt, and Iraq was a series of coups that reoriented domestic politics and foreign policy for decades. For challenger forces, the task at hand was figuring out a way to oust conservative elites from power. While multiparty elections were being held during these years, conservative elites (rightly) felt threatened by challenger forces and either rigged elections to ensure conservative victories or simply ignored their results if they were not favorable. Given that the electoral route to power was closed, challengers turned to the army—where officers and recruits often were sympathetic to challenger views and wielded the coercive power to overthrow existing regimes. Military coups unfolded in Syria in 1949, in Egypt in 1952, and in Iraq in 1958. The political systems established in their wake cut ties to the West, established ties with the West's Cold War rival, the Soviet Union, and pursued redistributive economic policies.

Regime Structure and Disposition After Independence

What did Middle East political systems look like and prioritize after the dust had settled in the wake of the imperial powers' departure? There were three basic types: single-party dictatorships, monarchical dictatorships, and democratic (or semidemocratic) regimes.

Single-party systems. Political systems dominated by single, preponderant political parties emerged in Syria, Iraq, Egypt, Algeria, Tunisia, and South Yemen—all of which were republics ruled in dictatorial fashion by presidents. In most cases, presidents hailed from militaries, which had been key institutions of upward mobility for the lower classes. The political support of the military was a core anchor for these political systems. But preponderant, ruling political parties also served presidents in their exercise of power. These parties were massive, with systems of branches organized throughout these nations' territories as well as, often, in universities and workplaces. Presidents typically drew from party cadres to fill key positions in the bureaucracy in order to ensure that those in charge of implementing policy were loyal. Presidents also used these parties to distribute patronage (jobs and other material perquisites such as food, attractive terms for loans, etc.) to supporters, to socialize young people into the ideals of the regime, and to mobilize people into demonstrations of public support for the regime on important political occasions. Finally, presidents typically structured elections such that their ruling parties won either all or the vast majority of parliamentary seats—making parliaments rubber-stamp institutions.

These regimes adopted a state socialist economic development agenda. They used the power of the state to restructure and grow national economies: they nationalized numerous industries; they invested capital in industrialization campaigns; they implemented land reform programs that broke up the estates of large landholders and redistributed them to peasants; and they built massive state bureaucracies to manage the economy and deliver social welfare services to the masses. Their twin goals were to augment national power by building a thriving economic base and to see to it that all citizens—not just the elite—benefited.

The single-party dictatorships in the postimperial Middle East subscribed to the ideals of pan-Arab nationalism as articulated by Egypt's president Gamal Abdel Nasser. He blamed the West for facilitating the emergence of Israel and for dividing Arabs into a number of artificial states after World War I. This weakened Arabs when, according to Nasser and many intellectuals in the region, Arabs in fact constituted their own nation and should have had their own comprehensive state. To restore Arab strength, and to return the whole of the Palestine Mandate to the Palestinians, the divisions wrought by European interference would need to be overcome, and Arab political systems would need to be unified. How this would be accomplished in practice was never clear—and an experiment with Egyptian-Syrian union begun in 1958 ended in failure just three years later—but the ideals resonated among Arabs, whose hopes were raised that a renaissance of Arab power and dignity would soon be in the offing. As these single-party systems matured through the 1950s and 1960s, the Cold War was building into a crescendo of bipolar competition. With the United States evolving into Israel's most important ally, the Middle East's single-party regimes moved in the direction either of strategic neutrality or of alliance with the Soviet Union.

Monarchies. In the Middle Eastern monarchies—Saudi Arabia, Qatar, Kuwait, the UAE, Oman, Morocco, Jordan, and Iran—the right to rule stemmed not from elections but rather from claims about the legitimacy of specific families' indefinite monopoly on power. Depending on the country, such claims revolved around a family's historic role in founding the state (Saudi Arabia and Kuwait) and/or a family's religious lineage (several ruling families trace their ancestry to the Prophet Muhammad). In addition to claims about the legitimacy of family rule, royal families relied on a variety of other mechanisms for staying in power.

Trusted individuals (often family members) headed up the army, the secret police, and the cabinet. And the oil-rich monarchies used portions of their wealth to provide their subjects with elaborate social welfare benefits (free schooling, health care, etc.) to bolster political loyalty.

Like the single-party dictatorships, Middle Eastern monarchies tended to pursue state-led economic development. The state took the lead in making investments and building industry. The (many) monarchies with oil wealth used those resources to establish large public sectors and extensive social welfare services. Yet while the monarchies followed economic strategies similar to those of the single-party regimes, they did so without the populist and redistributionist ethos that often characterized the single-party cases. Neither did the monarchies subscribe to pan-Arab nationalist ideals. Iran is not an Arab country and thus was marginal to that discourse. The Arab monarchies were threatened by Arab nationalism, in part because in two of the states that advocated Arab nationalism most ardently, Egypt and Iraq, monarchs had been dethroned in very recent memory. Moreover, the republican and socialist ethos of those regimes was anathema to traditional ruling royal families and their wealthy, elite political allies.

While Egypt, Syria, Iraq, and Algeria courted Soviet assistance during the Cold War years, Middle East monarchies tended to ally with the United States. Iran under Mohammad Reza Shah Pahlavi (1941–1979) became a US client in the Middle East, advancing US foreign policy objectives in the region and buying US military equipment. Resource-poor Jordan relied on the United States for economic assistance and security guarantees. The oil-rich monarchies relied on the United States for security guarantees. Rivalries between the Middle East's single-party dictatorships and monarchies constituted an important Cold War dynamic in the region.

Democratic and semidemocratic systems. In just three countries did citizens have the capacity to vote incumbents out of office through elections: Israel, Turkey, and Lebanon. All three countries' structures featured a president (with Lebanon's and Turkey's having more constitutional authority relative to Israel's primarily ceremonial post) alongside a prime minister and cabinet constituted from an elected parliament. In all three countries, parliamentary elections were organized in such a way that parliaments reflected domestic constituencies in proportional fashion. Israel and Turkey had multiparty systems wherein parties gained parliamentary seats proportionate to the percentage of the vote share each won in elections. In Lebanon, electoral districts and seat allocation practices were designed to represent the country's myriad religious and sectarian groups.

Israel and Lebanon were democratic, while significant military influence in politics made Turkey semidemocratic.

Israel and Turkey followed state-led economic development trajectories similar to those pursued by single-party and monarchical regimes. In both Israel and Turkey during the 1950s, 1960s, and 1970s, the state played a major role in the economy—owning substantial assets and directing the priorities and pace of development. Lebanon was a regional exception during this time as it preserved a largely market economy during the heyday of state socialism in the 1950s, 1960s, and 1970s. In terms of foreign policy, Israel and Turkey were part of the Western "camp" during the Cold War—Turkey as part of the North Atlantic Treaty Organization (NATO) alliance, and Israel with its superpower backer, the United States. Lebanon was split between forces seeking to orient politics toward the West and others seeking to make Lebanon part of the pan-Arab nationalist fold; this divide was one of many stresses that sent Lebanon into fifteen years of civil war beginning in 1975.

The (Poor) Performance of Founding Regimes Through the Late 1970s

While state socialist economic development, Arab nationalism, and the confrontation with Israel dominated the rhetorical and policy landscape beginning in the 1950s, by the 1970s their collective failure had become evident. State socialist economies did not produce growth and prosperity for the Middle Eastern countries that adopted them. Instead, many countries faced bankruptcy and the need, beginning in the 1970s and 1980s, to radically restructure their economies. Neither did pan-Arab nationalism produce its intended effects. Intra-Arab rivalries—including those between the conservative monarchies and the more radical single-party republics—undermined the dream of Arab unity and strength. The failure of pan-Arab nationalism was underlined—and the ideology discredited—when Arab states suffered another devastating loss to Israel in the 1967 Six Day War. Nearly two decades after Arab states had failed to vanquish the forces of the Jewish state in 1948, in the 1967 war Israel captured the Golan Heights from Syria, the West Bank and East Jerusalem from Jordan, and the Gaza Strip and Sinai Peninsula from Egypt.

These developments undermined the legitimacy of Middle Eastern regimes—especially the single-party republics. Many analysts have argued that Nasser and the leaders of other single-party states (Syria, Iraq, Algeria, etc.) had made an implicit bargain with their peoples: the regimes would provide their citizens with economic prosperity and victory over Israel—but not political participation, free elections, and accountable government. Now, with regimes failing to deliver on their part of this bargain, citizens in the Middle East became politically restive. Because the monarchies had promoted neither populism nor pan-Arab nationalism, they were not as jeopardized by their failure. Still, the resource-poor monarchies were in difficult economic straits. And all Arab monarchies' citizens saw themselves at least in part as Arabs rather than just "Saudis" or "Kuwaitis." Arabs' inability to overcome Israel perplexed, demoralized, and led many (in monarchies and republics alike) to attempt to diagnose the roots of Arab weakness.

The Iranian Revolution and the Rise of Political Islam in the 1970s

As citizens, intellectuals, and activists pondered the reasons Arab regimes failed to deliver, many settled on variations of one basic answer: that Arab governments and society had distanced themselves too much from the teachings and traditions of Islam. The Arab single-party regimes in particular, while paying lip service to Islam, were quite secular in outlook and practice. Meanwhile, Arab societies, especially their middle- and upper-class urban strata, had adopted Western, secular mores and popular culture—including with respect to ways of dressing, decorating, consuming, recreating, and relating to the opposite sex. To critics, these developments undermined Arabs' Islamic heritage, in turn corrupting and handicapping them in their quest for dignity, prosperity, and power. Such Islamist thinkers harkened back to the days when the Umayyads, Abbasids, and Ottomans—empires that explicitly incorporated Islam and Islamic law into the public sphere—were in their glory, reasoning that political success stemmed from Islamic foundations.

In countries across the Middle East, Islamic movements emerged. More accurately, they reemerged, because the Muslim Brotherhood—the region's first and for decades one of its most important movements—was founded in Egypt in 1928. Established by Hassan al-Banna, a schoolteacher who rejected British political, economic, and cultural penetration of Egypt, the Muslim Brotherhood sought to return Egyptians to more pious lifestyles through educational and charitable activities, with the long-run goals of liberating Egypt from European domination, reconstituting the Egyptian state according to sharia law, and pursuing social and economic development. Nasser outlawed the Muslim Brotherhood, but his successor, Anwar Sadat, allowed it to return to action in the late 1970s to counterbalance his leftist opponents. Egypt's Muslim Brotherhood inspired branches in Syria, Jordan, and Palestine. Similar movements appeared elsewhere, including Tunisia's Islamic Tendency Movement and Algeria's Islamic Salvation Front.

These movements were galvanized in 1979 when, in Iran, Shi'ite cleric Ayatollah Ruhollah Khomeini brought down the monarchy of Mohammad Reza Shah Pahlavi by building a broad political coalition under the umbrella of politicized Islam. From the late 1950s through the 1970s, the Shah had presided over a secular, repressive, Westernizing dictatorship that was tightly allied with the United States, had diplomatic relations with Israel, and gravely mismanaged the Iranian economy despite that nation's considerable oil wealth. In making those choices, the Shah alienated numerous sectors of Iranian society. Khomeini deftly drew upon Islamic symbols and values to formulate a powerful critique of the Shah's regime, temporarily unify a wide variety of political factions, and move millions of Iranians to protest the Shah's regime—at considerable personal risk—in wave after wave of demonstrations that ultimately wore down the will of the Shah's armed forces to resist. On January 16, 1979, the Shah left Iran and headed into exile. Khomeini proceeded to build a new political system: the Islamic Republic of Iran.

Iran's Islamic Revolution sent a shock wave through the Middle East. For incumbents, the success of an oppositional Islamist movement was grim news. For Islamists, the revolution supplied powerful encouragement that there was hope for their cause. Indeed, much of the "stuff" of domestic politics across the region from the 1980s to 2011 pitted regimes against oppositional forces dominated by Islamist parties or movements. The comparative strength of Islamist actors—vis-à-vis both incumbents and other oppositional groups—varied from country to country, as did the tactics Islamists espoused. Some groups chose violent trajectories and sought to directly overthrow incumbent regimes, while others rejected violence and bided their time, "working within the system" as they focused on building their influence in society and in the institutions of the state. With few exceptions, however, Islamists were—and are—a political force to be reckoned with, regionwide.

Economic Reform and Democratization Pressures

The rise of political Islam was not the only new reality in the Middle East in the 1970s. Regimes also confronted two additional phenomena that constrained rulers' options and put pressure on their positions. First, beginning in the late 1970s and continuing into the 1990s, nearly every Middle Eastern country had to reform its economy, decreasing the state's role and integrating with the global market economy. Countries did so to varying degrees—and always reluctantly, because loans from the World Bank and the International Monetary Fund designed to facilitate economic restructuring came with conditions attached, including policy changes that caused hardships for citizens at the same time that they deprived regimes of key tools of political control. Second, also beginning in the 1970s, a wave of democratizing regime change swept through Southern Europe, Latin America, the Soviet Union and Eastern Europe, and parts of Asia and sub-Saharan Africa. Everywhere, political freedom seemed to be on the march.

For the Middle East's incumbent dictators, a new global democratic ethos was unwelcome, as it served to further delegitimize regimes whose constituents were already discontented and who faced increasingly significant Islamist oppositions. Meanwhile, all rulers—democrats and dictators—struggled with painful economic reform processes and worried about how the "losers" would react politically. Yet in the face of these multiple pressures—from Islamists, economic reform, and global democratizing norms—the region's authoritarian regimes persisted (for decades) by employing a variety of political strategies. Leaders in oil-rich states distributed their largesse in ways that kept key clienteles loyal and muted socioeconomic grievances. Leaders in less wealthy states tended to combine systematic repression carried out by their intelligence and security services with "facade" democratization—licensing opposition parties and holding elections that looked competitive while in reality playing fields were uneven and the positions candidates were elected to were devoid of actual power. Leaders also exploited the fears of many constituencies, both domestic and foreign, who worried about Islamists' power and what they would do with it if allowed to rule. Their argument essentially was, "better the devil you know."

The Arab Spring and Beyond

In December 2010, Arab authoritarian regimes began, for the first time, to be vulnerable. In Tunisia, massive, peaceful demonstrations were triggered by the self-immolation attempt of a desperate young man, Mohammad Bouazizi, and then facilitated by labor activists and social media. These protests overwhelmed the security forces, and, when the Tunisian army refused to enter the fray on his side, President Zine el-Abidine Ben Ali fled to Saudi Arabia. A single-party dictatorship erected in 1956 and sustained for fifty-five years by just two presidents had crumbled in one month's time. The Arab public—indeed, the whole world—watched this breathtaking turn of events on satellite television, and within weeks similar protests erupted across the region, expressing economic grievances while demanding more participatory, less corrupt governance.

By the end of 2011, three presidents had fallen: Ben Ali in Tunisia, Husni Mubarak in Egypt, and Ali Abdullah Salih in Yemen. The regime of Libya's leader Muammar Qaddafi had crumbled as well. In each of these countries, the stuff of politics then shifted to rewriting the rules of the game. In Tunisia, Egypt, and Libya this process got under way via the election of new representative assemblies that took up the herculean task of crafting new constitutions. In Yemen, complex negotiations unfolded among various stakeholders under the auspices of the Gulf Cooperation Council. In Syria, President Bashar al-Asad faced serious nationwide protests. His regime, however, has survived both the protests and the bloody and protracted civil war that followed in their wake.

While the presidents of Arab republics that had been characterized by single-party rule were especially vulnerable during the Arab Spring, the region's monarchies weathered the storm. Only Bahrain (where a Sunni monarchy governs a majority Shi'ite citizenry) experienced protests on a regime-threatening scale. The Bahraini government violently repressed protesters—with help from Saudi and Emirati forces—and during the ensuing years responded to persistent dissidence with arrests, detention, trials, and occasional violence. In no other monarchy was the status quo seriously threatened.

The monarchies were not passive in the face of regional upheaval, however. They felt their grip on power weaken and mobilized their resources to quell further rebellions and influence outcomes in the most affected countries—Tunisia, Egypt, Libya, Yemen, and Syria—where political trajectories were uncertain as key actors sought to establish new governing norms and institutions. Saudi Arabia led the countercharge, suppressing its own dissidents, sending troops to Bahrain, brokering an agreement that eased President Salih out of power in Yemen, and shoring up the poorer monarchies, Jordan and Morocco, with financial and political support. The Moroccan king preempted more thoroughgoing political change by offering a set of constitutional amendments that liberalized—but by no means democratized—the monarchy, and then holding new elections. Jordan's king made multiple changes in the prime ministerial and other cabinet positions, and his regime oversaw the passage of several modest reform measures bearing on elections, parties, and the judiciary. Saudi Arabia, the United Arab Emirates, and Qatar intervened in domestic affairs in Tunisia, Egypt, Libya, Syria, and Yemen, providing resources to and positive media coverage of favored politicians, parties, movements, and/or military leaders (Lynch 2016).

For those who hoped that Middle East political systems might evolve in a more inclusive and plural direction after the Arab Spring, trends have been sobering. Tunisia's politicians crafted a new, more democratic constitution and held sequential national elections that saw that country's Islamist party, En-Nahda, first take—and then relinquish—power. There were numerous crises along the way, however, and continuing socioeconomic grievances threaten to delegimitize new political institutions and practices. In Egypt, after a turbulent transitional period wherein the Muslim Brotherhood squared off against the military establishment in a test of wills, Field Marshall Abdel Fattah al-Sisi seized power, banned the Muslim Brotherhood, and established a new iteration of military-led authoritarian rule. Transitions in Libya and Yemen deteriorated into violent conflict due to their weak state institutions and deep domestic political divides, coupled with the interference of outside actors. The repression of the (moderate) Muslim Brotherhood in Egypt together with the breakdown of political order in Libya, Yemen, and Syria in turn created opportunities for extremist Islamist actors, including ISIS and al-Qaeda, to recruit members and to gain and control territory.

Importantly, the Arab Spring's repercussions were not limited to Arab states. In hindsight, the Green Movement protests in Iran following a fraudulent presidential election in June 2009 may have been a precursor to the Arab Spring, and incumbent Iranian conservatives no doubt had the Arab Spring on their mind as the 2013 and 2017 presidential elections unfolded. The fall of Mubarak in Egypt and Ben Ali in Tunisia deprived Israel of two of its most moderate Arab interlocutors while temporarily empowering Islamists with a more critical position vis-à-vis the Jewish state. In mid-2011 Israel experienced its own set of mass demonstrations, which saw economic grievances take center stage. Meanwhile, the upheavals presented Turkey with diplomatic headaches as it tried to manage the impact of political change on its commercial relationships with Arab states. Civil war in Syria meant that Turkey (as well as other neighboring states) was burdened with significant refugee flows as well as worries about how the dynamics of the Syrian civil war would impact Turkey's fraught relationship with its Kurdish population.

In a time of transition and upheaval in the Middle East, then, this book equips the reader with the general and specific knowledge essential for making sense of contemporary Middle East politics. Part 1 of the book contains seven chapters that provide an overview of the patterns, trends, and dynamics that characterize the region as a whole, across a number of core topics. Chapter 2, "Governments and Oppositions," analyzes the extent to which citizens can—or cannot—hold their governments accountable through periodic, democratically meaningful elections and the alternation in power of multiple political parties. Chapter 3, "The Impact of International Politics," offers a framework for understanding how dynamics and pressures outside states' borders have shaped the domestic politics of countries in the Middle East. Chapter 4, "Political Economy," analyzes how states have tried to spur economic growth and development, how politics has influenced the substance of economic decisions, and how economic realities in turn impact political dynamics and decisionmaking.

Chapter 5, "Civil Society," examines how citizens in countries of the Middle East organize outside the explicitly political sphere for philanthropic purposes and to advance their political, economic, and social interests—as well as why and how the Middle East's mostly authoritarian regimes have sought to control, curtail, and contain such activities. Chapter 6, "Religion and Politics," explores the three monotheistic faiths that emerged in the Middle East, the extent to which states in the region are religious, and the main forms of politicized religious activism in the region. Chapter 7, "Identity and Politics," considers how various types of attachments—to religion, language, lineage, and geographic homeland—matter politically. Finally, Chapter 8, "Gender and Politics," looks at the ways that women's (and men's) roles in society have been constructed and contested in the Middle East.

Part 2 presents case studies of contemporary political dynamics in twelve of the region's twenty countries: Algeria, Egypt, Iran, Iraq, Israel, Jordan, Kuwait and the United Arab Emirates, Palestine, Saudi Arabia, Syria, and Turkey. Each case study chapter opens with a historical overview and description of the contemporary political structure of the country in question. Each then examines the seven issue areas presented in Part 1, explicating the specific dynamics that animate each arena.

As a whole, the text demonstrates that several key problems, dynamics, and issues dominate politics in the contemporary Middle East. First, wars (civil and otherwise) have resulted in tremendous physical destruction and humanitarian suffering in Syria, Yemen, Libya, and, for a time, the region of Iraq where ISIS challenged the Iraqi government for territorial control. In these spaces we cannot describe and analyze political systems, as multiple armed groups (with very different visions of what politics should look like) are fighting for the right to control territory and the state. This is an important reminder that stable governance—wherein only state authorities possess the means of violence (and use it sparingly), and no other group challenges the state via militia or guerrilla activity—provides the key public good of basic political order.

Second, after decades of authoritarian rule, Tunisia has joined Israel, Turkey, Lebanon, and Iraq in crafting a political system in which electoral competition determines who rules. In these five countries, leaders and citizens alike confront the arduous challenge of living up to the letter and spirit of constitutions that call for actors with very different political preferences to make decisions transparently and through the ballot box rather than via diktat, violence, or corruption.

We will see that they do so with varying degrees of success. In the meantime, authoritarian rule persists through large swaths of the region: the monarchical systems, Algeria, Egypt, and Iran. In these countries, those who rule and those who are ruled will continue to engage in political struggles that will determine the prospects for more participatory and accountable governance.

Third, citizens' self-identification with respect to language, lineage, place, faith, and sect informs their political goals and tactics. These identities can divide political communities, affect contests about the shape of politics, and make democratic compromise more difficult. Across the Middle East's Muslim-majority states and also in Israel, for example, actors debate whether political rules should be based on secular or religious principles. Until the Arab Spring uprisings, regional dictatorships tended to be quite secular but faced (and repressed) potent Islamist opposition movements; in many places, violent confrontations took place between the two. In the wake of the Arab Spring uprisings, once-banned Islamist parties won elections in Egypt and Tunisia and assumed key roles in governance and the writing of new constitutions. Given the gulf in political perspectives deriving from very different identities, Islamist-secularist interactions and negotiations have been complex, heated, and difficult. In Tunisia thus far, secularist and Islamist actors are finding a way to coexist peacefully; the same cannot be said of dynamics in Egypt. Religious, sectarian, and/or ethnic divides complicate pluralist politics in similar ways in Lebanon and Iraq. Sunni-Shi'ite tensions especially have grown in the region in the wake of the Arab Spring as Saudi Arabia, Bahrain, and other Gulf states have wielded sectarian appeals and accusations designed to weaken domestic opponents.

Fourth, the Middle East faces daunting economic problems that influence political dynamics and are in turn affected by politics. Regime type aside, the goal of generating sustainable prosperity that is broadly shared by citizens has eluded even the richest of Middle East states in recent decades. Socioeconomic grievances were a key driver of Arab Spring protests. Many observers worry that Tunisia's nascent democratic system will be threatened if it is not perceived by citizens as offering sufficient economic progress. Autocrats who survived the Arab Spring have more reason than ever to worry about economic performance, living standards, and unemployment. In the meantime, state fragmentation, insurgency, and war in Libya, Yemen, Syria, and elsewhere have destroyed infrastructure and lives, and reduced living standards.

Fifth, an important dilemma for the region's leaders and peoples is how to relate to the West, and particularly the United States. European actors exercised imperial control over the region in the nineteenth and early twentieth centuries, only to be overtaken by the United States as the major Western hegemon after World War II. Today, Western countries are major (and not always welcome) military players on the ground in the region at the same time that they control the purse strings of global financial institutions and offer democracy as a political model—one that some aspire to and others reject altogether. What the content of diplomatic relations with the West should be and whether Middle East states adhere to Western policy exhortations (regarding economics, family law, human rights, etc.) constitute extremely sensitive political issues that divide and antagonize political parties and civil society actors.

All of these domains—the shape of political regimes, identity politics, economic challenges, and regional relations with the West—influence women's status in the region and will continue to shape the outcomes of struggles over gender norms. Significant intraregional variation notwithstanding, women in the Middle East participate in the labor force and political institutions at a far lower rate than do their male compatriots; regional norms prescribe a primarily domestic role for women; and women's legal rights in the area of family law are distinctly circumscribed. While for many (male and female) this state of affairs is acceptable, others work to achieve increased legal parity, economic autonomy, and political voice for women.

While these dynamics and challenges animate politics in the Middle East, it is important to keep in mind that there is a diversity of experience in the region: stable countries and countries torn apart by civil war, democracies and dictatorships, rich states and poor states, countries that have cooperative relationships with the West and countries that vigorously confront the West. This text helps readers navigate complexity to comprehend both broad patterns and trends as well as the important differences and variation that also exist within the Middle East.

Note

1. These characterizations of political rights and civil rights are adapted from Freedom House's methodology statement, available at http://www.freedomhouse.org.

PART 1

Contemporary Dynamics

2

Governments and Oppositions

Mona El-Ghobashy
and Michele Penner Angrist

A central organizing focus of comparative politics is the study of political systems or political regimes—that is, understanding who wields the power to make laws and allocate resources in a country, how those individuals come to wield that power, and the extent to which they are constrained and held accountable by other actors. During the colonial period, French, British, and Italian officials controlled state administrations in most of the Middle East. Denizens of the region were governed by individuals from other places and cultures and had no ability to affect law or policy. Over time, this status quo became unacceptable. Nationalist movements emerged, demanding that foreigners exit the scene and that the keys to the state pass into the hands of native-born citizens. It was the hope of many that liberation from European control and sovereign statehood would usher in a new era of dignity and prosperity.

But that is not what occurred. Across the region, after the coming of independence, political systems settled into various forms of authoritarian rule. Leaders tended to come to power via military coup or hereditary succession rather than through competitive elections. Leaders tended to stay in power for long periods, buttressing their positions with the support of militaries, secret police, and international allies while ensuring that their opponents had neither the resources nor the political space to challenge them and hold them accountable. Where elections took place, they were rigged. Beyond an initial decade or two of rising economic fortunes, citizens in most Middle East countries enjoyed neither dignity nor prosperity. Increasingly, homegrown and sometimes arbitrary authoritarian regimes mismanaged economies and presided over cowed and fearful publics.

This was the situation in the region in late 2010. Then, an event in a small town in Tunisia set in motion a series of startling developments. A policewoman confiscated the cart of a twenty-six-year-old fruit vendor named Mohammad Bouazizi. When he went to the municipality to complain and retrieve his wares, he was barred from entering the building. He left but then returned and planted himself outside the municipality gates, doused his body with gasoline, and set himself on fire to protest how ordinary people like him are mistreated and then ignored by government officials. Bouazizi's plight resonated with his fellow townspeople and then with hundreds of thousands of Tunisians. Their protests led to a cascade of ever-larger demonstrations that spread from various Tunisian cities to the capital, Tunis, and from there to the provincial cities and capitals of Egypt, Libya, Yemen, Algeria, Morocco, Jordan, Syria, and Bahrain.

The Arab Spring brought hundreds of thousands of citizens out into the streets to demand social justice, freedom, and democracy. They were calling for democracy in its most essential form: the ability of citizens to have a say in the decisions that affect their lives. But this common-sense notion of democracy is very difficult to translate into concrete practices. It means that citizens should be able to control governments, usually by participating in periodic elections. For most of human history, however, it has been governments that have controlled their subjects. Governments possess armed forces, essential information, and the control over state organizations that give them huge advantages over ordinary people.

This chapter takes up the issue of how citizens come to control their governments, especially in circumstances where governments historically have had the upper hand, neither representing nor serving the people. Elections have become the primary method by which citizens choose their rulers, returning them to office if they serve their interests and removing them from office when they do not. What's more, during the time when elected officials are in office, they're kept in check by legislatures, opposition parties, and an independent press, all of which make it their business to monitor the behavior of the government to ensure that officials do not abuse their power. In all of the countries in the Middle East, including the non-Arab states of Israel, Turkey, and Iran, politics revolves around the struggle to make or keep governments honest and accountable, both through free and fair elections and through the creation of legal opposition political parties.

Distinguishing Among Three Key Political Science Concepts

State: The permanent organizations of bureaucracy, the military and police forces, the legislature, the judiciary, taxation structures, economic regulation agencies, communication agencies (e.g., postal services and railways), penal institutions, and so forth.

Government: The group of people who control and manage state organizations. Governments attain power in a variety of ways—through popular election, selection by a narrow elite, military coup, or hereditary rule—depending on the kind of relations they establish with the societies they rule.

Regime: The set of rules for determining how key public offices are filled. These rules are determined by governments through bargaining and struggle with opposition groups, societal interest groups, and even international actors, including foreign governments. Regimes can be democratic, nondemocratic, or somewhere in between.

The Idea and Practice of Opposition

The democratic idea that people should choose who governs them is ancient, but the practice is fairly recent. For most of human history, people had no say in who ran the political community they lived in. Even rarer is the practice of a government accepting opposition as a regular and protected feature of the political system. As political scientist Robert Dahl noted, "The fact that a system of peaceful and legal opposition by political parties is a comparative rarity means that it must be exceedingly difficult to *introduce* such a system, or to *maintain* it, or both" (1966: xiv, emphasis in original). If we assume that government officials seek to maintain their hold on power and minimize opposition, what would give rise to tolerated opposition parties? And how do such parties survive and become an accepted feature of a country's political life?

It seems reasonable to posit that governments would tolerate opposition only if they are compelled to do so. One circumstance in which governments may feel so compelled is when they recognize that in order to get things done, they need the cooperation of a broad segment of the population. Take the issue of taxation. All governments need taxes to fund public works projects such as roads and bridges and to underwrite massive ventures such as wars and systems of national defense. To induce people to pay taxes, governments need the consent of the governed—otherwise they risk antitax revolts or revolutions. Consent cannot be given orally or informally; instead, it must be hammered out within permanent institutions. Enter legislatures, the formal place where government officials bargain with representatives of the people over the terms of taxation. Hence the famous phrase from the American revolution: no taxation without representation. The process of negotiations over taxation and other major public policies is one concrete example of governments conceding the need for societal participation to get things done.

How does opposition come into play? Legislatures house representatives of the citizenry who negotiate on its behalf, but they are also places where critics of government performance bide their time until the next elections, when they can make a bid to become the government. Thus, opposition parties are not just groups of people who oppose the government. Their main goal is to win the public's confidence through elections and to become the government. The key idea is for different parties to compete before the public for the prize of exercising government power. Voters are the arbiters, choosing which of the competing groups will get to assume public office for a set term (usually four or five years). The party that wins the public's vote becomes the government while the party that loses moves into the ranks of legislative opposition until the next round of elections. Rotating government power in this way ensures that no single group captures state organizations and uses them to benefit only its supporters and clients.

It turns out that rotating political power—while desirable in theory—is very difficult to implement in practice. It took centuries of protracted crises, civil wars, and revolutions for today's advanced democracies to become countries where power changes hands peacefully and regularly via elections. As political sociologist Charles Tilly wrote, "Over the past few centuries of Western history, for example, whole clusters of regimes underwent a momentous shift from millennia of being simply unavailable for democratic change to frequent oscillation between democratization and dedemocratization" (2007: 17). Thus, even when a political system reaches the point of peaceful, regular transfer of power, there is no guarantee that it will remain there. Democratization is not a one-way street. It can be reversed, especially if a party refuses to abide by the rules of the game and decides to monopolize governmental power indefinitely. In the Middle East, on the eve of the Arab Spring uprisings, the majority of countries suffered from a monopoly hold on government power by a single leader and his family and cronies. They used this power to enrich themselves while the impoverished majority like Mohammad Bouazizi led hardscrabble lives, with no opportunities for political participation.

Clearly, elections are important for the distribution and rotation of power. But how can we tell if an election is free and fair? How do we know if elections are moments of real competition between rival parties? After all, it's easy for rulers to hold elections and then manipulate them so thoroughly that incumbents can never be defeated at the polls. In fact, all over the world leaders have so frequently manipulated elections and other ostensibly democratic instruments such as parliaments and constitutions that political scientists have coined a special term for such political systems: *electoral authoritarian regimes* (Schedler 2002). These are political systems that have regular elections, but the function of elections is to thwart rather than deepen democratization.

How is it possible that elections can subvert democracy instead of advancing it? Scholars have tracked the diverse tactics used by autocratic leaders to game elections so effectively that they can never lose. Among other tricks, rulers design electoral rules that discriminate against the opposition (Robinson 1998; Posusney 2002); write vast powers for themselves into the constitution (Brown 2002); and purposely structure elections in ways that make opposition forces appear weak and hapless in front of the public (Schmitter 1978). Steven Heydemann summarized these tactics as employed in the Arab world with the pithy phrase "authoritarian upgrading" (Heydemann 2007). He points out that Arab rulers were not cartoonish dictators who simply repressed their opposition. Over time, they upgraded outdated forms of dictatorship with smarter, more efficient versions of autocratic control using elections.

Since elections are so easily manipulated to ornament autocratic rule, it's crucial to be able to discern whether any given election is really democratic. The key to meaningful elections is that government power changes hands periodically and peacefully. Different groups of people ought to take turns being in power, so that no single group entrenches its dominance and monopolizes the political arena. To be even more concrete, political scientists have developed a four-part litmus test to assess the democratic significance of an election (Przeworski et al. 1996):

1. Can incumbent parties lose the election?
2. If so, would the winners be allowed to form a government?
3. Would the winners be able to govern (i.e., make and change laws)?
4. Are elections held repeatedly and regularly?

If you think about these four questions carefully, they all get at the same concern: Is there some entrenched power bloc behind the scenes that distorts elections and prevents the periodic transfer of power? This is all-important since, as we've seen, elections can be staged to give the appearance of competition while the outcome is predetermined and the ruler(s) can never lose. By asking if dominant parties can lose and challenger parties can govern, the questions appraise whether elections really are the currency of political power, or whether they're a sideshow and power is actually concentrated in the hands of irremovable, unaccountable individuals.

Governments and Oppositions in the Middle East and North Africa

Before considering how elections in the contemporary Middle East fare under our criteria, let's take a closer look at the political lay of the land. What types of political systems exist in the region? To what extent can opposition parties form and contest the conduct of the government, and what are their chances of having a go at being the government? The region's political systems can be classified into three main types: republics led by presidents and/or prime ministers; monarchies ruled by kings; and the hybrid system of Iran, which is led by both a president and a high-ranking Shi'a cleric (ayatollah), a very powerful figure dubbed "the Leader" in Iran's constitution.

Historically, republics such as Tunisia, Algeria, Egypt, Yemen, Syria, and Iraq all were governed by powerful presidents who often rose from humble social backgrounds to the summit of political power through service in the military or police forces. The presidents consolidated their rule through tight control over two principal organizations: the armed forces and a single ruling party that dominated the political scene. Ruling parties performed a variety of crucial functions and explain why many of these presidents remained in power for years on end. Using their control over government resources, presidents used single parties as a patronage delivery system that distributed jobs, money, import licenses, and a host of other perks to cronies and their constituents. Ruling-party branches were spread out over the country to monitor the population, recruit young people to fill the party's ranks, and provide a space where ambitious party cadres could compete with each other to rise through party ranks and gain access to the president's inner circle.

During national legislative elections, ruling parties swung into action, ensuring that opposition parties did not make significant gains at the ballot box. Ruling-party cadres organized campaign rallies for the party's candidates, bought off voters with cash or foodstuffs, and faced off with popular opposition-party candidates in the streets and at the polling booth to maintain the party's crucial majority in parliament.

Ruling-party legislators were the president's eyes and ears within parliament, controlling the post of parliamentary speaker, ensuring the smooth passage of all bills proposed by the president, and standing up to opposition legislators if they attempted to block legislation or assert their oversight role over the government.

Presidents in Tunisia, Egypt, Algeria, Syria, and Yemen even put themselves up for election in stage-managed contests with handpicked challengers. In 2004, Tunisia's president Zine el-Abidine Ben Ali extended his seventeen years in power by an election where he netted 94.49 percent of votes. Presidents engaged in such spectacles to legitimize their prolonged hold on power and claim broad popular acclaim for their rule. Ruling parties were indispensable on these occasions as well, organizing massive campaign rallies for the incumbent, orchestrating promotional appearances for him in the government-controlled media, and preventing independent monitors from observing the balloting on the ground to mask fraud, rigging, and voter intimidation. Finally, presidents frequently amended their countries' constitutions to prolong their rule, acts made possible by their ruling parties' majorities in parliament. For example, in 2000, Syria's constitution was amended to lower the minimum age for the president from 40 to 34, the age of current president Bashar al-Asad when he inherited the post after the death of his father Hafiz al-Asad.

In Iraq, the regime of Saddam Hussein fell in the wake of the 2003 invasion and occupation of that country by US and coalition forces. Eight years later, the Arab Spring uprisings altered politics drastically in several of the region's other republics. Dictatorial presidents fell in Tunisia, Egypt, and Yemen, while Syrian president Bashar al-Asad's determination to cling to power regardless of the cost plunged that country into a prolonged civil war. Libyan leader Muammar Qaddafi, who had constructed a unique political system with some republic-like characteristics, also fell from power. Tunisia, Libya, and Egypt went on to hold competitive elections for new assemblies and/or leaders to guide those countries through complex and uncertain transitions away from what had been long-standing authoritarian regimes. While hopes were high that democratic systems might be erected in their stead, as of this writing outcomes have been sobering. The region's republics today present a much more heterogeneous set of political conditions—ranging from external intervention and war (e.g., Yemen), to civil conflict and civil war (e.g., Libya and Syria), to quite authoritarian (e.g., Algeria, Egypt), to reasonably democratic (e.g., Tunisia, for now). This range is a reminder that the task of altering the rules by which governments operate in a more democratic direction is enormously difficult.

Moving on from the republics, one of the most striking facts about the Middle East is the presence of eight monarchies. The survival of monarchies in the Middle East is a puzzle because monarchs who actually rule and not simply reign have otherwise become extinct in the contemporary world. Yet far from being antique holdovers from a traditional age, Arab monarchies are quite modern in their origins and their techniques of rule. Arab would-be kings first gained a foothold on power by forming alliances with the British and French colonial states that wielded enormous power in the Middle East during the late nineteenth and early twentieth centuries. Indeed, the monarchies of Saudi Arabia and Jordan would scarcely have retained their power had they not been sponsored and supported first by the British and then by the US governments. The one exception is the Moroccan monarchy, which has ruled the country since 1649.

When they were anointed, monarchs built and sustained their hold on power using the "authoritarian upgrading" strategies identified by Heydemann. But there is one key difference in how monarchs manage the political arena as compared to the autocratic presidents of republics. Instead of establishing a large ruling party to dominate the political arena, monarchs often encourage pluralism among social groups and political parties, promoting ethnic, regional, and religious diversity. These "linchpin monarchies" (Lucas 2004), as in Morocco and Jordan, construct the position of the king as the essential node that holds the system together, standing above all societal divisions, protecting religious or ethnic minorities, and uniting the nation.

This familiar strategy of divide and rule is coupled with ideologies emphasizing the monarchies' noble origins in a storied past. Members of the Kuwaiti Al Sabah dynasty, rulers of Kuwait for over 200 years, underscore that their rule is responsible for the country's sovereign independence from the Iraqi threat (Herb 1999: 159). The Jordanian monarchy claims descent from the Prophet Muhammad, asserting on its official website, "Direct descendants of the Prophet Muhammad, the Hashemite family is a unifying factor interwoven into the life of modern Jordan."[1] By contrast, the Saudi monarchy does not claim descent from the Prophet but emphasizes instead its services to Islam: the Sauds title themselves "Custodians of the Holy Places," referring to the Muslim pilgrimage cities of Mecca and Medina. The Sauds also stress the exceptional qualities of Abdulaziz Al Saud, who united the Arabian Peninsula and proclaimed the Kingdom of Saudi Arabia in 1932, citing his "shrewdness, courage, farsightedness and horsemanship."[2] As with all founding myths of modern governments, the monarchies' official ideologies are best analyzed as instruments of rule rather than accepted as statements of fact.

The Islamic Republic of Iran is a hybrid system where political power is divided between elected politicians in the presidency and parliament, and indirectly elected clerics—one who serves as the Leader and others who populate the powerful institution of the Guardian Council. The six clerics (and six lay lawyers) on the Guardian Council vet all candidates for presidential and parliamentary elections often disqualifying opposition candidates. The Guardian Council must also approve all bills passed by parliament and has the power to block bills if it considers them inconsistent with the constitution and Islamic law. In this way, the scope of political competition is significantly limited to groups approved by clerical gatekeepers.

Beyond the republic–monarchy–Islamic Republic distinction, another major difference among the region's political systems is the extent to which they allow organized opposition parties to form and participate in honest elections. Historically, the two countries with the most well-developed competitive multiparty systems have been Israel and Turkey—though both countries possess antidemocratic qualities today. Israel's is a parliamentary democracy with a relatively large number of political parties. Of the 120 seats in the Israeli parliament (Knesset), 61 are required to form a government. Since 1948 when Israel was founded, no political party has secured the full 61 seats, and thus elections have instead produced coalition governments composed of several political parties. From 1948 to 1977, Israel was a "dominant-party democracy," where the same large party (the left-wing Labor party) repeatedly won elections and led coalition governments. This changed in 1977 when the right-wing Likud party displaced the Labor party as the winner, making Israeli politics more competitive by inaugurating the practice of power rotation between different parties. Right-wing parties have dominated the political scene for the past two decades, and Israel's power over the fates of the West Bank and Gaza Strip—where Palestinians experience occupation rather than democratic citizenship—means that two very different political systems exist in the territory Israel controls.

Turkey had a competitive multiparty parliamentary system after 1950, with political parties of various ideologies taking turns running government, often sharing power in coalition governments as in Israel. During this period, however, Turkish politics was constrained by the interventionist stance of the military, which aborted or attempted to manipulate the democratic process on average once per decade. In recent years, President Recep Tayyip Erdoğan's treatment of the press, political opponents, and other critics has raised troubling questions regarding the future of Turkey's competitive political system.

Before the 2011 uprisings, in none of the Arab countries could citizens choose their governments, much less control them. Arab kings and presidents alike thoroughly monopolized their countries' political systems, permitting some opposition parties while banning others, and ensuring that the tolerated opposition parties never threatened their hold on power. Indeed, their monopoly on the political system was so complete that the leaders of several Arab non-monarchies (ironically) were grooming their sons to succeed them. Syria's Hafiz al-Asad started the trend shortly before he died in 2000, and Husni Mubarak (Egypt), Muammar Qaddafi (Libya), Saddam Hussein (Iraq), and Ali Abdullah Salih (Yemen) were marching in al-Asad's footsteps before the 2003 US invasion toppled Hussein and the insurrections of 2011 toppled the other leaders. Indeed, the absence of any meaningful opportunities to replace the government via elections or make the existing government responsive to the public was one of the main grievances that motivated the Arab Spring uprisings.

In the wake of the Arab Spring, the status of opposition varies from country to country. There is a wide spectrum. In Tunisia, elections in 2014 saw a wide range of political parties given the freedom to compete. Jordan and Morocco, on the other hand, have semi-opposition parties that are neither fully repressed nor fully empowered. A handful of countries such as Saudi Arabia, Qatar, and the United Arab Emirates (UAE) ban all political parties. As the next section will demonstrate, the quality and competitiveness of elections also vary widely across Arab countries as well as within the same country over time—such as in Tunisia before and after the toppling of President Ben Ali in January 2011.

Iran is a very interesting halfway house between the cases of Turkey and Israel on the one hand and the (historically) noncompetitive Arab states on the other. Before 1979, Iran was ruled by a shah or king whom the people did not choose and could not replace. The Shah outlawed nearly all forms of opposition, which drove some of his opponents underground into armed groups (Abrahamian 1980). A spectacular popular revolution developed against the Shah's despotism in 1978–1979 and drove him out of Iran, establishing a new political system that marginally increased the Iranian people's ability to choose their government. Iranians simultaneously do and do not elect their leaders. Government power is divided between elected lay politicians (the president and members of parliament) and the indirectly elected Leader and Guardian Council. Presidential and parliamentary elections are vigorously contested by a variety of political factions. Yet the range of contestation is limited by the Guardian Council due to its power to vet candidates. All factions are loyal to the political system of the Islamic Republic; they differ over economic policy and the appropriate balance of power between the directly and indirectly elected institutions. Thus, unlike Arab citizens before 2011, Iranians are able to oppose and change some of their leaders.

Elections in the Middle East and North Africa

Now that we have a sense of the structure of political power in the region's countries, let's take a closer look at the quality of regional elections by subjecting them to the four-part litmus test used in this chapter (see Table 2.1).

It might come as a surprise to learn that even before the Arab uprisings, all of the region's countries held some form of elections. Saudi Arabia used to be the holdout, until it began holding municipal elections in 2005 and gave women the right to run and vote in the 2015 municipal elections. Still, it matters whether or not a country has full-suffrage elections for a national-level legislature. One strategy of electoral authoritarianism is to have elections only for municipal bodies, so that incumbents can monopolize both executive and law-making powers at the national level. Refer to the first column of Table 2.1 and note that all of the region's countries have held direct, full-suffrage national-level elections except three: Saudi Arabia, Qatar, and the UAE. Even within these three cases there are differences. In Saudi Arabia, there is a national legislature, but its 150 members are appointed by the Saudi king. Qatar has a legislature whose forty-five members also are all appointed; the country holds elections only for a municipal council. In the UAE, there are elections for a national legislature, but more than half of citizens can't vote in them; a restricted electorate chooses only half of the legislature's members—the other half are appointed.

Importantly, elections are not the only means of doing politics in the Middle East. Refer to the second column of Table 2.1 and note that in Syria, Lebanon, Libya, Yemen, and Palestine, various forms of political violence are also a prevalent feature of domestic politics. Political reputations and the distribution of power are determined not only at the ballot box but also in armed conflict between the government and insurgents, as in Syria; between a Saudi-backed government-in-exile and a rival insurgent government that controls most populated areas, as in Yemen; between rival administrations and their associated militias, as in Libya; between a fledgling government and an occupation force as in the West Bank and Gaza Strip; or between a would-be state and an existing state, as in (as of this writing) the lingering presence of ISIS (the Islamic State in Iraq and Syria) in Syria.

It is therefore important to add an additional question to those posed previously: Are elections the only currency of politics? If they are

Table 2.1 Democratic Significance of Elections in the Middle East

	Have Full-Suffrage, Direct National Legislative Elections Been Held?	Are Such Elections the Only Currency of Politics?	Are Elections Repeated at Regular Intervals?	Can Incumbents Lose Elections?	Can (Nonincumbent) Winners Form Governments?	Can Elected Governments Actually Govern?
Israel	✓	✓	✓	✓	✓	✓
Tunisia	✓	✓	✓	✓	✓	✓
Iraq	✓	✓	✓	✓	✓	✓
Turkey	✓	✓	✓	?	?	?
Morocco	✓	✓	✓	✓	✓	Monarch
Iran	✓	✓	✓	✓	✓	Leader
Kuwait	✓	✓	✓	✓		
Egypt	✓	✓	✓			
Algeria	✓	✓	✓			
Bahrain	✓	✓	✓			
Jordan	✓	✓	✓			
Oman	✓	✓	✓			
United Arab Emirates						
Qatar						
Saudi Arabia						
Syria	✓	Civil war	✓			
Lebanon	✓	Militias				
Libya	✓	Militias				
Yemen	✓	War				
West Bank	✓	Occupation				
Gaza Strip	✓	Externally imposed border closures, air and maritime controls, blockades, and boycotts				

not, and if foreign armies and/or domestic insurgents or militias figure prominently in politics, the democratic significance of elections clearly is tempered. One way to think about the development of democracy is as reflecting the extent to which political violence is minimized in a society over time. Political violence is never fully expunged from any political system, but in democratic states, armed conflict is reconfigured such that major policies and issues are decided by peaceful if hard bargaining between rival political parties—rather than by bullets.

Are Elections Repeated at Regular Intervals?

A key criterion for democratic elections is that they are repeated at regular intervals and not subject to cancellation or delay by incumbents (see the third column of Table 2.1). Unelected power holders can decide to delay or suspend elections at whim, so it is especially important for the electoral process to be predictable and organized at regular intervals. Elections lose meaning as a means of popular control over government if their scheduling is opaque or erratic. For example, Jordan's King Hussein postponed general elections from 1967 to 1989 and closed parliament from 1974 to 1984. In Algeria in 1992, military leaders canceled that nation's first competitive legislative elections after an Islamist political party, the Islamic Salvation Front (FIS), was poised to win. Tragically, this action sank Algeria into a decade-long civil war between the military-led government and armed insurgent offshoots of the FIS. Ironically, both presidential and parliamentary elections continued to be held during the civil war. But with such pervasive political violence, one must question how meaningful such elections were, not least since they were held under the supervision of a military that had already showed itself to be incapable of accepting the outcome of a free vote.

This brings us back to the issue of political violence. How do we make sense of elections in political systems where there is considerable political violence, waged either by armed forces of the state or armed militias outside state control? How do we classify countries where the currency of political power is both elections and political violence? Again, violence can never be fully expunged from a political community. The challenge is to prevent the conditions leading to violence so that it occurs at the margins of the political process, not at its core. That requires that the political process be inclusive enough to accommodate all of a country's interest groups and factions. Since most political violence involves struggles to control or get access to the state, the establishment of legal opposition parties is crucial for channeling competition over the state into peaceful forums. Power-sharing and the creation of opportunities for different groups to take turns being in government are key to reducing political violence. Table 2.1 demonstrates how rare such opportunities are in the Middle East, for, as we move from left to right, there are fewer and fewer countries that meet all of the criteria for meaningful democratic elections.

Can Incumbents Lose Elections?

To assess the democratic significance of any given election, perhaps the most important question that must be asked is, Can ruling elites or parties lose elections? For elections to be considered serious, the group of people who govern must be able to be unseated if they have lost the public's confidence. Otherwise, if elections are held (even regularly and repeatedly) but power-holders never lose despite widespread political discontent, then polls serve as grand spectacles that project the government's power rather than meaningful procedures that allow citizens to choose their governments. Elections-as-spectacle are precisely what many former Arab presidents engaged in. In 1989, Tunisia's then president Ben Ali staged elections in which he won 99 percent of the vote and his party, the Democratic Constitutional Rally (RCD), won all 141 seats in parliament. Such contests, in which opposition parties have no real chance of winning due to government manipulation, can be thought of as opportunities for the rulers to flaunt their power rather than occasions for citizens to choose their rulers.

The fourth column in Table 2.1 shows that fewer than half of the countries that hold legislative elections meet this criterion of incumbent parties losing. A defining moment in Middle East politics when a dominant party lost elections and gave up power peacefully occurred in Turkey in 1950, when the Republican People's Party lost to the opposition Democrat Party, ending the hegemony of the party established by the founder of republican Turkey, Mustafa Kemal Atatürk. A second such defining moment was in 1977 in Israel, when the dominant Labor party lost to the rising Likud party, established just four years earlier. In this regard, the post–Arab Spring era's defining moment came in Tunisia where, after winning a plurality in that country's first democratic election in 2011, the Islamist En-Nahda party came in second in 2014; it proceeded to relinquish its right to lead a coalition government to the plurality-winning secularist Nidaa Tounes party. Such moments are rare occurrences in the region, however.

In Iran, the 1997 presidential election was important because it was the first time that the candidate favored by the Leader lost. The relatively unknown reformist Mohammad Khatami won with 70 percent of the vote in an election that saw 80 percent turnout (the previous presidential election had only 50 percent turnout). This upset was followed by more victories for upstart reformists, who captured 75 percent of the vote in local elections in 1999, 80 percent of the vote in parliamentary elections in 2000, and a second term for Khatami as president with 80 percent of the vote in 2001 (Abrahamian 2008: 188). In 2009, perhaps seeking to avoid a reprise of the Khatami phenomenon, Leader Ali Khamenei and other conservative clerics in Iran's government blocked the popular reformist presidential candidate, Mir-Hossein Mousavi, from winning by engineering the victory of their favored candidate, incumbent Mahmoud Ahmadinejad, via vote-rigging. The maneuver led to massive street demonstrations and the formation of the Green Movement as an oppositional social movement. Perhaps as a testament to this movement's impact, presidential elections in 2013 and 2017 do not appear to have been tainted by electoral fraud.

Iran in 2009 is not the only example of incumbent leaders refusing to lose elections. Perhaps the most famous case of incumbent leaders refusing to lose elections was introduced above: that of Algeria in 1991–1992. After gaining independence from France in 1962, Algeria had a one-party political system that banned opposition parties. This changed in 1989 when massive protests against unemployment and inflation compelled Algeria's leaders to legalize opposition political parties and allow them to contest elections. The FIS captured 55 percent of the vote in local elections in 1990 and 47 percent of the vote in the first round of parliamentary elections in 1991. The FIS was poised to win an absolute majority of seats in the legislature in a second round of voting, but the military stepped in, canceled the elections, and banned the FIS. The ensuing civil war claimed 150,000 lives, demonstrating the lengths to which some incumbents will go to avoid being unseated in elections.

Can (Nonincumbent) Electoral Victors Form Governments?

It seems counterintuitive, but winning an election is no guarantee that the victorious party will actually get to form a government, that is, appoint cabinet ministers—or, if the country has a parliamentary system, seat a prime minister from the winning party. Refer to the fifth column of Table 2.1. The case of the constitutional monarchy of Kuwait is interesting here. Since its independence from Britain in 1962, the country has possessed the Gulf's most assertive parliament, elected in robust national elections. The fifty-member parliament has the power to vote cabinet ministers out of office, including the prime minister, but does not have the ability to appoint the government, a prerogative claimed by the ruling Al Sabah dynasty. Since 2006, the elected parliament has been locked in battle with the Kuwaiti emir over the right to fill top cabinet positions, a battle that has seen the resignation of several governments. The struggle spilled out into street demonstrations that peaked in November 2011, when 50,000 demonstrators demanded the resignation of the prime minister (a nephew of the emir). In a sign of the increasing influence of both parliamentary opposition and youth-led social movements, the emir acceded to the protesters' demands and replaced the prime minister with another royal family member. But that did not appease the opposition, which is not backing down from its core demand to appoint the government. Yet the Al Sabah are not prepared to make this concession and have battled back in a variety of ways, including by altering electoral rules to weaken its parliamentary opposition, harassing opposition leaders and critical media, and dissolving multiple parliaments.

Can Elected Governments Actually Govern?

The protracted power struggle in Kuwait reveals a fundamental dynamic of democratization: struggles between elected and unelected branches of government. Recall the theme of this chapter, how citizens come to control their government. We know that elections are one means by which citizens control governments, by choosing the people who exercise government power and holding them to account. But what about powerful institutions of government that are not elected, such as monarchs, judiciaries, clerics, and militaries? In theory, elected branches of government serve as watchdogs over these unelected institutions, but what happens when the unelected parts of the government control the elected parts?

This is the problem addressed by the final criterion of our litmus test. Refer to the last column of Table 2.1 and observe how rare it is for elected officials actually to be able to govern in the Middle East and North Africa. Why should this be? Remember that the underlying point of our criteria is to identify whether or not entrenched, unelected power blocs subvert the purpose of elections. We can imagine a scenario where elections are held, incumbents lose, winners are congratulated and even allowed to form a government—yet their efforts are short-circuited or their ability to govern is circumscribed by powerful unelected institutions or elites. Let's consider this dynamic of antidemocratic obstruction according to the type of elite that intervenes.

One familiar culprit is a politicized military elite that puts itself above the political fray but seeks to control the normal political process so that it always has the last word. Since canceling elections altogether—as the Algerian military did in 1992—incurs domestic and international condemnation, military generals who don't like the results of elections sometimes pursue more subtle means of intervention. One tactic is to let an election run its course, allow the winners to form a government, but then manipulate events to force the government out of office. This is what happened in Turkey in 1997 when the military high command engaged in a "postmodern" coup. Rather than deploy tanks to oust the elected prime minister Necmettin Erbakan, the generals compelled him to adopt unpopular policies that eventually forced him to step down. Soon after, the promilitary Constitutional Court closed Erbakan's Welfare Party. The unelected parts of the Turkish government colluded to overturn the voters' will because the party chosen by the electorate threatened the interests of entrenched state elites. Today the Turkish military's ability to intervene in politics is much reduced due to reforms demanded by the European Union (EU) that increased civilian control over the military and a steep drop in public support for military interference in politics.

A meddling military has more tricks up its sleeve to limit the reach of elected branches of government. It can allow an opposition party to win elections and form a government, but it can then "fence off" particular policy areas and government positions from oversight by elected officials. This is what political scientist Samuel Valenzuela calls creating "reserve domains" and "reserve positions" (1990). After Egypt's uprising, Egyptian military generals pursued these tactics when they realized that they could not rig presidential elections in 2012 the way their former leader Husni Mubarak had. Soon after polls closed, the generals issued a decree that stated that declaring war and appointing constitution-writers was their domain, not the elected president's, and that the minister of defense would be a position reserved for one of their own, not a civilian presidential appointee. Egyptian politics looked set to be a military-managed affair until the newly elected president, Mohammad Morsi, turned the tables on the generals a couple of months later and wrested back presidential powers. This did not last long, however: the military ousted Morsi from the presidency in 2013. Under the ensuing administration of President Abdel Fattah al-Sisi—former chief of military intelligence and minister of defense—the Egyptian military continued to enjoy significant autonomy from civilian control and oversight.

It is not only military generals who seek to limit the reach of elected officials. Monarchs too are very wary of elected parliaments and their demands to appoint and dismiss cabinet officials, as we have seen in the case of Kuwait. Thus, kings wall off sensitive government positions from control by elected bodies. A pertinent case here is Morocco, where King Mohammed VI hastily organized constitutional reforms and presided over parliamentary elections in 2011 to avoid the diffusion of regional protest to his country. Under the new constitution, the king relinquished his sacred status and agreed to pick a prime minister from the majority party in parliament. In legislative elections in 2011 and 2016, the Islamist Justice and Development Party won and its chief was duly asked by the king to form a government. But with that same constitution, King Mohammed VI reserved for himself key policy domains and positions, retaining control of the religious establishment, the military, and the security services, as well as veto power over all ministerial appointments. All laws must still be confirmed by the king (Lust 2011).

More unusual is interference by clerics in the workings of elected governments. The relevant case here is Iran. Unlike Turkey's and Egypt's military generals, who intervened in the democratic process after elections brought to power political parties that threatened their interests, Iran's clerics control key steps *before* elections. For example, in the 2004 parliamentary elections, to avoid a repeat of the 2000 elections when reformists won 195 of 290 Majles (parliament) seats, clerics disqualified 2,300 candidates out of more than 8,000 (Tezcür 2008: 58). In effect, Iran's clerics control both the input and output sides of elections, controlling who runs in elections and, for good measure, also having the final say on laws that elected bodies produce. The Leader has vast reserve domains, appointing the heads of the judiciary, the armed forces and police, radio and television, prayer leaders in city mosques, and the Supreme National and Security Council. It is no surprise that the dynamics of contemporary Iranian politics revolve around the struggle for freer and fairer elections as a pathway into the longer-term struggle to empower elected parts of the Iranian state over its unelected parts.

One of the most unusual and dramatic instances where an opposition party won general elections, formed a government, but was prevented from governing was in early 2006, when the Palestinian militia–cum–political party–cum–social welfare organization Hamas defeated the dominant standard-bearer of Palestinian politics, Fatah. The upset was particularly dramatic because Hamas had never before participated in national legislative elections, having rejected them as a charade of the Oslo peace process, which it had taken up arms to oppose. The obstructing actors here were not military generals, monarchs, or clerics threatened by an opposition party coming to power but rather a coalition of powerful international powers that had supported the losing incumbent Fatah party. The governments of the United States, Israel, and the European Union boycotted the Hamas government for its refusal to recognize Israel and give up its armed wing, depriving it of the international aid on which the Palestinian Authority government had historically relied. To further strangle the fledgling government,

Israel withheld Palestinian tax revenues, resulting in widespread discontent among 150,000 state employees (including doctors, teachers, and security personnel) who received only half their salaries in 2006. Power-sharing agreements between the losing Fatah party and Hamas failed, and a civil war ensued that split the Palestinian Authority into a Fatah-controlled Palestinian National Authority in the West Bank and a Hamas government in the Gaza Strip.

The 2006 Palestinian legislative elections and the 1991 Algerian elections illustrate the lengths to which entrenched powers will go to reverse the outcomes of democratic elections, even if the cost is a debilitating civil war. The ability of citizens to choose their governments unsettles established networks of power and upends existing hierarchies. It is no surprise that incumbent elites often do everything possible to limit the transformative potential of democratic elections.

Conclusion

Citizens who took to the streets in Tunisia, Egypt, Libya, and the rest of the countries that experienced massive popular protests in 2011 may not have explicitly called for free and fair elections (although many did). Their demands were phrased in more abstract and more basic terms, centering on popular participation in government and a say in how public policies are made. On the third day of the eighteen-day Egyptian uprising that would eventually topple Mubarak, a twenty-nine-year-old glass factory worker told a reporter, "It's our right to choose our government ourselves. We have been living 29 years, my whole life, without being able to choose a president. I've grown bald, and Mubarak has stayed Mubarak," he said, rubbing his bare scalp (Dziadosz 2011). Nearly two years later in Jordan, during large, unprecedented demonstrations calling for the ouster of King Abdullah II, a twenty-two-year-old medical student said to a journalist, "When the people choose their government, they will accept the government's decisions—even a price hike—because then it is a decision of the people, too. It is not just a matter of money. It is about the will of the people" (Kirkpatrick 2012).

When protesters did cite elections, they were keen to distinguish between the rigged polls used by autocratic leaders and the free, fair contests citizens wanted to see. In October 2011, thousands of Moroccans demonstrated against the parliamentary elections announced by King Mohammed VI. "It is obvious that the polls will bring to power the same figures who have for years been plundering the wealth of the country and holding hostage the future of the Moroccan population," an activist from the February 20 protest movement said. Protesters chanted, "The elections are a charade; you will not fool us this time" (Karam 2011).

Citizens in the Middle East and North Africa have long struggled against the abuse of elections by autocratic leaders, either resisting openly by protesting in the streets and braving government intimidation to cast votes for opposition candidates, or staying home and refusing to participate in sham contests. The extraordinary wave of popular empowerment that surged through the region beginning in 2011 for a time gave new momentum to long-standing efforts by citizens to control their governments and keep them in check. First-time honest, competitive elections in Tunisia, Egypt, and Libya raised citizens' hopes that such elections would be repeated until they became routine features of their countries' political systems, and that citizens could work toward empowering the elected institutions of government against the obstructionist, interventionist ambitions of unelected power centers.

As sociologist Charles Tilly would point out, the work of crafting representative, responsive governments is a herculean collective endeavor. Indeed, the varied outcomes of the Arab Spring demonstrate that that work can come up against persistent roadblocks (Libya), break down altogether (Yemen and Syria), or turn into forms of reconstructed autocratic rule (Egypt). Democracy is attractive in theory but very difficult to birth in practice, since it threatens very powerful interests and established hierarchies. As you read through the rest of the book and learn more about additional factors affecting government-opposition relations, keep in mind Robert Dahl's two key questions: What would it take to introduce a system of peaceful legal opposition in environments where it does not exist? And what would it take to maintain such a system?

Notes

1. "The Hashemites: Jordan's Royal Family," King Hussein I, February 28, 2013, http://www.kinghussein.gov.jo/hashemites.html.

2. "King Abdul Aziz Al Saud," The Saudi Network, February 28, 2013, http://www.the-saudi.net/al-saud/abdulaziz.htm.

3

The Impact of International Politics

F. Gregory Gause III and Curtis R. Ryan

Domestic politics can at times be influenced and even overshadowed by external factors in international politics. That seems to be particularly true of the Middle East, as a regional system that has so often been a focal point for local, intraregional, and global power struggles. In every country in the Middle East, therefore, domestic politics can be deeply affected by external factors as well as factors internal to that country. The Middle East has often been viewed as a "subordinate" system, incorporated into a global order largely by the imperial machinations of Western powers, which drew many of the borders and have continued to influence regional affairs even long after independence from European powers. This chapter examines the influences of international politics on the domestic politics of the contemporary Middle East. We do this in two ways. First, we examine how the region has been affected by global politics, and especially by the region's placement in the global order, from the international political economy to the geopolitics of the international system. Second, we examine how regional dynamics—from transnational dimensions to the Arab uprisings and regional wars—have affected internal politics across the Middle East.

The Global System and the Middle East

The Middle East is located in three intersecting global systems, each one exerting its own pushes and pulls on the local states: the international economic system, the international geopolitical system, and the new global normative structure in which Western standards of human rights and governance are increasingly enshrined in international covenants while their observance is considered the entrance price for participating in some international institutions.

The International Economic System and the Middle East

Globalization is not a new phenomenon in the Middle East. The region has a long historical role as an entrepôt and middleman in East-West trade. Since the beginning of the nineteenth century, more of its trade was directed toward an ascendant Europe than toward South and East Asia, which had been the dominant trading pattern previously. Middle Eastern and North African producers of agricultural and primary products geared production for the European market. Egyptian cotton, Syrian and Lebanese silk, and Algerian wine were exported to Europe. As noted in Chapter 1, European economic strength and political influence combined to open Middle Eastern markets to European manufactured goods, displacing local industry in many cases. European capital poured into the region in the nineteenth century, building the Suez Canal, railroads, and ports, and financing the deficits of the Ottoman, Egyptian, Tunisian, and Persian governments (Issawi 1982: chaps. 2, 4). These trade and capital flows pulled the region more closely into the European orbit, facilitating and justifying European interventions in local politics throughout the century.

Regions less integrated into the European-based global economy in the nineteenth century, particularly the Arabian Peninsula, became more so with the development of their oil resources in the twentieth century. While many of the newly independent Middle Eastern states adopted statist, if not autarkic, policies in the early and middle twentieth century to reduce the influence of outside powers in their countries (Turkey and Egypt are examples), Middle East oil exporters were becoming important parts of the global capitalist economy. Foreign capital developed the energy resources of Algeria, Libya, Iraq, Saudi Arabia, Iran, and the smaller Gulf states, providing governments with the money to build larger and more extensive states. While these governments benefited from their oil riches, the role of foreign oil companies in their politics excited nationalist opposition, which in turn led the home governments of these companies to intervene in local politics to protect these strategic investments. The most notorious of these efforts was the US-British operation in Iran in 1953 that led to the overthrow of Prime Minister Mohammad Mossadeq, who had nationalized the Anglo-Iranian Oil Company in 1951, and the restoration of the Shah of Iran to power. While the United States was motivated more by Cold War concerns, British intervention was aimed at preserving economic interests (Gasiorowski and Byrne 2004).

All of the Middle Eastern energy producers took control of their oil industries from the international energy companies in the 1970s and 1980s as part of the world energy markets revolution that drove up prices and shifted power from consumer to producer countries. They remain highly integrated into the world economy, though the levels of their exports as a proportion of their gross domestic product (GDP) fluctuate with oil prices and with political factors like civil and regional wars (see Table 3.1). Governments in oil states reaped enormous revenues from the price increases and their new control of their natural resources. These windfalls allowed them to build "rentier" states, relying on revenues that accrued directly to their treasuries from the international economic system to fund their budgets rather than having to tax their own populations. It is generally agreed that vast oil wealth strengthens authoritarian tendencies and reduces the chances of democratic development in rentier states (Ross 2001; Anderson 2001; Bellin 2004). Beyond that, there are important debates about the specific political consequences of oil wealth, referenced in Chapter 4, on political economy.

While the Middle Eastern oil states were being integrated into the world economy in the twentieth century, many of the nonoil states of the region were trying to decouple themselves from the world economy and pursue development strategies that emphasized local industrialization and de-emphasized reliance on international trade. However, as Chapter 4

Table 3.1 Exports as Percentage of GDP, 1970–2015

	1970	1975	1980	1985	1990	1995	2000	2005	2010	2015
Nonenergy economies										
Egypt	15	18	28	18	20	23	16	30	25[a]	13
Israel	31	33	44	44	34	29	38	45	37	37
Jordan	8	31	39	37	63	52	42	52	46[a]	38
Morocco	18	23	15	20	24	23	26	32	33	34
Syria	17	21	18	12	28	31	36	42	29[a]	n.a.
Tunisia	22	31	41	33	43	45	45	48	49	44[b]
Turkey	6	7	7	21	20	20	24	27	21	23[b]
Energy-exporting economies										
Algeria	24	34	34	24	24	27	42	48	38	23
Iran	20	41	13	8	15	22	23	29	28	20
Saudi Arabia	59	84	71	36	46	38	44	59	58	33

Sources: International Monetary Fund, *International Financial Statistics Yearbook 1994* (for 1970–1990 data), *International Financial Statistics Yearbook 2007* (for 1995–2005 data), and *International Financial Statistics Yearbook 2012* (for 2009–2010 data) (Washington, DC, 1994, 2007, and 2012). Percentages calculated from lines 90c and 99b of the country tables in these yearbooks; 2015 data are from https://www.theglobaleconomy.com/rankings/Exports.

Notes: n.a. indicates data are not available. a. 2009 data. b. 2017 data.

explains, these strategies, while generating impressive economic growth rates in the 1950s and into the 1960s, by the 1970s were unable to sustain the economic growth necessary to keep pace with population growth (Richards and Waterbury 2008: chap. 8; Henry and Springborg 2001: chaps. 1–2). A number of Middle Eastern states then shifted their development strategies toward export-led growth and sought to reintegrate into the global capitalist economy. The emirate of Dubai in the United Arab Emirates (UAE) has gone the furthest in this regard, attempting to become a global center for trade, tourism, and services on the model of Hong Kong and Singapore (Davidson 2008).

Among the larger economies, Israel, Turkey, Morocco, and Tunisia took the most dramatic steps to adopt the "Washington Consensus" by aligning their economies with the recommendations of international financial institutions like the International Monetary Fund and the World Bank. In each of these cases, outside actors played a major role in encouraging these policy changes and providing financial support for the transition. In the 1980s, the United States essentially midwived the Israeli switch by making emergency aid to Israel, which was mired in an inflationary economic crisis, contingent on the adoption of more liberal and market-oriented policies. The United States and the European Union opened their markets to Turkish exports and provided foreign aid to Turkey to cushion its economic transition, while the hope of EU membership pushed Turkish politicians to liberalize the economy further. Tunisia and Morocco benefited from preferential access to the EU market and various EU programs aimed at encouraging economic development along the Mediterranean rim (Richards and Waterbury 2008: chap. 9). (See Table 3.1 for the increasing role of exports in these countries' economies.)

While a few of the nonoil Middle Eastern states followed the zeitgeist of the late twentieth century and adopted Washington Consensus policies, many of them did not, or did so only in a halfhearted way. The Egyptian government, for example, feared the domestic political consequences of fully liberalizing its economy. Lifting food subsidies already had led to riots on more than one occasion. Opening the country fully to imports from abroad risked undercutting state-protected industrial manufacturers in Egypt and thus imperiling the jobs of Egyptians employed in this sector. So, Egypt moved very slowly on economic reform. One of the reasons it was able to avoid the kind of wrenching economic transition other countries have experienced is the amount of foreign aid it received from the United States since it signed a peace treaty with Israel in 1979. For decades, Egypt used its strategic position to extract military aid, economic aid, and other concessions from great powers and regional neighbors.

A good example of how Egypt was able to avoid the kind of fiscal crisis that frequently accompanies the statist policies it had followed, while dodging pressures for full-scale implementation of Washington Consensus policies, occurred during the Gulf War of 1990–1991. The government of president Husni Mubarak had run up a considerable foreign debt during the 1980s, postponing hard economic choices and subsidizing consumption. By the end of the decade, it was facing a serious debt crisis. Normally, the kind of debt relief Egypt needed would come only from international financial institutions, with stringent requirements for implementation of Washington Consensus policies. Then Saddam Hussein invaded Kuwait in August 1990. Egypt's support was so central to the construction of the US-led international coalition that expelled the Iraqis from Kuwait that Mubarak was able to get billions of dollars of official debt forgiven by the United States and European countries, negotiate more favorable repayment terms on Egypt's debt to Western private sector creditors, and garner billions in aid from the Gulf oil states. Economic crisis averted!

But Egypt's ability to play the strategic card was not unbounded. Pressures built for more serious implementation of Washington Consensus policies. After the appointment of Prime Minister Ahmed Nazif in 2004, Egypt took more serious steps to reduce consumer subsidies and dismantle the state sector of the economy. Egyptian exports as a percentage of GDP increased from the high teens and low twenties in the 1980s and 1990s to 30 percent in 2005 (see Table 3.1). The consequences included increased labor unrest and further limitations on political activism, preparing the ground for the upheaval of 2011 that forced Mubarak from office (Richards and Waterbury 2008: chap. 9; Henry and Springborg 2001: chap. 5).

It is interesting to note that the first two governments to fall in the Arab Spring of 2011 were Tunisia and Egypt, where economic liberalization had progressed further than in many other Arab countries. While the Washington Consensus agenda did lead to economic growth in both, it did little to address issues of unemployment, inequality, and corruption. Those exact issues ranked high on the list of grievances leading to the uprisings. In their aftermath, which saw the ouster of both the Tunisian and Egyptian presidents, Tunisia pursued more of a standard neoliberal economic model, working closely with Western powers and global economic institutions. Egypt, in contrast, remained mired in a chronic economic crisis, but its increasingly authoritarian regime—under President Abdel Fatah al-Sisi—continued to parlay Egypt's perceived geopolitical importance into vast amounts of US economic and military aid.

The Egyptian case illustrates the fact that most Middle Eastern states, because of their energy resources, strategic locations, or close ties with outside powers, retain some bargaining power in the international economy. They are not in a situation of dependency, where they are subject to the vagaries of international economic forces with little or no power to influence how those forces affect them. But they are not economic powerhouses. Their bargaining leverage is limited. They find themselves in a situation of asymmetric interdependence with the major players in the world economy, policy "takers" more than policymakers, but still able to affect the terms of their integration into the world economy.

Turkey's candidacy for membership in the European Union was the most far-reaching effort by a Middle Eastern state to integrate into the larger global economy by joining an international organization. Turkey applied for membership in 1987, with the EU officially granting Turkey candidate status in 1999. But the negotiations on actual membership bogged down, and Ankara began to give up hope of ever achieving full membership status. Still, in order to advance its candidacy, Turkey made substantial changes in its economic and legal systems to bring them into accord with EU standards. It also enjoyed the benefits of trade access to the EU, which since the mid-1980s had allowed Turkish industries to reconfigure themselves to serve the European market (see Table 3.1). With the rise of the Justice and Development Party (AKP) in Turkey, and in particular of Recep Tayyip Erdoğan (as prime minister, from 2003 to 2014, and president since 2014), Turkish-EU relations have soured, as has Turkish interest in joining the EU.

The Turkish effort to join the EU was the most important international integration step by a Middle Eastern country, but it was not the only one. The United States has negotiated free trade agreements with Bahrain, Israel, Jordan, Morocco, and Oman. Negotiations with other states are ongoing. Only five Middle Eastern states are not members of the World Trade Organization (WTO): Algeria, Libya, Syria, Iraq, and Iran—although each of these holds observer status within the WTO. These linkages have led to changes in the economic policies of the states involved, toward greater openness to the world economy. Iran, closed out of several international economic organizations and agreements for political reasons, has looked toward the Indian Ocean and East Asia for economic integration. Trade and other economic agreements with these states do not require the kinds of liberalizing domestic economic change that free trade agreements with the United States or the European Union do. Even Syria, one of the least "reformed" economies of the region, saw the role of exports in its economy grow, though almost 50 percent of its exports in the 2000s went to Iraq and Lebanon, two countries whose recent political circumstances gave Syria a larger role in their economies than would probably have been the case otherwise (see Table 3.1). The ongoing Syrian civil war reversed those tentative steps toward a more export-focused economy, however.

Trade and finance are not the only means by which Middle Eastern states are integrated into the world economy. Labor movements across regional lines also tie together the economies of sending and receiving regions. Sending countries usually receive labor remittances from their nationals working abroad; receiving countries frequently experience social problems when integrating large foreign worker populations into their societies. Foreign workers can also develop new political identities when living abroad. The fact that the September 11, 2001, terrorist plot was hatched in Germany among Arabs working there who were sympathetic to al-Qaeda indicates that labor migration is not just an economic phenomenon. Middle Easterners working in Europe are a key regional linkage. In the early 2000s there were an estimated 1.4 million Moroccans, 1.3 million Algerians, 436,000 Tunisians, and 3.2 million Turks living in the European Union. Remittances accounted for 8.5 percent of Morocco's GDP and 5.1 percent of Tunisia's GDP in 2004. A second important linkage is between the Arab states of the Persian Gulf and the Indian Subcontinent. In 2002 it was estimated that 3.2 million Indians, 1.7 million Pakistanis, 820,000 Bangladeshis, and 705,000 Sri Lankans were working in the states of the Gulf Cooperation Council (GCC) (Richards and Waterbury 2008: chap. 15).

The degree of integration of Middle Eastern states into the international economy has had a significant effect on their own economies and thus their politics. Oil countries have benefited from their integration into the world petroleum and financial systems, reaping windfalls during high price periods and being able to sustain programs that subsidize consumer goods and provide state employment to their citizens. However, oil states have suffered economically and, on occasion, found themselves victims of political instability when oil prices turned down. Some nonoil Middle Eastern countries, with the encouragement and assistance of international actors, adopted the liberal economic policies urged by Washington and the international financial institutions in the 1980s and 1990s, significantly changing their political economies. Other nonoil states resisted those pressures for liberal market reforms and received support from international patrons that helped them sustain elements of their more statist economies for longer than would have been the case otherwise. In all cases, both the position of Middle Eastern states in the international political economy and their relations with specific outside actors help explain their domestic political economies.

The International Geopolitical System and the Middle East

Because of geographical proximity and the importance of transit routes to the east, the Middle East has been entwined with the European international political system for centuries. Before the nineteenth century, the relationship was more between equals, with European intrusions into the region (the Crusades) balanced by Middle Eastern intrusions into Europe (from the Muslim conquest of Spain in the eighth century to Ottoman advances into southeastern Europe through the seventeenth century). But since Napoleon's conquest of Egypt in 1798, it has been the European powers (and the United States) that have been doing the intervening in the Middle East. Except for northern Yemen and central and western Arabia, every part of the Middle East was under European military control at some time in the twentieth century. In the second half of the twentieth century it was the United States and the Soviet Union that competed for influence in the region. The oil resources of the Persian Gulf have attracted great-power interest since the beginning of the twentieth century. The September 11 attacks on the United States, perpetrated by nineteen Arab men affiliated with al-Qaeda, led to further Western interventions in the region, with the United States invading Afghanistan in 2001 and Iraq in 2003. The United States justified its military interventions as part of a global "war on terror," and this rhetoric continued as the invasions were followed by instability, insurgency, and increased levels of terrorism. In 2014, a militant jihadist group declared itself a state—the Islamic State in Iraq and Syria (ISIS)—prompting outside intervention in both countries, from regional and global powers alike.

The most consequential effect of outside-power interventions on the domestic politics of many Middle Eastern states, dating back to the early twentieth century, was the very creation of those states in the first place. Libya, Jordan, Syria, Lebanon, Iraq, and the United Arab Emirates had never existed as independent political entities, in their current or any other borders, before they were created by Italian, French, and British colonial authorities. Even states that had some claim to an independent, precolonial history saw their borders drawn and their modern state governments created by European colonialism. Egypt and Iran, ancient civilizations with millennial state histories, were occupied by European powers whose interventions set the course of their modern politics. The same can be said of Morocco, a kingdom with a centuries-long history of independence before the twentieth century. Only Turkey and Saudi Arabia owe their modern foundations primarily to indigenous political movements—Mustafa Kemal Atatürk's nationalist movement in the wake of World War I and Abdulaziz Ibn Saud's religious-dynastic campaign in the first three decades of the twentieth century. In both cases, European pressures helped to determine the borders of the new states and European recognition cemented the two statebuilders' achievements. In the Saudi case, British financial support was an invaluable contribution to Abdulaziz's success. While history in the Middle East did not begin with European colonialism, European colonialism basically drew the map of the modern Middle East.

As described in Chapter 1, the age of direct European control of the region ended in the two decades after World War II, but the emergence of independent Middle Eastern states did not end the interest of outside powers in the region or their interventions in its politics. Great-power involvement did not have uniform consequences, however. In some cases outsiders overthrew Middle Eastern governments and, as in the case of the US occupation of Iraq in 2003, completely restructured a Middle Eastern state. But many Middle Eastern regimes were able to use outside powers' interest in the area to gain resources and support for their domestic and foreign policies, sometimes for their very survival. Skillful (and lucky) Middle Eastern rulers could play international politics in ways that bolstered their rule; unskillful (and unlucky) rulers lost their thrones, their offices, and even their lives because they crossed a world power.

The examples of outside-power interventions that brought down leaders are dramatic and clear. During World War II, British and Soviet forces occupied Iran in 1941 and deposed its ruler, Reza Shah Pahlavi (aka Reza Khan), whom they (rightly) suspected of contacts with Nazi Germany. The occupiers placed his young son, Mohammad Reza, on the throne as the new Shah. As mentioned, in 1953 US and British intelligence operatives coordinated an effort to bring down Iranian prime minister Mohammad Mossadeq, who had nationalized British oil interests in 1951 and who the United States feared would bring Iran into the Soviet orbit. Not all Cold War intelligence operations in the Middle East were so successful, however. Efforts by the Central Intelligence Agency (CIA) to destabilize what Washington saw as pro-Soviet leaders in Egypt and Syria in the 1950s and 1960s backfired.

The end of the Cold War did not end great-power meddling in the domestic politics of regional states. The US invasion of Iraq in 2003 was aimed at replacing the regime of Saddam Hussein and his Baath Party. Having accomplished that in relatively short order, the United States took on the more ambitious task of restructuring the entire Iraqi state, disbanding the army and gutting the bureaucracy through decisions made a few months after the invasion (Ricks 2007). US occupation authorities and military commanders attempted to rebuild Iraqi military and civilian institutions, with mixed success, up until the US military withdrawal in 2011. The ultimate results of the US occupation of Iraq remain to be seen, but there is no denying that the intervention has dramatically changed the course of Iraqi political history. Another example of outside actors altering the political trajectory of a Middle Eastern state is the US, British, and French air support that was essential to the victory of the Libyan rebels who brought down Muammar Qaddafi in 2011.

Less obviously but no less importantly, great-power policies have also on occasion contributed to the strengthening of Middle Eastern states and regimes. Middle Eastern states occupy important strategic locations, and they have been able to use great powers' interests in them to extract resources from those powers. The Cold War competition between the United States and the Soviet Union provided the context for a number of regional leaders to obtain economic and military aid and political support from the superpowers. Egypt is an excellent example of how local rulers exploited the Cold War rivalry to their benefit. In the 1950s, Egyptian president Gamal Abdel Nasser received economic aid from both superpowers and military supplies from the Soviet Union, as Moscow and Washington each tried to bring the largest Arab state into its orbit. When Egypt was attacked in 1956 by Israel, Great Britain, and France after Nasser's nationalization of the Suez Canal, both the United States and the Soviet Union supported him and helped him turn a military defeat into a political victory. As Nasser became more tightly allied with the Soviet Union in the 1960s, US aid dried up, but the Soviets supplied him with military equipment and helped him build the Aswan Dam (Rubinstein 1977). As the Soviet economic model faltered and Egypt's need for foreign aid grew, Nasser's successor, Anwar Sadat, skillfully repositioned Egypt as an ally of the United States. By making peace with Israel and cooperating with US political and military plans in the region, he was able to make Egypt the second-largest recipient of US foreign aid (after Israel) in the world (Karawan 1994).

While Egypt played the superpowers against each other in the 1950s and switched sides in the 1970s, benefiting all along, other Middle Eastern states picked a Cold War side early and were compensated for their loyalty. Under Soviet pressure for political and military concessions immediately after World War II, Turkey looked to the United States for support, which was forthcoming under the Truman Doctrine. Turkey joined the North Atlantic Treaty Organization (NATO) in 1951 and remains a member of the Western alliance to this day. During the 1950s, Turkey was a major recipient of US military and foreign aid. Morocco and Jordan are also longtime US allies and recipients of US foreign and military aid. Syria, beginning in the 1950s, and Iraq, beginning in the 1960s, were Soviet allies, exploiting the Soviet desire for strategic footholds in the region in order to extract aid from Moscow. Other Middle Eastern states also played the Cold War game and benefited from the superpowers' willingness to trade money and guns for political considerations.

Israel's relationship with the United States also developed in the Cold War context but is buttressed by the strong connections many Americans feel with the Jewish state. Substantial US military aid to Israel began in the 1960s and major economic aid began in the 1970s as Washington gave up hope of drawing Egypt away from the Soviet orbit. US policymakers saw Israel as a counter to Soviet allies in Cairo and Damascus and an asset in the larger contest for Cold War influence in the region. After the Egyptian-Israeli peace treaty of 1979, Israel became the largest recipient of US foreign and military aid in the world. The Cold War's end did not change the relationship: support for Israel among the US public generally and from important organized political groups like American Jewish and fundamentalist Christian supporters of Israel ensured that US aid would continue to flow. (For differing views on the drivers of US support for Israel, see Mearsheimer and Walt 2007 and Organski 1990.)

The US strategic interest in Middle East oil provided regimes in the Persian Gulf with military, economic, and political support from Washington. Saudi Arabia has been the centerpiece of US policy in the area since the end of World War II. US companies developed the Saudi oil industry and, from the 1940s through the 1960s, supplied the Saudi state with invaluable financial and technical assistance to consolidate Saudi family rule in Arabia (Vitalis 2007). The US government built and supplied the Saudi armed forces and provided military protection directly to Saudi Arabia when it was threatened by Egypt's involvement in the Yemen civil war in the 1960s and by Iraq's invasion of Kuwait in 1990. Indeed, Kuwait would not be a Middle Eastern state today had the United States not constructed an international military coalition to turn back Iraq's annexation of the country and fought the Gulf War of 1990–1991.

Yet strong external political support and military and financial aid were no guarantee of regime stability. Mohammad Reza Shah of Iran—installed on his throne by Great Britain and the Soviet Union, restored to power by US and British intelligence agents, recipient of US economic and military aid, and strong ally of the United States—was overthrown in the Iranian revolution of 1978–1979, and the United States, in the words of revolutionary leader Ayatollah Ruhollah Khomeini, "could not do a damn thing." The socialist government of South Yemen, an independent state from 1967 to 1990, relied heavily upon Soviet economic aid and political support. When Mikhail Gorbachev abandoned the Cold War competition with the United States, the South Yemeni leadership chose to unify with North Yemen and, in the process, lost its political clout. Egyptian president Husni Mubarak's close ties to the United States did not help him face down the popular uprising that led to his overthrow in 2011. In the end, the United States supported the Egyptian military when it removed Mubarak from office. So, close ties with great powers do not guarantee protection for Middle East leaders. But some have been able, at various times and in various ways, to exploit outside-power interest in the region in order to extract resources and gain political and military support from those powers, helping them to build their states and solidify their regimes.

The International Normative System and the Middle East

International norms are much less tangible than military interventions or economic aid, but they do have some effect on the domestic politics of some Middle Eastern states. By the "international normative system" we mean the growing belief that Western ideas regarding human and individual rights, international law, and governance standards have universal applicability. Some of these norms are embodied in international covenants (like the UN's Universal Declaration of Human Rights) signed by almost all Middle Eastern states. Others, like the global democracy trend, do not have an international legal basis but set a powerful normative standard that appeals to many people in the region. External governments hold Middle Eastern governments to account for their deficiencies in meeting these standards on occasion, but not frequently. Nongovernmental organizations like Human Rights Watch and Amnesty International call the attention of the world's media to violations by Middle Eastern governments of the rights of their citizens and try to support human rights activists in Middle Eastern countries. New communications technologies bring examples of democratic uprisings in other parts of the world directly to the citizens of Middle Eastern states. While very few Middle Eastern governments live up to these international norms, they can no longer ignore them as they formulate their domestic governing strategies.

For many years, the best example of how the international normative system can affect the domestic politics of Middle Eastern states was Turkey. The Turkish ambition to join the European Union meant that Turkish governments over several decades had to change a range of domestic laws and policies in order to comply with EU standards. Aside from political-economic change from the Atatürkist state-directed economy to a more liberal, export-oriented approach, Turkey also extended new legal rights to the Kurdish minority, abolished the death penalty, and adopted other social legislation to meet EU requirements. Of late under

Erdoğan's leadership, however, Turkey has reasserted a kind of defiant sovereignty, abandoning its attempts to join the EU, and rejecting Western complaints about its human rights record and increasing autocracy.

None of the other Middle Eastern states had as compelling a carrot as EU membership in front of it as a spur to accept these new global norms. But there are other efforts by outside powers to create institutional incentives for these states to better respect human rights and move toward democracy. The EU's Barcelona Process uses economic incentives to prod Middle Eastern states not only to reform their economies but also to improve their domestic governance and promote regional peace and stability (European Union 2008). After the September 11, 2001, terrorist attacks, the United States created a number of programs, including the Middle East Partnership Initiative and, with its Group of Eight (G8) partners, the Broader Middle East and North Africa Initiative, to encourage Arab states to liberalize and democratize (Wittes 2008).

Given the strategic importance of the region to outside powers, Middle Eastern governments are better positioned than their colleagues in other regions to resist external pressures for domestic reform. But Middle Eastern leaders have demonstrated that they do not think they can simply ignore these global trends. Indeed, numerous authoritarian Arab regimes have felt compelled to have "freer" elections than they had in the past three decades or to institute elections where none had existed. Direct US pressure post-9/11 explains some of this movement, but not all of it. Saudi Arabia reinstituted municipal elections in 2005. Bahrain, Qatar, Oman, and the UAE all instituted some form of elections to a national and/or municipal assembly after 1990. In 2005 Egypt conducted the freest parliamentary elections since the military coup of 1952 and changed its constitution to allow for direct election of the president. Jordan restored its elected parliament in 1989 and has since held eight rounds of national parliamentary elections. Algeria has conducted a number of elections for parliament and the presidency since its civil war wound down in the late 1990s. Morocco has held six rounds of parliamentary elections since the 1990s, including two since the start of a liberalization program that led to a new constitution in 2011. In all these cases, authoritarian rulers manipulated the rules and used their power to limit the effects of these democratic experiments (Brumberg 2002; Heydemann 2007). How important the global democracy trend and these tentative democratic steps were to the revolts of the Arab Spring remains an open question. However, it is important to note that every Arab Spring revolt was made in the name of democracy and that free and fair elections followed the fall of dictators in Tunisia, Egypt, and Libya. In the years that followed, Tunisia's tenuous democratization experiment continued, while Egypt slid back into even deeper levels of authoritarianism, and Libya struggled with division and civil strife.

The effects of global norms on Middle Eastern politics should not be exaggerated. Human rights are abused from the Atlantic Ocean to the Persian Gulf and from the Black Sea to the Indian Ocean. Women's roles in society and politics are buffeted among international standards, Islamist groups' interpretations of religion, and local cultural practices. Oil money and strategic location allow Middle Eastern leaders to resist and deflect external pressures for reform. We saw this most recently in Bahrain, where the government suppressed Arab Spring demonstrations with very few international repercussions. The political effects of the global communications revolution are not yet clear, but they do not seem to pressure uniformly in the direction of more democratic politics. Yet we must recognize these external pressures on Middle Eastern governments to adhere to global standards of governance and note that Middle Eastern activists themselves are increasingly using these global standards to call their leaders to account. These standards are now part of the global environment in which Middle Eastern states must function, but within the region, they vary dramatically from country to country.

The Domestic Effects of Middle East Regional Politics

The global system is not the only international context in which Middle Eastern states have to operate. Their own regional interactions can have powerful effects on their domestic politics as well. Middle Eastern states—particularly the Arab states but to some extent other members of the system as well—are tied together by cross-border linkages of ethnicity, language, religion, sect, and tribe. Identity crosses borders, as the dramatic spread of popular demonstrations across the Arab world during the Arab Spring attests. These trans-state identities are a cause of regional conflict and, to a lesser extent, of regional integration. Both the conflicts and the integrative effects are important for understanding the domestic politics of Middle Eastern states.

Regional War and Domestic Politics

There has been no shortage of regional conflict in the Middle East since the end of World War II (see Table 3.2): nine Arab-Israeli wars (depending on how one counts them); the Iran-Iraq War; Iraq's invasion of Kuwait; regional interventions in civil wars in Yemen, Oman, Lebanon, Iraq, and Syria; and border skirmishes and troop buildups at one time or another on almost every international border in the region. War can make the state, in that war forces a state to develop administrative

Table 3.2 Middle East Wars and Conflicts, 1948–2018

Conflict	Years of Conflict	Major Players
Arab-Israeli wars		
Israeli War for Independence	1948–1949	Israel, Egypt, Jordan, Syria, Lebanon
Suez War	1956–1957	Israel, Egypt, France, Great Britain
Six Day War	1967	Israel, Egypt, Syria, Jordan
War of Attrition	1969–1970	Israel, Egypt
Yom Kippur/Ramadan War	1973	Israel, Egypt, Syria
Israeli incursion into southern Lebanon	1978	Israel, Lebanon, PLO
Israeli invasion of Lebanon (final withdrawal in 2000)	1982	Israel, Lebanon, PLO
Israel-Lebanon border war	2006	Israel, Hezbollah
Israel-Hamas wars in the Gaza Strip	2008–2009, 2012, 2014	Israel, Hamas
Gulf wars		
Iran-Iraq War	1980–1988	Iran and Iraq
Gulf War	1990–1991	United States and international coalition v. Iraq
Iraq War	2003–2011	United States and Iraq
Civil wars		
North Yemen (Yemen Arab Republic)	1962–1970	Egypt, Saudi Arabia, Great Britain, United States, Soviet Union
Jordan	1970–1971	PLO, Syria, Israel
Oman	1970–1975	Iran, South Yemen, Great Britain
Lebanon	1975–1991	Syria, Israel, PLO, Iraq, Iran, Libya, Saudi Arabia, United States, Soviet Union
Algeria	1992–early 2000s	France
Iraq	2003–present	United States, Iran, Turkey, Syria, Saudi Arabia
Syria	2011–present	Turkey, Iran, Saudi Arabia, Qatar, United States, Russia
Yemen	2015–present	Yemen (government v. Houthi rebel militias), Saudia Arabia, Iran, UAE, United States
Other persistent militarized disputes		
Western Sahara	1975–present	Morocco, Algeria, Mauritania, Polisario
Kurdish issue	1920–present	Turkey, Iraq, Iran, Syria, and Kurdish groups in each country seeking autonomy and/or independence
Israeli-Palestinian issue	1947–1948, 1987–1991, 2000–present	Israel, PLO, Palestinian Authority, Hamas

capacities and can generate patriotic feelings that link society to the state. But war can break the state—or the regime—as well, particularly on the losing side.

War-making has undoubtedly strengthened the Israeli state and affected its development. Born in war and involved in war almost continuously since its birth, Israel has built a citizen army whose influence pervades Israeli political life. Service in the army is the path to advancement in Israeli society and politics. It has also served as an integrating mechanism for Israel's disparate Jewish communities. The Israeli state developed as a wartime state, with large-scale state control over the economy and society (Barnett 1992). It was only in the 1980s that Israel adopted more liberal economic policies. The particular history of the birth of Israel, in the wake of the Holocaust and amid Arab rejection, has forged a tight bond of patriotism between the state and its Jewish citizens. At the same time, this focus on the threat from the Arab world has made problematic the status of Israel's large Arab citizen minority within Israel's democratic political system. In addition, since 1967, the Palestinian question has been the dominant issue in Israeli politics. This includes questions of what to do with the territories captured in that war, particularly the West Bank and Gaza, how to govern the Palestinians who live in those territories, or whether to allow the creation of an independent Palestinian state as part of a two-state solution.

Defeat in war has shaped Palestinian political identity in a similar way. The loss by Palestinians to the Zionist movement in the civil war of 1947–1948 meant that they would not get their own state in their own territory. The refugee exodus from that war and the subsequent Arab-Israeli war of 1948–1949 dispersed Palestinians across the region, with substantial communities established in Jordan, Lebanon, Syria, and Kuwait. This experience of defeat and dispersion created a strong Palestinian identity, nurtured later by the Palestine Liberation Organization (PLO), founded in 1964. Palestinian communities in both Jordan and Lebanon provided a base for the PLO and its armed units to set up shop in those countries and contributed to tensions that eventually led to civil wars in both places. Like Israeli identity, Palestinian identity has been forged by war (Kimmerling and Migdal 1993; Khalidi 1997).

Israel and Palestine are states (or potential states) and identities born in war. The other Arab states do not owe their existence to Arab-Israeli wars, but the course of those wars has greatly affected their own political histories. While Israel's Arab neighbors have been motivated to become involved in the conflict by normal geopolitical incentives—such as territory, regional dominance, and balance-of-power concerns—popular support for the Palestinians also has driven them to fight the Israelis. The common Arab identity has led citizens in Egypt, Jordan, Syria, Iraq, and across the Arab world to sympathize with the Palestinians and see Israel's creation as an affront to Arabism. The Arab states were driven in part by popular pressures to enter into the war against Israel in 1948 (Rubin 1981). Defeat in that war contributed to political instability in Syria and to the Egyptian military coup of 1952. The Syrian government's desire to bolster its domestic credentials by escalating the confrontation with Israel helped to drive the crisis that culminated in the 1967 Arab-Israeli war, in which Egypt lost the Sinai Peninsula and Gaza Strip, Jordan lost the West Bank and East Jerusalem, and Syria lost the Golan Heights. Jordan's entry into the 1967 war was driven by King Hussein's belief that to stay on the sidelines while the Arab world confronted Israel would lead to a popular uprising against his regime. It was only with the weakening of pan-Arabism as a political ideology after the 1967 war that Egypt (1979) and Jordan (1994) were willing to risk signing peace agreements with Israel. (The 1993 Oslo Accords between Israel and the PLO also facilitated Jordan's willingness to sign a peace treaty with Israel.)

War also greatly affected the political development of the Islamic Republic of Iran. The revolutionary regime that came to power in 1979 was able to use the Iran-Iraq War, launched by Iraq in 1980, to consolidate its control domestically. With Iraq's attack, the regime's domestic opponents could be portrayed to the Iranian public as traitors to the nation. War mobilization allowed the government to extend its control over society and the economy while rallying the Iranian public to its side. The new regime's success in turning back the Iraqi attack and recovering lost territory by 1982 helped legitimate it to the Iranian public. Continuation of the war for six more years, in an (unsuccessful) effort to bring down Saddam Hussein's regime in Iraq, helped make the Islamic Republic—and make it in a particular way: as a centralized, dirigiste state (Milani 1994).

Regional conflicts gave Middle Eastern regimes a readily understandable, and for some of their population even an acceptable, pretext to consolidate authoritarian rule at home, under the slogan (coined by Egyptian propagandist Mohammad Hassanein Heikal) that "no voice could be louder than the voice of battle." Real and imagined threats from neighbors were used by other regional regimes as well to justify building police states and severely restricting political rights. War and preparation for war might help make a state, but they rarely lead to more liberal politics. War preparation also skewed the economies of Middle Eastern states toward more centralized control and led to high rates of military spending as a percentage of the total economy (see Table 3.3).

Table 3.3 Military Expenditures as Percentage of GDP, 2017

Middle Eastern countries	
Algeria	5.7
Bahrain	4.1
Egypt	1.3
Iran	3.1
Iraq	3.9
Israel	4.7
Jordan	4.8
Kuwait	5.8
Lebanon	4.5
Libya	3.6[a]
Morocco	3.2
Oman	12.1
Qatar	2.5[a]
Saudi Arabia	10.3
Syria	3.9[a]
Tunisia	2.1
Turkey	2.2
United Arab Emirates	5.3[a]
Yemen	5.8[a]
Middle East average	5.0[a]
Arab World average	6.4
Other countries and regions	
Brazil	1.4
China	1.9
East Asia and Australasia	1.7
NATO (excluding United States)	1.6[a]
Non-NATO Europe	1.0[a]
Nigeria	0.4
Pakistan	3.5
Russia	4.3
South and Central Asia	1.9[a]
United States	3.1
Global average	2.4[a]

Source: World Bank, 2017, https://data.worldbank.org/indicator/ms.mil.xpnd.gd.zs.

Note: a. Data for 2010 from International Institute for Strategic Studies, *The Military Balance* (New York: Routledge, 2012).

Trans-state Identities as Challenges to States

Identities cross borders in the Middle East, and the mis-fit between the borders of states and political communities creates important challenges to the consolidation of state authority and the development of citizen loyalty to the state (see Halliday 2005; Hinnebusch 2003; Lawson 2006; see Figure 3.1 for an outline of cross-border identities in the region). People in many Middle Eastern states do not see loyalty to their state as the ultimate expression of their political identity. Cross-border identities provide an avenue for intervention in the domestic politics of neighboring states. Ambitious leaders have used regional identities to mobilize support for themselves and against other leaders, destabilizing the

Figure 3.1 Transnational and Cross-State Identities and Organizations in the Middle East

Transnational identities
Pan-Arabism or Arab nationalism
- Arab Revolt/Hashimite Arab nationalist movement (1917–early 1950s, including Iraqi "Fertile Crescent" plans and Jordanian "Greater Syria" plans)
- Baath Party (founded in 1943 with branches in many countries of the Arab East and, as of 2013, still the ruling party in Syria, whose platform calls for Arab unity)
- Gamal Abdel Nasser's pan-Arabist movement (1954–1967, whose high point was the union of Egypt and Syria in the United Arab Republic, 1958–1961)

Islam
- Shi'i Islamist movements with ties to Iran (e.g., Hezbollah in Lebanon, Islamic Supreme Council of Iraq)
- Muslim Brotherhood, a centralized, Sunni political organization with branches in Egypt, Palestine, Jordan, Syria, Iraq, Kuwait, and elsewhere
- Salafi Sunni Islamist movements, including al-Qaeda
- Shi'i "sources of emulation" (*al-marja'iyyat*) (e.g., Ayatollah Ali al-Sistani of Najaf, who has followers not only in Iraq but also in Iran, Saudi Arabia, Bahrain, and elsewhere)
- Sufi brotherhoods

Cross-state identities
- Kurdish identity, with Kurdish communities in Turkey, Syria, Iraq, and Iran
- Palestinian identity, with significant Palestinian communities in Israel, the Palestinian territories, Jordan, Lebanon, and Syria
- Tribal identities (e.g., Shammar tribal confederation, with members in Saudi Arabia, Kuwait, Iraq, Jordan, and Syria)

domestic politics of their targets and sometimes bringing down other regimes. Here we use the terms *trans-state* and *cross-border* to indicate any such identity; *transnational* to indicate identities that are region-wide, or close to it, transcending existing state borders; and *cross-state* to describe identities that are of a state or substate character yet cross over one or more existing borders.

Arab identity was a serious challenge to state consolidation in the Arab East in the early decades of independence. In the immediate aftermath of the creation of the Arab states, important political movements argued that the division of the Arab world by the colonial powers was illegitimate and that the former Arab provinces of the Ottoman Empire should form a united Arab state. The Hashimite monarchs of Iraq and Jordan, whose family led the "Great Arab Revolt" against the Ottomans, put forward various Arab unity plans in the interwar years. The creation of Israel added an emotional, popular element to the pan-Arab agenda. Arab nationalism was used to justify interventions into the politics of weaker Arab states like Syria by Iraqi politicians looking to encourage "Fertile Crescent" unity. Gamal Abdel Nasser of Egypt took up the banner of "progressive" Arab unity in the mid-1950s, using the new technology of the transistor radio to speak directly to Arabs in other countries, urging them to oppose their own governments and follow the Nasserist line. Nasser was able to mobilize support across borders and destabilize fellow Arab governments. The high point of Nasserist pan-Arabism was the union of Syria and Egypt in 1958 in the United Arab Republic (UAR), with pro-Nasser officers in the Syrian army conducting a coup and in effect offering the country to Nasser. While it did not last long, breaking up in 1961, the UAR actually redrew the map of the Middle East. Even when they were not crowned with such success, Nasser's efforts to mobilize support for himself and his local allies in other Arab states encouraged domestic instability up to the 1967 war (Seale 1987; Kerr 1971). Even after the heyday of Arab nationalism, common Arab identity was used as a pretext by the Baathist regimes of Syria and Iraq to interfere in each other's domestic politics and in the politics of other Arab states (Kienle 1990). While the popularity of Arab unity has faded, common Arab identity remains an important element of regional politics. The speed with which the Arab Spring demonstrations of 2011 spread from Tunisia to Egypt, Yemen, Bahrain, Syria, Libya, and (less disruptively) elsewhere in the Arab world attests to the fact that Arabs look across their borders and are affected by what their fellow Arabs in other states are doing.

In a similar way to Nasser, Ayatollah Khomeini used the larger Islamic identity and the narrower, sectarian Shi'i identity to mobilize support in Arab states and pressure Arab governments that opposed the Islamic Republic of Iran. Revolutionary Iran encouraged fellow Shi'a abroad to oppose the secular Baathist regime of Saddam Hussein and the pro-US monarchies of the Persian Gulf. While Khomeini was unable to bring down any of these regimes, agitation among Iraqi Shi'a contributed to Saddam Hussein's decision to launch his war against Iran in 1980 and contributed to the heightening of sectarian identities in Iraq. Pro-Iranian groups in Kuwait and Bahrain launched attacks against those governments in the 1980s. After the Israeli invasion of Lebanon in 1982, Iran created Hezbollah in conjunction with local allies there as an arm of its Shi'i Islamic revolution (Ramazani 1986).

States with weak administrative structures and multiple identity groups are particularly vulnerable to this kind of cross-border political intervention. Almost every major regional state, at one time or another, sponsored a group or party in Lebanon. Iraq after the US invasion of 2003, with its army and state apparatus dismantled, was an open field for regional political interventions. Iran in particular took advantage of the weak Iraqi center and its ties to various Iraqi Shi'i political groups to increase its influence there. As Syria descended into civil war in 2011, an array of regional powers, including Iran, Turkey, and Saudi Arabia, sought to advance their interests by supporting local factions. We have seen similar dynamics in Libya since its 2011 uprising and the overthrow of the Qaddafi regime, with some local factions backed by Qatar, while their rivals are often backed by Saudi Arabia and the United Arab Emirates. Saudi Arabia and other regional powers have supported political and ideological allies in Yemen over the decades. In the violent aftermath of Yemen's Arab Spring, local government forces squared off against Houthi militias, with the government backed by Saudi Arabia and the UAE, while the Houthi rebels received support from Iran. In Iraq, Syria, Libya, and Yemen, as refugees flowed out, arms flowed in, with regional powers backing various sides within the local conflicts and also as proxies against each other. As these conflicts dragged on, they also saw the rise of nonstate militant groups challenging all sides of the local wars, including a resurgent al-Qaeda in Yemen and the emergence of ISIS—a jihadist movement declaring itself the "Islamic State in Iraq and Syria."

Strong nationalist sentiment among Kurds provides a ready point of access for states looking to pressure Iraq, Iran, or Turkey. The Shah's Iran, supported by the United States and Israel, encouraged Iraqi Kurds to oppose the Baghdad government in the early 1970s. During the Iran-Iraq War, both countries tried to stir up the Kurdish populations of the other. Both Iran and Turkey, fearful of the autonomy Iraq's Kurds have enjoyed since 1991, have intervened in Iraqi Kurdish politics by building client relations with local politicians and parties. Turkey has also intervened militarily in Iraqi Kurdistan on a number of occasions (McDowall 2004).

The importance of cross-state identities in the Middle East has made it more difficult for states to consolidate their control over their territories and to develop patriotic links between citizens and their government. These identities offer an avenue for intervention by outsiders in the domestic politics of targeted states. They make neighbors acutely interested in what happens across their borders, for fear that identity politics will spill back into their own domestic politics. Cross-state identities can exacerbate regional tensions and lead to conflicts, which in turn can have their own effects on the politics of the states involved.

Trans-state Identities and Regional Integration

Regionally, the destabilizing effects of cross-border identities far outweigh their integrative effects. However, Arab identity encouraged large-scale labor migrations within the Arab world during the oil boom of the 1970s and early 1980s. Millions of Egyptians went to work in Libya and Iraq, and hundreds of thousands went to the Arab Gulf states. Hundreds of thousands of Yemenis worked in Saudi Arabia. Hundreds of thousands of Jordanians and Palestinians found work in the Persian Gulf states, especially in Kuwait and Saudi Arabia. These massive migrations helped to redistribute some of the oil bounty from the resource-rich Arab states to the resource-poor states (Kerr and Yassin 1982). By lessening the pressures on domestic economies to employ their growing populations, the oil-fueled labor migrations took some of the political pressure off governments in the labor-exporting countries. Labor remittances helped to sustain balance-of-payments deficits in the labor exporters as well. Migrants also brought home new political ideas. The Saudi brand of Salafi Sunni Islam spread in the Middle East in part by Arab migrant workers picking up these ideas in Saudi Arabia and bringing them back home.

The second oil boom, of the 2000s, has not had the same effects in Arab labor markets. The political divisions created by the Gulf War of 1990–1991, with Iraq, Jordan, Yemen, and the PLO on one side and the Gulf states and Egypt on the other, disrupted the migration patterns that had developed in the 1970s. Egyptians left Iraq; Yemenis left Saudi Arabia. The restored Kuwaiti government made it clear that Palestinians were no longer as welcome, leading to the forced exodus of most of what had been a prosperous and long-established Palestinian community in the Gulf region. Since that time, the oil-rich Gulf states have looked more to South and Southeast Asia for labor. These foreign labor communities, unable to develop links with the local community through Arab identity and the Arabic language, are easier to control politically and present less of a threat to the ruling regimes in a crisis. However, there are still large numbers of fellow Arabs working in the oil-rich Gulf states, including almost 1.5 million Egyptians and hundreds of thousands of Palestinians, Lebanese, Jordanians, and Yemenis (Richards and Waterbury 2008: chap. 15).

Conclusion

It is important to understand the regional and international setting for any country in the Middle East in order to understand its domestic politics. International and regional effects are not, however, one-dimensional. They can help to solidify states and regimes; they can also weaken states and regimes. Recent global economic forces push toward more open and liberal domestic economies, but some Middle Eastern states have been able to trade their strategic positions for outside support, enabling them to sustain inefficient statist economies longer than would have been possible otherwise. The region is not immune to global normative pressures around human rights and democracy, as the Arab Spring demonstrated, but many Middle Eastern states have successfully avoided serious domestic political reform urged by outsiders. While it is not possible to present one simple argument about the overall impact of global and regional influences on any particular Middle Eastern state, no Middle Eastern state can be analyzed in isolation from those influences. The task of the analyst is to appreciate how global and regional forces specifically play into the domestic politics of each of the states in the region.

4

Political Economy

Pete W. Moore

When one talks about "bread and butter" politics, what is commonly implied is the ability to afford the necessities of everyday life. Paying for education, financing a home, buying medications, and getting from home to work define a great deal of the human condition. We engage in such tasks, focused on the here and now, but the conditions under which we work are shaped by far larger dynamics. Housing, education, health care, and the workplace are simultaneously points of exchange and arenas of political action. This is the core of the field of political economy, the mutual constitution of the political and the economic. It is a critical disposition in which the most common first step is the simple question: Where is the money going? But of course, once one starts pulling on the edge of that tablecloth, a lot more than just the bread and butter can start to fall.

In the Arab World of the late twentieth and early twenty-first centuries, issues of political economy have been front and center. A number of countries whose economies grew through the 1960s and 1970s stagnated in subsequent decades, resulting in lower standards of living for many. In the late 1970s, Egyptians angry at these conditions launched massive public protests known as "the bread riots." Similar outbursts of rebellion centered on socioeconomic grievances spread to other parts of the region in the 1980s and 1990s. Baguette-waving Tunisians termed their monumental protests in early 2011 "the Bread Revolution" partly in acknowledgment of this history. We can appreciate then that a political economy approach is transnational: what happens in one country can have ramifications for others. This approach also appreciates change that is long term and historical, since socioeconomic outcomes and political dynamics build in ways that are hardly linear or neat.

This chapter takes up that analytical tradition to stress the political foundations of economies and their effects. Specifically, we cover four themes that bind the Middle East region:

- *Political power and economic policies.* Since the end of World War II, political leaders in the Middle East have crafted and implemented economic policies with clear political imperatives to maintain their rule and the socioeconomic privileges of their supporters.
- *Oil and politics.* The discovery, exploitation, and protection of oil resources in the region have interacted with the domestic politics of countries as well as relations between states in the region.
- *Reform and liberalization.* Since the 1980s, there has been a growing tension between state-dominated economies, which were the norm for most of the post–World War II period, and international pressures to reform and liberalize those same economies. The politics of these shifts has rewarded well-positioned elites while increasing burdens on large parts of Arab society. Inequality is a significant political economy concern.
- *The 2011 uprisings and their aftermath.* While socioeconomic grievance was far from the only complaint to drive protesters in 2011, it was prominent. This should not be surprising, given that protests infused with bread-and-butter concerns have characterized the region since the late 1970s and early 1980s. Over that same period, the fiscal and regulatory capacities of many Arab states have deteriorated.

All the countries of the region have gone through similar periods of growth and stagnation. In the aftermath of World War II, optimism and enthusiasm for political independence drove political leaderships to embark on grand plans to catch up to the rest of the world in economic terms and with regard to infrastructure development. Many of these efforts were conditioned by the legacies of colonial rule and each country's particular social relations. From about the mid-1960s until the early 1980s, the region witnessed what can be termed "the boom period," in which increasingly high oil prices and growing public investment nurtured domestic economies with capital, finance, and planning. The clearest expression of this was the region's impressive annual growth in gross domestic product (GDP) in the 1970s (see Table 4.1). In particular, urban growth was significant, as was migration to cities. Highway systems, ports, and communications networks were put in place or expanded; public education spread; and state administration and regulation increased. As all of this investment was guided by

Table 4.1 GDP Growth in the Middle East and North Africa, 1976–2015 (average percentage per period)

1976–1980	1981–1985	1986–1990	1991–1995	1996–2000	2001–2005	2006–2010	2011–2015
6.2	–1.3	3.9	3.0	4.0	4.3	4.2	3.1

Sources: World Bank, World Databank, World Development Indicators and Global Development Finance, various years, includes all income levels, Middle East and North Africa, http://data.worldbank.org/data-catalog (Washington, DC).

unelected monarchs and presidents, there was a clear political subtext. Money and economic privileges could be used to buy loyalty or weaken one's political adversaries.

The lurking problem was that such political foundations proved unable or unwilling to build on these advances. Starting in the early 1980s, oil prices dropped quickly, public budgets went into debt, and in parts of the region with persistent violent conflicts, instability combined with these dislocations and led to what has been termed "the bust period." In basic terms this meant that economic expansion measured by GDP growth rates stagnated (see Table 4.1) and unemployment increased. Earlier promises of socioeconomic equality and advancement gave way to increasing inequality, both economically and politically. From the late 1970s and increasing into the 1980s, protests among workers and others adversely impacted by these shifts took place in Egypt, Morocco, Jordan, and Tunisia, foreshadowing the mass uprisings of 2011. In response, some states attempted austerity measures—like increases in prices and reductions in welfare subsidies—but often this led again to public disturbances and protests.

Not all countries, however, have succumbed to these types of developmental failures. For prolonged periods, Turkey, Israel, and Tunisia succeeded in building upon earlier advances to upgrade workforce skills and capitalize on exports in niche industries. Among the Gulf oil states, Dubai in the United Arab Emirates (UAE) has launched unprecedented but still incomplete efforts at diversification away from oil reliance. Similarly, in 2016 Saudi Arabia announced grand transformation plans under the banner "Vision 2030." Still, for most of the region boom and bust have gone hand in hand, and periodic economic growth has not led to productive or sustainable development. Since the turn of the century, the pendulum has again swung wildly. A new oil boom was followed by the 2008–2009 global financial crisis, which sent prices plunging and increased regional fears of financial contagion. The 2011 uprisings in turn put socioeconomic issues firmly back on the political table. The following sections examine the legacies of colonial rule, the early years of economic growth, the bust period that followed, oil politics, and the current situation of the region's political economies in the aftermath of the 2011 uprisings.

The Colonial State and Political-Economy Legacies

Chapter 1 chronicles how most of the region's states achieved formal political independence from the European powers after World War II. Prior to European imperialism and to varying degrees, the Ottoman Empire had controlled most of the region's people and economies. None of these external powers was interested in establishing responsible governance or developing productive economies. Instead, policies directed at the people and societies within a foreign power's control were designed to serve external strategic and commercial aims, often in competition with other outside powers. These legacies meant that newly independent rulers in the 1950s were hardly working from a blank slate when it came to their political economies. Hundreds of years of foreign rule, punctuated by two world wars in the twentieth century, left their impact in three ways.

First, when foreign governors and military forces departed, they left behind institutions that governed the collection of revenue, import and export practices, the distribution of investment, and the adjudication of property rights. Colonial rulers generally did not invest in developing states' administrative capacities to tax residents or businesses. Rather, grants from the European capital typically funded the operations of the colonial enterprises. This left an important legacy in that political elites had important leverage over merchants and citizens, since rulers did not rely on them to generate public funds. Colonial powers determined import and export monopolies whereby selected business elites were given special access to imported goods—often from the colonial homeland (Vitalis and Heydemann 2000). This weakened domestic producers of the same good (often agricultural products) as well as other domestic private sector elements, which were left out of the special deals. Where large European settler or foreign merchant communities existed (Algeria, Palestine, Egypt, and Turkey), colonial rule supported and extended those communities' economic privileges, thereby setting the stage for political backlash after independence. Colonial officials also favored the creation or continued existence of large landowning elites in the rural areas of countries like Egypt, Syria, and Iraq. The existence of these (often absent) landlords dampened development in rural agriculture, increased rural inequities, and provided resistance to industrialization and better collection of public revenues through taxation. But because these rural elites supported colonial rulers, their interests were protected (Gerber 1987). Finally, where external powers did establish profitable businesses within the indigenous economies (particularly in the oil sector and Egypt's Suez Canal, for example), continued foreign control even after political independence would ensure future political conflict.

Second, the creation of new states and borders limited the choices available in building economies or imparted strong incentives to build one's economy in a specific direction. In the most basic sense, the creation of new borders recognized by the United Nations (UN) meant some new states had natural resources while others did not—oil reserves being the most obvious. Where whole new political entities were created, as in Lebanon, Jordan, and Israel, labor markets, private sector alignments, and domestic markets were remade. In the preindependence years, for example, merchants (especially in the Gulf) could migrate to other areas if relations with local political rulers soured. Once new borders were established, this form of exit was cut off (Crystal 1995). In short, the regional state system determined by departing colonial powers meant local leaders inherited a geographic and political economy terrain that could be changed little or only at great cost.

Third, how political independence from colonial rule unfolded often left consequential political legacies. Turkey's achievement of independence under the leadership of Mustafa Kemal Atatürk proved an early model for the economic development of other states later in the century. Atatürk's policies of the 1930s that established significant state control over the economy and financial sectors would be replicated—but under different conditions—by Gamal Abdel Nasser in Egypt twenty years later (Richards and Waterbury 1990: 187–193). The costly Algerian war of independence from France (1954–1962) led to subsequent political arrangements in which a strong Algerian state dominated by the victorious National Liberation Front (FLN) would guide economic decisions. Another series of violent conflicts culminating in 1948, which resulted in the creation of the State of Israel and the expulsion of Palestinians, had profound and lasting effects on regional political economies—particularly impacting the neighboring countries of Jordan, Syria, and Lebanon.

All Middle East states inherited political economic institutions and factors shaping their future development. This did not mean trajectories could not be changed or that destinies were set; however, decisions in the new environment of political independence were circumscribed. Moving sharply against these legacies would not be easy or politically profitable in most cases.

The Boom Years, 1950s–1970s

For many in the Middle East, the end of World War II marked an optimistic change. The instability of the end of Ottoman rule and the dislocations from European dominance were in the past. Formal political independence seemed to promise control over the future. The challenges of building new states and economies, however, were daunting. Political leaders had to build new state bureaucracies from the remnants of previous colonial rule, craft national identities and attachments for populations that were sometimes very socially diverse, and construct national economies with a promise of higher living standards for all. Rulers often pursued all of these tasks simultaneously within a highly unequal global economy dominated by the victorious post–World War II Western powers. Moreover, attempts to address any one of these tasks would surely affect the prospects of completing the others. To add further complication, countries faced these challenges from different starting points or levels of preparation.

Some of the resource-poor countries, like Syria, Jordan, and Lebanon (as well as resource-rich Iraq), had complex societal divisions, which meant that economic decisions that favored one part of society over another were bound to have political repercussions. A number of the smaller Gulf countries did not face such acute divisions, but some having newly established political borders and limited urban populations brought other challenges. Where they enjoyed an advantage was with close European and US support for building their oil-based economies right from the start. By contrast, a state like Egypt had a more developed bureaucracy and civil service inherited from British rule, yet that same colonial legacy meant Egypt's finance and trade sectors were dominated by foreign interests (the British- and French-owned Suez Canal, for example). Perhaps the best-prepared states could be found in Turkey and Israel after 1948. In both cases, but for different reasons (Turkey because foreign rule was thwarted and Israel because foreign support undergirded Jewish rule), these states enjoyed comparatively more autonomy from external economic influences than did their neighbors. Domestically, political leaders in these states also faced less entrenched socioeconomic interests (particularly the absence of large landowning elites) that could block efforts at economic development and industrialization, as often occurred in other parts of the region. Despite different levels of preparation, all countries built their economies with significant state leadership. All would realize decades of economic expansion and growth, but uneven productive development would characterize the experience of most Arab countries.

In the 1950s, a consensus emerged that economic development required strong state guidance. The argument followed that investment and public finance would have to be injected to kick-start growth. Strong national leadership was required to guide the process and generate a national commitment to large-scale public enterprises. Again, Atatürk's Turkey provided the model that Egypt and a number of other Arab states would follow. Coupled with the rising tide of anticolonial movements in the region, these statist policies became wrapped in a collectivist ideology. State-led development and socialist means of production—meaning significant public ownership of leading economic sectors—had the declared goal of guaranteeing that all classes of Arabs would benefit from growth. Rural peasants would be liberated from serflike conditions and urban workers would join with students in moving toward greater social equality. That an Egyptian, Syrian, or Algerian state would control the key economic assets of the country would free countries from foreign economic control. These ideas were not particular to the Middle East; they generally were embraced across the developing world. Moreover, these views dominated economic policy discourse well into the 1970s and contributed to widely shared economic policies across the region, including growth of the public sector, state-directed finance and creation of state-owned enterprises (SOEs), nationalization of leading economic enterprises, and rural land reform and agricultural expansion. In fact, it is no coincidence that the 2011 protests often articulated commitments to equality and fairness, which have for so long gone unfulfilled for much of the region's people.

Building the capacity of the public sector entailed the wholesale expansion of government agencies and quasi-state institutions. In the 1950s and especially the 1960s, the size and scope of government ministries expanded. The logic was that since the economies of the region were "underdeveloped," modern civil servants and state capacities were needed to guide and encourage economic growth. An important complement to public sector expansion was the treatment of labor unions and professional associations. With few exceptions, labor unions and professional associations of doctors, lawyers, and engineers were brought under some form of state control (Moore and Salloukh 2007). In countries with mass-based political parties—like the FLN in Algeria, the Baath parties in Syria and Iraq, and the Arab Socialist Union in Egypt—unions and associations came under the sway of parties. To get a business license or practice in one's field, membership in such associations or the party was required. As a consequence, unions and associations in the Middle East were large but had limited autonomy and ability to influence economic development or worker rights. This does not mean labor or associational activity has been marginal; rather, their roles in domestic political economies have often been limited by political leaders (Posusney 1997).

In part, the significant role organized labor played in Egypt and Tunisia's 2011 uprisings was built upon a history of labor activism and state repression. Once that repression seemed to give way in 2011, labor, along with other social allies, was primed to keep pushing.

States also moved aggressively to nationalize leading industries and financial enterprises. Among the countries without significant oil reserves, the first sectors to be nationalized were industry, agriculture, and transportation. This typically entailed state purchase of company assets from foreign and domestic shareholders. The most famous of these nationalizations was Nasser's nationalization of the British- and French-owned Suez Canal in 1956. Such sequestrations were replicated across the region. While some countries, like Jordan, professed a "free market" commitment even in these early years, all countries, including Israel and Turkey, allowed for significant state involvement in the economy. The oil-exporting nations followed similar patterns; however, national oil companies that had been controlled by European and US firms were the primary targets of nationalization. By the 1970s, all major oil-exporting countries had completely taken over their oil industries. In addition to the takeover of resident firms, states also created wholly new public industries and utilities, such as national airlines, telecommunications, and transportation companies. These SOEs enjoyed subsidized inputs and protection from external competition. Located in urban areas, these industries were also designed to provide employment for growing urban populations. Once protected industries developed their own capacities and efficiencies, the idea went, protections could be removed and these domestic firms would then compete in regional and international markets.

Not all economic policies were directed at cities. A number of policies, generally referred to as *land reform,* targeted rural areas. While the small Gulf oil countries generally lacked populated rural areas and, therefore, focused on urban growth, Egypt, Syria, and Iraq had inherited significantly unequal and impoverished rural areas from colonial rule. Peasants (*fellahin*) often worked land—which was owned by large, mostly absent landlords—for increasingly marginal returns. In many countries, these landed elites had supported previous colonial rule and often inherited state institutions after independence; therefore, once revolutionary regimes took power, these elites became popular political targets. Land reform took many forms, but the aim was to break up large rural landholdings and redistribute the parcels to peasants. States were then to help small farmers prosper through the provision of irrigation, fertilizer, and road networks. Agricultural production would increase as a result and rural inequity would be alleviated—at least that was the idea.

Behind these ambitious policies and rapid changes, political constraints and opportunities were at work. As the great social historian Ibn Khaldun once remarked, no king is powerful alone; he requires people to support his rule. Economic policies, then, were a principal means of securing that support. Three basic political imperatives were at work: fashion a political coalition to support the ruling regime; weaken domestic rivals to that regime; and compete for ideological and sociocultural authenticity at home and abroad.

Expanding government agencies and the civil service directly employed large portions of the labor market. This gave people, especially in urban areas, a tangible stake in a regime's political rule. In countries with new revolutionary regimes, mass-based political parties evolved into gatekeepers to employment and economic gain. Party membership and civil service employment overlapped, so that the most likely path to social and economic advancement came through party allegiance. In the monarchical states and smaller Gulf countries, political parties were effectively outlawed or handicapped, so ruling families directly expanded public sector employment. By the 1980s, public sector employment, including in the military, was among the largest components of the workforce in most countries. Outside the public sector, state management of labor unions and professional associations limited the ability of political rivals or activists to mobilize through these venues. And while the letter of the law professed various labor rights in most countries, in practice these rights were not upheld, as strikes were not allowed and union leaders had little autonomy.

State control over leading economic firms, trade protection, and subsidies gave political leaders the tools to reward political allies. In the political economy sense, economic control translated into political patronage. Rulers could assign their allies, or clients, to sit on corporate boards and award public works contracts to favored businesses. By the 1970s, public-private shareholding companies formed in which the state would maintain a controlling ownership, with smaller—but very profitable—shares allowed for private sector allies. The sale or transfer of public land, particularly in booming urban areas, provided another way to route patronage to political allies. Finally, by controlling credit allocation and strictly licensing who was allowed to import and export, rulers could select allies to receive incredibly lucrative monopolies over luxury goods as well as basic staples. Imagine the money that can be made if one has the exclusive right to import, say, BMW motorcars or Apple computers to Saudi Arabia or Egypt. By signing one's name to the import bill, millions are made with little effort. Scholars refer to these mechanisms as "side payments," a euphemism for payoffs (Waterbury 1993).

Last, in tone and in proclaimed intent, these policies corresponded to broad ideological as well as local sociocultural sentiments of the day. Arab nationalism, equality, and collective advancement were more than just slogans for many in the region. Though separate from Arab nationalism, Turks, Israelis, and Iranians identified with this collectivist spirit as well. Consequently, state efforts to limit foreign capital and guide the domestic private sector comported with conceptions of fairness and justice. Early efforts at land reform and redistribution in rural areas in particular expressed these attributes. Since the situation of peasants and rural inequality had been aggravated under colonial rule, it was no surprise that revolutionary movements in Syria, Iraq, Egypt, and Algeria drew much of their early support from these areas.

Through these various forms of patronage, regimes built coalitions of support and sidelined rivals in ways that would be economically consequential (Waldner 1999). In Algeria, Iraq, Egypt, and Syria, private sector elites who had been aligned with the previous colonial regimes were pushed out or co-opted through state-mediated side payments. In the Gulf states, ruling families were able to build massive bureaucracies that left marginal room for the private sector. However, an important caveat is necessary. Highlighting the political, social, or cultural sources of economic policy is not to argue that such considerations automatically impair economic development or "interfere with the market." On the contrary, state provision of regulation, infrastructure, and investment is a requirement of productive market operation, not an impediment. Middle Eastern countries were, after all, emulating the policies and strategies that had led to Europe's successful economic development a century earlier (Gerschenkron 1962), and economic policies that reflect sociocultural conceptions of justice can be found in all national economies. The question of the political underpinning of economic policies is not about political direction per se, but about who is to benefit from such policies. Are investments designed to broaden economic participation? Increase opportunities and capacities to advance? Distribute resources so as to include more and more sectors of society? Or are policies designed to enrich only a narrow stratum of society? The 2011 uprisings focused in particular on this last question.

Despite looming problems, some of the optimism of these decades was rewarded. In terms of real GDP growth per capita, the Middle East outperformed all other parts of the developing world, excluding East Asia, until 1979 (IMF 2003). State policies in these decades led to the construction of urban infrastructure, expanded road networks, new power grids, and modernized port facilities. Expansion of public education succeeded in boosting literacy, and increased public employment allowed women into the workforce in large numbers for the first time. Unfortunately, these were gains that could stagnate or be reversed.

Oil Politics

Shaikh Ahmed Zaki Yamani, Saudi Arabia's second oil minister, was reported to have once remarked, "All in all, I wish we had discovered water" (Karl 1997: 188). Reference to the perils of oil may clash with the perceived wealth of many oil-producing countries today; however, the interaction between oil and politics is anything but a clear success story. As the Ottoman Empire came to an end and Western dominance took hold, a group of seven US and European oil companies (the so-called Seven Sisters) came to control the region's oil resources through what were termed *concession agreements*. Typically, these agreements meant oil companies would finance oil exploration, but in return the Seven Sisters essentially owned the natural resource, could dispose of it as they saw fit, and only remitted a small portion of the profits to the host government (Parra 2004). Additionally, these contracts could not be adjudicated under the host country's legal system, creating conditions ripe for exploitation by the oil companies. The history of Western oil companies in the Middle East, therefore, is hardly a happy one (Vitalis 2007).

After independence, oil-exporting countries gradually turned the tables and organized so that in 1960 the Organization of Petroleum Exporting Countries (OPEC) was founded in Baghdad. From 1970 to 1973, the last three major exporters, Algeria, Libya, and Iraq, nationalized their oil industries. States, not companies, now controlled the use of their oil resources. In the wake of the 1973 Arab-Israeli war and US support for Israel, the OPEC states embargoed oil shipments, sparking the oil crisis of the 1970s. The rapid spike in the price of a barrel of oil transferred historically high profits directly to rulers and the nationalized oil companies they controlled. This has meant that oil profits compose the largest part of gross domestic product as well as the majority of government revenue in these countries. However, not all oil exporters in the region are similar.

One of the basic distinctions is size. The larger oil states—Algeria, Saudi Arabia, Iraq, and Iran—all have populations over 20 million. By contrast, the smaller Gulf oil states average populations of 1 million or less (see Table 4.2). Distributing oil profits over a larger society versus a smaller one leads to important differences. Consequently, the smaller Gulf states are among the world's wealthiest in terms of per capita income and GDP, whereas Saudi Arabia, the world's largest oil exporter, has seen its per capita GDP decline since the 1980s as its population has grown. It is easy to appreciate, then, that with such wealth, politics is

Table 4.2 Oil Production and Population Statistics, 2018

	Production (million barrels per day)	Population (total residents/ nonnationals in millions)
Algeria	1.3	40/negligible
Iran	4.0	82/negligible
Iraq	4.4	39/negligible
Kuwait	2.7	4.4/3.0
Libya	0.87	6.6/0.79
Qatar	1.5	2.3/2.0
Saudi Arabia	10.4	28/5.5
United Arab Emirates	3.0	9.4/8.2

Source: CIA World Factbook, https://www.cia.gov/library/publications/the-world-factbook (accessed August 2018).

Note: Production is distinct from exports, which are lower in most cases due to domestic consumption.

close by. The interaction of oil and politics can be assessed from two vantage points: domestic and regional.

How oil has affected the internal politics of countries has long been a focus of scholarly debate. Until the 1970s, it was common for Western academics to argue that authoritarianism in the Arab Middle East was due to Islam or an unchanging "Arab character." Such simple connections persist today, but they have consistently been critiqued in the past several decades. A focus on the role of oil, instead of strictly religion or culture, informed one of these critiques. The most prominent set of these arguments, known as the "resource curse" or "rentier state" theories, holds that the way a state earns its money (in this case through oil export) determines its basic politics.[1]

Rulers with exclusive access to oil profits enjoy what are called soft budget constraints; that is, far more money than required for public expenditure is available year in and year out due to high oil prices. In turn, rulers are free to distribute this wealth through myriad means to co-opt political allies and sideline rivals. In the logic of the rentier framework, since rulers do not have to exploit domestic resources to fund their states (that is, tax citizens and corporations), they are not compelled to grant political representation either; hence the twist on a well-known maxim, "no taxation, no representation." The expectation is that such polities should experience declining political opposition and subdued civic association, since gaining individual favor with the ruler becomes the name of the game. In this way, rentier theory argues that lack of democracy was not caused by religion or culture, but by political economic factors, that is, easy oil profits controlled by unelected rulers. Lavish lifestyles for rulers, public budgets that dwarfed private interests, well-funded internal security apparatuses, and militarily powerful foreign patrons all gave the rentier state an appearance of fierce political strength. Yet here is where the "curse" part comes in, for there are costs to this type of political economy.

States built on distribution rather than extraction (i.e., an income or corporate tax) are argued to have underdeveloped administrative capacities. For example, consider all of the information a government needs to tax a paycheck. All of those deductions and accounting procedures require lots of information that is constantly updated; this in turn requires state agencies with vast administrative skills to generate, monitor, and authenticate that information. Straightforward revenue distribution does not require such information-gathering skills. So, while typical oil-state agencies appear numerous, expansive, and well staffed, they are flabby in terms of actual capacities and capabilities. They can't do much. Moreover, oil-dependent economies suffer from what economists term "the Dutch disease," a condition in which an economy is flooded with external revenue, depressing incentives to manufacture products while increasing the ability to purchase imported products. The result is a one-dimensional economy in which little is manufactured locally. Hence in theory, when the price of oil drops, the oil-dependent state does not have much to fall back on, and political crisis is expected to follow. What happens when the rentier state is then forced to turn to domestic taxes? Should we then expect a situation of no taxation without representation?

As far as these arguments go, there is a degree of logic and plausibility. However, scholars have lately come to question the simplistic formula that oil causes political outcomes. After all, oil does not spend itself; political rulers choose how to control and deploy these assets (Okruhlik 1999). As discussed previously, state-led development in the region has had clear political rationales. Likewise, Gulf rulers deployed their oil wealth not just to generate economic growth but also to secure political rule. Certainly, having exclusive control over massive oil monies makes it easier to thwart political opponents and reward allies, but something more than just oil revenue generated society's support for or acquiescence to nondemocratic rule in the Gulf and beyond. For one thing, though oil prices declined precipitously in the 1980s and 1990s, no oil exporters embarked on democratization, and where some political liberalization did take place, it was marginal (Gause 1993). And though the exportation of oil seems an important similarity between, say, Libya and Iran, oil exporters are hardly uniform. For instance, Kuwait, a small oil-rich state with a ruling family, has had a freely elected parliament with a well-organized opposition since 1961. Though the Kuwaiti parliament's legislative powers are circumscribed, its latitude of political action is far greater compared to legislative bodies in neighboring countries. And in 2006, Kuwait extended suffrage to its female citizens, the first among the Gulf Arab monarchies to do so. Indeed, Algeria, Saudi Arabia, Qatar, Oman, Bahrain, and the UAE all have nondemocratic regimes that enjoy monopoly access to oil and gas revenues, yet their politics and societies are hardly similar. That mass political protest in 2011 struck Libya and Bahrain to a greater extent than the other resource-dependent countries reinforces the point of divergence among the Arab oil exporters.

The oil boom of the 1970s also had profound effects on the region as a whole and the relations among its states. Since many of the smaller oil states experienced inflows of finance that they could not hope to fully invest domestically, there was much capital to invest elsewhere. From the 1970s onward, Gulf states provided billions of dollars in bilateral aid, loans, grants, and development assistance to other Arab states that lacked oil resources. This financial power has positioned donor states, like Saudi Arabia, as important players and decisionmakers regarding a number of regional diplomatic issues. Such funds also became important sources of external financing for Egypt, Syria, Lebanon, Palestine, Morocco, and Yemen. In return, as the oil boom fed growth and expansion, large numbers of citizens of these countries migrated to the Gulf states to staff professional and middle-management positions in the government and private sector. The money they earned was often sent back to their families at home. Like development aid, these worker remittances became important sources of finance for the resource-poor countries of the Middle East.

In short, oil and politics have historically been deeply intertwined, and since oil is a finite resource in continual demand, this relationship is sure to endure for many more decades.

The Bust Years, 1980s–2000s

Beginning in the early 1980s, most countries of the Middle East experienced stagnant or unstable economic growth and mounting public debt. Much of the dissatisfaction with socioeconomic conditions that was manifested in the 2011 uprisings originated in this period. While expansion and public investment took place until the late 1970s, more tangible development, through investments yielding productive returns and labor upgrading, failed to take root. After decades of mounting expectations, the economic crunch contributed to public discontent across the region. Sharp increases in the price of basic staples in Egypt,

Jordan, and Morocco led to public protests beginning in the late 1970s through the late 1980s, often ending in violent clashes with security forces. The increasing gap between rich and poor, and overt displays of elite consumption, contrasted sharply with regimes' rhetoric regarding equality and social justice. Where state programs and public investment were launched as means to fight inequality, they instead became exclusive venues for those few who had enough political access to realize significant benefit. Investment in education and in upgrading labor skills quickly atrophied, because while such expenditures pay benefits for many in the long term, they pay few short-term political benefits. State-owned industries failed to become competitive and instead siphoned off declining public assets to continue operation. The private sector, though surviving the nationalizations and restrictions of the 1960s and 1970s, reacted by investing little in domestic enterprises and instead sent its capital overseas. Cities that had grown rapidly became overburdened with new arrivals, social services weakened, and urban planning ceased in many areas.

Rural areas fared little better. Promised land redistribution either never materialized or was piecemeal. Where peasants actually took control of land, state support arrived infrequently, forcing farmers to turn for loans to some of the same large landowners whose land was sequestered in the first place. Instead of a productive agricultural sector developing, rural debt increased and countries were forced to import many food products. Rural discontent was reflected in growing political opposition as well as cultural critique. For example, Yusuf al-Qa'id's popular novel *War in the Land of Egypt* depicted the failure of Nasser's land reform and the peasant oppression that followed. Among the Gulf oil exporters, the financial cushions were greater, but for the first time since independence public debt became a reality. The conspicuous wealth of the ruling families led to critical questioning about the destination of oil profits. Here too, discontent expressed itself through popular novels like Abdul Rahman Munif's trilogy *Cities of Salt,* which depicted the social dislocations caused by oil exploitation in a small Gulf country.

These socioeconomic strains took place at the same time population growth remained high across the region. Since economic growth was not keeping up with the need to produce jobs, unemployment increased. Previous decades of growth and expansion without genuine economic development and investment succeeded in producing only low-quality jobs and uncompetitive industries. While sectors of the Turkish and Israeli populations achieved higher living standards in the 1980s, and previously underdeveloped South Korea and Taiwan began producing cars and electronics, Arab countries remained wedded to industries with low worker skills or sectors of economic activity that required little fixed investment (like transportation, trade, and services) and little upgrading or educational investment. Thousands of university graduates were coming into the labor market with few prospects beyond a mundane career in the public sector. Only for the few who were politically connected, or for the children of private sector elites, were there more opportunities for the future.

What explains such a big turnaround? The spark is commonly attributed to the long decline of oil and commodity prices from their highs in the 1970s to their lows in the 1990s. As oil producers witnessed reductions in their public revenue, bilateral aid and worker remittances to the resource-poor states declined accordingly. Egyptian, Palestinian, Jordanian, and Yemeni workers in the Gulf sent less money back home. The reduction in regional finances put serious strains on states' ability to continue their expansive economic policies. However, while oil prices certainly played a role, the problems of the bust decades went deeper.

A major reason for the economic downturn was found in the political rationales for the boom policies in the first place. As noted earlier, many economic policies corresponded to the needs of political elites to maintain ruling coalitions, thus the webs of political patronage that followed were not easily changed. Clients of political patrons were expected to deliver political loyalty, not more valuable goods, more skilled workers, or more efficient factories. SOEs and shareholding companies that had been fostered through state patronage and protection had no incentive to wean themselves or invest in upgrading. Instead, state-owned factories became employment vehicles of last resort and sources of easy profit for the politically connected. Private sector elites cushioned by trade protection and easy profits from public contracts had little reason to switch to more risky investments in domestic production.

Another reason for the bust was that competition in the international marketplace became fiercer. While the post–World War II global market was dominated by North America and a recovering Western Europe, the global economy of the 1980s saw the East Asian economies arrive as serious competitors. Exposing SOEs and shareholding companies to such competition would have had dire social ramifications. Domestic currencies that had been overvalued to aid industry and support urban consumer purchases of imports came to be an obstacle to economic adaptation. Lowering the value of one's currency (thus lowering the cost of exports but increasing the cost of imports) is one way to compete internationally, but it would carry political costs that rulers were not willing to undertake.

The region's economic decline could also be correlated with outbreaks of chronic political violence, domestically and regionally (Rodrik 1999). While interstate wars had plagued the region before the 1970s, complex and continuing violence since has impaired socioeconomic development. There are numerous, depressing examples. The Iran-Iraq War in the 1980s devastated both countries and negatively impacted neighboring countries and economies. In Yemen and Algeria in the 1990s, highly destructive civil violence reversed previous gains in those societies (Blumi 2018; Martinez 2000). Similarly, the wrenching civil war in Syria starting after the 2011 uprisings has brutalized Syrian society and imposed substantial costs for its economic future. Israel's increasingly violent occupation of the Palestinian territories in the wake of the 1987 intifada had dire consequences for the prospects of Palestinian development (Gordon 2008). Israeli blockades and frequent military interventions have scared away investment, leaving Palestinians worse off than before the Oslo peace process began in 1993 (Roy 2007: 250–293). Last but not least, a series of US-led military interventions beginning with the so-called war on terror and the 2003 invasion of Iraq have yielded widespread social and economic destruction. Large parts of Baghdad remain ethnically cleansed; hundreds of thousands of civilians have been wounded or killed; and over 4 million have been displaced. The impacts of similar US and European interventions in Libya and Somalia have contributed to socioeconomic devastation even beyond the region, including parts of East Africa (Eritrea), Central Africa (Central African Republic), and West Africa (Mali and Niger). Under such conditions, it has been easy for rulers to continue massive investments in the security sectors while starving infrastructure, education, and social welfare.

Stuck between the rock of political survival and the hard place of economic crunch, rulers and states responded by implementing selective and limited economic reform, reaching out to international lending agencies for support, and allowing elements of limited political liberalization. At first, nearly all states in the early 1980s avoided any reductions in public spending or price supports. They simply kept going in the hope that conditions would improve. Such avoidance is common to most governments in the world, because what politician wants to be the first to call for austerity? However, as the downturn in world oil and commodity prices continued, public debt mounted, particularly among the resource-poor countries.

Countries like Yemen, Egypt, Jordan, and Morocco had problems financing their debts. Controlled experiments to lower public subsidies and let prices rise resulted in public unrest, limiting those options. A number of countries announced economic reform policies, or what generally became known as *infitah* (economic opening). Egypt, Tunisia, and Turkey led the way by announcing policies to increase the role of the private sector, increase foreign investment, and boost exports. Eventually, most countries in the region announced similar intents, but their experiences varied. Whereas Turkey and Tunisia achieved some success in boosting manufactured exports and attracting investment, Egypt generally failed in its efforts. Openings to the private sector were selective and geared toward retaining political clients. Removing the modest welfare provisions that many states had created in the 1970s risked pushing more people toward the political opposition, which came to be dominated by the increasingly popular Islamist parties in the 1980s and 1990s. For rulers, the political costs of decentralizing economic control and resources were just too great.

By the late 1980s, some of the non–oil exporters were compelled to turn to international lending agencies like the World Bank and International Monetary Fund (IMF) for assistance. In what was known as the Washington Consensus, these international agencies offered funds to debt-burdened developing states, including Middle Eastern states, but required specific policy reforms in return. These reforms went beyond earlier *infitah* policies and included privatization of state assets, trade liberalization, currency liberalization, elimination of foreign investment restrictions, and public sector reductions. But such reforms could cut support to clients, increase unemployment, and endanger private profits, all of which threatened the political loyalty and social stability that these policies were intended to generate in the first place. Rulers were wary of going down this road, and—as critics of the Washington Consensus argued—it was far from clear that such policies would restore growth and lead to meaningful development (Rodrik 1997).

Nevertheless, a number of Arab states (Algeria, Egypt, Jordan, Morocco, and Tunisia) signed loan agreements with the IMF. Interestingly, these states have been able to avoid or limit implementation of many of the reforms required by the loan agreements. Since the Middle East is viewed as strategically crucial for the United States and Europe, which are the IMF's largest contributors, there was a geostrategic interest in advancing loans to lessen political pressure on friendly regimes. When push came to shove, there was little interest on the part of Western donor countries to compel reforms or withdraw funding in ways that might endanger the stability of friendly regimes, especially in Jordan and Egypt (Harrigan and El-Said 2009: 10–11). Just as regimes in the region relied on different forms of state involvement in the economy as one means to ensure their political rule, leaders in the West needed those same regimes to stay in place to ensure their own political interests, like guaranteeing access to oil and privileging the interests of Israel.

The resource-exporting countries faced similar financial pressures, but most did not need to turn to international lenders. Iraq survived its war with Iran but then faced decaying economic conditions at a time of declining oil revenues. Saddam Hussein was able to survive until 2003 in part because of oil smuggling and circumvention of import restrictions through neighboring countries. Saudi Arabia witnessed a dramatic reduction in per capita income as its population continued to grow while its oil profits plateaued. The smaller oil producers met hard times as well, but the Gulf enjoyed a larger toolbox of responses to avoid turning to the IMF. These states could endure longer periods of debt financing and avoid serious austerity as private lenders were all too happy to extend loans (without reform conditions) to countries with significant oil revenues. Thus, none of the oil states were forced to turn to international lending agencies.

Finally, faced with tough social dislocations, some states entertained limited moves toward political liberalization as a last resort. Jordan reinstituted its elected parliament in 1989; Kuwait did the same after being liberated from Iraq in 1991; and Yemen followed suit after its brief civil war in the mid-1990s. The more conservative Gulf states promised various forms of appointed consultative councils—though as Chapter 2 recounts these were well short of elected bodies. While not exactly a form of political liberalization, Saddam Hussein's Baath Party in Iraq devolved economic and political power to provinces in the south and west in order to cope with international sanctions in the 1990s. Finally, press freedoms were relaxed in a number of countries as new forms of media made their appearance in the 1990s. All of these shifts influenced some observers to expect that political liberalization would deepen as the economic downturn continued (Anderson 1995). Economic liberalization can be part of broader democratization, but in the case of the Middle East this was not to be.

Liberalizations remained limited and genuine political decentralization rarely occurred. In Egypt, Jordan, Morocco, Kuwait, and Tunisia, press and associative freedoms were reversed in the mid-1990s. State security agencies increased their surveillance of opposition groups, while periodic arrests of opposition figures and general intimidation silenced those who might voice more opposition. Consequently, the region's regimes survived the bust decades politically intact. Economically and socially, however, there were great costs. Infrastructure decayed in many cities, living standards stagnated, public education withered, and inequality increased. Though opposition movements were blocked, the socioeconomic reasons for discontent remained unaddressed and would make themselves felt in 2011.

A New Century and the Road to 2011

The turn of the century has seen a region seemingly accustomed to shocks and sudden shifts witness even more. In this period a new oil boom in the early 2000s took place, approaching the highs of the 1970s. The 2008–2009 global financial crisis had its effects, but the region largely escaped entanglement with the bursting US bubble. Instead, it was the 2011 uprisings that rocked the region, with ramifications that we have only begun to grasp. Three trends from 2000 to the present are consequential for the near future: (1) increased international and bilateral pressures to liberalize economies, (2) deepening socioeconomic decay and inequality in a number of countries, and (3) the mass political uprisings and regime instabilities that followed. Taken together, these factors are remaking the region in profound ways. No longer can we speak of a single regional economy, one developmental path, or shared strategies. Instead, different parts of the region are moving in diverse directions, and disparities in wealth among as well as within countries are growing more pronounced. The road to 2011 was paved with these tensions.

In one sense, the start of the 2000s seemed to have provided much-needed fiscal cushion to the region's states. External actors, international lending agencies, multinational corporations, and world trade organizations increased investment and aid. Rulers in strategically important Middle Eastern countries could expect to bide their financial time through increased bilateral and military aid from the West, particularly the United States. In pursuing the "war on terror," US financial assistance to Jordan, Egypt, Yemen, and Morocco increased significantly after 2000. Just like oil monies that flow to the Gulf's ruling families, Western budgetary and security assistance flows directly into the coffers of allied regimes, allowing them to shore up their rule without addressing underlying socioeconomic dislocations (Peters and Moore 2009). Indeed, depending on how it is measured, the Middle East is either the most aid-dependent region in the developing world or second only to sub-Saharan Africa (World Bank 2008: 366; Rivlin 2009: 33).

Additional external support has come from multilateral institutions offering potential benefits like membership in the World Trade Organization (WTO) and bilateral trade agreements with the European Union and the United States. The United States has signed free trade agreements with Israel, Jordan, Bahrain, Morocco, and Oman. These agreements require varying levels of openness to external investment, adherence to intellectual property rights, and even minimal labor rights. In theory, Arab countries that sign will gain privileged access to Western consumer markets, but in return Western exporters and investors should realize unfettered access to the signers' domestic markets. In general, these bilateral trade agreements signaled more political support than actual economic development, although Jordanian and Israeli exports to the United States have increased. Thus the general impression of the region on the eve of the 2011 uprisings was one of slow but progressing economic development—not great but better than some other parts of the developing world.

Returning to the theme of domestic political foundations of economic development, we can begin to appreciate a different perspective in the lead-up to 2011, one that emphasizes socioeconomic discontent built on decades of uneven development. After all, little of the external aid awash in the region since 2000 seems to have trickled down, a fact not lost on much of the region's peoples. Public opinion surveys over that same period consistently ranked the economy and corruption as the top two concerns of most Arab citizens. Countries that already had young and impoverished populations, such as Yemen, Egypt, and Morocco, remained the same. Syria and Jordan faced many of the same problems, as income levels, infrastructure, and overall development have not advanced much past their levels in the mid-1980s. For example, though on the eve of the 2011 uprisings the Middle East exported more fuel than any other region, it also exported fewer manufactured goods than any other region, including sub-Saharan Africa (World Bank 2018).

The region entered the new century with some of the highest unemployment rates in the world, particularly among youth. It was no surprise, then, that organized labor emerged as a prominent actor in the 2011 uprisings. Comparing the Middle East to other regions of the world shows it to be the most economically unequal (Alvaredo, Assouad, and Piketty 2017), which explains why other measures of poverty and living standards have worsened. For example, in Cairo, Amman, or Rabat today, it is easy to see pockets of wealth replete with conspicuous consumption, prestige vehicles, and Western retail chains. For the vast majority of citizens, however, these luxuries are far out of reach, leading to the conclusion that while new wealth is apparent in the region, it remains poorly invested and unevenly distributed. Those with political connections profit, and those profits tend to be spent on consumption and overseas bank accounts, not on productive domestic investments. Not surprisingly, then, among developing regions, Arab countries consistently rank high on indexes measuring perceptions of corruption (UNDP 2004: 136–141). Those without such connections struggle to give their families a better life.

All told, then, political opposition and discontent with socioeconomic conditions came together in 2011 across the region. As we have reviewed, few of these conditions were new; in fact, there was a long history of socioeconomic protest met with state repression. While a full account of the 2011 uprisings is not the charge of this chapter, it was clear that protests in every country were infused with popular anger at corruption, inequality, poor job prospects, and most importantly, the accumulated privileges of regime leaders and their cronies. In Tunisia, protesters targeted First Lady Leila Ben Ali and her real estate holdings and "Mr. 10%" Slim Chiboub and his Carrefour grocery chain. In Egypt, it was Ahmed Ezz's steel and the Mubaraks' Palm Hills. In Yemen, student protesters highlighted the ruling Salih family's trade monopolies; in Syria, the target was Rami Makhlouf's mobile phones and hotels; and in Jordan, public disgust was directed at Marouf Bakhit and his Dead Sea casino project. In these ways, decades of inequality and corruption came out into the open, linking places, monopolies, and regime cronies to give citizens no shortage of symbols of protest.

What then of the oil exporters for whom the socioeconomic context might be different? At first glance, the 2011 uprisings seemed to have bypassed the major Arab resource exporters: Saudi Arabia, Kuwait, Qatar, Oman, and the UAE. On the other hand, Bahrain and Libya witnessed large-scale protest driven by many of the same socioeconomic grievances of the less resource-rich countries. For Libyans, the corruption of the Muammar Qaddafi regime and vast inequality in how oil money was invested in the country animated protest. Bahrain had seen its resource exports decline at roughly the same time promises by the ruling Al Khalifas to allow greater political participation failed to materialize. That many of the country's poorest were also those most politically disenfranchised proved a combustible mix. Both countries attracted external intervention: North Atlantic Treaty Organization (NATO) intervention in Libya to hasten the fall of the Qaddafi regime, and Saudi and UAE intervention in Bahrain to preserve the ruling family there. And if we look more closely, Saudi Arabia, Kuwait, and the UAE were not as calm in the face of 2011 as is widely assumed. While the kind of sustained protests seen in Cairo's Tahrir Square did not sweep the Gulf states, these smaller societies did witness historically unprecedented unrest. Saudi Arabia responded to organized protests with violence in its eastern provinces; parliamentary and mass street protests took place in Kuwait, forcing the Emir Shaikh Sabah al-Ahmad al-Sabah to shut down parliament; and, in response to dissent voiced by some prominent Emiratis, UAE authorities arrested scores and exiled others. In the face of these protests, the oil exporters again benefited from a much larger set of tools with which to respond and survive.

Staggeringly high oil prices until 2008 buoyed public budgets across the Gulf and allowed new forms of investment such as sovereign wealth funds (SWFs). These funds consist of percentages of oil revenues put aside each year. The resulting fund is controlled by the state and invested, usually overseas and without transparency, to earn returns so that in a future without oil reserves, national wealth can be preserved. These SWFs have grown in value into the hundreds of billions of dollars, making Kuwait, the UAE, and Saudi Arabia important global financial players with significant investment in Western government securities and private equities. The new oil boom also ensured continued military purchases from the West at a high pace, reinforcing the deep financial ties between Washington and the Arab Gulf's ruling families. In addition to the use of force in responding to 2011, the oil exporters also deployed their new financial muscle to quell dissent. As Egypt's protests mounted in early 2011, Saudi Arabia, Kuwait, and the UAE announced massive new social spending and civil service pay increases. As protests spread from Egypt and Tunisia, the Gulf oil exporters then promised similar financial support to allied monarchies in Jordan and Morocco. The message was clear: continued ruling family control in the Gulf required the survival of monarchies in the entire region. The rentier state model discussed earlier has gone regional. And perhaps owing to the oil exporters' fiscal muscle, Washington and Europe have been content to pick and choose where to step in—supporting regime opponents in Libya and Syria but supporting the regimes in Bahrain and Saudi Arabia.

For the time being, revenue and repression have worked for the Gulf states and their allies in Jordan and Morocco. Yet, it's important to note that little of this addresses the underlying socioeconomic grievances that have been at play for decades and loomed large in 2011.

Conclusion

Arabs and Muslim society in general have historically been closely associated with commerce. Yet as post–World War II patterns demonstrate, the Middle East's tremendous potential for economic development has not been realized. While much of the region has experienced periods of economic growth and there were early socioeconomic advances, overall little productive development has been sustained. Much of the more recent growth has comprised increased consumption and expansion of money, coming and going with boom and bust. One of the few threads linking all of these phases has been that the groups who have benefited are mostly synonymous with rulers and their allies. More inclusive socioeconomic development, on the other hand, requires more public investment, greater support for competitive exporting, and an increase in the skills, education, and security of domestic labor. Once begun, this kind of development is harder to reverse and tends to build upon itself. With few exceptions, these benchmarks have not been achieved. The millions of Arab citizens who took to the streets in 2011 did so in defiance of a history of economic stagnation and political despotism. Their victory was to achieve tangible hope for meaningful change, but this change will not be easy in political economy terms. Rulers hardly want to embark on the kind of institutional and political changes required, and so coercion and oppression have been easy options. At the same time, periodic and popular protests in many countries since 2011 have proven tenacious and not easily ignored. Equality and justice are not just hopeful concepts; they are at the core of struggles over political and economic futures.

Note

1. *Rentier theory* refers to income in the form of rents. In the classic definition, rental income is viewed as reward rather than something that is earned. Rent often derives from monopoly control of an asset. Some forms of commodity extraction, especially oil, require very little labor and capital investment after the initial drilling, and hence the price of a barrel of oil far exceeds the actual cost of production. Given that oil is state owned in most countries (a monopoly), the difference between low production costs and high world prices is the rent income.

5
Civil Society

Sheila Carapico

Protests in a central Tunisian village in December 2010 initiated what many English speakers called the Arab Spring, but many Tunisians, Egyptians, Syrians, Libyans, and Yemenis envisioned them as revolutionary movements to unseat entrenched dictators. The mass, cross-national occupation of public civic spaces was unprecedented in the Middle East and seemed to inspire or animate the Occupy Wall Street movement in New York and other cities in the Global North. The Arab Spring and the Occupy demonstrations seemed, for a brief window of time, to take civic activism beyond the tame roundtable chambers of professional nongovernmental organizations (NGOs) into the streets. Yet, for different reasons, neither the Arab uprisings nor the Occupy movements achieved their stated goals. Several Arab autocrats were deposed, via popular mobilization or foreign intervention; yet civil war or renewed repression ensued in Syria, Yemen, Libya, and Egypt. Nor did Occupy movements in Europe and North America survive beyond an initial surge of civic activism.

These circumstances raise a key question. What role does civil society play in the mostly authoritarian polities of the Middle East? *Civil society* is broadly defined as an associational space situated between governments and households, and between the public state sector and the commercial economy. It is composed of professional associations, charities, universities, interest groups, media outlets, book clubs, and community betterment drives; of public gatherings or displays in civic-minded parades, concerts, or museums; and of suffrage, labor, civil rights, antiwar, and environmental movements. In times of war, depression, or disaster, activists mobilize relief, soup kitchens, or emergency supplies. Often called the nonprofit, nongovernmental, or "third" sector, civil society is driven by neither the profit motive nor the ambition of political parties or revolutionary movements to take over the state. The civic realm is a place for voluntarism, philanthropy, public-spirited participation, and civil discourse; it's a metaphorical public square.

According to some social scientists, civil society is a distinctively modern phenomenon that gradually replaced primordial associations grounded in ascriptive bonds of caste and clan with individuals' voluntary memberships in the organizations of mass, literate, largely urban, bourgeois society. In many conceptualizations, a vibrant civic associational network and a lively public intellectual domain are the sine qua non for democratic development; to function fully, democracy needs a watchdog "fourth estate" in the press, organized groups to articulate interests and protect rights, and the free flow of ideas and information. Some take this argument a step further to assert that the test of civil society is its enabling of democratic transitions. By this criterion, many regarded civil society in most of the Middle East as impotent, or perhaps disabled. Even after mass mobilizations drove several tyrants from power in 2011 and 2012, some insisted that the test of civil society was whether the uprisings led directly to liberal democracy.

Yet we have known all along that when circumstances demand, civic activism can enable communities to cope with physical or political adversity, to navigate bureaucratic obstacles, and even to breach authoritarianism. Comparative historical research in Europe, the Americas, and elsewhere shows that civil society is not a constant, unchanging cultural attribute but rather a variable that changes shape and scope according to political and economic circumstances. At different moments, German civil society marched for Nazism, cowered from a police state, and breached the Berlin Wall. American civil society was not constant from colonial days through the Jim Crow era, the Great Depression, World War II, the Vietnam protests, and the age of electronic networks; it still assumes different forms in rural Wyoming, urban Manhattan, and suburban Texas. Totalitarian institutions penetrated civic networks in the old Soviet Union; but writers, intellectuals, and regular folk found enclaves in scientific institutes, theatrical companies, or religious and cultural establishments. Histories of postcolonial Africa document ways in which churches, Sufi orders, ethnic associations, and folk traditions contribute to the public civic sphere even in the absence of democratic governance, and sometimes amid very dire socioeconomic conditions or bloody conflict. Finally, as these examples remind us, even if we insist that civil society practice some civility, we should not subscribe to a romantic fantasy of inherent, uniform liberalism; without ideological diversity and debate, tolerance is rather meaningless.

This chapter explores modes of activism in public civic spheres in the Middle East, even, or especially, in the absence of democracy. The main argument is that civic engagement responds to material and political constraints and opportunities. It isn't just "there" or "not there," and it can certainly persist in the absence of liberal democracy. The first section shows that, contrary to Orientalist stereotypes, strong traditions of voluntarism, philanthropy, and community activism in the precontemporary Middle East constituted public civic realms if not modern civil society. The next two sections consider mid-twentieth-century mobilization of civic associations—and how hard new national governments worked to contain, co-opt, or suppress independent public organizing. The ways that individuals and groups operate within, evade, and protest authoritarianism are the subject of the fourth section. Finally, we examine how the historic outpouring of public activism in 2011 constituted a civic revolution even if the near-term outcome was not liberal democracy, as well as how activism adjusted to dire circumstances in an era of counterrevolution.

The Traditional Public Civic Realm

One formerly prominent but now outmoded viewpoint insists that civil society is a product of Western civilization, inimical to the Islamic world. Whole societies and organizations either are or are not civic, according to this essentialist, nearly racist line of reasoning. For some Orientalists, that which is Islamic cannot be simultaneously civil, nor can either indigenous initiatives rooted in ethnic, kinship, or aristocratic identities or philanthropy based on Muslim or tribal impulses be seen as examples of civic spiritedness. This perspective eliminates most Middle Eastern religious and communal charities, libraries, academies, coffeehouses, guilds, foundations, and municipal services as inherently different from the forebears of Euro-American civil society. By contrast, French salons, parochial universities, Knights of Columbus, Jewish community centers, and other faith-based or sectarian institutions are considered civic because of their activities.

The essentialist view of civil society as a historical and cultural constant rather than a variable breaks down easily under scrutiny. So does the claim that Islam, in contrast with the Judeo-Christian traditions, lacks concepts of public spirit, civic engagement, and charity. Inside the Middle East, notably in Jerusalem, the three great monotheistic religions historically provided great and small public services in fundamentally similar ways. In Islam, the concept of *maslahah* (the common good) is well developed. So is *khayriyyah,* meaning welfare. Across the region, community welfare societies were common. *Zakat,* a charitable tithe, is one of the five pillars of Islam. In some places and times, the tithe was spent by community zakat committees. Philanthropy by wealthy men and women was, of course, political as well as pious. *Waqf* (or *hubus*) endowments historically supported public drinking fountains, baths, canal systems, schools, mosques, marketplaces, caravanserais, libraries, and universities. Waqf constituted social as well as economic capital. Educational facilities were important sites of the premodern public civic realm, insulated from state or imperial penetration by the benefactor's wishes. The concept of *sadaqah,* meaning alms or charity, is almost identical in its spelling and its meaning in Hebrew and Arabic. The point here is not that Islam is all about charity, but that Islam has a philanthropic tradition.

Regardless of religion, the regions south of the Mediterranean, down the Red Sea and the Persian Gulf, and stretching to the Indian Ocean, have a very rich urban history, traditions of municipal development, and legacies of local self-help. Clusters of religious scholars, judges, and officials interacted in architecturally rich public spaces. Chambers of commerce and guilds represented traders and tradesmen, offering services to members and their families. Villages, tribes, and neighborhoods collectively owned and supported meager but necessary water supplies, basic education, justice, and marketplaces. There were also judicial and scholarly communities, and Sufi orders. These inhabited a sort of public civic sphere whose role varied, considerably, across geographies and over time. The most profound changes occurred in the modern era alongside the expansion of state authority and big business.

The "development" of civil society was certainly not a linear evolution from a primordial civic realm of waqf, caravanserais, and tribal water management into a modern civil society of journalist syndicates and feminist advocacy. There was always political struggle in and over the civic realm. Colonial rulers and leaders of postcolonial nation-states strove to mobilize or constrain civic institutions and movements. The centuries witnessed constant, multilayered contestation for control of zakat revenues between and among Ottoman (and earlier) caliphates; the kings, muftis, and imams of vassal polities and provinces; and municipal institutions. While religious scholars on royal payrolls asserted the inseparability of Islam from governance as justification for state appropriation of the zakat, jurists in provincial academies often cited the "poor amongst you" clause of the quranic duty to tithe, to insist that revenues be spent locally. Tax revolts erupted when Ottoman and other rulers imposed nonquranic surcharges on the zakat. The centralization of independent foundations and their real estate under Ministries of Awqaf (the plural of waqf) was a long, politicized process everywhere, fraught with protracted disputes over control of waqf bequests, often vast downtown complexes of public buildings together with the commercial property whose revenues subsidized them. Struggles surrounded nationalization of formerly independent educational institutions, whose faculty-designed curricula were replaced by centrally determined lesson plans. Similarly, the amalgamation by colonial and postcolonial governments of heretofore locally autonomous judicial training institutes and religious and tribal courts met provincial resistance.

The mostly precapitalist public civic realm functioned, without a modern state, to provide goods and services—water, education, justice. Forms and practices were not identical to those in Italy or New England, where physical topographies, economic relationships, and political landscapes were very different. In the Middle East, for instance, ecological conditions necessitated complex institutional, legal, and infrastructural arrangements for managing scarce water resources. These varied across the Nile valley, Arabian Desert, Mesopotamia, Kurdistan's mountains, and the Mediterranean coast; among cities, towns, and villages; and according to rainfall and groundwater supplies available for households, animals, and crops. Yet nearly everywhere, water management accorded mosques a vital function beyond ablutions for prayer, gave special prominence to public baths, required complex cooperation among farmers, called for elegant engineering solutions, was continually litigated under Islamic and tribal law, and was often handled by specialized committees. These indigenous, nonprofit, extragovernmental practices had no direct counterpart in soggy Ireland.

In Yemen, disparaged by even Gulf and Mediterranean Arabs as a primitive backwater, residential, professional, and tribal communities acted collectively on social and political issues under changing political, economic, and legal circumstances. For instance in the mid-twentieth century students at a waqf academy in Hadramaut staged a protest play; political prisoners in Hajjah penned radical poems; labor unions staged strikes in Aden; migrant committees financed local schools and water projects in Hujuriyyah; merchants in Hodeida instituted commercial taxes to pay for street improvements; shaikhs mobilized volunteers to clear vehicular tracks up the mountains in al-Mahwit; thousands of men attended national and regional conferences; and exiles in Cairo established a dissident press. These were transitional initiatives, vacillating between customary and contemporary activism, both a sign of socioeconomic change and an engine of that change: community roads, for instance, radically remade the countryside and its relationship to ports and capital cities.

Modern Civic Associations

The interaction of European imperialism and regional dynamics transformed old social systems. New states were carved from the dying Ottoman Empire, and capitalist enclaves emerged in cities like Aden, Alexandria, Algiers, Basra, and Beirut. Political parties spanning the spectrum from the Communists on the left to the Muslim Brotherhood on the right appeared. The numbers of secondary and university students expanded exponentially. These and other changing circumstances expanded and shaped the space for civic activism, creating new exigencies, possibilities, and constraints.

Professional associations became strong, distinctly modern features of Arab civil society. The transition to capitalism stimulated some old trade guilds and merchants' associations to reorganize; more important, it produced new kinds of class- or work-based unions, associations, and cooperatives. Business associations promoted innovative public works conducive to commerce while cultivating contacts with transnational firms and national governments, often wielding political as well as economic clout. Syndicates representing the professions—physicians, attorneys, engineers, teachers, pharmacists, architects, journalists, and other educated, middle-class fields—rose to national prominence. Likewise, especially in and around cities like Baghdad and Cairo, labor unions organized to represent workers, particularly in large transportation and manufacturing enterprises. In rural areas, farmers formed agricultural cooperatives and peasants' associations. Student unions gave voice to university campuses that were growing into large public spaces. Among these, labor unions were especially well positioned to engage in large-scale actions such as strikes, but farmers, students, women, and professionals organized marches, petition drives, publicity campaigns, and the like.

Another noticeable advance directly connected to changing economies was the appearance of new kinds of charities and welfare societies. Many, but not all, were faith-based. Among those with a spiritual mandate, new and different Christian and Jewish models imported from Europe by missionaries and settlers made their mark in education, health, and the creation of the Jewish state. Muslim charities combining European, Ottoman, and indigenous practices expanded the range and number of their projects. Volunteers utilizing charitable donations provided free health clinics, Ramadan meals, women's centers, orphanages, parochial and secular education, and other welfare services. Although piety motivated many donors, teams of social scientists, feminists, and communists, among secular communities, joined social welfare movements in the Levant, North Africa, and Mesopotamia.

Civil society as a public realm for discussion and debate expanded with advances in education and the media. The print press, followed by radio, television, cassette tapes, cable stations, and the internet, all spawned new communities of information and of shared interest. Because it is the lingua franca of what became, in the interwar era, more than twenty countries, broadcasting and publishing in Arabic spread information and ideas out from Cairo, Baghdad, and Beirut, the media centers. Arabic-language radio and later television influenced public discourses, literally shaping something called modern standard Arabic.

Cities across the Arab world, Turkey, Iran, and what would become Israel experienced an intellectual renaissance. Communities of socially conscious artists, writers, performers, educators, and other professions formed clubs and salons, started schools, published newspapers, wrote treatises and manifestos, created art, and performed music or poetry. National and international conferences of intellectuals, such as international women's conferences held in Damascus and Baghdad, made special contributions to the public civic sphere.

The spread of sports leagues, recreational clubs, and large sporting events added to the new public civic realm. Teams, games, and fan clubs provide public experiences that generate social solidarity and social networks, within and across neighborhood and municipal lines. Fans flocked to huge soccer stadiums, cheering urban or national teams; boys played in empty neighborhood lots. These new public spaces established communities, expressed nationalism, and occasionally (as in the Egyptian uprising in 2011) contributed politically relevant modalities of mass expression.

Many or all of these civic repertoires were available for mobilization in moments of upheaval, disaster, or transition. Especially during the movements for national independence, syndicates, unions, sports clubs, medical charities, sororities, campuses, media, and other networks became sites of mass participation. Now and then, enthusiasts filled downtown streets. In the 1930s and 1940s, Cairo and Baghdad were hotbeds of public activism by intellectuals, workers, feminists, professionals, and others. The long anticolonial struggles in Algeria and South Yemen during the 1950s and 1960s engaged peaceful demonstrators alongside independence fighters. In Kuwait and Jordan, where sovereignty was granted rather than won militarily, the public civic sphere was galvanized by the pending transfer of power. Other places and moments of extraordinary, even frenzied, public civic involvement included Turkey in the early days of its republic, Iran in the dying days of the Shah's reign, Yemen immediately after unification, and Palestine in the mid-1990s when hopes were high that a state would be created in the West Bank and Gaza. But just as engagement overflowed around propitious historical events, it subsided at other times, especially in the face of ascendant police states.

Curtailing Civil Society

After independence, governments sought to rein in civic energies. Newly installed monarchs and strongmen often consolidated national power by attempting to obliterate alternative loci of legitimacy and harnessing community energies toward the central statebuilding project. In Turkey, Iran, Saudi Arabia, Egypt, and elsewhere, governments sought to undermine or curtail previously powerful clerical, judicial, academic, and commercial institutions. As explained elsewhere in this book, military officers gained power and established ruling parties in most of the newly established republics: Egypt, Algeria, Tunisia, Syria, Iraq, and both Yemens. The Baath Party in Syria and Iraq, the National Liberation Front in Algeria, the Socialist Party in South Yemen, and the Arab Socialist Union (later renamed the National Democratic Party) in Egypt laid claim to representing their entire populations via the parties' incorporation of civic organizations into their ranks. Although practices varied, the prevailing strategy was to give a veneer of legitimacy to centralized authoritarian governance by bringing most voluntary associations and other institutions under ruling-party control, and simultaneously to stifle existing or new autonomous organizations and media through regulation and censorship.

In effect, just as businesses like banks, industries, and the properties of the old aristocracies were nationalized, so too were universities, media enterprises, unions, syndicates, popular associations, charities, and even mosques. Agricultural cooperatives and community development associations were amalgamated into pyramidal nationwide federations with mandatory membership. National leagues of women, youth unions, and peasant associations were fused to ruling parties, sometimes in exchange for token parliamentary representation. Ruling parties or government agencies harnessed and regulated professional syndicates of the educated middle and upper-middle classes. With the nationalization of transportation and industry, port workers, rail workers, and factory workers became state employees, represented by national unions affiliated with or subsumed within ruling parties. In many fields, membership in the national federation or union, a precondition for employment or benefits, effectively mandated party membership. Charities were bureaucratized. Not only academic curricula but in many places even congregational sermons parroted government propaganda. Ministries of education, health, labor, agriculture, industry, and information wielded inordinate power in their sectors.

In a second prong of the same strategic centralization of social capital, independent civic organizing was effectively curtailed by draconian laws of association, known as nongovernmental organization (NGO) laws, and by ministries of social affairs that were empowered to approve or dissolve social organizations. Egypt generated the model for laws of association throughout the Arab region: North Yemen, Algeria, Jordan, and later the incipient Palestinian Authority and even the Coalition Provisional Authority in Iraq (in Order 45 of 2003) replicated language and restrictions from Egypt's associational law. Egypt's Ministry of Social Affairs (MOSA) was created in the 1930s to oversee social reform experiments and pilot community services operated by organizations as diverse as the Egyptian Society for Social Studies, the Muslim Brotherhood, the Communist Party, and the Daughters of the Nile. Law 49 of 1945 entitled the ministry to register, oversee, audit, and dissolve all associations. The nationalist military officers, who in the 1950s abolished the pro-British monarchy, promised free universal services, and embarked on a program of nationalizations, were suspicious of elitist charities, politicized associations, and independent social activism, whether foreign-influenced or indigenous, politically conservative or progressive. They banned both the Communists and the Brotherhood and enacted legislation to rein in freelance social work. The notorious Law 34 of 1964 suspended 4,000 associations already registered, pending their reorganization under new, complex regulations empowering MOSA to merge, suspend, reorganize, or freeze the assets of any organization for reasons not specified. The ministry did exercise this power.

In the 1990s the notion of the NGO came into vogue among international donors and democracy brokers. North American, European, and United Nations (UN) agencies budgeted funds for distribution as grants to civil society advocacy organizations, known in the aid industry as CSOs. Indeed, among professional development brokers and the staff of international NGOs, it became the convention to equate "civil society" with NGOs, and to use the two terms more or less interchangeably. The expression NGO, written and pronounced exactly as in English (or alternatively, in the French version, as ONG), entered written and spoken Arabic. Donor agencies developed precise criteria for NGOs' eligibility for small grants and inclusion in NGO conferences and networks. To register as an observer at a UN convention or obtain funds from European or US agencies, organizations had to submit paperwork documenting goals that were expressly consonant with the sponsors', at least three years' worth of financial records, elections for their boards of directors, and a suitable plan of activities. Those so qualifying for civil society funding—formal organizations with professional translators and accountants and a liberal organizational mandate—could compete for funds.

Authoritarian governments resisted this perceived intrusion by various methods. One strategy government ministries deployed to reinforce monopolies on both foreign aid and ideological discourse was known as cloning: the creation of state-backed nongovernmental organizations, also called GONGOs (government-organized NGOs). Yemen's ruling party, the General People's Congress, encouraged party members to found NGOs to compete with autonomous organizations in similar issue areas for international assistance and domestic publicity. The Tunisian government created a number of "front" NGOs, like Lawyers Without Borders, often infiltrated by security police. So-called RONGOs (royally organized NGOs) headed or endowed by members of the ruling Hashimite family, especially its princesses, multiplied in Jordan. A similar phenomenon took place in Morocco.

In Jordan, Morocco, Tunisia, Algeria, Egypt, Yemen, and the Palestinian Authority, NGO and other laws blocked access to foreign funds by counter-elites in order to maintain control of patronage networks and development assistance packages. The Egyptian government took particular umbrage with professional advocacy organizations like the Arab Women's Solidarity Association, the Egyptian Association of Human Rights, and the Ibn Khaldun Center, whose Egyptian-American director and Sudanese accountant were imprisoned for making a European-financed documentary that Cairo charged was "harmful to Egypt's reputation." Indeed, after several lawsuits, and despite vigorous criticism from Egyptian activists and international agencies, Law 34 was tightened explicitly to limit political activities and close loopholes that had enabled some associations to evade ministerial oversight by registering as non-profit civil companies. Associations Law 84 of 2002 specifically forbade NGOs from engaging in labor advocacy or political campaigning, tightened ministerial micromanagement, and empowered MOSA State Security to prosecute violations of the many specified restrictions.

Along with even cruder devices like spying on citizens, banning public meetings, outlawing criticism of the head of state, arbitrary detention, and physical brutality, these measures curtailed civic activism. In Syria and Iraq under the Baathis, in Libya and Turkey under the generals, in Iran under the Shah, in the Palestinian territories under Israeli occupation, and to a considerable extent in Tunisia, Egypt, Yemen, and the Islamic Republic of Iran, ever-watchful national security establishments penetrated deep into public civic realms. Gatherings of more than a handful of people outside their homes required a special permit in many countries. It was nearly impossible to operate under police radar. Progressive and left-leaning or labor-oriented politicking was stringently suppressed. In some circumstances, like occupied Palestine and Baathist Iraq, religious congregations or tribal associations, though not entirely insulated from government interference, were the safest outlets for civic impulses, charity, and self-help. This was true in Iran under the Shah, too, which helps explain why religious authorities gravitated to the center of the power vacuum created by the Islamic revolution; ironically, the Islamic Republic cracked down on religious institutions and associations for the same reason.

Civil Society in Action

Short of armed insurrection, how can ordinary people and educated elites challenge such constraints? This section considers various forms of civic engagement under conditions of authoritarian repression. They can be grouped under three headings: the quotidian ways that people engage in the public sphere, either within the system or by finding enclaves outside it; the more exceptional, take-to-the-streets moments of mass civic involvement; and ways in which citizens pursue their causes transnationally and in cyberspace.

Working Within the System

Some space exists for participating within the bounds of authoritarian political systems. First, millions of people belong to tens of thousands of licensed and registered labor unions, professional syndicates, women's federations, cooperatives, sports leagues, municipal betterment clubs, welfare funds, chambers of commerce, farmers' bureaus, alumni organizations, research centers, student governments, benevolent societies, theatrical groups, parent-teacher associations, and other voluntary organizations. Syndicates for faculty, journalists, physicians, engineers, and other professions are strong middle-class lobbying and voluntary associations. Members meet, elect officers, put out newsletters, recruit participants, march in parades, sponsor fundraising drives, host street fairs, and respond to humanitarian emergencies. Moreover, organizations of the sort we think of as the epitome of civil society—professional think tank–type advocacy groups dedicated to causes such as human rights, women's issues, or social reform—mushroomed across the Middle East, from Iran to Morocco. They hold authorized conferences and public service events. Staff or volunteers write essays and give lectures. While vocally political projects rankle authorities, people in cities, towns, and rural areas tackle less controversial projects on a regular, ongoing basis.

Second, cultural and customary venues offer a different sort of civic outlet in some settings and circumstances. Funeral processions or fortieth-day commemorations, normally apolitical ceremonies, can take shape as protest displays, as when the Shah's forces murdered protesting seminarians and then more students who gathered to mourn the seminarians, and again decades later when the same murder-mourning-punishment cycle was repeated under the Islamic Republic during the 2009 Green Movement protests: extraordinary circumstances infused a religious ritual with protest energies. Day-to-day social gatherings in coffeehouses may contain sustained intellectual exchange about public affairs. In the affluent Gulf monarchies, where formal organizations with any sort of political agenda are inhibited, the customary cultural institution of the *diwaniyya* is an important site for public-spirited debate and deliberation. A *diwan* is a room, typically adjacent to the main house, where guests gather; the *diwaniyya* is the name for that gathering. It's a space that is physically within the domestic realm of the household, or the private sphere—but also a public space where men or women (usually not both together) gather for coffee or tea and conversation. In Yemen the corresponding venue is the qat chew, also a public gathering inside a *diwan*, where the chewing of this slightly stronger stimulant elicits even livelier conversation.

These are informal institutions, unregulated societal customs authenticated by "tradition." What suggests that these rather quaint semipublic gatherings constitute a civic realm is not only the nature of the discussions but also the sheer ubiquity and frequency of the meetings, whose repetitive, alternating, and interlocking attendance seems to engage large segments of the public in a common conversation.

Another institution that is not inherently civic, but can be a vehicle for civic activism, is the tribe. Yemeni and Iraqi tribes are grounded in a region or locality; the tribe's members are the ranchers and farmers of the region bearing the tribe's name. When management of community property—water sources, grazing lands, market trails, and sometimes marketplaces—was organized historically through the tribe, committees formed to collect and spend the zakat or raise cash contributions or work crews via a tribal rallying call. Later, tribal institutions took charge of upgrading water delivery systems and roads, or lobbied the state to do so. Thus community betterment associations can be organized on tribal principles. During times of political ferment, tribal institutions organized protests, conferences, peace mediations, and demands for constitutional reforms. So, while almost no one considers tribes themselves civic associations, neither are they simply vestiges of a precapitalist primordial civic realm: tribal networks can sometimes be mobilized for grassroots organizing.

The charitable endeavors we hear the most about are the faith-based initiatives, especially Islamic welfare societies, many of which combine traditional motifs with thoroughly modern practices. As discussed in Chapter 6, the contemporary Islamist political movement is multifaceted. It includes legal and illegal political parties that attempt, either via elections or by use of violence, to assume local, provincial, or national leadership. Parts of the movement are situated, somewhat insulated, inside mosque congregations and religious academies. There's a violent wing, too, in many countries and across the region. As a definitional matter we should distinguish civic participation from either partisanship or religious worship, and also, obviously, from militancy. But old and new Islamic institutions do qualify as part of civil society in the same way that Jewish, Coptic, or Maronite welfare associations, think tanks, community centers, and philanthropic foundations do. The clampdown against leftists and progressive forces across the Middle East in the 1970s and 1980s indirectly empowered more conservative, pious institutions associated with the Islamist movement toward the turn of the millennium. Islamist institutions are many, varied, and vibrant, and they include both contemporary versions of traditional practices like zakat committees or waqf endowments and thoroughly modern hospitals, benevolent associations, and universities. Denominational charities and welfare associations have provided particularly crucial services where states failed to function as such—

particularly in Lebanon during the civil war, the West Bank and Gaza, wartime Iraq, and more recently in Syria and Yemen—but they also offer an essential social safety net in the poor countries of the Middle East.

People can network without joining formal organizations via small, short-term projects that marshal limited resources. Poor women join informal reciprocity networks of friends and neighbors. Unregistered, largely invisible, and comprising both men and women, these networks support rescue squads, community welfare funds, cleanup days, and neighborhood watch committees. Parents cooperate with or beyond schools and pool their resources for childcare, tutoring, playgrounds, and other youth-oriented educational and recreational activities.

Artists and other intellectuals find ways to articulate frustrations and aspirations within the bounds of censorship. Arabic and Persian verbal arts like poetry, song, storytelling, and jokes provide fictionalized satirical commentary on politics and society in the guise of parables about lions or pharaohs. These are passed by word of mouth; shared among friends inside homes, classrooms, or *diwans*; or distributed via cassette, CD, or, more recently, Facebook, Twitter, and YouTube. Nowadays, rap and *rai* musicians animate the imaginations of youth and concertgoers with their political lyrics. In addition, researchers and educators produce and disseminate socially and politically conscious materials for use by activists, and scholars hold workshops and seminars. Consider the work of women writers, scholars, and performers, for example, or a concert in Cairo in April 2008 by popular activist singer Marcel Khalifa, who performed songs with messages of labor solidarity and the works of Palestinian poet Mahmoud Darwish.

Organized interests find some room within semiauthoritarian systems to lobby parliaments for political reform. This is not easy, of course. In the century-long struggle of Egyptian women, there were suffragette marches in the 1930s, and women's groups staged a sit-in at the parliament during the ferment leading up to the 1952 revolution. Writers, performers, and political figures publicized women's issues in the 1960s, 1970s, and 1980s. In one of a long series of focused campaigns involving complex coalition building, feminists called hundreds of meetings and enlisted jurists, historians, and a new generation of young female scholars to find religiously based arguments to repeal clauses in Egyptian family law that prohibited women from initiating a divorce; in 2001 they won a modest but significant legislative victory.

Protest Activities

When the legal avenues for complaint and lobbying are exhausted, when conditions become intolerable, or amid crises, people take to the streets, often in organized fashion, sometimes spontaneously. Even prior to the phenomenal confluence of Arab uprisings in 2011, three sets of issues seemed to prompt mass protests, which usually started off peacefully but were often confronted by police armed with laws prohibiting mass gatherings.

First, and frequently, people gather to protest wars. Demonstrations erupt across the Middle East in response to Israeli and US military actions; some protests and rallies have government support, but others face riot police. For six weeks in March and April 2002, during the Israeli incursion into the West Bank, protesters streamed into Amman's streets, where they were confronted with tank cordons. The following spring, when the US-led coalition invaded Iraq, some 20,000 demonstrators filled downtown Cairo shouting antiwar slogans and scorning George W. Bush and Tony Blair; a few hundred activists, lawyers, journalists, and students then assembled in front of the national bar association to demand the release of protesters who had been dragged off to jail. Millions marched against Israel's incursion into Lebanon in 2006 and Gaza in early 2009. In the face of war, people don't just voice disapproval, however. Like Europeans or Americans, Middle Easterners also organize charitable and medical donations for war victims in Afghanistan, Bosnia, Palestine, and elsewhere.

Second, economic protests in defiance of government policies come in two forms: labor activism by employees and demonstrations against economic conditions by consumers. Both are mostly confined to the low-income countries, although there have been a few labor actions among usually passive immigrant workers in the Gulf as well. A wave of strikes gripped Egypt, the most populous country in the region, in 2006–2007. The most dramatic, protracted industrial action involved 30,000 textile workers at the Spinning and Weaving Company in Mahalla. In another episode, 2,000 members of the pharmacists' syndicate rallied to protest police raids on drugstores and privatization of the national pharmaceutical company. In June 2007, Al-Azhar University professors demonstrated for better pay. Over 50,000 Egyptian property-tax collectors engaged in a lengthy work stoppage and a ten-day sit-in in front of the national cabinet office, demanding salaries commensurate with other public sector white-collar workers. In 2008, a wheat and bread crisis led to more mass protest. In Yemen during 2005 and beyond, a series of demonstrations and protest marches, including a few that turned into riots, resisted policies like the lifting of subsidies on diesel fuel and the raising of taxes as the government passed the costs of its fiscal crisis on to consumers and citizens. All these and many other protests took different forms depending on context.

Third, people organize and agitate for political reform. Algerians wracked by economic crises and fed up with political conditions networked, protested, and lobbied in the late 1980s, pressing the ruling party for openly contested elections. In Yemen between unification in 1990 and the first national elections in 1993, and between the 1993 elections and the outbreak of civil war in 1994, tens of thousands participated in conferences leading to what became known as a national dialogue: a solidarity conference in 1990, a cohesion conference in 1991, half a dozen other tribal conferences in rural areas, and urban meetings in Ta'iz and other cities—all complete with working papers written by scholars and petitions for better public health care, local and national elections, proper judicial procedures, and other reforms. In between, scores of colloquia and academic workshops generated resolutions and proposals for nationwide publication and distribution. The National Dialogue of Political Forces, a broad coalition led by two or three dozen nationally prominent political figures from across the ideological spectrum, was supported by countless weekly seminars and antiwar vigils on university campuses.

Additional important protest movements and civic activities are described in other chapters in this book. The first Palestinian intifada was especially noteworthy. As well, three decades after Iranians deposed the Shah in a mass uprising only to find themselves constrained by a new form of authoritarianism, in 2009 students and others gathered repeatedly to protest the closure of newspapers, attacks on intellectuals, the fraudulent trial of an outspoken professor, and the less-than-transparent reelection of an increasingly unpopular president.

Neither the Algerians nor the Yemenis were able to thwart the eventual outbreak of domestic armed conflict in the early 1990s (a short war in Yemen and protracted murderous strife in Algeria). Civil society proved an insufficient bulwark against ruling military establishments, and activists became disheartened by the resort to violence. The crushing of the first intifada and the greater resort to violence in the second were very sobering. The multifaceted surge of activism by judges, workers, students, and others in Egypt during the middle of the first decade of the twenty-first century, including the Kifaya (Enough!) and April 6 movements, took years to reach a tipping point. The limits to the so-called Cedar Revolution in Lebanon, the brutal crackdown against protesters in Iran, the sporadic nature of demonstrations in Jordan, and the limited success of other popular movements analyzed elsewhere in this volume explain widespread pessimism in the region and abroad about the prospects for civil society to generate sustained, meaningful political reform. When crowds tried to initiate meaningful change, they were confronted by heavy-handed police and security establishments claiming to be defending law and order.

Transnational Public Civic Realms and Cyberspace

Besides the outlets for their civic energies people find in the everyday world of parent-teacher associations and in exceptional take-to-the-streets moments, two extraterritorial arenas for activism are available to speakers of multinational languages (Arabic, English, or French). First, at international conference circuits, rights defenders can take their complaints and claims to the transnational arena. Second, the internet offers new possibilities for expression and networking. Available mainly to elites, these very contemporary spaces for expression and agitation can at least partly evade state censorship and restrictions on assembly. Because of the lingua franca and a common media sphere, inter-Arab networks can—as in 2011—show particular vibrancy.

Sometimes relying on donor resources, Arab (and sometimes Turkish, Israeli, Iranian, or Kurdish) rights advocates from different countries find common cause in regional women's organizations, bar associations, journalists' clubs, and other groups via annual or more frequent conferences. Consider the conference circuit dedicated to gender issues and female empowerment, which was activated by the 1995 Beijing Conference on Women and a host of preparatory and follow-up meetings. Scores of intergovernmental, governmental, and nongovernmental organizations, machineries, and agencies connect with a vast associational complex operating on several scales simultaneously: global, regional, national, and local. This complex has specialized branches dealing with family law, honor crimes, labor rights, gender images in media, and other topics. Scores of Arab and other Middle Eastern women's groups participate in this network, attending global and regional plenary meetings and then conveying lessons learned once back home in workshops and training sessions. This material serves as the basis for national campaigns to reform divorce or criminal law or propose gender quotas for parliamentary elections. Even when conferences take place in Cairo, Amman, Doha, Ankara, or other Middle Eastern cities—and of course especially when women travel to Europe, North America, or Asia—the dialogue is extraterritorial and multilingual. This is an intermittent expansion of the public civic sphere beyond national boundaries.

Comparable networks unite judicial and rights communities in the Middle East and abroad that convene to discuss matters of national and international law. For instance, the Union Internationale des Avocats, a consortium of some 200 national bar associations, held its annual meeting at the Jnan Palace Hotel and the Fez Congress Centre in 2005 around the theme "Lawyers of the World: A Single Code of Ethics?" With simultaneous translation into French, Arabic, Spanish, and English, this was an event both in Morocco and in the transnational sphere. A 2006 conference titled "The Role of the Judiciary in the Process of Political Reform in Egypt and in the Arab World," organized by the Cairo Institute for Human Rights Studies in coordination with the Euro-Med Network, attracted judges, advocates, lawyers, and scholars from eleven

Arab states, France, Germany, and the United States. Scores of such meetings constitute a transnational community of Arab jurists and advocates with a common language, modern standard legal Arabic. They establish epistemic communities of legal practitioners who may be equally critical, for instance, of the egregious offenses of the Saddam Hussein regime and the US occupation that followed it. Pan-Arab and transnational solidarity-building networks thus enable some activists to take reform agendas outside the realm of sovereign dictatorship.

A second extraterritorial space for civic engagement exists on the internet and in the blogosphere. The World Wide Web, of course, is a virtual rather than a physical public sphere. People type on their devices, sitting at home or in an internet café, rather than conversing face-to-face or massing in the streets. Yet as others have noted, the scope and reach of websites, blog posts, and text messaging are wide, even infinite; the capacity to disseminate messages, in words and in video, including video captured on cell phones, is unprecedented.

In the early twenty-first century, Middle Easterners have deployed the power of the internet to communicate political messages to fellow citizens and foreigners. Examples include Riverbend, the Baghdad blogger who fiercely resisted the Anglo-American occupation of Iraq, and Egyptian dissidents who created the enormously famous "We Are All Khalid Sa'id" Facebook page to protest police brutality. Iranian and Israeli peace activists reached beyond linguistic and national boundaries to contact comrades abroad and even nearby. During Israel's Gaza campaign of early 2009, the Arabic blogosphere lit up with messages nearly as critical of Arab governments as of the Israeli Defense Forces.

Many outsiders dubbed the 2011 Arab uprisings a Facebook revolution. Inside Tunisia, Egypt, and other affected countries, people who communicated face-to-face or via cell phone found this silly, because the internet was really not a tool of mass mobilization domestically. Instead, the World Wide Web, YouTube, and even elite conference networks were mediums of international exchange. They helped communicate what was happening in Tunisia to Egyptians and then Yemenis, Bahrainis, Libyans, Syrians, and the world at large. Technology and globalization did not mobilize Yemenis, who by 2011 had been protesting for years, but direct contact with Tunisians and Egyptians emboldened the youth movement and broadened the pan-Arab discursive sphere.

Civic Revolutions

For years prior to 2011 Yemenis had been staging political rallies and finding other ways to challenge an increasingly authoritarian and corrupt government. Beneath the facade of stability Egypt had been in foment for a decade. Tunisians, Libyans, Bahrainis, and Syrians seethed with frustration. Across the region, flash protests appeared and vanished. Now and then seemingly apolitical soccer fans took over whole cities. Living standards had been deteriorating, except perhaps for members of bloated national security establishments and Gulf royal families. Meanwhile more human rights groups undertook professional investigations into instruments of repression wielded against dissidents and agitators. In recognition of millions of Arab citizens demanding social justice, the 2011 Nobel Peace Prize was awarded to Tawakkul Karman, head of an association called Women Journalists Without Chains. She had been arrested in Yemen and released shortly before emerging as a spokesperson for the movement to drive Ali Abdullah Salih from power.

In retrospect it was not surprising that a seemingly minor incident ignited mass indignation in Tunisia, that millions of Egyptians took to the streets after a blatantly fraudulent election and so much police and security abuse, that tens of thousands of Yemenis decided to camp out until basic political demands were addressed, or that, after peaceful marches were met with brute force, Libyan and Syrian dissidents took up arms against two of the most despicable of Arab dictatorships. The surprise was that all these things happened in such rapid succession, or simultaneously, and galvanized Arab civic imaginations and Western perceptions in heretofore unthinkable ways.

The improbable spark for the so-called Arab Spring was when a street vendor in provincial Tunisia set himself on fire after an all-too-common altercation with a police officer. His friends, their friends, their contacts, and others who heard of what happened decided to take a stand. An ordinary event spawned extraordinary public reaction. After a month of popular protests, a Tunisian dictator in power for more than three decades fled with his family to Saudi Arabia. Meanwhile the mother and friends of a young man murdered at a police station, Khalid Sa'id, invited Egyptians to show their defiance on Police Day, January 25, 2011. A video of this sad, soft-spoken mother speaking from her couch went viral. The turnout was huge. Three days later, on January 28, sports fans accustomed to claiming the streets joined political dissidents, civic activists, and other angry citizens in breaking through police barricades. Throngs of people occupied Cairo's iconic Tahrir Square for another fifteen days before another lifelong dictator abdicated. By this time Yemenis mobilized protests that blended slogans from Tunisia and Egypt—"the people want the downfall of the regime" and "leave!"—with indigenous national or local chants, symbols, performances, manifestos, and other forms of political expression. In all three cases, citizens acted collectively by gathering in public places and organizing to provide sanitation, protection, food, internet access, and safety to protest encampments. Cairo's neighborhood watch and cleanup committees engaged energies that may or may not have been sympathetic to the revolt against Husni Mubarak. Against incredible odds, Yemeni protesters persevered for months on end in tent cities in Sana'a, Ta'iz, and other towns before the dictator finally (and grudgingly) relinquished power.

Meanwhile, videographers, artists, bloggers, high school students, rappers, journalists, and others contributed socially conscious images, essays, and songs to the public civic sphere. Archivists collated these forms of creative expression for posterity. Public art and gallery exhibitions were commemorative, decorative, and inspirational. There were more job actions (organized employee protests) than ever. Labor and professional syndicates replaced leaders. Interest groups strategized. Human rights organizations worked overtime. University faculty insisted on electing deans. Schoolchildren demanded better lunches. More parents joined educational committees. Thousands of Web initiatives and YouTube videos were launched.

Activism Amid Counterrevolutionary Violence

The uprisings that in 2010–2012 swept Arab republics where presidents had overstayed their welcome and maneuvered to appoint family members as successors revealed the collective power of bilingual elites, sports fanatics, wage laborers, rural smallholders, women's rights activists, students and graduates, neighborhood watch volunteers, and others to assert custodianship of public spaces. Mass protests defied the power of national security states, the disproportionate influence of oil monarchies, and the smug theories of Western transitions-to-democracy experts. They demonstrated the power of the multitudes.

However, the multitudes—and the myriad civic microefforts—could not easily overcome the powers of deep states, regional monarchies, and their Western allies. Outcomes varied substantially. Saudi tanks crushed the uprising in Bahrain, which was the only monarchy deemed part of the Arab Spring. Protests toppled leaders in Tunisia, Egypt, Yemen, and Libya—but not Syria, where the regime of Bashar al-Assad survived a complex, ferocious civil war. In Tunisia and Egypt heretofore banned Islamist parties won astoundingly free and fair elections, although the Egyptian army overthrew the Muslim Brotherhood government in 2013. The North Atlantic Treaty Organization (NATO) facilitated the bloody demise of the Libyan tyrant Muammar Qaddafi and probably the ensuing civil war.

Postuprising Tunisia and Yemen stood out for both similarities and profound differences. Both entrusted the transition to widely praised national dialogue conversations. The Nobel Peace Prize committee recognized the outspoken opposition leader Tawakkul Karman in 2011, when it looked as if "revolutions" in several countries would succeed. The Tunisian National Dialogue Quartet, composed of important, well-established civil society organizations—two labor confederations, the Tunisian Human Rights League, and the Tunisian Order of Lawyers—won the 2015 Nobel Peace Prize for initiating the national dialogue. In both cases formal national dialogues engaged civic leaders and politicians from a wide political spectrum.

Tunisia is widely hailed as the (relative) success story of the wave of uprisings that originated there, largely (though not entirely) as a result of civil society activism. Representatives of twenty-one Tunisian political parties grappling with increased polarization in 2013—and conscious of the military coup d'état in Egypt—convened for six months of extragovernmental negotiations. They reached consensus on fundamental principles. Their pact laid the groundwork for a second round of openly contested elections in October 2014, and for a Truth and Dignity Commission. If anything, in this instance, civil society appears as the prerequisite for democracy, rather than vice versa. Nonetheless, journalists, human rights observers, and activists continue to encounter challenges and limitations, especially in reporting on the behavior of state institutions.

Yemen initiated its National Dialogue Conference (NDC) in 2013, when over 600 men and women representing a panoply of political parties and tendencies and every province began meeting at the Movenpick Hotel in Sana'a. As an experience—especially for the substantial female contingent (28 percent) and a smaller group of "youth," both of whom had been activists in the revolutionary movement but were previously more or less excluded from central decisionmaking—the NDC opened opportunities for meaningful national-level civic participation. But it also rested on a strange political agreement known as the Gulf Cooperation Council (GCC) Initiative that replaced the incumbent president, Salih, with his handpicked deputy, Abdrabbo Mansour Hadi, and granted immunity to Salih. The GCC monarchies, mistrustful and restrictive of civic initiatives and democratic institutions, held the purse strings. International consultants lectured conference delegates. In the end, outside the formal process, Hadi hastily appointed a committee to draft a new constitution without sufficient input from key constituencies. In a convoluted turn of events, fighting broke out, Hadi fled to Riyadh, and an international coalition led by Saudi Arabia and the United Arab Emirates and armed by the United States, the UK, and other NATO members intervened to reinstate Hadi. The coalition bombed mercilessly while armed militias occupied various towns and districts.

Thus while it initially resembled Tunisia, several years later Yemen's political and military situation was closer to Syria's and Libya's. Under circumstances of violence and desperation (and in Yemen mass food insecurity and rampant disease), a national civic realm collapses. Instead, communities cope with conditions ranging from punishing bombardment to occupation by jihadi groups to influxes of displaced persons to relative normalcy. Activism takes various forms, often localized or regionalized, sometimes sectarianized and/or partisan, drawing on past precedents or devising new mechanisms, according to exigencies and occasions.

Emergency medical response, familiar to Palestinian, Lebanese, Iraqi, and perhaps Algerian communities but not to most Libyans, Syrians, and Yemenis, necessarily depends on trained professionals working as volunteer ambulance drivers, nurses, and so forth. It also depends on financial contributions for medicines and supplies, and on the blood, sweat, and tears of neighbors and family members. Community-based rescue missions—vital initiatives amidst complex domestic conflicts—scarcely resemble the placid concept of civil society dependent on functioning democracy. Yet they epitomize voluntarism and philanthropy. Finding places and ways to bury the dead means tapping religious and primordial traditions while coping with very modern circumstances.

Similarly, some faith communities or municipal networks tapped communal solidarities in offering succor to orphans, displaced families, and other people enduring hunger and/or disease. Depending on capabilities and needs, towns, neighborhoods, or societies fragmented by multiple, localized wars converted schools to hostels, arranged food collection and distribution, found ways to deliver water, or mounted online GoFundMe campaigns. Yemen's competing factions—including the Southern-separatist Hirak, the Zaydi-militant Ansar Allah (better known as the Houthi militia), the Tihama solidarity movement, and an array of Salafi or self-declared Sunni groups in distinct locales—arranged relief for their followers, or to recruit followers. Hirak, Tihami activists, and others (hardly known outside) organized to communicate and advance regional interests. Whether they are movements, lobbyists, or primordial groups lies in the eye of the beholder. In some enclaves, they mount public demonstrations of the sort that engender a 2011-style sense of collective political expression. Mothers of the disappeared gather outside supposedly clandestine prisons—sometimes protected by chivalry, other times brutalized, always hoping to publicize brutalities.

Even in wartime—when roundtable discussions seem effete and removed from the brutality of everyday life—the sorts of initiatives envisioned by civil society experts in the democracy-promotion industry persist. Libyan, Syrian, and Yemeni activists—especially younger, English-speaking, tech-savvy campaigners—get their messages across. Activists in their home countries and abroad blog, post to social media, create documentaries or data sets, attend conferences or participate on televised panels, and grant interviews to journalists—all to call international attention to their plights or causes. Photographers and videographers posting on Facebook or other cybervenues spread messages of pathos and desperation. Importantly, as authorities in control of entry visas blocked visits from Amnesty International or Human Rights Watch, domestic or exiled war-crime monitors—some frankly partisan, others striving for an elusive "neutrality"—attempted to document abuses. This was true not only for the three countries engulfed in savage conflict, but also in Turkey and Egypt under martial law, Iran amid tumult and some reluctance to appeal to Western audiences, Palestinians in the West Bank and Gaza, and dissidents in the usually placid kingdoms of the Gulf.

Conclusion

Civic activism is a variable, not a constant. If it were an immutable cultural characteristic with no historical or geographical variation, as Orientalists used to assert, there would be no variations across time and place. Instead, in the Middle East, as elsewhere, civil society advances and retreats, and changes scope and shape, responding to constraints, openings, and emergencies. Historical antecedents in traditional public civic realms refute Orientalists' tropes presenting only the most Europeanized societies of Turkey and Israel, and nowadays perhaps Tunisia, as capable of proper civic activism. Late colonial and postcolonial civic efflorescence, usually centered on national independence, was subsequently co-opted to a centralized, hierarchical, often stifling nation-building project. As detailed in other chapters, governments resorted to banal repression to curtail civic activism.

Nonetheless, in ordinary ways and crisis-driven outbursts, people organized, animated, and debated, sometimes within legal channels and sometimes by challenging restraints on assembly and expression. New technologies and conference networks empowered some activists to transcend some confines of censorship, policing, and legal restrictions on associational life by organizing in extraterritorial, denationalized spaces or in cyberspace. More importantly, multitudes of ordinary people occupied public squares across much of the Arab world—and inspired "occupy" movements across the globe. These developments do not necessarily predict a gloriously teleological outcome of democratic development on the near horizon; reformist and revolutionary movements have mostly failed to bring about better governance. The evidence does not call for excessive optimism or lead us to expect a linear progression toward democracy and social justice. Neither, however, are there grounds for ruling out the possibilities for democratization in the Middle East. Rather, civil society operates, even within autocratic polities, because citizens continually do struggle for rights, liberties, and a decent life.

6
Religion and Politics

Jillian Schwedler

With media coverage of Middle East politics replete with headlines about the Islamic State in Iraq and Syria (ISIS), al-Qaeda, and other jihadi extremist groups claiming to be motivated by Islam, one might reasonably conclude that religious conflicts are the driving force behind politics in the region. Just as Arab nationalism loomed large across the region in the local struggles for independence from colonial and imperial powers during the first half of the twentieth century, by the late twentieth century and into the twenty-first century, Islam appeared to be the dominant framework for many movements that sought to change the entrenched and nondemocratic regimes of the Middle East. Upon closer inspection, the region is also home to liberal, secular, socialist, and nationalist movements. But the outsized role of opposition groups invoking Islam means that a careful examination of the role of religion is essential for understanding the politics of the Middle East.

Indeed, following the outbreak of Arab uprisings in late 2010, Islamist parties in Egypt and Tunisia won the largest parliamentary blocs in those states' first truly free elections, only to see their power quickly diminish. Politics, at its heart, is about power, and political actors of every ilk bring their own understandings of the causes of injustice and the appropriate means for political change. At the same time, religion is a central part of daily life in every Middle Eastern country, informing the ways in which most ordinary citizens understand politics as well as their own place in the world. But Western countries have also seen a resurgence of debate around religion, from its appropriate place in national politics to the growing number of religious revivalist movements. In this regard, politics in the Middle East is not necessarily about religion any more than is politics in Western countries.

In this chapter, I examine the major religions in the Middle East and the resurgence of politicized religion, from the creation of a powerful Islam-state alliance in early twentieth-century Saudi Arabia and the popular revolution in Iran that led to the creation of an Islamic state there in 1979, to the early Zionist movement that led to the establishment of the State of Israel in 1948, to the explosion of Islamic revivalist movements that emerged to challenge existing regimes in the latter quarter of the twentieth century, to the new roles in governance won by Islamist parties through free elections since 2011 and their subsequent demise.

I focus on two main categories of politicized religious activism, both of which advocate for political communities to adopt practices more closely shaped by their core religious values. The first includes religious groups working within existing regimes, a category that encompasses the vast majority of politicized Islamist groups. These groups engage in formal political processes to realize gradual political, social, and economic reforms. They do so in authoritarian states as well as in states that have adopted limited democratic institutions. The second category includes religious groups that reject existing regimes; these extremists seek immediate political change and frequently aim to rapidly overthrow the existing political order, through the use of violence if necessary. Though far fewer in number, extremists have left their mark on regional as well as global politics. Given that the vast majority of Middle Eastern people are Muslim—followers of the Islamic faith—both categories of religious activism are dominated by Islamist groups. However, it is important to remember that other religious groups also fall into each category.

The Historical Role of Religion in the Middle East

The Middle East is the birthplace of the world's three Abrahamic religions—Judaism, Christianity, and Islam—and thus the politics of the region have long been intertwined with struggles framed and inspired by religious differences. This does not mean that Middle East politics are religious in nature, but rather that political struggles—understood here as conflicts over the control of particular lands and the resources they hold—are often couched in terms of religion. As we will see, this distinction is crucial for understanding the historical role of religion in the Middle East as well as current debates about religious conflicts in general and Islamist groups in particular.

Judaism

Established more than 4,000 years ago, Judaism is the first of the three great monotheistic religions. According to Hebrew tradition, Moses led the Jewish people, with God's guidance, out of their slavery in Egypt and brought them to the Holy Land to establish a Kingdom of God (around 1450–1250 B.C.E.). Christians and Muslims share this vision of Judaism's origins, as each recognizes its faith as part of the same religious lineage (Judaism to Christianity to Islam) and believes in the same God. God revealed to Moses the first five books of the Hebrew Bible, called the Torah, which, together with the Talmud (a secondary text that includes interpretations of Jewish law, called the halakah, and the Torah), is the basic source of religious principles for the Jewish faith.

In 70 C.E., Jews were forced out of Jerusalem and Judea by the Romans, who also destroyed the Second Temple, which had been built on the site of Solomon's Temple (the First Temple). Exiled Jews settled in many directions yet maintained a strong identity as a single community that would one day reunite. In the Diaspora they maintained their religious practices and rituals, sustaining their identity through close-knit communities. In the late nineteenth and early twentieth centuries, increased violence and discrimination against Jews in Europe led to the emergence of a Jewish nationalist movement—Zionism—that aimed to establish a Jewish homeland and possibly even a Jewish state on the lands of historical Israel. Thousands of Zionists emigrated to Palestine over the next fifty years, sometimes living in peace with the indigenous Christian and Muslim Palestinians, and sometimes clashing, particularly over the control of land. The Jewish state of Israel was formally established in 1948.

Many of the first Zionists were secular and even Marxist in orientation, viewing Judaism as an identity and Zionism as a means for this religious-racial community to live on the land to which it felt strong historical connections. Today, the political left in Israel views the Israeli state more as a protector of the Jewish community than as a strictly religious state. On the right, Zionism is broadly viewed as an effort to realize God's intention that the Jewish people establish a Kingdom of God on that specific land. Today, Judaism has some 14 million adherents worldwide. In the contemporary Middle East, most Jews live in Israel, although small communities remain in Iran, Iraq, Morocco, Syria, Tunisia, and Yemen.

Christianity

Christianity is the largest religion in the world, with 2.3 billion followers. It finds its roots in the teachings of Jesus of Nazareth, a Jew whose followers later came to believe he was also the Messiah and the Son of God. Jesus was born in Bethlehem (circa 7–2 B.C.E.) and crucified by the Romans in Jerusalem (circa 26–36 C.E.). Jews (and thus early Christians) were exiled from Jerusalem in 70 C.E. by the Romans, migrating primarily to lands along the eastern Mediterranean, though often remaining under the repressive authority of Roman administrators. Christianity spread rapidly over the next 300 years and continued to thrive in Europe following the Islamic conquest of the Middle East beginning in the seventh century, though Christian communities remained active throughout the region.

The period before the Reformation was marked by the concerted efforts of European leaders to shape Middle Eastern politics in the name of religion. The Crusades were not a single campaign but nine major European military invasions into the region from the eleventh to the thirteenth centuries. Early successes were followed by numerous defeats. Following the capture of Jerusalem by Christian forces in 1099, the invading army formally pardoned those who surrendered, then continued on to massacre all remaining Muslim survivors. Muslims recaptured Jerusalem in 1187 under the leadership of Saladin, and the last Crusader stronghold in the Holy Land, in Acre, fell to Muslim control in 1291.

Foreign Christian intervention in the Middle East returned in great strength during the European colonial period. In addition to direct political intervention by the governments of the predominantly Christian countries of Britain and France, colonialism brought Christian missionaries, who opened schools, publishing houses, and hospitals, and who proselytized Muslims at every opportunity. Given this historical connection of Christianity and colonialism, it is not surprising that many struggles for independence from colonial powers in the Middle East were fought in the name of religion.

Today, Christians make up significant populations in Lebanon and the West Bank and Gaza, and have smaller communities in Egypt, Iran, Iraq, Jordan, and Syria. The number of Christians (and particularly Catholics) in the Middle East has increased significantly in recent decades as a result of the presence of large numbers of foreign workers, including laborers and domestic workers.

Islam

The third of the Abrahamic faiths is Islam, founded in the early seventh century when Muhammad of Mecca (570–632 C.E.) received the last revelations of God (beginning in 610 C.E.) via the angel Gabriel. Muhammad was ordered to spread a simple message: that there is only one God (in Arabic, Allah), and no other god is worthy of worship. This message was the same as that revealed to Abraham, Moses, and Jesus, among other prophets. Muhammad was to be the last prophet, however, delivering God's final set of instructions to humankind. A follower of the Islamic faith is called a Muslim, meaning "one who submits" to the will of God.

From the outset, Islam gained followers not only for the simplicity and clarity of its message but also because its orthodox strand declared—contrary to centuries of Christian domination in Europe—that individual believers needed no intermediaries between themselves and God. Following Muhammad's emigration (hijra) from Mecca in 622 C.E., the first Muslims recaptured Mecca against much stronger armies, a success that facilitated the first of many large-scale conversions to Islam by demonstrating that God was on Muhammad's side. Jews and Christians were declared to be protected religious communities, or dhimmi, and (at least officially) were not to be targets of conversion (though voluntary conversion was welcome). In practice, of course, Jews and Christians often experienced discrimination, though at times they prospered under Muslim rulers, many of whom were relatively more tolerant of Jews than were Christian rulers in Europe. Because literacy is central to Islam, Muslim leaders supported the creation of numerous centers of higher education. For example, the oldest continuously operating university in the world is Al-Azhar University in Cairo, still a major center of Sunni learning. Early Muslim scholars were also responsible for preserving the classic texts and histories of the Greek and Roman periods, and for reintroducing them to Europe during the Middle Ages.

There are several divisions within the larger Muslim *umma,* or global community, although Muslims view these differences as having varying degrees of importance. The most significant divide came early in Islam's history, when a dispute emerged over authority within the first Muslim community following the death of Muhammad. The majority view—what has come to be called the orthodox view by that virtue alone—was that authority should be shared and that a new leader, to the extent one was needed, should be selected from among the community. The followers of this view are called Sunni Muslims. The alternative view is that authority should have passed to direct blood descendants of Muhammad's family through his nephew, Ali. These followers or partisans of Ali, literally Shi'at Ali, are the Shi'a (or Shi'ites, as sometimes written). The series of leaders through this bloodline are called imams, and different Shi'i communities follow the line of imams to different points. For example, some follow only through the seventh imam, some to the tenth imam, and still others through the twelfth imam, who is believed to have disappeared from Earth and will return one day to bring justice to the world. Shi'a are today located throughout the Middle East, but have significant communities (and sometimes majorities) in Iraq, Bahrain, Saudi Arabia, Lebanon, Yemen, and Iran.

For all Muslims the basic text of Islam is the Quran, or "recitation," and unlike the Hebrew and Christian bibles, it is believed to be the literal word of God as conveyed to Muhammad through the angel Gabriel. The Quran and the Sunna—the sayings (hadith) and practices of the Prophet Muhammad—together provide all the guidance needed in life and form the basis of sharia. The term *sharia* is often translated as "Islamic law," but its meaning is more akin to a set of guiding principles derived from the Quran and the Sunna. Within Sunni Islam, there are four main schools of interpreting sharia. Individual Muslims may choose to follow the school they find most compelling, and while they may draw guidance from scholars who study sharia, they are ultimately responsible to Allah for making their own decisions. Islamic scholars of sharia, sometimes called jurists, clerics, or mullahs, are often asked by followers to issue an opinion, or fatwa, on a particular topic. Many Islamic scholars over time have cultivated personal followings, but their opinions and interpretations are never binding on individual Muslims.

The Islamic conquests that took place following Muhammad's consolidation of the first Muslim community in Mecca and Medina spread quickly throughout the Arab world and beyond; by the sixteenth century three great empires were Islamic: the Turkic Ottomans (who dominated the Arab world), the Safavids in Iran, and the Moguls on the Indian Subcontinent. While Muslim rulers gradually lost control of the far reaches of these empires—Muslim Andalusia in southern Spain was lost in 1492—the Islamic faith is today the world's fastest-growing religion, with 1.8 billion adherents approaching Christianity's 2.3 billion.

Religious States

Most countries in the Middle East can be defined as religious in the sense that a specific religion is given the status of official state religion. What this means in practice, however, varies dramatically. There are formal religious states (such as Saudi Arabia and Iran) that prioritize the full application of religious law in some combination of political, social, and economic matters. There also are more nominally religious states, where either the ruling elite claim authority based on direct descent from the bloodline of the Prophet Muhammad (as in Jordan and Morocco), or the constitution specifies an official state religion and requires the head of state to be a member of that religion (as in Egypt, Yemen, Syria, Iraq, Libya, Algeria, Oman, Saudi Arabia, Bahrain, Kuwait, the United Arab Emirates, and Tunisia). Israel is also a religious state to the extent that it claims legitimacy in part as a national homeland for Jewish people, though as we shall see, religious authorities do not dominate the political sphere.

Most regimes in the Middle East claim their legitimacy at least in part based on religion. We think of Saudi Arabia and Iran as Islamic states and of Israel as a Jewish state, but religion is actually written into the constitutions of most states in the region. It is crucial to remember that regimes as well as their challengers often seek to associate themselves with the most popular ideas of the time, and the language of religion is used in diverse ways by a wide range of actors, including state officials.

The State of Israel and the Symbolism of Jerusalem

In the late nineteenth century, the desire to establish a Jewish homeland spread among Jews throughout Europe, particularly after the first Zionist conference was held in 1897. When the Ottoman Empire was dismantled after World War I, Britain gained control of most of Palestine and was convinced by European Zionists to draw up the Balfour Declaration. This 1917 document, which was accepted by the League of Nations, called for the establishment of a Jewish national home in Palestine. Hundreds of thousands of Jews migrated to Palestine, largely from Europe but also from Arab, African, and other non-Western countries. The United Nations (UN) passed a resolution in 1947 that divided Palestine and called for the creation of the State of Israel. In the months before May 15, 1948, when the British mandate over Palestine was set to expire, Zionists and Arabs in Palestine fought a bloody civil war that drove many Palestinians into exile. Israel declared independence on May 15, forming a modern nation-state with an overtly religious identity.

The question of Israel as a Jewish state cannot be divorced from struggles over the sovereignty of Jerusalem, a city claimed by both Israelis and Palestinians as their capital, and by all three Abrahamic religions as historically and symbolically central to their faiths. With the establishment of Israel in 1948, Jerusalem was divided, with the western (Christian, Jewish, and Armenian) quarters under Israeli control, and the eastern (Arab) quarters (including the Western Wall and the site of the Temple Mount [which Arabs know as the Haram al-Sharif]) under Jordanian control. Israelis and Jews worldwide celebrated the reunification of the city when Israel recaptured the eastern quarters in the 1967 Six Day War. The status of the city remains contested under international law, and the Israeli claim of Jerusalem as its capital is not recognized by most nations.

For Christians, too, Jerusalem is a city of tremendous symbolic significance. Christianity originated in Jerusalem, where Jesus preached, died, and is believed to have been resurrected. Millions of Christians make pilgrimages to holy sites in Jerusalem each year, as well as to other holy sites in the West Bank (notably Bethlehem and Nazareth) and Jordan (notably the Baptismal Site on the East Bank of the Jordan River). Jerusalem is also the third-holiest place in Islam, after Mecca and Medina (both in present-day Saudi Arabia). Muhammad is believed to have ascended to heaven from the site of the rock on the Haram al-Sharif where Abraham was willing to sacrifice his son Isaac to God. (Jews built the First and Second Temples on the site for the same reason.) The loss of Jerusalem to Jewish control in the twentieth century is viewed by many Muslims as a dire warning from God to renew and deepen their faith. Indeed, many Islamic revival groups view the success of foreign powers in colonizing and dominating Muslim lands as a result of the widespread loss of faith among Muslims. Only by returning to the fundamental teachings of their faith, they argue, can Muslim peoples ever hope to regain dignity and control over their destinies.

Viewing Israel as a religious state, however, can sometimes obscure more than it illuminates. While it is true that its Law of Return grants citizenship rights to all Jews or those of Jewish lineage, at least 40 percent of Israel's Jewish population self-identify as secular and even atheist. While marriages and divorces are overseen entirely by religious courts (Jewish, Muslim, Christian, and Druze), Israel's legal system combines Jewish law with elements of British common law and civil law. Religious law does not dominate most issues in the political realm, from national security to the particularities of Israel's democratic system. The elected parliament, called the Knesset, is open to all citizens of Israel, including Druze and Arabs, both Muslim and Christian. But Israel's non-Jewish citizens—mostly Muslim and Christian Arabs but also Druze—are not given rights equal to those of Israel's Jewish population, which lends force to the claims of those who view conflicts in the region as religious in character.

Strongly Islamic States

Both Saudi Arabia and Iran were established in the twentieth century explicitly as religious states. The flag of Saudi Arabia includes the Islamic profession of faith, or *shahada* ("There is no God but God, and Muhammad is his Messenger"); the Iranian flag includes the phrase Allahu Akbar ("God is great") twenty-two times. But states like these may be described as "strongly Islamic" not only because they claim their legitimacy to rule on religious grounds, but also because they give religious leaders high levels of power and the authority to exercise control over certain spheres of governance and social practices. What this means in practice varies considerably.

The Kingdom of Saudi Arabia was established by the House of Saud in 1932 as an Islamic state. Although perhaps a marriage of convenience, the Saudi monarchy was formed through an alliance with a very conservative Sunni revival movement, Wahhabism, which called for adhering to the literal word of the Quran. King Abdulaziz Al Saud swept to power with the support of bedouin and Islamic extremists (the Wahhabis), whose fearlessness and commitment to an Islamic vision led them to conquer village after village. Indeed, these early extremists, called the Muslim Brethren (no connection to the Muslim Brotherhood discussed later, who are Sunni but not Wahhabi), were more zealous than Abdulaziz in terms of religion and the desire for political conquest. In 1929, Abdulaziz was forced to fight his own Muslim Brethren forces in order to stop their continued conquest of lands controlled by the British. Today the Wahhabi establishment in Saudi Arabia exerts near-absolute control over decisions relating to sharia, and it fully oversees the Islamic holy sites located inside the kingdom, including Mecca and Medina. But unlike in Iran, the Wahhabi clerics do not hold formal positions of state power, which remain fully in the hands of the Saudi royal family. The current crown prince of Saudi Arabia is Mohammad bin Salman, whose father, the king, lives in a state of mental demise such that the crown prince effectively rules. In his short time at the helm, the crown prince has declared his intention to modernize Saudi Arabia and lessen the power of the conservative religious establishment. While restrictions on women driving cars have been lessened, the eventual extent of the crown prince's reforms remains unknown.

Iran is also a strongly religious state. The revolution of 1978–1979, which brought the Islamic regime to power, is conventionally understood as Islamic because of its Islam symbolism and rhetoric, and also given the prominent role played by clerics and the mosques. The massive mobilization that brought down the regime of Mohammad Reza Shah Pahlavi, however, was realized only through a broad alliance of bazaar merchants, clerical elites, nationalists, intellectuals, feminists, students, and laborers (among others). More than a year passed before the clerics, under the leadership of Ayatollah Ruhollah Khomeini, emerged triumphant against the nationalists and established the Islamic Republic of Iran. Clerics further solidified their power through their control of the Council of Guardians, which passes judgment on all political matters by declaring whether policies are in line with sharia. In this sense, Iran is the only country in the Middle East directly ruled by members of the clergy.

Although Iran has a democratically elected president and legislative body, in practice the Council of Guardians uses its power to exert extreme control over political, social, and economic matters. Like the Wahhabi religious clergy in Saudi Arabia, the Council of Guardians decides what sorts of foreign investment are permissible, how citizens may dress, and even whether citizens may use contraceptives (only if married, in which case the state provides them for free). It also determines who may run for elected office, including the presidency, thus seriously limiting the range of candidates and rendering elections far less democratic than they might be. In addition, any legislative reform passed through the national assembly must be approved by the Council of Guardians. Of the hundreds of reforms passed by the popularly elected assembly during the term of reformist president Mohammad Khatami (1997–2005), not a single one was approved and implemented. For example, the assembly had passed several laws expanding the rights of women in divorce and child custody matters, but in each case the Council of Guardians vetoed the new laws as contrary to sharia.

The supreme authority in Iran belongs to the *velayat-e faqih,* an individual possessing superior religious knowledge in the absence of the twelfth imam, whom Shi'a believe to be in occultation: he has not died but is absent on Earth and will one day return to fill the world with justice. The office of the *faqih* was created after the 1979 revolution and was occupied by Ayatollah Khomeini until his death in 1989. The *faqih* is selected by the Assembly of Experts, composed of eighty-six clerics elected every eight years, with the Council of Guardians determining who may run for the seats. He holds his position for life, acts as the final authority in all political matters, and is not accountable to the public or any other authority. The *faqih* appoints half of the Council of Guardians as well as the head of the judiciary, who in turn supervises the election by parliament of the remainder of the Council of Guardians. In this sense, clerical rule in Iran is virtually absolute, with a range of mechanisms used to systematically exclude challenges to their rule.

One of the stated goals of the early Islamic Republic of Iran was the export of the revolution: to encourage and indeed support Muslims in other countries to rise up against and topple their regimes and establish Islamic states in their wake. This objective met with overwhelming failure, although the impact of this policy (which was largely pushed to the back burner following the death of Khomeini in 1989) continues to be felt in terms of the support Iran provides to a few Islamist groups, notably Hezbollah in Lebanon. Iran is also rumored to play a role in supporting Shi'i factions in postwar Iraq and a minor Shi'i movement in Yemen (the northern-based al-Huthi who are members of the Zaydi sect), though these connections have not been indisputably established.

Nominally Islamic States

Most other states in the Middle East accord some formal status to religion, often stipulating Islam as the official religion or requiring the president to be Muslim. Turkey was the notable exception: when Mustafa Kemal (later called Atatürk) established the modern state of Turkey in 1923, he advocated a program of forced secularism that included dismantling religious courts and outlawing religious or traditional dress. Most regimes in the region, however, now actively embrace an Islamic identity (and the center of gravity of Turkish politics has been steadily moving away from Atatürk's vision over the past few decades).

Many republics too have established in their constitutions that Islam is the official state religion and sharia is a source of law and legislation, including Algeria, Egypt, Tunisia, Yemen, and Iraq. What this means in practice varies considerably. Certainly, the president must be a Muslim, and it is not unusual on high Muslim holidays or during times of domestic or regional turmoil to see the president and other state officials praying prominently, televised for all to see. (Note that US presidents almost universally end their public addresses, in times of both war and peace, with the words "God bless America.") During the Gulf War of 1990–1991, Saddam Hussein even added the words "God is great" to the Iraqi flag. Although his religious credentials were thin at best, he perhaps thought that the phrase might give him greater legitimacy and, in particular, greater support from other Muslim countries.

In Egypt the office of mufti has long been filled by a prominent cleric from Al-Azhar University; his job is to judge whether state policies are in adherence to sharia. Unlike Iran's Council of Guardians, in Egypt this office (like similar ones in Jordan and elsewhere) is mostly symbolic; nevertheless, the regime's need to at least appear to conform to sharia underlines the power of Islamic symbolism in sustaining the state's authority to rule. In Egypt, the clerics, or ulama, from Al-Azhar University continue to function as a conservative (but not extremist) force in Egypt; they control the religious courts and provide imams (prayer leaders) to each of the country's tens of thousands of mosques.

Overall, the vast majority of states in the Middle East accord some official status to religion. Some regimes use religion to expand the perceived legitimacy of their rule, while others maintain an official status for religion out of popular pressure. In the early 1970s, for example, Syrian president Hafiz al-Asad tried to remove from the constitution the condition that the president be Muslim; he abandoned this aim in large part due to strong societal pressure. After the Arab uprisings, the role of Islam in the new regimes and constitutions was a hotly debated issue and is likely to continue to be, as a range of religious and nonreligious political actors struggle over what the new political institutions will look like.

Is Lebanon a Religious State?

Lebanon is a confessional state, meaning that seats in parliament and the offices of president, prime minister, and speaker of parliament are distributed according to sect, an affiliation based on membership in a confessional community. Lebanon's confessional system, which was established in 1942 as a means of preventing sectarian conflict by ensuring representation of all communities, also works to preserve (rather than overcome) sectarian differences of the sort that tore the country apart during its fifteen-year civil war beginning in 1975. That conflict formally ended with the Ta'if Accord, signed in 1989, which expanded parliament from 99 to 128 seats; these seats are now evenly divided between Muslim and Christian sects (the previous allocation provided for 54 Christian and 45 Muslim seats). This system ensures broad representation in government, but also affords Christians a disproportionate number of seats, as the demographics have changed: Muslims are estimated to now make up at least 60 percent of the population. Ironically, the adoption of a similar confessional system in post-Saddam Iraq has exacerbated sectarian tensions by institutionalizing sectarian divisions in the structure of the parliament.

Executive branch

President: Maronite Orthodox Christian
Prime minister: Sunni Muslim
Speaker of parliament: Shi'i Muslim

Parliament

Muslim seats	64
Sunni	27
Shi'i	27
Druze	8
Alawite	2
Christian seats	64
Maronite	34
Greek Orthodox	14
Greek Catholic	8
Armenian Orthodox	5
Armenian Catholic	1
Protestant	1
Other Christian	1

Religious Revivalism

The contemporary Middle East has seen an expansion of religious revivalist groups, in part inspired by anticolonial struggles and the desire for a politics that can be locally recognized as authentic. Much of the Arab world remained under Ottoman control in the late nineteenth century, although the farther reaches of the empire were gradually gaining local autonomy. For many parts of the Middle East the spread of European colonialism meant the exchange of one foreign occupier (the Ottoman Turks) for another (France, Great Britain, or Italy). The lack of Arab autonomy was viewed both as humiliating and as the cause of innumerable economic and political hardships, and it was in this context that a diverse range of revivalist movements emerged, first in the early twentieth century and then in a broader wave beginning in the 1970s. In much of that century, the dominant political narratives in the region were Arab nationalism, socialism, and Islamic revivalism; each offered a means of imagining alternative political arrangements in which Arabs would regain dignity through control of their own destinies.

Islamic revivalism took many forms, but a common theme was that Muslim peoples had diverged too far from their faith and that a return to the core values of their religion would restore the community's rightful dignity—along with political, social, and economic control of their lives. This narrative gained popularity as more or less secular regimes—many espousing the language of socialism and Arab nationalism—failed to provide economic prosperity, meaningful political participation, or even a sense of pride and dignity. In the face of such ignominious military defeats as the 1967 Six Day War—which saw the routing of the Egyptian, Syrian, and Jordanian armies and the loss of much Palestinian land, including East Jerusalem, to Israeli control—Islamic revivalist groups provided an alternative vision to that of state socialism and Arab nationalism and saw their numbers swell over the next decade. Islamic revivalism took diverse forms, ranging from legal political parties that sought to contest elections to underground militant groups that aimed to use arms to defeat incumbent regimes. Jewish religious revivalism also took several forms but was primarily framed in relation to Zionism and the need to establish (and later defend) the State of Israel as a national homeland for Jews.

In the broadest terms, religious revivalist movements seek to reform or replace existing political structures and social practices with those viewed as more in line with core religious values. But how is this change to be realized? Most revivalist groups seek to enact change gradually, by working within existing political structures and through education and socialization programs. Other groups are characterized by their full rejection of existing regimes, which they seek to overthrow, if necessary through the use of political violence. The following sections examine the dominant trend of seeking gradual reform, the minority trend of advocating the immediate overthrow of existing regimes, and the new trend of working with a range of political actors to shape the post–Arab uprisings regimes. The leaders of Islamic revivalist movements hail from diverse social and economic backgrounds, though they most frequently have strong middle-class and professional roots: they are engineers, doctors, lawyers, teachers, and civil servants. The social bases of those who support Islamic revivalist groups are likewise diverse, ranging from the disenfranchised poor to the social and political elite. But in all cases, the educated middle class makes up a significant portion of group leadership and the rank-and-file.

Islamist Groups Working Within Existing Regimes

Even prior to the Arab uprisings, the vast majority of Islamist revivalist groups sought to realize their visions for a more Islamic society by working within existing regimes, often by fielding candidates in local, municipal, and national elections, and by forming local nongovernmental organizations to advocate change at the grassroots level through education and social services. In this sense, most religious political activism in the Middle East can be readily characterized as moderate rather than extremist. In fact, the region is flush with religious revivalist groups from all the Abrahamic faiths that advocate gradual reform, organize political parties (and strive for legal status), and cooperate with groups across the ideological spectrum. In much of the region, for example, Islamic groups routinely cooperate with communists, socialists, liberals, Christians, and nationalists. Indeed, the range of religious activism is so diverse that this chapter could not possibly mention every group and examine every dimension of religion and politics.

Islamist groups that work within existing regimes justify their gradual or integrative approach on Islamic terms. Many believe that, as long as one adheres to the spirit and values of the Quran and the hadith, a wide range of political systems, from socialism to liberal democracy to monarchy, are acceptable. Contemporary justifications for gradual reform and for participation in pluralist or democratic political systems frequently reference the thinking of Hassan al-Banna (1905–1949), who founded the Muslim Brotherhood in Egypt in 1928. Al-Banna was a schoolteacher who advocated a return to Islam's core values through reading and study groups and by working within existing political structures. Rather than focusing exclusively on political participation, for example, the Muslim Brotherhood was an early advocate of literacy programs for men as well as women to ensure that all Muslims were able to read the Quran and thus produce a more robustly Islamic society.

Since at least the 1990s, most debates among Islamists about political participation have found sufficient overlap in democratic and Islamic notions of participation so as to have little or no difficulty justifying participation in pluralist politics, particularly democratic elections. Branches of the Muslim Brotherhood in Egypt, Jordan, Tunisia, and Yemen have for decades sought to participate in multiparty elections—with varying degrees of success and regime permission. In Yemen, the Brotherhood participated in elections as a segment of the legal Yemeni Congregation for Reform, or Islah party, from 1993 until the outbreak of civil war in 2015. While Brotherhood members were sometimes at odds with other trends within the Islah party, they strongly supported pluralist politics and held numerous cabinet positions in the mid-1990s as a result of the party's success at the polls and its alliance with the ruling party, the General Popular Congress (GPC). With the defeat of the Yemeni Socialist Party during the 1994 civil war, the Islah party saw a decline in its political influence, as the ruling GPC of then president Ali Abdullah Salih came to dominate the political field much the way the National Democratic Party did in Egypt. The Islah party subsequently became a strong partner in the Joint Meetings Party (JMP), a bloc of secular as well as religious parties that emerged in the early 2000s in opposition to the GPC. The JMP played a formal role in Yemen's attempted transition to a new, post-Salih regime after the 2011 uprising, although as a part of the formal opposition it remained distant from much of the popular opposition mobilization on the street. The 2011 Nobel Peace Prize laureate Tawakkul Karman was an Islah member who had been elected to that party's primary governing body, or Shura Council.

In Jordan, the Muslim Brotherhood has been engaged in electoral politics since the 1950s, and since the 1970s several of its prominent leaders have held cabinet positions. With the first full parliamentary elections in two decades held in 1989—the assembly had been suspended following Jordan's defeat in the 1967 war until 1984—the Muslim Brotherhood fielded candidates and together with some independent Islamists won twenty-seven seats (out of eighty), or 40 percent of the assembly. In the early 1990s the group was granted five cabinet positions, largely in recognition of its success at the polls. When political parties were legalized in 1992, many of its prominent members joined forces with independent Islamists to form the Islamic Action Front (IAF) party. The IAF competes regularly in local and national elections and has forged strong relations with other opposition parties, including nationalists, communists, socialists, and liberals. Like Yemen's Islah party, the

IAF also engages in democratic practices internally and has seen prominent party leaders defeated in their bids to retain top party offices.

Islamist parties in Turkey have participated in elections since the 1970s but only relatively recently have become a strong political force. This development has come in the context of a process wherein Turkey's Constitutional Court repeatedly closed down Islamist parties for threatening the state's secular foundations. After winning only 7 percent of the vote in 1987 (Turkey's proportional representation system requires parties to win a minimum of 10 percent of the vote to gain seats in parliament), the Islamist-oriented Welfare Party reached out to conservative and pious middle-class Turks who were hurt by economic liberalization. The party continually gained strength, winning 17 percent of the vote in 1991 and 21 percent in 1995, all under the leadership of longtime Islamist leader Necmettin Erbakan, who became prime minister in 1996. The Constitutional Court outlawed the party in 1998, however, and the Virtue Party emerged in its place. It did not fare well in the 1999 elections, and the party suffered from internal divisions about the direction of the party, particularly concerning its commitment to democratic and pluralist norms. The Constitutional Court closed Virtue in 2001.

The Virtue Party was replaced by the Justice and Development Party (AKP), whose early stated commitments to European Union (EU) membership and pluralism were viewed by many Islamists as having strayed too far from core Islamic beliefs. The party proved highly popular, however, and won 34 percent of the vote in 2002, securing two-thirds of the parliament with 363 of 550 seats (only one other party surpassed the 10 percent threshold). After a contentious presidential election in 2007 in which AKP leader Abdullah Gül was victorious, the AKP won a remarkable 47 percent of the vote and 341 seats (fewer than in 2002 because another party passed the 10 percent threshold) in parliamentary elections that same year. The AKP has dominated Turkish politics ever since, with control of the parliament, presidency, and prime ministry. In 2018, AKP leader Recep Tayyip Erdoğan was reelected as president with 53 percent of the vote, further entrenching not only AKP power for the coming years, but also his increasingly personalistic and authoritarian style of rule. Many view recent events in Turkey as a process of democratic backsliding, where populist leaders utilize their power to consolidate their personal rule and purge rivals from office. The disturbing trend in Turkey has brought a weakening of secular institutions in favor of increased Islamization, but in practice the larger picture is one of authoritarian consolidation rather than religious rule.

What do these examples have in common? Beyond the language of Islam as a frame for political opposition, these groups have taken very different paths as they have engaged with formal political processes. The experiences of the Muslim Brotherhood in various countries are in many ways typical of other Islamist groups that seek to realize their reforms gradually and by working within the existing political systems. Some of these parties have been outlawed (e.g., an-Nahda in Tunisia until the 2011 revolution and the Muslim Brotherhood under Husni Mubarak's rule and again following the 2013 coup that ousted Mohammad Morsi, the Muslim Brotherhood leader who served for a year as Egypt's only democratically elected president). Some are legal political parties (e.g., the Islah party in Yemen, Hezbollah in Lebanon, and the IAF in Jordan). Kuwait has multiple Islamist groups that hold seats in its parliament, and Islamist groups are active in parliamentary politics in Iraq, Lebanon, Algeria, and Morocco.

In addition to formal participation in elected national assemblies and local elections, many Islamist groups are known for their provision of social services, particularly where state services are nowhere to be found. Hezbollah provided significant services in southern Lebanon during the civil war and after; Egypt's Muslim Brotherhood provided earthquake relief in 1992 in the face of a state that did not know where to begin. Most moderate Islamist groups are also engaged in literacy programs and schools, although the curriculum is carefully controlled. Islamist groups also frequently carry out charity work and provide health care services. Some scholars have questioned the depth and effectiveness of these social programs, arguing that they are championed for public relations purposes but in practice are far less effective. One study shows that Muslim Brotherhood–run health clinics in Cairo, for example, are seldom staffed by a medical doctor (Clark 2004). Nevertheless, these moderate Islamic activists—those who have sought to participate peacefully and legally in economic, political, and social realms—constitute the vast majority of Islamic revivalist movements. Their popularity largely stems from the fact that they provide an alternative—ideologically and substantively—to the corruption, ineffectiveness, repression, and failed economic projects of incumbent regimes.

Islamists Who Entirely Reject Existing Regimes

Even though they make up a small proportion of Islamic revivalist groups, extremist religious groups garner the most headlines, and the impact of their activities can be profound. The term *extremist* is used here to refer not to ideas that fall well outside the norm but, more specifically, to those who adopt militancy and the use of violence as a strategy for redressing their grievances. Extremists tend to emerge out of the most repressive contexts and aim to achieve political change by directly attacking those in power. Their targets include foreign agents—including troops and diplomats, but also foreign-owned businesses and tourists—as well as regimes they believe to be illegitimate. The latter include those they see as having been imposed by colonial and imperial powers (Israel would be an example) as well as regimes deemed to have abandoned Islamic values and teachings.

In Egypt, the Muslim Brotherhood supported Gamal Abdel Nasser and the Free Officers movement, which overthrew the Egyptian monarchy in 1952. When Nasser sought to consolidate his power, however, he viewed the Muslim Brotherhood as a primary threat and outlawed the organization in 1954 after accusing its members of attempting to assassinate him. From that period until Nasser's death in 1970, thousands of its members were jailed and many were executed. Among them was Sayyid Qutb, whose experiences of repression led him to abandon al-Banna's commitment to working within existing Muslim regimes to realize change. In his book *Signposts Along the Road* (Ma'alim fi-l-Tariq), Qutb argues that, contrary to a common interpretation of sharia, Muslims are not obligated to accept the legitimacy of the leadership of Muslim rulers if those leaders are not ruling in accord with Islam. Emancipation of Muslim communities must come through movement, he argued, rather than through works (teaching) alone. This position was radical because it justified, on Islamic grounds, attacking and overthrowing Muslim regimes. Qutb was executed by hanging in 1966 along with two others for allegedly plotting against Nasser's regime; many viewed these charges as a setup. Regardless, the impact of Qutb's teachings and his martyrdom at the hands of the Egyptian state has been profound.

Indeed, Qutb inspired the emergence of extremist groups in Egypt and later throughout the Muslim world. In the early 1970s, Egyptian president Anwar Sadat released hundreds of Muslim Brotherhood members from prison as part of his effort to distinguish his rule from that of Nasser, who had imprisoned thousands of political opponents, including many Islamists. Among the hundreds of Muslim Brotherhood members released over the course of several years were a number of Qutb followers, who formed small groups that advocated the violent overthrow of the regime. These included the Islamic Group (Al-Gama'a al-Islamiyya) and Islamic Jihad (Jihad al-Islami). In 1981, Islamic Jihad member Khalid Islambuli assassinated Sadat, hoping that his death would spark an Islamic revolution in Egypt and the Arab world, following the one in Iran just two years earlier. No popular uprising emerged, however, and Islambuli and his co-conspirators were arrested. Islambuli was executed but a number of others were exiled, including several who found refuge in Afghanistan and later joined al-Qaeda. In Egypt, the Islamic Group and Islamic Jihad regrouped and mounted a series of violent acts throughout the country, culminating in the 1997 massacre of tourists in the Valley of the Kings, which claimed the lives of four Egyptians and fifty-eight foreign tourists (along with six responsible for the attack). Islamic Jihad leaders who were already imprisoned at the time dissociated themselves from that attack, condemning it and formally disbanding their organization. Egypt has experienced little extremism since then, though the potential for a revival of religious extremism remains considerable as long as the Egyptian state continues to be repressive and nondemocratic in nature.

Egypt is not the only country that has suffered from domestic Islamic extremism. Algeria experienced a civil war by and among Islamist groups in the 1990s, although notably this bloodshed began after the Islamic Salvation Front (FIS) legitimately won parliamentary elections in 1992 that the military quickly annulled. Yemen has seen violence by extremists against tourists and missionaries, as well as against the holy shrines of minority Muslim groups and a former brewery in the south. Beginning in the 1970s, Islamist extremists from North Yemen assassinated hundreds of socialists from South Yemen; even after unification in the 1990s, assaults against socialists continued, particularly as the 1993 elections approached. Although these attacks subsided somewhat during the remainder of the 1990s, in 2002 the prominent socialist leader Jar Allah Umar was assassinated: he was shot point-blank as he left the stage after addressing an assembly of the Islamist Islah party's general membership. Since the late 1990s, a group calling itself al-Qaeda in the Arabian Peninsula has launched several attacks, including the 2009 murder of four Korean tourists in Yemen and the failed Christmas Day attack on an airplane bound for Detroit that same year. With the outbreak of civil war in 2015 following disagreements about the shape of Yemen's government after the ouster of President Salih in 2012, Islamic extremists have found fertile ground in the war-torn country. With the Yemeni people suffering a catastrophic humanitarian crisis, al-Qaeda and ISIS have been able to control small swaths of land because of their ability to provide much-needed resources and some semblance of local security.

Islamic extremists justify their use of violence as jihad, a legitimate use of force necessary to defend one's faith against threats. Conventional wisdom in the West holds that holy war is specific to Islam in the contemporary period, although it was famously waged by Christians during the Crusades, and the idea of holy war also emerged early in Judaism and continues to exert a strong influence in Israeli political affairs. Some Zionist groups believe that they are obligated to use violence if necessary to bring about God's desire for all Jews to return to the Holy Land (modern-day Israel, including the West Bank). In February 1994, for example, an

Israeli American named Baruch Goldstein opened fire on a crowd of Muslim worshippers in a mosque at the Cave of the Patriarchs, a site in Hebron (known to Arabs as Khalil) that is sacred to Jews, Christians, and Muslims alike. At least 39 Muslims were killed and 125 were injured. Goldstein was a member of the outlawed Kach party, which along with a spin-off group, Kahane Chai, is considered a terrorist organization by Israel and many other nations, including the United States.

Islamist Groups Since the Arab Uprisings

The Arab uprisings that began in southern Tunisia in late 2010 changed the equation for many Islamist groups by creating opportunities for meaningful participation in governing institutions. Tunisia's president Zine el-Abidine Ben Ali was the first regional dictator to fall, on January 14, 2011. The banned an-Nahda movement, while not a central player in the protests, reconstituted quickly with the return of its leader, Rachid Ghanouchi, who for decades had been exiled to London. A moderate revivalist group, an-Nahda had long espoused support for a democratic and liberal political system but, like all opposition, had been outlawed by Ben Ali. In Tunisia's first free elections for its Constituent Assembly in October 2011, an-Nahda won 37 percent of the seats—the largest bloc—and party member Hamadi Jebali was appointed Tunisia's first postrevolution prime minister. In the 2014 elections, an-Nahda saw its share decline to just under 28 percent, with the ascendance of the nationalist Nidaa Tounes party taking the largest share with nearly 40 percent of the vote.

In Egypt, the Muslim Brotherhood was long the most important nongovernmental group in the country, able to mobilize thousands for (largely) peaceful protests against the regime's policies and the dominance of the National Democratic Party in national politics. Under Mubarak's regime it remained an illegal organization, although it frequently fielded "independent" candidates for the People's Assembly as well as in local elections. After years of winning few seats, during the 2005 elections it won eighty-seven seats (nearly 19 percent of the assembly). During Egypt's January 25 revolution in 2011, the Brotherhood did not emerge as a significant actor until the protests had reached revolutionary levels, although some members joined the protests early on as individuals. In fact, the group had first instructed its followers not to join the protests at all. With Mubarak's resignation and the ensuing struggles over what the new Egypt would look like politically, the Brotherhood emerged as a major player. This is not surprising given the group's decades-long presence in communities and its institutional resources. It formed the Freedom and Justice Party in April and won 47.2 percent of the seats in parliamentary elections held between November 2011 and January 2012. Although the group had previously declared that it would not field a candidate for president, it revised its position, and in June 2012, Muslim Brotherhood member Mohammad Morsi won Egypt's first free presidential elections.

The initial success of Islamist parties after the uprisings is not surprising. In addition to possessing established constituencies, these groups presented stark alternatives to the corrupt regimes of Ben Ali and Mubarak. Islamists are often seen as highly moral and, owing to years suffering under severe state repression, unconnected to the old regime.

In addition to these moderate revivalist Islamists, Tunisia and Egypt have seen Salafi groups emerge onto the political scene since the uprisings. The term *Salafi* refers to a broad category of Islamist revivalists who seek to adhere closely to the practices and beliefs of the earliest Muslims, or *salaf* (meaning ancestors or predecessors). Salafi groups exist across the region and are not a united or cohesive movement. In many states, such as Jordan, Salafi groups have long been quiescent: they restrict their activities largely to Islamic study and take no position on the legitimacy of the ruling regime. Following the uprisings in Tunisia and Egypt, however, some Salafi groups (but not others) altered this position and formed formal political parties to contest elections. In Tunisia, Salafis openly criticized an-Nahda for cooperating with secular groups and for not moving quickly to implement sharia. In Egypt, the Salafi an-Nour party won 27.8 percent of the parliamentary votes in the November 2011–January 2012 contest. Since most of these groups have engaged with existing regimes even less than groups like the Muslim Brotherhood, they are perceived by many as entirely pure and uncorrupt. The future role of Salafism on the formal political scene will likely continue to range from formal political engagement to quiescence.

While an-Nahda continues to engage in parliamentary politics in Tunisia, developments in Egypt took a starkly different path. Following the legitimate victories of the Muslim Brotherhood in securing a majority in parliament and the presidency in 2012, its elected officials set about implementing their agenda. Although they were woefully inexperienced, they moved toward a number of reforms that led some in Egypt to fear that the group would turn Egypt into an Islamic theocracy. Hundreds and then thousands took to the streets to call for limits on their ability to effect lasting change, such as by amending or rewriting the constitution. The leaders of the army, however, were already working behind the scenes to limit the powers of the presidency. As demonstrations against the Muslim Brotherhood escalated in summer 2013, the army stepped in and removed Morsi and Muslim Brotherhood members of parliament from power. The army did so in the name of responding to the protesters and protecting the revolution, but from the very first days of the uprising in 2011 military leaders had been scheming for ways to insure they maintained a firm grip on power. Thousands of Muslim Brotherhood members and supporters took to the streets in August to protest the coup. The army, under the direction of Abdel Fatah al-Sisi—who would go on to take over the presidency and lead Egypt's retreat from democracy—ordered troops to attack the demonstrators. Nearly a thousand were massacred in a few short hours, decisively putting an end to Egypt's democratic opening.

Because Egypt's first democratically elected parliament and president were led by the Muslim Brotherhood, it is impossible to know whether the army would have reacted so strongly to remove elected officials had the Muslim Brotherhood not dominated the elections. Signs indicate that al-Sisi likely wanted to hijack the democratic process anyway, and the fact that some protesters called for Morsi's removal may have merely provided a convenient excuse to intervene.

Transnational Connections

The question of connections among Islamist groups in different countries has gained greater importance since the rise of groups like al-Qaeda, whose targets are not limited to a single state. The question of transnationalism, however, is fraught with difficulty, because the nature of "connections" among groups is highly varied. Islamist groups with similar goals, agendas, ideological commitments, or practical problems—but that hail from different countries—routinely dialogue with each other for purposes of sharing experiences, organizing conferences, building membership, and so on. A parallel would be the human rights groups based in a large number of countries that coordinate, cooperate, and share information (and sometimes resources) to advance goals shared by all the groups but that remain distinct and separate organizations. Many branches of the Muslim Brotherhood and other moderate Islamist groups conform to this pattern: they operate primarily within their own countries, but they dialogue with similar groups in other countries. Indeed, moderate revivalist groups frequently attend conferences organized by other Islamist groups, to discuss and debate such topics as elections, democracy, *dawa* (outreach) activities, education reform, and so on. Other transnational connections include those forged by both educational exchange programs and financial institutions, particularly banks that facilitate investments that do not violate the Islamic injunction against charging interest.

The primary concern with transnationalism, however, has less to do with these sorts of connections than with groups that are truly transnational—meaning groups that cross borders organizationally as well as with respect to their political objectives—particularly extremist groups. Indeed, Islamic extremism is not confined to domestic attacks, as the acts of violence that have gained the most attention internationally are those that target Israel and US troops in the Middle East, and of course the attacks of September 11, 2001, that targeted the Pentagon and World Trade Center in the United States. Palestinian militants have launched attacks on Israel since the 1960s, but it was not until the formation of Hamas in 1987 during the first intifada that Palestinian Islamist groups began using political violence operating inside Israel and the Occupied Palestinian Territories. Lebanon's Hezbollah has also launched numerous attacks on Israeli troops and Israeli soil. Hamas and Hezbollah differ from many other militant Islamist groups, however, in that their attacks are aimed at ousting what they view as foreign troops illegally occupying their land. In this regard, their activities, instead of being considered transnational in nature, might better be viewed as concerned with protecting and restoring what they view as legitimate sovereign borders.

Al-Qaeda and ISIS are the most famous and active transnational extremist groups, and both justify attacking not only governments but also foreigners and civilians deemed responsible for perpetuating the conditions that oppress Muslim peoples worldwide. Following Sayyid Qutb, al-Qaeda emerged in the 1990s and advocated attacking even Muslim rulers and regimes globally if they are not deemed to be acting in full accordance with Islam. While the activities of al-Qaeda represent an escalation of Islamic extremism in the scale of its tactics and the boundlessness of its targets, the movement has never enjoyed popular support within the Arab or Muslim world. Indeed, following the September 11 attacks, dozens of Muslim countries immediately expressed condolences to the citizens of the United States, and millions of Muslims worldwide organized candlelight vigils in neighborhoods and mosques in remembrance of the victims.

ISIS—the acronym for the Islamic State in Iraq and Syria, also referenced by its acronym in Arabic, Daesh—emerged around 2014 in Iraq and postuprising Syria out of a collection of dissidents from al-Qaeda and Iraqi Baathist officers who were purged from their positions following the US-led invasion of Iraq in 2003. The turmoil of the uprisings provided this incipient group with an opportunity to seize pockets of territory and declare the reestablishment of the Islamic caliphate, an event viewed as the harbinger of the End of Days, when the Messiah would return to Earth and believers would be immediately transported to heaven in the Rapture. Al-Qaeda leaders argued that the time was not ready for the return of the caliphate, but ISIS's message resonated with some small pockets of the larger Muslim community. For a few years, ISIS controlled a modest corridor across Syria and parts of Iraq, but the group has subsequently lost much of that territory. Like al-Qaeda, groups elsewhere in the region claimed the name and established small strongholds, particularly in war-torn Libya and Yemen.

The influence of extremist groups like al-Qaeda and ISIS appears to be diminishing across the region, and both were always fringe groups that never enjoyed widespread support. But each still enjoys the support of modest numbers of loyal followers in many parts of the Middle East, and war and foreign intervention create conditions in which they could see resurgence in the future.

Conclusion

Religion plays a central role in Middle Eastern politics, in part because political struggles have for centuries been understood as religious conflicts (e.g., the Crusades, colonialism's connection to Christian proselytizing, Western support for Israel, and the targeting of Muslims in the "war on terror"), and in part because of the intimate ties of the three Abrahamic faiths to the region. The great diversity of religious experiences and practices—from whether minority religious communities enjoy inclusion or endure repression, to the ways in which states accept or reject religious political parties, to the diverse means of invoking religious symbols and rhetoric in expressions of dissent—is a core feature of the region. Religion will undoubtedly continue to be a central component of politics in the Middle East for decades to come. As some recent trends of inclusion and tolerance illustrate, that reality need not necessarily entail violence.

As this chapter has illustrated, the fact that religion and politics have a long history in the Middle East does not mean that religion is always, or even most of the time, a crucial factor driving political conflicts. Indeed, most conflicts are classically political in character, in that they are at the most basic level conflicts over control of land, resources, or peoples. The Crusades were about the conquest of empire, not about core religious beliefs. The Arab uprisings that began in late 2010 also underline that while religion plays a role in political debates, popular political struggles more often concern demands for freedom, economic equality, and justice. This is not to suggest that religious motivations are superficial but to draw attention away from religion as a primary explanatory factor—as in "these religions have been fighting each other for centuries!"—and toward more complete understandings of struggles for power in the Middle East. In this regard, the expanding role of moderate Islamist revivalist groups in electoral politics—even within nondemocratic regimes—merits at least as much attention as do the exceptional extremist groups of the likes of al-Qaeda.

7

Identity and Politics

David Siddhartha Patel

Identity figures prominently in descriptions of and explanations about the Middle East. Open almost any news page or book and count the instances: Muslims and Christians; Sunnis and Shi'ites; Arabs and Turks; Israelis and Palestinians; Saudis and Iranians. But, far too often, identities in the Middle East are assumed to be basic, fundamental, and fixed. Scholars of the region are increasingly coming to a consensus that identity—how people perceive themselves and how they differentiate self from other—is constructed in some way. This chapter explores the variety of identities in the modern Middle East and how groups and relations between groups change over time in response to political, economic, and social processes. The following vignette illustrates the complexities involved.

Abbas Haydar lives in Basra, a city in southern Iraq. In the turbulent period following the US-led overthrow of Saddam Hussein's Baath regime in 2003, numerous groups tried to gain Abbas's support by telling him how he should think about Iraqi politics and his own identity. A local judge promised to represent "the people of Basra" and use revenue from nearby oil fields to develop the city. Several new political parties told Abbas to think of himself, first and foremost, as an Iraqi. One of these parties flew an old Iraqi flag with a design that had not been used since 1963. Other parties said that he was a member of an Arab nation of more than 300 million people that stretches 3,000 miles west from Iraq to Morocco. A preacher in the local mosque reminded Abbas that he was a member of the Islamic *umma,* the global community of more than 1 billion Muslims. Previously banned political movements said that the Shi'ite Muslim clergy knew what was best. Abbas's granduncle reminded him of his responsibility to support his extended family, including his distant cousins.

Like all people, Abbas has multiple identities. His religion (Islam), his sect (Shi'ism), the language he speaks at home (Arabic), his lineage (al-Kanaan clan of the Banu Tamim tribe), and the country (Iraq) and city (Basra) in which he lives are each a characteristic that he shares with some people but not others. Each characteristic and the group it defines could conceivably be important for Abbas's political choices, including for whom he votes, to whom he turns when he needs government services, and for whom he might willingly die or even kill. These political communities are "imagined," because Abbas will never meet, or even hear of, most fellow members (Anderson 1991). Yet they matter. In the 2005 parliamentary elections, the first held after the overthrow of Saddam, Abbas ignored appeals from Arab nationalist, tribal, and regional candidates and joined the vast majority of Iraqi Shi'ites in casting his ballot for an electoral list dominated by Shi'ite Islamists. That election ensured that ethnic and sectarian cleavages would play an important role in Iraq's nascent governing institutions, and Shi'ite Islamists have dominated the government ever since.

This chapter will help us make sense of Abbas's and the Middle East's multiple identities (Lewis 1998). We will assume that an individual's political identity is not fixed but is socially and politically constructed; it can change over time through manipulation or perhaps individual choice. In other words, we will reject the assumption that ancient and "essential" religious antagonisms and mentalities characterize Middle Eastern politics. This might be controversial, because the language we use to discuss the Middle East often assumes that some identities inherently matter more than others. For example, calling a region "the Holy Land" automatically implies that religion is important for its politics. When newspapers describe a regional rivalry between "Shi'ite Iran" and "Sunni Saudi Arabia," the adjectives condition us to believe that sectarian differences explain relations between these states when perhaps disagreements over oil policy or balance of power principles offer a better explanation.

All societies possess multiple lines of ethnic and religious division along which political competition and conflict might occur. Most of these divisions are politically unimportant; intergroup coexistence is always far more common than intergroup conflict. We want to understand variation in the political importance of particular identities within countries, between countries, and over time. In Jordan, for example, Transjordanian voters have tended to vote for family members or tribal candidates while Palestinian-Jordanian voters have been more likely to vote for Islamist candidates than for tribal ones (or not vote!). Why? Although bloody fighting occurred between Sunni and Shi'ite Arab armed groups in Iraq from 2004 to 2007 and again when the Islamic State in Iraq and Syria (ISIS) took control of much of northern Iraq from 2014 to 2017, sectarian violence was very rare in twentieth-century Iraq. Why did many Sunnis and Shi'ites in Iraq come to see members of the other sect as rivals or even enemies? In the aftermath of the Arab Spring, why did much of the violence in Iraq, Syria, Yemen, and Bahrain take on sectarian overtones while relations between Sunnis and Shi'ites remained relatively peaceful in Kuwait, Iran, Oman, and Saudi Arabia? In the 1950s and 1960s, Arab and pan-Arab nationalist movements grew dramatically and either came to power or formed the most powerful opposition movements in and across most Arab countries. Yet the political saliency of Arab nationalism declined quickly; many scholars and observers now consider it "dead" or at least unable to consistently mobilize large numbers of Arabic speakers. What explains this change? The purpose of this chapter is to provide a framework for understanding identity and intergroup relations in the Middle East. It describes these divisions and presents theories that might account for why countries differ with regard to which identities are most important for political behavior.

Ethnic and Religious Cleavages in the Middle East

Identity Groups and Identity Categories

It is useful to differentiate between identity groups and the categories those groups fit within (Sacks 1992; Posner 2005). Identity groups are the specific labels that people use to define who they are. Depending on the context, Abbas Haydar might describe himself as "Muslim," "Shi'ite," "Arab," "Iraqi," "member of Banu Tamim tribe," "member of al-Kanaan clan," "Basrawi," or "resident of al-Fursi neighborhood." Each of these is an identity group for which a specific imagined political community could exist. Identity categories, by contrast, are the broad cleavages of social division into which these identity groups can be sorted, such as religion, sect, native language, country of origin, tribe, clan, city of origin or residence, and neighborhood. Individuals can be assumed to have one identity group (e.g., one form of religion) from each identity category.

It is often claimed that Iraq today is divided among Sunnis, Shi'ites, and Kurds. As this framework immediately makes clear, however, this description conflates two identity categories. The identity group "Kurds" is part of the identity category of language; the identity groups "Sunnis" and "Shi'ites" are in the identity category of sect. Since most Kurds are also Sunni Muslims, the identity group "Sunnis" should include them. What people who make this claim mean to say is, "Iraq today is divided politically among Arab Sunnis, Arab Shi'ites, and Kurds of all sects." This is an important clarification, because it reveals how political alignments in Iraq might change in the future—perhaps Arab Sunnis and Kurdish Sunnis could ally along their shared sect, or perhaps Arab Sunnis and Arab Shi'ites will put aside their sectarian differences and align along their shared language as Arab Iraqis, a possibility that many Kurdish Iraqis fear.

Membership in a particular identity group might differentiate someone from other people in the same country, but not necessarily. Abbas and an Iraqi Christian share a nationality, but not a religion. Abbas speaks Arabic; other Iraqis speak Kurdish at home. Abbas traces his lineage to the Kanaan clan of the Banu Tamim tribe, while most other Iraqis are from different tribes or from other clans within the Banu Tamim tribe. For some countries, there is only one group in a particular category. Arabic is the native language of almost all citizens (but not all residents) in Egypt, Jordan, Saudi Arabia, Qatar, the Palestinian territories, Yemen, and Tunisia, and it is the overwhelmingly dominant and official language in several other states. Similarly, the government of Saudi Arabia presumes that all of its citizens are Muslims. The identity category of religion encompasses all Saudi citizens, but other categories could divide them. The category of sect would divide Saudis into Wahhabis, non-Wahhabi Sunnis, and Shi'ites. The category of regional identity differentiates Saudis from the Hijaz, Najd, 'Asir and Jizan, and the coast of the Persian Gulf. Citizenship, of course, divides Saudi citizens from the approximately 20–30 percent of the Saudi population who are noncitizens.

The Multiple Identities of the Middle East

The people of the Middle East differ in a number of ways that do matter, have mattered, or in the future could matter for politics. We turn here to exploring the cultural diversity of the Middle East in the framework of identity categories and groups, focusing on identity groups larger than family for which some sense of political community could exist. Each group might have associated cultural practices, such as cuisines, personal or family names, idioms, or art forms. Although not described here, these cultural practices often form the boundaries of group membership and help individuals identify who is and who is not a member of the group.

Ascriptive identity categories in the Middle East fall under four broad headings: religion and sect, language, lineage (tribe, clan), and geographic homeland (city, region, country). It is easier for individuals to move between groups in some categories than it is in others. Categories based on shared descent or ancestors' residence are probably the most difficult to change, although tribes do occasionally "re"discover lost lineages. An individual can change his language or religion; this can be difficult, but it occurs. Also, minority religious and linguistic groups in the Middle East are often concentrated in mountainous areas, such as Lebanon. This is unsurprising. Homogenizing pressures are less likely to affect communities in difficult-to-access mountains and isolated areas.

All population numbers presented here are estimates. Governments often manipulate demographic data for political reasons, especially when the size of identity groups is sensitive. Lebanon, for example, has not conducted an official census since 1932 because a new one would undoubtedly reveal that the Shi'ite Muslim proportion of the Lebanese population has increased relative to the Sunni Muslim and Christian proportions. Since the Lebanese political system allocates government jobs according to sect, acknowledging demographic changes would upset the existing agreed-upon balance. Similarly, the Jordanian government does not release data on the size of the Palestinian-Jordanian or Transjordanian populations. King Faisal of Saudi Arabia purportedly doubled the estimate of his kingdom's population after seeing the results from the country's first census, in 1969 (Wright 2006: 176); demographic data on Saudi Arabia have been inflated ever since.

Religion and sect. The Middle East is much smaller than the Muslim-majority world. Although approximately 92 percent of the residents of the Middle East are Muslims, 70 percent of the world's Muslims live outside the region. Indonesia, India, Pakistan, and Bangladesh have the four largest Muslim populations in the world; none is in the Middle East. Yet Islam remains closely associated with the Middle East because Islam's most sacred sites are in the region and Arabic is the sacred language of the Quran. All countries in the Middle East except Israel have Muslim majorities. Shi'ite Muslims are a majority in Bahrain, Iraq, and Iran. They are a plurality in Lebanon and a sizable minority in Yemen, Kuwait, Syria, and the United Arab Emirates (UAE). Few Shi'ite Muslims live in North Africa today. With the possible exception of Oman, Sunni Muslims predominate in the other Muslim-majority states of the Middle East. Each sect could be further divided into subgroups, most commonly into schools of Islamic theology and jurisprudence (called *madhahib*). The Amman Message, a prominent 2004 statement of tolerance within Islam, recognized eight such schools: four Sunni, two Shi'ite, and two others.

Christians constitute a significant minority in Lebanon and smaller communities in several other states. Although the percentage of indigenous Christians in the region has declined in recent decades as a result of emigration and relatively low fertility rates, many Christians have come to the region in recent decades as foreign workers. Jews were a significant minority in several Arab countries before the founding of the State of Israel. For example, Jews constituted 35 percent of Baghdad's population at the turn of the twentieth century (Batatu 1978: 248). From 1948 until 1972, perhaps 800,000 to 1 million Jews left Egypt, Iraq, Iran, Yemen, Syria, Lebanon, Turkey, and North Africa and settled in Israel. Today, sizable Jewish populations remain in Iran, Turkey, and Morocco.

Other, smaller religious groups survive throughout the Middle East, including Druze, Alevis, Alawites, Bahais, and Yazidis. Some face persecution. In 2014, ISIS massacred and enslaved large numbers of Yazidis in northern Iraq, leading to international condemnation and a US-led military intervention. Although most Yazidis speak Kurdish, the category of religion is the most salient one for the majority of the community.

Language. The Middle East is much larger than the Arab world. Almost 50 percent of the approximately 530 million residents of the Middle East speak a language other than Arabic at home, such as Turkish, Farsi, Kurdish, Azeri, Hebrew, or Berber (see Table 7.1).

Arabic is an official or national language of every country in the Middle East except Turkey and Iran; Arabic shares its official status with Hebrew in Israel, English and French in Lebanon, and Kurdish in Iraq. Modern standard or "formal" Arabic is a modernized version of the "classical" Arabic of the Quran; it is used for formal speeches, for official documents, and in most books, magazines, and newspapers throughout the Arab world. News broadcasts are in modern standard Arabic, which is why both Moroccans and Iraqis can understand pan-Arab satellite news channels such as Al-Jazeera and Al-Arabiyya. Yet this masks tremendous linguistic variation among the approximately 242 million first-language speakers of Arabic. Most educated Arabs can understand and many can speak modern standard Arabic, but it is awkward for everyday conversation. It would be similar to a modern English-speaker using Shakespearean English in his or her daily life. Instead, Arabs speak colloquial or "informal" Arabic vernaculars that can be unintelligible across regions in the Arab world. Linguists disagree on how to categorize Arabic dialects, but generally the closer two Arabs live to one another, the more likely they are to understand one another. Unless they spoke modern standard Arabic, it would be very difficult

Table 7.1 Languages and Religions of the Middle East

Country	Population	Languages	Religions
Algeria	41,657,488	Arabic (majority) 14% Berber languages (Kabyle and Tachawit)	99% Sunni Muslim 1% Christian and Jewish
Bahrain	1,442,659 (roughly 50% citizens and nonnationals)	Arabic (vast majority) Perhaps 50,000 Farsi speakers (not including nonnationals)	70% Shi'ite Muslim 29% Sunni Muslim 1% Other (not including nonnationals, many of whom are Christian or Hindu, perhaps 20% of the total population)
Egypt	99,413,317	Arabic	Approximately 90% Sunni Muslim <1% Shi'ite Muslim 8%–12% Christian
Iran	83,024,745	50% Farsi 22% Azeri and Turkmen 10% Kurdish 7% Mazanderani and Gilaki 6% Luri 2% Arabic 2% Balochi 1% Other	89% Shi'ite Muslim 9% Sunni Muslim (mostly Turkmen, Arabs, Baluchs, Kurds) 2% Other (mostly Bahai and Christian and small communities of Zoroastrians and Jews)
Iraq	40,194,216	Arabic (majority) 20% Kurdish 2% Azeri 1% Farsi 1% Turkmen	60%–65% Shi'ite Muslim 30%–35% Sunni Muslim 5% Other (mostly Christian, but also small communities of Yezidis, Sabean-Mandaeans, Bahais, etc.)
Israel	8,424,904 (includes settlers in the West Bank, Golan Heights, and East Jerusalem)	50% Hebrew (native speakers) 18% Arabic 15% Russian 2% Yiddish 15% Other (including Romanian)	76% Jewish 16% Muslim 2% Christian 6% Other (Druze, Bahai)

(continues)

Table 7.1 continued

Country	Population	Languages	Religions
Jordan	10,458,413 (includes up to 2,000,000 refugees)	Arabic	93% Sunni Muslim 6% Christian
Kuwait	2,916,467 (30% citizens, 70% nonnationals)	Arabic	65%–70% Sunni Muslim 30%–35% Shi'ite Muslim (real numbers unknown; many nonnationals are Hindu or Christian)
Lebanon	6,100,075 (includes up to 3,000,000 Syrian refugees)	Arabic (vast majority) Armenian (287,000)	28%–45% Shi'ite Muslim 28% Sunni Muslim 22% Maronite 8% Greek Orthodox 5% Druze 4% Greek Catholic 5% Other Christian denominations (all figures are estimates as no census has been taken since 1932)
Libya	6,754,507 (12% nonnationals)	Arabic (majority) 3% Berber dialects	97% Sunni Muslim
Morocco	32,314,130	Arabic (majority) 23% Berber languages (Tachelhit, Tamazight, Tarafit/Rifi)	99% Sunni Muslim 1% Christian <1% Other (mostly Jewish)
Oman	3,494,116 (55% citizens, 45% nonnationals)	Arabic (vast majority) Balochis (197,000)	Unknown, but most Ibadhi or Sunni (estimates vary widely regarding which is a majority) <5% Shi'ite (in capital and along northern coast)
Palestine	4,635,207 (1,836,713 in the Gaza Strip, 2,798,494 in the West Bank, not including Israeli settlers in the West Bank and East Jerusalem)	Arabic	Gaza: 100% Sunni Muslim West Bank: 90% Sunni Muslim, 10% Christian

(continues)

Table 7.1 continued

Country	Population	Languages	Religions
Qatar	2,363,569 (12% citizens, 88% nonnationals)	Arabic (majority) Farsi (219,000)	95% Sunni Muslim <5% Shi'ite Muslim Many nonnationals are Christian or Hindu
Saudi Arabia	33,091,113 (63% citizens, 37% nonnationals)	Arabic	90% Sunni Muslim 10% Shi'ite Muslim
Syria	19,454,263 (not including approximately 5,000,000 refugees outside the country)	Arabic (majority) 7–10% Kurdish 2% Other (Armenian, Aramaic)	74% Sunni 14% Alawite and Ismaili 3% Druze 9% Christian
Tunisia	11,516,189	Arabic	99% Sunni Muslim 1% Shi'ite Muslim
Turkey	81,257,239	70%–75% Turkish 15%–20% Kurdish 10% Other (Arabic, Azerbaijani, Bulgarian, Zaza)	99% Muslim (mostly Sunni, but an unknown number of Alevis) <1% Other (mostly Christian)
United Arab Emirates	9,701,315 (12% citizens, 88% nonnationals)	Arabic (vast majority) Up to 1,000,000 speak Pashto Balochi, or Farsi	85% Sunni Muslim 15% Shi'ite Muslim
Yemen	28,667,230	Arabic (vast majority)	Unknown 45% Zaydi Muslim 55% Sunni Muslim <1% Other (Jewish, Christian, and Hindu)

Sources: Population: Central Intelligence Agency (CIA), *World Factbook*, https://www.cia.gov/library/publications/resources/the-world-factbook. Languages: Principally, F. Simons and Charles D. Fennig, eds., *Ethnologue: Languages of the World*, 21st ed. (Dallas: SIL International, 2018), http://www.ethnologue.com; also country-specific sources. Religions: CIA, *World Factbook*; National Geographic Society, *Atlas of the Middle East*, 2nd ed. (Washington, DC, 2008); Vali Nasr, *The Shia Revival: How Conflicts Within Islam Will Shape the Future* (New York: Norton, 2006); and Vali Nasr, "When the Shi'ites Rise," *Foreign Affairs* 85, no. 4 (2006): 58–74; country-specific sources.

for a Tunisian and a Jordanian to understand one another in Arabic. Because of the popularity of Egyptian movies, our Iraqi friend Abbas might understand most of what an Egyptian says, but an Egyptian would probably understand less than half of what Abbas said in his Iraqi-Arabic dialect. Cities and villages within countries often differ in pronunciations and vocabulary, which means that dialect often overlaps with another identity category—city or region of origin. Abbas's Basrawi accent would mark him as a southern Iraqi if he traveled to Baghdad.

Although Arab nationalism was a powerful political force in the 1950s and 1960s, it is not readily obvious why Arabic should have generated an imagined political community. In the early twentieth century, calling a resident of Cairo an "Arab" would probably have been interpreted as an insult. At the time, the vast majority of Egyptians did not see their political fate as linked to residents of the Levant or Arabian Peninsula, much less residents of Morocco. Yet Arab nationalism, a political ideology directed at Arabic-speakers, emerged as one of the region's most powerful political identities.

With over 70 million speakers, Turkish is the second most spoken language in the Middle East. Although Turkish is rarely spoken in the Middle East outside of the Republic of Turkey, 2 million Iranians and perhaps 200,000 Iraqis speak related Turkic languages. Turkish was written in a variant of Perso-Arabic script until 1928, when Mustafa Kemal Atatürk replaced the Arabic script with a modified Latin script and purged many Arabic and Persian terms from Turkish. Today, therefore, the vast majority of Turks cannot read Arabic or the Ottoman Turkish script of their ancestors that was used for centuries in the Ottoman Empire.

The Iranian plateau is the most linguistically diverse region of the Middle East, with more than a dozen distinct dialects and languages widely spoken. Iran is losing this diversity, however, as an older generation, born before the spread of centralized education, dies out. Persian, or Farsi, is the first language of ever more Iranians.

Modern Hebrew is a revived form of an ancient language that had largely vanished as a spoken language but had survived as a written language due to its religious importance. Its revival and spread were a result of efforts by members of the Jewish nationalist movement in the nineteenth century. Within the Middle East, modern Hebrew is spoken in Israel and among Jewish settlers in the Occupied Territories. Although not all Israeli Jews speak Hebrew (especially since the post-1989 influx of almost 1 million Russian or Romanian speakers from the Soviet Union and post-Soviet states), it plays an incredibly important role in uniting Jews who emigrated to Israel speaking different first languages.

Arabic and Hebrew are related Semitic languages, and there are numerous similarities across the two. The term *Semitic* refers to a language group and is not a racial designation. Therefore, it is inaccurate and meaningless to claim that "Jews and Arabs are both Semites," although it is correct to say that "Hebrew and Arabic are both Semitic languages" (Lewis 1998: 46–47).

European Jews who came (or whose ancestors came) to Israel (or to Palestine, if they arrived before 1948) initially spoke different languages than Jews who came from Arab and Muslim lands. Differences between Ashkenazi Jews from western, central, and eastern Europe, and Sephardic and Mizrachi Jews from southeastern Europe, northern Africa, and the Middle East, are now more akin to a racial divide within Israeli society than to a linguistic one. Like many racial cleavages, this one overlaps with class. Although Sephardic and Mizrachi Jews are culturally and socially heterogeneous, they tend to be less well-off than their Ashkenazi compatriots.

Although Berber is often considered a single northern African language with many dialects, it varies enough to be mutually unintelligible across most dialects. Berber dialects are spoken by millions of Moroccans and Algerians and tens of thousands of Libyans and Tunisians. Approximately 23 percent (8 million) of Moroccans speak a Berber dialect, the most important of which are Tamazight (in central Morocco), Tachelhit (in the High Atlas region), and Tarafit or Rifi (in the Rif mountains). Approximately 14 percent of Algerians are considered Berber-speakers; the two largest dialects are Kabyle and Tachawit.

For centuries, speakers of Kurdish have lived in the mountains and plateaus where the modern states of Turkey, Iraq, Iran, and Syria meet. There are two main Kurdish dialects that are grammatically distinct from one another: Kurmanji (spoken by northern Kurds) and Surani (spoken by southern Kurds), and several smaller ones, notably Gurani and Zaza. Worldwide, there are perhaps 30–45 million Kurds; in comparison, there are approximately 17 million Jews and 12 million people of Palestinian descent in the world. Although estimates vary widely, about 12–20 million Kurds live in Turkey (constituting about 17 percent of the population of Turkey). Another 8 million live in Iran and 5 million in Iraq, constituting 10 percent and 15 percent of those countries' respective populations. The overwhelming majority (about 75 percent) of Kurds are Sunni Muslims; most of the rest follow varieties of Shi'ism. Kurds have increasingly thought of themselves as a distinct ethnic community since World War I, and Kurdish national identities continue to evolve among populations both within and across Turkey, Iraq, Syria, and Iran. The Kurdish-majority region of Iraq has been de facto autonomous from the Iraqi central government since 1991 and has been relatively stable and prosperous since the US-led invasion in 2003. Since the beginning of the Syrian civil war in 2012, Kurdish political movements have established control in northeast Syria and along much of the border with Turkey. They declared an autonomous Democratic Federation of Northern Syria in 2016; this region is known as "Rojava" (literally "the Western") in Kurdish, implying that it is part of a greater Kurdistan.

Lineage (tribe and clan). Kinship ties are often the basis of social and political solidarity. Yet the size, structure, coherence, and modes of livelihood of tribes vary across place and over time in the Middle East. Tribes usually, but not always, share some common imagined ancestry and territoriality. In general, tribes are pyramidal and segmentary. Family units aggregate into larger clans, lineages, tribes, and tribal confederations. Yet each unit or segment of the tribal structure could be an identity group and become a distinct political community. Ties to siblings and cousins tend to be strong and robust, while ties to more distant relatives are less likely to mobilize.

Before the rise of states, kinship or "tribal" forms of organization were a principal way in which individuals defended themselves and jointly provided other public goods. Tribal ties are often seen as being at odds with an individual's obligations to the global community of Muslims or patriotic loyalties to modern states. Yet some regimes use the image of tribes and familial relationships to reinforce their rule. Hafiz al-Asad of Syria, for example, was often portrayed on billboards and in the state-controlled media as the "father" of the Syrian people and, occasionally, of the Lebanese and Palestinians. In Saudi Arabia, the Saud family portrays itself as the head of a vast confederation that encompasses all citizens of the country. Kinship-based social and political organization and symbols associated with "tribes" remain important in many Middle Eastern states.

Geographic homeland (city, region, and country). The Arabic term *watan* means homeland, country, or place where one's family historically resides. Yet the idea of "place" in the Middle East has changed over time. Before the rise of nation-states in the twentieth century, *watan* could refer to a village, town, neighborhood, or province, but not to a "country" in a modern sense (Lewis 1998: 57). Boundaries were not always strictly demarcated; many of today's state borders are a colonial legacy. Since the writ of the decentralized Ottoman Empire often did not extend far beyond major cities, some provincial towns operated as de facto city-states. Powerful families and locality-based organizations provided order and public goods, and neighborhood-level affiliations could be politically important. Urban quarters in medieval Iraqi and Iranian cities, for example, were often controlled by neighborhood gangs or, as described by Juan Cole and Moojan Momen (1986), local mafias.

The breakup of the Ottoman Empire and emergence of modern Middle East states not only redrew the regional map but also redefined the identities available to the residents of those lands. These new states, often under colonial "tutelage," wrote laws that defined nationality and citizenship. People living within a new country's demarcated boundaries were told that they were now citizens of that state. A resident of the town of Irbid in the 1920s, for example, would eventually learn that he or she was now a citizen of the newly created Emirate of Transjordan. A trip north to Damascus or west to Haifa soon involved crossing an international border to Syria or Palestine. Furthermore, this resident was told to direct any grievances and aspirations to the new capital of Amman and the British-installed emir who governed from there.

The Middle East's new states differed in how they cultivated national identity among their citizens. This national patriotism or civil nationalism (*wataniyya*) contrasts with other conceptions of political community based on descent-based identity categories, such as pan-Arab nationalism (often called *qawmiyya*). Throughout the region, the rise of national identities was controversial. State officials often used pre-Islamic civilizations to create a distinct "modern" patriotic identity (Lewis 1998). The Egyptians, for example, used Pharaonic history to cultivate an Egyptian identity, and the Iraqi state rediscovered Babylon.

Country of origin is not necessarily the same as citizenship. For example, the term Palestinian-Jordanian commonly refers to the 60–70 percent of Jordanian citizens who trace their origins to (extant or destroyed) towns and villages west of the Jordan River in what had been the Palestine Mandate. Transjordanians, by contrast, are Jordanian citizens who trace their origins to groups considered native to lands east of the Jordan River. Despite efforts to create a "Jordanian" identity that unites Palestinian-Jordanians and Transjordanians, country of origin arguably remains the most salient identity category in Jordan. Since at least the early 1970s, Transjordanians have dominated government jobs and the military. Furthermore, the gerrymandering of electoral districts results in severe underrepresentation of Palestinian-Jordanians in the lower house of the Jordanian parliament. Despite being a majority of the population, it is common for less than 20 percent of the deputies in the Jordanian parliament to be Palestinian-Jordanians.

Explaining the Political Importance of Identities

Why do some identities, but not others, become the axes of political competition and conflict? Why do individuals "choose" one identity from their repertoire rather than another? Abbas Haydar voted for a sectarian (Shi'ite) political list instead of one based on Arab nationalism, local or provincial interests, or tribal ties. Why? There are several perspectives that may give us some insight into these questions.

Primordialism

Perhaps some identities garner inherently deeper and more emotional attachments than others. Theories of primordialism, or "essentialism," imply that "so profound are the sentiments of peoplehood, so securely are identities and loyalties transferred between generations, that even when they appear to subside they can readily be reignited" (Esman and Rabinovich 1988: 12). Journalists often describe Middle Eastern politics in primordial terms. Thomas Friedman, for example, once partly attributed authoritarianism in the region to the "primordial, tribe-like loyalties [that] governed men's identities and political attitudes so deeply" (1990: 91). Primordialism is frequently used either to account for the continued relevance of identity categories that might appear to have become less important over time in Western industrialized societies—such as tribe, religion, and sect—or to explain contemporary antagonisms as the continuation of conflicts that occurred centuries or even millennia ago.

Lisa Anderson points out that many advocates of democracy assumed that the failure of the Middle East to embrace it could be "explained by assigning some kind of handicap or immaturity to the people themselves" (1995: 77). Such arguments often rely on uninformative tautological reasoning, such as the claim that "tribalism remains important because people have deeply held loyalties to tribes; we know people have deeply held loyalties to tribes because tribalism remains important." There is a tendency to look for mysterious primordial "essences" that prevent democratization rather than to investigate verifiable factors that promote or hinder this process (Sadowski 1993). Similarly, journalists often describe contemporary conflicts as a continuation of age-old rivalries between groups. References to Cain and Abel, for example, are far too common in analyses of conflict between Israel and the Palestinians.

Aside from being circular, often unfalsifiable, and overly simplistic, primordialist perspectives cannot explain change or variation. Identities do change over time for individuals and societies. Abbas Haydar's ancestors were nominally Sunni tribesmen in southern Iraq who settled in towns in the mid-eighteenth century and converted to Shi'ite Islam. The most salient identity for Abbas (his Shi'ism), therefore, would be deeply alien to his great-great-great-grandfather, who was not a Shi'ite and would have relied on his tribal kinsmen for most social, economic, and political needs. The area that is now known as Iraq probably did not have a Shi'ite Muslim majority until the late nineteenth or even early twentieth century. Similarly, sectarianism appears to be a fairly recent political cleavage in Lebanon (Makdisi 2000). Yet these facts do not stop scholars and journalists from describing sectarian conflicts in those countries as continuous intra-Muslim conflicts that date to the seventh century. A final shortcoming of primordialist perspectives is that they overpredict conflict: that is, they cannot explain why intergroup coexistence is much more common than intergroup conflict.

Modernization and Socioeconomic Conditions

Another set of perspectives links identity to the socioeconomic conditions in which people find themselves and portrays "traditional" and "modern" identity categories as competing for the loyalty of individuals. Modernization theory, for example, posits that traditional parochial loyalties, such as to religion and tribe, gradually lose their salience as occupational and class differences become more important. Tribalism is seen as an anachronistic remnant of a previous age; it was an effective form of social organization only until centralized state governments were able to regulate economic, social, and political relations.

Urbanization and education are often linked to the weakening of tribalism and the strengthening of nonkinship identities. Although cities have long dominated the Middle East, urbanization has increased dramatically in recent decades. Today, as Table 1.1 indicates (see Chapter 1), only Yemen and Egypt have more than 50 percent of their populations living in rural areas. In many countries, the proportion of people living in urban or suburban areas is in the range of 75 to 95 percent. Despite stereotypes, pastoral nomadism is now exceedingly rare. Educational opportunities and literacy rates have also increased dramatically. Yet despite the predictions of modernization theory, tribal and religious identities appear to have strengthened in some societies. Puzzlingly, support for Islamist movements is often strongest among the most "modern" citizens in Arab societies—young, upwardly mobile university students and professionals (Wickham 2002). Similarly, tribal identities can coexist and even thrive in the context of "modern" states.

A related perspective comes from fourteenth-century scholar Ibn Khaldun, one of the forefathers of social science, who developed an explanation for changes in the saliency of tribal identity in a group over time. In his work *Al-Muqaddimah* (literally, "The Introduction" or "The Preface"), Ibn Khaldun describes how nomadic individuals living in harsh desert environments are driven to develop social bonds and a group solidarity or consciousness that he calls *'asabiyah*. United by *'asabiyah,* these bedouin conquer and replace sedentary city-dwellers. Within a few generations, they acquire wealth and adopt a life of ease and luxury that corrupts and undermines their group solidarity. Soon, another nomadic group united by *'asabiyah* arises to conquer the city, and the cyclical rise and fall of dynasties continues. Ibn Khaldun's argument focuses on variation in the importance of tribalism and says little about when we would expect an identity category other than tribalism, such as religion, to become salient.

These perspectives share certain claims, most notably that some identity categories (especially lineage-based or "tribal" identities) will weaken as states come to dominate people's lives. The persistence of kinship-based forms of mobilization, however, suggests that other factors, such as state policy or institutions, also play a role.

Historical Legacies

Perhaps history can bestow a hegemonic status on a particular identity group for an individual or on an identity category for a society. Many scholars argue that the saliency and resiliency of religious, linguistic, or tribal identities are a legacy of Ottoman-era institutions and policies or of European colonial efforts to "divide and rule" the people of the Middle East.

The Ottoman Empire was a vast, multiethnic, multireligious, Islamic polity ruled by a Turkish dynastic family. The subjects of the Ottoman sultan were organized into religious communities called *millets*. Muslims, Christians, Jews, and Druze were each given a significant degree of autonomy and had their own courts to administer religious and personal status law (e.g., regarding marriage, divorce, custody, and inheritance). Although not equal to Muslims under the *millet* system, local non-Muslim religious leaders enjoyed considerable leeway to manage the affairs of their co-religionists. Access to different legal infrastructures under this system gave the Middle East's indigenous Christians and Jews significant economic advantages compared to Muslim subjects of the sultan, which helped them dominate new economic sectors such as banking and insurance (Kuran 2004).

Kemal Karpat (1988) and others argue that the primacy of religious identity over ethnic or linguistic group solidarity in the Middle East is a function of Ottoman state policy. In other words, residents of the region think of themselves and others, first and foremost, as Muslims,

Christians, Jews, and the like, because that is how their ancestors' lives were structured in Ottoman times. However, the *millet* system varied considerably across groups and regions and changed over time; the Ottomans did not attempt to create an empire-wide *millet* structure until the nineteenth century, and the Young Turks formally abolished the *millet* system in 1909. It is unclear why we should expect the Ottoman *millet* system to continue to have such a profound influence 100 years later, after the dissolution of the Ottoman Empire, the rise of territorial states, Arab nationalism, industrialization, and the promotion of patriotic identities based on citizenship.

Other scholars look to the colonial era to account for the resiliency of particular identities and identity categories. Many boundaries of today's Middle Eastern states were drawn with little regard for tribal, religious, and linguistic groups. The Kurds, for example, are divided among Iraq, Iran, Turkey, and Syria. The Druze are divided among Lebanon, Syria, Israel, and Jordan. Several tribes and clans straddle the porous border between Syria and Iraq. Smugglers used these cross-border tribal connections to move goods into and out of Iraq during the sanctions period from 1990 to 2003, and insurgents fighting the US-led occupation of Iraq in 2003–2007 utilized these same cross-border tribal connections to move fighters, money, and arms into the country. These flows reversed themselves in 2011 as men and military equipment flowed to Syrian rebels. In mid-2014, ISIS released two videos showing its troops breaching and erasing this "colonial" border.

The predicted effect on identity of artificially dividing groups across borders, however, is unclear. Is a coherent Kurdish national identity more likely to develop if Kurds are united in a single "Kurdistan" or if they share the grievance of having their homeland divided and living as disadvantaged minorities in different states? If a greater Kurdish state existed, might a different identity category become increasingly salient and divide Kurds along tribal, regional, or dialect lines?

In addition to drawing borders, colonial powers sometimes pursued "divide-and-rule" policies that might have had effects that resonate today. Colonial legislatures frequently reserved seats for religious minorities, a practice that continues in several contemporary legislatures. For example, seats are reserved in the Jordanian lower house of parliament for Christians and Circassians/Chechens. In the mandate period, the French established autonomous states for the Druze and Alawite religious minorities in what is today Syria. The political instability that characterized postindependence Syrian politics and the rise of the Alawite-dominated military regime are often linked to colonial-era policies. Similarly, Arab Sunni domination in twentieth-century Iraq is often linked to Ottoman and British policies that favored Sunnis for administrative and military positions. In some cases, colonial policies "invented" tribal and linguistic identities that survived past independence; colonial administrators' understandings of tribal organization were codified and disseminated in ways that made them "official." French administrators in Morocco and Algeria, for example, emphasized the distinctiveness of Berber identity from Arab and Muslim identities (Gellner and Micaud 1972; Eickelman 2002: 205).

These perspectives suggest that identities are "sticky" and not a result of individuals' choices and that the broad axes of societal division are difficult to change once established. Colonial policies and decisions made during the process of state formation shape a society's trajectory. Either individuals do not choose their identity, or the past determines the choices available.

State Institutions

If rulers promote identities that enable them to maintain their authority, perhaps different types of regimes promote different types of identities. Alan Richards and John Waterbury (2008: 291–316) argue that the socialist republics of the Middle East deliberately fostered different identities than did the region's monarchies. In general, the socialist republics have been "purposeful states" bent on development and military might. They have emphasized unity and cohesion among citizens and often repressed religious or linguistic minority movements for autonomy or group rights, especially in the early years of state formation. Atatürk, for example, promoted Turkish nationalism and ruthlessly crushed a Kurdish rebellion in 1925. The Turkish government for decades officially referred to the Kurdish minority as "mountain Turks."

Richards and Waterbury argue that, in contrast, most monarchs in the Middle East have handled diversity and pluralism differently than the socialist republics. Monarchs rule by dividing and balancing competing interests. Richards and Waterbury write, "Monarchs speak in terms of the nation and decry the fractious elements in society that impede national unity, but they do not deny these elements legitimacy so long as they behave according to the rules of the game as the monarchy defines them. What the monarchs want is a plethora of interests, tribal, ethnic, professional, class-based, and partisan, whose competition for public patronage they can arbitrate" (2008: 312). Successful monarchs position themselves above competing identity groups in such a way that those groups fear chaos if the monarch is overthrown. The Jordanian and Saudi monarchies, for example, are often described as balancing competing tribal and regional loyalties.

Finally, states might delegate some government powers to the leaders of identity groups, which privileges certain identity categories over others. Religious authorities, for example, oversee personal status law in Israel and Lebanon. Arab nationalists and political Islamists have played prominent roles in designing or reforming educational systems. All of these perspectives suggest that state policy can influence how individuals think of themselves.

Political Entrepreneurs and Political Violence

As Abbas Haydar learned, aspiring political entrepreneurs seeking to develop a political following often try to convince people that one identity matters more than others. Maybe some individuals are craftier or more charismatic than others and, therefore, more likely to mobilize people around a particular identity. This line of argument implies that grievances alone are insufficient for mobilization, which also requires intellectuals and charismatic leaders who can articulate group demands and organize a vanguard of the masses. This makes sense. Grievances and unfulfilled aspirations are ubiquitous, but mobilization is not. The rise of Arab nationalism, for example, is often referred to as an "awakening" or "renaissance," which implies that mobilization along linguistic lines had long been possible for the Arab subjects of the Ottoman Empire. Arab nationalists later popularized the idea that "sleeping" Turkish and Arab nations existed under the Ottomans and that the Arabs needed a linguistic and cultural intellectual revival to spark a widespread independence movement. Pan-Arabism did not gain widespread popular support until the 1950s, when it found its champion in the charismatic Gamal Abdel Nasser.

Sunni Islamists in the early twentieth century sought to organize Muslims against colonialism by appealing to Islam instead of Arab nationalism or national histories. They presented a contrasting vision of what identity category is best to mobilize around. Yet it took the organizational innovations of Hassan al-Banna and his Society of Muslim Brothers to consistently mobilize large numbers of Muslims as Muslims.

Perhaps violence leads individuals to mobilize along particular identity categories. The creation of the State of Israel in 1948, the partition of Palestine, and the defeat of Arab armies might have contributed to the rise of a shared sense among Arabs that their fates are linked. Similarly, the decline of Arab nationalism and rise of Islamism closely followed the Israeli victory in the 1967 Six Day War. Maybe military defeats delegitimize particular identities or otherwise create opportunities for political entrepreneurs to encourage mobilization along a different identity category. Many scholars of Iraq argue that

Saddam collectively punished Shi'ites for the 1991 uprising, leading to a strengthening of Shi'ism as a mass group identity.

Some actors might use violence to deliberately politicize a particular identity category. The radical Sunni Islamist Abu Musab al-Zarqawi deliberately tried to foment sectarian violence in Iraq from 2003 until his death in 2006 by targeting Shi'ites in ways that he hoped would provoke Iraq's Shi'ites to retaliate against Sunnis. In February 2004, US officials in Iraq circulated a letter purportedly written by Zarqawi (Coalition Provisional Authority 2004). The letter advocates attacking Shi'ites because doing so "will provoke them [Shi'ites] to show the Sunnis their rabies . . . and bare the teeth of the hidden rancor working in their breasts. If we succeed in dragging them into the arena of sectarian war, it will become possible to awaken the inattentive Sunnis as they feel imminent danger and annihilating death at the hands of these Sabeans."[1] The plan worked; sectarian violence in Iraq escalated considerably following the February 2006 bombing of the Shi'ite 'Askariyya Shrine in Samarra. Zarqawi's organization renamed itself "The Islamic State of Iraq" eight months later and in 2011 became ISIS when it expanded operations into Syria. ISIS would engage in the wholesale slaughter of Shi'ites in northern Iraq in 2014, leading senior Shi'ite religious authorities to encourage followers to take up arms to fight ISIS and defend their holy places. A strategy to provoke sectarian violence worked once again.

Many observers witness intergroup animosity and "hatred" during periods of violence and assume that the hatred predates the violence and explains why it began. But intergroup hatred is often a product of violence and did not exist before the conflict began. Political violence is fairly common in twentieth-century Iraq, but that violence was not sectarian in nature until 1991, or even 2003. The hatred that exists between Sunnis and Shi'ites in Iraq today is largely a result of post-2003 violence, not its cause. Similarly, as the Syrian Civil War continued, the regime led by Bashar al-Asad became reliant on Alawite-dominated paramilitary forces and Shi'ites from abroad: Lebanese Hezbollah, fighters from Afghanistan and Iraq, and Iranian troops. The sectarian nature of the violence in Syria and the brutality of the regime have made a negotiated settlement particularly difficult to imagine. How can the Sunni-dominated rebels promise not to seek revenge on the minority Alawite community after the regime falls? The Alawites, or Nusayris, follow a syncretistic religion that combines elements of different religions but is widely considered a form of Shi'ism. They fear persecution, for good reason, if Sunni Islamists come to dominate post-Asad Syrian politics. That fear has led many Syrian religious minorities to tolerate, or even support, a brutal dictator.

Clientelism and Elections

If politics is about the contest for power and the distribution of scarce resources, perhaps some identities are more useful than others because they help power-holders limit access to the spoils that successful mobilization generates (Bates 1983). Writing about sub-Saharan Africa, Daniel Posner (2005) argues that group size, not depth of attachment, drives individual-level identity choice and thus determines which identity category becomes politically important at the society level. Such a perspective suggests that individuals will choose an identity that allows them to share the spoils of power with as few others as possible. Milton Esman and Itamar Rabinovich express a similar notion when they write that "ethnic and confessional solidarities survive only as long as they pay—as long as they provide more security, status and material rewards than do available alternatives" (1988: 13). In other words, individuals choose their identity based on expectations of benefits, not emotional attachments.

Tribal or religious minorities dominate several Middle Eastern regimes. The rise to power in Syria of Hafiz al-Asad, for example, allowed Alawites to enjoy privileged access to state resources and positions in the military under his regime. However, it is inaccurate to say that Alawites as a group "seized" the Syrian state. Al-Asad consolidated his power in 1970 by ousting the two other Alawite members of the triumvirate who had shared power with him since their coup d'état seven years earlier, and not all Alawites benefited from the Asad regime. Furthermore, the Syrian regime relied on the support of the Sunni urban business class. One scholar of Syria wrote, "The [Syrian] Ba'ath recruited from all those who were outside the system of connections, patronage or kin on which the old regime was built: the educated sons of peasants, the minorities, the rural lower middle class, the 'black sheep' from lesser branches of great families" (Hinnebusch 1979: 17). Nevertheless, violence during the Syrian Civil War has made the conflict a sectarian one.

Finally, several Arab states have held regular competitive parliamentary elections since the early 1990s. Until the so-called Arab Spring, none of these elections led to a transition to democracy, and they may actually have strengthened authoritarian regimes by regularizing competition over scarce resources. Ellen Lust-Okar (2006) argues that voters want representatives who will channel government resources to them personally. In such a system, tribal leaders might be more effective and credible conduits of state largesse than other candidates because of the size of tribes and the information flows among members. Tribal or other kin-based ties might make it easier for candidates to get out the vote and give their relatives greater faith that they will do their best to deliver jobs and services to them instead of others.

Conclusion

The history of the modern Middle East is often described as a series of sequential eras characterized by the prominence of particular identities. Until the twentieth century, religious affiliation was the most important identity category for subjects of the Ottoman sultan. The breakup of the Ottoman Empire into separate states ushered in a new identity category (state citizenship) that competed for citizens' loyalties. Pan-Arab nationalism flourished in the 1950s and early 1960s. After 1967, however, many scholars believe an era of political Islamism replaced the era of pan-Arab nationalism. Some scholars argue that the region recently has moved from an era of Islamism to something else (Roy 1994), perhaps an era characterized by local solidarities or sectarian cleavages (Nasr 2006). It is as yet unclear which identity categories, if any, will characterize the post–Arab Spring Middle East. The one identity that remains meaningless to the residents of the Middle East is that of Middle Easterner, a term that, as explained in Chapter 1, has literal and figurative meaning from a Western perspective but not from within the region.

In this chapter, I have provided a framework for making sense of the multiple identities of the Middle East, described the most important identity categories, and offered several theoretical perspectives that might account for why some identity categories—but not others—become or remain salient. The country chapters in Part 2 of this volume further describe the identity categories and groups within the various countries of the Middle East. While reading about these countries—their histories, their institutional structures, their track records regarding economic development, and so forth—consider, for each particular case, which theoretical perspective seems to best explain the nature of identity politics.

Note

1. The author of the letter uses *Sabean* as a derogatory term for Shi'ites, implying that they are not true Muslims. Some analysts argue that the letter was most probably not written by Zarqawi (see, for example, Novikov 2004).

8

Gender and Politics

Diane Singerman and Danielle Higgins

Political change in the Middle East is multidimensional and the product of many forces. This chapter explores comparative politics in the Middle East through the lens of gender, looking at how understandings of femininity and masculinity are socially constructed, institutionalized, appropriated, and contested. In this sense, the chapter privileges gender as an analytic concept. Gender refers not to a fixed biological notion of sex but rather to the "appropriate" social and cultural roles that society values as normal or desirable. In every society, many factors shape gender norms and socialize mass behavior, including long historical processes influenced by the state, religion, culture, law, morality, sexuality, ideology, and economic forces, as well as contemporary changes and challenges. Individuals and activists also shape norms and laws as they imagine new aspects of their own identity and demand the right to express themselves and engage in the larger polity, as full citizens and subjects. Out of these struggles, larger political movements grow to reform laws and alter political arrangements. The struggle for gender equality, which is itself a contested norm in the Middle East, necessitates utilizing political resources as activists try to build movements that target legal, economic, social, religious, or political reforms.

Throughout the globe and within many academic disciplines, there are raging debates about whether patriarchy, or the institutionalized domination and subordination of women, is universal or not. Lerner argued the good news about patriarchy was that because it had a historical beginning in laws that institutionalized the legal, economic, and sexual subordination of women, it could also have an end at another historical moment by reversing female subordination (1986). Men and women have waged many political struggles to end patriarchy by transforming the institutions, norms, and laws that have sustained it. While gender is not a synonym for women, it has typically been the contradictions and discrimination that women face in their daily lives that become so onerous at a certain point that they rebel to chip away at patriarchy, although male allies have also been extremely important at certain moments (Carver 1998).

In the last quarter of the twentieth century, women and gender studies in the Middle East exploded, producing a profusion of scholarship, reports, and surveys on the "question of women." Scholar-activists and intellectuals searched archives and reinterpreted legal and religious texts to analyze the position of women from their standpoint and their experiences. Reexamining and challenging long-held male-centric histories, reinterpreting sacred texts and religious law, and reimagining political possibilities infused intellectual debates about gender and women's history and fueled political activism as well. This chapter draws from this pioneering scholarship.

Global Rankings, Education, Employment, and Political Empowerment

Global efforts to improve the status and well-being of women, themselves a consequence of women's movements, have produced many techniques to measure gender equality and compare nations universally. A prominent example of a universal approach to analyzing the inequality between men and women is the World Economic Forum's (WEF's) Global Gender Gap Report. The 2017 report ranked 144 countries using economic, educational, health, and political criteria, measuring disparities between men and women. Overall the Middle East region ranked lowest (and Nordic countries highest). Of the bottom ten countries, seven are in the Middle East: Jordan, Morocco, Lebanon, Saudi Arabia, Iran, Syria, and Yemen (Leopold, Ratcheva, and Zahidi 2017: 11). Besides Israel (which is ranked 44th overall), Tunisia is ranked the highest (117th) in the Middle East region, while Yemen is ranked 144th, the very last spot of all of the countries included in the report.

Low rates of female labor force participation and political representation are the major factors driving down the rankings for Middle Eastern countries, but the Gender Gap Report also considers other rights and norms such as legislation protecting women from discrimination or violence, parental authority in marriage, inheritance rights of daughters, and women's access to credit and land ownership. These sorts of rights fall under the legal category of personal status law. In the early twentieth century, centralizing Ottoman codes and colonial, Western, and secular law influenced the creation of new civil and criminal legal systems. However, laws regulating the private spheres of marriage, divorce, child custody, and inheritance remained largely under the purview of Islamic jurisprudence. The mere existence of personal status law in Middle Eastern countries is one factor that damages rankings. For example, if personal status laws do not grant equal inheritance to men and women, this automatically downgrades the overall score. Scoring does not take into account implementation, which is a problem because context-specific practices may create variation in the extent to which personal status law restricts women.

Universal approaches have the effect, perhaps unintended, of making the "referent" or starting point for an observation the most "liberated" countries, in this case those in the more egalitarian Western Europe and North America. The "rest" or the "worst" are then expected to "progress" toward the achievements of the referent countries. Labdaoui argues that universalist norms "impos[e] criteria of classification regardless of local will and interests. It is a grammar which crosses national frontiers and which is scornful of national, cultural, or political considerations" (2003: 148). Because many non-Western parts of the world have experienced centuries of colonial domination, universal comparisons concerning women's status obscure important historical circumstances that partially explain why resistance to the idea of formal legal equality for women—as well as many other remaining obstacles to gender equality—still exist.

While Western Europe could close its gender gap in 61 years, it will take the Middle East 157 years at the current rate of progress. Interestingly, North America will take about a decade longer than the Middle East to close its gender gap, in spite of the fact that its gap is smaller than that of the Middle East (Leopold, Ratcheva, and Zahidi 2017: viii). This is a testament to the speed at which Middle East and North Africa (MENA) countries have made reforms, particularly with regard to education. Progress in increasing basic literacy and girls' education at all levels has been impressive in the MENA region in the past few decades, largely because the gender differential between men and women had been so great and because postcolonial governments have invested heavily in girls' education, as well as public education more generally. While European Union countries spend an average of 12 percent of their total government expenditure on education, the MENA region averages 15 percent, with Tunisia, Syria, and Saudi Arabia investing more than 20 percent (UNESCO 2017a).[1] These efforts have paid off. In 1980, only one-third of women (ages 15+) in the region were literate; forty years later, about three-quarters are (UNESCO 2017b). The gender gap in primary and secondary school enrollment has also steadily decreased over this time period: from 30 percent in 1980, to 20 percent in 1990, to less than 5 percent in 2016 (UNESCO 2017c). By 2006 the region as a whole reached gender parity in tertiary enrollment, and today in many MENA countries there are more women than men enrolled in universities (UNESCO 2017d). In Qatar, where female tertiary enrollment has been significantly higher than men's since the 1970s, there are *seven* women enrolled in university for every one man. Even Yemen, the lowest-ranking country in the region and overall, has closed 73 percent of its gender gap in educational attainment (Leopold, Ratcheva, and Zahidi 2017).

While these are significant achievements, there are important ways in which they reflect constraints on women's opportunities as much as they reflect a commitment to equality of educational opportunity for women. High university enrollment rates for women in the Gulf, for example, stem from the fact that protective families are far more likely to allow their sons, rather than their daughters, to attend prestigious universities abroad. The disproportionate number of women who seek higher education is also due to very low female labor-force participation rates, legal and cultural constraints on female mobility, the lack of jobs that are considered "appropriate" or safe for women, and skyrocketing female unemployment rates in the region.

Gains in female education in other global regions have been associated with gains in female employment, but far less so in Middle Eastern countries. In a sense, public investment in education may not be paying off in economic terms, as women are not as engaged as men in the economy and thus are also not earning wages and salaries. As neoliberal reforms in the 1980s and 1990s slashed public sector employment and privatized public sector firms, female unemployment and withdrawal from the labor force in the region increased. The MENA region has a larger gender gap in labor force participation than any other world region, except for Southern Asia. Today, only about 22 percent of women between the ages of fifteen and sixty-four participate in the labor force (ILO 2017a). Meanwhile, 78 percent of men do—a 56 percentage point gap—which is more than double the world average (ILO 2017b). The Middle East also has the highest unemployment rates for women: 18 percent at the regional level, while globally female unemployment stands at 6 percent (ILO 2017c). The MENA region is the only area of the world where there are more than two unemployed women for every unemployed man (ILO 2018).

High female unemployment rates are a major problem because "women's participation in the labor force can significantly improve the level of household income (by 25 percent) and bring many families out of poverty" (Livani 2007: 6). Yet if women predominate in low-wage labor and if childcare is expensive, the economic benefits of working outside the home are less appealing and it is thus understandable why many conservative men, as well as women themselves, support a vision of female gender roles centered on motherhood and raising children. A common, religiously inflected argument heard in the region suggests that men and women are not equal but instead are "complementary," each with particular natures rooted in their biological differences. This position reinforces a woman's primary duty as a wife, mother, and caregiver and suggests that the interests of her family and community are paramount to her individual needs, goals, and desires.

The financial implication of this "patriarchal gender contract" is that men are the breadwinners and are legally and morally responsible for financially supporting their wives, children, and elderly parents (Moghadam 2003: 41). This view shares a functionalist rationale that links women to their reproductive roles and suggests that these "natural" attributes should define women's lives. The biological determinism implicit in this position is not limited to the Muslim world but is found in other religions, including Christian and Jewish perspectives on gender, as well as in gender ideologies that move beyond religion to define women by their reproductive and maternal roles. The salience of calls for complementarity varies over time and with economic prospects. When economic recession and high male unemployment hit the region, conservative gender ideologues redoubled their message that women should "stay at home" for their children and families, so that men could fill the scant jobs and support their families.

Empirically, lower levels of female employment are associated with lower rates of female political representation, and female political representation in the MENA region trails much of the rest of the world. Female labor force participation and political representation are linked through both "supply-side" and "demand-side" explanations. When women are better educated and can participate in the economic sector, their credentials are more comparable to the men that they must compete against in elections. In other words, there is a larger "supply" of qualified female candidates. Though many studies indicate that men in politics do not necessarily have "conventional qualifications," the *belief* that men are more qualified than women for politics is strong in developing countries (Hoodfar and Tajali 2011). As women climb the socioeconomic ladder, negative attitudes toward women begin to change, opening up space for women's participation in the political sphere and creating more of a "demand" for female representation (Inglehart and Norris 2003).

Some scholars argue that oil production is to blame for the low levels of female labor force participation and political representation in the region (Ross 2008). When economies develop around extractive industries such as oil, they do not develop their manufacturing sector. Manufacturing jobs, such as those in textile factories, tend to employ more women, as employers can and do pay them lower wages compared to men. Very often this employment is precarious, characterized by low incomes, a lack of job security, little control over the labor process and access to trade unions for negotiating working conditions or wages, and few regulatory protections (Rodgers and Rodgers 1989: 11). Precarious employment rarely provides economic stability but it does provide income for women, and scholars argue that any female labor force participation increases the chances of political mobilization (and mobilization may in fact come as a result of low wages and poor working conditions). Oil-dependent economies do not experience this development so long as women remain excluded from the labor force.

Only one development has worked to increase female political representation in spite of low levels of labor force participation in the MENA region. Gender quotas for legislatures have helped to "overcome constraints traditionally posed by economic underdevelopment, authoritarianism, cultural influences, and even the electoral system" that keep levels of female representation low, not only in the Middle East but globally (Tripp and Kang 2008: 359). The largest wave of quota adoption occurred between 1995 and 2005, when more than fifty-five countries adopted gender quotas. Today, more than 110 countries have adopted quotas in some form, and female representation has increased from 11 percent of parliamentarians worldwide in 1995 to 24 percent in 2018 (IPU 2018).

Table 8.1 shows the increases in women's parliamentary representation in the Middle East over the past decade. The biggest increases took place in countries that adopted gender quotas. Several countries have also adopted quotas at the subnational level, increasing women's representation at the local level. Many quotas emerged via constitution-making processes, and these varied regarding their level of participation. Iraq's 2005 constitution, which guarantees women 25 percent of parliamentary seats, was drafted quickly under US occupation without much citizen input (Morrow 2005). Women used Tunisia's participatory constitution-making process "as a vehicle for mobilizing local efforts, connecting with gender rights advocates in other MENA countries, and participating in a transnational dialogue" (de Silva de Alwis, Mnasri, and Ward 2017). Beginning with the 2011 elections for the Constituent Assembly that was tasked with drafting a new constitution, Tunisia implemented a zipper list system that requires every other name on the list be that of a female candidate. The progressive gender quota as well as other guarantees of women's equality enshrined in the Tunisian constitution are an outcome of bottom-up feminist organizing and activism interacting with accommodating elites.

Some of these quotas emerged from top-down measures, with male political elites pushing for inclusion of women in the political realm without much demand from below. Single-party regimes or authoritarian

Table 8.1 Gender Quotas and the Percentage of Women in Parliament

	% of Women in Lower House of Parliament (2008)	% of Women in Lower House of Parliament (2018)	Change from 2008 to 2018	Quota Type	Year of Quota Adoption	Subnational Quotas
Algeria	7.7	25.8	+18.1	Reserved seats	2012	Yes
Bahrain	2.5	7.5	+5	None	n.a.	No
Egypt	1.8	14.9	+13.1	None currently, but quotas were in place in 2010 and 2012 elections	n.a.	Yes
Iran	2.8	5.9	+3.1	None	n.a.	No
Iraq	25.5	25.5	0	Reserved seats	2005	Yes
Israel	14.2	27.5	+13.3	None	n.a.	No
Jordan	6.4	15.4	+9	Reserved seats	2001	Yes
Kuwait	3.1	3.1	0	None	n.a.	No
Lebanon	4.7	4.7	0	None	n.a.	No
Libya	7.7	16	+8.3	Legislated candidate quotas	2012	Yes
Morocco	10.5	20.5	+10	Reserved seats	2002	Yes
Oman	0	1.2	+1.2	None	n.a.	No
Qatar	0	9.8	+9.8	None	n.a.	No
Saudi Arabia	0	19.9	+19.9	Reserved seats	2011	Yes
Syria	12.4	13.2	+0.8	None	n.a.	No
Tunisia	22.8	31.3	+8.5	Legislated candidate quotas	2014	Yes
Turkey	9.1	17.4	+8.3	None	n.a.	No
UAE	22.5	22.5	0	None	n.a.	No
Yemen	0.3	0	–0.3	None	n.a.	No

Sources: Data for female parliamentary representation come from the Inter-Parliamentary Union (IPU 2018). Information on gender quotas is from "The Quota Project," an initiative of the International Institute of Democracy and Electoral Assistance (International IDEA 2018).

Note: n.a. indicates not applicable.

leaders can unilaterally make the decision to bring women into political office, often for ideological or signaling purposes. For example, Turkey experienced single-party dominance during the interwar period, and male politicians pushed for the inclusion of women in the political realm as part of a larger movement toward secularization and Westernization, although few countries in Western Europe had yet achieved much by way of women's political participation (Arat 1989). State feminism—activism that depends on persuading regime elites and institutional actors to bestow rights on women rather than allow mass mobilization and electoral representation for women—has had only modest success in the region and elsewhere. Saudi Arabia's quota and Kuwait's appointment of women to office without a quota are examples of such "state feminist" pushes, but these may be little more than smokescreens, seemingly "empowering" women through inclusion in the political process, while excluding them from the more consequential rights to organize and to speak freely, among other political rights.

Quotas vary with regard to the legitimacy they provide. Reserved seats are generally viewed as the least empowering form of quotas, largely because parties are unlikely to allow women to contest open seats outside of the number already reserved for women, effectively setting a secondary glass ceiling for women. This may reinforce women's marginality in the political realm rather than contribute to their political agency and autonomy (Chowdhury 1994). Reserved seats are much more common in the Middle East, Africa, and Asia, while Western Europe promotes voluntary party quotas and Latin American countries tend to use candidate quotas, mandating a certain percentage of women on party lists (Clayton 2016). Algeria, Iraq, Jordan, Morocco, and Saudi Arabia reserve seats for women.

The adoption of gender quotas might signal a sincere commitment on behalf of the state to work toward women's equality, but gender quotas can also allow countries to mimic a commitment to women's rights and equality, without necessarily changing policies. This allows countries to reap the reputational benefits of being a "reformer," without having to reform. Consider Saudi Arabia's appointment of thirty women to the Shura Council in 2013, via a 20 percent reserved seat quota. Although the Shura Council is an unelected, advisory body with no legislative powers, the appointment of thirty women dramatically affected the kingdom's score on the United Nations Development Program's Gender Inequality Index (GII). The GII measures gender equality across five variables: maternal mortality ratio, adolescent birth rate, gender gaps in secondary education and labor force participation, and women's share of seats in parliament. Because of its wealth, Saudi Arabia does particularly well in the areas of female education and women's health; however, female participation in the labor force as well as in government has always been low. In 2012, prior to the adoption of the gender quota, Saudi Arabia ranked 145th out of 148 ranked countries, with an index value of .682 (a score of 1 being the most unequal) (UNDP 2017). In 2013, its ranking jumped to 56th, with an index value of .321, even though women in Saudi Arabia did not have the right to drive or vote at the time. Today, Saudi Arabia ranks 50th out of 160 countries on the GII, which should give us some pause about the validity of this measure for capturing the de facto experience of gender inequality (UNDP 2017). Authoritarian regimes can capitalize on the flaws of measuring gender inequality to present themselves in a particular light without a real commitment to improving the rights, representation, or standing of women.

Public opinion shows that people support gender equality in some realms and not others. The most recent Arab-Barometer (2016) survey shows that 83 percent of respondents reject the idea that a university education is more important for men than it is for women. About three-quarters of respondents (72 percent) answer that it is "acceptable in Islam" for male and female university students to attend classes together. The political sphere is where the public expresses the most resistance toward women's participation, indicating that even if people believe women have an equal right to education, they do not think that women are necessarily cut out for politics. Nearly 70 percent of respondents strongly agreed or agreed with the following statement: "In general, men make better political leaders than women." Over 80 percent of respondents in Algeria expressed a preference for male politicians in spite of the fact that Algeria has one of the highest rates of female political representation in the region, with women making up more than a quarter of the legislature (the People's National Assembly). Even as MENA countries introduce measures to bring more women into parliament, there is no guarantee that attitudes will change.

While comparisons of the gender gap or gender equality are important, they do not adequately reveal the political struggles surrounding gender from a variety of ideological perspectives and in different historical moments that live on in the contemporary period. Collective life is still inflected by the history of the women's movement in the region and those that have raised questions about patriarchy, gender inequality, or the status of women.

Women, Colonialism, and Islam

> *The degradation of women in the East is a canker that begins its destructive work early in childhood, and has eaten into the whole system of Islam.*
>
> *—Stanley Lane-Poole, 1908*
> *(quoted in Earl of Cromer 1908: 134)*

> *America's message to other women in the Middle East is this: You have a great deal to contribute, you should have a strong voice in leading your countries, and my nation looks to the day when you have the rights and privileges you deserve.*
>
> *—former US president*
> *George W. Bush, 2008*

In the nineteenth century, the intellectual and political roots of feminism and activism for women's rights were appropriated by Western colonialists and Orientalists, whose public discourse as "reformers" suggested that Westerners needed to "rescue" Middle Eastern women because of their supposed subordination and degradation by Islam and "Oriental Despotism" (Ahmed 1992: 152). Whether in the rhetoric of George W. Bush in 2008 or in that of Stanley Lane-Poole (a famous Orientalist) a century earlier in 1908, historians point out that Europeans and more recently Americans have utilized the "question of women" to legitimize foreign intervention, occupation, and influence in the region while promoting their "civilizing mission" through the rhetoric of progress, development, modernization, economic growth, and neoliberalism (Ahmed 1992; Abu-Lughod 2002). After all, the material and political motives of foreign powers for acquiring land, oil, resources, and influence are not nearly as laudable as the "noble" desire to rescue a supposedly oppressed part of the population.

Many of these same colonial officials never supported the liberation of women or women's rights in their own societies. When Lord Cromer, a British colonial official, returned from his diplomatic post as consul-general in the Anglo-Egyptian Condominium, he became a founding member and officer of the Men's League for Opposing Women's Suffrage in England. Furthermore, his policies as consul-general actually restricted the educational and professional opportunities of women (Ahmed 1992: 153). It was thus ironic that colonial feminism needed "white men [to] sav[e] brown women from brown men" (Spivak 1988: 297). George W. Bush certainly was not a feminist icon during his presidency (2000–2008), yet he partially justified the US intervention in Afghanistan after September 11, 2001, in terms of liberating Afghan women from the yoke of the repressive Taliban. Years later, this war and this discourse still continue, although foreign powers have withdrawn many of their troops even as Afghan violence and fatalities have increased.

When colonialists raised the "question of women" and spoke about the need to educate women, to employ them, to "unveil" them, and to reverse gender segregation in public spaces, these ideas and policies were perceived locally by many people as inauthentic, externally driven, and politically suspect. At the same time that Westerners used feminism to defend colonialism, indigenous leaders, intellectuals, and the ulama (clerics) often viewed external attacks on veiling, gender segregation, and other indigenous cultural practices as attacks on Islam. As a result, resistance to colonial domination could be waged over women, morality, and culture. As Parvin Paidar explains, "The family and women [became] the subject of a power struggle in the battle between the Western intervening powers and indigenous resisting forces. In this setting, women have become the bastions of Muslim identity and preservers of cultural authenticity" (1995: 23). The burden of bearing national identity and being the symbol of cultural and religious authenticity often meant that as women tried to change these norms and practices, they were seen as attacking or altering their culture and religion, particularly Islam.

One result of this has been that those seeking to change gender norms and grant women increased equality have found it strategic to assert that oppressive practices in the Middle East are not rooted in Islam (Kandiyoti 1991). That way, they avoid accusations of assaulting Islam itself. For example, the early Muslim reformer Mohammad Abduh (1849–1905) called for the elevation of women's status and legal reforms in divorce laws and polygamy. As he did so, he argued that Islam was not responsible for the oppression of women—indeed it recognized the "full and equal humanity of women" in its "ethical voice." Abduh argued that Islam had given women important legal protections such as the right to own property (Ahmed 1992: 139–140), but that the "practice" of Islam—reigning interpretations, customary practices, and local cultures—had prevented women from claiming the rights they had within Islam. Throughout this reformist discourse, which continues today, many scholars and activists blamed local cultural or customary practices—not the canon, laws, and message of Islam—for discrimination against women (see Sonbol 2003). Abduh and many of his contemporaries argued that reforming Islam from within and "restoring" the rights for women that Islam provided, rather than imitating Western ways and ideologies such as secularism or feminism, would strengthen Egyptian and Muslim societies.

The early women's movement in Egypt fought for women's rights not from within a religious framework but rather from within a secular, liberal framework of women's rights, equality, modernization, and development. When Huda Sha'rawi (1879–1947), a wealthy Egyptian woman and wife of a prominent political figure, founded the Egyptian Feminist Union in 1923, its main agenda was to fight for suffrage and other legal rights. Britain had granted nominal independence to Egypt in 1923, but the nationalist party, the Wafd, did not give women the right to vote when it came to power. Soon, the Egyptian feminist movement's public and substantive identity was enmeshed in symbolic struggles over Muslim identity as Sha'rawi publicly "de-veiled" at a train station upon her return from an international feminist conference in Rome. She and her colleagues built a women's movement that fought alongside other Egyptian nationalists to end British control of Egypt, but they primarily fought for women's rights, encouraging the growth of female leadership in the media, political movements, political parties, and civil society.

Indeed, ending gender segregation, educating women, enhancing opportunities for employment, and adopting more equitable marriage and divorce laws were objectives taken up by nascent feminist movements throughout the Middle East, from Morocco to Lebanon, Turkey to Iran. Women and allied men built these movements within the political spaces that were available to them. Since so many issues surrounding gender equality necessitated legal changes, and lawmaking is usually the domain of those in power, women had to build organizations and movements to raise these demands and mobilize support for new laws and policies—whether the regime in power was a monarchy, a liberal democracy, a military or authoritarian regime, or some combination thereof. As women mobilized, they contended with Islamic religious authorities who often took a conservative, more patriarchal stance on these issues and were reluctant to support additional women's rights. In a similar vein, leftist movements were typically blind to gender issues, and nationalist politicians encouraged women's movements and the new cohort of educated women to subordinate their demands to national unity, development, and progress.

Until the advent of colonialism, religious authorities supervised schooling and Islamic law governed the spheres of morality, sexuality, marriage, inheritance, childcare, and family (i.e., personal status). To change personal status law meant engaging, if not confronting, religious authorities, jurists, legal scholars, and court officials. We can see this dynamic playing out in dramatic fashion in early twentieth-century Iran. As far back as the Safavid Empire (1502 to 1722), religious leaders had established a monopoly over the domain of lawmaking, "while the political power of the state was there to enforce their laws" (Hoodfar and Sadr 2009: 5). As Iranians resisted Russian influence and new British taxes on tobacco in 1887, a constitutionalist movement emerged that demanded popular participation rights from the Qajar dynasty (1794–1925). European influence also sparked campaigns for modern education, secularism, and citizenship rights; yet the ulama were vehemently opposed to these ideas, since they threatened their sphere of influence and their control of education and law. Women joined protests against the state and its foreign indebtedness, started to publish in literary journals and the media, and supported public education for women. This movement was ahead of its time and established a constitutional monarchy and an elected parliament in 1905, limiting the power of the reigning Qajar monarch.

The "question of women," however, reached a critical juncture in Iran, and religious leaders blocked the extension of women's rights, even though there had been much public debate about women, fueled in part by the unusual participation of women in public demonstrations. "They, along with children, criminals and the mentally unfit, were deprived of the right to elect and be elected since women's participation in politics was supposedly against Islam" (Hoodfar and Sadr 2009: 8). Despite their supposed commitment to secularism, leaders of the 1905 constitutional movement "agreed to the insertion of a clause in the constitution that demanded that no laws be passed by parliament that would contradict Islam and that there should be a committee of five mojtaheds who would over-see the laws" (Hoodfar and Sadr 2009: 8). As in many other countries, and during many other nationalist, anti-imperialist, and anticolonial struggles, in Iran the constitution now had a religious character, and "significant compromises . . . were made in order to save the coalition of modernists and ulama against the Monarchy . . . at the cost of women" (Hoodfar and Sadr 2009: 8). Fast forward decades later to the 1979 Iranian Revolution when the Iranian ulama returned in force to create the *velayat-e faqih*, or Guardianship of the Jurist, insisting that religious clerics have the power to veto any laws made by the new elected parliament. Their newfound power and their repression of the Iranian feminist movement along with many other progressive forces led to a precipitous decline in women's rights and political freedom in Iran.

Political struggles in Iran, and in other Middle East countries, are often contests over the boundaries between what is public and what is private. As Seyla Benhabib has argued, "All struggles against oppression in the modern world begin by redefining what had previously been considered private, non-public, and non-political issues as matters of public concern, as issues of justice, as sites of power" (1992: 84). Yet, who has the legitimacy and power to redraw the public/private dichotomy? Why, for example, have conventions around dress, particularly women's dress, in the Middle East become so deeply controversial, politicized, and contested as a symbol of larger public issues? An older example of the politicization of women's dress that still resonates today unfolded shortly after Mustafa Kemal Atatürk led the Turkish "War of Liberation" against European attempts to carve up the Ottoman Empire into its own spheres of influence in 1920 after World War I. The government banned veiling in public institutions, instituted civil marriage, reformed divorce law to give women the right to initiate divorce (ending the unilateral male right to divorce), forbade polygamy, extended suffrage to women, and abolished the caliphate. Atatürk embarked on a path of radical secularization, or laicism, which subordinated religion to the state and dispatched Islam from the public sphere into the realm of private observance. Building the new Turkish republic involved dismantling the power structure and influence of the Ottoman elite and its institutions, including the ulama.

In barring women from veiling in public institutions (along with banning fezzes for men), Atatürk was redefining what had been private, nonpolitical practices as unacceptable or unjust according to the tenets of his own new radical political ideology. Yet more recently in Turkey, following the growth of Islamist political parties, a new generation of Turkish women, hailing largely from provincial, rural areas or who are recent migrants to the cities, are "covering" and wearing head scarves (*tesettür*), often accompanied by a long coat (manteau) (Saktanber 2002; Gole 1996). Turkish law forbade veiling in public spaces such as the parliament, universities, public hospitals, and state offices. A resilient Islamist party in Turkey, the Justice and Development Party (AKP), encouraged the public presence, rights, and loyalty of "head-scarved" women in the 1990s, and these women, in turn, promoted the party and its electoral strategies (White 2002; Arat 2005). Within the past decade "covered" women in Turkey have succeeded in contesting these dress codes that barred them from public institutions, and even the police and armed forces (the latter formerly the defender of secularism) now allow women to wear head scarves with their uniforms. In 1999 after her election from the Virtue Party, Merve Kavakçı entered parliament wearing a head scarf but was forcibly evicted from the hall in close to a brawl. She lost her citizenship (she had not disclosed that she held dual American citizenship) and left for exile in the United States for several years, but after the AKP consolidated its power in recent Turkish elections, her citizenship was restored and she now serves as the Turkish ambassador to Malaysia.

Contemporary Issues in Saudi Arabia, Tunisia, and Yemen

Saudi Arabia, Tunisia, and Yemen represent three cases where women's organizing efforts have had various degrees of success. Although there is a complex web of factors shaping mobilization, policy, and state-society relations across these three cases, comparing them helps us to see the importance of political opportunities. In Saudi Arabia, repression limits the space for women's organizations to operate, although mobilization does occur. The regime has co-opted feminist issues, jailing organizers while adopting some of their suggested reforms. In Yemen, women's groups had some successes in the aftermath of the Arab Spring, only to have their concerns sidelined by conflicts between regions that spun into civil war. Tunisian women have had the most success, in part because of comparatively strong civil society organizations prior to the Arab Spring and the commitment of political elites during the transition process to pursue gender equality.

One of the few countries where veiling is mandatory in public is Saudi Arabia. Few Saudi women see dress as a major area for reform but rather have been organizing and campaigning around other issues that they consider far more important and relevant. Cracks are beginning to appear in the Kingdom of Saudi Arabia's strict gender regime, especially under the youthful Crown Prince Mohammad bin Salman; however, policy changes are limited in scope and may serve to uphold the monarchical regime under the illusion of reform. All are taking effect against a backdrop of violence, with some of the most important women's rights activists detained on thin legal grounds or no charges whatsoever, and many alleging ill-treatment, abuse, and torture at the hands of the monarchy.

The first major gains for women came in the political realm, in spite of the fact that women still face major barriers to participation in society at large. In 2015, Saudi Arabia granted women the right to vote, becoming the last country in the world to do so (although Vatican City is the final holdout on women's suffrage since women cannot vote in papal elections). It is important to note, however, that men did not truly have suffrage in the kingdom until recent years either. The first municipal elections were held in 2005, but this development was limited in the sense that municipal councils have jurisdiction over only a few issues, such as sanitation and road repairs, and government appointees still make up a large proportion of these local bodies. Although 82 percent of registered voters cast ballots in the first municipal election, turnout declined to just 39 percent of registered voters (5 percent of the electorate, and 2 percent of the total population) in the second municipal elections, held in 2011. Just before the second election, King Abdullah announced that women would be able to run and vote in 2015. While approximately 20 percent of the male electorate registered to vote in 2015, less than 2 percent of eligible women did (Quamar 2016: 438).

When elections take place in monarchical or authoritarian contexts, they often function as tools for leaders to maintain their power, rather than opening legitimate spaces for challengers. Elections also serve as a signal to the international community, however empty, that the regime is willing to allow some degree of popular participation and democratic contestation, which may garner them reputational benefits (Hyde 2011). Allowing women to run for office carries the dual reputational benefit of being seen as a "reformer" on both the democracy and women's rights fronts. Still, women running for office in Saudi Arabia are encumbered by significant constraints, such as the inability to publish their pictures in their campaign materials. The most significant constraints facing Saudi women are guardianship laws that often require a male relative to consent for women to enroll in school, travel, marry, work outside of the home, or obtain a loan.

Guardianship laws are legitimated through strict interpretations of Islam, but they are also thoroughly "modern" reactions to Westernization and the rise of ultraconservative religious movements that gained influence in the region in the 1970s. Although personal status law based on religious teachings, traditions, and jurisprudence is common across the MENA region, in many places outside of Saudi Arabia there are far fewer restrictions on women, less power given to male guardians, and often, much more contestation about the concept of guardianship itself.

In February 2018 the Saudi government announced one of the most significant changes to the guardianship law to date, granting women the right to start their own businesses without a guardian's permission. This is part of Saudi Arabia's "Vision 2030" plan, which calls for increasing female labor force participation from 22 to 30 percent. Entertainment is also part of the plan, and women can increasingly access public spaces, although gender segregation is still in effect to varying degrees: the kingdom put on its first women-only concert in 2017 as well as sponsored a Comic-Con (comic convention) where men and women were permitted to mingle in the main tent. In 2018 women were allowed into soccer stadiums for the first time, albeit via designated entrances and only in designated family stands. In June 2018 Saudi Arabia lifted its ban on women drivers—a policy that had been a long-standing target of international criticism and ire for the severe limitations it places on women's mobility and ability to participate in social and economic life.

The first public protest of the driving ban took place in 1990 when four dozen women drove around Riyadh until police arrested them. Many of them were fired from their jobs and publicly shamed and shunned by family members; their reputation as "drivers" followed them for decades (Murphy 2008). In recent years, women's rights activists harnessed social media to draw international attention to the issue, including a 2011 Facebook campaign that featured widely shared videos of women, such as activist Manal al-Sharif, openly defying the driving ban. Many female organizers became targets of the regime, often experiencing repeated arrests and smear campaigns. For example, Loujain al-Hathloul, a young woman who was imprisoned for seventy-three days for driving her car from the United Arab Emirates to the Saudi Arabian border in 2014, was detained along with a number of prominent women's rights activists in a major crackdown in May 2018. The activists were denied access to lawyers and held in solitary confinement for the first three months of their detention and have described experiencing torture and sexual harassment to extract false confessions (Amnesty International 2018). Recall, 2018 was a "model year" for reforms on women's rights issues, from changes to the guardianship laws, to the opening of public spaces to women, to the lifting of the driving ban. Despite this, al-Hathloul and other activists detained in the May crackdown, as well as some who were arrested in the ensuing months after the end of the driving ban, remain imprisoned as of December 2018 (Amnesty International 2018). The regime appropriated the women's driving movement as a key issue of its reform program, while jailing the very women who led it.

The Crown Prince's treatment of activists and accusations regarding his role in the 2018 murder of journalist Jamal Khashoggi have created international scrutiny of the depth of his reforms. Are they merely a distraction from the violent repression that still underpins the Saudi coercive apparatus? The chipping away of certain obstacles to women's participation in public life will likely increase their economic participation and perhaps create the economic growth that Vision 2030 aims to achieve. But when it comes to substantive rights for women, and political rights for Saudis as a whole, these seem much further on the horizon.

Tunisian women and their male allies have been the most successful in realizing women's rights in recent years. Many scholars have argued that Tunisia made the greatest gains improving women's rights through changes in personal status laws shortly after independence. Because the women's movement's promotion of education and female employment coincided with nationalist goals to develop society and build the state, Tunisia enjoyed the largest percentage of working women in MENA, had a national trade union federation, and had high rates of educated women. Yet, as in many other Arab countries in the postcolonial period, Habib Bourguiba's regime seriously constrained the ability of any movement, whether Islamist, leftist, feminist, or liberal, to organize and contest the regime's policy. Zine el-Abidine Ben Ali's soft presidential coup in 1987 deepened the authoritarian regime. Activists had to work within the confines of what was politically possible—yet there was some room for maneuver by state feminists, or those who had worked with government elites to enact women's rights under authoritarian constraints and with a hobbled civil society.

Women played a major role in both the Arab Spring protests and the transitional moment of redesigning institutions and the constitution. Women were also active supporters of En-Nahda and the Islamist movement, which had been repressed for decades in Tunisia and was eager to promote its particular gender ideology during this new political opportunity. In the first truly free elections in Tunisia in October 2011, women won 49 of the 217 seats in the Constituent Assembly, due to the "zipper" list system of alternating men and women candidates on party lists. Forty-two of those women were affiliated with the Islamist En-Nahda party. As Tunisia took the slow, more inclusive road to a new order, debate soon arose about how to frame gender equality in the constitution. The first draft of the equal rights clause declared, "The state shall guarantee the protection of the rights of women and shall support the gains thereof as true partners to men in the building of the nation and as having a role complementary thereto within the family" (Charrad and Zarrugh 2014: 235). The notion that women were "complementary" to men was met with immediate resistance from many Tunisian activists and reflected the predominant position of En-Nahda (approximately a quarter of the seats) in Tunisia's Constituent Assembly. However, the controversy generated by this debate eventually led to a new final draft of the equality clause that stated that "all citizens, male and female, have equal rights and duties, and are equal before the law without any discrimination" (Article 21, under Title Two: Rights and Freedoms). Mounira Charrad and Amina Zarrugh argue that the activism and mobilization generated by the Jasmine Revolution, as well as the hard-fought deliberation and politicking in the Constituent Assembly, "illustrate a transition in Tunisia from a 'politics from above,' in which decisions regarding gender policy were determined by political elites, to a 'politics from below,' in which individuals organize, associate, and make demands upon the state" (2014: 240).

While a constitutional guarantee of gender equality may not change cultural norms and many regimes evade the lofty commitments of new constitutions, it has forced the rationalization of other laws. One of the most controversial issues for women's movements in the region has been a demand to reform inheritance laws that allocate women half the share of inheritance available to men who have the same degree of relation to the deceased. Such laws deprive women of intergenerational financial assets that have lasting effects on their economic and social position. In 2018 Tunisian president Beji Caid Essebsi and the Individual Freedoms and Equality Committee (COLIBE) recommended equalizing inheritance, but he suggested strangely "that families wishing to continue observing the existing laws surrounding inheritance may continue doing so" (Allahoum 2018). The ambiguity of his remarks suggests that political battles for equality remain in Tunisia. The draft inheritance law (not yet passed by the parliament) also led to Muslim religious scholars and officials in other countries denouncing this reform. Nevertheless, like other struggles and reforms from the women's movement, it will likely have an important demonstration effect and influence other groups to take on inegalitarian inheritance laws in their own legal systems.

Activism, campaigns, and legal reforms are all avenues for improving women's position, but the case of Yemen points to the damaging effects of war, violence, and foreign intervention on women's struggle for equality and rights. As discussed at the beginning of this chapter, Yemen currently and consistently ranks as the "worst" country when it comes to women's rights in the Middle East region. There, women face major obstacles in accessing education, labor market participation, and political representation. High levels of poverty, corruption, political conflict, and legal discrimination all work in tandem to produce a social, cultural, and political environment where women have few opportunities to organize and advocate for basic rights and protections, let alone full-scale gender equality.

The 2011 Arab Spring represented a brief window of opportunity for organizing around women's rights and political rights in Yemen. Women were at the forefront of the protests, including Tawakkul Karman, "The Mother of the Revolution," who won the Nobel Peace Prize later that year at the age of thirty-two for her nonviolent struggle for women's rights. By the end of the year, President Ali Abdullah Salih signed an agreement brokered by the Gulf Cooperation Council (GCC) to transfer power to his vice president, Abdrabbo Mansour Hadi, and begin the transition process, in return for legal immunity. The GCC initiative set up the National Dialogue Conference (NDC), which brought together the new, youthful revolutionary forces and historical challengers to the state with key government stakeholders in a participatory constitution-making process. Half of the NDC's 565 seats went to the South, 30 percent to women, and 20 percent to "youth" (delegates under the age of forty).

Women did make major inroads in these negotiations: The 2015 draft constitution includes an equal rights clause stating that women have full civil, political, economic, social, and cultural rights without discrimination. Other articles committed the state to the promotion of women in economic development, the elimination of negative cultural and social norms that demean the dignity of women, the protection of women from violence, the provision of equal access to public sector jobs, and the granting of greater equality in political representation via 30 percent women's quotas for certain elected bodies and offices. However, major political, internal, and regional conflict arose and the constitution was never finalized. The Yemeni Civil War and concurrent Saudi-led offensive have left at least tens of thousands dead since 2015 and millions of women and girls are even more vulnerable to child marriage, maternal mortality, sexual and gender-based violence, and sex trafficking. Combatants often utilize rape and sexual violence as a weapon of war that supranational institutions have increasingly recognized as a war crime. The consequences of civil war, indiscriminate violence, displacement, and migration often have deadly consequences for women, as we have seen in the aftermath of the Syrian, Libyan, Palestinian, Iraqi, and Kurdish conflicts and the waves of refugees they produced.

Conclusion

The struggle for gender equality and women's political participation and representation in the Middle East is diverse, complex, and deeply influenced by a range of factors. Creative and dedicated activists, intellectuals, professionals, and government personnel deploy their resources and skills within what is politically possible. In the past few decades, public education has expanded women's access to knowledge, knowledge creation, and theorizing about their lives, but political campaigns were often risky and illegal, and economic difficulties and the lack of widespread support for political struggles made radical success elusive. The regional change in 2011 after the Arab Spring offered both opportunities and challenges to activists, as electoral competition has become more important in some countries, at different scales, including subnational elections. Women's movements will have to move out of the main cities to build more robust national and local electoral strength and create coalitions with others. Women continue to expand their "voice" as writers, bloggers, bureaucrats, politicians, intellectuals, journalists, religious leaders, media pundits, novelists, and poets across a range of media, particularly social media. Yet, the region has seen only limited political openings following the Arab Spring, and civil wars, foreign intervention, and the return or reinforcement of monarchical, authoritarian, and military regimes have also stalled many forms of collective action. Syria, Libya, Yemen, Palestine, and Iraq have experienced widespread violence, and waves of refugees, migrants, and displaced persons have suffered greatly. Demands for gender equality and parity are rarely heard when violence predominates and is indiscriminate. Understanding the history of the women's movement and the construction of gender in its diversity throughout the region contextualizes these struggles and hopefully allows us to understand them better. As we saw in 2011, change often comes from unexpected quarters. When long-standing injustices are framed in legitimate ways and resonate deeply in society, and activists have a political opening to exploit, previously subdued forces in society may find their voice—and more.

Notes

We are very grateful for the research and editorial assistance of Kendall Dorland.

1. All education and labor force statistics for the Middle East region are based on the World Bank's classification, which includes Algeria, Bahrain, Djibouti, Egypt, Iran, Iraq, Israel, Jordan, Kuwait, Lebanon, Libya, Malta, Morocco, Oman, Qatar, Saudi Arabia, Syria, Tunisia, the United Arab Emirates, the West Bank and Gaza, and Yemen. This classification scheme differs slightly from how this volume defines the Middle East. It does not include Turkey, and it adds Djibouti and Malta.

PART 2
Cases

9

Algeria

Yahia H. Zoubir

Algeria dominated the news twice in its contemporary political history. The first event was the seven-year War of National Liberation against France (1954–1962). The war resulted in the deaths of hundreds of thousands of Algerian Muslims, victims of one of the most intensive settlers' colonizations in modern times. The colonial period (1830–1962), which reduced Algerians to second-class status, and the war of liberation remain the determining factors of national identity. The nationalist movement that emerged in the 1920s and the war of liberation have also been instrumental in shaping the postindependence political system, in which the military has played a key role. The second event spanned the 1990s. This was a civil conflict that pitted the regime's security forces against armed Islamist groups. This period witnessed gruesome massacres committed against the civilian population by Islamist extremists and harsh repression by security forces responsible for the disappearance of hundreds of individuals. The Algerian "red decade" of the 1990s finds its roots in the intricacies of the war of liberation and the nature of the political system that the nationalists instituted following independence.

Historical Background and Contemporary Political Structure

Algeria's history, though complex, is extremely rich. The country, whose native inhabitants are the Berbers (or Amazigh, meaning "the free"), has been prey to numerous foreign invasions, including by the Phoenicians, Romans, Vandals, Byzantines, Arabs, Ottoman Turks, and the French. The Arab-Islamic culture had the largest impact and would play a critical role in unifying the local Arab-Berber population against French colonial domination. In fact, Algerians considered the war against the French a jihad (holy war) and the combatants were called mujahidin (holy warriors). At the same time, French culture played an important role in shaping the nationalist movement, most of whose leaders were francophone.

French colonization had devastating effects on Algeria (McDougall 2017). Though it claimed to have a "civilizing mission," France uprooted entire populations, dispossessed farmers of their lands and gave them to European settlers, transformed mosques into churches, and provided education only to the children of local notables. Access to education improved over time but ultimately remained very limited. The famous French political philosopher Alexis de Tocqueville asserted that the rate of literacy among Algerians was quite high prior to colonization. Yet after 132 years of French control, at independence the overwhelming majority of Algerian Muslims were illiterate. The injustices and blatant discrimination colonial France was responsible for explain Algerians' stiff resistance to foreign domination. Indeed, it took France decades to establish its total control over the territory and crush the resistance of the very first anticolonialists and nationalists.

On November 1, 1954, the newly created National Liberation Front (FLN) began the Algerian war for liberation against French occupation (Horne 2006). The FLN and its armed wing, the National Liberation Army, fought a bloody, eight-year war against a very strong enemy, ultimately achieving Algerian independence in 1962. The price, however, was very heavy, as hundreds of thousands of Algerians lost their lives. The war would also have concrete political consequences for the shape of postindependence Algerian politics. During the war, all other existing political parties, such as the Democratic Union for the Algerian Manifesto, the Algerian Communist Party, and the influential Association of Algerian Muslim Ulama, were forced to dissolve their organizations and submit to the FLN's authority. Their integration into the FLN came not as parties but as individuals. The war of independence thus led to the creation of a nationalist political party with hegemonic status and ambitions.

After independence, an authoritarian political regime emerged in which the FLN became the sole legal political party. In August 1963, Decree 63-297 prohibited political associations other than the FLN from forming. The country's presidents came from the FLN, and FLN members dominated the bureaucracy while they monopolized parliament. The regime distrusted autonomous associations whatever their nature; even the Boy Scouts fell under the control of the state. Thus, the bureaucracy and the FLN—two key pillars of the postindependence regime—absorbed most independent or potentially independent associations. The few remaining autonomous associations were restricted to athletic, parenting, or religious activities (Zoubir 2003). The media, too, were subordinated to the state and the single party, serving as a propaganda tool for the regime.

True power in the postindependence Algerian political system lay in the hands of the military, the third but most important pillar of the regime. The FLN was a subordinate, minor apparatus relative to the military and its overpowering hegemony (Roberts 2003). Although constituting the backbone of the system, the army did not rule directly. Instead it acted as the guardian of the regime, defending Algeria's borders but also watching over the FLN and the domestic political arena. Under Houari Boumediene's rule, Algeria's military in the mid-1960s and 1970s ensured national security from foreign attack but also took the lead in developing Algeria's economy and society.

During the three decades following independence the authoritarian Algerian regime presided over state-led economic development and the creation of a generous socialist welfare state. However, it came under great stress in the 1980s as Algerians increasingly accumulated grievances against the regime. Many were angered by the regime's complete domination of state and society—specifically its repression of opposition to its rule, and the influence of the FLN. Meanwhile, state-led economic development (import substitution industrialization) failed as a strategy, and inflation and unemployment began to mount while the government was forced to cut back on the welfare state as it pursued poorly managed economic liberalization. A scarcity of affordable housing, as well as food and medicine shortages, also plagued the country. Corruption, incompetence, nepotism, and inefficiency permeated the economy and the political sphere. Finally, while many Algerians' grievances were economic in nature, others criticized the regime for its secularism and demanded the Islamization of the public sphere.

During the presidency of Colonel Chadli Bendjedid, political opposition came to a head. Lacking democratic channels to express their demands and grievances, Algerian dissident groups organized protests that the authorities severely repressed. The most influential such event occurred in October 1988 when widespread riots—met first with repression—eventually moved regime elites to open the political system and institute a degree of political liberalization. The key reform was a constitutional amendment that legalized the creation of political parties other than the FLN. This amendment ushered in the establishment of a multiparty system, theoretically terminating the FLN's hegemony. Thereafter, more than sixty political parties emerged into the political arena.

The regime had hoped that its liberalizing reforms would provide a democratic facade for incumbent rulers, increasing their legitimacy. It counted on none of the new parties being able to amass sufficient support to truly challenge the military-backed FLN. But it had miscalculated, for an Islamist party, the Islamic Salvation Front (FIS), was organizing itself and rapidly increasing its support base. After winning municipal elections in 1990, the FIS performed so well in the first round of multiparty parliamentary elections in December 1991 that it looked to be poised to form a majority after the second round. However, the second round was never held. The military stepped in and annulled the elections, because it was not willing to tolerate an opposition party taking power in parliament—especially not an Islamist party whose rhetoric regarding its ultimate political ambitions often was illiberal and hegemonic.

This cancellation of the civilian elections pushed Algerian politics into a showdown between the regime and its primarily Islamist opposition. The military forced the resignation of President Bendjedid, dissolved parliament, appointed historic figure Mohammad Boudiaf as the new president, and declared a state of emergency, which was not lifted until February 2011 after the Arab uprisings swept through the region. In the wake of the annulment of the elections and in response to the military's actions, various Islamist factions turned to violence against the regime. The regime's security forces responded in kind, and the result was that Algerian politics for much of the 1990s was characterized by what some call civil strife (others refer to it as civil war) (Mundy 2015). This was an era of high instability, assassination campaigns, disappearances, and grave violations of human rights by Islamists and security forces. Although there exist no reliable figures, certainly tens of thousands of Algerians lost their lives, while the country suffered the massive destruction of infrastructure and factories.

In the new millennium, Algeria began to emerge from this crisis environment. A constitutional revision in 1996 initiated new institutional arrangements that form some of the bases of Algeria's contemporary political structure. Algeria now has a bicameral parliament, encompassing a directly elected 462-member lower house, the National Assembly, and a partly appointed and partly indirectly elected upper chamber, the Council of the Nation. Local and regional assemblies elect two-thirds of the membership of the Council of the Nation; Algeria's president directly appoints the remaining third. The security services and segments of the military hierarchy remain pivotal actors behind the scenes of politics, however. With the support of the military, in 1999 former foreign minister (1963–1979) and FLN candidate Abdelaziz Bouteflika was elected president in a campaign that, while rich in political debate, was not truly competitive. Anticipating that the election would be rigged, Bouteflika's six competitors withdrew from the race.

Bouteflika's major challenges were to bring about political stability (Mortimer 2004), reestablish security in the country, revamp the economy, and break Algeria's international isolation. To reduce the level of violence, Bouteflika initiated an amnesty law, which the population approved overwhelmingly via referendum in September 1999. The law encouraged armed Islamist groups to renounce violence and lay down their arms. It exonerated individuals from legal proceedings, reduced the terms of existing sentences, imposed probation or the annulment of civic rights rather than prison sentences, and so forth—all at the discretion of the authorities. The law also protected security forces from prosecution for abuses they might have committed. Although the law resulted in the surrender of thousands of armed Islamists, large sections of civil society saw the law as a betrayal, especially since it granted legal impunity to the perpetrators of atrocities. From the government's perspective this was the only means to end the civil unrest.

Following his reelection in 2004, Bouteflika initiated yet another amnesty law, inscribed in the 2005 Charter for Peace and National Reconciliation. The text provided the terms of financial compensation to the families of the victims on all sides, as well as amnesty for security forces accused of human rights abuses and for Islamist groups implicated in terrorist activities. This prompted severe criticism from human rights organizations, which argued that crimes against humanity should not go unpunished. Furthermore, the fact that the charter forbade any questioning of the terms of the law was in direct contradiction to the country's constitution, which guarantees freedom of expression. Victims' families on both sides felt that the charter denied the right to truth and justice concerning the thousands of massacred and disappeared. Others, however, felt that the amnesty was the only way to move Algeria forward from the violence of the 1990s. Regardless of the criticism leveled against them, these laws brought peace and a large degree of stability to the country.

The 1996 Algerian constitution limited presidential mandates to two terms. However, Bouteflika introduced amendments to the constitution, adopted overwhelmingly by parliament in 2008, that removed the limit on the number of presidential terms in office (see Figure 9.1 for a political cartoon inspired by this maneuver). This allowed Bouteflika to run for and win another term in 2009 despite his age, poor health, and the mixed results of his presidency. Given the means at his disposal and the support of the parties that dominated the parliament, no one doubted who the winner would be. Bouteflika generally uses the parliament as a rubber stamp for his policies. Still, to ensure support for the constitutional revisions and for his candidacy for a third term, parliamentary deputies—and later governors and high government officials—received a 300 percent salary increase two months prior to the election, even though their salaries and benefits were already considerable compared to those of the average citizen (the cartoon in Figure 9.2 satirizes this).

Opposition political parties—secular and religious—exist, but they have no aspiration to accede to power. They are content with having representatives in the parliament in part because a portion of their salaries goes to the parties' coffers. The population at large has lost all hope of seeing political parties play a consequential role in politics or bring about any real change; the low turnout for the 2012 and 2017 legislative elections and the 2014 presidential election illustrates (and confirms) this pessimism toward the political system and its capacity to effect consequential transformation. Furthermore, Bouteflika has attempted to tame civil society and tolerates only those associations that support the incumbent president. Worse still, he has ensured that he remains president for life, although a 2016 constitutional amendment reinstituted the two-term limit, which does not affect him.

Figure 9.1 Spoofing the End of Term Limits for the Algerian President

"Draft constitutional amendment adopted by Parliament"
"Caesar for life!"
Dilem, *Liberté* (Algeria), November 15, 2008 (used with permission).

Religion and Politics

Politics and religion in Algeria have always been intertwined; the Islamic religion and its traditions permeate both civil society and the state. Islam in Algeria constitutes the basis of identity and culture, and Islamic norms to a large extent govern social relations. Despite its secularist inclinations, since independence the state has always resorted to Islamic symbols to establish and reproduce its legitimacy. Paradoxically, social movements and the religious opposition have used Islam not only to wage their struggles against the established regime but also to challenge the religious claims of the state. By denying the state one of its fundamental bases of legitimacy, radical Islamists have sought to delegitimize the state and the elites in charge of governing the country. Islam and Islamic references, rather than "imported" foreign ideologies,

Figure 9.2 Satirizing the Algerian Parliament's Willingness to Extend the Presidential Term in Office

"The deputies vote"
Deputies vote in favor of the revision of the constitution to allow President Abdelaziz Bouteflika to seek a third term in office (in return for raises).
Dilem, *Liberté* (Algeria), November 16, 2008 (used with permission).

have been the source of identity and authenticity. Here lies one of the main reasons for the emergence of radical Islamism and its popularity in the 1980s and early 1990s.

Neither Islam nor the Islamist phenomenon can be dissociated from the history of the country's nationalist movement. It would be no exaggeration to assert that the Islamist movement is one of the belated progenies of colonial rule in Algeria. While the movement is the product of the socioeconomic failure of the 1980s, its doctrinal aspects draw partly from the crisis of identity caused by 132 years of colonial rule. The colonial authorities did not content themselves with exploiting Algeria's natural and human resources. They also targeted the principal local religious institutions: mosques and religious schools were closed, religious lands were expropriated, and Islamic culture was projected as inferior to Western Christian civilization. The colonial state carried out a systematic uprooting of Arab and Islamic culture. Algerian Muslims lived in poverty and were denied basic religious, cultural, political, and economic rights—rights that Europeans, albeit a minority in the country, enjoyed. This explains why Islam became—and still is—the most salient component of Algerians' national identity as they sought—and still seek—to regain what European imperialism tried to destroy.

Islam, Nationbuilding, and Statebuilding

After independence, the authorities manipulated Islam for political purposes. To build a modern identity and gain legitimacy, successive governments sought to integrate what they defined as a modern type of Islam into revolutionary, vanguard perspectives. Islam, understood in its modernized form, was decreed the religion of the state in the 1963 and successive constitutions. State elites conceived of Islam as the foundation of the identity of Algerian citizens. They encouraged the construction of mosques, the teaching of the Arabic language, and the creation of religious institutions. The state established a monopoly over religious life and repressed interpretations that deviated from state-propagated official norms and the country's traditional Maleki Sunni school of law, which it seeks to preserve. The authorities thus incorporated Islam as a key component of the ideological and political apparatus of the regime. That tactic was part of a broader vision to build a modern nation-state through a developmentalist strategy. Islam as a system of values, or a set of rational principles, was to coexist with modernity in a model that French sociologist Henri Sanson defined as *laïcité islamique* (Islamic secularism).

In this context, then, largely secularist elites held a monopoly of power in postindependence Algeria. Yet Islam played an ever-greater role with respect to the legitimacy of successive governments. The regime used Islam not only as an instrument of national integration in an ethnically heterogeneous society, but also as a tool of political legitimization. Over time, the importance attributed to Islam in the country's sequence of constitutions paved the way for the emergence of competing understandings of Islam's proper role. While some elites saw Islam as a religion open to modernity, others viewed it through a traditionalist prism, resulting in very conservative readings of Islam's proper role in state and society. Conservative forces, including those within the regime itself, constructed an understanding of Islam that was at loggerheads with the socioeconomic and cultural policies espoused by dominant (secular) elites. In other words, the ostensibly secular state and its structures incorporated many Islamists—including some influential ulama. Faced with an internal ideological struggle between secular "progressives" and Islamists, the regime sought to achieve a balance between irreconcilable visions, contenting itself with excluding the most extreme Islamists to preserve national unity and depict the regime as an indispensable arbitrator.

The Islamist Challenge to the State

Islamist organizations have challenged the regime at various periods and to different degrees since the country's independence. Thus, it would be erroneous to attribute the emergence of Islamism to late twentieth-century socioeconomic factors alone, though the latter undoubtedly contributed to its eruption. Islamism can also be situated in the context of colonization and decolonization, in that one can view Islamism in Algeria as the latest reawakening against Western domination and Western-inspired modernity following the failure of postindependence authorities to create a prosperous Muslim society.

The early Islamist organizations challenged the state on the socialist options it had chosen. The first such organization was El-Qiyam al-Islamiyya (Islamic Values), founded in 1963—just one year after Algeria's independence. It was tolerated until 1966 but then banned by the government. El-Qiyam and religious personalities such as Shaikh Ahmed Sahnoun put forth demands that future Islamists would include in their agendas, like the full implementation of the sharia (Islamic law). They also advocated the closure of stores during Friday prayers (a demand satisfied in 1976) and called for a ban on the sale of alcohol, the exclusion of non-Muslims from public jobs, the separation of beaches into men's and women's sections, the introduction of religious teaching in schools (instituted in 1964), the interdiction of women's participation in sports, as well as parades celebrating national holidays. Although they failed to achieve many of these demands, they later compelled the government to establish the weekend as Thursday and Friday rather than as Saturday and Sunday. To the relief of the business community in its dealings with international partners, however, in 2009 the authorities decided—without debate—to change the weekend to Friday and Saturday.

The authorities tolerated some of the Islamist organizations but then eventually banned them. Yet many of their members remained anchored in the system, exerting pressure to extract further concessions from the state on moral, socioeconomic, and cultural issues. In response to those demands, the state launched its own campaign to "prevent the degradation of morals" resulting from the loosening of mores, alcoholism, and Western influence in the country. In other words, the state decided to contribute to the "re-Islamization" of Algeria and to the rehabilitation of the Arab-Islamic identity that the French colonial state had denigrated. Consequently, francophone intellectuals and Westernized elites, particularly women, would become the main targets of Islamist attacks. Moreover, Islamists' ideas affected the state's legislative agenda about language policy (in the early 1970s it ruled that all university education, except scientific curricula, would be administered in Arabic rather than French) as well as regarding gender matters (in 1984 it enacted a new personal status code that sharply constrained women's rights in marriage, divorce, and the like). At the societal level, Islamist ideology influenced the dress code of Algerians. Beginning in the late 1970s, many Algerians increasingly abandoned Western clothing styles, with women donning the hijab while many men wore the *kamis* (a traditional loose, flowing, floor-length robe).

The Radicalization of Political Islam

In the absence of democratic channels, marginalized Algerian youth, feeling betrayed by the state, found in the mosque a moral substitute for alcohol, drugs, and violence, which had constituted their main pursuit hitherto. Alienated youth in the 1980s communicated with the state through violence, expressed in the form of cyclical riots. In general, the state lost its authority and its raison d'être in the eyes of a disenchanted population. The almost total failure of social, economic, and cultural modernization was one of the main reasons for the rise of radical Islamism—without discounting the painful colonial history whose effects continue to influence the evolution of Algerian society.

So long as Islamists did not threaten the survival of the system, the regime allowed them to freely operate and even encouraged them in order to curb the secularist left, which also had its allies, albeit less powerful, within the bureaucracy. Whenever it opposed the Islamists' ideology, the regime did so in the name of Islam, because religion was a necessary, even though increasingly contested, component of its legitimacy. In fact, the regime facilitated, perhaps unwittingly, the spread of Islamist ideology not only by allowing the building of thousands of public and private mosques, but also by establishing Islamic institutes, flooding television with religious programs, and allocating substantial resources for hosting international seminars on Islamic thought. Secularist state elites were unwilling to leave religious activities to the realm of civil society; instead, they wished to control the terms of religious discourse. To have permitted the existence of a public sphere independent of the state would have curtailed the power of the regime and diminished its hegemonic rule.

In the 1980s, violence was present in the universities, with bloody encounters between Islamist students who mobilized around cultural, linguistic, and moralistic themes, on the one hand, and leftist or secular students, Berberists, and others who did not share the Islamists' interpretation of Islam, on the other. Ironically, it was the state's acceleration of its Arabization campaign in the public education system that led to further contestation, owing to the growing cultural distinctiveness and absence of professional opportunities for Arabic-educated emerging elites relative to francophone Algerians. Islamist groups couched their socioeconomic demands within an ideological discourse garbed with religion. Various (small) armed groups targeted bars, breweries, police stations, and Soviet citizens and interests in Algeria. They represented a real challenge to the state, which responded with equal violence. But to confirm its religious credentials, the state also responded with an expansion of religious programs and the introduction of Islamist-inspired legislation. The objective of Islamists, of course, was to take Islam away from the regime to undermine one of the essential pillars upon which it had built its legitimacy.

By the late 1980s, the FIS had emerged as the party that represented oppositional Islamist sentiment in Algeria. When the regime pursued political liberalization by legalizing the formation of parties other than the FLN, the FIS was the main beneficiary. It was successful because its leaders presented the party as the only potent alternative to the FLN-dominated system, even claiming that it incarnated the true, historical FLN of the war of national liberation, thus delegitimizing the postindependence FLN. The FIS convinced major segments of society that the FLN had usurped and betrayed the nationalist movement—and its Islamic principles—in the pursuit of power and self-enrichment. And because it identified itself with Islam in a profoundly Muslim society, the FIS was able to repudiate the secular pretensions of the parties that resisted its ambitions and its societal projects. By the June 1990 municipal and departmental elections, it became apparent that the other parties, whether secular or (moderate) Islamist, could not halt the ascension of the FIS. These parties failed to establish a common strategy or united front with which to meet the FIS's challenge.

Political liberalization in Algeria in the late 1980s and early 1990s would not lead to democratization, therefore, in part because of the actions (or lack thereof) of the non-FIS parties in the new, multiparty political arena. But the FIS, too, bears significant responsibility for derailing prospects for a genuine democratic transition. While part of the FIS's leadership was moderate and publicly supported the ideal of pluralistic political competition, a significant segment of the party sought to impose the party's hegemony and delegitimize the existence of any other party. FIS leaders contended that they expressed the general will of the Algerian people and promised to implement Islamic law once in power. Such a promise implied a disregard for the republican constitution and inaugurated the "divinization" of politics, hence implicitly precluding the expression of secular views and the development of a democratic polity. The claims of its leadership to represent the only legitimate path did not bode well for the future, especially for the Westernized middle class and women. Furthermore, promises of radicals within the party to create popular tribunals and to punish the "enemies of Islam," and even to punish those opposed to the FIS, scared not only officials in the regime but also secular intellectuals and ordinary citizens. Therefore, large segments of society did not oppose—indeed they even encouraged—the banning of the FIS after its victory in the first round of the December 1991 legislative election.

Although the FIS was banned in 1992, and despite the violence that then unfolded, many of the ideas the FIS propagated continue to be advocated today by moderate, legal Islamist parties like the Movement of the Society for Peace (MSP), the National Movement for Renewal (Islah), and the Islamic Renaissance Movement (En-Nahda), which grouped together in the spring of 2012 under the Alliance of Green Algeria—along with two more recently formed parties, the Justice and Development Front (El Adala) and the Front for Change (FC). The two new parties (El Adala and FC) gained eight and four seats, respectively, in the 2012 legislative elections. In the 2017 elections they ran in a coalition with bigger Islamist parties. Though these elections showed a sharp decline in the number of votes cast for Islamist parties, it does not follow that society is becoming more secularized. On the contrary, society has grown more conservative as Salafism, with its rigid interpretation of Islam, has gained ground.

Today's remaining armed groups have lost popular support; their violent campaigns have discredited them in the eyes of the population. The main armed group, al-Qaeda in the Islamic Maghreb (AQIM), which in late 2006 grew out of the Algerian Salafi Group for Preaching and Combat (GSPC), carried out some spectacular attacks against government structures and innocent civilians in 2007, but it has been weakened by the security services and forced to establish its base in northern Mali along the border with Algeria. The few operations AQIM occasionally executes are now limited to the Sahara Desert and the mountains in Kabylia in the north. As for the Islamic State in Iraq and Syria (ISIS), it failed to establish a presence in the country; the security forces destroyed the few cells it had set up. While disgruntled youths feed AQIM's ranks to some extent, a popular new strategy for today's alienated youth is to emigrate illegally to Europe by crossing the Mediterranean Sea at great risk to their lives.

Government and Opposition

While at the outset some hoped that Bouteflika's tenure in power would bring about democratization, instead Algeria has undergone a transition from military authoritarianism to presidential authoritarianism. Although Bouteflika was elected in 1999 because he was chosen by the military hierarchy and the intelligence services, he gradually gained a degree of autonomy from the military and removed some of the most influential senior officers in the military hierarchy from office, usually through forced retirements or by replacing them with officers loyal to his person. Bouteflika serves as both commander in chief and minister of defense. Following his reelection in 2004 to a second term, Bouteflika strengthened his control over the armed forces by appointing a close associate as secretary-general of the Ministry of Defense and appointing other loyalists as heads of Algeria's six military regions. In recent years the Algerian armed forces have distanced themselves from politics and concentrated on professionalization and modernization.

Until recently these developments had not translated into civilian control over the intelligence services, whose power had been strengthened by the domestic war on terrorism as well as their involvement in the global war on terrorism. This international cooperation provided them with additional power. Traditionally, the security services, collectively known as the Department of Intelligence and Security (DRS), had great influence over the appointments of ministers and ambassadors. They were said to determine elections by manipulating the private and public media as well as political parties. Whenever a political party split, the opposition accused the DRS of having stage-managed dissent within the party to break up the organization. Any president had to bargain with their leaders over policy issues and about the extent of his prerogatives. Thus, though the political role of the armed forces had greatly diminished, elected officials—including the chief executive—did not have final say over legislation and policy, given the political weight of the DRS. In 2015, however, Bouteflika forced into retirement the all-powerful head of intelligence, Mohammad Mediene. Bouteflika then dismantled the DRS in 2016 and replaced it with the Directorate of Security Services (DSS), which is under the direct authority of the presidency. This marked the decisive control of power by the Bouteflika clan.

What of parties and parliament? We have already seen that the security forces exercise important, undemocratic influence over parties and elections. The regime also has set up a multiparty system in which parties play the role of mediators between their constituents and the authorities—but have no aspiration to come to power and replace the current system with a new, more democratic polity. From 2004 until 2012, the party system was dominated by three parties referred to collectively as the Presidential Alliance because they supported Bouteflika and his political agenda. These included the nationalist FLN and the technocratic-modernist Democratic National Rally (RND), which some call a clone of the FLN because both it and the RND receive massive support from the state administration, are present throughout the country, and have considerable means at their disposal. The third party in the alliance was the moderate Islamist MSP. It withdrew from the alliance in 2012, however, accusing the other two partners of having emptied Bouteflika's reforms of their substance (Zoubir and Aghrout 2012).

In the run-up to the 2012 legislative elections, the regime allowed the formation of twenty-one new political parties, resulting in the participation of forty-four parties in the election. Given the staunch refusal by the government to authorize new parties for more than a decade prior, the shift was most probably caused by the Arab Spring uprisings, official statements to the contrary notwithstanding. The proliferation of political parties was also intended to increase participation and to thwart the emergence of a powerful, genuine opposition party that could challenge the incumbent as the FIS had in 1990–1991. In the 2012 election—against the trend in neighboring countries where Islamist parties performed well—the government parties took nearly 63 percent of the seats. The FLN obtained 221 seats while the RND obtained 70; both enjoyed an increase over their 2007 representation. The Alliance of Green Algeria led by the MSP, by contrast, obtained a mere 47 seats, though in 2007 the MSP alone had garnered 52 seats. Several smaller parties allowed to form in fall 2011—many of which up to this point were practically unknown to the public—also "earned" seats in parliament (Dessi 2012).

In the 2017 legislative elections, the Islamist parties did not do well at the polls; however, together they still hold about 80 seats in the parliament. Clearly, the fragmentation of the parties that the regime concocted since 2012 has borne fruit. The key dynamic to understand here is that the regime essentially decides ahead of time how many seats each party—including even those in the Presidential Alliance—will win. The regime uses parliamentary seats to reward individuals and parties that are loyal to the political status quo; it also seeks to provide the illusion of genuine pluralism.

Though critical on some issues, the Islamist parties are tamed organizations relative to what the FIS represented in the 1990s. They use their involvement in national political institutions to advance the interests of their constituents: mainly urban arabophone (i.e., solely Arabic-speaking) teachers, many of whom were educated in Middle Eastern universities, and civil servants who belong to the middle class. Their moderation and participation in the system have been exploited by the regime to demonstrate that Islamist parties that are opposed to violence, and that do not aspire to replace the incumbent regime, are welcome in the state's institutions—inside of which they can act as pressure groups to advance their demands. And while the current regime does not give in to demands for democracy, it has made concessions on moral issues that Islamist parties have raised in parliament (for example, a ban on alcohol imports). In sum, Islamist parties have been co-opted and now serve as support for the regime's facade democracy.

Other non-Islamist, democratic, secularist parties of note following the 2017 elections include the Front of Socialist Forces (FFS, fourteen seats); the Algerian Popular Movement (MPA, thirteen seats); and the Workers Party (PT, eleven seats), led by the charismatic, outspoken woman Louisa Hanoune. Before 2017, the FFS had boycotted all national elections over their allegedly fraudulent character. By contrast, the Rally for Culture and Democracy (RCD), which held nineteen seats in the 2007 parliament, boycotted the 2012 election, but decided to run in 2017, obtaining nine seats. These parties represent important minorities. They are made up of francophone and Berber members, many of whom are employed in the liberal professions (law, medicine, engineering, etc.) or serve as cadres in the various structures of the state. Even though they are critical of the regime, except for the FFS they have often played into the hands of the regime and have allowed themselves to be co-opted on occasion. They constitute no real threat. The PT, for instance, supported the constitutional amendment that permitted a third presidential term for President Bouteflika.

Given the ongoing role of the security services behind the scenes of the political arena and the rigged nature of a party system that lacks real, active political opposition, it is not surprising that Algerians are increasingly indifferent to parties and politics in general. Illustrating this sentiment, the 2007, 2012, and 2017 legislative elections elicited very low turnouts. While the authorities announce good turnouts, many assume correctly that the real participation rate is much lower than the official figures. For example, the authorities declared that participation in the 2012 election reached 43 percent; most observers, however, concur that the reality is at best about half that figure. In 2017, official participation was 37 percent, hence even lower than in 2012.

The fear of Arab Spring "spillover" into Algeria resulted in calls by some political parties, from the FFS to the FLN, for increased voter participation, warning that low turnout would threaten the unity of the country—possibly triggering foreign intervention similar to what occurred in neighboring Libya. On May 8, 2012, Bouteflika warned of such a scenario. In 2014, Bouteflika won a fourth mandate with a clearly inflated 52 percent of the vote. On February 10, 2019, the presidency announced that Bouteflika would seek a fifth term in the election scheduled for April 18. The resulting indignation and shame among the population led to millions of Algerians demonstrating peacefully against their incapacitated, rarely seen president. They understood that Bouteflika's cronies wanted a fifth term, in violation of the constitution, to continue their predation. His regime's corruption had reached such levels that Algerians from all walks of life decided to stand up against it, breaking through fears that regime change would lead to chaos. Algerians demanded an end to the system in place since independence. Persistent demonstrations by millions every Friday beginning on February 22 resulted in the military forcing Bouteflika to resign on April 2, 2019. Millions of peaceful protesters continued, however, to call for an end to the entire political system.

Civil Society

Although severely restricted, an Algerian civil society existed under French colonial rule. Countless civic, religious, sports, and even political associations animated organizational life throughout the country. However, after independence, except for sports or parents' associations, all other autonomous organizations were absorbed by the nationalist party, the FLN. Regardless of the repression used to muzzle dissent and the emergence of autonomous associations, independent organizations blossomed throughout the country to advance the interests of a wide variety of citizen-driven concerns (Zoubir 1999). These included cultural organizations (e.g., the Berber Cultural Movement), feminist groups (e.g., the Association of Independent Women), unions, human rights groups (e.g., the Algerian League of Human Rights), trade groups, and Islamist associations (e.g., Orientation and Reform [Al-Irshad wa'l Islah]). This development, coupled with cyclical revolts, forced the regime to pay more attention. Thus, a year before the 1988 riots, the government acknowledged the right of citizens to create nonpolitical associations around several issues, such as consumer defense and cultural activities (Zoubir 1995).

The emergence of a genuine civil society occurred in 1989 following the approval of a new constitution in February of that year. Literally thousands of associations sprang up, publicly expressing their opposition to such practices as the torture and imprisonment of individuals without due process of law. Other associations, whose members focused on such concerns as ecology, religion, and consumer protection, multiplied throughout the country. Women created associations to proclaim their right to full citizenship and to demand the abrogation of laws they felt were discriminatory, like the 1984 Family Code. Trade associations, such as the Association of Chief Executive Officers, the General Confederation of Algerian Economic Operators, and the Algerian Confederation of Businessmen, also emerged. Artists, writers, and peasants forged specific organizations to advance their interests. Even retired military personnel created their own association.

Although some of the autonomous associations gave birth to political parties—as the Berber Cultural Movement and Al-Irshad wa'l Islah did to the RCD and MSP, respectively—most today do not necessarily have a political nature. Instead they tend to react to the various societal problems that the country has faced (unemployment, the promotion of market economics, the advancement of the Arabic language, or the inclusion of Islamic teachings in education, for instance). The regime, however, has sought to undermine or co-opt these associations. It tries to mobilize them to support the election of the president; in return, co-opted associations receive financial support. Today, civil society lacks the means and the opportunity to hold discussions on the revision of the constitution or other matters of national interest. To hold a public meeting, an association needs an authorization—which is refused in most cases, unless the nongovernmental organization or association in question is close to the government. Other serious handicaps for the close to 100,000 associations that exist are their lack of democratic experience, lack of adequate funding, and, for most of them, dependence on the regime for survival.

Although there is an independent press, President Bouteflika sought to discredit it and has shown that he will not tolerate harsh criticism of him or his government. The authorities have used various means to intimidate journalists, including imprisoning them under the pretext of their alleged defamation of officials or collaboration with foreign entities. Journalists also engage in self-censorship on issues that could implicate powerful members of the regime, to avoid trouble with the law. Algerian television, watched in practically all households, is an important political medium through which the president used to propagate his views and policies unobstructed by opposition perspectives—though his last speech was in May 2012. Algerian television is virtually the voice of the government, and it is no surprise that the government long opposed the creation of private television stations—something it reluctantly approved only in 2011. As a result, most Algerians turn to European—mostly French—or Gulf Arab channels, through satellite dishes.

Political Economy

In the mid-1960s the regime of President Houari Boumediene inaugurated an ambitious economic program that gave priority to industrialization and heavy industry, while encouraging the creation of socialist, agricultural villages. The main objective of the regime was to get Algeria out of its underdevelopment as rapidly as possible. To achieve that goal, the authorities launched a widely acclaimed model of "industrializing industries," following a theory developed by French economist Gérard Destanne de Bernis. State-owned enterprises (SOEs) in sectors such as mining, hydrocarbons (oil and natural gas), banking, insurance, iron and steel, and construction materials constituted the vehicle for the industrialization effort. The state also nationalized several foreign assets to assert its economic independence. It established control over foreign trade and retail networks while nationalizing nearly all industries and businesses. SOEs run by Algerian executives, known as cadres, in cooperation with foreign nationals, covered most important industries. The authorities established multiyear economic plans, and the financing of capital-intensive industrialization was made possible thanks to Algeria's hydrocarbon revenues. Finally, the institution of free health care and free education allowed the regime to rule unchallenged.

Boumediene was convinced that heavy industry would be the locomotive that would haul behind it agriculture and other light industries. The initial results in education, health, and many other areas were impressive. Industrial growth from 1970 to 1979 was higher than growth of gross domestic product (GDP) (11.7 percent compared to 6.9 percent); in the same period, industry outside the hydrocarbon sector created 15 percent of the total number of jobs in the national economy. Indeed, from 1970 to 1980, 250,000 jobs were created every year.

Unfortunately, this model of development presented many problems, due largely to its reliance on capital-intensive technologies. Industry became a predator that devoured all available resources. The other sectors, especially agriculture, were sacrificed on the altar of modern industry. Under inducement from the authorities, a great number of peasants gathered into collective farms. This socialist experiment ultimately proved disastrous, however. Other peasants left their meager lands and settled in the already overcrowded major cities or their peripheries. The agricultural sector suffered from insufficient funding and the irrational use of scarce water. In part because of failures in the agricultural sector, but also due to a demographic explosion, Algeria continues to this day to import close to US$8 billion worth of foodstuffs.

Meanwhile, unemployment remained high, disillusioning those who had moved to the cities and their vicinity in the hopes of attaining higher living standards. Living conditions were simply miserable. The good intentions of Boumediene notwithstanding, demographics aggravated the socioeconomic shortcomings of his chosen development strategy. Furthermore, although many planners became aware of the necessity of involving the private sector in agriculture and in light industry, for political and ideological reasons the regime failed to encourage that sector to partake in the process of development. This is not to say that a private sector did not exist; on the contrary, such a sector existed and benefited from state-determined, artificially high prices for its goods. But the private sector played a parasitic rather than a productive role in the strategy of development.

So, despite initial euphoria about the "industrializing industries" projects, reliance on heavy industry did not produce the expected effects. The country failed to produce a diversified economy capable of sustaining long-lasting development. Moreover, reliance on hydrocarbon revenues to finance this ambitious development project meant that the strategy was vulnerable to fluctuations in oil prices. The authorities were inspired by economic nationalism and hoped that it would reduce their dependence on the capitalist economies. Unfortunately, fluctuations in the price of oil, the need for foreign (capital) assistance, and a lack of skilled labor—coupled with the cost of the welfare state (free education and free health care)—had dire consequences. The failure of the economic strategy and the socioeconomic problems that arose from this failure compelled the regime of Chadli Bendjedid to initiate economic reforms.

Increasing debt and failure of the authorities to sustain public investment compelled the government to introduce reforms intended to give Algeria a market-economy orientation. However, the reforms were quite timid, hampered by a nationalist ideology that still disapproved of large-scale privatization of the economy, especially in sectors deemed strategic. The regime dismantled state-owned enterprises, breaking them down into smaller units—but this did not translate into their privatization. The way this pseudo-liberalization was effectuated resulted in social and political upheavals. Liberalization was also hampered by the unwillingness of the population to give up the welfare system (which had hitherto provided a respectable degree of social justice) as well as by popular perceptions of the regime as corrupt and inefficient. Rising discontent in the mid-1980s was an indication of the turmoil that was yet to come. Indeed, the decline in oil prices in 1986 and the socioeconomic crisis that ensued provided the ammunition for the 1988 riots. In the aftermath of the riots, the regime had no choice but to initiate political liberalization, but it also introduced additional economic reforms.

To this end the regime called on technocrats capable of managing a transition to a market economy. However, transforming the economy was no easy task in view of Algeria's balance of payments. The country, which imported most of its needs and was also trying to finance its growth investments, could not pay the required installments on its foreign debt. The political instability of the late 1980s, aggravated in the 1990s due to the armed Islamist uprising, resulted in the near-bankruptcy of the state. In 1994 the Algerian government concluded an International Monetary Fund (IMF) agreement and a Paris Club rescheduling of $5.3 billion. A year later, the central bank rescheduled its commercially held foreign debt. Under its extended fund facility, the IMF agreed to a $1.8 billion structural reform credit for a three-year period (1995–1998).

IMF-inspired economic policies continued under the presidency of Bouteflika. By 2000, macroeconomic indicators were quite good and enticed some foreign investors outside the traditionally attractive hydrocarbon sector to explore the Algerian market. By 2005, inflation was down to 3 percent. At the same time, high oil prices helped Algeria overcome its budget deficit and contributed to the trade balance tilting in the country's favor. In 2005–2006, owing to huge hydrocarbon revenues and impressive external reserves, Algeria made the strategic decision to repay its external debt. The government made early debt repayments of $10.5 billion, including to Paris and London Club creditors; this helped reduce Algeria's external debt-to-GDP ratio from 17 percent in 2005 to 4.5 percent in 2006. In 2012, Algeria's debt was less than $5 billion, around 2.4 percent of GDP. In 2014, the external debt was a mere $307 million, while in 2017 it amounted to $3.7 billion, or 3 percent of GDP. By way of comparison, in 1994 the total external debt was close to $30 billion, corresponding to 70 percent of the country's GDP.

The main fear, of course, is that Algeria remains a one-commodity producer and thus its economy is dependent upon the price of and demand for oil. Although this commodity may be finite, the national oil company, Sonatrach, discovered eighteen new oil sites in 2006 alone and others in 2007–2008. Given the importance of oil, it is not surprising that Algerians decided in 2006 to reverse a 2005 law on liberalization of the oil sector that had allowed foreign ownership up to a maximum level of 70 percent. The new law compels Sonatrach to have the majority share (51 percent) in all contracts relating to research, exploitation, and refining. In addition, an amendment to the law imposes a tax of between 5 and 50 percent on exceptional nontaxable benefits, to be applied to partnership contracts when the price of oil surpasses $30 a barrel. This would represent additional revenue to the state of $1–$2 billion a year.

At the end of 2006, Algerian authorities emphasized the need to lessen dependence on hydrocarbons. They decided to launch a debate on a new industrial strategy, to begin in 2007 (Aghrout 2008). In the meantime, to avoid social conflicts resulting from the liberalization process, an economic and social pact was signed in October 2006 by three actors: the government, the private sector, and the national trade union (General Union of Algerian Trade Workers [UGTA]). The rationale for this pact was that, to give time for reforms to bear fruit and ignite the economy, an understanding among all parties needed to be reached so that the reforms were not undermined. Under the terms of this agreement, the government pledged to work toward improving workers' employment opportunities, incomes, purchasing power, and legal rights; the private sector promised to increase competitiveness and reduce corruption; and workers agreed to refrain from striking or creating "social tensions" in any industrial sector, or demanding raises—all for a four-year period.

In 2007, GDP growth remained at around 5 percent, again owing mostly to hydrocarbon exports. But growth in the nonhydrocarbon sector also progressed noticeably in 2007, reaching 11 percent, largely due to the booming construction sector. Algeria's foreign currency reserves reached $110 billion at the end of 2007 and $205 billion by mid-2012, making Algeria the country with the second-highest reserves in the Arab world (after Saudi Arabia). Because this circumstance owed primarily to hydrocarbon revenues, Prime Minister Ahmed Ouyahia declared in September 2008 that a drop in the price of a barrel of oil below $70 would prove catastrophic, especially since Algeria continues to import not only capital goods but also food products. However, the ensuing, momentary drop of oil prices to $40 a barrel did not impact the Algerian economy. The authorities remained quite worried about high levels of imports, especially of consumer products. In 2008 imports of foodstuffs amounted to over $6 billion, a 70 percent increase over foodstuff imports in 2007. This situation compelled the government to devalue the Algerian dinar to discourage imports. This was relatively successful; indeed, Algeria's food import bill amounted to $4.53 billion in the first nine months of 2009 compared to $6.15 billion during the same period in 2008. In 2012 the figure reached close to $9 billion.

The sharp depreciation of crude oil prices in 2014, accompanied by a contraction in oil production, presented Algeria with major challenges. According to the IMF, despite steady growth in the nonoil sector, unemployment rose to 11.7 percent in September 2017 and remains particularly high among young people (28.3 percent) and women (20.7 percent). The average inflation rate stood at 5.6 percent, against 6.4 percent in 2016, due to the slowdown in inflation for manufactured goods and services; it was 3.4 percent year-on-year in April 2018. Since 2014, Algeria has sought to address these challenges by restricting imports. Regardless, Algeria still imports more than $7 billion worth of foodstuffs per year. The authorities resorted to unconventional means (printing money) to address the treasury's deficit; they have also made efforts to improve efficiency and public expenditure management, as well as expand subsidy reforms. And Algeria's foreign exchange reserves are still substantial ($96 billion in 2018). Under Bouteflika's rule, the private sector has gained in importance; however, the new business class remained parasitic with close links to the regime, so much so that this class has increasingly displayed clout in influencing political decisions. In sum, although the private sector holds a major share of the market, the economy is still hydrocarbons-dependent, and the structural reforms promised repeatedly have yet to be set in place.

Identity and Politics

Out of a population of 42 million, the Berber-/Amazigh-speaking people represent about 10 million (23.8 percent). The Berbers are the native inhabitants of North Africa, concentrated mostly in Morocco, Algeria, and Tunisia. In Algeria, they are found primarily in the Kabylie and Aurès mountain regions, and in the Mzab and other Saharan oases. The most famous Berbers are Saint Augustine and today the soccer player and coach Zineddine Zidane; the most famous Berber dish is couscous, which in the Berber language means "well-rolled," in reference to the semolina of which it is made. During the colonial era, many leaders of the nationalist movement were Amazigh. However, successive regimes have refused to recognize either the Berber language or the Berber identity—allegedly in the name of national unity. Algerian Berbers have long sought this recognition. They have protested both their lack of political influence and the state's disregard for their culture and identity, particularly concerning the place of the Amazigh language in Algerian politics and society.

Amazigh militancy in Algeria has had a long tradition. In the spring of 1980, Berber militants called a general strike, first in Tizi Ouzou and then in the entire region of Greater Kabylia. In the ensuing days, the populations of surrounding Berber villages joined the protests in Tizi Ouzou, building barricades to confront the police. In response to this "Berber Spring" upheaval, the government launched a military operation to regain control of Tizi Ouzou; harsh repression was exerted against Berber students and workers. The government also blocked roads and isolated the region from the rest of the country. Many students, workers, and activists were arrested. To appease the situation going forward, the government took several measures and promised to promote Berber culture, including through the creation of university chairs of Berber studies.

The political liberalization launched in 1989 resulted in the mushrooming of hundreds of Berber associations focused mostly on their locality around issues such as language, village history, archaeological research, ancestral poetry, handicrafts, and music, as well as the organization of cultural festivals and galas. Their objective was to raise the consciousness of Berbers and assert their identity. But it would be erroneous to see the movement solely in its cultural dimension; Berbers had substantial political demands, as they felt discriminated against not only culturally but also politically and economically. Although many political parties include the Amazigh question in their platforms, two parties draw their primary support from the Berbers: the FFS and the RCD. The Movement for Autonomy in Kabylie, a more extremist, insignificant wing of the Berber movement that attracts little following, has called for the autonomy of or even independence for the Kabylie region.

In the decades after independence, with few exceptions, regime authorities claimed that Algerian identity rested solely on Arab-Islamic oneness. They denied the multiplicity of other factors that also contributed to Algerians' identity—such as Berber, African, and Mediterranean influences. For decades, state elites did not seem to discern the obvious contradictions within their ideology. On the one hand, they held a secular, modernistic, and socialistic discourse. On the other hand, they held a political-religious discourse that rested on an ideologized Islam that they sought to impose upon society. Basing Algerian identity in large part around Islam was part of that discourse, and it undermined the regime's secular principles while encouraging the emergence of Islamist opposition forces. Perhaps not surprisingly then, Islamists mirrored regime elites in the 1980s and 1990s in that they, too, denied the Berber, African, and Mediterranean components of Algerian identity.

In more recent years the government has addressed some Berber grievances, for instance creating in 1995 the High Commission for Amazighity, which introduced measures supporting the teaching of the Berber language in Berber areas. The 1996 constitution recognized Tamazight as one of the three constituent elements of Algerian identity in addition to its Arab and Islamic components. But Berbers felt that this was an administrative measure designed to deflect the Berbers' main demands: the recognition of Tamazight as an official language (i.e., that of official documents, speeches, correspondence, etc.) and as a national language (i.e., one that can be taught in Algerian schools). While the government eventually acceded to the second demand in 2002, it did not agree to the first one until 2016. Furthermore, many Algerians consider that the Algerian dialect of Arabic, the Berber dialects, classical Arabic, and French are all part of their cultural heritage, and they thus resist the regime's policy of Arabization, wherein it gradually eliminated French and made Arabic the sole language of instruction in Algerian primary, secondary, and tertiary education.

In 2001, another crisis erupted after the death of a secondary school pupil in police custody close to Tizi Ouzou. His death resulted in an important protest movement, notably among youth frustrated by difficult economic conditions. The repression of these protests resulted in 100 deaths and led to an Amazigh revolt that spread to several parts of the country. The protesters made various demands, including the recognition of Tamazight as an official language (Willis 2008). They also protested the lack of economic opportunities in the region and growing governmental hostility. A fifteen-point platform, adopted in June 2001 by the local movement Coordination des Archs, Dairas, et Communes (CADC),[1] served as a basis for dialogue with the authorities.

The government held a series of meetings with those in the CADC movement who were willing to talk (some were opposed to dialogue). The dialogue produced positive results, such as the recognition of Tamazight as a national language in March 2002 and the holding of partial new local elections in November 2005. The framers of the platform avoided regional particularism other than the language issue; generally, their demands related to national issues, including good governance and the democratization of political life. The government's agreement to the CADC's demands helped ease tensions in the region; however, questions related to the status and mission of the CADC delegates remained unanswered. CADC delegates continued their action on other issues of contention, such as making Tamazight an official language. President Bouteflika rejected this demand until 2016, arguing that recognizing two official languages was neither rational nor possible (even though numerous countries have more than one official language). However, Bouteflika finally understood that the regime needed to make amends if it wished to preserve national unity. Thus, in 2016, an amendment to the constitution finally recognized Tamazight as an official language. In January 2018, Bouteflika declared the Berber New Year, Yennayer, a national legal holiday, a decision that parliamentarians supported unanimously.

Gender and Politics

Despite their active role in the war of liberation, even as fighters, Algerian women did not obtain the status that they anticipated in postindependence politics. Not only did traditional values weigh on that status, but also the state did relatively little to create opportunities for them. The state has encouraged the education of women though: in 2004, 90.9 percent of girls between six and fifteen years old were educated and 65 percent of baccalaureate graduates were females. In 2007, two-thirds of university students were women (compared to only 39.5 percent in 1991), and while in 1966 the rate of illiteracy among women was 85 percent, that figure had dropped to 35 percent in 2002 (Dris-Aït-Hamadouche 2008). Despite this progress in the education of women, laws passed by the state reduced their role to that of minors.

A case in point was the Family Code of 1984, which restricted the rights of women, especially divorced women, who lost their right to the conjugal residence regardless of whether they had custody of the children. In addition, while men could easily initiate and obtain a divorce, women did not enjoy that right. Women in Algeria have demanded the abrogation of this law ever since parliament passed it. In fact, even some women's associations affiliated with Islamist parties have sought its dissolution, because they have found it to be contrary to Islam. The women's associations that mushroomed in the post-1989 era made abrogation of the Family Code one of their main demands. Facing pressures to democratize and in its fight against radical Islamism, the government has endeavored to improve the status of women. Specifically, in 2005, authorities revised the text of the Family Code. Although the revised text does not meet all the demands that women's associations have made, the new code makes polygamy more difficult, forces divorced fathers to financially support their ex-wives and their children, compels them to secure housing for mothers who retain custody of their children, and confers upon the mother the status of a parental authority, which was previously denied to her.

What of the economic and political realms? In terms of employment, notwithstanding the relatively high rate of literacy among women, the labor market remains rather discriminatory toward women. According to the 2005 Arab Human Development Report, women's activities constituted 31.6 percent of all economic activity in Algeria. The government passed legislation in 2005 to protect women in the workforce, ensuring that women receive pay equal to that of men for equal levels of qualification and performance. However, according to the World Bank, in 2017 only 15.2 percent of adult women participated in the labor force (2018).

In politics, too, the representation of women remains limited, although gradual progress has been made in recent years. Women represented a mere 7.7 percent of members of the National Popular Assembly elected in 2007 and less than 5 percent of the Senate. In the executive branch of government, the percentage is at 7.2 percent. The Inter-Parliamentary Union had ranked Algeria 117th in the proportion of women in parliament in 2011. This, however, changed when the government introduced new legislation to increase women's participation in elected bodies. Thus, in the 2012 election, a record 146 women were elected, making Algeria the first and only Arab country where women hold more than 31.4 percent of the seats in parliament, as opposed to 7.7 percent in the departing chamber. The Organic Law passed in November 2011 requires that 20–50 percent of the seats on party lists be reserved for women so they cannot be excluded from the ballot. This law, resisted by some (mostly Islamist) parties, came as part of a package of reforms that Bouteflika introduced following the uprisings that shook the Arab world. In the May 2017 election, women contenders won 118 seats and represented virtually all 63 political parties that participated in the ballot. Out of the 164 seats won by the FLN, 50 are held by women. Likewise, 32 out of the 97 seats won by the Democratic National Rally went to women. Today, more than one-third of judges are women. Regardless, Algeria remains a patriarchal society and the realm of politics is overwhelmingly male-dominated.

The Impact of International Politics

Over the course of the 1990s and 2000s, the main vector by which the international arena influenced Algerian politics was Western reactions to the cancellation of the second round of legislative elections in Algeria in early 1992. Divisions existed within European governments as well as inside the US administration as to how to deal with the Algerian political crisis (Darbouche and Zoubir 2008). The Islamists' distrustful attitude toward the West, on the one hand, and the West's skeptical perspective on the Islamists, on the other, not only resulted in mutual antipathy but also forced many Western powers to adopt contradictory postures. In Europe, Islamism has never been a question of foreign policy, as it is in the United States, but it might well be considered a domestic issue, not only because of the presence in Europe of millions of Muslims, but also because of the prospect of floods of new immigrants "marching" into Europe. The waves of refugees generated by the conflicts that erupted after the Arab Spring strengthened those apprehensions. Their democratic credentials notwithstanding, most Western countries, in varying degrees and with various reservations, were supportive of the cancellation of the electoral process in January 1992 by the Algerian military.

By 1995, the main initiative taken by France, the former colonial power that dominated policy on Algeria within the European Union (EU), consisted of urging the EU to infuse massive economic aid to Algeria, while at the same time finding a way of bringing together all the various Algerian political forces that were favorable to a democratic process. Fearful of Islamism, the EU's northern Mediterranean countries (France, Italy, and Spain) expressed support for the Algerian regime by advocating macroeconomic assistance as a remedy for what was viewed as a crisis essentially emanating from socioeconomic roots. Thus, the main European policies focused on rescheduling Algeria's debt through an IMF structural adjustment program and supporting the Algerian regime in its fight against radical Islamists, while at the same time advocating dialogue with those political forces outside of the regime that renounced violence.

For its part, the Algerian government promptly engaged in talks with the IMF that culminated in the "re-profiling" of Algeria's debt in

April 1994, reducing its external debt-servicing ratio by about two-thirds from where it then stood—at around 95 percent of its foreign currency income. The government also engaged in macroeconomic reforms imposed by the IMF, reforms that resulted in an increase in unemployment and socioeconomic hardship (due to the elimination of subsidies on staple goods, the closing of inefficient state-owned enterprises, etc.). Indeed, both France and the EU conditioned the release of allocated financial assistance to Algeria on its conclusion of an IMF agreement. The EU went a step further by initially giving only a lukewarm reception to Algeria's request for the opening of negotiations toward an association agreement in the framework of the European Community's Euro-Mediterranean Partnership. This is an EU initiative that seeks, through diplomatic engagement and trade agreements, to increase prosperity, good governance, cultural exchange, and security in the EU-Mediterranean arena.

Although the necessity of democratization was part of the EU's discourse, European governments were careful not to allow the Algerian government to collapse. They extended support to the regime while urging it to introduce economic reforms and undertake dialogue with a variety of Algerian political forces, including "moderate" Islamists. The United States also pushed for a compromise between "moderate" Islamists and the authorities. To that end, Algeria's main opposition parties—including the FIS, FLN, and FFS—met in Rome under the auspices of the small Catholic community Sant'Egidio in November 1994 and then again in January 1995. They agreed on a joint platform for peaceful political resolution of the Algerian crisis. The platform, deemed constructive by the international community—particularly the United States (Zoubir 2002)—set out a roadmap for a return to the electoral process and the renunciation of terrorist violence. But the Algerian government resisted the initiative and decided to proceed with its own policy of reforms and reconciliation. Under Bouteflika's presidency, the government launched a process of civil concord in 1999 and a law on national reconciliation in 2005 (Tlemçani 2008). Thus, the pressure applied by the United States and the EU resulted in the Algerian government's integration of moderate Islamists, who have now become part of the political system.

Since the events of September 11, 2001, Algeria has been co-opted into the security system that the United States launched in the Maghreb-Sahel region to fight the presence of armed Islamist groups that have settled there (Zoubir 2009). September 11 represented a significant event that focused US attention on the Maghreb in general and on Algeria in particular, as some perceive the latter as a pivotal state in the region (Zoubir

2018). Considerable concern exists among some US and European government officials that the Maghreb, and by extension the Sahel, has become a recruiting area for al-Qaeda, ISIS, and other jihadist groups—and a potential back door into Europe. Several events—including kidnappings of Westerners for ransoms, attacks on UN forces, and the erection of training camps for jihadists—in the Sahel region, which borders the southern extremities of the Sahara, provided further justification for the presence of US and other forces in the area. The existence of AQIM since 2007 also strengthened the rationale for the Pan-Sahel Initiative (PSI), launched by the US government in the aftermath of 9/11. The Trans-Sahara Counterterrorism Partnership (TSCTP), which succeeded the PSI in 2003, includes the Maghreb-Sahel states; US-led joint maneuvers under the Flintlock program are conducted annually with those states.

However, although Algeria refuses to serve as a proxy for the United States and EU in the Sahel, Algerians, in general, were not supportive of their country's involvement with the United States in the "war on terror" initiated under the administration of President George W. Bush. Algerians' hostility toward such cooperation stemmed from their perception of the United States as an enemy of the Muslim world due to its overwhelming support for Israel, its unjustified war in Iraq, and its involvement in Libya, Syria, and Yemen. Furthermore, some Algerians believe that the regime's close security cooperation with the United States has been an impediment to genuine democratization, because Washington needs Algeria to combat terrorism globally and thus will not be likely to pressure the regime to pursue genuine democratic reforms. Under the administration of President Barack Obama, relations with Algeria, particularly in the military and security realms, developed exponentially. Events in northern Mali since January 2013 further strengthened Algeria's cooperation with the United States in the fight against AQIM and other terrorist groups, such as the Movement for Oneness and Jihad in West Africa, and against drug traffickers in the region. The United States and EU have supported Algeria's mediation roles in Libya and Mali. Furthermore, the United States has praised the reforms that Algeria took following the Arab uprisings—especially regarding participation of women in political life—even though there is no evidence yet that those reforms are authentic. What is certain is that, because of the experience of the 1990s, Algerians have preferred stability to any perceived destabilizing reforms that the Arab Spring has generated.

Note

1. *Archs* are traditional clans or tribes; *dairas* are administrative units at the subprefectural level; and *communes* are local village councils.

10
Egypt

Joshua Stacher

In April 2018 the head of Egypt's election authority announced that President Abdel Fattah al-Sisi, a general and former defense minister, had been reelected for a second four-year term in office. Almost 60 million registered voters, or 41 percent of the electorate, reportedly participated in the vote. Sisi secured an unbelievable 97 percent of the valid votes cast. His formal opponent, Mousa Mostafa Mousa, won just 2.92 percent of the vote. More people wrote in Egyptian soccer star Mohammad Salah for president than voted for Sisi's opponent. This was supposed to be Sisi's last term. Yet, parliament has since changed the law allowing for Sisi to have two more six-year terms, which means that the current president can stay in the presidential office until 2034. Should this come to pass, Sisi would be president for twenty years.

Eight years after a national uprising that ended the presidency of longtime president Husni Mubarak and likely prevented the hereditary succession of Gamal Mubarak, Sisi's presidency has been taken to mean that politics has returned to "normal" in Egypt. After all, since takeover of the state in 1952 by military officers, Egyptians have only experienced just over two years of nonautocratic rule. In fact, some scholars argue that Sisi's presidency indicates that "new authoritarianism" is the best way to understand the disastrous wake of Egypt's national protests and fraught political transition. The state under Sisi, who arrived to the office on the back of a military coup d'état against a democratically elected president, has orchestrated a massive crackdown against anyone remotely active before, during, or since the uprising. People languish in newly built prisons housed to warehouse dissenters, sit heartbrokenly in exile around the world, or watch helplessly as the state revokes their ability to leave the country.

Did Egypt's uprising or revolution fail? Was the military's takeover of the state inevitable? How can we understand the darkness that now envelops the politics of Egypt where hope briefly reigned supreme? A student of the politics of Egypt might conclude that the balance sheet of the regimes of Gamal Abdel Nasser (ruled 1954–1970) as well as Anwar Sadat (1970–1981) and Mubarak (1981–2011) led to the 2011 impasse between those who govern and those who are governed. The poor fiscal health of the state and a perpetually weak economy ground people to the nub, while the slow but constant drip of state violence built symbolic enclosures around people as ruling elites worked to discourage the airing of organized discontent. Having had enough, Egyptians rose up in 2011. The protesters collapsed the routine and predictable balance of power between the state's coercive forces and a society's clamoring for greater economic opportunities, more democracy, and reversal of the social injustice that permeated daily life in Egypt.

The protests of January 25, 2011, morphed into a rebellious uprising that paralyzed the ability of politicians to govern. The uprising moved politics from an arena where elites spoke and the masses followed for fear of state repression to one where many voices made demands and the state elites were impotent to respond. People began to believe in a more hopeful future. There would be no option for those trying to govern Egypt but to open up the political system.

A flurry of activities followed Mubarak's forced resignation after eighteen days of protests around the country. There were five national elections between March 2011 and June 2012. Constitutional amendments were added to restrict executive power; groups that had been illegal won the largest blocs in parliament; new political parties formed; and the world's only superpower talked about the importance of democracy succeeding in Egypt. Furthermore, in what is likely the biggest surprise of the entire postuprising period, a former political prisoner and leader from Egypt's Muslim Brotherhood, Mohammad Morsi, became president and moved into the presidential palace once occupied by Mubarak. Yet divisions abounded. Many of the elites in Mubarak's disbanded National Democratic Party (NDP) used their connections to international capital to remain relevant politically. The army, which had not been politically active since the 1970s, made a return in the form of the Supreme Council of the Armed Forces. The body became the arbitrator of politics as well as the leading force coordinating the use of state violence against civilians demanding more rights. Liberals distrusted the Muslim Brotherhood. The Brotherhood and the military distrusted each other. The military began to surmise that the only way to safeguard its position and economic interests was by ending the rowdy period of protests, elections, and economic freefall.

In July 2013, the military arrested Morsi and handed the state over to a former judge named Adly Mansour to govern on an interim basis. Five weeks after the coup, the military's special forces and militarized police violently cleared ongoing sit-ins by the Muslim Brotherhood. It is unclear how many people died, but Human Rights Watch called the dispersal of Rabaa al-Adawiyya Square the largest state massacre of its own citizens since, at least, Tiananmen Square in Beijing in 1989. Some claim Rabaa might have been larger.

The army then nudged a reluctant Sisi into the presidency. In the space of three short years, the leadership of Egypt's armed forces went from being one of the institutions consulted by Mubarak on big policy initiatives to governing from in front of the curtain without many allies to help anchor its rule. All the corridors of state power now lead to and emerge from its offices. The cult of personality surrounding Sisi dominated the landscapes around the capital and country. His image appeared on cupcakes, ladies' underwear, and posters put up everywhere. Sisi struck a deal with the region's most reactionary political forces in Saudi Arabia, the UAE, Kuwait, and Israel in order to solicit favor and gain protective cover from successive administrations in Washington, DC. The state banned protests, threw people in prisons, exiled others, and placed travel bans on activists who were too prominent to jail because of their foreign constituencies.

Sisi borrowed money from the International Monetary Fund (IMF) and began cutting subsidies and other social spending. Military intelligence organized parliamentary elections, which produced the most feckless parliament in Egypt's modern history. It remains entirely unclear if Sisi has managed to recalibrate the state in terms of basic coherence, to develop a predictable regime where practices and norms have been established with society, or if the Egyptian state has finished shedding its administrative capabilities yet. The steep increase in state violence and even more laughable election results compared to the rule of previous dictators might be a new wrinkle on an older, familiar refrain. However, if this situation is seen as a process rather than the outcome, we are better positioned to analyze the ongoing struggle between the state and society that is unfolding in Egypt.

Historical Background and Contemporary Political Structure

A group of army officers from Egypt's lower and middle classes overthrew King Farouk in July 1952.[1] The Free Officers ended the monarchy and reconstituted Egypt as a republic. The 1952 military coup was a political earthquake that ushered in a social revolution for Egyptians. It unsettled the unsteady political order and became the first time in centuries that Egyptians governed Egypt.

Egypt's political path under monarchical rule during the previous 150 years left peculiar political arrangements. A family of Albanian origin held the monarchy, and it had tried to rule Egypt independently since the early 1800s even though the country formally remained a province of the Ottoman Empire until 1914. Some rulers from the family had plans to modernize Egypt, introducing new institutions such as a military, constructing railroads, digging canals, and encouraging profitable new crops in the country's dominant agricultural sector. But by the late 1870s the country had borrowed more capital to finance these ambitious projects than it could repay. Egypt's debt holders in Europe insisted that European officials be given a role overseeing Egyptian finances—a step that provoked domestic criticism and unrest. This bankruptcy became a site of struggle against the prospect of European colonization, which was developing momentum in the region. Nevertheless, Egypt would fall under its yoke. In 1882 Great Britain occupied the country to put down an Egyptian rebellion but kept the ruling family in place. Britain also opted to maintain the link with the Ottoman Empire, preferring to administer Egypt from behind the scenes. During World War I, Britain finally declared a protectorate over Egypt and detached it from the Ottoman Empire. British officials contemplated incorporating Egypt more fully into their own empire at the close of the war. But another nationalist uprising convinced them that this act would be too costly.

The leaders of the 1919 uprising formed a political party called the Wafd. British representatives in Cairo tried to work with the Wafd and, when those negotiations failed, simply ceded nominal independence to Egypt in 1922. The hope was to keep Egypt in Britain's sphere of influence. The following year, the Egyptian king issued a constitution that allowed for an elected People's Assembly—a parliament that was generally dominated by Wafd leaders. As a result, from 1922 to 1952 Egypt merged democratic and monarchical features; it was legally an independent state, but the British controlled Egypt's foreign policy as well as its most important strategic asset—the Suez Canal. The resulting system produced constant rivalry among the British, the Wafd, and the king. Politics grew more instable as new actors emerged and began to participate in national politics in the 1930s and 1940s. Several new mass political movements—such as the Muslim Brotherhood (established 1928) and more protofascist groups such as the Brown Shirts—all had established militias alongside their parties. They and the state were as likely to engage in violence as they were in nonviolent politics during this period.

Inclusive and Exclusive Authoritarianism

On July 23, 1952, a group of military officers seized state power. The officers' working principle was that the politics of Egypt had grown violent because of British interference, but also due to the weakness of the king and the democratic unruliness of the parliament and political parties. The military officers exiled the king, closed parliament, and abolished party pluralism. They buttressed these maneuvers by exposing the old system as a corrupt one that outside actors had used to interfere with politics in Egypt.

The officers did not stop their alterations to the political system there. In the years after launching their revolution from above, the military also moved against many other independent political and social organizations, ranging from the Muslim Brotherhood to labor unions. After Mohammad Naguib's brief presidency, Gamal Abdel Nasser became president. Nasser established a highly centralized presidential system with a single political party called the Arab Socialist Union (ASU). While the new regime repressed those trying to remain politically active, the state under Nasser also catered to popular needs. The new rulers did this partly on a symbolic level—by abolishing titles and claiming to be much more egalitarian—but also on a policy level, through measures such as land reform and nationalizations of industries (and eventually by pursuing populist, state-led economic development).

A debate had raged among the Free Officers about what kind of state they should design to assert Egypt's independence in their postcolonial world. While Naguib had favored a return to parliamentary politics, Nasser viewed democracy as inefficient and unhelpful in the quest to economically develop and distance Egypt from the bad old days under colonial rule. Thus Nasser established a presidency that was above checks on its authority from state institutions or ordinary civilians. Nasser also recruited politicians from a terrain that he knew well: the military. Nasser effectively steered Egypt away from democracy in favor of officer rule in Cairo. He tapped his friends from the military to lead ministries and establish redundant intelligence offices. The military became the ultimate source of authority during Nasser's presidency. Indeed, some scholars have claimed that when Abdel Hakim Amer was the minister of defense, he oversaw a military that became "a state within a state." Those civilians willing to do the bidding of Nasser's regime found themselves as ASU heads of labor unions, colleges, universities, and newspapers.

Nasser's single-party state used the ASU as a proxy for filtering loyal followers into service to the state. The ASU was the only party allowed to enter parliament. Although this situation was wholly undemocratic, many Egyptians—especially those not arrested by Nasser's overlapping intelligence agencies—supported Nasser's presidency. He rallied people to his base by arguing for independence from Egypt's previous colonial minders as well as by rhetorically supporting pan-Arab nationalism to unify the region. In practice, when Egypt unified politically with Syria in the short-lived United Arab Republic (1958–1961), Nasser proved that Egypt would always be the central focus of his political attention; Syrians felt fleeced and exploited by the union, prompting their exit.

Nasser's charisma enticed people to his side while his policy priorities provided pride and upward mobility for millions of Egyptians. Nasser nationalized the Suez Canal in 1956 and earned a political victory by withstanding a coordinated military attack by the UK, France, and Israel. His state pursued land reform, which broke up large landowners' holdings and redistributed them to landless tenant farmers. The new president also nationalized all major industrial companies. Nasser oversaw the expansion of education and the widening ability of Egyptians to not only receive a university education but also find employment afterward. Nasser expanded health care as well. Given how Egyptians had been treated by their previous colonial masters, this was a dramatic improvement in their life chances.

As noted above, Nasser was no democrat. His regime contained and crushed labor activism. Citizens who publicly disapproved of Nasser or his policies usually were arrested. Nasser also was wary of mass movements like the Muslim Brotherhood, which he outlawed in 1954. Political repression, land reform, and nationalizations allowed Nasser and his courtiers to sideline the political and economic elites from the pre-1952 era. These practices also facilitated the building of a regime that purportedly championed classes of Egyptians that had been marginalized previously. Indeed, the authoritarian regime Nasser built has been called an inclusive populist regime because of the wide coalition the state propped up.

Nasser died of a heart attack in 1970, just three short years after Egypt's humiliating military defeat to Israel. Millions poured into the streets from Alexandria to Aswan to mourn his passing. He was succeeded by his vice president, Anwar Sadat. Sadat too was a Free Officer from the 1952 intervention, but he was categorically different from

Nasser. He was not nearly as charismatic as Nasser but had a flare for surprising his political opponents. At the outset of Sadat's presidency, the Nasserists who made up the state had him cornered. The ASU was hostile to him. The labor unions were suspicious of him. Even the farmers distrusted Sadat. It was in this context that Sadat launched a "corrective revolution" in May 1971. Sadat argued that Nasser's state had produced a class of people who abused the system for their own gain. He moved against the so-called centers of power in the army, party, and security services. After outfoxing them, he introduced party pluralism to dilute the power of the ASU. Starting in 1976, Egypt had a right, left, and center party. Sadat also tolerated and allowed the reintroduction of the Muslim Brotherhood as a way to counteract the influence of the ASU and the Nasserists. These political maneuvers were accompanied by a movement away from state capitalism to limited economic liberalization.

Sadat's corrective revolution was about sidelining potential rivals. In addition to using party pluralism to dilute the ASU, none of the parties were permitted to have strong or independent leaders or given much room. This effectively left the president as the only voice that mattered in politics. Sadat took over control of the center party and named it the National Democratic Party (NDP). The party was a paean to his personality and reflected his policy preferences. Sadat used these changing governing structures and policies to develop his own base of his rule. He made cronies rich through business opportunities. He enjoyed support from the Brotherhood, which developed mechanisms for delivering social services but did not challenge him politically. Sadat also eliminated most of the military officers—who under Nasser had comprised the central recruiting ground for government ministers—from the cabinet. He attacked the active armed forces with similar vigor. He seemed to reshuffle the military's commanding officers annually during the 1970s. By the end of that decade, the military brass, which had played a major role as political actors, were reduced to superfluous advisers for the president's initiatives. This encouraged loyalty among the military officers toward Sadat personally. One officer who survived this slow-moving transformation of the armed forces was an unthreatening general named Husni Mubarak, whom Sadat designated vice president in 1975.

The combination of shifting policies, alterations to the political system, the emergence of fat-cat businessmen, and the purging of Nasserist allies produced a response from society. Liberalizing economic policies jeopardized the social guarantees of the Nasser presidency. Foreign investment and selective cuts on social spending generated social discontent. Major foreign policy initiatives like unilaterally signing a peace treaty with Israel led citizens to publicly criticize and question the president. Sadat was incensed that the public might question his authority, yet he had created as many enemies inside the political establishment as he had outside of it. The more people started to dissent and criticize him, the more he responded with state repression. During the last years of his presidency (1979–1981), Sadat launched periodic crackdowns against those in the opposition. In the midst of one of those crackdowns, a member of a violent Islamist organization, who was also an army officer, assassinated Sadat in October 1981 during a military parade. If Nasser oversaw inclusive authoritarianism, Sadat introduced exclusive authoritarianism as he signaled that the wide coalition propping up the state would be shaved over time.

Vice President Mubarak assumed office after Sadat's assassination. A career air force officer, Mubarak's presidency would go on to be longer than Nasser's and Sadat's combined. Ruling for nearly thirty years (1981–2011), Mubarak proved to be an able leader who seemed to know when to liberalize and when to crack down. Yet, in the final analysis, the system was unsustainable and produced a revolutionary attempt from a society clamoring to dislodge the repressive order. Mubarak was less polarizing than Sadat, uncharismatic, and is best known for not really innovating anything he inherited from Sadat. He refused to alter the structural design of politics because he was obsessed with amassing as much presidential authority as possible. While more opposition parties were allowed, the judiciary was partially independent, and the media was somewhat more open in the mid-2000s, politics remained the purview of a hegemonic executive—as evidenced by regularly rigged elections. Mubarak's durability hinged on a wide network of regime officials that he consulted with and developed consensus among. His weakness was that he spent so long as a dictator that he lost the ability to directly negotiate with opposition forces. In fact, by the end, Mubarak was downright dismissive of them, suggesting that they did not matter. These deficiencies ended his presidency after demonstrations overwhelmed his security forces and left him unable to stop their protests during the 2011 uprising.

During Mubarak's presidency, an economy dependent on Suez Canal profits, expatriate remittances, tourism, and international aid necessitated state repression to ensure citizen compliance, produce favorable electoral outcomes, and keep the regime afloat. Mubarak proved to be a survivor in terms of navigating regional upheaval and economic shocks, but over time the domestic contradictions bubbled to the surface. The economy never produced enough revenue to improve the life chances of many or most Egyptians. There simply was not enough money to revive Nasserist state-led economic development and its associated social supports. To keep macroeconomic growth going consistent with the neoliberal demands of the international financial institutions (a process Sadat began), the state under Mubarak was forced to repeatedly and selectively privatize its state-owned industries as well as cut subsidies on the staple goods that made the lives of Egyptians possible. The repeated cuts year after year produced an economy of social revolt, where life got incrementally more difficult. The difficulties compounded over time. If and when an uprising would occur was never clear, but Mubarak's presidency spent nearly thirty years pouring kerosene on an already flammable situation.

Before the uprising, the Egyptian political system sported all the aspects of a constitutional and democratic political system—a parliament and a president, both elected by the people, and a judiciary able to ensure that the law is applied fairly. But in practice, regime interference always produced regime-friendly electoral results, constraints on freedom of speech and assembly were omnipresent, and expansive presidential appointive powers created a political environment in which no actor except the president had autonomy or agency. Additionally, the interior ministry's extensive security apparatus surveilled and harassed opposition figures and groups in an attempt to prolong an untenable status quo. By 2009, one in fifty Egyptians was in the employ of the security forces. The system was not as openly authoritarian as under Nasser—some opposition parties were allowed, the press was more open, and the judiciary was more independent—but there was no likelihood that political power would change hands as the result of an election. Furthermore, the notion that political officials would be held accountable to anyone other than the president and his coterie of close advisers was unthinkable.

The 2011 Uprising and Afterward

A national uprising began on January 25, 2011. It brought Egyptians from all over the country into public squares in villages, towns, and cities throughout Egypt. Tahrir Square in Cairo might have developed as the symbol of the uprising, but uprisings against autocracy were in many spaces, including homes, offices, factories, and farms. The demands were simple and clear: more democracy, better economic opportunities, and a redistribution of wealth.

After the 2011 uprising, Egyptians were forced to drink from a poisoned chalice. Egypt had developed a political history that was buttressed by strong, centralized presidential rule. Besides the Muslim Brotherhood, there was no effectively organized opposition that reached into all the corners of the country. While it is conceivable that the protesters could have created lasting movements, this required time that they did not have. The state was the only organization that touched the lives of most Egyptians. The ministries, bureaucracy, and other arms of the state had cloned autocratic logics throughout their operations. All communication led to and from the office of the president. Despite the bravery and tenacity of the protests in 2011, the state and its hierarchies survived the initial disruptions caused by the mobilization.

Yet to say that Mubarak's regime survived intact would be inaccurate. The ruling party, the NDP, dissolved into thin air. The police—initially concerned they would be blamed for the orders they carried out—rebelled. The president's son Gamal, who had been eyeing the presidency for at least a decade, watched his succession chances end as he was carted off to prison on corruption charges. The military leadership, which had been marginalized as political agents since the 1970s, returned to the scene. As shocked by the national uprising as everyone else, the military authored a fiction that it would save the Egyptian revolution and see it through.

The centralized authority of the president was diluted because of the revolutionary protests. The military's high command, the Supreme Council of the Armed Forces (SCAF), forced Mubarak from power on February 11, 2011, and began ruling as an interim governing body. All of the generals on the SCAF were Mubarak appointees. The leader of the SCAF during the transition, Field Marshall Hussein Tantawi, had been referenced in US government documents as "Mubarak's poodle." Tantawi made key appointments, presided over the cabinet, ordered constitutional declarations, and oversaw key decisions about the order of events during the nearly eighteen-month transition.

The SCAF tried to regain control over the state and quell the multiplying demands from society. In so doing it oversaw a violent transition that satisfied none of the protesters' core demands of more democracy, better economic prospects, and a redistribution of wealth. For example, many workers went on strike during the first eighteen days of protest, and their demands increased after Mubarak was ejected from power. The head of SCAF began to speak about the "crisis of the state" and demanded that all special interest protests cease so the wheels of production could turn again. The goal was simple: get people to stop protesting and back into predictable routines so that SCAF could stabilize the political system. The SCAF's most damaging actions were a 6.5-time increase in the use of military trials against civilians in eleven months compared to in Mubarak's nearly thirty-year presidency. The army also oversaw "virginity tests" on female protesters and unleashed tremendous quantities of tear gas, rubber bullets, and live ammunition, in addition to running over protesters with armored personnel vehicles.

The SCAF also used elections to structure a more familiar Mubarakist strategy of governing, which was to pose the question: Do you want us or the Islamists? The SCAF oversaw five national elections between March 2011 and June 2012, which saw the Muslim Brotherhood secure the largest bloc of seats in the upper and lower houses of parliament in addition to winning the presidency. Along the way, revolutionary actors were sidelined and marginalized from the halls of representation as the political system defaulted to a competition between people from the old regime (*feloul,* lodged in SCAF and the state) and the Brotherhood (*ikhwan,* lodged in parliament and the presidency). When the Brotherhood's bloc of nearly 50 percent of the parliament entered the doors of the assembly, its members noticed how weak the body was. The parliament could not check the executive (SCAF), make durable policy, or appoint cabinet ministers. Every law that parliament passed had to be approved by the SCAF. While at first saying it was not interested in the presidency, the Brotherhood changed course when it saw that the generals would not allow a parliamentary democracy to materialize. Mohammad Morsi, a leader within the Brotherhood, won the presidency over a former general close to Mubarak, Ahmed Shafiq, in June 2012. Morsi claimed 51.7 percent of the vote in Egypt's first and only democratic presidential election to date. Many revolutionaries claimed they had to hold their nose and vote for Morsi because they hated Ahmed Shafiq more.

To ensure that Morsi would not govern with institutional support, a court dissolved parliament and the SCAF issued another constitutional declaration that gutted the powers of the presidency. Morsi was forced to govern without a constitution, without a parliament, and from a state apparatus that deeply mistrusted his intentions to govern. The Brotherhood had fought for over eighty years to get near the presidency, and when it arrived, all of the authority had been vacuumed out of the corridors of power. Morsi was a president in name only. The SCAF, the bureaucracy, and the courts began to line up against his ability to exercise power. Morsi realized the system was cornering him, so he tried to respond. Rather than assent to the demands of skeptical voters who hesitatingly had cast their votes for him, he sided with the security forces and military. He tried to placate them. He appealed to their importance. He signaled that he could be their president while throwing the revolutionaries under the proverbial bus. Morsi even let the military reshuffle its leadership as it chose a young general named Abdel Fattah al-Sisi to be the new minister of defense in August 2012. A very tentative pact between the president and the military seemed to be emerging.

With this assurance, Morsi began to act out in ways that hurt his ability to rule. He rammed through a new constitution that the disbanded parliament had worked on without public debate. In November 2012, after helping to broker a cease-fire between Hamas and Israel, Morsi issued a constitutional declaration that tried to streamline decisionmaking in an attempt to offset the fact that the courts had dissolved parliament and SCAF declarations had gutted the authority of the presidency. Morsi's declaration was not popular. It was publicly understood as a power grab by the new president. Morsi began to develop the popular reputation that he was a new pharaoh or an updated Mubarak. Protests erupted against the president in front of the presidential palace in Cairo. Supporters of the Brotherhood made citizen arrests of protesters and in some cases tortured them. If Morsi had a honeymoon with Egyptians, it ended quickly. As the protests began to take place against him, the army began to walk back its support. At one point in December 2012, the new defense minister claimed that Egypt might collapse. The final six months of Morsi's rule were fraught, and as protests increased, mysterious gasoline shortages started to occur (the military supplies the gas) and electrical outages became frequent and sometimes daily occurrences.

By late May 2013, a raucous atmosphere gripped Egypt. A new organization called Tamarrod (Rebel) began to collect petitions for Morsi to step down or hold new elections. Months later, some Tamarrod leaders claimed that military intelligence had organized them and their petition campaign. Tamarrod reportedly amassed over 22 million petitions, but this has never been independently verified. A protest was called for June 30 to force Morsi to step down. The protests on June 30 enjoyed wide coverage from the state media. At one point this media circulated footage of protests across twelve major Egyptian cities. Morsi refused to budge. The following day, Defense Minister Sisi delivered an ultimatum to Morsi to vacate the presidency or face consequences. Morsi balked. On July 3 an organized military coup took place. Bridges and state radio and television were taken over by the army. Helicopters flew over Tahrir Square and dropped Egyptian flags in celebration. Sisi had Morsi arrested on July 3.

Supporters of Morsi, who mostly were members of the Muslim Brotherhood, began sit-ins to demand the release of the elected president. The most famous of these was in Rabaa al-Adawiyya Square in Nasr City. For five weeks, protesters sat in. In the meantime, the state began to kill more and more protesters. Sisi, who had called for a political roadmap to reset the country's politics, appointed a judge as interim president. Sisi took to giving addresses in front of popular rallies where he was clad in his sunglasses and military uniform. He asked for a popular mandate to combat terrorism, which was code for the Muslim Brotherhood. The Brotherhood became dehumanized as citizens. Liberals and the old state practically dared Sisi to crush them. Famous celebrities like Alaa al-Aswani and Bassem Yousef signaled their approval.

On August 14, 2013, the special forces from the military as well as militarized police sealed the exits to Rabaa al-Adwiyya Square and launched a military assault that resulted in the deaths of at least 800 people. The Brotherhood supporters not killed were left seeking refuge in exile or imprisoned in one of Egypt's many newly built prisons. The military calculated that if it launched an attack against the Brotherhood, then it would be improbable that Brotherhood members could return to society as the political opposition. Therefore, the military decided to crush the movement with repression on a much more expansive scale than the crackdowns by Nasser in the 1950s and 1960s.

Egypt drifted for the following year until Sisi decided to retire his military uniform in exchange for a civilian suit. Buttressed by a well-organized and distributed cult of personality that would make any dictator smirk, Sisi ran for president in 2014 and was elected with 97 percent of the vote. Installed by this seeming landslide, Sisi began to govern. He borrowed money and favors from allied Gulf states such as Saudi Arabia, Kuwait, and the United Arab Emirates (UAE). He signed a controversial economic loan package from the IMF in exchange for cutting social subsidies for Egyptians. Egyptian territory in the straits of Tiran was given away to Saudi Arabia, which caused massive protests. Sisi then outlawed all protests. Having run out of Islamists to jail or exile, he turned to civil society activists. People active in the 2011 uprising—from journalists to human rights lawyers to college professors to members of the LGBTQI (lesbian, gay, bisexual, transgender, questioning, intersex) community—all were labeled as threats to the Egyptian regime. Sisi also conducted a war against an insurgency in the Sinai.

Sisi ran for reelection in 2018 and once more won in a landslide. Because the most pliant parliament in Egypt's history abolished term limits for Sisi, he—like Nasser, Sadat, and Mubarak—seems to be set up to be president for life or until another national uprising can dislodge him from office.

Many want to look at this history and suggest that Egypt experienced nearly sixty years of military rule. There was a brief interlude before the generals reassumed what they understand to be their natural right to govern. Yet, as can be seen, the path has not been easy or straightforward. Furthermore, popular protests and social struggle have a way of changing political dynamics. The state that Sisi oversees is not nearly as robust or capable as the one Mubarak ran into the ground. The foundation of the state is narrowed. It remains without a viable ruling party or political opposition. Elections can only be conducted with the money and logistical support of military intelligence. Foreign governments and international financial institutions like the IMF own huge portions of the country's debt. The military, which until 2011 operated a business empire, has been shoved into governing the country from in front of the veil of state power. The military now uses its economic profits to buy allies and cement allegiances. The state sheds its administrative capacities each year. The economic lives of Egyptians continue to deteriorate. None of this suggests that another uprising is inevitable; repression, foreign diplomatic cover, and a bit of luck can keep the generals in power and moving forward. Yet, if another uprising took place tomorrow, few would be surprised. The grievances that animated the 2011 protests have been accentuated and remain present in the lives of all but the globally wealthy. Beyond the military generals, it is unclear who, what, or where constitutes the base of Sisi's regime-in-formation. If Nasser oversaw inclusive autocracy while Sadat and Mubarak managed exclusive authoritarianism, Sisi can only manage to repress the citizenry into acquiescence. Egypt's state has likely never been on such a narrow foundation, nor have state elites wielded more violence, than in the current era.

Government and Opposition

Before the 2011 uprising that ejected Mubarak from the presidency, Egyptians struggled against the strong centralized executive with minor and contained successes. During Mubarak's presidency, three categories of opposition existed: legal opposition parties, a tolerated but illegal opposition group, and a small protest movement.

With respect to legal parties, Egypt had twenty legal parties in addition to the 2.2-million-person ruling NDP. While some parties, such as the Wafd, had long and storied histories, they lacked the abilities or space to serve as formidable or actual opposition. The Wafd might win a handful of parliamentary seats in elections, but it had no street presence beyond its outdated newspaper and run-down party offices. The other legal parties were even weaker. Outside the historic political parties of the Wafd, Nasserists, and Tagammu', around seventeen other minor parties existed. As late as 2005 commentators and newspapers in Egypt referred to all of the opposition parties as "brain dead." Most Egyptians could not even name most of the legal opposition parties. For example, the al-Umma party existed, and one of the core platform issues for al-Umma was to bring back the Ottoman fez hat. When al-Umma ran a presidential candidate against Mubarak in 2005, its candidate Ahmed al-Sabahy was famously asked by a journalist what he would do if he beat Mubarak in the election. He reared back and replied, "God forbid, if I win, I will give the presidency to Mubarak." The legal opposition parties remained a facade or decoration to stand alongside Mubarak's NDP.

There was also an illegal but tolerated opposition group. This was the way people characterized the participation of Egypt's Society of Muslim Brothers. Founded in 1928 by a schoolteacher named Hassan al-Banna, the Muslim Brotherhood was the largest opposition force in Egypt. It had grassroots support around most of the country and remained a mainstream party of the professional middle class. In exchange for being let out of prison by Sadat during the 1970s, the leaders of the Brotherhood agreed to compete for minimal political gains while providing social services in spaces from which the state was withdrawing. During the nearly thirty-year period of Mubarak's presidency, the Brotherhood experienced a revolving door of parliamentary election victories and prison. The high point for the Brotherhood in parliament came in the 2005 elections, when it won 20 percent of the seats in parliament. Yet calling the Brotherhood contentious opposition would be inaccurate. The Brotherhood had internalized the repression of the state as well as the norms of the ruling regime. It was careful not to directly challenge the state and remained in frequent contact with the Mubarak regime's intelligence agencies.

When the 2011 uprising occurred, the Brotherhood did not join the demonstrations at first. Rather, the group waited until Mubarak was vulnerable and joined in to tip the momentum toward the crowds. On January 28, 2011, the Brotherhood sent its ranks out into the streets to join the revolution. In addition, the Brotherhood dispatched teams of people to calm bouts of sectarian strife around the country during and in the immediate aftermath of the uprising. The group played a complicated two-faced game with the protest movement. The Brotherhood did not respect the unorganized protest movement and kept its focus on the military and the shaky regime. After Mubarak's fall protesters were quickly sold out by the Brotherhood, which tried to negotiate with the army over the need for speedy elections (which would favor the Brotherhood). As described earlier, the Brotherhood failed to manage the transition from being the only real political party structure in the country to governing. Prior to the uprising, the group served the Mubarak-run state as a tamed opposition party. Unlike the toothless legal opposition parties, the Muslim Brotherhood actually had substantial grassroots connections and national coverage and support.

The last group of opposition that existed in pre-2011 Egypt was the contentious protest movement. Its contemporary origins date back to the US invasion of Iraq in 2003. While the protests started in relation to foreign affairs, the movement adopted domestic targets shortly thereafter. By December 2004, the Kifaya (Enough!) movement began staging nearly weekly protests. Other groups such as April 6 emerged and tried to cooperate with contentious labor protests, which had increased following the installation of Ahmed Nazif's cabinet in July 2004. The connections did not come easily because labor tends to focus on working conditions rather than view itself as an opposition force for democracy. Still, Egypt experienced more protest incidents between 2004 and 2010 than at any time since the period around World War II. The protest movement differed from the other kinds of opposition because it rejected the norms of the ruling regime. Its leaders rejected the regime's institutions, national media, and police brutality. In a very harsh organizing climate and unable to develop a strategy for effecting political change, the protest movement shifted its demands and group names changed frequently. This group was small but unruly. The routine of engaging in protest normalized protesting. The Mubarak regime would try to surround the mobilizations but not stop them. In some cases, the demonstrations were so small that the government must not have worried about their efficacy. Yet the act of protesting made January 25, 2011, possible.

After the 2011 uprising, political power moved and shifted. Power was redistributed in the fragmenting regime and state as it flowed away from the presidency and other institutions and toward the military. The collapsing status quo enhanced the effect of protests, which expanded in number, frequency, and location in the wake of Mubarak's resignation. With political parties in shambles and the Brotherhood locked in a game of expanding its influence without threatening the military, and with the lines of authority and hierarchy fraying, the military and the police became the arbitrators of repression as they used force and violence to contain the continuing protests.

The deteriorating situation, which was brought on by the SCAF's inability to meet the demands of the protesters, led to a preemptive coup against President Morsi in July 2013. Following the coup, the amount and intensity of state violence increased. Mass killings by the state became a recurring feature of the politics of Egypt while arrests, exiling, and the use of travel bans all spiked to stop another attempt at revolutionary political change. After the accession of General Sisi to the presidency, there has been no opposition to speak of. The Muslim Brotherhood is in disarray while the legal parties have evaporated into thin air. There have been attempts to build Sisi a ruling party, but one has not materialized yet. Protests still happen, but they are rare. For example, in April 2015 thousands marched against Sisi's plan to give two islands of Egyptian sovereign territory to the Kingdom of Saudi Arabia. There were also bread protests in Upper Egypt during 2017. Protests, however, are not serialized as they were during Mubarak's final decade. Furthermore, the number of actions has decreased since the military's coup.

The political climate is dangerous for those organizing protests. This is a response to the extent of repression. The state's violence drives opposition underground and away from public view. This means that it is hard for researchers to assess how much dissent there is against Sisi's government, but it also means that the state cannot see or understand the dissent that is present in Egyptian society. Perhaps more damaging for Egypt's state moving forward is the difficulty in accurately measuring political support because people in repressive contexts frequently lie about their allegiances to prevent a blow from the state's hammering fist.

Prior to the uprising, Mubarak sat atop a rickety but robust state apparatus. He had clear authority over the state's moving parts. The president was supported by a massive ruling party, which decorated its democratic credentials by coexisting with twenty legal opposition parties. The Mubarak regime also was bolstered by the opposition Muslim Brotherhood, which could be counted on to behave in predictable and nonthreatening ways. The protest movement was small but visible. Protesters gave the regime a way to access and understand the dissent of those unwilling or unable to participate in politics through formal institutions. In the wake of the uprising and the tumultuous political transition, Egypt has not upgraded to new authoritarianism or returned to Mubarakism. President Sisi sits atop the weakest state Egypt has seen since the 1952 military intervention. While Sisi can remain president by expanding state repression, the lack of tools like a ruling party, a facade legal opposition, illegal opposition, or a visible contentious protest movement means that Sisi and the state are weak and flimsy. What remains unknowable is if another uprising will happen and when to anticipate its arrival. The 2011 uprising targeted and changed a much stronger state and economy than operates currently, a fact that should keep the military brass awake at night.

Political Economy

When it intervened into politics in July 1952, the Free Officers inherited a colonized economy that was woefully underdeveloped. Outside powers—namely, Britain—had structured Egypt's economy and mainly its cotton industry to help the UK profit. The military officers felt that the existence of too many domestic inputs into policymaking was to blame for not having a cohesive economy. If Egypt was to develop, it needed to streamline its economic objectives. The officers viewed an independent state as the necessary engine of economic growth. Nasser and his colleagues proceeded to merge the state's political field with its economic decisionmaking processes. Over time political considerations would undermine sound economic planning, and Egyptian society would become the victim.

Through state intervention and economic populism, which was popular at this time, the postindependent state began to win followers. State elites nationalized privately owned assets and redistributed land and wealth. New incumbents attacked existing capital holders in the country and handed over the gains to previously marginalized groups. The state pursued land reform, seizing land from large landowners and giving small lots to many landless tenant farmers. State elites also took over factories. This helped them eliminate political rivals that might be independent of them. Income from these assets provided a onetime boon to the state in terms of revenue, which it used to provide social entitlements. For the first time in history, the state in Egypt provided universal health care, free university education, and guaranteed employment for graduates. Public sector employment grew by leaps and bounds. The population became healthier and gained access to medical care unavailable to previous generations. Public schools and universities were full. These policy innovations provided upward mobility for millions of Egyptians despite the repressive political framework.

What had emerged was an unstated political deal: the state would take care of its citizens materially, but there would be no democracy. This bargain allowed Nasser to eliminate political competitors while winning the population's support. One of the outcomes of this approach was that political and economic considerations were combined into one indistinguishable entity that led to and from a strong, centralized executive. Yet after a few years of growth, the state-led economic development model stagnated. Rather than liberalize the economy, Nasser doubled down on the populist experiment. When Nasser died of a heart attack in September 1970, Egypt owed about $6 billion in debts to external creditors. In addition to the debt, there was a capital-accumulation crisis and a chronic imbalance of loan payments. The state-led development model had revealed its tensions and contradictions.

Like Nasser, Sadat prioritized political stability over uncontrolled economic development. Yet, Sadat was uncomfortable with all of the Nasserist politicians who seemed to want to contain his presidency. To break these constraints, Sadat moved Egypt into the US sphere of influence. Sadat wanted US political support and investment. Liberalizing the economy in the direction of a free market system became his plan. In 1974, Sadat launched his Infitah (Open Door) economic liberalization program. The president pursued economic opening with reckless abandon. In January 1977 he shockingly announced the end of government subsidies on staples such as bread. This immediately produced an insurrection from Alexandria to Aswan that lasted three days and nearly ended his presidency. In fact, the military had to reestablish control around the country before Sadat withdrew his declaration. The population's mobilized response to these actions guided economic decisionmaking regarding price controls on gas, bread, and utilities throughout Mubarak's presidency. Sadat also created a group of capitalists who were dependent on his patronage. Egyptians popularly called these businessmen "Fat Cats." Political loyalty became the fastest route to business success.

Sadat's *infitah* policies, coupled with state spending to continue populist commitments (education, health care, etc.), produced a mixed system that was neither state-run nor driven by capitalist principles. This led to a crushing increase in the national debt. In Sadat's eleven years in office, Egypt's debt multiplied fivefold, to $30 billion. The invasion of foreign goods rapidly eclipsed the market for low-quality, locally produced domestic ones. Money fled the country in exchange for foreign goods. Crony capitalists grew fabulously wealthy while the many poor became more impoverished. The professional middle classes also felt the squeeze on all ends as prices and the cost of living went up, Egyptian currency weakened in value, and state support receded. Moreover, Sadat's reforms produced a service-dominated economy rather than an industrial one, while Egypt became a net importer of grain for the first time in history. By the end of the decade, Sadat had signed a peace agreement with Israel and, as a result, was receiving over $2 billion a year in much-needed aid from the United States.

Husni Mubarak inherited Sadat's large external debt and client relationship with the United States. During his first decade in power, Mubarak was extremely cautious about rolling back the social contract for fear of inciting another popular revolt. Despite attempts by the IMF to pressure Egypt to pursue a macro-structural-adjustment package beginning in 1986, Egypt stayed the course as economic stagnation became a way of life for the citizenry. Egypt's debt jumped to $48 billion by 1990. Economists in Egyptian newspapers began to prophecy an endgame for the 1952 state. It was running out of money and favors. Egypt was financially exhausted.

Egypt received a lifeline when Saddam Hussein's Iraq invaded Kuwait in August 1990. When US officials assembled a military coalition to expel Iraqi forces from Kuwait in January 1991, they strongly lobbied Egypt to join the first war after the Cold War. Mubarak agreed to contribute troops to George H. W. Bush's military campaign. In exchange, the US and international financial institutions forgave over half of Egypt's external debt. Mubarak subsequently approved an IMF structural adjustment program in 1991 in order to reorder Egypt's macroeconomic policies. Land reform and tenant laws were reversed, which left many poor farmers excluded from the government's constituency. Union activity and labor rights were reined in, which produced wildcat strikes. Public sector ventures were privatized. Egypt's textile industry lost nearly half its jobs as a result. Nevertheless, Mubarak's economic reforms were not a decisive break from the years of Nasserism or the model Sadat pursued. Rather, the president erred on the side of caution. His prevailing concern was the social unrest that economic disruptions and dislocations might invite, so Mubarak tried to do as little as possible. Thus, before long, economic growth slowed and debt began to creep upward again.

At the beginning of the late Mubarak presidency, Gamal Mubarak persuaded his father to turn over the nation's economic portfolio to him. An investment banker, Gamal introduced a new group of technocrats to address the problems of Egypt's economy. Beginning in June 2004 with a cabinet led by Canadian-trained prime minister Ahmed Nazif, Gamal Mubarak and his group pursued Egypt's most aggressive economic experiment. From a strictly statistical perspective, the policies were a success. Egypt produced a 7 percent annual growth rate and was frequently named one of the World Bank's top reformers between 2005 and 2010. The major international financial institutions declared victory and held up Egypt as a model for others.

Beyond the corridors of the World Bank and IMF, the view from inside Egypt was quite different. The wealth gap expanded radically. Nearly all of the wealth generated by 7 percent annual growth rates concentrated in the wealthiest part of society. There was no trickle-down, despite different ministers spinning promises otherwise. The growing poverty was not lost on anyone. Even the then sitting US ambassador noted in a cable to Washington that 35 to 40 percent of the population lived in intractable poverty. Demonstrations and labor activism grew.

When the attempted revolution began in January 2011, nearly all economic growth stopped. The economy contracted by 4.2 percent during the first quarter of 2011, and Egypt experienced its highest level of unemployment in over a decade. Tourism, which is one of Egypt's highest revenue earners, dried up because of foreign perceptions of political instability. In the transition's first sixteen months, Egypt used up over $21 billion of reserves. The SCAF put all economic policy initiatives on hold.

When it became clear that the elected president from the Muslim Brotherhood was not going to be able to reduce the frequency of protests in Egypt, the military took to the streets to whip up support for a military intervention. Yet, it was not just the local population that had to be on board with the military intervention; the military had to be careful because the United States cannot legally provide aid to a government that overthrows a democratically elected president. The US government has never labeled what occurred in July 2013 as a "coup," and instead stands by its argument that legally the US government does not have to make a determination over what the event was. Bypassing this determination, US aid was temporarily suspended—and then it was resumed. To date, the Egyptian military continues to receive about $1.3 billion in US aid annually. Other countries were less concerned about engaging in bad optics. Days after the 2013 coup, Saudi Arabia, the UAE, and Kuwait contributed lavish amounts of aid that totaled over $12 billion in cash injections to stabilize the country. Egypt has since signed agreements with international financial institutions to secure loans in exchange for deeper cuts to social spending. The Egyptian pound has been floated on the open exchange and in 2016 lost over 50 percent of its value. While macroeconomic indicators have improved slightly, they do not compare to the preuprising growth rate.

Similarly, economic life is not getting better and may very well be the Achilles heel of Sisi's regime, which is still being consolidated. While Sisi faces a number of challenges, the economy is his biggest obstacle. Although the engine for the 2011 uprising was not only economic, the economy and the growing divide between rich and poor provided the environment that allowed the protests to congeal. While the economy might be improving at the margins, the state's fiscal health remains weak. Egypt continues to spend more than it takes in as revenue. While the state's repressive arm has mostly focused on political dissent, force will eventually be needed to help contain the consequences of ongoing economic collapse. For now, especially as seen with bread protests in Upper Egypt in 2017, the state is not exacerbating the situation by using state violence to contain protests over food. Nevertheless, this dynamic is a losing proposition for the Egyptian state. Precarious economic circumstances will continue to require the state to funnel extra resources to shore up the security services, which compounds the problem. This means that while there is more money for security, there is less for providing goods and services for Egyptians, who have no means to sustain themselves or their families. Egypt has never had a president who has been able to develop a plan to address the fiscal weakness of the state.

Civil Society

Unlike some colonized parts of the Global South, Egypt has had a strong and active civil society since the early 1800s. Mohammad Ali's reign (1804–1848) was a period of modernization and statebuilding. Yet because the state was not particularly strong, Egyptians filled the void by starting all types of citizen-led organizations. Over time, civil society's growth in Egypt has flourished during periods when the state either was incapable of policing its growth or allowed space for civil society to expand its reach. On the eve of the 2011 uprising, according to government figures Egypt had over 18,000 registered organizations. Whether in a state of expansion or coerced contraction, Egypt's civil society has acquired a tremendous amount of diversity within it with organizations that are religious, charitable, profession-based, or focused on economic and political development advocacy. Moving between periods of greater and lesser efficacy, civil society is currently being decimated under President Sisi after a brief opening ushered in by the weakening of the state in the wake of the 2011 protests.

Although we tend to think of civil society as a complement to modern governance, Egypt has a long-standing tradition of religious and social organizations working to develop a sense of community and coexistence. Whether religious or profession-based, many formal and informal organizations provided their fellow citizens social or economic services. Civil society organizations founded schools, places to worship and come together, hospitals, or other social infrastructure to build a sense of community. Given that Coptic Christianity and Islam both have traditions of aiding the poor and almsgiving, a tradition of private donations funded many activities over the centuries.

Beginning in the nineteenth century as Egypt began to take on many features of a European state and society, newer kinds of organizations were established. As local elites developed a state structure, the result was that the state acted more autocratically than democratically. Therefore, mimicking their counterparts in Europe, Egyptians (and a small group of expatriates) developed societies to protect and advance their interests. For example, the Greek population established an association in 1827. Egyptians founded a Geographic Association in 1875. The Islamic Philanthropic Association was formed in 1878 and was followed by the Coptic Charitable Efforts Association three years later. Other professional associations were established during the first twenty years of the twentieth century, such as the Lawyers Syndicate in 1912. Organizations that advanced women's rights began to take off in the aftermath of the 1919 uprising, as can be seen in the establishment of the Egyptian Feminist Union by Hoda Shaarawi.

Stepping back to assess the larger pattern, Egypt's liberal phase (1923–1952) proved to be a golden age for Egypt's civil society. With an embattled king, a rambunctious parliament, and the British colonizing hand slowly losing its grip, the 1923 constitution allowed for the establishment of civil society organizations and granted them legal status. The law promised that the state would recognize groups and then refrain from interfering in their operations. Egypt's civil society prospered in this environment. Unions proliferated. Professionals organized guild syndicates to promote their collective interests. Other philanthropic and charity-based organizations emerged. What explains the wide berth given to civil society during this era? The Egyptian state had gained nominal independence from the British in 1922. Britain overtly supported the Egyptian monarch. Thus, the monarch was careful not to repress civil society because he would look like an external agent trying to counter Egyptians' desires for full independence. The monarch and other elites had to let Egyptians organize beyond their control because civil society had monopolized the anticolonial political ground. Egyptians took this opportunity and civil society facilitated political and civic participation. But if Egyptian civil society prospered under British colonial rule through a governing proxy, it would be curtailed after the 1952 military intervention and the ending of British influence.

After the Free Officers captured the state in 1952 and exiled King Farouk, they began to crack down on civil society because they felt it made Egypt too unruly to govern. Nasser and his colleagues saw Egypt as backwards, both politically and economically. They believed that only through top-down political leadership and a disciplined state-centered development program could Egypt develop into a strong independent state on the European model. This did not allow for political dissent. As Nasser implemented his vision, he sought to establish the state's control over civil society. After cracking down on civic organizations during the 1950s, Nasser issued Law 32 of 1964, which placed restrictions on civil organizations' activities and their ability to operate without government interference. The law also granted the executive branch the authority to license new organizations. The state could also close down organizations. The number of civil society organizations dropped dramatically. Some people watched their civic talents get neutralized by being absorbed into the state. Others were left in a suspended state because their organizations were deemed illegal. Organizations that the state deemed as apolitical, or at least not directly a challenge, continued to provide social services. This was mostly in the field of charitable or religious organizations. For nearly five decades, the Egyptian state under Nasser, Sadat, and Mubarak weakened autonomous groups run by ordinary citizens.

Of the three presidencies, Nasser's was the most repressive for civil society. Despite keeping Nasser's Law 32 of 1964 on the books, both Sadat and Mubarak gave more space to civil society—likely because forever shutting down spaces for citizens to contribute is an unwinnable strategy for a state over the long term. Other imperatives also informed opening. Sadat tolerated more civil society freedoms because he was intent on attracting foreign investment, and investors are wary of closed political systems. Furthermore, state repression of civil society rarely kills off organizing; rather, the organizing goes underground and is largely hidden from state elites. Sadat allowed more civil society organizing so that his political apparatus could assess who were potential opponents.

Mubarak was in no position to implement a draconian crackdown. Lawyers, engineers, pharmacists, and doctors were getting more active. Islamists, especially from the Muslim Brotherhood, were winning professional syndicate elections. Given that the Muslim Brotherhood and other charismatic individuals were not allowed to form political parties, they drifted into leadership in the syndicates and other civic groups. If civic leaders were not active in the syndicates, it was not uncommon for them to establish nongovernmental organizations (NGOs) that worked on democracy, human rights, or journalism. Given that establishing political parties was so tightly controlled by the state, people started operating syndicates and NGOs as pseudo political parties. These groups articulated demands over reforming the regime, ending the state of emergency (in place from 1967), expanding speech and assembly protections, and asking for more transparency in national and local elections. It was also common for these groups to take positions on foreign policy issues like the 1991 Gulf War, the Palestinian intifadas, relations with Israel, and the US invasion of Iraq in 2003. Such positions usually broke from the Mubarak government's stated policies.

Mubarak's governments (between 1981 and 2011) existed in a perpetual state of fiscal crisis. They never had enough money to expand services for society despite running a debt that ballooned year after year. This meant civil society organizations largely made up for what the state could not provide. The Mubarak state and its security and intelligence agencies calculated that as long as groups were not "too political," they could provide all the social services they wished. If, however, they crossed over the line of politics, the regime would shutter their offices. An unrelenting economic crisis meant that civil society expanded. In 1986 it was reported that Egypt had 7,593 registered NGOs. By 1999, Egypt had over 16,000 civic organizations. Civil society groups targeted poverty alleviation, unemployment, women's empowerment, street children, professional training, and development. They operated in the open. Other groups formed to work on human rights, education, and policy advocacy. Given the shifting economic terrain, business associations also gained prominence in the late Mubarak period. Civil society became populated by groups that wanted to advance, maintain, or resist the status quo.

Mubarak's regime always seemed to be balancing the different groups and their demands, but he and his intelligence agencies worried that some of these groups were operating beyond their control. One of the persistent demands of civil society was to abolish Nasser's 1964 NGO law. During the late Mubarak period, the state was more interested in fashioning Law 32 into something more restrictive as the state tried to close loopholes for political activism. Law 84 of 2002 thus was enacted to give the state greater control over licenses as well as to grant the state a wider perch from which to shut down organizations it deemed to be too vocal.

Civil society enjoyed a brief period of expansion between the 2011 uprising and the 2013 military coup. Yet civil society organizations proved to have internalized authoritarian habits from the context they had grown up in. For example, many civil society organizations had a prominent personality at their center that ran the organization like an autocratic political party. Therefore, many organizations were neither democratic nor grassroots-based. In addition to this aspect, the groups also compromised their financial operations because they did not invite in the masses to build the organizations together. This left most of these personalized civil society organizations to compete for donor money from Western aid agencies. Under this scenario, donors' programmatic emphases on election monitoring and transparency, women's empowerment, and civic training made these organizations susceptible to the allegation that their groups were set up to grease Western interference into Egyptian affairs.

This is not to say that all civil society organizations operated in this way. A huge number of organizations that formed in the wake of Mubarak's forced resignation tried to fill the role of Egypt's shaky state. With the state in retreat and space emerging for civil society, the turbulent transition let many Egyptians experiment with different groups. For example, when state agents organized mobs of men to separate women and sexually molest them in big crowds like those assembled around Tahrir, ordinary citizens developed mobile phone applications to alert people of problems and erected scaffolding where observers with binoculars watched the crowds in order to protect their ranks.

Any gains made by civil society between 2011 and 2013 have been erased by the presidency of Sisi, which is revealing itself to be the most repressive period for civil society in the history of modern Egypt. Since Sisi's election in 2014, civil society in Egypt has been decimated. In addition to all Islamist organizations being labeled as connected to the Muslim Brotherhood and thus dismantled, the Sisi-led state has cracked down on human rights attorneys, judges' clubs, and women's organizations. In order to lubricate his crackdown, Sisi ratified a new NGO law in 2017. This law, which has eighty-nine different articles, is the most restrictive NGO law in Egypt's history. Rather than force NGOs to register with the relevant government ministry, Sisi has established and appointed the

National Authority for the Regulation of Non-Governmental Foreign Organizations. This allows the executive branch to monitor all foreign and local donor contributions. Furthermore, while the previous law claimed that the state had sixty days to respond to requests or else NGOs were legal, now the law states that the state's failure to respond equals a rejection of an organization's application. Never before have Egyptians had to struggle so much for the basic right to organize beyond the grip of the state. Sisi is cracking down so intently on civil society because he sits atop a weakened state that lacks a wide foundation; a strong civil society thus is seen as a serious political threat. State violence is forcing civil society to change and morph in ways that will likely produce new innovations. These struggles are laying the groundwork for the next phase of state-civil society relations in Egypt. While politics look dire at the moment, Egyptians continue to organize even if we cannot always see the fruits of their labors.

Religion and Politics

Religion—whether it is Sunni Islam or Coptic Christianity—is a prominent feature of Egyptian society. Egyptians tend to be religious and allow popular interpretations of religion to influence social norms. Yet religion is not the main force galvanizing Egyptians to organize politically. While groups do mobilize in the name of religion, few such groups are doing anything beyond using religion to reflect on their broader political priorities—be they economic concerns, ideas about education, or how Egypt should interact with imperial countries.

If one observes Egypt's political trajectory since Nasser, there is an unmistakable trend of religion becoming more prominent in politics. Nasser never referenced his religiosity. It was a private matter for him. Instead, Nasser pushed a strong pan-Arab message predicated on secularism and state-led national development. Sadat introduced religion into the public sphere in more obvious ways and was often photographed praying or sporting a prayer mark on his forehead. He even became known as the pious president. Mubarak played this dynamic in a centrist manner. Around holidays, he would be seen praying at the mosque. But when Islamist groups seemed to challenge him, he portrayed himself as the secular stalwart against an Islamic revolution. Thus, over time, religion has gained social prominence in Egypt, especially compared to the 1950s or 1960s. Yet Egyptian identity is so strong that during moments of upheaval like the 2011 uprising, the protesters were conscious and careful to integrate all religions into a national movement for rights as opposed to pushing for a narrow sectarian state. Most Egyptians are in agreement that religion should play some role in public life. Many would hesitate before claiming they were secularists. The biggest challenges for Egypt since the 1970s have been deciding to what extent religion should be in public life, who interprets the scriptures, and what role non-Muslims should play in this design.

The 1971 constitution claimed that Egypt's state religion is Islam and sharia law serves as the principle for laws—but the state also allows for religious freedom for Coptic Christians. This formula was maintained with the 2011 constitutional declarations as well as the constitution promulgated in 2014. The official role for religion can mainly be seen in personal status law, which allows one's religion to oversee and be responsible for matters of marriage, divorce, and inheritance. Islamic sources of law govern Muslims. The Coptic Church, which has its own pope, oversees these aspects for Christians. Besides personal status, most areas of life are governed by laws that have nothing to do with Islam or Christianity. Rather, the state in Egypt has mimicked European laws (especially France's) in order to develop civil law.

To safeguard itself from opposition groups that would use Islam for political purposes, the Egyptian state co-opted and controlled traditional Islamic institutions. The state under Nasser absorbed Al-Azhar, which is one of the oldest mosque-university hybrids in the world. Hence, it is common for Al-Azhar to weigh in on controversial legislation or social practices. Al-Azhar always takes the position of the president. Furthermore, the state also controls Dar al-Ifta', which was established in the nineteenth century to provide guidance to Egyptian leaders on questions about the law and Islam. Finally, through the Ministry of Religious Endowments, the state can oversee and regulate the many trusts and foundations that are religiously defined in order to maintain control over them. The Egyptian state also promotes official versions of Islam and Coptic Christianity. Students in public schools attend religion classes (there are separate classes for Copts), and state-run television carries religious programming across the country.

What does this mean for the roughly 10 percent of the population that is not Muslim? Egyptian Copts are one of the world's oldest Christian communities in the world. In fact, "Egypt" is related to "Copt" in terms of its etymology. Even though Egyptian Christians can detail with evidence the ways in which the state discriminates against them, few seem to desire a separation of religion from state affairs. From the 1970s until the present, the existing state has allowed Christians religious autonomy. Rather than see religion removed from public life, the Coptic Christian establishment wants to be better represented. During the uprising, Egyptian Copts frequently protested against what they viewed as autocratic practices in the Christian community. There were demonstrations by Coptic Christians that explicitly wanted to democratize the church's hierarchy. These calls fell on ears unwilling to listen or contemplate such demands.

Outside of official, state-sanctioned religion, groups often adopt religious frameworks to participate in politics. Beginning in the 1920s, many groups formed that eschewed secularism as their organizing principle. Given that the colonial powers that parasitically preyed on Egypt advertised themselves as nationalist and secular, some Egyptians were skeptical that national liberation and development could be facilitated by ideas with European origins. Instead, they believed that Egypt would achieve political, social, and economic development by relying on the greatness of Islam as well as Islamic values. The most successful of these societies was the Muslim Brotherhood, which was founded by a schoolteacher in 1928. Hassan Al-Banna felt that a Boy Scouts–type organization could teach young men to be God-fearing, educated, civic-minded, socially conscious, charitable, and physically fit to overcome the challenges facing a developing Egypt. He organized cadres around the country into small blocs that supported one another and educated those around them. Because the Brotherhood hoped to develop Egypt, its organizational framework remained loose in order to accommodate the many forms and activities the group adopted across space and over time. For example, the Brotherhood had a charity wing, provided tutors to university students, organized field trips around the country, emerged as a mass movement, and acted like a political party. While the Brotherhood had a paramilitary unit during the 1940s, so did many groups of all ideological persuasions.

Immediately following the 1952 military intervention, the Brotherhood felt it would play a more constructive role in developing Egypt. Yet Nasser and his colleagues grew suspicious of the group and its many members. The Free Officers refused to allow groups they didn't control to have political autonomy. In 1954, after one of its members was accused of trying to shoot Nasser (a charge the Brotherhood denied), the president declared the Brotherhood illegal and opened a campaign of repression against it. Some Brotherhood members spent nearly twenty years in prison. Others, like Sayyid Qutb, were hanged by the state in 1966.

The situation was dire for the Brotherhood until the arrival of Sadat, whose presidency allowed the Brotherhood space to return to society as long as it did not directly challenge the president's regime. By the time Mubarak became president, the Brotherhood was running candidates for parliament. When Mubarak initially shut this activity down through the use of military trials and prison sentences for leaders, the group got more involved in the syndicates. By the 2000s the Brotherhood began to participate in elections again and won eighty-eight seats, or 20 percent of the People's Assembly, in 2005. Between 2006 and 2010 the Brotherhood was again a target for the Egyptian state, which seemed like it was contemplating a hereditary succession from Husni to Gamal Mubarak. In the wake of the 2011 uprising, the Brotherhood was the most robust civilian institution in the country. It had the largest capacity to reach citizens around the country even if its message was frequently marginalizing to non-Muslims and non-Brotherhood members. The group would win 49 percent of the parliament as well as the presidency before the military coup of 2013. After the coup, the Brotherhood was recast as a social ill and dehumanized. This allowed for a campaign to destroy the Brotherhood, which was largely cheered on by so-called liberals.

While there is a lot of talk about extremist Islamist movements, and Egypt has seen its share of these movements, the overwhelming dominance of the Muslim Brotherhood historically says something important about Egyptians and religion. Egyptians do not mind groups using religion to expand a political presence in society, but they prefer institutional and peaceful means rather than rigid or strict groups willing to engage in violence to bring religion into the public sphere. Although in power for only twelve months, Morsi developed legions of critics. Neither Morsi nor the Brotherhood could commandeer the political system or state after the election. Morsi's bid to expand his authority only elevated the calls for his resignation. For a movement that prided itself on a slow, long march to political power, all of its successes and achievements came crashing down after winning the presidency. After the coup, Sisi tried to liquidate the movement. While Sisi has proven to be an equal opportunity agent for repression, the Brotherhood has been the most prominent target because it was the most organized political force before and after the uprising. Sisi, for his part, has emulated the approaches of both Nasser and Sadat/Mubarak. He has opted for extreme repression against the Brotherhood, while bolstering his Islamic credentials as a pious president whenever he can.

Identity and Politics

Compared to most Arab countries, Egyptians have a cohesive and strong sense of national identity. The early statebuilding project of Mohammad Ali between 1804 and 1848 included constituting an army that integrated people from around the country, thus Egyptians developed a sense of national identity before many of the other countries of the region that formed out of the Ottoman Empire, British colonial rule in the Gulf, or French colonialism in North Africa. Still, the Egypt of the nineteenth century was a diverse place, especially in the urban centers of Cairo and Alexandria. By the time of the collapse of the Ottoman

Empire, Egyptian intellectuals were openly accepting European models of national identity and translating them into Egyptian Arabic. As Britain refused to leave Egypt's political scene for good, more anticolonial sentiment came to the fore and further strengthened Egypt's identity. Schools and universities multiplied, banks proliferated, and large numbers of people debated an independent future.

Egypt is overwhelmingly homogenous with respect to ethnicity and linguistics. While prior to 1952 there were significant minorities such as Italians, Greeks, and Jews in cities such as Cairo or Alexandria, Egyptian law did not apply to them. The different legal treatment, which also extended to Armenians, Lebanese, and others, was a product of a weak, colonized Egypt being forced to capitulate to the dictates of outside powers. The post-1952 Nasserist state could decide to either integrate these minorities or nudge them to depart. Nasser chose the latter, and over time these minorities largely took their leave.

Egyptians had a strong sense of themselves when the military intervention occurred in 1952. The borders were fixed and stable. The country proved to be further along in terms of national political institutions (such as a constitution, a judiciary, and a parliament) than most Arab countries. People were connected to one another in an imagined community. Nasser, surveying the scene and observing decolonization of the Arab world, opted to promote his political development project under an ideology of pan-Arabism. This had a number of advantages. First, pan-Arabism accepted Muslims and non-Muslims alike. If you spoke Arabic and grew up with an Arab civilizational backdrop, Arabism was an expansive tent from which to include people as well as construct a domestic political regime and a foreign policy. Second, Egypt is one of the most homogenous countries in the Middle East. The population is 90 percent Sunni Muslim and 10 percent Coptic Christian. All speak Arabic at home. While there are Shi'ite Muslims or Protestant Christians, their numbers are so small they barely register. What this all means is that Egyptians could develop a strong national identity while also being supportive of a transnational identity frame. Other places, such as Syria, were not as lucky. The borders were not set, the cities of Syria were not necessarily grouped together naturally, and few in the 1940s emphasized their Syrian identity over their Arab identity. In fact, it took Syrian leaders decades to construct a national identity.

The various regions and cities in Egypt do have some different characteristics and popular stereotypes. For example, most Upper Egyptians (Sa'idis) are treated as not as cosmopolitan as those from big cities or the delta. Sa'idis are the butt of innocent jokes. The Sinai has also been historically detached from "mainland" Egypt. In fact, Sisi has battled a violent insurgency in the Sinai. The origins of the troubles in Sinai are Mubarak policies of the early 2000s where the Cairo-based regime funneled as many tourist dollars as possible out of the Sinai to Cairo.

Because everyone can communicate and most share a dominant historical frame about the country, it is easy for Egyptians to know one another and think of themselves as Egyptians first. While Nasser might have injected pan-Arabism into the political sphere, it is fair to claim that pan-Arabism was never deeply adopted by Egyptians, who easily shed this coat in exchange for an Egyptian-centered national identity when pressed by their leaders. This fluidity permitted Sadat to move Egyptians from believing in pan-Arabism to being part of an "Egypt First" campaign during the 1970s. While Nasser had wrapped his development program and his social spending around an ideology seeking to unite Arab states, the 1967 defeat to Israel shattered his program. Nasser spent his last three years as president trying to rein in dissenting institutions like the judiciary or the military. People and bureaucrats saw Nasser's blustering rhetoric as empty despite its achievements, such as nationalizing the Suez Canal in 1956. The famous novelist Naguib Mahfouz even wrote a novel called *Adrift on the Nile* that commented on the failure of Nasserism and pan-Arabism.

Sadat adopted an "Egypt First" ideology in the 1970s. Signs around the country encouraged Egyptians to think of home first. Egyptians shed pan-Arabism easily in favor of Mother Egypt. Ultimately, this allowed Sadat to sign a peace treaty with Israel to get occupied Egyptian lands back while leaving the Palestinians isolated diplomatically as a consequence. This change of emphasis on national identity for Egyptians has remained a mainstay of politics even if some chant pan-Arab slogans at demonstrations. Egypt's strong national identity has been used by Mubarak, Sisi, and the Muslim Brotherhood. In fact, with the exception of Palestine, the Muslim Brotherhood in Egypt is obsessed with Egyptian political, economic, and social development to the point that references to the Islamic nation almost feel perfunctory.

Despite Egypt's stable borders, its linguistic and ethnic homogeneity, and its lack of diversity in terms of religion, there have been growing tensions between Egypt's Muslim and Christian communities in recent years. With religiosity making new inroads into Egyptian society since the 1970s, religious tensions are easier to spot. Something that has grown more frequent over time is sectarian clashes stemming from disagreements between individuals in the Muslim and Christian communities. These clashes tend to disproportionately affect the Christian community. While community leaders in both religions try to find peaceful ways to resolve conflicts, clashes and bombings do occur from things as trivial as rumors about conversations or cross-sectarian romances to disagreements between neighbors. While sectarian clashes do break out between Muslims and Copts, the state has chosen to not criminally prosecute the aggressors. Therefore, there is no legal deterrent to stop future attacks. Instead, the state sends in intelligence and security officials to oversee reconciliation councils, which rarely establish justice or peace between the conflicting parties without a threat of state repression dangling in the air. Thus, for many, particularly in Upper Egypt, sectarian clashes are becoming more routine than in the past. Egypt's laws are clear that Coptic Christians are full citizens. Yet, according to most Coptic Christians, there are obstacles to their ability to fully participate in some sectors of the state or society.

Gender and Politics

Most Egyptian families situate the father as their central figure.[2] Despite this very real nod to patriarchy, vigorous debates—especially over the relationship between the individual and the family and appropriate roles for men and women in society—are constantly taking place. Egyptians from different classes and backgrounds approach such issues in different ways.

The 2014 constitution, like its predecessors in 2012 and 1971, proclaimed the family "as the basis of society" founded on "religion, morality, and patriotism." It also promised that the state would strive to "protect its cohesion and stability, and the consolidation of its values." The preamble also promises gender equality as a principle, though no implementing mechanism is elucidated. Children are taught that the family is most valued in society. Individualism comes after the family's needs. They are raised to respect elders and accept specific roles within the family and society generally. These roles are defined by gender, socioeconomic status, and age. With respect to gender, men and women have expectant sets of rights and duties that are shaped by tradition and religion. For example, husbands are supposed to provide materially for the family's needs, a role that allows them some dominance but also makes it possible for wives to make demands of their husbands. Wives can even seek divorce if the husband is unable or unwilling to fulfill his financial obligations. Extended families are still very strong in Egypt, but one's immediate nuclear family is growing in importance. It is legally permissible for a husband to have more than one wife, though this is rare and there have been attempts to discourage the practice in recent decades. Marriage is a major life milestone for men and women and underscores the importance of the institution and of establishing a family. Financial barriers are making it tougher for young couples to marry, and marriage is being put off later into adulthood.

The urge to get married is being complemented by another rising trend. Divorce in Egypt is on the rise. Since the 1970s several revisions have been made to the personal status code that favor women. The code ended a man's unilateral right to end a marriage as well as his right to take a second wife without the consent of his first wife. It also grants women the right of *khul'*, to divorce the husband after paying financial compensation. The latest statistics reveal that while marriage rates increased by 4.3 percent in December 2017 (compared to the same month in 2016), the divorce rate increased by 6.5 percent. While Muslim women can seek divorces, Coptic women cannot. Even if most women have earned the right to divorce, there are massive risks involved for a woman seeking a definitive separation. For example, a woman is required to return all gifts and presents from the husband. Given that the husband is employed and is the chief breadwinner, this means the wife must hand over assets. A woman seeking a divorce must be prepared to strike out on her own—potentially without housing, money, or a job. While the father would have to take care of any children financially, for many women, to realize a divorce is to give up financial security and social privileges. Divorce does not affect a man's position in society nearly as dramatically as it does a woman's.

Speaking generally about family values and practices in Egypt is difficult. Class, size, educational level, religious values, and geographic origins all structure relationships within the family and produce and replicate gender roles. Among middle-class, poor, and rural families, girls usually do not enjoy treatment equal to that of boys. They might not receive the same levels of education and it appears that girls are less valued than boys. Girls are expected to assume household chores and might even receive less food and medical care. Nationwide, the literacy level is lower among women than men (68.06 percent compared to 83.6 percent in 2015 among the age bracket of fifteen years and older). This percentage is even more disparate in rural areas and in Upper Egypt. Female circumcision is not uncommon as a way to curb female sexual desires, despite the government's attempts to eliminate the practice.

The economic opening that began in the mid-1970s had a major impact on the family unit because liberalization whet Egyptians' appetite for consumption as the cost of living also rose. Fathers sought extra jobs while wives began to work outside the home to increase the family's income. Millions of Egyptian workers, peasants, and middle-class professionals moved to the Gulf states as expatriates because the pay was better than they could earn in Egypt. It became a typical story for an Egyptian family to muddle along as an absentee father stayed away for long years as an expatriate. All these developments have affected the cohesion of the family while the social welfare system has gotten less prominent or was dismantled because state expenditures outpaced revenues each year.

Over the past few decades, women have become increasingly visible in public life. Yet, they are still woefully underrepresented. Women have a constitutional right to receive wages and opportunities equal to those of men. However, in practice, women might not receive the same opportunities. For example, the workforce has been open to women since the 1950s, yet today while women constitute 49 percent of the total population, they represent just over 23 percent of the labor force.

Women won the right to vote and run for parliament in 1956. They entered parliament beginning in 1957 and have assumed cabinet positions since 1963. However, by 2008 during the late Mubarak presidency, there were only two women in the cabinet out of thirty posts. In the 2005 parliamentary elections, the NDP nominated only 6 women out of 444 candidates. The uprising and subsequent military coup has not magically solved this problem, but the situation for women in public life has improved. In the current parliament, women occupy 75 out of the 568 seats in the assembly, which means 14.9 percent of the parliament is female. It is the highest female representation in the parliamentary history of Egypt.

Irrespective of the promises of state elites or constitutions, Egyptian women have had to continuously protest their mistreatment in society. The revolution hardly brought an end to complaints. In fact, the brief two-year window of the uprising and transition produced more women than ever making public claims to rectify their position in society. This came as the number of incidents of sexual harassment and assault ramped up in areas around protests. The breakdown of public security, along with the security forces targeting prominent women wanting revolution, left many Egyptian women realizing that public spaces remain hostile places for them.

The Impact of International Politics

Egypt has always been attractive to foreign powers and conquering imperial armies. Whether for its glorious past (symbolized by pyramids or pharaonic tombs) or contemporary riches or strategic sites (such as its cotton industry or the Suez Canal), Egypt matters to the world. Furthermore, its size as the largest Arab country and its strategic location at the corner of Africa and Asia makes it desirable. Whether Egyptians like it or not, foreigners look to Egypt and take actions that affect domestic politics.

When Nasser came to power in the 1950s, he joined the nonaligned movement and tried to side with neither the Soviet Union nor the

United States, who were making the Cold War a global competition for influence. Yet Nasser's development projects forced him into negotiations with both superpowers over the most favorable terms for loans to help construct the Aswan Dam, which when completed increased the electrification of Egypt and stopped annual floods. While Egypt under Nasser chose the Soviet Union, the Soviets were not intrusive patrons. They provided advisers and assistance but were not as obsessive about political loyalty as the US government is with respect to the conditions that are placed on foreign aid. By the 1970s, however, Sadat had made his intention clear to move Egypt away from the Soviet orbit and into the US one. Since signing the Camp David Peace Treaty with Israel in 1979, Egypt has been a client state of the United States. Not only does the United States treat Egypt as a dumping ground for excess grain, it also allows aid to Egypt to serve as a domestic subsidy on US arms manufacturing. The United States routinely has provided diplomatic cover for whatever autocratic leader occupies the presidential palace. While at times the United States might push Egyptian leaders to undertake various cosmetic reforms, such as multicandidacy presidential elections, rarely has Washington wavered in its support of Egypt under its different leaders, all of whom came out of the military.

During the initial eighteen days of Arab Spring–era protests in early 2011, the Barack Obama administration fought bitterly over a strategy as Mubarak's position became more tenuous. Originally repeating lines about not labeling Mubarak as an autocrat, the argument became focused on what US allies would think if Washington abandoned Mubarak. When it became clear that the Egyptian military was going to force Mubarak to resign, the United States claimed victory, proclaimed its support for democracy, and accepted the actions of the military. There are times when the United States disagrees with what Egyptian politicians are doing yet still galvanizes support behind a general. For example, as momentum built against Morsi in 2013, the United States made it clear that it was more in favor of an early election than a coup. The military launched its coup regardless. The United States then spent five weeks not calling it a coup so that it would not have to suspend Cairo's aid package. In the lead-up to the state massacre at Rabaa al-Adawiyya Square, the United States dispatched negotiators to prevent the killings. Yet Sisi and company did it anyway. Not long after, in a statement issued in Pakistan, Secretary of State John Kerry celebrated the Egyptian military's commitment to safeguarding democracy.

This does not mean the relationship does not continue to change. In the wake of the 2011 uprising, Egypt's regional profile has diminished. Some observers note that Egypt's classic conception of itself as a leader in the African, Arab, and Islamic worlds has not been true since the days of Nasser. This is certainly the case following the uprising. Before the uprising, the United States was largely responsible for protecting Egypt with diplomatic and financial support. Egypt now receives additional, significant financial support from the UAE, Kuwait, and Saudi Arabia. These countries were alarmed when a member of the Muslim Brotherhood was elected president of Egypt; as a result, they have a stake in propping up the Sisi regime. Furthermore, Israel has repeatedly defended Sisi as president. Compared to twenty years ago when Egypt required absolute attention, now it has been bundled together with the most counterrevolutionary states in the region. Once a regional leader with its bold, independent foreign policy, Egypt after the uprising has become a dependent, rentier state. Now other smaller but richer states, as well as its global superpower patron, keep Egypt afloat but weak and dependent.

Notes

1. This section relies on a previous edition of this chapter authored by Nathan Brown, Emad Shahin, and Joshua Stacher.
2. Many ideas in this section, as well as some of the language, appeared in previous editions.

11

Iran

Arang Keshavarzian

In 2017 Iranians participated in multiple political arenas in quick succession. In May, over 41 million Iranians, or over 73 percent of eligible voters, cast ballots in elections for the presidency and local councils. This massive turnout was integral to Hassan Rouhani's reelection and the defeat of the conservative candidate aligned with Ali Khamenei, the Leader of the Islamic republic (Keshavarzian and Sohrabi 2017). For over a week at the end of the year hundreds of Iranians took to the streets of dozens of cities and provincial towns to protest everything from dire economic conditions to the corruption and neglect by the state (Bayat 2018). In rallies that sometimes turned into clashes with security personnel, some chanted "Down with the Dictator" and others mentioned the Pahlavi monarchy nostalgically. Politicians responded by diverting blame and deploying coercion, but other than the deaths of twenty-five people, little was done to address grievances or channel these voices into decisionmaking.

Both before and after these elections and protests, there have been a steady stream of strikes, sit-ins, and gatherings in front of government institutions by highly skilled and semiskilled workers as well as panicked customers whose savings were lost in poorly regulated and bankrupt financial operations. In certain regions farmers chafed under prolonged drought conditions and policies diverting water, and in other locales citizens opposed administrative redistricting that threatened to channel state funds away from their provincial towns. This list of examples can be expanded to include truck drivers, industrial workers, nurses, teachers, pensioners, the unemployed, and women protesting state-imposed veiling.

In short, Iran's 80 million citizens seize political opportunities to both participate in state-sanctioned politics, such as elections and associational life, and carve out channels to express their demands and hold decision-makers to account despite the looming threat of state violence. Iranian politics is anything but static and stable, and this has been the case since the 1979 revolution, which toppled Mohammad Reza Shah (ruled 1941–1979) and in doing so centuries of monarchical rule. The current juncture is particularly volatile since elite rivalries and factionalism have intersected with an admixture of discontent born out of a sense of social injustice on the one hand, and escalating international conflict, spearheaded by the Donald Trump administration and its allies in Saudi Arabia and Israel, on the other. Figures in the US government believe that exerting "maximum pressure" either will force Tehran to the negotiation table to make greater concessions with regard to a range of issues, including its regional policies and its nuclear capabilities, or will generate enough discontent for Iranians to overthrow the regime. While neither may happen, Iranians are experiencing hardship and losing trust in their rulers and state institutions.

Still, the regime has withstood past challenges from more organized opposition and elite-led mobilizations (e.g., the reformist movement from 1997 to 2005 and the Green Movement of 2009). In these cases supporters of the Leader, Ali Khamenei (r. 1989–present), not only have organized rallies but also have deployed targeted repression and indiscriminate violence to fend off political elites calling for institutional reform and social formations challenging state policies. At the same time, these regular political protests expose the contradictions within the Islamic Republic. These aspirations and forces are manifestations of the Islamic Republic's policies and semiauthoritarian structure that have produced an educated, urban population with basic welfare that now clearly is demanding more adequate political representation. Many practices and institutions, such as competitive elections, encourage participation and reflect diversity within the official political class, but at the same time, restrictions exist on the range of views expressed. In addition, the power and resources vested in the office of the Leader detract from the efficacy of popularly elected branches. The limited success of protests illustrates the resources of the regime and organizational weaknesses of oppositional politics. In this chapter, we will explore these matters and place them in their historical and comparative contexts. Hope and frustrations have ebbed and flowed together in the past four decades. This approach reframes the dominant narrative presented by many observers, who treat domestic Iranian politics as a mere sideshow to their own concern over Iran's nuclear program or Washington's continued military threats.

As we have seen in this book, specific histories, geographies, and demographics have often made political and social developments in the Middle East dissimilar from those in other regions. Yet difference does not mean that analytical concepts and political logics are unhelpful in analyzing Iran. In fact, what is often described as the "Persian paradox" or "Persian puzzle" is less perplexing if we study politics in Iran as a product of historical processes and concrete institutions, rather than religious ideology and essential cultural characteristics. For on closer examination, what is striking about Iranian politics is that it is multivocal and malleable—despite the persistence of dictatorship, international conflict, and utopian ideals.

Historical Background and Contemporary Political Structure

For almost four decades Iran has been governed by a regime that is part republic and part "Islamic government," as theorized by Ayatollah Ruhollah Khomeini (1902–1989). As such, it is a radical departure both from Iran's two millennia of monarchy and from centuries of Shi'ite theology, which accepted and even legitimated the temporal powers of the shahs. To fully understand both the magnitude of this discontinuity and the social forces that have molded this polity, one needs to reflect on the historical processes that resulted in the Islamic Republic and persisting battles over it. In Iran, as in many other countries in the developing world, modern politics has been a struggle to create a state that is simultaneously effective and accountable to its citizens.

Contemporary Iran is the successor to a series of empires headed by shahs (kings) who have ruled the Persian plateau for over two millennia. As such, its current boundaries are a product of centuries of battles and negotiations with neighboring powers, including the Ottomans, Moguls, Russians, and British colonial forces in India. While it was one of a handful of non-Western states not to be formally colonized, ironically Iran's independence was due to a compromise between Britain and Russia to maintain it as a buffer between the two great nineteenth-century imperial powers. Thus Iran escaped the more direct and formalized imperialism experienced by Algeria, Egypt, or Iraq but did not escape the influence of great powers on its domestic politics and economy—including Britain's 1901 oil concession.

Another factor that sets Iran apart from much of the region is that the vast majority of Iranians are Shi'ite Muslims. Despite considerable ethnolinguistic and regional diversity, approximately 90 percent of Iranians are Shi'ite (see section on Identity and Politics). Iranians did not adopt Shi'ite Islam in large numbers until after the sixteenth century, when the Safavid dynasty made Shi'ism the official religion and Sunni and non-Muslim Iranians converted to the minority branch of Islam. Over the centuries, Shi'ite clerics were willing to accord the shahs temporal authority and legitimate monarchical rule; meanwhile the clergy maintained educational and legal institutions and sources of revenue that were independent of the royal court. This autonomy from the state allowed politically oriented clerics to periodically participate in politics. So, while Khomeini's assertion that Shi'ite clergy should dislodge lay rulers was radical, the clergy did have a history of parlaying their religious authority into political muscle. An early example of this was the Constitutional Revolution (1905–1911).

The Constitutional Revolution: An Early Salvo Against Absolutism

After a series of military defeats at the hands of the Russians and economic concessions to Europeans, a broad but unwieldy alliance of Iranians challenged the absolutist monarch, who was increasingly viewed as incompetent and unjust. Western-educated and -inspired intellectuals joined the urban mercantile class and some clerics to confront the Shah, who was supported by landed aristocrats and certain high-ranking clerics. In local associations and newspapers, these activists accused the Qajar dynasty (1798–1925) of being unable to defend the nation's interests against British and Russian imperial ambitions and unable to implement the economic and social reforms necessary to achieve equal footing with foreign powers. Iranians began seeing constitutionalism as a means to limit the monarchy's power and improve the quality of citizens' lives. After a series of nationwide protests, the Shah relented and established a parliament (the Majles) and signed the constitution (1906). Yet internal differences within the constitutionalist camp, British and Russian opposition to the movement, and the chaos and misery of World War I colluded to mute the achievements of the constitutionalists. The monarchy gradually wrested powers from the parliament, leaving many social and economic reforms unrealized. Despite these failures, the Constitutional Revolution succeeded in establishing the principles of rule of law and participatory government that continue to be referenced by ordinary citizens today.

Reza Shah: Statebuilding and the Origins of the Pahlavi Monarchy

The Constitutional Revolution may have failed to achieve its objectives, but it succeeded in delegitimizing the Qajar dynasty. As with the collapse of the Ottoman Empire and the establishment of Turkey in the 1920s, a military man, Reza Khan, came to power with the promise of bringing order and development to Iran. After heading a military coup and displacing the Qajars, the coup leader proclaimed himself Shah and founded the Pahlavi dynasty (1925–1979). The primary objectives of

Reza Shah were to centralize power by suppressing powerful landowners, tribal leaders, and clerics, and to monopolize authority in the hands of the expanded army and the nascent bureaucracy in Tehran—while extending the reach of that authority to the frontier lands on Iran's geographic periphery. It was under his direction that, for the first time, Iran had a centralized government with the capacity to commence large-scale projects, such as building railroads and initiating industrialization.

To legitimate his statebuilding the Shah cobbled together an ideology including aspects of nationalism, secularism, and modernism. A national education system and uniform dress code were implemented to fashion a culturally uniform and disciplined citizenry. Iranians and Western intellectuals were recruited to promulgate and instill a partly mythical understanding of pre-Islamic Iranian history that both justified monarchy and privileged Persian language and culture while subordinating non-Persian languages. The powers and social functions of the clergy were restricted through the establishment of state-run courts, schools, and property and marriage registration offices. For the Shah and his advisers, modernization was associated with adopting Western culture as much as with replicating Western industrial models. For instance, it was argued that to modernize Iranians must dress in the same manner as Europeans, and this included a law forbidding women from wearing the veil (this law was repealed by Mohammad Reza Shah).

However, unlike the constitutionalists, Reza Shah did not see accountable government as essential to development and something that should be imported from the West along with factories and fashion. He ruled as a dictator and retained an exclusive grip on power, turning the constitution into a dead letter and the parliament into a rubber stamp. Yet Reza Shah's ability to enhance Iran's independence and curtail foreign interference in its domestic affairs was limited. In fact, his 1921 coup enjoyed the tacit (if not active) support of the British, and in 1941, fearing German aspirations to dominate Iran, the Allied Powers removed him from power and replaced him with his son, Mohammad Reza Pahlavi.

A Parliamentarian Interlude and the Resurrection of Monarchical Modernism

Unlike his father, the young Shah was too inexperienced to suppress political debate and politicians who sought greater accountability from the monarch. From 1941 to 1953, Iran experienced more pluralistic politics, with liberal nationalists, pro-Soviet communists, conservative landlords, and others participating in various ways. Out of this mix, the National Front coalition marshaled the support of old constitutionalists, the emerging educated middle class, and merchants to control the parliament and elect their popular leader, Mohammad Mossadeq, as prime minister in 1951. One of the main issues that galvanized Iranians and endeared Mossadeq to them was his staunch opposition to British control of Iran's oil resources and to Iranians' limited input in the management of the Anglo-Iranian Oil Company (later renamed British Petroleum and BP). Once he became prime minister and the parliament passed a bill nationalizing Iranian oil and redirecting oil profits from the British to the Iranian government, Mossadeq faced British ire. The battle over Iran's oil ended only in 1953 when the newly formed US Central Intelligence Agency (CIA) helped orchestrate a military coup overthrowing Mossadeq and returning Iran to royal autocracy. This marked the CIA's first covert operation (Abrahamian 2013).

The coup was a watershed in Iranian international and domestic politics. After decades of direct and indirect British and Russian interference in Iranian domestic affairs, it was a shock to many Iranians that it was the self-proclaimed anti-imperialist United States that intervened in the most blatant manner. After the coup and during the early Cold War years, the United States and the Shah aligned with one another. Although initially still weak, the Shah presented himself to the United States as a loyal leader of a strategically important frontline state in the struggle against the Soviet Union as well as a protector of US interests in the oil-rich Persian Gulf. In return, the Shah received economic and military assistance and political patronage from the United States. From 1953 to 1960 Iran received $450 million in military aid and $557 million in economic aid to help stabilize the monarchy (Bill 1988: 114); by the oil boom years of "the mid-1970s Iran was spending approximately $5 billion a year on arms and materiel" (Bill 1988: 196). At the governmental level this relationship was mutually beneficial, but within Iranian society the United States and the Shah were seen as two sides of the same dictatorial coin. Over the subsequent quarter century, the mutual dependence between the US government and the Shah only increased and blinded them to Iran's social reality. A half century after the Constitutional Revolution sought to simultaneously build an accountable government and uphold Iranian independence, monarchy reinforced itself through foreign patronage.

The 1953 coup derailed Iran's first meaningful parliamentary government and with it an attempt at creating a competitive party system. Once the Shah returned to power he lost no time suppressing dissident groups, union activists, journalists, and politically active merchants while at the same time placing Mossadeq under house arrest for the rest of his life. In particular, secular political organizations, both liberal and Marxist, were identified as threats and subsequently suppressed and monitored by the regime. In this pursuit, the government initially curried the favor and assistance of clerics, who were equally threatened by these ideologies. Mosques and religious organizations enjoyed greater freedom than did secularly oriented politics in the 1950s and 1960s. This helped set the stage for the development of political Islam in Iran.

Some Iranian intellectuals became disillusioned with liberalism and socialism, for they failed to bring about political change. In response, a small but growing number turned to Islamic thought as a "native" and "authentic" means to challenge dictatorship, negotiate Western cultural influence, and garner greater popular support. Concurrently, in 1963 a little-known cleric, Khomeini, publicly began to criticize the Shah. The next year, his vociferous opposition to the extension of diplomatic immunity to US military personnel led to his arrest, exile, and eventual resettling in the seminaries of southern Iraq. The government silenced Khomeini, but he and his supporters, both inside seminaries and beyond them, did not forsake politics.

The Shah and his advisers, meanwhile, hoped that economic prosperity would dampen demands for political participation and create a social base for the regime. Flush with oil revenue, Iran enjoyed impressive growth rates during the 1960s and 1970s. The Shah developed an elaborate system of patronage to cultivate cronies and consumerism to maintain the acceptance (if not support) of the burgeoning middle class. As in the rest of the region, urban bias spurred large numbers of landless peasants and their children to migrate to the cities in search of employment and opportunities for social mobility. While oil wealth, US aid, and the large development projects of the 1960s and 1970s may not have achieved the "Great Civilization" that the Shah imagined, they did restructure Iranian society. Iran went from being a largely rural, agrarian, and illiterate society in the first half of the twentieth century to one that by the 1970s had a predominantly urban population, an economy that was integrated into a global capitalist economy through oil exports and imports of consumer and industrial goods, and a growing, educated middle class aspiring to enter the industrial and service sectors.

Yet this socioeconomic modernization did not come with parallel "political modernization," or the restructuring of relations between government and the governed through the building of institutions and organizations for articulating and aggregating interests. The Shah would neither accept the formation of independent political parties, trade unions, and professional associations nor tolerate meaningful debate in parliament or the media.

The Revolution of 1979: More Than Islamic

It was unthinkable to the Shah, political activists, and US policymakers that in the midst of economic growth the monarchy would be overthrown by a mass national movement that included liberal democrats, leftists, Islamists, women's rights activists, bureaucrats, laborers, merchants, and students, and that was ultimately led by an elderly cleric (Kurzman 2004). But this is exactly what happened in the course of a little more than a year. By the time the Shah left Iran and Khomeini returned in early 1979, the well-rehearsed alliance of intellectuals, *bazaari* merchants, and politicized seminarians was joined by new social groups such as university students, industrial workers, and the bureaucratic middle class. Some were motivated by economic hardship and political repression, while others were angered by the adulation of all things Western and the disregard of Iran's Islamic culture. Despite dissimilar grievances and goals, these groups realized that coordination would lead to the downfall of monarchy.

This politicization was made possible by the successes of the Shah's modernization policies as much as by the grievances that his authoritarian hubris generated. The building of universities and a large state bureaucracy had created an urban middle class that many aspired to join. Industrialization and consumerism gave birth to a working class and a mercantile class aiming to expand their enterprises and share of profits. State-led secularism simultaneously inspired women who wanted more meaningful gender equality and angered conservative and religious men and women. The Shah produced these new demands, sensibilities, and social constellations, but tried to keep them at bay. Finally, because Iran was a rentier state, it has been argued that the Shah's regime depended on revenue from the world economy and was autonomous from domestic forces (Shambayati 1994). This direct access to revenue left Iran's state institutionally weak and ill-equipped to monitor, incorporate, and bargain with social groups.

The vehicles of the revolution were not opposition parties, for they had been driven underground. Instead, would-be revolutionaries inventively used the limited public space available to transform social venues, such as mosques and poetry readings, into places for gathering, coordination, and protest. In 1978 existing cultural practices were reconceived for the purpose of political dissent. For instance, Middle Easterners of many faiths commemorate the fortieth day after a person's death. These are nonpolitical social rituals. However, when government troops murdered several protesting seminarians in January 1978, political dissidents who regarded the victims as "martyrs" transformed fortieth-day commemorations into political rallies. When troops killed protesters attending these rallies, an opportunity for another commemoration cum political rally took place and a forty-day cycle of protests was unleashed.

The mobilization repertoire was increasingly religiously inflected, but so was the message. Prior to the revolution, Khomeini's theological writings were largely unknown, but his political sermons, captured in pamphlets and on cassette tapes, were brought from Iraq, where he was residing in exile. Borrowing from the normative agenda of popular lay political Islamists such as Ali Shariati and Jalal Al-e Ahmad, who themselves had been influenced by Marxist and other ideas, Khomeini's rhetoric synthesized anti-imperialism and egalitarian messages with a call for political activism and sacrifice that he associated with Shi'ism. In his unforgiving speeches and writings, Khomeini blamed the overly didactic and quiescent clergy, the tyrannical Shah, and imperial forces for exploiting Iran and undermining Islam.

Yet, like all revolutions, Iran's 1979 uprising is too complex a social event to be captured by a single adjective. It has come to be known as the Islamic Revolution because it authored a new utopian regime ruling in the name of Islam and with the mission of creating a just Islamic society. A cleric, Khomeini, became the principal face and spokesperson of this project. However, characterizing the revolution as "Islamic" threatens to misconstrue the motivations of the millions of Iranians who went on strike, marched in rallies, and distributed flyers in opposition to the monarchy. The speedy and relatively bloodless success of the revolution was due to its cross-class and ideological inclusiveness rather than singularity of purpose. Self-professed leftists, nationalists, and constitutionalists from almost all social classes fashioned the revolution. Only a minority of clerics supported the revolution, and many of the high-ranking ayatollahs publicly distanced themselves from Khomeini's political theory of legitimate religious rule. The diversity of actors and political ideologies is important because even after Khomeini and his followers monopolized power (1979–1981), these forces persisted, produced many unintended outcomes, and challenged the ruling elites.

Islamic Republic: A Hybrid Experiment

While the revolutionary coalition agreed that the Shah must go and chanted "freedom, independence, and Islamic republic," it was not entirely clear what these concepts meant, who would define them, and how they would be instituted. In the end, Khomeini and his close associates were able to take advantage of the cleric's charismatic authority, along with their organizational advantage over secular groups, to consolidate power. The seizure of the US embassy (November 1979) and Iraq's invasion (September 1980) were critical junctures that allowed the Khomeinists to suppress opposition voices in the name of national unity and against real and imagined foreign threats. However, more liberal and non-Islamist voices were not quashed until after they were able to leave imprints on the structure of the Islamic Republic.

In his writing in the 1970s, Khomeini rejected republicanism and instead envisioned a system of government headed by a single clerical guardian ("guardianship of the jurisconsult," *velayat-e faqih*) who would ensure that God's will, as reflected in the scripture and interpreted by religious scholars, was fully applied. For the first time in Shi'ism, this ruling jurist, known more commonly as the Leader, would fuse religious and worldly authority. Yet the 1979 constitution married Khomeini's concept of Islamic government with republican principles, which were championed by secular democrats and more liberal Islamists. As such, under the Islamic Republic's constitution, sovereignty belongs to God but is delegated to all humans (Article 3: 8, 57). Executive and legislative power is formally divided between popularly elected branches of government and unelected offices and councils that are entrusted with maintaining the dominion of God and the will of the Leader (see Figure 11.1). After Khomeini's death (1989), the religious standing of the Leader was greatly diminished because his successor's religious stature was markedly less substantial; consequently, the theological premise of overlaying popular sovereignty with clerical representation of God's will became more suspect under Khamenei.

Like democracies, the Islamic Republic includes institutions that allow citizens to participate in making and executing the rules governing their lives. Elections for various offices and levels of government (e.g., the president, parliament, city councils, and Assembly of Experts) are regularly held and—except for the 2009 presidential election—have been largely free of violence and allegations of vote-rigging. Even though only approved candidates can run for office, elections are competitive and often result in surprises, such as when Mohammad Khatami defeated the candidate aligned with the Leader in 1997 and Mahmoud Ahmadinejad defeated Akbar Hashemi-Rafsanjani, a powerful cleric and former president, in 2005. Given the populist and revolutionary roots of the regime and the existence of universal suffrage, voter participation has become an integral means for politicians, factions, and the regime to claim legitimacy. For instance, elections are moments when state-run radio and television call on citizens to be "ever-present in the political arena" and demonstrate their opposition to the "enemies of the Islamic Revolution." In Iran, in contrast to many of the region's countries, voting is encouraged and not thwarted. Indeed, voter participation in Iranian presidential and parliamentary elections is substantial (as high as 85 percent in 2009 and over 72 percent in 2013 and 2017), even if it is uneven over time and across provinces. Iranian elections have been a means for citizens to either punish the establishment by voting incumbents out of office or express displeasure by abstaining and implicitly undermining the popular credentials of the regime (Keshavarzian and Sohrabi 2017). Moreover, parliamentary debates over policies are heated, and criticism of various branches of government is common, with the parliament frequently exercising its power to reject presidential appointments and censure ministers.

Figure 11.1 Structure of Power in the Islamic Republic of Iran

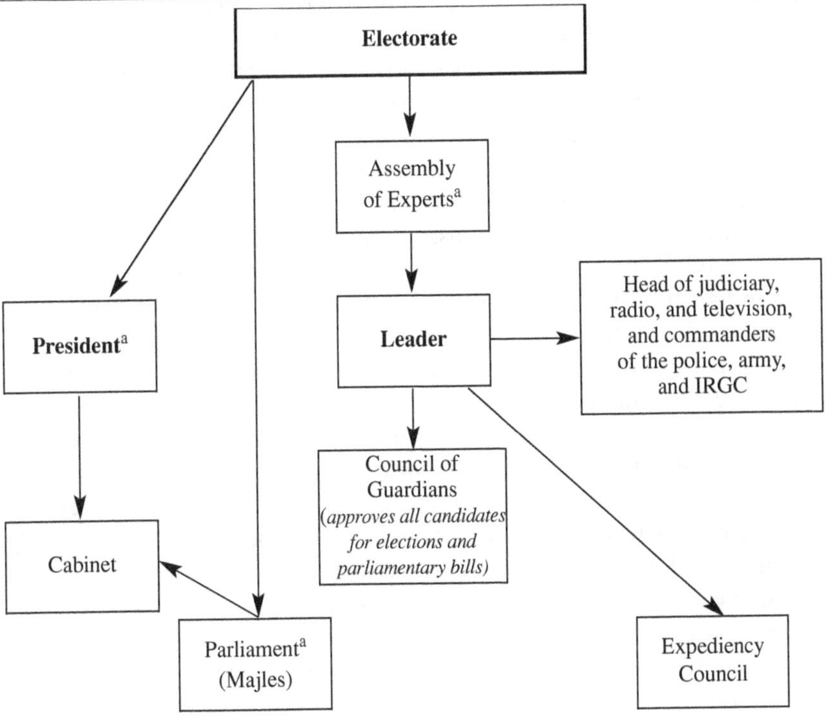

Note: a. Candidates in these elections are vetted by the Council of Guardians.

During the tenures of both Presidents Ahmadinejad (2005–2013) and Rouhani (2013–present), for instance, multiple cabinet members were impeached and several others resigned after public criticism.

However, these democratic practices and institutions are limited by a whole host of mechanisms that mute contestation and meaningful participation. The doctrine of *velayat-e faqih* has come to be defined in personal and absolute terms, wherein the Leader (Khomeini, 1979–1989, and Khamenei, 1989–present) wields extensive supervisory and executive powers.[1] The Leader is not expected to participate in everyday politics and under Khomeini acted as a father figure who remained above political squabbling and factional clashes. Yet the Leader has extensive executive powers to which Khamenei has increasingly resorted. Article 110 of the constitution stipulates that the Leader is authorized to "determine the general policies" of and "supervise over" the regime, declare war and peace as the supreme commander of the armed forces, and appoint and dismiss the heads of the judiciary and the commanders of the Islamic Revolutionary Guard Corps (IRGC) and police forces. While Khomeini's charismatic authority endowed this post with particular power, with the support of conservative allies in other branches of government, the less religiously authoritative Khamenei has also wielded decree powers, for example to sanction negotiations with the United States or publicly and quickly side with Ahmadinejad in the disputed 2009 election. Another critical component is the Leader's discretion over the budget for various religious, cultural, and security organizations, which diminishes oversight by the president and parliament.

In addition, the Leader directly appoints half the members of the Council of Guardians; the remaining six are selected by the parliament from a list of nominees drawn up by the head of the judiciary, who is appointed by the Leader (Article 91). The Council of Guardians is entrusted with two critical responsibilities. First, it reviews all legislation to ensure that it is compatible with Islamic law and the constitution. When the Council of Guardians rejects a parliamentary bill, the legislative dispute is resolved by the Expediency Council, an unelected body composed of all branches of the government, including representatives of the Leader. Second, the Council of Guardians is authorized to supervise presidential and parliamentary elections (Article 99); it uses this approbatory power to vet candidates. In 2018 the powers of the Council of Guardians and Expediency Council were displayed when the Council of Guardians rejected the election of a Zoroastrian member of a city council, but several months later the Expediency Council stepped in and voted to overrule the Council and reinstate the councilman.

Furthermore, despite constitutional protections (Articles 19–42) and claims made by public officials, political and civil rights (e.g., freedoms of assembly, speech, and the press) are routinely violated by administrative regulations and extralegal practices. An opaque court system convicts political activists, journalists, academics, artists, and even members of the government whom hard-liners deem as threats to the regime or their individual interests. These legal and administrative impediments to free and fair political participation are reinforced by the use of targeted violence and indiscriminate intimidation by vigilante squads and a multilayered law enforcement apparatus. These methods were critical in combating the Green Movement that emerged in the wake of the 2009 election and have been deployed again against more recent protests.

The heterogeneity of the revolution laid the foundation for a unique attempt to accommodate God's will and popular sovereignty in a single regime. Simultaneously, Iran is governed by one of the many types of "hybrid regimes" that combine democracy and authoritarianism. The result is that Iran's rulers are not accountable to its citizens, although they can be responsive.

Government and Opposition: Fragmented Ruling Elites, Disjointed Opponents

With its dualism in sovereignty, Iran's hybrid regime is coupled with an equally pervasive fragmentation of power that has led to a contradictory outcome (Keshavarzian 2005). On the one hand, the fragmentation of state institutions makes rivalry and conflict, even among regime supporters, endemic and public. However, the balance of power is such that neither reformers within the state nor opponents in society at large have been able to push through radical changes using social protest or by unifying in order to bargain with hard-liners to extract compromises and usher in regime-led democratization—a phenomenon that has been documented by political scientists studying cases in Latin America and Southern Europe.

The Architecture of Governance and Its Realignments

A patchwork of parallel institutions creates overlapping authorities, competing interests, and checks and balances in the Islamic Republic. In sharp contrast to the highly centralized Pahlavi monarchy, the postrevolutionary state consists of multiple and competing bodies. Below the office of the Leader a disjointed bureaucratic grid persists, engendering elite competition and allowing factionalism to flourish.

For instance, paralleling one another are the army and the IRGC, the Housing Foundation of the Islamic Revolution and the Ministry of Housing and Urban Development, and the Organization for Islamic Propaganda and the Ministry of Culture and Islamic Guidance. The judiciary is composed of myriad courts, with alleged press violations being directed to branches of either the revolutionary court or the press court. Even the power associated with the office of the Leader has been fragmented in the years since it has been occupied by the less religiously qualified and politically powerful successor to Khomeini (Schirazi 1998: 79–80). This constellation of institutions makes it almost impossible for a single ministry to decide and execute policies unilaterally or without criticism from social forces. This elite fragmentation and contestation continued even after the sidelining of reformists after 2005 and the purges after the 2009 election; divisions among the conservatives were exposed and sharpened, creating space for a centrist-reformist alliance to sweep Rouhani to power in 2013.

The origins and persistence of fragmented state structures are rooted in the nature of the revolution and the Shi'ite clergy. The initial creation of parallel bodies was due to the revolutionaries' mistrust of the ancien régime's entities and their decision to hastily create countervailing military, economic, political, and cultural institutions. A strong single party might have added cohesion to this decentralized authoritarianism, as the National Liberation Front did in Algeria. Indeed, the Islamic Republic Party was established shortly after the revolution in order to unify the pro-Khomeini forces against their rivals. Yet the party was unable to create consensus or impose a uniform platform on important issues—let alone mobilize the masses, a task that was left to local Islamic associations, Friday prayer leaders, and revolutionary-era committees. Finally, the absence of a formal ecclesiastic hierarchy and the historical independence of individual Shi'ite clerics from one another have fueled the factionalism (Mottahedeh 1985). Despite initial attempts, the Islamic Republic could not create a centralized chain of command within the clergy to link the minority of clerics working for the state with the aloof majority (Chehabi 1991).

However structurally diffuse, the regime has enjoyed considerable material and ideological resources that have allowed it to withstand domestic and international pressures. For much of the first decade following the revolution, the political establishment enjoyed and manipulated its revolutionary credentials. The mass nature of the revolution allowed the government to claim legitimacy and argue that it represented the entire nation. This position was only amplified by the Iran-Iraq War and US-Iranian conflicts. Given that the revolution and much of twentieth-century Iranian politics sought greater independence from foreign powers, the government welcomed international tension as a means to exhibit its nationalist stature and restrict domestic dissent. The regime also bolstered its social base in the 1980s by expanding state employment and various welfare systems for the poor, veterans, and families of martyrs from the revolution and the war.

However, by the late 1980s this revolutionary and religious rhetoric of solidarity and sacrifice became less compelling to a growing number of Iranians. Khomeini passed away and by definition his charismatic authority ended; he was replaced by Khamenei, who lacked religious stature and political gravitas. The war with Iraq resulted in enormous human and financial costs but did not achieve territorial gain or the removal of Saddam Hussein from power. Meanwhile, a whole host of material concerns such as unemployment, a deteriorating urban and petroleum infrastructure, and international isolation affected Iranians.

Beginning with the 1989 presidential election of Hashemi-Rafsanjani, the political establishment had to resort to more conventional resources to secure support, manage dissent, and demobilize and reintegrate those who fought in the war. Although diminishing in per capita terms, petroleum exports ensured that the security apparatus was funded, regime cadres were cultivated through patronage, and government spending could dampen grievances. Critically, in the first two decades pathways for upward mobility were developed by expanding education and access to health care, subsidizing basic goods (e.g., gasoline), and maintaining employment in the public sector. In this era in which a growing percentage of Iran's population had not experienced the monarchy, revolution, or war, politicians offered new platforms to garner votes and restructure the regime. Hashemi-Rafsanjani rolled back certain cultural restrictions and championed economic liberalism to garner greater support from the urban middle class created after 1979.

It is at this moment that the Islamic Revolutionary Guard Corps, which played a critical role in the eight-year war with Iraq, was encouraged to take a greater role in postwar reconstruction by winning contracts for infrastructural projects. Over time the active and retired IRGC leadership expanded their activities to include banking, telecommunications, and other key sectors. Their age profile and belief that their sacrifices during the war with Iraq entitled them to a greater role in political decisionmaking emboldened them to run for elected office, take ministerial posts, and act as a lobby group with a direct line of communication to the Leader. Thus, their recent political rise is reflective of a generational shift and their key socioeconomic position dating back to the 1990s rather than an organized political rupture.

If the rise of the IRGC represents one trajectory since the 1980s, the reformist movement offers a distinct alternative that also grew within the contours of the regime. In the 1990s intellectuals and technocrats proposed coupling socioeconomic liberalism with deep political reforms designed to curtail the privileges of political oligarchs as well as state enterprises, but preserve the Islamic Republic as a polity. This platform, which attracted independent political voices among university students and secular-oriented intellectuals, helped a liberal-minded cleric, Khatami, win two terms as president while his followers were victorious in parliamentary (2000) and city council (1999) elections. The real limits of reformism were also illustrated during this era when the Leader utilized the judiciary, Council of Guardians, and security apparatus (including the *basij*, a voluntary paramilitary organization) to blunt legislative changes and muzzle reformist newspapers and spokespersons.

With the reformist agenda shackled and given apathy among the reformists' social base, the stage was set for a new and younger conservative current to take center stage. Mahmoud Ahmadinejad came to power through a coalition of support from religious conservatives attracted to his avowed support for the *velayat-e faqih,* junior members of the security-military apparatus produced by the Iran-Iraq War and the conflict with the reformist movement, and members of the working class in urban and provincial areas who gravitated to his anticorruption message and redistributive promises. While both the reformists' message of democratization and Ahmadinejad's populist neoconservativism had their supporters, until recently (and unlike the reformists), the latter also had the personal and institutional support of Khamenei and the coercive might of the state.

Factionalism: The Islamic Republic's Opposition from Within

The original opponents of the Islamic Republic were crushed in a series of purges shortly after the revolution. These democrats, leftists, and liberal Islamists were either imprisoned and executed or driven underground, abroad, or out of politics (Abrahamian 1999). However, the state's fragmented institutions provide opportunities for factional expression and elite regeneration and have yielded a new category of opponents to the regime. Given the limited but real space for participation and competition, opposition to the status quo exists within the regime itself. All chief executives, from reformist president Khatami to hard-line conservative president Ahmadinejad to the centrist president Rouhani, have faced criticisms and challenges from members of parliament (MPs), members of the judiciary, and the media.

Rivalries have formed into factions rather than official and socially embedded parties. By the 1990s these factions were typically described as comprising three main blocs: hard-liners (or conservatives), reformists, and centrists or pragmatists. The first faction tends to support a more authoritarian interpretation of the Islamic Republic, with the Leader enjoying greater power and deference at the expense of elected officials. These self-described "principlists" hold a highly literal understanding of Islamic law to counter those who understand Islam in less legalistic and static terms. The members of the Council of Guardians and judiciary, the current IRGC leadership, and the Leader and his entourage are the core of this camp. While Ahmadinejad emerged out of and was backed by these conservative circles, he fell out of favor over a number of positions he took, including his comments about religion; indeed, he and his associates have been labeled a "deviant current" by most conservatives. Conservativism in Iran is built on the office of the Leader, the military-security apparatus, and clerical supporters of "guardianship of the jurisconsult" in the seminaries and judiciary.

Reformists seek to empower elected institutions, civil society, and a more pluralistic understanding of the regime. They have called for improving relations with Arab and European states, and welcomed greater dialogue with the United States. Members of this camp have impeccable revolutionary credentials; many were among the lay and clerical founders of the regime and even former members of the IRGC. Reformists can also be found among technocrats, independent-minded clerics, and intellectuals seeking to synthesize secular and religious thought. One scholar describes the reformist movement as "post-Islamist": "by embracing a fusion of faith and freedom, religion and rights, post-Islamism transcended the Islamist polity. It called for individual choice, pluralism, and democracy, as well as religious ethics" (Bayat 2007: 55). The conservative backlash during Khatami's second term and under Ahmadinejad consisted of the judiciary and the Council of Guardians clamping down on the press, disqualifying many reformist candidates, and confronting reform-oriented nongovernmental organizations (NGOs) and academics.[2]

During the 2009 election and subsequent protest movement that contested the results, reformist leaders and citizens sympathetic to their platform supported the call for a recount of ballots and questioned the legitimacy of Ahmadinejad's victory (Ehsani, Keshavarzian, and Moruzzi 2009). In the wake of the regime's crackdown on what came to be known as the Green Movement, reformists were imprisoned, put under house arrest, or went into exile, while many organizations associated with this trend were disbanded. After these setbacks reformists have debated how to approach the imperfect electoral process, if they should engage more pragmatic elements among the conservatives, and if they should sequence and prioritize political, social, and economic reforms. In recent years, analysts have wondered aloud if the reformist movement exists in any coherent and meaningful way.

While the 2000s featured intense and often bloody rivalry between reformists and conservatives, since 2009 an amorphous cohort of politicians and technocrats has emerged. They have articulated a centrist platform, building bridges with powerful hard-liners, including the Leader, while adopting some of the vocabulary and policy agenda of reformists. Critical to their objective to "moderate" conflicts within Iran has been the goal of diminishing international tensions. With this in mind, Rouhani and his cabinet spent much time and political capital negotiating a nuclear agreement (Joint Comprehensive Plan of Action, JCPOA), which was signed in 2015. An indication of the popular support for this diplomatic breakthrough was Rouhani's almost 20-percentage-point election victory over a conservative candidate in May 2017. Since then, however, despite monitors repeatedly concluding that Iran has abided by the rules of the agreement, Donald Trump withdrew from the JCPOA and imposed wide-reaching sanctions that have undermined Iran's ability to sell its oil and control its financial system.

These political rivalries are undergoing an unpredictable phase since none of these political blocs has been able to formulate a cohesive plan to move beyond the breakdown of the nuclear deal, the economic and monetary crises created by sanctions and mismanagement, and the plethora of social dissent. Meanwhile, Khamenei has not drawn a clear and consistent agenda, preferring to balance different forces to maintain his superiority. With the Leader aging, Iranian politics is entering a moment of limbo, with many waiting for the impending struggle over succession.

Opposition Outside the Regime

In 1989 when Khomeini passed away, many opponents outside of the regime believed this was an opportunity to seize the state. They were mistaken, as succession proceeded relatively smoothly. The issue of opposition has resurfaced in the contemporary era. Given that the reformist opposition operates within the regime, its oppositional or "outsider" credentials are compromised in the eyes of a politicized society that has been disappointed with the pace and extent of changes to policies and institutions. Yet beyond the boundaries of this elite factionalism, opponents to the regime as a whole have little space or resources to either formulate clear platforms or present them to citizens. Party formation is heavily regulated and not an option for groups unwilling to pledge loyalty to the constitution.

Yet criticism is not something heard only in the privacy of homes or with hushed voices in taxis. Government officials and policies are taken to task in print media, via a plethora of online and social media platforms, and as mentioned earlier, there has been a steady stream of direct actions by citizens. These brave acts have not dislodged Iran's rulers or forced them to share power, but they have made government-opposition relations more polyvocal than is often recognized.

Opposition among Iranian expatriates living in the United States and Europe to date has been limited, disorganized, and unpopular inside Iran. Even so, some US pundits and government officials periodically suggest that these groups (especially those with an ethnic-separatist agenda) can be bolstered to destabilize the regime. Under the Trump administration, monarchists, the Mojahedin-e Khalq (People's Mojahedin Organization of Iran, an armed Marxist-Islamist group that has fought both the Shah's regime and the Islamic Republic), and other expatriate opposition actors have sought to curry favor from Washington and take advantage of political protests and economic hardships in Iran. It is difficult to evaluate how popular they are or may be in the future, but reports of the United States and other governments allocating funds to these groups allow a fearful Islamic Republic to punish any and all critics as traitors and tools of imperialism, with dual-national Iranians often being targeted.

Political Economy: A Mixed Record and Uneven Society

One of the chief criticisms of the Shah was that his policies did not benefit the majority of Iranians. In response, policymakers and activists in the Islamic Republic paid particular attention to human and rural development so as to redistribute resources to a larger share of the population (Harris 2017). Because of this social justice ethos, at least initially the new regime was able to recruit young, idealistic men and women for national and local projects. Many new officials were from humble rural backgrounds, making them more attuned to local needs and giving them local clout.

In terms of basic indicators of literacy, access to health care and clean water, infant and maternal morality, and life expectancy, policies have been impressive—especially considering the Iran-Iraq War, international sanctions and isolation, and declining oil revenue in real terms. Rural areas have been transformed by construction and electrification projects. In the two decades after the revolution, rural roads increased from a total of 8,000 to 59,000 kilometers, while the proportion of villages with access to electricity increased from 6 to 99 percent (Hooglund 2009). These improvements knit rural communities into the national fabric by giving villagers access to urban markets, social service facilities, and television. At the national level, education and health care have seen marked improvements. Literacy rates have continuously risen, by 2014 reaching 90 percent for men over fifteen years old and 80 percent for women, while the gap between sexes has narrowed from 1976 levels, when 48 percent of men over fifteen were literate in comparison to only 25 percent of women. High school and university attendance for both genders has similarly increased. A system of volunteer-led health clinics has helped dramatically reduce maternal and infant mortality while increasing access to cheap and affordable vaccinations and contraception. The combination of improved access to health care and higher levels of education has lowered the fertility rate and dampened economic and political pressures associated with rapid population growth in the 1970s and 1980s. These policies and achievements have garnered support for the Islamic Republic among the middle and lower classes, especially those living outside Tehran.

There are additional burdens and escalating problems, however. This increasingly educated and young society demands greater job opportunities. Yet it faces mounting challenges associated with urban living and global competition, high levels of unemployment, and inflation. International sanctions and the lack of a transparent legal framework threaten to discourage long-term investment in productive sectors, and a lack of job opportunities undermines social welfare gains. Comprehensive and sustained development requires making the state more accountable and Iran's foreign relations less confrontational. Neither has happened; instead strikes, cost-of-living protests, and other social justice–inspired actions have proliferated across the country and especially in some of the provinces and towns that were social bases of support for the revolution, war, and the Islamic Republic.

Changing course is easier said than done, however, for there are profound obstacles to restructuring Iran's economy. The state has been heavily dependent upon oil exports—rather than taxing and borrowing from the domestic economy—for revenue. This has freed politicians from having to confront social classes or borrow from international lending institutions. Yet unlike small-population rentier states such as Kuwait and the United Arab Emirates, whose oil revenue per capita is extremely high, Iran has a much larger population and thus needs to diversify its economy beyond the petroleum sector to generate employment, exports, and revenue. Like most other late-developing countries, Iran first adopted import substitution industrialization (ISI) (1950s–1980s) and later sought to liberalize and privatize its economy (1990s–2000s) as means to achieve development objectives (Ehsani 2009; Khosravi 2017). Nonetheless, there are important caveats to this narrative.

First, the oil boom years (1960s and early 1970s) ensured that Iran could import industrial and commercial goods more freely than ISI regimes could normally manage. This ensured that commercial and service sectors were profitable, with urban consumerism flourishing at the expense of agricultural and industrial production. Each round of oil price hikes has reinforced this dynamic. Politically, it meant that the private commercial community (*bazaari* merchants) has been wealthier and more pivotal in Iran's economy than in Egypt, Turkey, and other large industrializing economies. These resources have made merchants important political actors, as was exhibited in the Islamic Revolution (Keshavarzian 2007).

Second, while many of the economies in the region began to adopt liberalizing economic policies as a response to budget deficits and pressure from international lending agencies in the 1980s, Iran's tight regulation of its economy persisted and even expanded in that decade. Cajoled by a politicized society, the new regime rationed hard currency, set prices for consumer goods, maintained many labor protections, and distributed loans to key sectors of the economy. Policymakers were compelled to increase the state's profile because many industrialists were exiled after 1979, the regime promised to redistribute wealth, international investment had come to a standstill, and the war required the state to direct resources for the front. Ministries, parastatal organizations, and the IRGC took on major roles in production, finance, and commerce. This resulted in multiple, sometimes competing state organizations and institutions becoming involved in the economy. Once the war ended, these vested interests resisted attempts to liberalize policies and break up oligarchies. Thus, neoliberal policy packages were adopted later and more haphazardly than in comparable cases.

Still, economic liberalization was initiated, with regime allies such as members of the IRGC seizing this opportunity to secure government assets and contracts. Higher oil prices since 2003 along with some policy reforms did improve growth rates and benefit certain export-oriented sectors; however, inequality and youth unemployment have persisted, while increased sanctions since 2011, the collapse of the value of the rial, and the restructuring of subsidies have fueled inflation. Meanwhile, to address sanctions-related contingencies or factional rivalries, short-sighted programs devoid of oversight have been initiated that neither address welfare needs nor enhance accountability (Ehsani 2009; Habibi 2014; Salehi-Isfahani 2008, 2015).

International sanctions, spearheaded by the United States, are another factor shaping Iran's political economy. These broad sanctions limit Iran's ability to import goods and technologies essential for manufacturing. Meanwhile, oil exports have been crippled both by lack of foreign investment in petroleum industry infrastructure and by expanding third-party sanctions that discourage companies and countries from importing Iranian crude oil. Additionally, when Iran can export commodities, financial restrictions have resulted in a monetary crisis and the rial losing well over half of its value in 2018. While the lives of ordinary Iranians have deteriorated, it is highly questionable whether sanctions will achieve the goal of influencing regime elites to end the nuclear program or to adopt radically different foreign policies. In fact, regime-aligned businesses have profited from the restricted economy.

Finally, state regulations, international sanctions, and high unemployment have fueled a large informal and quasi-illegal economy, including the smuggling of restricted goods and illicit commodities. This trade is reinforced by sanctions and Iran's proximity to Dubai's commercial hub and to states with porous borders and devastated economies (Iraq, Afghanistan, and the former Soviet Union). The informal economy has provided some income for marginalized people and ensured that Iranians have access to foreign goods, but well-placed agents and middlemen, many of them with connections to state officials, are the primary beneficiaries of this uneven gray economy. This contributes to inequality and undermines the cause of building sustainable development.

Gender and Politics: Battleground for Contending Visions

The contradictions between socioeconomic accomplishments and political limits in the Islamic Republic are strikingly evident when examining gender relations. Policies toward women and the family also reveal much about the shift from the modernist and Western-oriented Pahlavi monarchy to the Islamist and populist Islamic Republic. For the Shah, women needed to be rescued from the "traditionalism" of the clergy and Islam. By reforming marriage and divorce laws and presenting an image of the ideal Iranian woman without a veil and in a miniskirt, the monarchy sought to demonstrate that Iran was "Westernizing" and hence modernizing. Similarly, the founders of the Islamic Republic believed that women needed saving; for them, Western immorality and consumerism were the blights, with women becoming symbols of Islamic authenticity and national independence. At least since Reza Shah's law that forbade the wearing of the veil, Iranian women's bodies and rights have been a battleground between contending visions of the nation and modernity.

The Islamic emancipation of women from "immorality" resulted in dramatic changes in the legal structure after the Islamic Revolution. Based on their patriarchal understanding of Islamic law, lawmakers' working premise has been that women are principally mothers, wives, or daughters, rather than independent citizens. To conform to these gender roles, laws were changed to lower the minimum age of marriage for women, enhance men's powers in divorce and child custody cases, mandate veiling, and allow husbands to deny their wives the ability to travel abroad or work outside the home. This reversal shocked urban, educated women, many of whom had fought for these rights and used them to participate in the labor market, family decisionmaking, and the revolution itself.

Paradoxically, however, this blatant and categorical discrimination against women created a common ground for protest by women, regardless of their political attitudes, age, or religiosity (Kian-Thiébaut 2002). At first defensively, but subsequently proactively, women of different social backgrounds and generations established associations and journals to articulate policy demands as well as women-centered approaches to Islam, law, and development, replacing an earlier discourse of family, loyalty, and responsibility with one about rights, choice, and opportunity (Osanloo 2009). Indeed, Iran's "Islamic feminism" has been one of the areas of dialogue between Iranian and other Muslim intellectuals.

While it would be an exaggeration to say that Iran has developed a powerful women's movement to challenge the forms of institutionalized and societal patriarchy that exist, women activists have enjoyed political power and social presence. As Zhaleh Shaditalab, a university professor and specialist on women's affairs in Iran, reminds us, "In Iran, elections constitute one of the rare occasions when women, half the voters, can determine the fate of men" (in Kian-Thiébaut 2002: 57). This power was exhibited in the electoral victories of reformists, who often highlight many of the concerns of women, as well as the highly visible role played by women in the Green Movement and other protests. At the same time, this does not mean that all women support reformists or that conservative women do not pressure hard-liners and clerics (Sadeghi 2009; Shahrokni 2009).

Still, radical and socially penetrating change via political institutions alone is unlikely. Laws and policies are experienced by women in very different social and economic contexts. For instance, mandatory veiling has been viewed as both oppression and liberation because it operates differently across society. For urban and secular women, the imposition of the veil represents a public and daily instrument for gender segregation and denial of individual choice. However, for women in more religious settings in middle- and lower-class neighborhoods and smaller towns, the veil is not viewed as an alien imposition. Rather, the veil and the "Islamicized public sphere" at least initially helped them participate in society without the admonishments of paternalistic and religious family members and their communities. In the years after the revolution, it became more dubious for fathers, brothers, husbands, and others to tell women that they should not go to university, work, and parks, or ride public transportation, because these were sites of irreligiosity and cultural corruption.

The religious nature of the regime has simultaneously curtailed rights *and* allowed larger numbers of women to access higher education and the job market, which has altered gender roles at large. But as a 2018 government study shows, attitudes toward state policies toward women, and mandatory veiling in particular, have changed. Specifically, unlike earlier decades, the majority of men and women oppose state imposition of dress codes. In recent years, this has been reflected in actions taken by individual women to challenge the laws mandating the wearing of the veil in public and calling for women to have greater control over their bodies and lives.

This new politics of gender relations is built on dramatic sociological shifts. As noted earlier, female illiteracy has dramatically declined. By 1999, an equal number of women and men were enrolled in universities (Kian-Thiébaut 2002: 63). Higher rates of literacy and education have led to Iranian women marrying later and to a declining age gap between husbands and wives (Moruzzi and Sadeghi 2006). These changes, combined with a policy shift in favor of family planning, dramatically reduced the population growth rate in the 1990s. The decline in fertility rates will ease the burden on the state and economy to provide education, health care, and jobs, and it should also affect female labor force participation rates, which have not increased at the same rate as educational achievement (Salehi-Isfahani 2001). Policymakers did not intend to empower women when they implemented education and health programs, but these policies, which have often depended on the active volunteerism of women, seem to have done exactly this (Hoodfar 2009). Today, Iranian women are more educated, marrying later in life, working more outside the home, having fewer children, and struggling to make relationships within marriage more egalitarian. Not only has the behavior of women changed, but so have attitudes of Iranian women and men. Studies show that women desire to work in the labor force (even after marriage) and aspire to greater gender equality in society, in the family, and between husbands and wives (Kurzman 2008; Moaddel and Azadarmaki 2002).

Thus a widening gap has emerged between the legal system's view of women and the self-perception and social reality of women. These social changes and ideological struggles have helped women confront social norms and traditional forms of patriarchy in households. However, women face new challenges, familiar to women around the world: "The decline of formal traditionalism has meant that gender inequality has evolved into specifically modern forms: sexual harassment on the street, gender discrimination in the workplace and sexual double standards in the bedroom. . . . If women no longer experience explicitly patriarchal authority on a daily basis, what they experience is definitely still a 'masculinist' structure of social authority: not necessarily the dominance of the father, but definitely still the preeminence of men" (Moruzzi and Sadeghi 2006: 24).

Religion and Politics: Unexpected Experiences

The Islamic Republic certainly left many of the secular and democratically oriented supporters of the revolution alienated, yet clerics and the pious also have reason to be dissatisfied. For instance, within a year of becoming president, Ahmadinejad closed a Sufi (mystic) lodge in Qom, the city where Khomeini studied and taught. The leader of the revolution himself angered clerics when he ruled that the eating and producing of caviar were permissible under Islamic dietary law, contravening the prevailing view among religious scholars.[3] Given that caviar production and exports are an important sector in the Iranian economy, it seems that once Khomeini took over the reins of the state, profits trumped purity laws. These examples force us to contemplate how religious institutions and practices have fared under political Islamism.

Khomeini's political innovation of cleric-led government has reconfigured "church"-state relations. For instance, job opportunities and income are available to clerics in the judicial system, in the ministries, and as Friday prayer leaders. Clerics and their kin, especially former students of Khomeini, have been prominent in the higher reaches of the regime, yet the actual running of the state has never been monopolized by seminary graduates and their presence has declined since the 1980s. One indication is the decline in the number of clerics in parliament. In the very first parliament, almost half of members were clerics, but by the mid-1990s clerics constituted less than 20 percent of MPs, and in the current parliament the figure is just 6 percent.

The majority of clerics can be found in seminaries, teaching and studying religious texts, and they remain indifferent and even disdainful of their peers employed by the government. In turn, the state has monitored seminaries by dictating curricula, and the Leader has used his office to support seminaries and clerics sympathetic to the concept of the guardianship of the jurisprudent and the regime's interpretations of Islam. In theory there should be no distinction between state and mosque, but in practice they remain apart despite the infusion of seminarians and religion into the state. The state can never be sure that the seminaries are producing "appropriate" clergy for the government or socializing Iranians in the official doctrine.

As the caviar example illustrates, there are tensions between religious law and the practicalities of running a modern nation-state. These conflicts were directly confronted by Khomeini at the end of his life when, after a series of disputes wherein the parliament legislated economic and social policies and the Council of Guardians struck them down in the name of Islamic law, Khomeini amended his doctrine of guardianship of the jurisprudent to allow the state to override religious law when that was deemed expedient.[4] He declared that this "absolute mandate (*velayat-e motlaq*) was the most important of divine commandments and has priority over all derivative divine commandments . . . even over prayer, fasting, and the pilgrimage to Mecca" (Arjomand 1988: 182). Needless to say, most traditionally oriented Muslims and clerics were horrified by this subordination of religion to the interests of the state, as the whole purpose of setting up an Islamic government had been the exact opposite.

Unlike in most of the Middle East, political Islam in contemporary Iran is not a movement of the opposition but rather an ideology and policy agenda of the state. Religious tests exist for college entrance and government positions; gender segregation and mandatory veiling are instituted to maintain "Islamic dignity"; and laws, such as inheritance and criminal law, are based on Islamic doctrine. Official speeches and pronouncements are peppered with religious expressions and quotations, the calendar is full of religious holidays, and religious observance is often public and conspicuous. All of this is in order to "Islamicize" society and ensure that Iranians live in a religiously observant manner.

It is difficult to judge to what extent these policies have made Iranians (more) devout, and the limited available evidence presents a very complicated picture. While most Iranians consider themselves religious and consider religious matters and practices as important aspects of their lives, results from the 2000–2001 World Values Survey suggest many dimensions to religiosity. Based on these results, Iranians are no more "religious" than Jordanians and Egyptians, and along certain dimensions significantly less so (Moaddel and Azadarmaki 2002).

Notably, in comparison to Egypt and Jordan, a larger portion of Iranians self-identify in nationalist terms. Also, while 79 and 60 percent of surveyed Egyptians and Jordanians, respectively, indicated that "religious authorities sufficiently respond to the country's problems," only 47 percent of surveyed Iranians felt this way. When considering the findings from national public opinion polls in the 1970s, we observe that levels of personal religiosity (e.g., frequency of prayer) have remained relatively constant, but participation in organized religion (e.g., attending congregational Friday prayers) has declined, reflecting a growing ambivalence toward state-sponsored public religious practices (Kazemipur and Rezaei 2003). The increasingly urban, educated Iranian society has helped generate new interpretations of faith and new demands on clerics. Religious belief and practice have become more individualized and personalized. This helps explain the popularity of books and lectures on meditation, self-help, and mysticism.

Finally, public opinion research shows that, on average, Iranians who attend communal Friday prayers tend to be less religious than those who do not attend (Tezcür, Azadarmaki, and Bahar 2006). Participation in these public and state-regulated religious events seems to be more an indication of one's political attitudes and approval of the regime than of religiosity. Since the establishment of the Islamic Republic, there also has emerged a class of Iranians that can be described as "politically dissatisfied Islamists." These people are religious and even favor clerical rule and state enforcement of Islamic law and principles, but disapprove of the regime's performance and responsiveness.

This religious disillusionment with the system is reflected in multiple ways: by those who want to strengthen republicanism, by those who want to impose Islam from above more strictly, and by theologians who call for separating "church" and state—not because they advocate secularism per se, but out of concern for personal piety and social morality. For over a century, Muslims have advocated the separation of "church" and state, but they have always been Western-oriented secularists. In Iran, for the first time, religious arguments are being made for this separation, on the grounds that coercively imposed religion harms religious knowledge and spirituality. These types of arguments garnered religious support for the reformist movement and have spurred opposition to hard-liners in the past couple of decades.

Identity and Politics: Inclusions and Exclusions

If clerics and pious Muslims have reasons to criticize the regime's religious policies, it is not surprising that non-Muslims (approximately 2 percent of the total population) have grounds for anxiety. As small communities, Bahais, Christians, Zoroastrians, and Jews have faced long-standing social discrimination and local persecution, with protection being an extension of the will of state leaders rather than legal equality. Yet for centuries these religious minorities have lived and often flourished in Iran, their identities being informed by Persian language and history as they contributed to Iranian culture and society. The Pahlavi regime's secularist policies, emphasis on pre-Islamic history, and close ties with Western governments were reassuring for some in these confessional groups. Non-Muslim elites were more evident in the economic and cultural realms than in state institutions; nonetheless, significant numbers (especially among Armenians) were involved in various political currents, including the 1979 revolution.

As the constitution of the Islamic Republic was being drafted, leaders of the Christian, Zoroastrian, and Jewish communities, in cooperation with sympathetic Shi'ite clerics, were able to acquire certain protections for religious practices and personal matters (Sanasarian 2000). These rights are extended because Muslims consider Islam as emerging out of the same tradition as these religions and believe that these "people of the book" are entitled to protections. Parliament reserves two seats for Armenian Christians and one seat each for Assyrian Christians, Zoroastrians, and Jews. Yet the office of the president and other top posts are reserved for Shi'ite Muslims, the penal code systematically discriminates against non-Muslims, and the law against apostasy threatens death for Muslim converts to other faiths. Iranian Jews, the largest Jewish community in the region outside of Israel, face a particular dilemma. Since its founding the regime has been virulently anti-Israeli, and politicians, such as Ahmadinejad, have questioned the veracity of the Holocaust. Yet public officials are typically careful to draw a distinction between Judaism, which is lauded as part of the Abrahamic tradition, on the one hand, and Zionism as a political ideology of the State of Israel, which is accused of usurping Palestinian land and oppressing Palestinians, on the other. While this critical distinction may have encouraged some Jews to remain in Iran, where they have lived for over two millennia, it also burdens them with demonstrating their loyalty to Iran.

Unlike the "people of the book," the faith of Iran's largest non-Muslim minority, Bahais, is unrecognized as an official religion. The estimated 350,000 Bahais living in Iran have faced discrimination since the emergence of the new faith in the nineteenth century (Brookshaw and Fazel 2008). To Muslims, who believe that Islam is the last revelation, the Bahai faith's belief in a new prophecy is heresy. The Islamic Republic has institutionalized this view, systematically discriminating against Bahais; to this day they may not attend university, for instance.

The treatment of these religious minorities is and should be a concern of Iranians and the international community; however, given that their numbers are small and the populations are not geographically localized, religious sectarianism is not a threat to the territorial integrity or political power of the state. By contrast, ethnolinguistic cleavages and the relatively large Sunni population (8 percent) are potentially politically volatile. Barely over half of Iranians are ethnically Persian. The native tongues of the remainder are Azeri (25 percent), Kurdish (8–9 percent), Arabic (3 percent), and other languages. While there have been instances of localized ethnic conflicts and moments in history when separatist movements have gained traction, what is striking about the Iranian case is the lack of ethnic politicization and protracted conflict that have been common in neighboring Iraq and Turkey.

Several factors have depoliticized ethnic cleavages and enabled Iranian national identity to be inclusive of diversity. As a former empire with a polyglot and culturally diverse population distributed over a diverse territory, Iran and Iranian identity have been constituted by history and land as much as by language and religion. In Persian poetry, mythology, and historical narratives, "Iran" is primarily associated with a land, rather than a language or religion (Kashani-Sabet 1999). Nationalists thus have available to them a conception of Iranian identity that is inclusive of people of different languages, cultures, and religions. Recent historical events also have created a shared mass experience. The Islamic Revolution included and attracted the support of Iranians of all ethnic backgrounds; in fact, Kurds were particularly supportive of overthrowing the monarchy, although this enthusiasm did not lead to collaboration in the construction of the Islamic Republic. Similarly, the eight-year war with Iraq and the wartime experience of hundreds of thousands of young men from all corners of Iran helped reinforce national solidarity and consciousness. The war was also important because it forced the nascent Shi'ite regime to simultaneously adopt a more hybrid nationalism. Given that the majority of Iraqis are Shi'ite,[5] the leaders of the Islamic Republic had to validate the war in the name of Iranian brotherhood and defense of territory, not just Shi'ite unity and duty.

Moreover, the very categories of ethnicity and religion are replete with crosscutting cleavages. While a majority of Kurds in Iran are Sunni (an additional identity setting them apart from the majority), approximately 30 percent are Shi'ite. The central government has recruited Shi'ite Kurds both as a way to reach out to the Kurdish community and as a method of divide and rule. The large Azeri population, meanwhile, is entirely Shi'ite, making religion a bridge with the larger Persian population. In turn, the Azeri population itself is divided geographically across large population centers in Tabriz, Ardebil, and Tehran, with noticeable rivalries and cultural differences existing among them (Chehabi 1997). While the small religious minorities tend to be united, Sunni organization and cooperation face serious challenges, since the population is fragmented into three distinct and geographically distant ethnolinguistic groups—Kurds in the northwest, Baluch in the southeast, and Turkmen in the northeast.

Unlike the Persian-centric brand of nationalism that prevailed under the Pahlavi monarchy, the current regime has initiated state policies recognizing and to some extent accommodating ethnic differences. Persian is the official language, but state law also permits and even financially supports the limited use of local languages and dialects on television, radio, and in the print media, and allows universities to offer a few programs in the study of the Azeri and Kurdish languages. "The ethnic fact is openly acknowledged in Iran, and the central government is more willing than the previous regime to allow the expression of cultural particularism" (Chehabi 1997: 247).

Finally, economic, cultural, military, religious, and political elites increasingly reflect Iran's ethnic heterogeneity. Urban Iranian society is quite mixed, with marriage across ethnic groups common. Many Iranians acknowledge their polyglot and multiregional backgrounds and thus it is relatively unremarkable that the previous mayor of Tehran is believed to be half Kurdish; a former IRGC commander and minister of defense is Arab; and Khamenei, the Leader, was born into an Azeri family.

If multiethnic coexistence is a possibility and ethnic conflict is not inevitable, the reverse is also true. There are forces that lead to greater politicization of ethnic and Shi'ite-Sunni cleavages, as they have at certain moments in the past. First, state policies have exacerbated as well as ameliorated ethnic conflicts. Iranian nationalism under the Pahlavi monarchy was not as virulent as Mustafa Kemal Atatürk's Turkish nationalism or the Baath Party's pan-Arabism, yet it did alienate non-Persians because Persianization was frequently imposed by the strong hand of the state. That resentment was reflected in the rise in the 1940s of Kurdish and Azeri nationalism and the brief creation of Kurdish and Azeri states when Iran was occupied by allied troops at the end of World War II. In the wake of the Islamic Revolution, Kurdish groups openly mobilized for greater autonomy and even independence—only to be brutally suppressed.

The Islamic Republic's privileging of Shi'ism has overlain the existing Sunni-Shi'ite cleavage with the weight of the state. Iran's Sunni population does not have equal access to government jobs, and their religious institutions are treated in a discriminatory manner. The Sunni population in Tehran, for instance, has not received permission to build a Sunni mosque. To date, mobilization in the name of Sunni Islam is limited in Iran, but regional dynamics may change this. The upsurge of sectarianism in the region and the development of transnational

Islamic networks over the past three decades may enable Iranian Sunnis to envision and articulate their grievances in a more sectarian fashion (Ghaffari 2009). Sunni-Shi'ite strife in post–Saddam Hussein Iraq, and Sunni Arab governments speaking of a rising threat from the "Shi'ite crescent," can only embolden those seeking sectarian violence.

These examples also allude to the role of international and cross-border dynamics. Iran's ethnic minorities live mostly in the country's periphery and all have ethnic kin across the border. Thus, Iran's ethnic dynamics are informed by the actions of neighboring states and peoples. For instance, the formation of an independent Azerbaijan, after the collapse of the Soviet Union, strengthened Azeri consciousness and enhanced Iranian Azeris' bargaining power vis-à-vis the central state (Chehabi 1997). Similarly, the emergence of a semi-independent Kurdish region after the 1991 Gulf War and debates about federalism and Kurdish autonomy in post-2003 Iraq have unnerved Iranian officials and may be an inspiration to some Kurds in Iran. With the exception of a few isolated armed attacks, ethnic groups have been either uninterested in or unable to organize popular and resilient parties and militias; political activism has been mostly directed at acquiring greater rights and resources from the state rather than independence. Consequently, the reformist-oriented candidates have been particularly popular in minority regions.

The biggest cause of tension between Persians and non-Persians as well as between Shi'ites and Sunnis is socioeconomic inequality. As detailed earlier, major improvements in rural and socioeconomic development have occurred under the current regime. Yet development, including environmental sustainability, remains highly uneven. For instance, the provinces of Kurdistan and Sistan-Baluchestan, whose populations are largely Kurdish and Baluchi, respectively, have the lowest human development rankings of Iran's twenty-six provinces. The variation in human development across Iran's provinces is closely correlated with government expenditure, thus giving socioeconomic inequality a profoundly political dimension (UNDP and Plan and Budget Organization of the Islamic Republic 1999: 23, 156–157). Given that the central government is composed mostly of Shi'ite Persians, the disparities in rates of literacy, unemployment, and access to health care and education have politicized ethnic difference. Socioeconomic inequality, political strife, and ethnic mobilization are less pronounced in Azeri- and Arab-dominated areas, which enjoy far better standards of living, a fact that reinforces the point that development is critical for ethnic coexistence. In sum, while the Iranian polity has a long way to go to fully integrate its populations as equal citizens, critical social and political steps have been taken to imagine the Iranian community in a more inclusive manner and dampen the prospects of interethnic and sectarian violence.

Civil Society: Potentials and Limits

One of the lessons of both the revolution and contestation under the Islamic Republic is that nongovernmental organizations in civil society can be consequential. Prior to the revolution, formal associations were controlled by the state to recruit clients and co-opt elites and were not the organizations that made the revolution. Instead, a whole host of informal associations operating under the radar of the state were instrumental for social mobilization. Given that the media were restricted and professional associations were dominated by the state, informal gatherings and relations functioned as transmission belts for sharing information and forging social bonds and trust.

Mass participation in the revolution itself strengthened the sense of national engagement in politics. The Iran-Iraq War reinforced the spirit of collective participation, as large numbers of Iranians were recruited to fight and volunteer their professional expertise as doctors, nurses, and cameramen. Occurring so soon after the revolution, the war enabled the regime to redirect the politicization of Iranians away from domestic politics and toward foreign enemies and then reconstruction. Additionally, the regime demobilized civil society by integrating it into the state bureaucracy. The Islamic associations and volunteer organizations (e.g., *basij*) that mushroomed during the revolution and war were gradually transformed from voluntary community-based groups into paid representatives of the Leader (Sadeghi 2009). These "governmental NGOs" were deployed by conservatives against reformists during the backlash against Khatami as well as against protesters after the 2009 election.

While the activities of political parties were limited by the regime, the two-headed nature of sovereignty and fragmented nature of the state created a space for advocacy NGOs to formulate independent views and participate in a nascent public sphere. The majority of these associations focused on various aspects of human rights. The Society for Protection of the Rights of the Child, created by 2003 Nobel Peace Prize winner Shirin Ebadi, is an example of such an initiative among legal activists. Alongside were print media covering politics and social issues from a critical perspective and representing intellectual debates, some of which have facilitated dialogue between secular and religious activists, who previously had been largely uninterested in or wary of one another.

Many of these journalists, lawyers, and activists are young university students and recent graduates. Their energies have helped continue the prerevolutionary tradition of university activism. Student groups have been important in protesting the closure of newspapers and attacks on intellectuals, as well as challenging the privatization of education.

Independent media and NGOs have mobilized voters for reformist and centrist-oriented candidates and helped keep them relevant even after the conservatives shunted many of them out of government during the Ahmadinejad years. While many of their efforts and successes have come in the area of changing the terms of public debate, they have also helped push through modest legal changes, in family and inheritance law for example. These organizations are vulnerable, however, because they are easily prevented from developing horizontal connections across locations or constituencies. This is one of the main reasons why neither civil disobedience nor reformists' electoral victories are able to scale up and translate into political power with which to negotiate with authoritarians in the regime.

The Impact of International Politics: Real and Imagined Fears

Because Iran was not part of the Ottoman Empire, does not have Arabic as its main language, and is majority Shi'ite rather than Sunni Muslim, the country is often treated as distinct from the Middle East. Yet regional forces have been immensely important in the past and present. This is partly related to the movement of people and goods. Economically, Iran has been trading a greater share of goods and services with countries in the Middle East and the rest of Asia than it previously did. Some of this is driven by the economic growth of East Asian economies, but it also is an outcome of sanctions and reflects the desire of Iranian leaders to participate in the world economy without being dependent on Western European and North American economies, as was the case under the Pahlavi monarchy. Additionally, commercial relations have been forged with Dubai's entrepôt economy and the war economies of Iraq and Afghanistan. Alongside this trade, weapons, drugs, and humans have been trafficked to, from, and through Iran. Conflicts in neighboring countries also have resulted in Iran becoming home to one of the largest refugee populations in the world. Finally, ordinary Iranian citizens have turned to new destinations for tourism, pilgrimage, and study. Given tight visa restrictions for travel to Western Europe and North America, vacationers and pilgrims increasingly head to Dubai, Syria, Turkey, China, Malaysia, and Indonesia, only to encounter Iranian businessmen and politicians on their voyages. Contemporary Iran's economy and society hence are more integrated and engaged with regional dynamics than was the case during the Pahlavi era.

Iran's eight-year war with Iraq was arguably as significant as the Islamic Revolution. Its impact was felt most in the war zone along Iran's western border, but the whole society and economy were transformed by an event that mobilized over 2 million Iranians, killed and injured 1 million people, and consumed a substantial share of government resources (Ehsani 1995: 51). Politically, the impact of the war—which was officially termed the "imposed war" or the "sacred defense"—can be summed up as follows: "While the revolution brought a multiplicity of voices, at times emphasizing contradictory aspirations (e.g., submission to Islam and the spiritual leader as well as democracy and freedom), the war offered a univocal venue for both crushing domestic opposition to the newly emerging political order as well as 'sacred defense' against international aggression" (Farhi 2004: 104). Out of the war has emerged a "war generation" of young men and their families who were shaped as much by their experiences at the front as by the revolution. Now that many of these soldiers and IRGC officers are in their fifties and sixties, those who have been politically inclined are demanding a bigger say in national and local politics. Although differences exist, the tendency of these veterans has been to call for more "social order" and a greater state role in providing for lower-class citizens, disproportionately large numbers of whom volunteered for the war. Even though the war generation is divided politically and economically, conservatives claim to represent a large portion of this constituency by valorizing them and their sacrifices.

Since the Arab uprisings, Tehran has tried to position itself in the shifting regional terrain by helping allies stay in power and championing insurrections against other governments it has viewed as foes (Bajoghli and Keshavarzian 2017). Most significant has been Iran's military and financial support for the ruling Baath Party in Syria. Indirectly and with advisers at first and subsequently more overtly after the civil war began to rage, the IRGC has helped train Bashar al-Asad's forces, sent its own troops, and coordinated various militias drawn from Lebanon, Afghanistan, and Iraq to bolster Asad as he faced his own people's demands for revolution and armed groups funded by Turkey, Saudi Arabia, Qatar, the United Arab Emirates, and the United States. This bloody intervention may have helped prop up one of the few Arab regimes aligned with the Islamic Republic and defeat the Islamic State in Iraq and Syria (ISIS), but it has left Iran's decisionmakers open to criticism at home, with Iranians asking why resources are spent in foreign lands at a time when many Iranians face economic hardship.

Yet when one thinks of Iran and international relations, one thinks primarily of international geopolitics, and for over half a century this has meant US-Iran relations. From the Shah to Rouhani, from barely literate shopkeepers to ivy league–trained engineers, Iranians believe that politics in Iran can be and is altered by decisions made beyond its borders and by politicians not their own. Like most societal phobias, it is based on fact and disempowerment. As this chapter's introductory discussion of twentieth-century Iran illustrates, the facts are clear. British, Russian, and US intrigues and interests have repeatedly influenced Iranian domestic politics. Foreign forces have been involved in the toppling of rulers (e.g., Reza Shah in 1941 and Prime Minister Mossadeq in

1953) and have undermined the development of pluralism and democracy. Economically, international interests have often impinged on Iran's independence and access to technology (e.g., railroads, telegraph, and nuclear technology). Hence the Iranian government's argument that Iran has "a right to nuclear technology" resonates with much of Iranian society. International politics has not only undermined and destabilized regimes in Iran, but it has also helped strengthen them, as was the case with US patronage of the Shah after 1953 and the 1980 Iraqi invasion and the consolidation of Khomeinists in Tehran. US foreign policy was so important that when the administration of Jimmy Carter called for greater human rights in Iran, both the Shah and political dissidents believed that the US government had turned against the regime.

The US approach to the Islamic Republic since 1979 has been bellicose and confrontational in part because of the 1979–1980 taking of the US embassy in Tehran. But US policies enable regime leaders to call for unity and smother criticism. For instance, the authoritarian backlash against the reformist movement was bolstered by the US government's decisions to invade two of Iran's neighbors (Afghanistan and Iraq), include Iran in the "axis of evil," expand economic sanctions, and threaten military action. Iranian politicians have used these US actions to deflect attention away from their responsibilities and accuse all critics of being instruments of US imperial ambition. This has often been the response of conservative spokespersons to the social justice protests of recent years. Thus, while the military and security sector is bolstered, Iranian journalists, activists, and academic researchers have all been targeted with accusations of treason. The reality and fear of foreign meddling in Iran's domestic affairs not only enhance Iranians' sense of vulnerability vis-à-vis more powerful foreign states but also are used by autocrats to actually disempower Iran's polity.

Notes

1. The Leader is selected by the Assembly of Experts, which is a popularly elected chamber of clerics with ten-year terms. In theory, the Assembly of Experts is more powerful than the Leader, since it elects him and has the power to dismiss him if it deems the Leader incapable of fulfilling his role. Yet in practice the Assembly of Experts is beholden to the Leader, since candidates for the assembly are themselves subject to the approval of the Council of Guardians, whose members are in large part chosen by the Leader.

2. From 1997 to 2002 the courts banned 108 daily newspapers and periodicals, and from 2000 to 2003 the Council of Guardians vetoed over fifty parliamentary bills (Bayat 2007: 120, 123).

3. According to Shi'ite (and Jewish) dietary laws, fish must have scales in order to be eaten. Yet caviar is the roe from sturgeon, which have no scales.

4. This ultimately led to the creation of the Expediency Council, which is mandated to resolve disputes between parliament and the Council of Guardians. It is unelected and consists of members from various branches of government and representatives of the Leader.

5. Given that Saddam Hussein and many of the leading members of the Baath Party were Sunni, Shi'ite iconography and history were integral to the Iranian government's war effort.

12
Iraq

Fred H. Lawson

Iraqi politics have displayed a high degree of turbulence for more than half a century. Iraq as it exists in its current borders came into being at the end of World War I, as a British-controlled monarchy under a mandate from the League of Nations. After independence in 1932, Iraqi politics involved intense rivalry between conservative elites who dominated the electoral system and an assortment of more radical parties and movements that pushed for fundamental change. These tensions culminated in a military-led uprising in July 1958 that brought down the monarchy. After that time, Iraq endured forty-five years of authoritarian rule, sometimes headed by a single individual—usually a military commander—and at other times by collective leaderships governing in the name of the Socialist Arab Renaissance (Baath) Party.

Historical Background and Contemporary Political Structure

Iraq's 1958 revolution was orchestrated by a cluster of military officers who soon fell out with one another, ushering in years of bloody skirmishing among factions of the armed forces, Communists, Muslim Brothers, oil workers, farm laborers, and students. Indeed, the decade between 1958 and 1968 was one of extreme instability until the Baath Party was able to consolidate power.

According to the terms of the September 1968 constitution, executive and legislative authority was vested in the Revolution Command Council (RCC), which was led at the time by President Ahmad Hasan al-Bakr and the commander in chief of the armed forces, Hardan al-Takriti. The RCC was reconfigured in early 1969 to replace military officers with senior figures in the Baath Party's security forces. The new council installed party commissars at all levels of the armed forces to instill loyalty to Baathi principles and keep track of potential dissidents (Hashim 2003: 23). After an attempted coup d'état in June 1973, President al-Bakr took charge of the ministry of defense and subordinated the military's intelligence branches to the Baath Party's security apparatus. A month later, the RCC reached an agreement with the Iraqi Communist Party, which authorized Baathi cadres to take over the country's workers', students', and women's unions.

In January 1976, the head of the Baath Party security apparatus, Saddam Hussein (a cousin of President al-Bakr), was awarded the rank of general, despite having no previous military experience. The Baath Party militia doubled in size; under its new name, the People's Militia, it was placed under the command of a protégé of Saddam Hussein, Taha Yasin Ramadan. The party and its security forces then initiated a drive to impose Baathi ideology and forms of organization on the country's major institutions, most notably university campuses.

Immediately after acceding to the presidency in 1979, Saddam Hussein purged the RCC of rivals. The resulting body consisted entirely of longtime colleagues and relatives of the new president. In March 1980, Saddam Hussein issued a law that created a 250-member National Assembly. The first elections took place that June and resulted in an overwhelming victory for Baath Party candidates (Baram 1981). In September 1980 Iraq invaded Iran (then in the throes of its Islamic revolution), kicking off a bloody eight-year war that cost Iraq dearly in terms of blood and treasure without netting it any territorial gain.

With the war against Iran winding down, Saddam Hussein and his allies in August 1988 purged the armed forces of all commanders who showed any sign of disloyalty (Hashim 2003: 20). As part of the postwar reconstruction effort, a new ministry of industry and military industrialization was created and placed in the hands of the president's son-in-law, Husain Kamil al-Majid. The ministry was given charge over the state-run petrochemical sector, which provided it with revenues to carry out a variety of industrial and infrastructure projects. Nevertheless, the local economy continued to stagger, prompting the RCC to loosen restrictions on elections to the National Assembly. In the April 1989 balloting, independent candidates were permitted to run for the first time.

Iraq's occupation of Kuwait in August 1990 tightened the hold of the president and his closest allies over the political system. The elite Republican Guard and Baath Party security forces crushed popular uprisings that erupted in March 1991. Thereafter, national politics became a family affair. One half-brother of Saddam Hussein was minister of the interior; another half-brother headed the security directorate; a cousin took over as minister of defense; al-Majid remained in his post; and another son-in-law commanded a key security force. Another security agency was put in the hands of the president's younger son, Qusai. The older son, 'Udai, became minister of information, youth, and sport.

On a number of occasions after the 1990–1991 Gulf War, discontented military officers tried to overthrow Saddam Hussein. In retaliation, the Republican Guard was purged in the summer of 1995 and command was given to the president's cousin Kamal Mustafa Al Bu Sultan. Saddam Hussein's son 'Udai was severely injured in an assassination attempt in December 1996, and an attack on Qusai took place in early 1997. Nevertheless, in 2000 the president announced that Qusai would act as caretaker president in the event that he became incapacitated. In April 2001, Qusai was elected to a seat in the Regional (Iraqi) Command of the Baath Party.

As United Nations (UN) economic sanctions weakened the central administration during the late 1990s, the Baath Party apparatus distributed food and other vital goods to the population. Ration coupons issued by the party became the primary means whereby citizens acquired staples. Still, party membership dropped precipitously. The regime then turned to tribal leaders (shaikhs) to administer local affairs (Baram 1997). The shaikhs maintained public order and collected taxes in urban neighborhoods and rural districts, which were officially designated "tribal areas." Representatives of the shaikhs dominated the National Assembly after the March 2000 elections.

In April 2003, the Baathi regime led by Saddam Hussein collapsed in the face of a massive military assault orchestrated by the United States and United Kingdom. The Coalition Provisional Authority (CPA), which took charge of the country's southern and central provinces, immediately dismantled Iraq's regular armed forces and internal security apparatus and prohibited Baath Party members from holding positions in the administration and state-run economic enterprises. The CPA relied instead on a loose collection of political movements known as the Iraqi National Congress (INC) to govern the country. The INC formed the core of the Iraqi Governing Council (IGC) that was set up by the CPA in July 2003, along with an assortment of liberal democratic parties, the Iraqi Communist Party, the Kurdistan Democratic Party (KDP), the Patriotic Union of Kurdistan (PUK), and two predominantly Shi'i organizations that had long opposed the Baathi regime: the Supreme Council for Islamic Revolution in Iraq (SCIRI) and the Party of the Call to Islam.

Within weeks it became clear that the IGC was fatally tainted by its links to the CPA. The most prestigious figure in the country's Shi'i religious hierarchy, Grand Ayatollah 'Ali al-Sistani, demanded that the IGC be replaced by local leadership and that an elected assembly draw up a new constitution for the post-Baathi era. Opposition to the IGC at the same time spread among the Sunni population and resulted in the formation of the militant Association of Muslim Scholars and an armed group made up of displaced Baathis called the Army of the Men of the Naqshbandi Order. Popular discontent flared after US soldiers shot into a crowd of protesters in the city of Fallujah, killing more than a dozen unarmed demonstrators (Hashim 2006: 23).

Politics in Iraq in the immediate aftermath of the Baathi era reflected rivalry among three factions of the country's majority Shi'i community. Grand Ayatollah 'Ali al-Sistani had been a longtime critic of religious rule, particularly as it was practiced in the Islamic Republic of Iran. Al-Sistani had urged Shi'ites not to resist the advance of US and UK forces and expected the CPA to solicit his guidance in setting up the new order. He was furious when the CPA announced that it intended to write the new constitution, and despite his general sympathy for liberal forms of governance he became an outspoken critic of the institutions and procedures created by that document.

Al-Sistani's main adversary was the radical preacher Muqtada al-Sadr, who mobilized poorer neighborhoods in Baghdad, Najaf, and Kufa after the collapse of the Baathi regime and won widespread support for his efforts to restore order and provide public services. Al-Sadr was contemptuous of al-Sistani for failing to stand up to Saddam Hussein prior to 2003, and equally dismissive of INC members for spending their careers outside the country. He insisted that Iraq be ruled by Iraqis, rather than by figures like al-Sistani, whose family background lay in Iran. He advocated replacing Iraq's existing Shi'i hierarchy with popular seminaries that emphasized political and social activism. His followers, who formed the Mahdi Army, attacked liquor stores, video shops, and brothels and patrolled the sprawling Baghdad suburb that took the name Sadr City.

Somewhat less influential was Ayatollah Mohammad Sa'id al-Hakim, a cousin of the head of SCIRI, Mohammad Baqir al-Hakim. SCIRI broke with the United States in January 2003, when Washington announced that the CPA would run Iraq and resumed its longtime partnership with Iran. SCIRI's militia, the Badr Brigade, had been trained by Iran's Islamic Revolutionary Guards Corps and enjoyed close ties to Iran's supreme leader, Ayatollah Ali Khamenei. In May 2003, Baqir al-Hakim marched into the southern city of Basra from southwestern Iran. He called for a legal system rooted in Islam, but one that protected the rights of dissidents and women. He told supporters that the government "must be chosen by Iraqis and be totally independent. We will not," he continued, "accept a government that is imposed on us" (Macintyre 2003). A month later, however, the chief UN representative in Iraq persuaded Baqir al-Hakim to join the IGC.

In August 2003 Sa'id al-Hakim was wounded by a bomb blast in Najaf. Shortly thereafter, a truck bomb exploded outside that city's shrine of al-Imam 'Ali, killing Baqir al-Hakim. The Badr Brigade then took up positions throughout Najaf, prompting the Mahdi Army to move into the city as well. In the adjacent pilgrimage city of Karbala, Mahmud al-Hasani al-Sarkhi raised a rival Shi'i militia called Husain's Army. Sunni militants formed the 1920 Revolution Battalions. Competition among the various militias escalated, accompanied by more frequent and intense exchanges of fire across the barricades.

In April 2004 the CPA launched a campaign to suppress the Sadrist movement. The Mahdi Army responded by attacking US patrols and occupying government offices in Sadr City, Najaf, Kufa, and Nasiriyyah. US troops counterattacked in August and, with al-Sistani's blessing, forced the Mahdi Army to give up the struggle. Former Baathi activists and Islamist radicals in Fallujah proved more obdurate. Heavy fighting raged from April to December, undermining the effectiveness and legitimacy of the Interim Iraqi Government led by Prime Minister Iyad 'Allawi, which had supplanted the IGC in March 2004. Sunni resistance gained traction in Ramadi and Samarra over the following months. Sunni Islamist radicals claimed to be cooperating with a leader of the global militant organization al-Qaeda, Abu Musab al-Zarqawi, and took credit for indiscriminate attacks carried out in the name of al-Qaeda in the Land of the Two Rivers.

Elections took place in January 2005 for a successor to the Interim Iraqi Government, called the Transitional National Assembly (TNA). The Sadrist movement orchestrated popular protests against the balloting and called on the authorities to restore water and electricity instead of wasting time and resources on elections. Influential Sunni movements boycotted the proceedings as well, while radical Sunnis attacked police stations and provincial offices. Candidates representing SCIRI, the Party of the Call to Islam, and the KDP and PUK emerged victorious. The TNA named the PUK's Jalal Talebani as president of the republic and the Party of the Call to Islam's Ibrahim al-Ja'fari as prime minister. SCIRI's energetic minister of the interior, Bayan Jabbur, allowed the Badr Brigade to take over the internal security forces.

Radical Sunni activists expressed their fears of a Shi'i-dominated order through a wave of suicide bombings. The Sunni speaker of the TNA appealed to his community to abandon violence and take part in the electoral process, to no avail (Hashim 2006: 55). Such entreaties were undercut by the actions of Prime Minister al-Ja'fari, who refused to appoint Sunnis to key ministerial positions (Hashim 2006: 78).

In October 2005 a new constitution was approved by popular referendum, despite receiving almost no support from the Sunni community (al-Istrabadi 2009). It provided for an elected Council of Representatives, which would select a president of the republic from among its members. The presidency was to be largely ceremonial, although with the right to invite the leader of "the parliamentary majority" to act as prime minister and form a council of ministers. Whether this meant the leader of the largest single party or of the largest bloc of representatives was left vague. The constitution also declared Iraq to be a federation of "regions and governorates," in which any discrepancies between national and regional laws would be resolved in favor of the regions. These terms enabled the Kurdistan Regional Government in the north to maintain its de facto autonomy and opened the door to separatist claims by Sunnis in the central provinces and Shi'ites in the south.

Government and Opposition

Elections for the Council of Representatives took place in December 2005. This time, Muqtada al-Sadr urged his supporters to vote, and the major Shi'i parties campaigned in Baghdad and the southern provinces as the United Iraqi Alliance (UIA). Several Sunni parties took part in the balloting as well, including the Iraqi Islamic Party, the National Dialogue Council, and the General Conference of the Iraqi People. In all, 228 parties put forward candidates (Dawisha 2009: 252). The UIA won 128 of the 275 assembly seats; Kurdish parties, 53; and an alliance of Sunni parties led by the Iraqi Islamic Party, 44 (Marr 2007).

UIA representatives nominated al-Ja'fari to stay on as prime minister, but objections from Kurdish and Sunni representatives convinced him to step aside. Nuri Kamal al-Maliki of the Party of the Call to Islam became prime minister in April 2006. The most experienced figures in the government were affiliated with the Kurdish parties. High-level posts were distributed along sectarian lines: Since Talebani retained the presidency, a Sunni and a Shi'ite were appointed vice presidents; al-Maliki was balanced with one Sunni and one Kurdish deputy prime minister; and the speaker of the Council of Representatives was a Sunni, with a Shi'ite and a Kurd as deputy speakers (Dawisha 2009: 260–262).

Prime Minister al-Maliki took steps to consolidate power in the premiership. He set up a new Office of the Commander in Chief to oversee the armed forces, put it in the hands of a trusted ally, and incorporated it into the Office of the Prime Minister. He appointed his son to be deputy chief of staff in charge of the military security forces, appropriated the power to appoint district police commanders, and used state funds to resurrect the network of tribal "support councils" that US commanders had created to combat Islamist militants. In the spring of 2008, he launched a military campaign against the Sadrist movement, imposed the central administration's authority over Sadr City, and pushed the Mahdi Army out of the cities of 'Amarah and Basra. The offensive alienated SCIRI, now known as the Islamic Supreme Council of Iraq (ISCI). In the January 2009 provincial council elections, al-Maliki formed a new alliance called the State of Law Coalition (SLC), which gained control of all but one of Iraq's provinces.

Parliamentary elections in March 2010 pitted al-Maliki's SLC against an alliance of liberal parties called the Iraqi Patriotic Movement, headed by former prime minister 'Allawi. The SLC came away with 89 seats, while the Patriotic Movement won 91, the Sadrists 40, and an ISCI-led grouping 30. Al-Maliki initially refused to accept the outcome, and negotiations delayed the formation of a new government for almost nine months. In the end, al-Maliki retained the premiership, as well as the minister of the interior post, and placed a longtime ally in charge of the ministry of national security. The council of ministers took control of the previously independent Higher Electoral Commission, the Integrity Council (an anticorruption agency), and the central bank, effectively putting these agencies in al-Maliki's hands. At the same time, pivotal Sunni commanders in the military and security forces were let go and replaced by Shi'i officers loyal to the SLC.

Popular protests erupted in Baghdad and the northern metropolis of Mosul in February 2011. The demonstrations, led by the lawyers' union and university students, demanded that the internal security forces respect constitutional guarantees of citizens' rights and that steps be taken to root out pervasive official corruption. After police officers shot into a demonstration in Kut, protesters stormed the governor's office and set it on fire. Rioting subsequently spread to Basra, Fallujah, Najaf, and Tikrit. Prime Minister al-Maliki announced that funds allocated to purchase warplanes from the United States would be used to assist the poor, then cut electricity rates and distributed food to low-income districts.

Attacks against government officials nevertheless persisted. Responsibility was claimed by a clandestine organization with ties to al-Qaeda called the Islamic State of Iraq. Meanwhile, the Sadrists organized mass demonstrations to demand that all US troops leave the country by the end of 2011. On a single day in mid-August, forty-two bombings occurred across the country. That September, Sadrist movement cadres took to the streets to demand reliable public services and an end to corruption. A month later, the leadership of Salah al-Din province voted to become fully autonomous after the security forces targeted local Sunni activists.

US forces pulled out of Iraq in December 2011. Prime Minister al-Maliki immediately ordered the arrest of dozens of his political adversaries and sent commandos to surround the houses of the three most prominent Sunni politicians: Vice President Tariq al-Hashimi, Deputy Prime Minister Salih al-Mutlaq, and Minister of Finance Rafi' al-Issawi. In early 2012, a Shi'i rival of the Sadrists, the Bands of the People of Truth, announced that it would give up the armed struggle and engage in the electoral process (Mohammed 2012); the organization made overtures to Prime Minister al-Maliki, who permitted it to organize a rally in the heart of Baghdad (al-Amiry 2012). Cadres of the Bands of the People of Truth then assaulted politicians who criticized the prime minister and harassed civil rights activists. Collaboration between al-Maliki and the Bands elicited condemnation from the Sadrists, and protests continued throughout the country.

In June 2012, members of the Council of Representatives tried to call a vote of no confidence in the prime minister. President Talebani demanded to see a list of persons who backed the measure, and the list ended up in the hands of al-Maliki. Enough sponsors withdrew their support that the effort failed. That summer, the Islamic State of Iraq launched a wave of bombings that prompted the government to rely more heavily on the Bands of the People of Truth. Minister of Finance al-Issawi delivered an inflammatory speech against al-Maliki to a crowd in Ramadi in December, which sparked renewed demonstrations in Mosul, Fallujah, Samarra, and Ba'qubah. Government forces shot into a protest in Fallujah on January 25, 2013, killing nine people. Protests then erupted across the central and southern provinces, and armed militants, including the Army of the Men of the Naqshbandi Order, began to accompany the demonstrators.

In May 2013 Muqtada al-Sadr called on Prime Minister al-Maliki to bring the chaos to an end and demanded the dissolution of the Bands of the People of Truth. His sentiments resonated with civil rights activists in al-Anbar province and opened the door to a cross-sectarian challenge to the government. Sensing that his authority was eroding, al-Maliki encouraged the formation of new pro-government militias. During the closing weeks of 2013, al-Maliki ordered the internal security forces to obliterate the protest encampment at Ramadi and declared martial law. These moves set the stage for parliamentary elections in April 2014, in which the State of Law Coalition won 95 of 328 seats. Opposition parties displayed a high degree of fragmentation, which delayed the process of confirming a new prime minister. While negotiations continued, the

Islamic State in Iraq and the Levant (ISIL) and the Army of the Men of the Naqshbandi Order launched a major offensive in the northern and central provinces and pushed the Iraqi army out of Mosul, Tikrit, Fallujah, and parts of Ramadi. Pro-regime forces managed to prevent the advance from overrunning Samarra, Ba'qubah, and Baghdad. As the battle raged, al-Sistani issued a pronouncement calling for a unified national response to the danger; scholars close to al-Sistani urged the Shi'i community to take up arms to protect itself, and al-Maliki encouraged localities to set up defense committees to supplement the armed forces, under the auspices of the Popular Mobilization.

By July 2014, it became clear that al-Maliki intended to put himself forward for a third term as prime minister, despite the fact that the Council of Representatives had passed a law that limited premiers to two terms in office. The leadership of ISCI threatened to stop working with the State of Law Coalition if he went ahead with his plans, and reconciled with the Sadrists to block the effort. In a rare comment on governmental affairs, al-Sistani issued a statement that called on senior officials not to cling to their posts. Incensed, al-Maliki wrote to al-Sistani that he should "limit [his] role to the provision of religious and moral guidance to [his] followers and leave politics to politicians." Army units loyal to al-Maliki took up positions in the capital. Refusing to be intimidated, President Fuad Ma'sum nominated Haidar Jawwad al-'Abadi of the Party of the Call to Islam to be the next prime minister. Al-Sadr, al-Sistani, and Iran's Supreme Leader Ali Khamenei all voiced approval of the choice, and al-Maliki relinquished the premiership.

Prime Minister al-'Abadi nominated a prominent Sunni figure to be minister of defense and the leader of the Badr Brigade (now known as the Badr Organization) to be minister of the interior. The nominations were rejected by the Council of Representatives, but after protracted bargaining a representative of the Sunni National Forces Coalition ended up as minister of defense, and a representative of the Badr Organization took charge of the interior ministry. In September the prime minister proposed the creation of a new military formation, the National Guard, to act as intermediary between the regular armed forces and the various progovernment militias and bring an end to sectarian violence by components of the Popular Mobilization. He also urged the United States to send troops to fight ISIL, but this entreaty was rejected out of hand by the Sadrists, the Badr Organization, and the Bands of the People of Truth.

Fighting dragged on throughout the winter of 2014–2015. Prime Minister al-'Abadi repeatedly proposed to integrate the Popular Mobilization into the regular armed forces but was rebuffed by the militia commanders. Setbacks on the battlefield prompted the heads of the

Badr Organization and the Bands of the People of Truth to express doubts about the prime minister's ability to command. Such criticisms were echoed by former prime minister al-Maliki, who claimed credit for setting up the Popular Mobilization and made frequent public appearances with the leaders of various militias.

Persistent electricity outages during the summer of 2015 sparked popular protests in Baghdad, Basra, Hillah, Najaf, and Nasiriyyah. The demonstrators blamed the lack of essential public services on official corruption and mismanagement. Al-Sistani joined the chorus and called on al-'Abadi to appoint officials on the basis of competence rather than party or sectarian affiliation. In response, the prime minister pledged to scale back government spending, terminate sectarian quotas for administrative posts, and replace several senior officials with "independent" figures. The initiative was ratified by the Council of Representatives, despite the possibility that it would reduce the number of Sunnis in the state apparatus. When anticorruption protests resumed in October 2015, the Council of Representatives reversed itself and rescinded authorization for al-'Abadi's reform program.

As resistance to governmental reform gathered steam in the Council of Representatives and among militia commanders, Muqtada al-Sadr took up the campaign to put government agencies in the hands of skilled administrators. His supporters marched to the main gate of the exclusive administrative zone in Baghdad in March 2016 and staged a sit-in to demand a reshuffling of ministers. A month later, the Sadrists pushed into the so-called Green Zone and occupied the national assembly chamber. Cadres of the Bands of the People of Truth and Popular Mobilization confronted the Sadrists and persuaded them to withdraw peacefully. Meanwhile, al-Maliki reemerged as a political actor: His allies set up the Reform Front and charged that al-'Abadi's government had "failed to manage the country and fulfill his promises." Al-Sadr at the same time proposed that the Popular Mobilization be incorporated into the regular armed forces and that the electoral law be changed to reduce the influence of smaller parties. These proposals were welcomed by prominent Sunni politicians, as well as by the Iraqi Patriotic Movement.

As parliamentary elections approached in the winter of 2017–2018, the State of Law Coalition put forward an amendment to the electoral law that permitted both Prime Minister al-'Abadi and former prime minister al-Maliki to campaign as leaders of the Party of the Call to Islam. More important, al-'Abadi issued a regulation that prohibited militia members from running for seats in the Council of Representatives. The Badr Organization then announced plans to draw up a list of approved candidates called the Conquest Alliance. As the year ended, al-'Abadi worked out an arrangement to cooperate with the Conquest Alliance under the auspices of Iraqi Victory. The Sadrists joined the Iraqi Communist Party and several Sunni parties in a countercoalition called the Marchers Toward Reform.

Voting took place in May 2018, with almost 7,000 candidates competing for 329 seats in the Council of Representatives. The Conquest Alliance, which distanced itself from al-'Abadi's Iraqi Victory, received support from the Popular Mobilization, the Bands of the People of Truth, and a number of Iran-sponsored militias. Public enthusiasm for the election nevertheless flagged, and only 45 percent of eligible voters participated. The Marchers Toward Reform—which had campaigned on a platform of reforming government, ending sectarian politics, and eliminating foreign interference—came away with 54 seats, while the Conquest Alliance won 47 and Iraqi Victory ended up with 42. A list of candidates associated with al-Maliki gained 25. Muqtada al-Sadr did not run for a seat and thus could not become prime minister, but he emerged as the pivotal actor in the negotiations that followed.

Popular protests once again erupted across the south during the summer of 2018. In Najaf, rioters set the local headquarters of the major Shi'i political organizations on fire; government offices in Basra, Karbala, 'Amarah, Kut, and Nasiriyyah were attacked as well. Al-Sistani expressed sympathy for the protesters, prompting the government to dismiss the minister of electricity and allocate US$3.5 billion for new infrastructure projects in Basra province. As the disorders continued, Barham Salih of the PUK was installed as president in early October. The Marchers Toward Reform and Iraqi Victory then joined the Conquest Alliance and al-Maliki's supporters to nominate 'Adil 'Abd al-Mahdi to be prime minister, the first since 2003 not to hail from the Party of the Call to Islam.

Civil Society

Iraq enjoyed a flowering of civic activism and public expression during the 1930s and 1940s (Davis 2005), but associational life contracted soon after the 1958 coup d'état that overthrew the monarchy. By the mid-1980s, regimentation and surveillance permeated the domestic arena. More than any other Arab country, late Baathi Iraq approximated a totalitarian regime: public initiatives of any kind—political, economic, artistic—were ruthlessly quashed (al-Khalil 1989; al-Khafaji 1994).

Civic activism revived fitfully after 2003 and took a distinctly sectarian form. Neighborhood and village associations that were not tied to religious parties and movements proved unable to compete with the Sadrists and other Islamists, particularly after the UN's humanitarian mission—which had sponsored a number of nongovernmental organizations (NGOs)—pulled out of the country in August 2003.

Industrial and infrastructure workers set up the Iraqi Federation of Trade Unions (IFTU) in May 2003. Thirteen labor unions affiliated with the IFTU, giving the federation a total membership of almost 200,000 (Tripp 2007: 298). The IFTU's efforts to improve working conditions and protect jobs attracted the attention of US military commanders, who considered worker unrest a security threat. Consequently, US troops shut down IFTU headquarters from mid-2003 to July 2004 (Tripp 2007: 299). Trade unions were subjected to further restrictions in August 2005, when the al-Ja'fari government enacted a law that allowed the newly created Committee for Labor and Social Rights to supervise all aspects of worker organizations. As Charles Tripp (2007: 299) points out, "Government attempts to interfere in union elections, as well as to retain overall control of their finances and to enforce a restrictive legal framework for their operation, indicated that the impulse to curb the potential of an independent union movement was strong in the Islamist parties of the UIA."

Predominantly Kurdish districts, particularly in the northern provinces of the Kurdistan Regional Government (KRG), provided a more hospitable environment for civic activism. Rivalry between the KDP and PUK opened a space in which civic associations could take root (Tripp 2007: 309). Survivors of the Halabja massacre organized a demonstration in March 2006 to remind the authorities of the continuing poverty of the area and took to the streets yet again that summer to protest the inefficiency and corruption of the local administration. Such protests elicited strong responses from the KDP and PUK militias, which used force to break up peaceful marches.

Civic associations in post-Baathi Iraq exhibit features similar to those that characterized state-affiliated popular organizations during the Baathi era. NGOs survive and flourish if they enjoy close connections to government agencies or operate under the auspices of powerful external patrons, but they face sustained official harassment if they do not. These organizations are required to be licensed by the state, and their leaderships make decisions and supervise day-to-day activities in a heavily top-down fashion.

Political Economy

For most of the Baathi era (1963–2003), Iraq boasted a socialist economic program. Large agricultural estates were broken up and land was haltingly distributed to former laborers. June 1972 saw the nationalization of the Iraq Petroleum Company. As oil revenues skyrocketed, state officials set up Soviet-style collective farms and constructed dams and irrigation works to support them. Both large-scale, capital-intensive and smaller-scale, labor-intensive manufacturing plants were created to form a public sector in industry (Marr 2004: 162–163).

By the late 1980s revenue shortages led the government to encourage the expansion of private enterprise. Forty-seven public sector companies were sold to private interests in 1987. Such measures failed to resolve Iraq's growing economic crisis (Chaudhry 1991). Meanwhile, Baghdad complained that Kuwait and the United Arab Emirates were robbing the Iraqi treasury by exporting oil in excess of their Organization of Petroleum Exporting Countries allotments and driving down world prices. Economic problems, therefore, lay at the heart of the 1990 Iraqi invasion of Kuwait.

In response to the invasion, the UN Security Council froze all Iraqi assets outside the country, imposed an embargo on Iraqi oil exports, and tightly restricted imports. Furthermore, the 1990–1991 war destroyed almost all of the country's power plants, fertilizer factories, iron and steel works, oil production and distribution facilities, and transportation infrastructure. The local economy received relief in April 1995, when the Security Council set up a system whereby Iraq was permitted to sell a limited amount of oil to purchase food and medical supplies. The first shipment of oil under the terms of the so-called oil-for-food arrangement took place in March 1997. Yet, as Abbas Alnasrawi (2001: 213) observes, "it is obvious from the data that, while the oil-for-food programme provided some relief, it failed to change the underlying conditions of a deteriorating economy."

Out of the chaos arose a scrappy group of private businesspeople whom Christopher Parker and Pete Moore (2007: 9–10) call "the cats of the embargo." This group, which attracted risk-taking entrepreneurs from all communities, included mid-level state officials and Baath Party cadres along with individuals who had long opposed the regime. Operations controlled by "the cats" employed a broad spectrum of drivers, mechanics, security guards, warehouse workers, and clerks.

These actors had little incentive to rally to the defense of the Baathi order in the spring of 2003, but they faced severe challenges on two fronts in the wake of the US-led assault. The CPA announced plans to create an open marketplace built on formal guarantees of individual property rights (Medani 2004). The remaining public sector enterprises were put up for auction, tariffs and customs duties were abolished, and the state-run banking sector was dismantled. CPA officials encouraged foreign companies to move into manufacturing and trade. Such measures alienated "the cats" and tribal leaders alike and posed a direct threat to the livelihoods of their employees.

Militants linked to the Sadrist movement and SCIRI confiscated all sorts of economic assets during 2003–2004. In the impoverished suburbs of Baghdad, the Mahdi Army shut down businesses that dealt in "indecent" items or operated in an exploitative fashion. Cadres of the Badr Brigade and the Party of the Call to Islam oversaw the influx of Iranian goods into the southern provinces. Armed groups attacked the newly rebuilt petroleum pipelines in a bid to force the government to ship oil by truck (Parker and Moore 2007: 13). In late 2006 SCIRI activists demanded that the oil-producing districts outside Basra be turned over to the provincial administration, just as the oil sector in the far north had fallen under the control of the KRG.

Officials in the Kurdish region had already signed new contracts with foreign oil companies to increase production in the fields around Kirkuk. Such contracts elicited strong objections from the petroleum ministry in Baghdad, who joined the Sadrists and Sunni politicians alike in insisting that Iraq's natural resources belonged to the nation as a whole. The KRG administration countered that the US-sponsored constitution of 2005 explicitly allowed compensation for "the damaged regions that were unjustly deprived [of revenues] by the former regime." In July 2008 the oil ministry announced that foreign companies would be invited to submit revised bids for long-term contracts to rejuvenate the oil industry.

By 2011 local entrepreneurs and international investors had created a network of profitable manufacturing and financial companies. One example was the family-run Shamara Holding Company, which owned steel mills and electricity-generating plants and had begun to operate state-of-the-art petroleum refineries (Myers 2011). Another was the Iraqi branch of the British-based Hong Kong Shanghai Bank Company, which transformed the Dar al-Salam Investment Bank from a US$91 million enterprise to one worth more than US$400 million. Most of this private activity was orchestrated by the Task Force for Business and Stability Operations, an agency created in 2006 by the US Department of Defense. Connections to government institutions accompanied pervasive corruption (Looney 2008).

Four years of intense fighting against ISIL left large areas of Iraq destroyed. In January 2018 the government called on foreign investors to provide US$100 billion to rebuild crucial infrastructure and industrial plants. To encourage such investment, state officials cut back regulations on economic activity. Yet a meeting of potential investors in Kuwait pledged only US$30 billion for reconstruction, much of which took the form of loans. Desperate for resources, the Council of Representatives introduced a 10 percent sales tax on most activities. The new tax played a role in triggering the popular unrest that flared during the summer of 2018. At the same time, severe drought devastated local agriculture, particularly such food crops as rice and wheat.

The Impact of International Politics

Iraq is tightly integrated into the global economy. Yet the country's exports remain concentrated in only one area, hydrocarbons. Reliance on petroleum exports actually increased between 1970 and 1985, despite the government's efforts to diversify the local economy (Lawson 1992: 191). Consequently, the economy prospers when oil prices rise and suffers when they drop, no matter what government is in place.

External threats helped to consolidate authoritarian rule by channeling an inordinate share of the country's resources into the armed forces. Military spending kept pace with oil revenue throughout the 1970s, and expenditures during the 1980–1988 Iran-Iraq war eclipsed all other budgetary outlays. After the destruction of the oil facilities at Mina al-Bakr and Khawr al-'Umayyah during the war reduced oil income, grants and loans from Saudi Arabia, Kuwait, and the United Arab Emirates filled in the gaps (al-Khafaji 2000: 273).

Iraqi politics have been equally affected by foreign actors in the post-Baathi era. The CPA created the ground rules for political life in the new order and established institutions and agencies rooted in the principle of sectarian representation (Younis 2011; Jacoby and Neggaz 2018). More important, the CPA set a precedent of discouraging forms of political mobilization that it deemed inappropriate. Whereas Baathi-era restrictions on students' and women's associations were abolished, equally restrictive regulations on workers' unions were preserved. Such policies highlighted the neoliberal ideology of the CPA, as well as the US government's commitment to remake Iraq in its own image (Tripp 2007: 289–290).

During the battle against ISIL, Iran sharply increased its influence in the domestic affairs of Iraq. Armed formations sponsored by the Islamic Republic proliferated and steadily sidelined the regular armed forces. Goods produced in Iran took a greater share of the local market, and electricity generated in Iran became crucial for the southern provinces. Imports and investments from Iran tended to be channeled through militias linked to the Islamic Republic in a bid to strengthen those forces' role in the Iraqi political economy (Badawi 2018). Widespread resentment against Iran's growing presence played a significant role in propelling the Sadrist movement to victory in the May 2018 elections.

Religion and Politics

Shortly before the 1958 coup d'état, Shi'i notables in Najaf formed the Society of Religious Scholars to resist the spread of atheism and communism. The organization was headed by one of the most prestigious figures in the Shi'i hierarchy, Grand Ayatollah Muhsin al-Hakim (Wiley 1992: 31–32). It undertook no overt political activity, although it did claim that the proposed land reform program violated Islamic principles that respect private property. Similar positions were espoused by the more activist Shi'i Party of the Call to Islam, which emerged in late 1957 under the leadership of Sayyid Mohammad Baqir al-Sadr, as well as by the much smaller Sunni Muslim Brothers. They were joined in 1961 by the militant Shi'i Islamic Action Organization, which more closely approximated a political party.

After Baath Party officers seized power in 1963, and particularly after Baathi radicals declared themselves Marxist that November, the Party of the Call to Islam redoubled its efforts to resist the regime. The organization gained widespread support after the government nationalized banks, insurance companies, and factories as part of a socialist initiative in 1964.

Religious activism surged again in the spring of 1969, after the government signed an agreement with the Soviet Union to develop oil fields in the southern, Shi'i-dominated provinces, and the Baathi regime expelled longtime residents of Iranian descent. Muhsin al-Hakim publicly denounced these policies, sparking demonstrations in Najaf and Karbala. Baathi officials then confiscated the endowments of the religious institutions located in Najaf. This move provoked rioting in Najaf, Karbala, and Basra.

Muhsin al-Hakim's outspoken opposition to the Baathi regime raised the profile and popularity of the Party of the Call to Islam, but it was Mohammad Baqir al-Sadr's organizational skills that gave it the capacity to challenge the authorities. Baqir al-Sadr's efforts to mobilize the Shi'i community coincided with a series of innovative lectures on religion and politics composed by exiled Iranian scholar Grand Ayatollah Ruhollah Khomeini, at the same time that the Islamic Action Organization was advocating armed struggle against the Baath. Before these disparate currents could converge, Muhsin al-Hakim died, and the Shi'i Islamist movement split between the more activist Mohammad Baqir al-Sadr and the resolutely apolitical Grand Ayatollah Abu al-Qasim al-Khu'i, who succeeded al-Hakim as the most respected figure in the Shi'i hierarchy.

Following mass protests in Najaf and Karbala in 1977, the Party of the Call to Islam and the Islamic Action Organization became more active. Popular support for these organizations deepened after the 1978–1979 Iranian revolution. Mohammad Baqir al-Sadr led a public celebration of the Shah's overthrow and was subsequently placed under house arrest. In April 1980 a member of the Islamic Action Organization attempted to assassinate the deputy prime minister, Tariq 'Aziz. In retaliation, Baqir al-Sadr and his sister were taken to Baghdad, tortured, and killed. Ayatollah al-Khu'i was put under house arrest, and the government appointed Mohammad Sadiq al-Sadr to be head of the Shi'i religious hierarchy.

In 1982 the Supreme Council for Islamic Revolution in Iraq was created in Tehran under the leadership of Mohammad Baqir al-Hakim.

When Shi'i districts in southern Iraq rose in revolt at the end of the 1990–1991 war, SCIRI leaders called for the establishment of an Islamic form of government along the lines of the Islamic Republic of Iran. Prominent Shi'i figures were systematically eliminated after the revolt was crushed. Embittered by the repression, Mohammad Sadiq al-Sadr began building an underground network of religious institutions, supervised by his son Muqtada al-Sadr. By early 1998, Sadiq al-Sadr had started to give Friday sermons demanding the release of imprisoned Shi'i activists. Such outspokenness led to his assassination in 1999, leaving Grand Ayatollah 'Ali al-Sistani as the senior figure in the Shi'i hierarchy.

In the wake of the 2003 overthrow of the Baathi order, those who rejected the notion that religious scholars should manage the affairs of the state gravitated around al-Sistani. Those who had looked to Mohammad Sadiq al-Sadr as a source of inspiration leaned toward Muqtada al-Sadr. The main proponent of rule by religious scholars was Mohammad Sa'id al-Hakim. Nevertheless, doctrinal matters often gave way to political expediency: Anthony Shadid reported in August 2003 that Muqtada al-Sadr had formed an alliance with the Sunni Islamist Ahmad al-Kubaisi. Both leaders stood squarely against the US-backed Iraqi Governing Council and had common interests with the Sunni Association of Muslim Scholars.

Rivalry among Shi'i and Sunni Islamist movements escalated sharply in the spring of 2004. That March the previously unknown group al-Qaeda in the Land of the Two Rivers detonated bombs outside major Shi'i shrines in Karbala and Qadimiyyah, killing more than 250 people. Four months later, the Unity and Struggle Group, another militant Sunni organization, took over Samarra and massacred its Shi'i and Kurdish inhabitants. Yet another radical Sunni formation, the Consultative Council of Fighters, forged ties to al-Qaeda in the Land of the Two Rivers in early 2006 and most likely carried out the bombing of a historic Shi'i pilgrimage mosque in Samarra that ignited eighteen months of brutal warfare among Islamist militias.

Clashes between the Mahdi Army and the Badr Brigade culminated in full-scale confrontations in Karbala, Najaf, and Baghdad during the summer of 2007. The Badr Brigade ended up prevailing, and at the end of August Muqtada al-Sadr declared a unilateral cease-fire. In January 2008 the Sadrist movement joined the Party of the Call to Islam and a number of Sunni organizations in releasing the Baghdad Charter, which denounced sectarianism as a basis upon which to construct the Iraqi political system. Muqtada al-Sadr returned to Iraq in January 2011 after spending four years in the Iranian seminary city of Qom. His supporters then set up a new, avowedly nonsectarian organization, called the Helpers, to push for full independence from foreign control.

Sectarian tensions mounted, nonetheless. Attacks on Christian-owned liquor stores in Baghdad multiplied, and Sunnis in Samarra grumbled about plans to expand the Shi'i pilgrimage mosque complex in Samarra, which would displace large numbers of nearby residents. In June 2011 radicals of the Battalions of the Party of God, a previously unknown Shi'i group, attacked a US military outpost in Baghdad. Indiscriminate bombings took place more frequently as the year passed. Meanwhile, radical Shi'ites, who chafed at Muqtada al-Sadr's new-found moderation, filled the ranks of a rival movement, the Bands of the People of Truth, led by Qais al-Khaz'ali. By the spring of 2012, fighting had become rampant not only between the Sadrists and the Bands of the People of Truth but also between supporters of al-Sistani and cadres of Husain's Army (Waleed 2012).

May 2014 saw a coalition of radical Sunni Islamist forces led by the Islamic State in Iraq and the Levant launch a large-scale offensive that overran extensive areas of northern and central Iraq. Fighters affiliated with the Sadrist movement organized a new militia called the Peace Companies to resist the assault, while the Party of the Call to Islam created the Battalions of Fury. These forces joined the Badr Organization, the Bands of the People of Truth, the Battalions of the Party of God, and a handful of Iran-sponsored militias to combat ISIL. The prominence of these forces gave a sectarian coloring to the conflict. The May 2015 campaign to regain control of Ramadi, for instance, was assigned a distinctively Shi'i code name: "We Obey You, O Husain." The commander of the Bands of the People of Truth declared that his organization constituted the core of "Islamic resistance" against the country's foreign enemies from Britain in the 1920s to ISIL today.

As Shi'i militias advanced into predominantly Sunni districts north of Samarra, residents complained that they were targeted for not having resisted ISIL with sufficient vigor. Radical Sunni Islamist groups like the Supporters of the Tradition and the Supporters of Islam revived in Salah al-Din and Diyala provinces and were joined by new formations like the Army of the Free of the Tradition. The reemergence of these local forces coincided with an initiative on the part of Ahmad al-Kubaisi to create a unified Sunni religious authority parallel to the Shi'i religious hierarchy (Mamouri 2018b). This proposal was rejected by the major Sunni political parties.

Religious figures played an unprecedented role in the 2018 elections. Scholars close to 'Ali al-Sistani repeatedly warned against the return of Nuri al-Maliki; preachers allied with Muqtada al-Sadr told worshippers to reject politicians who had failed to keep their promises; other influential clerics urged their followers to boycott the voting entirely, on the grounds that the electoral system had been imposed on the country by nonbelievers. Immediately prior to the balloting, al-Sistani's office publicly castigated the Conquest Alliance for trying to use the prestige it had won in the struggle against ISIL for selfish political gain (Mamouri 2018a).

Identity and Politics

At first glance, Iraq appears to be made up of three distinct ethnosectarian regions: a Shi'i Arab lowlands in the south, a Sunni Arab central plain, and a mountainous Kurdish north. About 60 percent of the country's population consists of Arabic-speaking Shi'ites, while about 35 percent are Arabic-speaking Sunnis and 15–20 percent are Kurdish-speakers (who are predominantly—but not exclusively—Sunni) (Hobbs 2009: 263–264). Smaller groups of Sunni Turks, known in Iraq as Turkomans, and Christian Armenians, Chaldeans, and Assyrians can be found in the northern cities of Kirkuk and Irbil and in villages scattered across the northern highlands. Finally, northwestern Iraq harbors reclusive clusters of Yazidis, an ancient sect whose beliefs derive from Zoroastrianism.

Yet this summary masks important distinctions. The Shi'ites of the south include cosmopolitan urbanites in Basra and Samarra, marsh dwellers along the confluence of the Tigris and Euphrates Rivers, bedouin tribespeople, and Iranian expatriates who are longtime residents of Najaf and Karbala. Similarly, the Sunni Arab population consists of notable families (some of whose members trace their lineage to the Islamic conquest and others whose forebears arrived in 1920 with the British-sponsored Hashimi ruling family), a commercial and intellectual bourgeoisie that provided the foundation for the Arab nationalist movement of the late nineteenth century, urban factory workers and rural smallholders who formed the initial backbone of the Baath Party, and bedouin tribespeople of the western desert. Kurds are divided not only into Sunnis, Shi'ites, and Alevis, but also into Kurmanji- and Sorani-speakers and, more important, supporters of the rival Barzani and Talebani clans.

Sectarian affiliation played only a minor role in politics during most of the history of the Iraqi state. Prominent Shi'ites were outspoken advocates of a unified, independent Iraq in the 1920s and 1930s (Visser 2005). Nascent Assyrian nationalism was crushed in August 1933 by a coalition of Arab troops and Kurdish auxiliaries (Husry 1974). More recently, the Shi'i population of the south not only ignored appeals by the revolutionary regime in Iran to rise up against the Baath Party but also stood united in defense of the Iraqi homeland during the 1980–1988 Iran-Iraq War. As late as the 1990s, the Baath Party prided itself on promoting Sunnis, Shi'ites, and Christians alike to senior positions.

The exception to the rule has been the Kurdish community, whose domain spills over the country's borders into Turkey in the north, Iran in the east, and Syria in the west. The Iraqi Communist Party mobilized large numbers of Kurdish workers in the oil fields around Kirkuk during the 1950s, and clashes between Kurds and Turkomans prompted the armed forces to crack down on the party in July 1959. Two years later, Mustafa Barzani of the Kurdistan Democratic Party demanded an end to authoritarian rule and autonomy for the Kurdish provinces. Clashes between the KDP militia and the Iraqi armed forces erupted that fall; by the end of the year the faction of the KDP that was loyal to Jalal Talebani had joined the battle. Both wings of the party welcomed the February 1963 coup d'état that brought the Baath Party to power (Tripp 2000: 172).

Negotiations over Kurdish autonomy quickly broke down, however, and the KDP initiated a campaign of armed struggle against the Baathi regime. The Barzani and Talebani wings of the KDP fragmented: in 1975 Barzani led his supporters into Iran; Talebani then set up the Patriotic Union of Kurdistan. The bifurcation of the Kurdish national movement enabled the authorities to transfer large numbers of Kurds from the northern countryside into poorly equipped suburbs of the central and southern cities (Tripp 2000: 214). During the final stage of the 1980–1988 war, Iraqi troops carried out a military offensive against Kurdish fighters, which culminated in poison gas attacks against the towns of Halabja and Sayw Senan (Yildiz 2007: 27–28).

Kurdish activists took advantage of the 1991 uprising in the south to seize control of Sulaimaniyyah, Zakho, Irbil, and Kirkuk ('Abd al-Jabbar 1994: 109–110). Iraqi troops recaptured the northern cities, but in April the US Air Force announced that it would enforce a "safe haven" for Kurds in territory north of the 36th parallel of latitude. Refugees from Sulaimaniyyah and Irbil flocked to the safe haven, and that October the high command in Baghdad pulled Iraqi troops out of Sulaimaniyyah, Irbil, and Dohuk provinces. The withdrawal of central authority set the stage for elections in May 1992 to choose a popular assembly, which evolved into the autonomous Kurdistan Regional Government (Yildiz 2007: 44–50).

When the Iraqi Governing Council was set up in July 2003, the CPA allocated membership on a strictly sectarian basis. Five seats were reserved for Kurds, thirteen for Shi'ites, five for Sunni Arabs, and one each for the Turkomans and Assyrians. The KDP's Mas'ud Barzani and the PUK's Jalal Talebani joined the IGC at the outset and stayed on as members of the Interim Iraqi Government. Talebani's appointment to the presidency confirmed both the influence of the Kurds as a political force and the role of sectarianism as the organizing principle of the new order (Visser 2008; Younis 2011; Jacoby and Neggaz 2018).

The Kurdish leadership's success in promoting that community's interests had a dark side. Kurdish activists annexed districts adjacent to the territory administered by the KRG, most crucially around the city of

Kirkuk. Kurdish militias systematically harassed Turkoman and Arab residents of the cities under the KRG's control and did their best to force non-Kurds to abandon their homes and property. As a result, leaders of the Chaldean, Assyrian, and Yazidi communities demanded that a larger number of seats be guaranteed to their respective constituents on the provincial councils that were created at the end of 2008.

Relations between the KRG and the central administration in Baghdad plummeted at the end of 2010, when Vice President Tariq al-Hashimi fled northward on his way out of the country. The Kurdish officials who welcomed al-Hashimi took the opportunity to complain that Prime Minister al-Maliki had reverted to the authoritarian practices that had characterized the Baathi era, and at least one prominent Kurdish figure declared that the time had come for Kurds to set up an independent state.

ISIL's 2014 offensive further inflamed intercommunal tensions. The previously docile Iraqi Turkoman Front organized a militia to protect the Turkoman community in Kirkuk from ISIL and threatened to turn against the KRG after Kurdish fighters seized control of the city. In late 2016 members of Kirkuk's Circassian community requested official recognition, so that their citizenship and property rights could be guaranteed (Salloum 2016). The Yazidi community splintered into a pro-KRG faction and an anti-KRG faction after Kurdish forces pushed ISIL out of the districts around Sinjar and Tal 'Afar (Jalabi 2017). And the tiny Christian Shabak community complained that Kurdish fighters blocked its members from returning to their homes once ISIL had been expelled from the villages outside Qaraqosh (Neurink 2017).

Gender and Politics

Baathi socialism in principle champions the interests of women and promises to protect families from the injustices inherent in capitalist patriarchy. The Baath Party created the General Federation of Iraqi Women (GFIW) in 1968 and gave it the responsibility "(1) to work for and fight the enemies of a socialist, democratic Arab society; (2) to ensure the equality of Iraqi women with men in rights; [and] (3) to contribute to the economic and social development of Iraq by co-operating with other Iraqi [popular] organizations and by raising the national consciousness of women" (Joseph 1991: 182). The GFIW set up centers to train women for skilled jobs in manufacturing, disseminate new agricultural techniques, and promote literacy among poor women and girls (Ismael 1980; Rassam 1992; Al-Ali 2005). It also worked with the party-affiliated trade union federation to find employment for women, although as late as 1977, females made up no more than 7 percent of all wage laborers (Joseph 1991: 183).

Women moved into a wide range of professional and technical jobs during the course of the 1980–1988 war with Iran. New laws were promulgated to support women who sacrificed family life in order to contribute to the war effort (al-Jawaheri 2008: 21–24). A female accountant recollected that "the Iran-Iraq war had a big effect on society. It showed the efficiency of women in a very clear way. Most of the men were fighting at the front. There was a great dependence on women. And women proved their strength and their resourcefulness. You could even see women at gas stations or women truck drivers" (Al-Ali and Pratt 2009: 37). Nevertheless, wartime rhetoric highlighted the role of women as mothers of prospective soldiers and glorified the masculinity of male soldiers at the front (Al-Ali and Pratt 2009: 38). Women were thus pushed out of the labor force as soon as the fighting ended.

When the Baathi regime was overthrown, the CPA made few overtures to the representatives of women's organizations. The head of the CPA, Paul Bremer, rejected a quota for women on the Iraqi Governing Council, although three women were eventually appointed (Al-Ali and Pratt 2009: 90–91). In December 2003 the IGC, chaired by SCIRI's 'Abd al-'Aziz al-Hakim, overturned the Baathi personal status code and reinstated Sunni and Shi'i religious law (Al-Ali and Pratt 2009: 93). The decree lapsed when Bremer refused to sign it. Five women were given posts in the Interim Iraqi Government, and six female ministers were nominated following the December 2005 elections.

Women's rights occupied a central place in debates surrounding the drafting of the permanent constitution. In the end, however, the document left personal status matters to be determined later and in accordance with each person's "own religion, sect, belief, and choice." By incorporating notions of federalism, the constitution "devolved authority to the regions to specify family law, thereby allowing regional differences in family law" (Al-Ali and Pratt 2009: 114). More important, ongoing warfare among Islamist groups trapped professional women in their houses and forced them to devote their energies to caring for their families (Ismael and Ismael 2008).

By 2012, there remained only one female minister in the government, the minister of state for women's affairs. This individual, Ibtihal al-Zaidi, took over after her predecessor resigned to protest the reduction of the ministry's annual budget to the token sum of US$1,500. Prime Minister al-'Abadi abolished the ministry in August 2015 as part of his reform initiative but maintained a women's department in the office of the prime minister. Squeezed out of the top of the political arena, women ran in unprecedented numbers for the 2018 parliamentary elections (Bellingreri 2018). Suhad al-Khatib, a Communist Party member, won in Najaf on the Marchers Toward Reform ticket.

13

Israel

Alan Dowty

One of the puzzles of Israeli politics is how the nation managed to establish and maintain a stable competitive political system. Consider the obstacles: relatively few of the Jewish immigrants to Palestine or to Israel were from countries with a viable democratic tradition; most came as refugees dominated by a sense of insecurity; and those who came were plunged into an ongoing conflict requiring total mobilization and a constant state of high readiness. The country was plagued by serious internal cleavages, both between Jews and Arabs and within the Jewish community itself. Meanwhile, the economic pressures created by security demands and massive refugee flows were staggering.

In meeting these challenges, however, those who established the new Jewish *yishuv* (community) in Palestine drew upon a rich Jewish experience in politics. Numerous historical Jewish communities in different settings exercised a high degree of autonomy, governing their internal life in defense against a hostile environment. In Tsarist Russia, from which most of the early settlers came, Jewish communities held their own elections, passed their own laws, taxed themselves, had their own courts and welfare systems, and even conducted their own diplomacy. Though not democratic by modern standards, this "Jewish politics" created a foundation for the growth of competitive politics (Dowty 2001: chap. 2).

Consequently, Israel has been classified as a democracy in all the major listings of democratic states (Rustow 1967; Dahl 1971; Powell 1982; Lijphart 1984, 1994; Vanhanen 1991; Coppedge and Reinecke 1991; Przeworski et al. 2000; Unified Democracy Scores 2014; Economist Intelligence Unit 2016; Marshall and Elzinga-Marshall 2017; V-Dem Institute

2017). Freedom House gives it the highest ranking on political rights and the second-highest ranking (citing "deficiencies in a few aspects") on civil liberties (Freedom House 2017). There are fundamental problems in practice with the status and rights of the Palestinian Arab minority in Israel, and there are challenging issues regarding the role of religion in politics. But within its own borders, Israel meets the criteria that define competitive politics: the right to vote and to run for office, elections without a predetermined outcome, and freedom of expression. In terms of the four criteria of the "litmus test" for democratic elections posed in Chapter 2, incumbent parties can lose elections, the winners are allowed to form a government, the winners actually govern, and the elections are repeated at specified intervals.

Following the general framework of this volume, in this chapter I discuss only the domestic politics of Israel. International political dynamics, though they perhaps affect Israel more than most other nations, are considered only in the context of their impact on Israel's domestic politics. Likewise, I deal only with the territory that is juridically part of Israel and not the West Bank and the Gaza Strip, Palestinian territories occupied by Israel since 1967 and governed under the international law of belligerent occupation. (For analysis of the differing status and reality of Israeli rule in the occupied Palestinian territories, see Dowty 2001: chap. 10.)

Historical Background and Contemporary Political Structure

Modern Jewish settlement in Palestine—the "Return to Zion"—began from Tsarist Russia in the early 1880s. Russia was then home to half the world's Jews and was itself in great turmoil. As a result, Jews became targets of a vicious, officially tolerated anti-Semitism. In the course of four decades (1880–1920), an estimated 4 million Jewish refugees fled to more hospitable shores. Most left for Western Europe or the New World, but a small handful—perhaps 2 percent of the whole—concluded that the time had come to rebuild Jewish life in the historical homeland.

Historically, Jews had often fled lands of persecution to find haven elsewhere. But anti-Semitism produced a different reaction this time, because of an important difference in context. On the eve of the twentieth century, nationalism, and the model of the nation-state, had become the dominant idea in political thinking and had been extended from France, Germany, and Italy to the peoples of Central and Eastern Europe. But reestablishing a Jewish community in the Palestinian provinces of the Ottoman Empire, against daunting physical obstacles and the hostility of both the Turkish rulers and the Arab inhabitants, was a formidable challenge. Not surprisingly, success in the first twenty years was very limited: seventeen new settlements with a few thousand inhabitants (added to an existing Jewish community of 20,000–30,000). Had nothing changed, this would have remained a minor footnote in history. But two developments altered the course of history.

One was the emergence of the first effective Zionist political movement. The label of "Zionist" had come into use during the 1880s to identify those who supported the reestablishment of a Jewish homeland (not necessarily a state at this stage) in Palestine. This early movement lacked organization and definition, but at the end of the 1890s this lack was remedied by a very unlikely founding figure. Theodore Herzl, a thirty-five-year-old journalist and would-be playwright, was stung into action by the rise of anti-Semitism in France (where he served as a newspaper correspondent) and in his own city of Vienna. In 1896, Herzl published a hugely influential manifesto, *Der Judenstaat* (The Jews' State), and in 1897 he organized the World Zionist Organization, whose declared aim was "to create for the Jewish people a home in Palestine secured by public law" (in deference to the governing Ottoman Turks, the word *state* was avoided). This declared aim received important international support during World War I, when Great Britain announced in the Balfour Declaration (November 2, 1917) that it favored "the establishment in Palestine of a national home for the Jewish people." This support became operative when the declaration was written into Britain's Palestine Mandate by the League of Nations.

The other new development was a renewed wave of anti-Semitism, ignited by the first Russian revolution of 1905, which produced another wave of refugees. By the eve of World War I, Jews in Palestine had grown to an established community of about 80,000, with the organization and resources needed to absorb later influxes. This pattern repeated again and again, as each outbreak of persecution produced a new "wave" (*aliyah* in Hebrew) of settlers. Civil war in Russia in the 1920s brought the third *aliyah*. Anti-Semitic government policies in Poland in the mid-1920s led to the fourth *aliyah*. The rise of Nazi Germany and other fascist regimes in the 1930s drove the fifth *aliyah*. The Holocaust—the Nazi genocide of European Jews—made Zionists out of nearly all Jews, with refugees and survivors struggling to reach Palestine. Roughly 80 percent of those who came to Israel over the years meet the standard international definition of "refugees," a fact that is basic to understanding Israeli political attitudes and opinions.

After the creation of Israel in 1948, the influx of Jews fleeing from Arab countries almost doubled the population of the country in its first decade, while the massive outflow of Arab refugees during the war that led to Israel's independence reduced the Arab population to about 19 percent within the new armistice lines—roughly the same proportion of the population as today.

There was no enforceable central authority in the Zionist movement or in the Jewish *yishuv* during the days of the Palestine Mandate (1921–1948). In Mandatory Palestine, British administration covered all areas of government, including defense, police, courts, and economic and social regulation. Only in areas where it did not conflict with Mandatory law could the *yishuv* govern itself, and then only by voluntary consent. This reality reinforced a remarkable capacity to encompass totally opposed worldviews that could have torn the *yishuv* apart. There were revolutionary and nonrevolutionary socialists who combined Zionism with theories of class struggle, religious Zionists who demanded adherence to traditional Jewish law, and "General Zionists" who advocated Jewish statehood but rejected both socialism and traditional religion. Later on, a fourth strand, "Revisionist" Zionism, imitated militant nationalism elsewhere and advocated an expansionist territorial vision for the Jewish state. In addition, there was in Palestine an existing Jewish "ultra-orthodox" (*haredi*) community that rejected Zionism in principle.

But Zionists of different persuasions were able to work together in a system of power-sharing that owed much to historical experience. For example, beginning in the 1930s Labor Zionist leaders (secular socialists), who dominated at that time, made explicit arrangements with religious Zionist parties on a proportionate division of jobs and other benefits. This initiated a forty-year period of partnership between Labor Zionists and religious Zionists.

By the end of World War II, Jews in Britain's Palestine Mandate were able to maintain a level of organization and self-defense extraordinary for a community without formal government powers. This community levied and collected taxes, established an army, represented its own interests internationally, administered welfare and educational services, and set its own economic and social policies—all on a voluntary basis. The strength of this social cohesion was apparent in the 1948 war that led to Israel's independence.

During the first two decades of statehood, roughly up to the 1967 war, the basic patterns of Israeli politics were set under the leadership of David Ben-Gurion, the dominant figure from the 1930s until his resignation as prime minister in 1963. Central to Ben-Gurion's thinking was the concept of *mamlachtiut*, a term of his own devising that is best translated as "a sense of public responsibility" or "civic-mindedness." Ben-Gurion accomplished the first task of *mamlachtiut*—bringing all elements of the Jewish community under government authority—

quickly and with little need for coercion. This involved important concessions to the ultra-orthodox *haredi* community, which comprised strictly religious Jews who were ideologically opposed to Zionism.

Ben-Gurion centralized authority by combining the parliamentary model with centralized political parties and coalition politics, producing a government with strong executive powers. Since no single party ever captured a majority in an election, control was achieved by assembling a workable majority coalition and imposing the principle of collective responsibility. Most of the governing institutions established in the new state were based on pre-state institutions. These included a parliament (Knesset) of 120 members, elected to four-year terms by party-list proportional representation, with the entire nation as an undivided electoral district—an expression of power-sharing in perfect accord with Jewish politics. Israeli citizens thus vote for a party, not for individual candidates. The government or cabinet represents a majority in the Knesset, and since no single party has ever won a majority of the seats, all governments have been based on coalitions. The Knesset elects the president, a ceremonial head of state, to a seven-year term. Due to the lack of consensus between religious and secular parties, no written constitution was adopted, but over the years a series of "Basic Laws" that constitute most of a projected constitution have been passed.

The remarkable political stability that existed during this period was expressed in the consistency of voting behavior. In the seven elections that were held from 1949 to 1969, the Labor Zionist parties as a bloc consistently gained about half of the 120 available Knesset seats (from 59 to 65 seats, or 49 to 54 percent). The center-right parties (a category that combined General Zionists and Revisionists) consistently received a little less than a third of the seats (from 31 to 35 seats, or 26 to 29 percent). Religious parties received from 12.5 to 15 percent of Knesset seats, divided between the religious Zionists and the ultra-orthodox. A fourth bloc of parties included the radical left (primarily Communists) and Arab parties; they received from 5 to 9 percent of Knesset seats.

As time passed, the gap between a secular, socialist elite, mainly of Eastern European origin, and a significantly more traditional public, much of it of Middle Eastern origin, was bound to assert itself. "Traditional" in this context refers to those valuing existing family ties, ethnic identity, folkways, religion, gender stereotypes, and social roles, as opposed to the "civic" Israel—the "New Israel" created in the century since Herzl—that is more universalist, modernist, secular, liberal, and dovish. In "traditional" Israel one is usually a Jew first and an Israeli second, while in "civic" Israel the order is reversed.

The 1967 war, by reviving dormant territorial issues, contributed to the rise of more ethnically assertive and nationalist forces. These trends culminated in 1977 when the inconceivable occurred and a center-right government, under prominent Revisionist Zionist figure Menachem Begin, came to power after half a century of Labor Zionist hegemony.

Government and Opposition

The "upheaval" of 1977 marked an increased resurgence of ethnicity and nationalistic thinking. There was a loss of consensus on the most basic issue: the very definition of the state that Zionism pursued. The gulf that opened between competing territorial and demographic conceptions of Israel also corresponded to a great extent with communal divisions between Jews of European and Middle Eastern backgrounds, which had been less politically significant before. Voters from Middle East countries—about half the electorate during these years—tended to be strongly anti-Arab and attracted to the more hawkish parties. This tendency was reinforced by the identification of Labor Zionism with the privileged elite and the perception that socialism was an alien, Western doctrine not linked to the Jewish tradition. After a period of incubation, alienation from the Labor establishment grew quickly among the younger Middle Eastern generation who had grown up in Israel.

Security issues—the Arab-Israel conflict—have always been the most important axis of Israeli politics, pitting hawks who favor more assertive policies against doves who advocate conciliation and negotiation. But before the 1967 war, socioeconomic issues and the secular-religious divide also were prominent and, to some extent, independent of positions on security. Some leftists on economic issues took hawkish positions on security questions, and there were parties with conservative economic positions that were dovish on security. Religious parties, by and large, were not markedly hawkish or dovish; rather, they focused on religious issues.

After the 1967 war, however, the issue created by that war—the future of the occupied Palestinian, Syrian, and Egyptian territories—came to dominate Israeli politics. Religious parties became much more predictably hawkish, and socioeconomic issues were subordinated to security issues. Choosing between parties on economic issues became more and more difficult as their positions became incoherent or indistinguishable. Israeli politics can best be described not as left-right, as in most nations, but as dovish-hawkish. In fact, since lower-income Israelis are disproportionately of Middle Eastern origin, there is even a kind of "reverse correlation": lower-income groups vote disproportionately for the "right" (hawkish) and higher-income groups vote disproportionately for the "left" (dovish).

Post-1977 Israeli politics can thus be interpreted, in large part, as a resurgence of the more "traditional" sector of society. The immediate result was polarization and deadlock between the opposed blocs. Elections from 1977 to 1999 were marked by a fairly even balance between the left, dominated by a unified Labor party, and a bloc on the right led by the newly formed Likud party, with religious parties often holding the balance. Elections in 2003, 2009, 2013, and 2015 (though not 2006) registered a distinct shift to the right, in reaction to the second intifada, the rise of Hamas, the perceived failure of the peace process, and by demographic trends favoring sectors tending to hawkish positions: Jews of Middle Eastern background, religious Jews, and immigrants from the former Soviet Union.

As Table 13.1 shows, parties of the right grew from 39 seats (of 120) in 1973 to 45 in 1977, while parties of the left fell from 54 to 33 seats (analyzing Israeli elections by blocs of parties shows patterns more clearly than a focus on individual parties, which split and merge with kaleidoscopic complexity). The 1977 upheaval was not just a change in parties but also a watershed in Israeli politics. It brought a new orientation, with new values and political symbols, into equal political legitimacy and at least equal electoral potential with Labor Zionism. It marked the emergence of a truly competitive system, with clearly opposed options, as well as Israel's first successful transfer of power between parties. The thought that the 1977 elections might have been an aberration was put to rest by the 1981 elections. Likud continued its slow but steady climb, gaining an additional five seats over 1977.

In defiance of expectations, the 1984 elections produced a balance even more delicate than in 1981, forcing Labor and Likud to embark on an era of power-sharing as a "National Unity Government," with Yitzhak Shamir and Labor leader Shimon Peres taking turns as prime minister. The elections of 1988, like those of 1984, were again a potential turning point that turned nowhere: the two blocs again emerged nearly equal in the number of seats won. As a result, Labor was forced to agree to a renewed National Unity Government on less than equal terms, with Shamir projected as prime minister for the full four-year term of office.

In early 1990 the National Unity Government finally fell, marking the end of five and a half years of power-sharing by the two major blocs. After long and intricate maneuvering, Shamir emerged as head of a "narrow" Likud-led government with a bare majority. But this government was also unable to serve out its full term. The 1992 elections produced a narrow margin of victory for Labor together with other parties on the left. On the basis of this slim edge, the Labor-led government of Prime Minister Yitzhak Rabin opened up direct negotiations with the

Table 13.1 Knesset Seats by Blocs, 1973–2015

	1973	1977	1981	1984	1988	1992	1996	1999	2003	2006	2009	2013	2015
Arab[a]	8	8	4	6	6	5	9	10	8	10	11	11	13
Left[b]	54	33	48	47	47	56	43	38	28	24	16	21	29
Center[c]	4	17	4	7	2	0	11	18	15	36	28	27	11
Religious[d]	15	17	13	13	18	16	23	27	22	18	16	18	13
Right[e]	39	45	51	47	47	43	34	27	47	32	49	43	54

Notes: a. Arab parties: Hadash (formally binational party whose voters are predominantly Arab) (1973–2013), Progress and Development (1973), Bedouin and Arab Village List (1973), United Arab List (1977, 1992–2013), Progressive List for Peace (formally binational party whose voters are predominantly Arab) (1984–1988), Arab Democratic Party (1988–1992), Balad (1999–2013), Joint List (2015).

b. Left parties: Alignment/Labor (1973–2013), Civil Rights Movement (1973–1988), Mapam (1988), Meretz (1992–2015), Am Echad (1999–2003), Zionist Camp (2015).

c. Center parties: Independent Liberals (1973–1977), Democratic Movement for Change (1977), Telem (1981), Shinui (1981–1988, 1999–2003), Yahad (1984), Ometz (1984), Yisrael B'aliyah (1996–1999), Third Way (1996), Center Party (1999), Kadima (2006–2013), Gil (2006), Yesh Atid (2013, 2015), Hatnuah (2013).

d. Religious parties: National Religious Party (1973–2003), Religious Torah Front (1973), Agudat Yisrael (1977–1988), Poalei Agudat Yisrael (1977), Tami (1981–1984), Shas (1984–2015), Morasha (1984), Degel Hatorah (1988), United Torah Judaism (1992–2015).

e. Right parties: Likud (1973–2009, 2015), Shlomzion (1977), Tehiya (1981–1984), Tsomet (1984–1988), Kach (1984), Moledet (1988–1996), Ha'ichud Haleumi (1999–2009), Yisrael Beiteinu (1999, 2006–2009, 2015), Habayit Hayehudi (2013, 2015), Likud-Yishrael Beitenu (2013), Kulanu (2015).

Palestine Liberation Organization (PLO), initiating a process that led to the Israel-PLO Declaration of Principles in September 1993, agreement on Israeli withdrawal from Gaza and Jericho in May 1994, and an interim agreement on Palestinian autonomy in October 1995.

But Israel remained deeply divided between a secular, modernizing, more dovish half and a more traditional, conservative, hawkish half. This was underlined by the 1996 elections, which inaugurated an experiment of electing the prime minister directly in a vote separate from that for the Knesset. In a two-way race, Likud's Benjamin Netanyahu defeated Labor's Peres by less than 1 percent of the vote. The unintended consequence of the electoral reform was that voters abandoned Likud and Labor in large numbers in the regular party-list vote. The two major parties together gained only sixty-six seats, down from seventy-six in 1992.

The elections of 1999 continued this process of fragmentation, with Likud and Labor dropping to forty-five seats between the two of them, leading them to agree rather quickly on scrapping the direct election of the prime minister and returning to the prior system. In the meantime, however, Labor's Ehud Barak was elected prime minister in 1999 by a wide margin (56 vs. 44 percent) but then, in a specially called prime ministerial election (without a vote on Knesset seats) in February 2001, was soundly defeated (62 vs. 38 percent) by Likud leader Ariel Sharon.

Sharon also gained a solid victory in the next scheduled Knesset elections, in January 2003. But in 2005 his plan for unilateral withdrawal from Gaza sparked considerable opposition within his own party, leading him to split from Likud and found a new centrist party, Kadima (Forward), and call new elections for March 2006. In January 2006, however, Sharon suffered a massive stroke and was succeeded as party leader by Ehud Olmert. Under Olmert, Kadima emerged as the leading party and formed the core of a new government that included Labor and Shas, an ultra-orthodox party of Middle Eastern Jews.

For the first time in Israel's political history, a centrist party had formed a government. The center in Israeli politics has usually been weak; centrist parties have tended to make impressive debuts their first time out, gaining 10 percent or more of the vote (in 1977, 1996, 1999, and 2003), but then fade from the scene within one or two elections. Olmert's government was severely weakened by a two-front confrontation in the summer of 2006, against Hamas in the Gaza Strip and Hezbollah in southern Lebanon, in which Israel's military performance was sharply criticized. At the same time, Olmert's personal position was undermined by no fewer than five ongoing investigations for alleged personal corruption, forcing him to agree to elections for a new Kadima leader in September 2008. When the new leader, Tzipi Livni, was unable to reconstitute a government, elections were called for February 2009.

In the 2009 elections, against expectations, Livni managed to hold Kadima together and lose only one seat, even managing to beat Likud by one seat. For the first time in Israeli political history, a strong centrist party had actually lasted for more than one election. But the real import of the election was the clear victory of the right; in essence, the 2009 election erased the impact of the 2006 election that followed Ariel Sharon's defection from Likud and the establishment of Kadima. In 2006, center and left parties won seventy seats, while right-wing and religious parties held the remaining fifty. In 2009 the center and left were reduced to fifty-five seats, including eleven held by Arab parties, while right and religious parties grew to a combined sixty-five seats, thus reestablishing the clear majority won by these two blocs together in 2003.

The government established after elections was dominated by Likud, since together with two religious parties (Shas and United Torah Judaism) and two other right-wing parties (Yisrael Beitenu and Habayit Hayehudi) it commanded a majority. Labor, under Ehud Barak, also joined the coalition, giving the government seventy-four seats and leaving Kadima—the center party—rather illogically as the main opposition, despite its having won one more seat than Likud (twenty-eight to twenty-seven).

The 2013 election showed that the center in Israeli politics was there to stay, but that center parties could change rapidly. Kadima almost disappeared, shoved aside by the new party Yesh Atid (There Is a Future), led by television personality Yair Lapid. Yesh Atid gained much of its appeal by challenging the exemption of young ultra-orthodox Jews from military service. The aim was to form a government without the ultra-orthodox parties that would curtail the exemption from the draft and reduce generous government funding of ultra-orthodox institutions. At the time Benjamin Netanyahu was forced to follow the script, forming a government with Yesh Atid and without the religious parties. But friction between the two major parties led Netanyahu, sensing a drop in support for Yesh Atid, to call new elections in early 2015.

The 2015 elections were marked by a warning by Netanyahu on election day that Arabs (now unified in one party) were flocking to the polls in huge numbers. He called on all right-wing supporters to unify behind Likud. The ploy was effective as Likud emerged as the single largest party, largely at the expense of the religious parties and other right-wing parties. This enabled Likud to form a narrow right-religious government, without Yesh Atid, that reversed many of the measures aimed at curbing religious power and privilege that had been enacted by the previous government. The election also demonstrated that, because of demographic trends and other factors, right-wing and religious parties as a bloc had acquired clear dominance, having won a majority of the seats in all elections in the new century save the exceptional case of 2006.

Political Economy

Early Jewish settlers in Palestine had been exposed not only to the currents of nationalism and liberalism then prevalent in Europe but also to the ideas of socialism. Labor Zionists (as socialists came to be labeled) urged Jews to move out of such accustomed trades as commerce, finance, and the professions, and to create a Jewish proletariat based on manual labor, a return to the soil, and self-reliance in all spheres of production. In the words of the Zionist slogan, Jewish pioneers came to Eretz Yisrael (the Land of Israel) "in order to build and to be built in it." The establishment of the kibbutz, or rural communal settlement, was a perfect expression of these ideals.

The agrarian image of a return to the soil, as fostered by kibbutz ideology, was always exaggerated. A majority of new immigrants settled in cities; at its peak, in the 1930s, the agricultural sector accounted for less than a third of the Jewish population. The puzzle, then, is not the eventual decline of Labor Zionism but rather its long hold on power. Labor Zionists dominated the politics of the *yishuv* from the early 1930s, and socialist and agrarian thinking likewise dominated economic planning. In the circumstances of building a new society, the need for strong centralized planning was not seriously disputed, and both ideology and institutions carried over into the new state when it was established. As noted, the left-right spectrum on socioeconomic issues was not particularly prominent, being overshadowed by the Arab-Israel conflict. The roles of the public and private sectors were basically settled by the end of the first decade of statehood; there was considerable latitude for private enterprise (given the urgent need to attract capital), but in the framework of strong government direction and an extensive social welfare system.

Before the 1970s, Israel was judged to be an economic success story. With the help of reparations payments from Germany and private aid from Jewish communities, economic growth averaged around 10 percent a year. This was achieved despite the pressures of massive immigration and a level of defense spending (8 to 10 percent of gross domestic product [GDP]) heavier than that in any other democratic state. Israel did suffer from a chronic negative balance of trade, however, as well as from an overall negative balance of payments, which helped to fuel inflation.

The wars of 1967 and 1973 ratcheted defense spending up to new levels. It rose to over 20 percent of GDP after 1967 and to 28 percent or more after 1973, peaking somewhere above 30 percent (by most calculations) in 1975 (Berglas 1983). Yet there was no offsetting reduction in governmental social spending; in fact, public services continued to expand, with real spending rising by 60 percent per capita on health and 80 percent per capita on education during the 1968–1978 decade. By 1978, Israel ranked fifth in the world in public education expenditure as a proportion of GDP, at 8.5 percent (Ofer 1986).

The results were entirely predictable. The economy's annual growth rate fell to an average of 3.2 percent in the 1976–1989 period, with a low point of 1 to 2 percent in the early 1980s. Israel was not keeping pace with other developed countries; while per capita income stood at 83 percent of the average of the twenty-three most developed economies in 1960, this figure had dropped to 48 percent by 1978. The weight of public spending in Israel had always been impressive by world standards, running at around 50 percent of GDP, but by the early 1980s this had risen to 75 percent or more of GDP by most accounts, and for some years and by some measures even exceeded the official GDP.

By the mid-1980s, inflation was running at a 300–400 percent annual rate. Despite its supposed commitment to a market economy, Likud, after its 1977 victory, found itself no more able than Labor to tame the runaway economy (indeed, Likud's base of support was disproportionately, and paradoxically, among those most dependent on a continuing high level of government subsidies and services). The need for a massive restructuring of the economy was one of the major incentives for the formation of the National Unity Government after the elections of July 1984. This forced the two major blocs to share responsibility for the unpopular steps required, thus removing the issue from politics.

After some false starts, the National Unity Government used its emergency powers in July 1985 to impose a sweeping economic stabilization plan that was, like most large economic policies, the result of hard bargaining among the government, labor, and industry. The stabilization plan included dramatic cuts in government spending and subsidies, strict price controls, severe wage restraints, and devaluation, as well as measures to encourage private sector growth and the liberalization of trade restrictions in order to expose more of the economy to open competition.

The economic stabilization plan set in motion a gradual turnaround in the Israeli economy. In the short term it accelerated the deterioration of public services and threatened to collapse the agricultural sector, but it was a textbook success in curtailing inflation and reviving economic growth. A second round of market-oriented reforms took place in 2003–2005, when former prime minister Benjamin Netanyahu served as minister of finance in the Likud-led government of Ariel Sharon. These measures included reduction of the public sector, acceleration of privatization, a more competitive banking system, and welfare reform. With these changes, Israel completed a transition, similar to many developed economies, to a market economy integrated more closely with the globalizing world economy.

By 2007, Israel had matured as a modern, diversified economy with a very strong high-technology component, as indicated by the invitation that year to join the Organization for Economic Cooperation and Development (OECD). GDP by 2018 grew to $373.75 billion, or $42,120 per capita: in terms of purchasing power parity, on a par with developed European states (IMF 2018). The annual growth rate in 2018 was 4.4 percent, with almost no inflation. Israel ranked nineteenth in the world in 2016 on the UN Human Development Index, which the United Nations uses to measure social and economic well-being (UNDP 2016). Since 2002 Israel has been a creditor, rather than a debtor, nation, owing less than is owed to it. Its position will be further strengthened by exploitation of large natural gas reserves discovered offshore in 2010.

Globalization has been an integral feature of Israel's economic development, with a special significance because of the lack of regional economic ties. The Swiss Economic Institute's 2018 annual globalization index, which measures a nation's integration into the world economy, ranked Israel thirty-seventh among the countries of the world, ahead of every other Middle East nation (KOF Swiss Economic Institute 2018). One expression of this is that Israel now has free trade agreements with the European Union (EU), the United States, the European Free Trade Association (EFTA), Turkey, Mexico, Canada, Jordan, Egypt, and Mercosur (indeed, it is the only non–Latin American partner of this South American trading bloc). Another measure is that direct foreign investment in Israel grew from $532 million in 1992 to $32.2 billion—sixty times as much—at the beginning of 2018 (Trading Economics 2018).

Globalization of course brings problems as well as benefits: the sharpening of internal divisions between traditional and modernizing sectors, the loss of control over social and economic policies, and the threat to local cultures. In Israel's case there has been growing concern about inequality, with roughly a quarter of the population below the official poverty line. The OECD ranks Israel as having the highest poverty rate among its members, except for the United States (OECD 2018). Other analyses of the inequality issue argue that Israel ranks roughly as predicted by its level of development (Sharkansky 2004), but the issue receives considerable attention because of the obvious conflict with classic Labor Zionist ideology.

Civil Society

In analyzing Israeli politics, a focus on the formal structure and powers of institutions is misleading. Most important policy decisions have been the product of a bargaining process in which not only various branches of the government but also other public institutions and major social groups participate.

A notable feature of Israeli public life is the importance of nongovernmental public institutions performing what would ordinarily be considered governmental functions. In the past, Israel's Histadrut (Labor Federation) determined much public policy in such areas as health care, welfare, pensions, and wage policies. This is less the case today, but the Histadrut remains a key participant in broad economic decisionmaking. The Jewish Agency, which represents the World Zionist Organization in Israel and was the central Jewish body before statehood, remains active in the areas of immigration, settlement, economic development, and relations with Jewish communities abroad. The Jewish National Fund is deeply involved in the purchase and management of public lands.

Interest groups in Israel also reflect this state of affairs. There is relatively little legislative lobbying of the traditional sort, since the important decisions are not made in the Knesset. Interest groups bargain with, or pressure, the governmental ministries, parties, and other bodies that together make the important decisions. For this purpose, they not only approach decisionmakers directly, as they would in most pluralist democratic systems, but also sometimes become an integral part of the process. For example, the kibbutz and moshav movements, representing communal and cooperative settlements, have been closely tied to the Ministry of Agriculture; similarly, the Israeli Manufacturers Association works closely with the Ministry of Commerce and Industry. To an unusual extent, in comparison to like situations elsewhere, doctors are consulted on the policies of the Ministry of Health, bus drivers on those of the Ministry of Transport, and teachers on those of the Ministry of Education. At a minimum, many such groups are able to informally veto proposals that they consider inimical to their interests.

Another dimension of this pattern is the tendency to deal with outside challengers by trying to bring them within the system. The history of the gradual, step-by-step inclusion of the ultra-orthodox (*haredi*) community has, in a sense, been an essay in the co-optation of a potentially alienated and disruptive force. Initially the *haredim* had refused to participate in the institutions of the new Zionist *yishuv*. After the establishment of the Palestine Mandate, there was a compromise providing for some funding of *haredi* schools, leading later to an agreement on formal cooperation in 1934. When the state was established, Ben-Gurion gave assurances to *haredi* rabbis that Israel would not publicly violate religious law, thereby gaining their consent to join the new government on a de facto basis.

The level of political awareness and knowledge in Israel has traditionally been high. In a study comparing Israeli "civic culture" with that of the five nations studied in Gabriel Almond and Sydney Verba's classic 1963 study, 79 percent of the Israeli respondents reported reading a newspaper at least once a week (the highest figure in Almond and Verba's study was 53 percent, in West Germany). Also, 76 percent of the Israeli sample followed political news on radio or television at least once a week (the highest elsewhere was 58 percent, in the United States). In terms of political knowledge, 74 percent of the Israelis surveyed could name at least four government ministers and party leaders (the highest elsewhere was 40 percent, in West Germany) (Golan 1977; Almond and Verba 1963).

Access to the media was more limited in the early period, since radio and television, which began in the late 1960s, were under state control, and most of the press was party affiliated. This became more pluralistic and more flexible over time, however. In 1965 the establishment of the Israel Broadcasting Authority brought more autonomy to the electronic media. A variety of viewpoints are heard, especially during election campaigns, when each party is given free broadcast time in proportion to its electoral strength. Over the years, the press has become increasingly variegated and critical, with much of the party press disappearing.

The intimate scale of Israeli politics should also be taken into account. The exposure of Israeli leaders to their own public is extensive: a prominent Israeli party leader, in or out of government, will spend many hours every week in direct and unrehearsed contact with the public in various forums, all open to media coverage. Those at the very top appear almost nightly on Israeli news programs (watched by a vast majority of the nation), either in live interviews or in films of appearances elsewhere. The aura of office is eroded to a great extent by this close contact.

The level of protest and extraparliamentary political activity was relatively low during the early years, when the political system was still able to cope with the relatively few challenges that it faced by resorting to the traditional tool of co-opting protest leaders into the system. During the 1948–1977 period, Israel ranked about average compared to other nations on indicators of political protest, and well below average on indicators of political violence (Taylor and Jodice 1983). Underneath the seeming stability, however, were signs of a basically confrontational view of politics that was only temporarily submerged. From the early 1970s there was a steep rise in direct public participation in politics. By the 1980s the incidence of protest and demonstration in Israel surpassed that of almost any other democratic regime. One analyst concluded that Israel was "the most protest-oriented polity in the democratic world today," pointing out a 1981 survey showing that 21.5 percent of Israelis had taken part in a protest event, while the highest proportion anywhere else was 11 percent in the United States (Lehman-Wilzig 1986). In 2016 the number of Israelis reporting participation in a public protest had risen to 29.5 percent (Central Bureau of Statistics 2016).

Social protest took on a new dimension with the outbreak of massive demonstrations in mid-2011. The background was the skyrocketing cost of housing, an erosion in public services, and growing inequality, coupled with the concentration of key sectors of the economy in the hands of powerful conglomerates, resulting in artificially high consumer prices. It began with a massive outcry over a huge jump in the cost of cottage cheese but took definitive shape when residents unable to afford high rentals began pitching tents on a Tel Aviv street. Soon there were thousands of tents in all major cities, and hundreds of thousands participated in marches and demonstrations (the largest, in September, attracting an estimated half a million nationwide, or about 10 percent of the adult population).

The protest was similar in some respects to Arab Spring unrest elsewhere in the Middle East, including the importance of social networking, the predominance of youth, and the role of economic grievances. But the Israeli protest was primarily of domestic origin, and its demands were almost entirely economic: better and cheaper housing, changes in taxation, more free schooling, lower prices, and an end to privatization. There was less of a call for political change: while some protesters called for Prime Minister Netanyahu's resignation or a change of government, protest remained within the system. Inevitably it drew disproportionate support from the left, but at least initially it enjoyed broad public support. Here it should be recalled that, given the "reverse correlation" in Israeli politics (see Government and Opposition section), the party of the "right" (Likud) draws disproportionately from lower-income groups likely to identify with the protesters' demands.

Netanyahu's government responded by announcing a new housing program and by appointing a governmental commission to be chaired by an academic economist (Manuel Trajtenberg). The Trajtenberg Commission took only a month to present an extensive set of recommendations covering all areas of contention. Though rejected by many protesters as insufficient, many of the recommendations were in fact enacted over the ensuing months: changes in taxation, free schooling from the age of three, and measures to strengthen antitrust enforcement and increase competition to hold down prices. In the years since, the real wages of Israelis have increased significantly, in part because of the success in curbing inflation. The cost of housing has increased, however, by about 30 percent, meaning that this basic issue remains largely unresolved (Bahar 2016).

Religion and Politics

Israel is a "Jewish" state, but most Jews do not understand "Jewish" to imply a state based on religious law or theocratic principles. In its broadest interpretation, Jewishness is seen as a common national or ethnic identity of a historically developed community of people with distinct cultural attributes, including a distinct Judaic religion. But nonobservant Jews are still considered Jews, and Israel demonstrates that a "Jewish" state can operate largely by secular rather than religious law—precisely the major criticism of Israel made by religious Jews.

Israel does not match the Western ideal of separation between religion and state, but neither is it a theocracy governed by religious clerics or religious laws. Israel ranks somewhere in the middle of the spectrum, together with European states that feature established, state-supported religions but strong respect, at the same time, for religious freedom.

Israel does not even have a single state religion, as legally Judaism is but one of fourteen established and state-supported religions (together with Islam, Bahai, the Druze faith, and ten Christian denominations).

Thus, despite the absence of formal constitutional guarantees, the protection of minority religions is not the major issue. The main controversy involves the application of Jewish religious law to the Jewish public. Secular Israelis characterize existing arrangements (such as the orthodox rabbinical monopoly over Jewish marriage and divorce) as a form of religious coercion. Nonorthodox (Conservative and Reform) Jewish movements complain that only in Israel, among all democratic states, are they subject to legal discrimination. On the other hand, orthodox advocates argue that without protection by the state (for example, the guarantee of the right not to work on the Sabbath), those faithful to religious precepts are effectively denied equal rights and full integration into the nation's social and cultural life.

This debate is complicated by conflicting readings of Jewish law, by lack of precedent on this law's relationship to the state, and by the preexisting pattern of religious governance in the Middle East—the millet system of autonomy for religious communities—that carried over into Zionism and the State of Israel. Furthermore, both major groups within the religious population refused in principle to recognize the supremacy of state law over religious commandments: religious Zionists did so because their Zionism was linked to the state's religious mission, while non-Zionist "ultra-orthodox" Jews disputed the state's legitimacy from the outset.

In reality there are many degrees of religious observance in Israel. In 2016, 14.1 percent of Israeli Jews identified themselves as "ultra-orthodox" (*haredi*), 15.5 percent as "religious" or "very religious," 25 percent as "traditional," and 45.4 percent as "secular" (Central Bureau of Statistics 2018: 40).

Most Jewish religious authorities initially rejected Zionism as a theological error and as an institutional threat. While religious Zionists came to terms with the movement by ascribing messianic significance to the Jewish state as the "beginning of Redemption," anti-Zionists turned this on its head by labeling Zionism a "false Redemption." Genuine redemption—that is, God's final salvation of the world—could not take place in a secular framework. Cooperation and accommodation with the Zionist state were regarded by many anti-Zionists as a practical or tactical necessity but did not necessarily indicate recognition of its legitimacy.

After the Holocaust, most of the ultra-orthodox came to accept the practical necessity of an independent Jewish state, even if that state was not religiously correct. Before supporting Zionist goals even on this

Religious Divisions in Israel

Ultra-orthodox: Strictly religious Jews who refer to themselves as haredim, meaning "those who tremble in awe" (before God). Historically, *haredim* were anti-Zionist or non-Zionist on religious grounds, but most participate in Israeli politics on a de facto basis.

Religious Zionists: Jews who combine orthodox Jewish religious practice with Zionism. Also known as national religious, modern orthodox, or simply "religious" (*dati*).

Traditional (masorti): Jews who follow many Jewish religious traditions, but more as custom than as law. "Traditional" describes the religious practice of many Jews of Middle Eastern background.

Nonorthodox movements: Movements such as Conservative or Reform Judaism that challenge orthodox interpretations. Such movements are small in formal membership in Israel but may overlap traditional or secular Judaism in practice.

Secular: Israeli Jews who do not follow orthodox Jewish law in their daily life, though they may observe holidays and other rituals as part of the national culture.

conditional basis, however, they sought assurance that this "Jewish" state would not publicly desecrate religious law. David Ben-Gurion provided such assurance in a June 19, 1947, letter that became the basis of a "status quo" with which both sides could live. This status quo included recognizing the Jewish Sabbath as a day of rest, maintaining kashrut (Jewish dietary laws) in governmental institutions, providing state funding of religious public schools, and leaving jurisdiction over marriage and divorce in the hands of religious authorities.

Religious parties have been part of nearly every government coalition since 1948. Throughout most of this time the National Religious Party (NRP), representing religious Zionists, was the most consistent coalition partner. More recently, as the NRP has been absorbed into right-wing parties, the coalition partner has usually been Shas, the Sephardi Torah Guardians, who represent the ultra-orthodox among Jews of Middle Eastern origin (Sephardim).

Discontent about the role of religion in Israeli life is quite audible, but it needs to be seen in perspective. The status quo represents no one's preferred solution but is simply a compromise that most Israelis accept for want of a better option. Clearly the long-term goals of secularists and the orthodox are incompatible, but in the meantime the level of mutual dissatisfaction has been in reasonable balance. Despite dissatisfaction, there is little actual challenge to the basic elements of the status quo or to the general division of territory between the secular and religious spheres of life.

The primary religious arrangement that impinges on the "freedom of conscience" of a secular Israeli is the monopoly of marriage and divorce matters in the hands of the orthodox rabbinate. All Israeli Jews wishing to be married in Israel must meet the orthodox definition of who is Jewish and who is eligible to be married to whom (for example, *kohanim*—considered to be descendants of Aaron—cannot marry divorcees). On the other hand, marriages performed in other countries are recognized, providing an alternative for many secular Israelis. Most other examples of religious legislation either are matters of minor inconvenience, are unenforced, or in practice affect only religious Jews. Furthermore, there is widespread support, or at least tolerance, among secular Israelis for many of the symbolic expressions of Judaism in public life.

Strikingly, there is not even agreement on which side is gaining. Both secular and religious Israelis tend to perceive themselves as losing ground to the other side. Both sides claim defeat. This accounts for some of the bitterness in the confrontation, despite the balance of mutual dissatisfaction. But the major threats to the stability of secular-religious relations in Israel are the rise of ultra-orthodox influence within the religious camp and the strong link that has been forged between religious Zionism and territorial nationalism.

Religious Zionists often lament what they term the "retreat" of modern orthodoxy before a resurgence of ultra-orthodoxy. The results of the three 2009–2015 elections were especially alarming, as two ultra-orthodox parties remained in sole possession of the religious camp, while the remnants of the National Religious Party merged into right-wing parties. There is evidence that the classic power-sharing pattern in Israeli religious politics is declining and religious-secular conflict is on the rise, in large part because of the rise of the ultra-orthodox within the religious community. There is, consequently, a more explicit rejection of pluralism as a model and less willingness to compromise on religious issues (Cohen 2004). Others argue, however, that as Shas has taken the place of the NRP as an available coalition partner, the basic accommodation is still alive (Sandler and Kampinsky 2009).

The second major problematic aspect of religion and politics in Israel is tied to broader political issues. Many Israelis have felt threatened by orthodoxy not because of religious issues per se but because of the linkage between religious fervor and militant nationalism. The highly charged issues connected with Israeli-Arab relations, including such questions as Jewish settlement in the territories held by Israel after 1967, are widely seen as religious issues, since many of the more fervent nationalists come from religious Zionist circles.

Identity and Politics

Israel is marked by a communal division between Jews of European background (Ashkenazim) and those from the Middle East, Africa, or Asia (Sephardim), and by an ethnic division between Jews and Arabs. In addition, a large influx of immigrants from the former Soviet Union since the 1970s has created a new subculture that has become a lasting feature of Israel's society.

The communal split in Israel developed from the reality that members of the founding generation were predominantly secular Zionists from Eastern Europe, and that most Jews from non-European backgrounds arrived after the social and political framework of the state had been established. The European elite tended to regard Sephardi (Middle Eastern) Jews patronizingly, assuming that they would have to assimilate to the prevailing model. However, gaps between the two communities persisted into following generations in social, cultural, political, and (to a lesser extent) economic terms. The political awakening of second-generation Sephardim, beginning in the late 1960s, was marked by deep resentment toward the existing Labor establishment and contributed greatly to the upheaval of 1977.

But while its grip has been loosened, the Western, secular model of Zionism is still the officially sanctioned version taught widely and systematically in schools. In addition, the categories of Ashkenazim and Sephardim (or "Western" and "Eastern") have become increasingly irrelevant as intermarriage has risen steadily. (In fact, the Central Bureau of Statistics has stopped trying to keep track of intercommunal marriages.) Officially, in 2017, 25 percent of Israeli Jews were born in, or had fathers born in, Asia or Africa; 31 percent were born in, or had fathers born in, Europe or America; and 44 percent were born to fathers also born in Israel (Central Bureau of Statistics 2017). Remaining communal differences are likely to blur yet further. Also, there is a strong sense of commonness among Jews in Israel; in the end, the communal split is less of a threat than other divisions (ethnic or religious), because both communities regard it as a transitory division. There is no significant opposition to integration into a common society and culture, though communal subcultures may remain.

Middle Eastern Jews, by integrating into Israeli life, have to a great extent adopted the patterns of Western society. Families have become smaller and less patriarchal, fertility rates have decreased, women have entered the job market, "Western" consumer patterns and leisure activities have been adopted, and religious observance and traditional customs have declined. Differences remain, of course: residential patterns are still segregated to some degree, religious observance and traditional gender roles are still stronger among Eastern Jews, and families are still somewhat larger.

But the "social distance" between the two communities has diminished dramatically. For example, the percentage of high school students with reservations about "intermarriage" between the two communities dropped from 60 percent in 1965 to 21 percent only ten years later; in 1991 only 6 percent of an adult sample opposed marriage of their son or daughter to someone from a different community (Smooha 1978; Levy, Levinsohn, and Katz 1993). Thus it is not surprising that communal identity is not considered very important to most Israelis; when asked to rank nine different components of collective identity, only 2.7 percent ranked their communal identity first, while 75.3 percent said it was not important at all (Kimmerling 1993).

To use Knesset membership as an index, only 6 percent (7 seats out of 120) in the first Knesset (1949) were of non-European origin, and in the eighth Knesset (1973) this had risen to only 10 percent (12 seats). With the electoral "upheaval" of 1977, this number rose to 23 seats, and thereafter increased steadily: 30 in 1981, 32 in 1984, 38 in 1988, 40 in 1992, 41 in 1996, and 40 in 2009. By this time, due to intermarriage it became difficult to offer precise numbers in the Knesset, as it had become earlier in the general population. But with about one-third of Knesset members having Middle East origins, representation there was roughly in line with the nation as a whole.

Israel has had a Sephardi president, chief of staff, deputy prime minister, speaker of the Knesset, and chairman of the Histadrut. Representation in the top echelons of the civil service, the Histadrut, party central committees, and other centers of power, while not yet proportionate to numbers in the population at large, also has increased substantially.

The Sephardi percentage of the population has actually decreased given the large influx of immigrants from the Soviet Union in the 1970s, and from the former Soviet Union after its collapse in 1991. These two groups constitute about 20 percent of Israel's population and have "changed Israel forever" (Gitelman 2004: 106). Arriving with a higher level of education than most immigrant groups, they have contributed greatly to Israel's economic advance, especially in high technology. They have also created a lively Russian subculture—newspapers, magazines, educational and cultural institutions, entertainment, shops, and so forth—that continues to thrive. Politically, the immigrants from the former Soviet Union have favored hawkish positions on security issues and secularism on the religious front. Russian parties were the first "immigrant" parties to succeed in the Israeli political system, securing several seats in elections from 1996 onward. In the 2009 election, the largely Russian Yisrael Beiteinu party, which takes a very hawkish position, won fifteen seats and emerged as the third-largest party in the Knesset. However, it dropped to thirteen in 2013 and to only six in 2015.

The ethnic division between Jew and Arab poses a more basic challenge to Israel as a Jewish state. The place of the Palestinian Arab minority in Israel—about 21 percent of the population—is quite different from that of any part of the Jewish population. While Arabs in Israel possess formal rights of citizenship, including the right to vote, and have access to the political system, they stand outside the sphere of mainstream Jewish politics. There has been no meaningful power-sharing with the Arab community and, despite great absolute progress made since 1948, no proportionate distribution of economic gains, government services, or other public goods. Until the early 1980s there was no independent nationwide Arab political party or organization dedicated to the vigorous pursuit of Arab rights within the Israeli political system and speaking credibly for the Arab community as a whole. In short, in the bargaining process that characterizes Israeli politics, the Arab community has not been invited to participate as a negotiating partner and has not coalesced on a strategy for pursuing this status.

Though Israeli Arabs are not partners in the political system, the overall trend has been toward gradual, if halting and incomplete, liberalization. The starting point, in 1948, was one of overwhelming suspicion and de facto domination on one side, and overwhelming alienation and demoralization on the other, with enormous economic, educational, and other gaps between the two communities. A military government established in Arab areas was phased out by the early 1970s. Expropriation of land within Israel (as opposed to the occupied Palestinian territories), beyond legitimate public need, came virtually to a halt after 1976. By the early 1990s there was visible representation of Arabs in some fields of public life, especially health, education, police, media, arts, and the Histadrut. But the peace process of the 1990s brought few tangible improvements in their position (al-Haj 2004). An "equality index," devised by the leading organization working for equality, put inequality in 2009 at 0.3361 on a scale of 0 to 1 (0 being complete equality and 1 complete inequality); this represented an increase of 6.1 percent in inequality since the index was first established in 2006. Large gaps remained, in order of increasing severity, in health, housing, education, employment, and social welfare (Sikkuy 2009).

Government policy alone does not explain such things as the underrepresentation of Arabs in the Knesset. Even though there are informal barriers and national political organization is weak, there is no formal obstacle to Arabs voting for Arab party lists and achieving a level of representation proportionate to their share of the population. Only one proposed Arab party list—the El Ard movement in the 1960s—has been disqualified from competing in elections (on grounds that it rejected the legitimacy of the State of Israel as a Jewish state).

The Arab public was politically fragmented until 2015, when a higher threshold for entry into the Knesset forced Arab parties to unify. Their "Joint List" won thirteen seats, emerging as the third-largest party in the Knesset. This election also raised the turnout among Arab voters, which had been dropping and fell to 57 percent in 2013 (compared to 67 percent in the Jewish sector). In 2015 it rose to about 64 percent. The number of Arab Knesset members reached an all-time high of seventeen: the thirteen Joint List members and four on other party lists.

Palestinian Arab citizens of Israel have recently become more assertive in their demands for transforming Israel into a "state of all its citizens." In an important series of documents issued in 2007, leaders of this community challenged the basic legitimacy of a Jewish state, calling for the elimination of all elements that reflect an ethnic character—such as the right of Jews to return to Israel, or even the national anthem and flag. But while they may be demanding basic changes in the political system, Arab citizens of Israel clearly want to remain a part of the state. Suggestions that Arab-populated areas of Israel be transferred to a Palestinian state have met with vociferous opposition from these very inhabitants.

Gender and Politics

Classic Labor Zionist ideology included strong advocacy of women's rights, invoking the socialist image of men and women fighting shoulder to shoulder in the struggle against oppression and injustice. The image of the founding generations, especially in such settings as the progressive kibbutz movement, pictured women in frontline roles tilling the soil, driving trucks, and even bearing arms. The Israeli Defense Forces (IDF) became the world's only army that drafted women, and Prime Minister Golda Meir was one of the first, and one of the best-known, female heads of state.

In truth there was always a considerable gap here, as in other respects, between ideology and reality. Early settlers came from societies that were still fairly traditional in gender and family terms, and

The Islamic Movement in the Knesset

Among the movements active in the Arab sector of Israeli society is the Islamic Movement, which sees itself as part of the Islamist resurgence throughout the Middle East. Israeli Islamists have been especially active in local politics and have gained control of a number of Arab municipalities. The movement debated at length whether to run in Knesset elections, which are closed to any party that negates "the existence of the State of Israel as the state of the Jewish people." But beginning in 1996 the southern branch of the Islamic Movement ran on a joint Knesset list (the United Arab List [UAL]) with the Arab Democratic Party. Since 2003 the United Arab List has formed an electoral alliance with the Arab Movement for Change (Ta'al); in 2009 and 2013 UAL-Ta'al won four seats, two of them held by Islamic Movement leaders. In 2015, when the threshold for representation was raised, the UAL joined the other three major Arab parties in the Joint List, winning thirteen seats—four of them held by UAL representatives. The party's eligibility to run in Knesset elections has often been challenged; in 2009 it was disqualified by the Central Elections Committee, but the ban was overturned by Israel's Supreme Court.

they tended to continue familiar patterns; even in the kibbutzim, women were relegated to cooking, laundry, and childcare. Women in the IDF were not assigned to combat duty, and in fact certain military occupations (for example, clerical or communications posts) also became "women's work," while the overwhelmingly masculine ethos of the military establishment actually worked to reinforce traditional gender roles and the subordination of women.

Israel was in the forefront as far as legal equality was concerned; legislation to date includes measures for equal pay, affirmative action, and tough penalties for violence against women. But Israel lagged behind many other states regarding de facto equality in public life, in the marketplace, and in society at large (Swirsky and Safir 1991). Even some of the advances made were rolled back as progressive ideology yielded ground to more traditional attitudes associated with growing religiosity or imported non-Western folkways. The decline of classic Labor ideology, reinforced by increasing religiosity and the large immigration from Middle Eastern societies with very conventional gender roles, led to further slippage in achieving gender equality. There was a visible revival of traditional femininity.

Religious law had always presented serious obstacles to the achievement of gender equality. In Israel, control of all marriage and divorce by the orthodox rabbinical establishment means that all women, regardless of personal beliefs, are subject to the discriminatory provisions of these laws. One ongoing problem, for example, is the plight of *agunot*, women who are "chained" to husbands who have disappeared or who are recalcitrant, but without whose consent no divorce can be granted. In 2018 the Knesset was considering a bill that would expand the power of rabbinical courts to deal with such cases. But the rise of ultra-orthodox influence has also led to attempts toward further segregation or restriction. For example, there are now bus routes in ultra-orthodox neighborhoods with "modesty buses," in which women voluntarily (in theory) segregate themselves in the back of the bus.

On a political level, the number of women members of the Knesset fell from twelve (10 percent) in the first two Knessets to only eight in the 1981 Knesset. Only in 1999 did the number rise appreciably, to eighteen; it rose to twenty-four in the 2003 elections, fell to seventeen in 2006, and rose again to twenty-four in 2009, to twenty-seven in 2013, and to twenty-nine in 2015—which increased to thirty-four by 2018 due to replacement of party representatives. In all Israeli governments from 1948 to 2018, only eighteen women served as ministers. The government formed after the 2015 election included five women (among twenty-eight ministers), more than any of its predecessors.

In 2007 the Israel Women's Network, the leading lobbying force for women's rights, submitted to the Knesset's Committee on the Status of Women a lengthy study on women in the economy. The study documented the fact that, despite legal guarantees, women are paid on average one-third less than men for the same job. This gap has remained unchanged since 1967; in 2017 it was measured as 31.7 percent (Central Bureau of Statistics 2017). The United Nations Development Programme, however, ranked Israel nineteenth in the world in gender equality in its most recent "Gender Inequality Index"—ahead of most European nations (UNDP 2016).

One area of progress was the judiciary, where by 2011 women composed nearly 51 percent of lower court judges and held five of the fifteen Supreme Court positions. Most political parties had adopted affirmative action goals for leadership positions, though this did not apply to the religious parties, whose twenty-two Knesset members were all males. In the civil service nearly 60 percent of employees were women, but they were concentrated in the lower levels of the bureaucracy (Chazan 2011).

One development that increased awareness of gender issues in Israel was the appearance of high-profile cases involving charges of sexual harassment and sexual crimes. The most prominent case involved the president of Israel, Moshe Katsav, who was accused of repeated sexual harassment and rape, and who was forced from office (near the end of his term) in a plea bargain that he later repudiated. As a result Katsav stood trial and in December 2010 was convicted on two counts of rape and other sexual offenses. After exhausting all channels of appeal, he entered prison a year later to begin a seven-year sentence.

The Impact of International Politics

The international context has been a dominant force in the shaping of Israeli history and politics. Events in other lands impelled the waves of immigration that created the Jewish community in Palestine. Relations between the major powers and the Ottoman Empire greatly influenced the development of this community, and the establishment of Britain's Palestine Mandate was instrumental in its consolidation. After statehood, Israel was dependent on outside powers for economic and military support; this support came from the French during the 1950s, and then from the United States after the 1967 war.

In some respects, Israel's international standing is at an all-time high. In 1985 only 68 states maintained diplomatic relations with Israel; in 2018 the number was 159, including several Muslim nations. In the United States support for Israel remains strong, with public opinion favoring Israel by a three-to-one margin (64 percent to 19 percent) over the Palestinians in a February 2018 poll (Gallup Polls 2018). Strategic cooperation—spurred by the "war on terror"—remains as high as ever. The US focus on the terrorism threat has played to Israel's advantage by strengthening agreement on the definition of common enemies.

The most important external influence, however, is regional, not global. The dominant issue in Israeli politics is, and always has been, the conflict with Palestinians and with Arab states over the creation of a Jewish state and, since 1967, over Israel's occupation of lands then forming parts of Jordan, Syria, and Egypt. In recent years this conflict has entered a new stage with the emergence of radical Islamist movements. The shift began with the appearance of Hezbollah, a non-Palestinian Shi'ite Arab movement in Lebanon inspired and supported by the Islamic Republic of Iran. This was followed by the Palestinian movement Hamas—the Islamic Resistance Movement—which came into existence with the onset of the first intifada, at the end of 1987. In 2006 this process culminated in the victory of Hamas in Palestinian elections in January, and the war between Israel and Hezbollah in July and August. In June 2007 Hamas took over complete control of the Gaza Strip, meaning that any agreement between Israel and the Palestinian Authority would at best apply only to the 60 percent of the Palestinian population who reside in the West Bank.

In some ways the regional setting is less threatening to Israel than it was in decades past. Neighboring Arab states have, since 1967, engaged in a gradual disengagement from the Arab-Israeli conflict, and Israel now has peace treaties and normal relations with two of the four bordering Arab states. There have been no state-to-state wars since 1973; the Arab boycott of those who deal with Israel is defunct; the Iraqi threat no longer exists; and Egypt and Jordan—before the Arab Spring—had even become, in a limited way, strategic partners. But in other respects, the regional setting seems more ominous, with renewed calls for Israel's destruction from the leaders of Iran and other extremist religious figures in the Muslim world.

Iran's threats were seen in light of its nuclear technology development, which brought that nation within months of producing nuclear weapons should it choose to withdraw from the Nuclear Non-Proliferation Treaty. This "breakout" time was lengthened by at least a year by the nuclear agreement reached between Iran and the world's six leading powers in 2015, though the Israeli government opposed that agreement as inadequate (and the United States subsequently withdrew from it). The issue remains central in Israeli perceptions. Indeed, it is part of a bigger issue: the reality of the proliferation of weapons of mass destruction in the Middle East. Chemical and biological weapons are a part of the equation between Israel and Syria, for example. A regional "balance of terror" already exists.

The outbreak of the second intifada, in 2000, together with the rise of Hamas and the events of 2006–2007, pushed the Israeli electorate in a hawkish direction. Prime Minister Ariel Sharon, long regarded as a superhawk, had carried out the evacuation of Israeli settlements and forces from Gaza in late 2005, and disengagement—or "consolidation"—was the declared objective of the government formed, under the new Kadima party, after elections in early 2006. But with the intensification of attacks and threats from evacuated areas—Lebanon in 2000 and Gaza in 2005—support for further withdrawals disappeared, and elections in 2009, 2013, and 2015 confirmed a shift to the right that had already registered in 2003. Continuing rocket attacks on Israeli cities and towns near the Gaza Strip created great pressure on the government to act, leading finally to military campaigns in Gaza in 2008–2009, 2012, and 2014.

The emergence of the Arab Spring at the end of 2010 posed new challenges to Israel and put greater pressure on its political system. In theory, a more democratic Middle East would work in Israel's favor by removing aggressive autocrats and providing a better long-term platform for lasting peace agreements. But this is the long-term view; the turbulent transition to stable democracy promised, in the short term, some rough passages.

The truth was that some autocratic regimes were less hostile to Israel than their own publics, and that this had provided some stability, over the decades, in their relations to Israel. The primary case was Egypt, which had observed a peace treaty with Israel since 1979. The fall of the Husni Mubarak regime and the election of an Islamist president in Cairo rang alarm bells at all levels in Israeli public life. Though Muslim Brotherhood leaders, including the new president Mohammad Morsi, promised to maintain the peace treaty with Israel, there were already signs that Morsi would test the limits and act more unilaterally. Of special concern was the future of Hamas-controlled Gaza, where Egypt had cooperated with Israel's partial blockade. Given that Hamas defined itself as a branch of the Muslim Brotherhood, it seemed likely that the new Egyptian regime would open up its frontier with Gaza and thereby undercut Israel's strategy on this critical issue.

Another case of major concern was Jordan, where King Abdullah's peaceful relations with Israel ran counter to prevailing attitudes among much of his public, a majority of them Palestinians. The Arab Spring also pushed the Palestinian Authority and Hamas to engage in serious talks aimed at unifying Gaza and the West Bank. Though none of the unity agreements achieved were immediately implemented, the specter of a renewed Hamas presence in the West Bank gave Israeli policymakers another reason to view the Arab Spring with misgivings.

The outbreak of civil war in Syria was also a source of concern. Though the Asad regime (father and son) was among the most hostile to Israel, it had since 1970 avoided direct war and had kept the mutual border quiet. Should the regime fall, there was fear that what might follow—an Islamist government?—might be a bigger threat. Moreover, there were fears that the chaos itself would spill over into Israel, or that Syria's chemical weapons might fall into irresponsible hands.

All of this made a renewal of the peace process less likely. Israelis tended to see greater risks in the new situation, leading to support for more far-reaching security demands and less readiness for concessions. When new US Secretary of State John Kerry made the third major effort (after 2000–2001 and 2007–2008) to settle the Israeli-Palestinian conflict, the government of Netanyahu added new demands for the stationing of Israeli forces on the Jordan River and requiring that the Palestinian Authority recognize Israel as the nation-state of the Jewish people in any future agreement.

Since the major axis of Israeli politics is Arab-Palestinian relations, the terms *left* and *right* should be read as "dovish" and "hawkish" more than as positions on socioeconomic issues. To clarify this, let us look at the spectrum of positions toward the conflict, proceeding from left (dovish) to right (hawkish).

The Joint List of four Arab parties, in its 2015 electoral platform, backed a two-state solution with an independent Palestinian state in the entire West Bank and Gaza along pre-1967 lines, including East Jerusalem as its capital. It supported the right of return for all Palestinian refugees to their former homes in Israel itself as set out in UN Resolution 194 of 1949.

Jewish parties on the left, Meretz and the Zionist Union, also support a two-state solution but leave room for modification of the pre-1967 borders on strategic or demographic grounds. Meretz emphasizes the need for Israel to integrate itself into the Middle East, while the Zionist Union stresses defensible borders and Jerusalem remaining the capital of Israel.

In the center, Yesh Atid supports "two states for two peoples" with provisions to include large Jewish settlement blocs in the West Bank within Israel's borders. The party also supports a regional approach to peace negotiations based on cooperation with moderate Arab regimes.

The ultra-orthodox religious parties historically have not taken strong positions on foreign policy and security, given their ambivalence toward the Zionist state. This is still true for United Torah Judaism, the Ashkenazi party, although it is sympathetic to the right of Jews to settle anywhere in the historical Land of Israel and its voters tend to oppose any territorial withdrawal. Shas, the Sephardi ultra-orthodox party, has opposed the Oslo peace process as well as unilateral disengagement and is strongly opposed to any redivision of Jerusalem.

Right-wing parties oppose unilateral territorial concessions and reject a return to the pre-1967 borders or any territorial compromise on Jerusalem. Likud has issued a highly conditional acceptance of a two-state solution but argues that any future borders must be based on security considerations and that any negotiations must involve only "sincere" partners. Yisrael Beiteinu, with its base in immigrants from the former Soviet Union, takes a somewhat heterodox view in arguing for territorial exchange rather than concessions; the party has even proposed swapping Arab-inhabited areas of Israel proper for settlement blocs in the West Bank. The smaller parties on the far right, representing primarily religious nationalists and strongly linked to Jewish settlers in the territories, continue to oppose any Palestinian state and would offer negotiated autonomy to Arabs in the West Bank and Gaza.

It is important to note continuing strong support in Israel for negotiation and a two-state solution, despite the bleak prospects. A 2018 poll showed 55 percent of Jewish Israelis supporting a two-state solution (Institute for National Security Studies 2018). However, at about the same time 79 percent felt the chance of establishing an independent Palestinian state in the next five years was low or nonexistent (Palestine Center for Survey and Policy Research 2017).

14

Jordan

Curtis R. Ryan

The Hashimite Kingdom of Jordan is one of the smaller and more resource-poor states in the Middle East, yet its regional influence seems often to belie these factors. The Kingdom can be seen as weaker than its neighbors by almost any measure—politically, economically, militarily—yet it tends to be more stable than most of them. Jordan is one of only two countries in the region to maintain a peace treaty with Israel, and it has long-standing alliances with powerful international actors, such as the United States, the United Kingdom, and the states of the European Union. Jordan's kings, and indeed the country at large, have each developed a reputation as a regional "survivor" by pursuing moderate policies and at all times ensuring that the kingdom has a strong set of regional and global allies to rely on. In an otherwise tumultuous region, Jordan has managed to survive multiple Arab-Israeli wars, a civil war, and wave upon wave of refugee flows from neighboring states into the Hashimite Kingdom, including Palestinians, Iraqis, and since 2011, Syrians.

When the "Arab Spring" spread across the region, Jordan did not see a revolution, coup d'etat, or civil war, unlike many of its neighbors. But it did see protesters in the streets, and tensions between government and opposition. Although Jordan can be seen to have survived this set of challenges too, at least during the era of the Arab uprisings, most of the issues that brought people into the streets remain unresolved. In many ways, and for many years now, Jordanian domestic politics has been dominated by struggles over the meaning and depth of reform in the kingdom.

Historical Background and Contemporary Political Structure

Jordan's King Abdullah II ascended the Hashimite throne in 1999, succeeding his long-serving father, the late King Hussein, who had ruled from 1953 to 1999. Abdullah became only the fourth king in the Hashimite dynasty, and indeed the Hashimites only came to rule the area now known as Jordan in the third decade of the twentieth century. Thus both the Jordanian state and the monarchy itself are relatively modern creations on the world stage.

Like so many states in the Middle East, the modern state of Jordan first emerged from the imperial machinations that divided the Middle East following the collapse of the Ottoman Empire in World War I. After the war, Britain, under the League of Nations mandate system, carved out Jordan's borders and set up the Hashimite regime under the Emir Abdullah (who later became King Abdullah I). The Hashimite family, however, actually hailed from Mecca in western Arabia (in what is today Saudi Arabia). During World War I, the Hashimites had allied themselves with the British, helping to launch the "Great Arab Revolt" against the Ottoman Turkish Empire. But in the years immediately following the war, the Hashimites plunged into another conflict, this time with the rival Al Saud family and its allies. The Saudis defeated the Hashimites, consolidated control over much of the Arabian Peninsula (which they thereafter renamed Saudi Arabia), and expelled the Hashimite family.

Despite their defeat and ouster from Arabia, the Hashimites, with strong British support, reemerged as the ruling dynasties in two newly created Arab states: Transjordan and Iraq. The Hashimite dynasty in Iraq was overthrown and eliminated in a bloody coup in Baghdad in 1958. Yet more than fifty years later in neighboring Jordan, the Hashimite monarchy continues to both reign and rule. Following its emergence as a British mandate in 1921, Jordan evolved into the Emirate of Transjordan at the time of independence from Britain in 1946 and finally, in 1949, into its current form as the Hashimite Kingdom of Jordan (Wilson 1987). In its origins, then, Jordan can be seen as among the most artificial states in the modern Middle East, with a highly contested national identity (Fathi 1994; Layne 1994; Lynch 1999; Massad 2001). Over time, however, a sense of nationhood has developed within the kingdom so that the notion of "Jordanian" does carry very real meaning for most Jordanians.

From the 1950s to 1999, King Hussein was the key figure to lead Jordan's political development, creating many of its institutions and ensuring that the Western "great powers" would view the kingdom as of vital geopolitical and geostrategic importance in both the Cold War and the Middle East peace process. From the foundation of the Hashimite state onward, Jordan maintained close strategic ties to Britain. After World War

II, and with the onset of the Cold War, Jordan also established increasingly strong links to the United States, as the Western powers came to view Jordan as a conservative bulwark against communism and radical forms of pan-Arabism, and potentially as a moderating element in the Arab-Israeli conflict. King Hussein, for his part, played on these concerns and his regime's conservative and anticommunist credentials to solidify ties with the United States in particular (al-Madfai 1993). From the beginning, then, Jordan has held close ties to powerful Western states and has in fact depended heavily on foreign aid from these countries to keep the economy stable and to support the survival of the Hashimite regime itself.

The regime emphasizes that Jordan is a constitutional monarchy, with the roles and responsibilities of governing institutions established in the 1952 Jordanian constitution. In Jordanian politics, executive power is invested mainly in the hands of the king but also in those of his appointed prime minister and cabinet (the Council of Ministers). The political system also includes a bicameral legislature, with a royally appointed upper house (Majlis al-'Ayyan, or House of Notables or Senate) and a popularly elected 110-member lower house (Majlis al-Nu'ab, or House of Representatives). In addition to these national institutions, the kingdom is divided into twelve governorates, each with a royally appointed governor.

The most important change to the machinery of government in Jordan began when the regime initiated its program of limited political liberalization in 1989. Yet that process is rooted mainly in national legislative and local municipal elections and hence has not really extended to the executive branch of government. The prime minister remains a royal appointee, and cabinet ministers are not necessarily drawn from among the elected members of parliament.

In some respects, as in many other political systems, the upper house of parliament is designed to serve as a check on the lower house. Even the leadership of the two bodies underscores this point, for the speaker of the House of Representatives is elected from and by members of the House, while the speaker of the Senate is appointed by the king. Perhaps not surprisingly, the Senate speaker tends to be a conservative royalist drawn from one of the more powerful families in the kingdom. The membership of the Senate overall, in fact, is actually constitutionally required to consist of top regime veterans. The constitution, for example, notes that Senate membership is to be extended only to former prime ministers or other ministers, ambassadors, former top military officers, and so on. As a result, the Senate often appears to be a who's who—or who was who—of Jordanian politics. In sum, this chamber remains unaffected by the political liberalization process, at least institutionally. The parliamentary effects of political liberalization, therefore, can be seen almost exclusively within the lower house.

The members of the lower house are divided among various multimember constituencies. The regime also reserves a number of seats for specific minority constituencies, all of which have traditionally been strong supporters of the Hashimite monarchy. These include six seats for the rural bedouin, nine seats for the Christian community, and three seats for the Circassian and Chechen communities collectively. Jordanian opposition figures, especially those from Jordan's majority Muslim community, have long argued that such set-asides overrepresent ethnic and religious minorities. In contrast, many members of these minority communities see the reserved seats as critical to the preservation of their rights. This type of formula, originally intended to ensure religious and ethnic representation, has now also been applied to the kingdom's gender politics; in 2003, the regime added a quota of six seats to guarantee women's representation in the legislature. That number increased in later electoral laws, and by 2013 fifteen seats were reserved for women's representation in parliament.

Jordan's judiciary is slowly becoming a more independent entity, as the regime attempts to streamline judicial proceedings, improve the training and salaries of judges, and professionalize the court system. Yet judges remain appointees of the Higher Judiciary Council, whose members are—in turn—themselves royal appointees. The judicial system includes criminal, civil, and religious courts. The religious courts provide for separate proceedings for Muslims and Christians, in order to accommodate different religious traditions and approaches to such matters as marriage, divorce, and family law.

While Jordan did not see revolutionary fervor in 2011 or 2012, the regime did clearly feel the pressure to make changes in all the institutions and governing structures noted above. Alarmed at the sight of large demonstrations across the country (as regimes fell in Tunisia and Egypt), the monarchy dismissed the government. A series of cabinet reshuffles and changes in prime minister followed, so that Jordan had five governments from January 2011 to December 2012. The regime also responded with a series of reform measures, including a new electoral law, a new law on political parties, multiple amendments to the constitution, the establishment of a constitutional court, and an independent electoral commission. Yet many in the opposition regarded these as minimal changes and demanded far deeper structural reforms.

Pro-reform parties and movements called for a more constitutional monarchy, beyond the current model, in which the king cedes some of his powers to the elected parliament. Reformers also demanded that the Senate should be elected rather than appointed, that the judiciary should be more fully independent, and that there should be more checks, balances, and separation of powers between the government, the monarchy, and the parliament. The government itself, they argued, should emerge from parliament after elections (as in a truer parliamentary system) rather than be royally appointed, and the election law should be changed to eliminate gerrymandered districts and allow greater opportunities for political parties to win elections and secure representation in parliament.

Government and Opposition

King Hussein, who led Jordan's political development from the early 1950s to his death in 1999, set a pattern for Jordanian politics by developing the power of the Jordanian state while also allowing intermittent and minimal levels of pluralism. Thus the Jordanian state under the Hashimite regime never developed the level of authoritarianism found in neighbors such as Saudi Arabia, Syria, or (for most of its existence) Iraq. But neither was pluralism allowed to flourish if it in any way challenged the state. For that reason, Jordan was often regarded as a semi-authoritarian or, to use a more recent phrase, a "soft" authoritarian regime. It is in this sense a "hybrid" regime, with both authoritarian features and some level of liberalization (Ryan and Schwedler 2004).

Jordan's process of political liberalization began defensively in 1989 as a then-precarious regime responded to rioting and political upheavals in many parts of the country (Brand 1992; Brynen 1992; Robinson 1998; Ryan 1998). The waves of political unrest had been triggered by an International Monetary Fund (IMF) austerity program in the spring of 1989. The kingdom had reluctantly agreed to IMF adjustment measures following a prolonged economic crisis that had featured the rapid devaluation of the Jordanian dinar, a skyrocketing national debt, and rising inflation and unemployment. But the policies intended to address the economic crisis set off a corresponding political crisis as rioting spread from the south of Jordan to parts of the capital. Reductions in state subsidies on staple foods and other goods had led to rapid price increases just as many Jordanians were already having trouble making ends meet.

Out of this sequence of negative developments, however, emerged the liberalization process itself. In the first several years of the program, liberalization included easing government controls over the media, restoring parliamentary life and electoral democracy for the lower house of the legislature, and lifting martial law for the first time in more than twenty years. In 1993—following the 1991 creation of a new national charter dedicated to pluralism, liberalization, and loyalty to the Hashimite monarchy—the regime allowed for the legalization of political parties for the first time since the 1950s. This process involved extensive intra-elite bargaining and hence underscores a key feature of political opposition in Jordan: It has tended to be peaceful and reformist, rather than violent and revolutionary (Mufti 1999). Indeed, the national charter was meant to institutionalize this long-standing idea of loyal opposition within the Hashimite Kingdom.

Since the reform program began, Jordan has seen fairly routine national parliamentary elections (1989, 1993, 1997, 2003, 2007, 2010, 2013, and 2016). But Jordan has also unveiled a new electoral law for every election. Since 1993 Jordan's electoral system has usually featured uneven electoral districts that overrepresent rural (and often more conservative, royalist, and East Jordanian) areas, while underrepresenting more urban (and often more Palestinian and sometimes more Islamist) areas. Jordan's opposition parties sometimes call for an end to this type of districting, but they always call for a mixed electoral system, with proportional representation included to strengthen parties in the kingdom.

In Jordan, political opposition has traditionally come from two broad categories: secular, left-leaning activists (including Communists as well as Baathists and other pan-Arab nationalists), and Islamist activists. The latter category is by far the more influential and historically the best-organized opposition element in the kingdom. The Islamist sector in Jordan is based mainly in Jordan's Muslim Brotherhood, an Islamist movement as old as the Hashimite regime itself, and the movement's political party, the Islamic Action Front (IAF) (Wiktorowicz 2000b). Political parties in general have tended to be weak in Jordan, with most Jordanians having no partisan attachment. Opposition has, therefore, emerged institutionally not only in the form of parties but also from within professional associations and trade unions. In addition, since 2011 Jordan has seen a rise in largely youth-based "Popular Movements" (known as the Hirak) that have emerged in almost every town and city in the country.

For its part, the Jordanian regime heralded the political liberalization process that began in 1989 as the most extensive in the entire Arab world, and in many respects that assessment was accurate. The process began to change, however, as the kingdom secured its 1994 peace treaty with Israel. Thereafter, regime tolerance for dissent declined precipitously. The opposition had surprised regime loyalists by taking more than half the seats in parliament after the first elections in 1989 (with Islamists taking thirty-four of the eighty seats). In response, the regime changed the electoral law for the 1993 elections, switching to a one-person, one-vote system. The previous electoral law had allowed citizens a number of votes matching the number of representatives for their respective (multimember) parliamentary districts. The new electoral law ended this practice, forcing voters to pick just one candidate even in multimember districts. Many voters responded by supporting candidates with a family, clan, or tribal connection. They, therefore, voted not for parties, platforms, or even particular candidates that they might otherwise have supported, but instead voted strategically for representatives they were more personally connected to. The new law also featured a set of uneven electoral districts that favored rural pro-regime constituencies over the more urban bases of support for opposition groups from the secular left to the religious right.

In a sense, the regime was both mobilizing and containing political opposition. The strategy worked, and not surprisingly the Islamists as well as secular leftist parties lost seats in the 1993 elections. Jordan's opposition parties then threatened an electoral boycott in 1997 unless the electoral law was changed. When no such revision took place, the IAF led an eleven-party bloc in boycotting the 1997 elections, yielding a 1997–2001 parliament dominated by pro-regime conservatives and tribal leaders—and very few opposition voices. That parliament, pliant though it was, was dissolved by the king in 2001 in preparation for new elections. Yet the elections themselves were postponed several times, rendering the kingdom without an active parliament for more than two years. In the absence of parliament, the palace ruled by decree, issuing a series of controversial emergency and temporary laws.

In June 2003 the new elections were finally held, under still another electoral law. The new law, announced in July 2001, lowered the age of voting eligibility for men and women from nineteen to eighteen and increased the number of parliamentary seats from 80 to 104, with new (but still uneven) electoral districts. As noted, King Abdullah later added a new decree creating six more parliamentary seats in a specific quota to ensure minimal representation for women. The 2003 elections were also important in that they were the first under King Abdullah, and they represented a return of the opposition (after the 1997 boycott) to electoral and parliamentary politics. In those elections, pro-regime conservatives, as usual, won most of the seats, but the Islamic Action Front did manage to gain seventeen seats, with five more going to independent Islamists.

The next round of elections, held in November 2007, produced a resounding defeat for Jordan's Islamist movement. But this came with considerable controversy about the process itself, as there were widespread allegations of vote-rigging. When the vote-counting was completed, the Islamists had dropped from seventeen seats to a mere six, having lost even in districts where they enjoy substantial support, such as Irbid and Zarqa. It may be that both sides—the Islamist movement and the Hashimite regime—were reacting to the 2006 electoral success of Hamas in the Palestinian territories. The government reacted with alarm and attempted to thwart any sign of a Hamas-like turn within Jordan's own Islamist movement. Yet simultaneously the IAF was inspired by the nearby elections and may have overplayed its hand (Susser 2008). The 2007 elections, in short, may have signaled a change in the regime's approach to its opponents, especially its Islamist opposition. For most of their existence, the Hashimites had pursued strategies of dividing or containing their political opponents (Lust-Okar 2004, 2006). Now there seemed to be a more confrontational tone emerging both from the state and from more hawkish elements within the Islamist movement itself (Ryan 2008). This level of mutual distrust continued well beyond the 2007 election, leading to Islamist boycotts of the national polls in both 2010 and 2013.

The Muslim Brotherhood, however, has seen its fortunes change radically across the region since 2011. After the military coup that overthrew the Egyptian Muslim Brotherhood government in 2013, the group was banned in Egypt, Saudi Arabia, and the United Arab Emirates—all allies of Jordan. Within the Hashimite Kingdom, however, the Brotherhood remains mainly legal, but it is split between an official version, recognized by the state, and an unofficial and unlicensed version that is as old as the state itself and continues to operate. Historically a major component of political opposition in Jordan, the Islamist movement, in short, now amounts to multiple different elements.

Regarding political opposition in general, despite differences in ideological or even religious orientation, opposition parties of all types in Jordan actually agree on several things. Most have been sharply critical of the peace treaty with Israel. They demand that the regime cease normalizing relations with Israel, and some even demand the abolition of the treaty itself. Within domestic politics and policy, the opposition parties also insist that future prime ministers and cabinets be drawn from parliament in a truer model of a parliamentary system, rather than be royally appointed pending only the formality of parliamentary approval. Still, whether rooted in Islam, in pan-Arab nationalism, or in secular leftist ideas, the political opposition in Jordan has tended to struggle with the regime over policy and the direction of the state (including demands for greater democratization) but has rarely challenged the nature of the state itself as a Hashimite monarchy.

Religion and Politics

Islam is the official state religion within Jordan, with the overwhelming majority of the population following the Sunni Islamic tradition. Throughout its existence the Hashimite monarchy has pointedly emphasized its Islamic lineage. King Hussein in particular made clear the direct Hashimite family line descending from the Prophet Muhammad. Yet despite its Islamic familial credentials, Hashimite Jordan remains largely a secular state, without the religious overtones that one finds in Saudi Arabia or Iran.

Jordan also has a long history of religious tolerance and support for religious minorities. Jordan's Christians, who account for perhaps 5 percent of the country's population, enjoy full political rights, including freedom of religion and the right to attend churches and Christian religious schools if they so desire. The Hashimite kings have tended to rely on strong support from Christians and other minorities and have supported various centers, conferences, and institutes focused on Christian-Muslim understanding. King Abdullah II in particular has emphasized interfaith tolerance not just on a national but also on a global level. In 2005 Jordan hosted a major conference of more than 200 leading Muslim theologians from fifty countries and all schools of Sunni, Shi'i, and Ibadi thought. Together, they produced the "Amman Message" against sectarianism, militancy, and questionable practices such as *takfir* (excommunication) in Islam. This was followed in 2007 by the release of "A Common Word," a message to all Christian denominations to create greater Christian-Islamic understanding. Finally, in 2010 King Abdullah addressed the UN General Assembly and proposed World Interfaith Harmony Week, which was approved and is now celebrated in the first week of February in many places throughout the world.

Within Jordan, while many Jordanian Christians are stalwart supporters of the Hashimite regime, others have played major roles in Jordan's opposition movement, especially through left-wing political parties. Indeed it is in the politics of opposition that one finds the most extensive levels of religion-based activism in the kingdom. As noted, Jordan's Islamist movement remains the largest and best-organized component of political opposition in the kingdom, and it is as old as the Hashimite monarchy itself. Unlike the Muslim Brotherhood in Egypt, the Jordanian movement has enjoyed a more cooperative relationship with the Jordanian state as a loyal opposition organization. And unlike Hamas, the IAF and Muslim Brotherhood do not have militant wings; instead, they focus on civilian party and interest group organization and remain very much a part of the pro-democratization movement in the kingdom (Schwedler 2006).

Jordan's Muslim Brotherhood, therefore, stands in sharp contrast to more militant and even terrorist religious organizations, such as al-Qaeda. This point was brought home in a particularly horrible way on November 9, 2005, when al-Qaeda suicide bombers simultaneously attacked several Jordanian hotels in central Amman. The attacks killed sixty while wounding hundreds and thereafter have been considered "Jordan's 9/11." The terrorists turned out to be Iraqi nationals who had crossed the border into Jordan on the orders of Abu Musab al-Zarqawi, a former Jordanian national who became the head of al-Qaeda in Iraq. Yet most Jordanians—secular and religious, royalist and Islamist, regime supporters and opponents—united in condemning these attacks. In doing so, and despite the many divisive issues in Jordanian politics, they also underscored two major features of Jordanian political life:

that the kingdom has a long tradition of moderation and tolerance between and among religions, and that opposition has rarely turned to violence or terrorism but rather has been based in grassroots activism for reform and change. While peaceful opposition has remained the norm in Jordanian politics, the kingdom has, unfortunately, seen a rise in Salafi jihadist militancy and even terrorism, with security forces occasionally battling terrorist cells within Jordan itself. But this kind of religious militancy continues to be condemned by government and opposition alike.

The Impact of International Politics

When political power in Jordan shifted in 1999 from King Hussein to the current king, Abdullah II, the new regime was quickly reminded of the often intense impact of international affairs on Jordan's domestic politics and security. Indeed, the succession came at a particularly challenging time in regional politics, which would soon see the collapse of the Arab-Israeli peace process, a renewed Palestinian intifada, and US wars in both Iraq and Afghanistan. Given its political and geographic location at the very heart of the Middle East, Jordan has for its whole existence found itself wedged between the Israeli-Palestinian conflict to the west and Iraqi and Persian Gulf tensions to the east. The Hashimite Kingdom of Jordan has been deeply affected by the Arab-Israeli wars of 1948, 1956, 1967, 1973, and 1982, and the Persian Gulf wars of 1980–1988, 1990–1991, and 2003–2009, in addition to the country's own internal conflict in 1970–1971. Given Jordan's long border with Israel, its peace treaty with the Jewish state, and its large Palestinian population, the kingdom has also felt the impact of Palestinian uprisings in the West Bank and Gaza from 1987 to 1993 and again after September 2000.

Jordan's very centrality in Middle East politics and geography has, therefore, also carried with it a real strategic vulnerability. This has even led to overuse of an old English-language pun in some Jordanian political circles to the effect that Jordan resides "between Iraq and a hard place." And indeed regional conflicts, coupled with Jordan's central location, have led to repeated and massive population shifts across Jordan's borders. In both 1948 and 1967, Arab losses in wars with Israel led hundreds of thousands of Palestinians to cross the Jordan River into the Hashimite Kingdom. Even today, the kingdom includes several million Palestinians among its citizens. In 2003 the US invasion of Iraq and the severe political unrest that followed led several hundred thousand Iraqis to flee to Jordan. In 2011 and 2012 more than 750,000 Syrian refugees fled to Jordan to escape the violence of the Bashar al-Asad regime and the Syrian civil war. The Jordanian government, in fact, argues that the number of refugees is closer to 1,300,000. Each wave of refugees, whether from the west, east, or north, has put severe strains on Jordan's infrastructure and social services and sometimes its domestic security. Regional conflict, ideological challenges, and domestic regime insecurity are in many ways almost constant features of Jordan's existence as a small state in a very difficult neighborhood.

Even in the 1950s, when the kingdom was still young and viewed by many pan-Arab nationalists as an artificial "paper tiger," some Jordanian officials feared that another regional conflict might eliminate the Hashimite state entirely. In that decade Arab politics became intensely radicalized, with the Cold War and Arab-Israeli conflicts looming large in political discourse. Radical trends from communism to pan-Arab nationalism were at their peak, challenging the legitimacy of Western-leaning conservative monarchies like Jordan. In 1957 Hussein headed off an attempted coup d'état (inspired by external radical and nationalist ideas), while in 1958 a bloody military coup overthrew the Hashimite monarchy of King Hussein's cousin, Faisal, in neighboring Iraq. The new regime in Baghdad killed the king and his family before consolidating control over the country. The effects of these ideological challenges and external events are important, because the regime reacted to them by disbanding parliament, banning political parties, and closing the door on liberalization for decades to come.

By the late 1960s, the regime was forced to focus outward once again as regional tensions escalated—especially between Israel and the Gamal Abdel Nasser regime in Egypt. Those tensions soon led to the defining event of the decade: the 1967 Arab-Israeli war. Known as the Six Day War for good reason, the conflict began when Israeli forces launched what they viewed as a preemptive strike on Arab forces in Egypt and Syria, effectively destroying the Arab air forces while they were still on the ground. With no air support, the land battles that followed produced an overwhelming Israeli victory not only against Egypt and Syria, but also against Jordan, whose forces had joined the fighting.

That fateful decision and the complete failure of the Arab war effort led to Israeli occupation of the Sinai Peninsula, Egyptian territory, and the Golan Heights, Syrian territory. For the Jordanians, the domestic result of the military failure in the 1967 war also was the loss of territory to Israel, specifically the agriculturally rich West Bank and religiously significant East Jerusalem. In addition to territorial losses, the 1967 war resulted in tens of thousands of Palestinian refugees crossing the border into Jordan, changing the demographics and ultimately impacting the domestic stability of the kingdom.

That uneasy situation exploded in September 1970, when guerrilla forces of the Palestine Liberation Organization (PLO) fought the royalist forces of the Hashimite government. This Jordanian civil war resulted in a bloody Hashimite victory and the expulsion of PLO guerrilla forces from Jordan. What looked like a particularly vicious internal struggle became internationalized, however, when Syrian forces launched an unsuccessful invasion of northern Jordan in support of the PLO. Many feared that Israeli or US intervention would also soon follow, but those very threats, coupled with the efforts of the Hashimite army, repelled the Syrians and defeated the PLO.

In October 1973, with the kingdom still recovering from the war of 1967 and the internal conflict of 1970, Egyptian and Syrian forces launched an initially successful surprise attack on Israel, starting an event known variously as the Yom Kippur, Ramadan, or October War. Having lost all of the West Bank and East Jerusalem to Israel just six years earlier, Jordan stayed largely out of the 1973 conflict. As Egypt and Syria fought Israel on northern and southern fronts, Jordan never opened an eastern front and instead sent a small contingent of troops to aid Syria in its (unsuccessful) attempt to recover the Golan Heights.

What is perhaps most amazing about those years is that Jordan survived at all as a state and as a Hashimite monarchy despite international wars, internal conflict, and revolutions toppling monarchies in neighboring states. Awareness of this strategic vulnerability led Jordanian policymakers to focus on ensuring international allies and domestic military prowess despite the small size of the state and its coffers. Many regimes fear external conflict or internal upheaval, but for the Hashimite regime these fears have been far from hypothetical.

In the 1980s the Jordanian regime became deeply concerned about the challenges posed by the Iranian revolution. Revolutionary Iran was a successful example—and indeed an active supporter—of the overthrow of conservative, pro-Western monarchies. Iran, therefore, seemed also to threaten the Arab Gulf monarchies (and hence Jordan's main sources of oil supplies and Arab foreign aid). When Iraq invaded Iran in 1980, King Hussein's regime supported Baghdad for all eight years of the war, and indeed Jordan came to serve as Iraq's main supply source.

Even when that war finally came to an end, however, the region would know very little peace. After a mere one-year hiatus, Jordan's now-close ally, Iraq, launched a surprise invasion of Kuwait on August 2, 1990. Once again, international affairs deeply affected Jordanian domestic politics. By this time, the kingdom's own liberalization process was well under way, and a newly energized public rallied in support of Iraq against the emerging US-led coalition. Feeling the domestic political pressure, King Hussein's Hashimite regime attempted to straddle the fence, neither aiding Iraq nor joining the coalition against it. But the result of that strategy was a sudden loss of US, British, and Gulf foreign aid; the loss of oil supplies; and the expulsion of half a million Jordanians working in the Gulf. Yet again, hundreds of thousands of suddenly displaced people descended on Jordan's capital, Amman.

That nightmarish episode has in many ways cast a shadow over Jordanian policy ever since. It was with that scenario in mind that the Hashimite regime of King Abdullah attempted to prevent its most powerful ally, the United States, from attacking Iraq once again in 2003. But having failed in that effort, the Jordanians were determined to avoid the devastating effects of opposing the United States. Thus, after the invasion, Jordan supported Iraqi reconstruction efforts and trained police officers for the new Iraq, thereby avoiding the painful dislocations and penalties of the early 1990s. But well into the twenty-first century, the reputation of the Hashimite Kingdom of Jordan as a kind of geographic oasis of stability was challenged repeatedly by the spillover of other conflicts, including the recurrent violence of the Israeli-Palestinian conflict, insurgency and terrorism in Iraq, and civil war in Syria.

In 2014 yet another security challenge emerged across Jordan's borders, this time in the form of the self-declared "Islamic State" in Iraq and Syria (better known as ISIS or by its Arabic acronym, Daesh). As a small and relatively weak country by most measures, Jordan is always influenced by regional events and especially by regional insecurity. But the period since the rise and fall of the Arab Spring has proved to be something of an insecurity overload for the Hashimite Kingdom. Jordan has focused on countering both ISIS and al-Qaeda, and on eliminating militant jihadist cells when they emerge even from within Jordan itself. The kingdom has also pushed for an end to the Syrian civil war, even as it has struggled to deal with hundreds of thousands of Syrian refugees.

The external effects on Jordan's internal politics really couldn't be more profound. The influx of Syrian refugees, for example, has been a challenge for Jordan's economy, but also for society and politics. It has been costly in terms of housing, food, and water supplies, but it has also added another layer of tension to Jordan's already delicate social balance and hence its identity issues. Meanwhile the many external security threats, especially from jihadist terrorism, have led the regime to focus first and foremost on security, at times sacrificing reform efforts in the process. In terms of its own foreign relations, the kingdom has tried to avoid getting dragged into regional wars (in Syria, Yemen, the Israeli-Palestinian conflict, or even the regional "cold war" between Saudi Arabia and Iran) as it attempts to concentrate on domestic political issues from reform debates to recurrent economic crises.

Political Economy

Given its minimal resource endowments, throughout its history the Hashimite Kingdom of Jordan has been dependent on foreign assistance to keep its economy afloat. With limited arable land and chronic problems of adequate water supply, agriculture remains a small part of Jordan's overall economy. Indeed, given the small agricultural base in the country, Jordan imports far more food than it exports. That pattern actually applies more broadly, since a chronic trade deficit is a standard feature of the Jordanian economy.

Like the agricultural sector, the manufacturing base is small, with the bulk of the economy concentrated in the service sector. The kingdom has few natural resources, but manages to exploit those minerals it does possess, particularly phosphates and potash. It also manufactures and exports cement and fertilizers. Under King Abdullah II, Jordan has moved steadily away from a state-dominated or public sector economy toward economic openness *(infitah),* increasing levels of privatization, and an overall emphasis on neoliberal economic policies.

Jordan's main resource has been and remains its people. Jordanians tend to have very high levels of education and have, therefore, been able to take advantage of skilled labor and service sector job opportunities in other countries in the region, especially those in the Gulf. Worker remittances are thus a major component of the Jordanian economy. So many Jordanians work outside the country, in fact, that the kingdom is both a major labor importer and a labor exporter. Laborers from Sudan and especially Egypt, for example, work in many of the lower-skilled jobs within the kingdom, while Jordanian citizens are more likely to work for the state, in private businesses in the skilled service sector, or in jobs in the Gulf states.

With foreign aid remaining a large part of state revenue, and hence a critical source of state expenditures, the Jordanian economy is highly vulnerable to regional and global tensions affecting its labor and aid partners. Jordan is, in short, a semi-rentier economy, meaning that it relies heavily on external sources of income or "rents." The rentier concept is usually associated with extensive natural resource endowments and extractive industries. But in the Middle Eastern context, with the regional political economy of oil, even nonoil states have become deeply linked to the overall petroleum economy. Jordan is thus a semi-rentier economy not because of its own minimal oil endowment (it remains an importer of oil) but rather because its major sources of both expatriate remittances and foreign aid are based in the Gulf oil states (Brand 1992; Brynen 1992).

Since 1989, when Jordan's debt crisis had triggered IMF restructuring (and political unrest), Jordan has pressed forward with economic liberalization. King Abdullah has made clear his conviction that Jordan's future lies in economic development—including foreign investment and privatization of the state's companies. In doing so, he is challenging a resistant and to some extent entrenched elite of state managers. But he is also creating an alternative constituency of like-minded elites who share his enthusiasm for neoliberal approaches to Jordan's development. This has been reflected increasingly in the king's political appointments and the tendency for many top cabinet posts to go to technocratic elites with experience in Jordan's industrial and trade zones.

The makeup of the government thus underscores the absolutely central emphasis of Abdullah's regime on economic development, continuing privatization, expanding trade, and luring international investment. With these goals in mind, the regime also aggressively pursued trade agreements with its key Western allies. In 2000 Jordan entered the World Trade Organization (WTO), and later that year the kingdom signed a free trade agreement with the United States. Jordan also relies on extensive trade with and investment from the countries of the European Union. In addition to his emphasis on free trade, King Abdullah has pushed for Jordan to become a regional center for information technology and communications.

The government's overall economic development aims are, therefore, clear, but restructuring remains a colossal task, and one with profound social and political ramifications. As Western stores, fast food chains, and other businesses continue to multiply in Jordan, and as the capital continues to expand rapidly, the larger questions that still remain are not just those of trade and investment but also those of poverty alleviation, uneven development, and continuing high levels of unemployment. These latter questions are the focus of many opposition parties and activists who hope to push the political liberalization process forward, in part to alleviate some of the hardships of economic liberalization. Indeed, economic grievances have led to recurrent unrest in the south of Jordan, especially among the tribal East Jordanian communities that have historically been counted on as bases of loyalty to the regime.

By 2018 Jordan's national debt was almost as large as its gross domestic product (GDP), leading the state to engage in yet another round of austerity measures and tax hikes. This led to massive protests across the country, as professional associations, trade unions, and the Hirak groups staged the first general strike in Jordanian history. The protests soon expanded well beyond the initial labor stoppage and came to include people from all walks of life, protesting by the thousands the high costs of living, corruption in public life, and the general sense that the population had continually made adjustments and sacrifices and now had nothing left to give. As in the days of the Arab Spring, the government was dismissed, and a new reformist government emerged under Omar al-Razzaz, himself already a longtime advocate of reform. But the task ahead was daunting, given Jordan's chronic fiscal crisis and the many popular demands for political and economic reform.

Identity and Politics

One of the major features of Jordanian identity politics is the ethnic divide between Palestinians and East Jordanians (also called Transjordanians), or between those originally of West Bank and East Bank origin, respectively, within modern Jordan. This division has sometimes been given far too much importance in writings on Jordan, especially when used as the social explanation for domestic politics, or when reduced to a "Palestinian versus bedouin" type of image. The nomadic bedouin account for less than a tenth of the kingdom's population, but they are an important part of the social construction of national identity for many Jordanians, underscoring "traditional" roots. Family, clan, and tribal links and lineages remain real and important for many Jordanians. In addition, there are other ethnic groups within Jordan, such as the Circassian and Chechen communities, who are mainly Muslims whose ancestors fled the Russian Caucasus region in the 1860s and 1870s and who have since played prominent roles in national politics, often as strong supporters of the Hashimite regime.

Many Jordanians reject divisive forms of identity politics and instead embrace more inclusive and pluralistic visions of modern Jordan. Yet the division between the Transjordanian and Palestinian communities persists for some and is often utilized by anti-reform forces to divide potential coalitions for reform and change. While the estimated percentages vary greatly depending on one's source, it is likely that more than half the population of the kingdom today is of Palestinian origin. The Jordanian government, however, maintains that Palestinians are at most 40 percent of the population. Although this West Bank–East Bank ethnic divide is sometimes overstated, it remains a significant feature of Jordan's society and political economy, and of the Jordanian state itself. Much of the Jordanian government, public sector, and military is dominated by East Bank Jordanians, while much of the private sector is dominated by Palestinians. Before 1970, the Hashimites had regarded their monarchy as more solidly a union of the West and East Banks of the Jordan River and had strived for some level of balance in the political system. Yet this general ethnic division of labor (so to speak), and hence of power, became more pronounced as a political issue in the wake of the 1970–1971 internal conflict within the kingdom (when Palestinian guerrillas fought the Jordanian authorities).

It is difficult to imagine, in fact, a more contentious and touchy issue within Jordanian politics. Even the Palestinians who are most closely associated with the Hashimite establishment are not immune from intraethnic controversy. In 1999, Adnan Abu Odeh, one of the most powerful Palestinians in the kingdom, a consummate insider, and former adviser to King Hussein, found himself under attack from many social and political quarters for his views on Palestinian-Jordanian relations within the kingdom. Abu Odeh had published a book on the topic and then delivered a series of lectures at various venues in Jordan (Abu Odeh 1999). His theme in these writings and speeches was the ethnic imbalance of opportunities within Jordanian society and politics. Abu Odeh was thereafter asked to resign from the Senate. Similarly, in 2001, Jawad Anani, who just two years earlier had served as chief of the Royal Hashimite Court, published an editorial in an Arabic daily in the United Arab Emirates (UAE) arguing that the ethnic divide represented Jordan's main political hurdle to achieving real inclusion or democracy. Shortly afterward, Anani too was forced out of the Senate.

Yet such acts of exclusion are neither systematic nor universal. For example, Taher al-Masri, a former prime minister who is of Palestinian origin, has been similarly critical of the ethnic divisions and of the limits of the political liberalization process. He was also one of the most prominent politicians associated with the 1997 electoral boycott. Yet Masri has frequently been appointed to the Senate and to lead key national committees and served for many years as Speaker of the Senate. And Jawad Anani, who had been forced out of the Senate, later returned to government, holding several key cabinet posts. It is important to note that these prominent Jordanians of Palestinian origin are not separatists; all, in fact, are integrationists, and all support the regime. But they remain critical of specific disparities in representation—especially in government—for Palestinian Jordanians as opposed to East Bank Jordanians.[1]

The renewed attention to ethnicity within Jordanian national identity is to some extent rooted in regional politics. With the signing of the 1993 Israel-PLO accords and the 1994 Israeli-Jordanian peace treaty, the question of Palestinian citizenship, rights, and loyalties resurfaced within Jordanian politics. With the collapse of the peace process and the onset of the second Palestinian uprising against Israel, beginning in September 2000, these questions became still more intense.

Many Palestinians clearly feel that they are second-class citizens. But this cannot be taken in a strictly material or economic sense, for the communities do not neatly fall into an economic hierarchy that parallels the political hierarchy. Rather, in addition to impoverished Palestinians in refugee camps (which today are usually urban neighborhoods), the bulk of Jordan's poorest population can be found especially in rural Transjordanian communities across southern Jordan. Much of the private sector economic elite, in contrast, is Palestinian. That said, much of the public sector elite and most top government officials are Transjordanian. Since the abolition of the national military draft in 1992, Transjordanian dominance of the armed forces and the security services has only increased. Many Transjordanians, in turn, point to the enormous wealth of many Palestinian business families and to their lavish villas in neighborhoods like Abdun. They point out that of all the Arab countries, only

Jordan has extended citizenship to Palestinians. And they note that many of the kingdom's prominent ministers and politicians are of Palestinian origin. Accordingly, this line of argument tends to arrive at the issue of gratitude—or perhaps more often, ingratitude.

For their part, Palestinians—even including many who have reached the pinnacle of the kingdom's economic and political elite—say that they are still treated on a day-to-day basis as second-class citizens. They argue that in interactions with bureaucrats, police officers, soldiers, and other officials, they are treated differently and negatively. Family names give much away for anyone in Jordanian society—since the family name usually signals the owner's ethnicity and religion. Many Palestinians then argue that no matter how long they have lived in Jordan, they still feel that they are treated as foreigners—that despite their full citizenship status, they nonetheless do not enjoy full political rights. They feel that they are still seen as temporary residents by many Transjordanians. And indeed, right-wing Transjordanian nationalists agree with them—at least in the sense that these nationalists see Palestinians as essentially foreign and not as "real" Jordanians. For these nationalists, Jordanian identity is rooted in East Bank heritage and often in real or imagined bedouin traditional values. For them, Palestinians are indeed temporarily in the kingdom, and of highly suspect loyalty. The nightmare scenario for such ultranationalist Transjordanians would be a new wave of Palestinian refugees, forced across the Jordan River in the face of an Israeli military offensive.

Thus both successes and failures in the peace process have actually exacerbated some of these domestic tensions. After the 1993 accords, the creation of the Palestinian National Authority and the possibility of a sovereign Palestinian state raised questions in Jordan about which state Palestinians would be loyal to, which state they would live in, and what any of these decisions and scenarios would mean not just for Jordan's survival as a state but also for its very identity as a nation and as a people.

On this issue, as on many others, many Jordanians are looking to their leadership for hope and direction. Some point, for example, to the potentially unifying symbolism of the Hashimite regime itself, particularly in the form of Abdullah II as the Hashimite Jordanian king and his wife, Queen Rania, who is of Palestinian origin. Certainly some Palestinian Jordanians are hopeful that this translates to more than symbolism, with a king and queen literally representing a marriage of Transjordanian—and Palestinian—Jordanians. For his part, King Abdullah has made clear his belief that the major factor in integrating Jordanian society will be the same factor intended to dampen hostility toward normalization of relations with Israel: expanded economic development. The broader question for Jordanian politics and society will remain, however, not only one of equality of economic opportunity but also one of equality of political representation. The additional question, of course, is whether increased international investment, privatization, and trade will prove sufficient as economic solutions to social problems.

Gender and Politics

The preceding discussion of interethnic divisions within Jordan has something of a parallel in gendered divisions in Jordanian society, because here too the emphasis is on de jure legal equality, coupled with de facto differences in empowerment. Jordanian women are not subjected to restrictive national dress codes, as they are in Iran and Saudi Arabia; neither does one find in Jordan the strict sex segregation and constraints on women's movement that are so much a part of Saudi society. Indeed, women in Jordan are equal to men before the law and have full rights to education, work, and political participation. The state's commitment to public education for both sexes has, for example, yielded an overall literacy rate of 96 percent, the highest in the Middle East. While the legal and political systems guarantee equality of the sexes, Jordan also remains a fairly conservative society, and hence patriarchal norms do tend to dominate within family life and in society in general.

Certainly the most controversial gender issue in Jordanian politics is that of killings over "honor crimes." The reference here is to family members killing female relatives suspected of adultery or of otherwise offending "family honor." This often amounts to little more than a woman being the subject of rumors, wherein male family members have then acted to "cleanse" the family's honor by killing the woman in question. This contentious issue has received media attention globally, with specific exposure within Jordan provided by such journalists as Rana Husseini of the *Jordan Times*.

The issue has turned not only on the act of violence itself and its dubious "traditional" roots, but also on its legal status. Article 340 of the Jordanian penal code specifically allows leniency in sentencing for men convicted of murder in cases of honor crimes. While conservative nationalists have claimed that this practice is rooted in bedouin traditions, their erstwhile Islamist opponents are actually on the same side on this issue, arguing for their part that the practice is rooted in Islamic law, or sharia. In contrast to these more reactionary positions, human rights activists have waged a campaign to highlight this violence and to repeal Article 340. Women's rights activists are correct when they argue that the practice is in no way rooted in Islam, but they tend to run into a wall of tradition, in which misogyny is sometimes mistaken for tradition, culture, and religious authenticity (Sonbol 2003).

The Hashimite royal family directly joined this debate, and both Queen Noor and later King Hussein condemned the practice. Since then,

King Abdullah and Queen Rania have lent their voices to this campaign. Even more directly, Prince Ghazi (King Abdullah's adviser on bedouin and tribal affairs) helped lead protests against honor killings and leniency within the penal codes. The practice has thus been condemned by a large grassroots movement as well as by the palace itself. It is possible, however, that the state's very emphasis on privatization and neoliberal economic reforms has unintentionally triggered a reactionary backlash among conservative Jordanians, including holding on to even the most suspect of "traditions" in the name of defending authentic Jordanian life in the face of what they see as an overwhelming pace and scale of change.

In the struggle for gender equality and social justice in Jordan, the honor crimes issue will clearly continue to be one of paramount concern in any analysis of women's rights in the kingdom. The struggle for equality also takes place, of course, in the public sphere, as women attempt to make their legal rights match social, economic, and political practice. In that regard, Jordanian women activists have argued that attention needs to focus also on private and public sector employment opportunities and continuing struggles for political representation.

In terms of the government, women are not entirely absent from top positions (such as cabinet posts), but they remain underrepresented nonetheless. This is certainly not due to a lack of qualified candidates, since Jordan, to its credit, has an extensive public education system, with a small gender gap in literacy between men and women, and one of the best-educated populations in the entire Arab world. It is precisely because of the education level of Jordan's workforce that so many Jordanians have been employed as skilled professionals in Gulf economies. Most of these migrants, however, are men. Within Jordan, despite their education levels and qualifications, Jordanian women are more often found as clerical staff, clerks, and administrators in ministries, offices, banks, and so on, rather than as ministers or directors (Brand 1998; Amawi 2000).

Jordan's women's movement scored a significant success in 2001 when its efforts to secure a women's quota for parliamentary representation finally succeeded, although not to the extent that activists had hoped for. The new law added six more parliamentary seats in a specific quota to ensure representation for women. In the previous three elections (1989, 1993, and 1997), only two women were elected to parliament.[2] In 2010, the women's quota was increased to twelve seats, and then to fifteen for the 2013 elections.

Still, while glass ceilings have been broken in terms of educational opportunities, and sometimes in elections, the fact remains that women continue to be underrepresented in both houses of parliament as well as in the cabinet ministries. Although it is clear that women lack full empowerment with respect to the key levers of power in Jordanian public life, it would be misleading to attempt to draw a general picture of the status of all Jordanian women, given the vastly different circumstances of women's lives in the kingdom. For here the intersectional variables of social class, ethnicity, religion, urban or rural circumstances, and so on each deeply affect a woman's status and opportunities (in both the public and private spheres). It is fair to say, however, that the various transitions confronting Jordanian society—especially in terms of the political and economic liberalization programs—each have had gendered impacts that can be disproportionately negative for women. As Laurie Brand has suggested in her study of women and liberalization, women are more likely than men to find themselves unemployed as a result of IMF restructuring programs (1998: 120).

Civil Society

When the Hashimite Kingdom of Jordan first emerged, the monarchy immediately established itself as the premier and centralized political power in the emerging Jordanian state. As the Jordanian state developed, civil society, like the economic basis for the new state, was weak. And hence the government almost immediately filled these gaps, establishing a large role for the public sector in the economy (a legacy undergoing transformation only today), ensuring a similarly large role for the military in backing the political regime, and, finally, co-opting the fragmented aspects of much of civil society into the new Hashimite political order (Brand 1995).

Civil society has nonetheless continued to emerge in Jordan, especially in the wake of the political and economic liberalization process. There are times, however, when "political society" and "civil society" in Jordan are actually difficult to distinguish from one another. In 1997, for example, after the Islamist movement led the opposition boycott of the parliamentary elections, the resulting parliament naturally proved to be overwhelmingly conservative, nationalist, and pro-Hashimite. With only six independent Islamists in the new parliament, and none whatsoever from the IAF, Islamist strength and strategy shifted away from parties and parliament toward the professional associations instead. Thus a key element of civil society became instantly politicized. In short order, Islamist candidates won the leadership posts of almost every professional association in the kingdom (e.g., engineers, pharmacists, medical doctors), thereby creating a basis for Islamist political activism outside the halls of parliament, but very much across Jordanian civil society.

Beyond the numerous legal political parties and professional associations within the kingdom, the key facets of Jordan's still-emerging civil society (as opposed to more explicitly political society) include the many nongovernmental organizations (NGOs) within the kingdom. Yet while these civic organizations are themselves independent, they nonetheless retain legal links to the state, since all NGOs register with the General Union of Voluntary Societies. State regulations also constrain the NGOs from exercising complete independence, as charitable NGOs come under the jurisdiction of the Ministry of Social Development, while cultural and social NGOs are regulated by the Ministry of Culture. Islamic NGOs are also permitted (and indeed have proliferated) in Jordan, but only if they pursue civic and social—rather than political—activism. Islamic NGOs, for example, may distribute religious literature or offer religious classes, but they may not campaign for Islamist candidates (Wiktorowicz 2002).

While NGOs have proliferated in Jordan, especially since the 1989 liberalization process began, the largest and most active organizations in the kingdom are actually royally organized NGOs—also known as RONGOs. These are organizations headed by a member of the royal family, a prince or princess who acts as royal patron of the group. These Hashimite NGOs include, for example, the Women's Resources Center (led by Princess Basma), the Arab Thought Forum (Prince Hassan), the Noor al-Hussein Foundation (former queen Noor), and the Jordan River Foundation (Queen Rania). Thus in the Jordanian context, civic and social activism is based not only on NGOs but also on RONGOs, which in turn provide myriad services to the population but also maintain a level of social and political control over civil society (Clark 2004; Wiktorowicz 2000a, 2002). Similarly, Jordanian workers are allowed to organize through trade unions, but these must then be approved and incorporated into the General Federation of Jordanian Trade Unions. In short, seemingly pluralist forms of social, economic, and civic activism are perhaps best seen as corporatist in organization, as the state both mobilizes and contains the participation of citizens in public life.

While Jordan's NGOs can be counted among the most democratic organizations in the country, at times they have been the subject of maneuvers to curb their potential influence. Since 2000 especially, the government has sometimes focused on the "foreign connections" of these groups. Most, of course, have global connections and just as obviously draw on sources of funding outside the kingdom. But some government officials, followed dutifully by many of the more pliant organs of the Jordanian media, have continued to characterize these groups virtually as foreign infiltrators. This type of maneuver is, of course, quite old in Jordanian politics. Internationalist left-wing parties, from the Communists to the Baathists, found themselves subjected to similar charges from the 1950s onward. But in the modern era of liberalization, and under a regime that openly embraces globalization, it seems particularly odd to criticize organizations for having global links. It is still odder that Jordanian Islamists sometimes fall in step with this critique themselves, despite the fact that it has also been used against them. Yet just as they tend to be suspicious of the Communist and Baathist parties, the Islamists are also suspicious of what they see as the too Western links of many NGOs, especially feminist, pro-democracy, and human rights organizations.

Another key aspect of civil society is independent media, and indeed the loosening of restrictions on the media beginning in 1989 was a central pillar of the initial liberalization program. The immediate proliferation of weekly publications and the emphasis of some of them on exposing scandals apparently tried the patience of regime officials—many of whom were skeptical about the very idea of democratization. A new press and publications law in 1993 was heralded by some as a step toward democracy, since it replaced legislation in effect since 1973 and hence during the martial law period. But the law also required that journalists be members of the Jordan Press Association—a government body. Individual journalists have continually criticized this feature of the many different versions of press laws that have been handed down since 1989, since they see it as compromising their independence and hence running counter to civil society.

While print media came under fairly tight restrictions, Jordan developed a regional reputation for its openness regarding the internet. This was in keeping with King Abdullah's goals of opening the economy and making Jordan a regional center for internet and communications technology. Yet in the midst of the Arab Spring, in September 2012, regime conservatives pushed through a new media law to restrict internet news sites (which had proliferated) and bring them under rules similar to those for print media. In addition to the concerns regarding the stifling of news reporting in both electronic and print media, free speech advocates in the kingdom feared that the new rules might be extended to include blogs, Facebook, Twitter, or other forms of social media.

In many respects, Jordan's struggle for greater liberalization and openness seems to continually advance and retreat. But while the process has slipped since the mid-1990s, it has not yet slid backward to the pre-1989 period. Today, unlike the era before 1989, extensive polling data are produced by such impressive institutions as the University of Jordan's Center for Strategic Studies. Detailed analyses of the press, parties, associations, and other aspects of the liberalization process are produced and disseminated from the independent Al-Urdun al-Jadid (New Jordan) Research Center. NGOs such as the Arab Archives Institute now link to global human rights organizations such as Transparency International and the Euro-Mediterranean Human Rights Network. These can be counted as among the most positive and hopeful features on the Jordanian political landscape.

Within the state, in 2005 King Abdullah appointed the kingdom's former foreign minister Marwan Muasher as deputy prime minister for reform. In that capacity, Muasher led a broad-based committee of Jordanians (drawn from government and society) in creating an ambitious program called the National Agenda for Reform. That effort called for deep reforms within the kingdom, including changing the electoral laws, loosening restrictions on the press, expanding the rights of women, and strengthening Jordan's nascent civil society (Muasher 2008). The National Agenda, however, was met with overt hostility by many antireform hard-liners within the regime, with suspicion by the Islamist movement, and with considerable indifference on the part of a Jordanian public that seemed to have grown tired of new initiatives and new slogans. Despite its comprehensive approach to many of Jordan's problems, the National Agenda was essentially shelved in the face of conservative resistance. Today, perhaps ironically, liberal and progressive Jordanians are calling for many of the same reforms.

Despite such public cynicism and what may be called "slogan fatigue," many Jordanians are looking to a young and reformist king to tip the scales back toward liberalization and away from the conservative retrenchment that has undone much of that same reform process. Others, however, no longer count the king in the reformist camp. The lack of faith in the overall process is palpable, and it was especially so during 2011 and 2012 when Jordan reshuffled cabinets so often that it had five governments in that two-year period.

What is perhaps just as compelling about Jordan's struggles over reform, however, is the determination of many independent activists, organizations, and social movements to press on in their attempts to build civil society and more meaningful democratization. The efforts of these individuals and groups nonetheless run headlong into a core of the ruling elite who see democratization and all its trappings as a completed mission. For many regime conservatives the liberalization process already occurred, and it includes strict parameters intended to give a showy and pluralist facade to an established pattern of power and privilege. But even the cynicism on the part of old guard or hard-line elements within the Jordanian state, coupled with various moments of backsliding or deliberalization, should not be allowed to obscure the fact that there are real reformers within the state, as well as energetic democracy activists independent of the state who are working to create a more effective civil society and a return to more extensive liberalization.

Notes

This chapter draws, in part, on Ryan 2002 and Ryan 2009.

1. A detailed and thorough discussion of the public-sphere debates within Jordan over ethnicity, identity, and democracy can be found in Lynch 1999.

2. In 1993 Tujan Faysal was elected to a parliamentary seat (in a Circassian constituency in Amman), and in 1997 Nuha Ma'atah was elected in a special election called to fill the seat of the late Lutfi Barghuti.

15

Kuwait and the United Arab Emirates

Michael Herb

Kuwait and the United Arab Emirates (the UAE) are two small Arab monarchies located on the eastern margins of the Arabian Peninsula. Both are blessed by an extraordinary abundance of oil wealth. They have much in common, including their shared monarchism, their wealth, the Arab background of most of their citizens, and a legacy of British colonial rule. In recent decades, however, they have increasingly followed different paths in responding to the opportunities provided by their oil wealth. The UAE has diversified its economy away from oil, while Kuwait has not. Kuwait holds competitive elections to a parliament that wields real power, while the UAE has nothing of the sort. The UAE has seven emirates, each with its own ruling family, while Kuwait is one emirate. And the UAE has an increasingly activist foreign policy.

Historical Background and Contemporary Political Structure

Kuwait and the UAE lie along the coast of the Persian Gulf, Kuwait at the far northern end and the UAE along the southern shore. The climate in both Kuwait and the UAE is dry with blazingly hot summers: Before oil the area supported only a modest amount of agriculture and thus a small population. Those who lived on the shoreline made their living from the sea, mostly through trading and the harvesting of pearls from the offshore seabed. On land, pastoral nomads raised sheep and camels; in scattered oases, settled or seminomadic populations raised dates. The lack of population density and the absence of a large agricultural surplus discouraged the development of large, strong centralized states in the pre-oil era. We can contrast the situation along the Gulf littoral with that of Egypt, where the Nile provides fresh water for the fertile land along its banks, which in turn supports a dense population and a very large agricultural surplus. Ease of movement along the Nile facilitated the exploitation of this surplus and the construction of a relatively stronger central government. It also made Egypt a target for foreign powers. Along the Gulf shore, by contrast, there was no comparable agricultural surplus to support a large population or to attract sustained foreign interest. The hinterlands were loosely governed at best, while the seaside towns typically maintained a fair amount of autonomy, even if their rulers gave allegiance to one outside power or another.

Kuwait's modern history dates back to the eighteenth century, when a group of Arab families of Sunni tribal origin, hailing from the Nejd in what is now Saudi Arabia, settled on the site of what is now Kuwait City. The families formed the core of the Kuwaiti elite, which was a merchant rather than landowning elite as a consequence of the lack of extensive agriculture. These merchant families selected from among themselves one family, the Al Sabah, to rule (Crystal 1995). In the 250 years since, the Kuwaitis have established relationships of various sorts with outside powers, most notably the Ottoman Empire, Great Britain, and the United States. Yet throughout, the Kuwaitis have largely ruled themselves under the leadership of the Al Sabah (the exception being during the Iraqi occupation of 1990–1991). Foreign powers have typically confined their influence to matters of foreign policy: There was little economic gain to be had from a more extensive European involvement until the age of oil, by which time European empires were in full retreat.

British rule came earlier to the small emirates that later became the UAE, and this area was one of the parts of the Arab world that never came under Ottoman rule (Anscombe 1997). The British drew up treaties with local rulers (all of them Sunni Arabs), and it was as a result of this treaty-making habit that the UAE, before independence, came to be known as the Trucial Coast. Piracy was a central concern of Britain in its relations with the Trucial Coast rulers, along with prohibiting the trade in slaves, but in general the British were far more interested in maintaining order and excluding foreign powers than in exploiting the limited resources of the coastal areas of the Gulf. These treaties strengthened the authority of the ruling families against their rivals, and over time British recognition came to be a crucial element in each ruling family's claim to rule over its emirate. There were changes in the number of ruling families (and thus separate emirates) recognized by the British, but by the 1950s the current lineup of seven emirates had emerged. The southernmost, and largest, emirate is Abu Dhabi; moving north and east along the Gulf coast we find Dubai, Sharjah, Ajman, Umm al-Quwain, and Ras al-Khaimah. Fujairah lies on the Indian Ocean coast. When the British announced their withdrawal from the area before independence in 1971, the ruler of Abu Dhabi offered to pay the British to keep a military presence in his emirate, fearing his neighbors. The British withdrew anyway, and the seven emirates, along with Bahrain and Qatar, entered into negotiations to form a federation. Bahrain and Qatar eventually decided to go it alone, and thus was born the UAE as a confederation of seven separate emirates, each with its own ruling family.

Oil and the Creation of Ruling Family Institutions

The Gulf monarchies today have a distinctive form of monarchical rule: Members of the ruling family are found throughout the senior posts in the government and monopolize many of them (Herb 1999). This is in sharp contrast to the traditions of monarchical governance in Europe, where relatives of the king or queen were generally expected (and very often constitutionally required) to avoid holding positions in the government. Thus in the Gulf states the prime minister (where there is one), the minister of foreign affairs, the minister of defense, and the minister of interior are almost universally members of the ruling dynasties. This style of monarchical rule is new to the Gulf, if only because formal ministerial governments (those with ministers of foreign affairs, defense, interior, and so forth) did not exist in the Gulf before the oil era. Before oil, and before the possibility of the construction of large states, the ruler shared little power with other members of his family. Sometimes he would send a male relative to rule distant dependencies. For example, in 1946 the ruler of Abu Dhabi sent his brother to govern the oasis of Al-Ain, about a hundred miles away across the desert. And the ruler might have a trusted lieutenant or two from among the members of his family. The rest of his relatives, however, lacked formal offices in the state.

The modern sharing of high posts in the government among members of the ruling dynasties emerged first in Kuwait in 1939. In the previous year the Kuwaiti merchant elite, drawn from Sunni Arab families who had migrated to Kuwait with the Al Sabah in the eighteenth century, held elections among themselves for members of a legislative council, or *majlis*. The Al Sabah had ruled much more autocratically since the reign of Mubarak the Great, who killed his brothers and seized power in 1896, and the merchant elite sought to return to the days of merchant predominance before Mubarak. The merchant elite also wanted to use Kuwait's available resources to create a more effective set of state institutions for education, the police, and so forth, and this the *majlis* did after its members were selected in 1938.

The ruler had no desire to see his wings clipped by the merchants, however, and he closed their *majlis* in 1939 with support from his family, desert tribes, and Kuwait's Shi‘a. Some shaikhs of the Al Sabah supported the *majlis* movement initially, largely because the ruler had previously refused to share power with his relatives. The shaikhs of the ruling family helped the ruler close the *majlis* and then divided up among themselves the various departments of the Kuwaiti state. One shaikh took over the treasury, another the town police, a third the armory, a fourth the precursor to the Kuwaiti army, a fifth the department of education, and so forth. Before the *majlis* movement, the ruler ruled; afterward, the ruling family ruled.

This set a precedent in the Gulf that was followed, to one degree or another, by most other Gulf ruling families. Ever since, the shaikhs of the Al Sabah have monopolized the key posts in the state, which today include the prime minister and the ministers of interior (that is, police), foreign affairs, and defense. The formation of a family regime in Kuwait, as elsewhere in the Gulf monarchies, was followed by the construction of strong, modern state institutions capable of exerting rule across the entirety of the territory claimed by the state. Oil paid for it all.

In Abu Dhabi the development of a family regime came much later, in 1966. The ruler—Shaikh Shakhbut—refused to share power with his immediate relatives and he also refused to spend Abu Dhabi's surging oil revenues. The ruler's brother, Shaikh Zayed, overthrew his brother and secured the support of his relatives by promising them various departments of the Abu Dhabi government. Some of these hardly existed at the time, since Abu Dhabi was little more than a dusty village—there was, for example, but one clinic, with one doctor, in all of the town of Abu Dhabi. After becoming ruler in 1966, Zayed transformed Abu Dhabi into a modern city with blinding speed.

These family regimes are founded on consensus and tradition. They are not encoded in constitutions, most of which can be changed by the ruler at will except in Kuwait. This creates an opening for monarchs to use their formal powers to undermine the family nature of monarchical rule in the Gulf. We see this today in Saudi Arabia where the crown prince, Mohammad bin Salman, has executed a coup against much of his family, imprisoning some. None of the other Gulf rulers has followed suit, but Mohammad bin Salman's success, so far, provides a model that might be emulated by other Gulf rulers. Both Abu Dhabi and Dubai are currently ruled by strong rulers. In Dubai, Mohammad bin Rashid has ruled since his brother's death in 2006. Mohammad bin Zayed is Abu Dhabi's crown prince, while his older brother holds the office of ruler and president of the UAE; there is no doubt, however, that Mohammad bin Zayed rules. In Kuwait the aging emir, Sabah al-Ahmad, is unlikely to upset the family nature of rule. The next emir will need to deal with a fractious parliament and his family together: Kuwait's constitution, which is much stronger than any other among the Gulf monarchies and gives the parliament much more power, will make it very difficult for a future Kuwaiti emir to follow the example of Mohammad bin Salman of Saudi Arabia.

Kuwait's political system. The Gulf monarchies, by and large, do not pretend to be democratic. Most, including Saudi Arabia, do not even need to figure out clever ways to steal elections because they do not have elections (for national offices) at all. Kuwait is an exception: Kuwaiti citizens elect their National Assembly in reasonably free and fair elections, and the National Assembly actually has some power to constrain the emir and the ruling family. Why does Kuwait have a strong parliament? An important part of any explanation lies across the border, in Iraq. In two crucial periods in Kuwaiti history the Iraqi threat pushed the ruling Al Sabah family toward political reform. In 1961 Kuwait gained its independence, and Iraq immediately claimed Kuwait as its nineteenth province. The Al Sabah could not defend Kuwait against its much larger northern neighbor and had little option but to seek support from outside powers. In particular, the Al Sabah needed to join both the Arab League and the United Nations (UN), and to accomplish this the emir needed to dispel, or at least qualify, the widespread opinion outside Kuwait that the Al Sabah were oil despots ruling over a resentful population. The ruler thus appointed a well-known Arab nationalist to a leading post in what became the ministry of foreign affairs; sent a delegation of leading Kuwaitis—including opposition figures—on a tour of Arab capitals to make Kuwait's case; and held elections, in late 1961, to a constitutional convention. The emir also had a liberal streak, and his interventions ensured that the new constitution gave the parliament relatively expansive powers.

The 1962 constitution remains in effect today, without amendments. The constitution divides power between the ruling family and an elected parliament, and in this it resembles the constitutions of nineteenth-century European monarchies, written in a period when it was thought that the people should have some voice in governance but that full democracy was dangerous. These European political systems gave the king—and not the elected parliament—the power to appoint the ministers who directed the executive branch of government. These countries democratized only when the leading parties in the parliament demanded the right to appoint the prime minister and other ministers themselves, rendering the monarch a figurehead.

In Kuwait the parliament is freely elected, but the emir appoints the prime minister, who has always been a shaikh of the ruling family. For decades the crown prince was appointed prime minister; the two posts were separated only in 2003. The prime minister, with the advice of the emir and other senior members of the family, selects the government. At least one member of the government must be drawn from among the fifty elected members of the parliament; the other members of the government become members of parliament by virtue of their government posts. The constitution limits the size of the government to sixteen total members. This arrangement allows shaikhs of the Al Sabah to hold seats in the parliament without sitting for election (the shaikhs of the family on principle have never subjected their authority to election); it also in effect gives the government up to fifteen wholly appointed members of the parliament, the total membership of which can rise to a maximum of sixty-five members. Since the government votes as a bloc, this gives it the ability to pass ordinary legislation even when a majority (though not a large majority) of the elected members vote against the legislation.

In standard parliamentary democracies the parliament must provide the government with a vote of confidence when it first takes office. The Kuwaiti constitution does not require this, and the practice has not emerged by tradition. Nonetheless the constitution allows the parliament to vote no confidence in individual ministers. Members of the government cannot vote on motions of confidence and thus a majority of the elected members of parliament can dismiss a minister from his position. By contrast, ministers can vote on ordinary legislation, and thus it requires substantially more than a majority of the elected members of parliament to pass a bill over government objections. The prime minister himself can also lose what amounts to a vote of confidence. Should this happen (it hasn't yet), the emir can either dismiss the prime minister or hold new elections. If he calls new elections and the new parliament again votes against the prime minister, the latter must resign.

Kuwait's Supreme Court is composed of five judges selected by the High Judicial Council and appointed by decree of the emir. In practice the judiciary enjoys a good deal of independence. The Supreme Court has the power to declare laws and decrees unconstitutional. The legislative and executive branches have the standing to bring constitutional cases directly to the Court; like the US Supreme Court, the Kuwaiti Supreme Court hears cases brought by ordinary citizens only on appeal from lower courts. In practice the Court displays occasional independence from the government, such as its 2006 overturning of a restrictive law on public assemblies. But the court also invalidated the two parliamentary elections held in February 2012, providing convenient relief to a government facing serious opposition from deputies in the National Assembly.

The UAE's political system. The dominant political institutions in the UAE are the seven ruling families, one for each emirate. The families, however, are not equal in stature, because some have oil and others do not. Each emirate owns the oil resources in its territory, and the individual emirates, rather than the federal government, receive the income from oil sales. The vast oil wealth of Abu Dhabi, some of which is redistributed to the federation and to the poorer emirates, is the glue that holds the UAE together. Other emirates produce oil—including Dubai, Sharjah, and Ras al-Khaimah—but their combined production in 2010 amounted to only around 5 percent of Abu Dhabi's production. The federal budget relies largely on contributions from the individual emirates rather than on taxes. In practice this means that Abu Dhabi pays the bulk of federal expenses. The poorer emirates contribute much more modest amounts, and Dubai's contribution, while larger, is not on the scale of that of Abu Dhabi. The imposition of a value-added tax (VAT) of 5 percent in 2018 will provide the federal government with some direct revenues: It will receive 30 percent of the funds generated. This, however, is unlikely to substantially dilute the financial influence of Abu Dhabi in the federation.

Under the 1971 constitution the dominant political institution at the federal level is the Supreme Council, which consists of the rulers of the seven emirates. The rulers of Abu Dhabi and Dubai have a veto, reflecting their predominance within the federation. One of the chief functions of the Supreme Council is to elect the president, who serves as head of state. By tradition, the rulers have always elected the ruler of Abu Dhabi to this post, a tradition that continued when Shaikh Zayed died in 2004 and his son Khalifa became ruler of Abu Dhabi.

Beneath the Supreme Council is the Council of Ministers; each minister heads up one of the federal ministries. The Council of Ministers includes members of each of the seven ruling families, along with some "commoners." By custom, the ruler of Dubai serves as prime minister. The federal government includes the full panoply of ministries that one would expect to find in a modern state. In practice, however, the ministries are constrained, to one degree or another, by the power and influence of the governments of the individual emirates. To give one example, the minister of defense is by tradition a member of the ruling family of Dubai, but also by tradition the minister has little power: the Emirati military is headquartered in Abu Dhabi, paid for by Abu Dhabi, and run by the ruling family of Abu Dhabi (Davidson 2007: 37–38). Some government services are provided by the individual emirates, others by the federal government. The richer emirates, especially Dubai and Abu Dhabi, tend to provide their own services, but the individual emirates enjoy substantial autonomy in many fields. Thus the federal ministry of interior pays for the salaries of police in all emirates except Dubai; the individual rulers appoint the chief of police in their emirates. In health care, Dubai and Abu Dhabi operate their own health care authorities while the other emirates rely on the federal health ministry—although even Dubai leaves prescription drugs to the federal government.

The federal institutions also include a representative body of sorts, the unicameral Federal National Council (FNC). Abu Dhabi and Dubai have eight members each on the council, Ras al-Khaimah and Sharjah have six members each, and the three smaller emirates have four members each, for a total of forty members. The rulers appointed all FNC members until 2006 when half of the members were elected. The electorate in that election, however, consisted of only 6,000 or so Emiratis who were hand-selected by the rulers of each emirate. The method of selection was anything but transparent, and the process inspired mostly cynicism: Turnout was only 63 percent even among the handpicked electorate. In 2011 the electorate was expanded to 130,000 citizens (and 224,000 in 2015), but the elections similarly suffered from poor turnout.

Compared to the Kuwaiti National Assembly, the FNC has exceedingly modest powers: It cannot remove confidence in ministers, and it has only advisory power on legislation. Its only notable power lies in its ability to publicize issues. In the 1990s, an Emirati graduate student surveyed the forty members of the FNC: Thirty responded, and twenty-four of those agreed that "the FNC has virtually no powers" (Khalfan 1997). These were the views of those whom one would expect to have a positive view of the institution, having been handpicked for membership by the rulers of their respective emirates.

The UAE Supreme Court can review laws for their constitutionality, but only the emirates, the federal authorities, and lower courts have the ability to ask the Supreme Court to rule on the constitutionality of laws. The UAE has a civil law legal system that was influenced, like Kuwait's, by Egyptian practice, which in turn has sources in French and Roman law. Family law issues are heard in special courts that apply the sharia, or Islamic law; these courts are Sunni, though there is a Shi'i court in Dubai. Three emirates—Dubai, Abu Dhabi, and Ras al-Khaimah—run their own court systems independently of the federal courts. The judiciary is weakened by the fact that many judges are foreigners working under renewable, fixed-term contracts that make them reliant on maintaining the favor of the authorities.

Government and Opposition

The Ruling Family and the National Assembly in Kuwait

Kuwait has two powerful political institutions, the monarchy and the National Assembly. The two share power, often uncomfortably. The central question of Kuwaiti politics is the balance of power between the two, which changes over time, and the ultimate possibility that one day the balance might tip permanently and decisively in favor of one or the other. Since 1962 this has not happened, though there were times when it appeared that the ruling family would vanquish the National Assembly. Between 2006 and 2012 the balance tipped toward the National Assembly, to the point that there was talk of a transition to democracy. In subsequent years, however, the monarchy regained its footing, and while it did not undo some of the gains achieved by the National Assembly, it has prevented further movement toward parliamentary government.

During the first decades after independence, the ruling family was assertive about maintaining the limits of parliamentary power, and in some periods sought to change the constitution to permanently limit the National Assembly's authority. The family's efforts to undo the constitution started with election fraud in 1967, which excluded leading members of the Arab nationalist opposition from the parliament. Fair elections were held in 1971 and 1975, but in 1976 the ruling family unilaterally suspended the parliament, providing as an excuse the outbreak of civil war in Lebanon, which was seen as an example of the dangers of too much participation. The Al Sabah held fair elections again in 1981, although only after a unilateral redistricting and an unsuccessful attempt to revise the constitution. Kuwaiti voters in 1985 returned a parliament much more obstreperous than its predecessors, in part because of an economic crisis involving a bubble in the stock market and in part because Islamists—who had entered the parliament in force in 1981—shifted toward the opposition. In 1985 the parliament forced a member of the ruling family from his cabinet post, and in 1986 opposition deputies directed interpellations at three prominent members of the government. In response the ruling family unconstitutionally suspended the parliament a second time.

Initial public reaction to the suspension of 1986 was muted, in part because many felt that the parliament had overstepped its bounds. By 1988, however, the opposition reemerged, circulating petitions demanding a resumption of parliamentary life. This was followed in 1989 by a series of large public gatherings at *diwaniyyas* around Kuwait, including some in the outlying bedouin areas of Kuwait City. The protests brought together the main ideological currents and identity groups in Kuwait, encompassing Sunnis and Shi'a, the nationalist left and Islamists, liberal merchants, the bedouin of the outer districts and Kuwaitis from old town families, and so forth. As the number of attendees grew into the thousands, the ruling family alternated between tolerance and repression. At one meeting, held in the outlying town of Jahra, the police beat up a number of participants, including some notable Kuwaiti figures, one in his seventies. The ruling family responded to the protests by announcing elections to a new assembly, but one stripped of many of the crucial powers granted to the National Assembly by the 1962 constitution. Most Kuwaiti political figures—those who had served in previous parliaments especially, and members of organized political groups—boycotted the elections, as did many citizens. The new assembly first met in July 1990, shortly before Iraq invaded Kuwait on August 2.

Most of Kuwait's ruling family and political class fled into exile during or after the invasion. As the United States prepared to liberate Kuwait, its lack of democracy became awkward, and so too was the tension between the ruling family and the opposition. The United States did not want to appear to be restoring a group of despots to power. To address this problem, Kuwaitis in exile convened a conference in Jedda, Saudi Arabia, to reaffirm their support for the family. The price, however, was a promise by the Al Sabah to resume parliamentary life under the 1962 constitution after liberation. Having made this promise, and with the world watching, the Al Sabah had little choice but to hold elections after liberation, though long procrastination (a full year and a half) betrayed the family's reluctance.

In 2006 the National Assembly started to assert its authority against that of the ruling family with some persistence, resulting, by 2012, in a noticeable expansion in the power of the National Assembly and a dilution in the authority of the ruling family. In early 2006 the emir, Jabir al-Ahmad, died. The crown prince at the time, Sa'd al-Abdallah, suffered from dementia: It was said at the time that he might not have been able to pronounce the oath of office before the parliament, an oath of only twenty-six words. The obvious candidate to replace Sa'd was the prime minister, Sabah al-Ahmad, who had been the dominant member of the ruling family in the later years of Jabir's reign (Jabir had been very ill before his death in 2006). Sa'd, however, belonged to the Salim branch of the ruling family, while Sabah came from the Jabir branch of the family. The branches are named after two brothers who ruled in the early twentieth century, and there had been a tradition in Kuwait that rule would alternate between the branches (see Figure 15.1).

Shortly after Jabir's death, Sabah and his allies in the ruling family and in the parliament prepared to depose Sa'd. It is here that the constitution became important. Sa'd—or those in his immediate family who spoke for him—refused to resign. The ruling families of the Gulf have jealously guarded their prerogative in selecting rulers, rejecting any interference by outsiders. The shaikhs of the Al Sabah met together—absent a handful of Sa'd's diehard supporters—to proclaim their support for Sabah al-Ahmad. Yet the constitution specified that only the parliament, and not the ruling family, could depose the emir. Sabah al-Ahmad thus had a stark choice between maintaining the prerogatives of the ruling family to select the emir and following the letter and spirit of the constitution. He chose to abide by the constitution, and the emir was deposed by a unanimous vote of the parliament on January 24, 2006.

Figure 15.1 Family Tree of Al Sabah Rulers of Kuwait

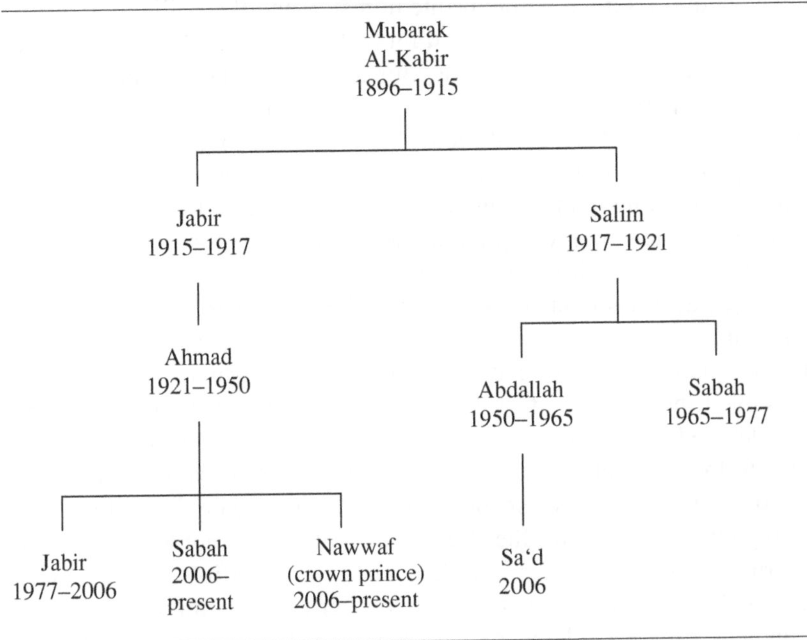

The new emir, no one would forget, came to power via a vote of the parliament, and not merely by the selection of the ruling family.

A second major political crisis, a few months later, further demonstrated the ascendance of the parliament and the relative decline in the authority of the ruling family, at least in comparison with its Gulf counterparts (including the ruling families of the UAE). From the 1963 elections to the 1975 elections, Kuwait had ten electoral districts, each of which elected five members to the National Assembly. In 1980 the ruling family increased the number of districts to twenty-five, each returning two members to the parliament. The ruling family hoped that this would make it harder for opponents of the family to win election to the National Assembly. Demands for a reduction in the number of districts grew in the years preceding 2006, and the issue came to a head in May 2006 when twenty-nine members of parliament (MPs) stormed out of a parliamentary session in protest of the government's refusal to address electoral reform. Supporters of redistricting (who had settled on a demand for five districts) demonstrated in front of the parliament, adopting orange as the color of their movement, following the example of Ukrainian Orangist protesters earlier in the year. Opposition MPs declared their intention to interpellate and perhaps vote no confidence in the prime minister. This was the first time that the parliament had demanded to interpellate the prime minister, and the willingness of the opposition to take this step owed much to its role in the deposition of the emir earlier in the year. The emir headed off the interpellation by dismissing parliament and calling new elections, a maneuver that was legal under the 1962 constitution. The campaign focused on the redistricting issue, and the opposition won decisively, building its majority from twenty-nine to approximately thirty-four seats. The ruling family, recognizing defeat, gave up its opposition to redistricting, and an electoral law with five districts was promptly passed.

Several years later, in the spring of 2009, several deputies in the National Assembly again moved to interpellate the prime minister. Fearing that this would lead to a vote of no confidence, again the emir dissolved the parliament. Before the dissolution the ruling family met and debated whether or not the suspension should be constitutional (and thus followed by elections) or unconstitutional. According to reports in a prominent Kuwaiti newspaper, the debate focused on the ability of the ruling family to "control the streets" and whether or not Kuwaitis could be ruled "in this manner" (al-Abd al-Hadi, al-Sa'idi, and al-'Aydan 2009). The consensus was that it was wiser to stay within the constitution, and a few days later the emir announced a constitutional dissolution of the National Assembly, followed by elections.

Later in 2009, the ruling family finally consented to an interpellation of the prime minister by the National Assembly and a subsequent vote of confidence. The prime minister won the vote of confidence with a solid majority. But this set a crucial precedent: The ruling family recognized that the prime minister and the government required the support of a majority in the National Assembly. When the prime minister lost majority support, he would then presumably be removed.

At the end of 2011 the prime minister appeared to lose the support of a majority in the National Assembly following a corruption scandal in which it was revealed that some deputies in the National Assembly had large sums (in the millions of dollars) in their bank accounts, the origins of which they could not explain. There was little reason to think that the funds were anything but bribes given in return for support for the government in the National Assembly. Faced with a lack of support for the prime minister in the parliament, the emir again dissolved the National Assembly and called new elections. He then replaced the prime minister with a different member of the ruling family. This was a clear victory for the Kuwaiti opposition.

Kuwaiti candidates aligned with the opposition—which is a somewhat amorphous group of politicians and activists who seek to limit the influence of the ruling family—did very well in the February 2012 elections, winning around thirty-five of the fifty elected seats. This set off a particularly contentious several years in Kuwaiti politics. The Majority bloc, as the opposition members of the National Assembly took to calling themselves (with some accuracy), demanded that they be able to select nine of the sixteen members of the cabinet, which raised the prospect of National Assembly control over the government. The prime minister refused, and the National Assembly backed down.

Tensions continued, and in the summer the Constitutional Court invalidated the elections of February 2012, forcing new elections. The emir then issued a controversial decree that unilaterally put in place a new electoral system. Under the former system voters had cast ballots for four candidates from among all of the candidates running in their district, with the top ten vote-getters winning a seat. The emir's decree reduced the number of votes cast by each voter from four to one.[1] The effect was to make it more difficult for electoral blocs—be they ideological or tribal—to coordinate their voters and build coalitions. For some voters it made it difficult to cast a ballot both for a member of their family or tribe and also for candidates more closely aligned with their political ideology.

In response to the decree, the opposition called a boycott of the new elections that were held in late 2012. The opposition, the public face of which was a Twitter account named Karamet Watan (dignity of the nation), organized a series of protest marches in an effort to force the emir to back down. The effort did not succeed. The Constitutional Court ruled in favor of the constitutionality of the emir's decree, and the boycott partially crumbled when the next elections were held in the summer of 2013. The opposition did not help its case much by making maximalist political demands, beyond the resurrection of the four-vote system. A number of prominent politicians demanded parliamentary government, which is to say a government appointed by the parliament, not by the emir and a prime minister who is also a member of the ruling family. This, along with some attacks directed at the emir personally, turned the moderate middle in Kuwaiti politics against the opposition (Albloshi and Herb 2018).

By 2014 the regime felt confident enough to crack down decisively on the opposition, stripping citizenship from several prominent members and their families. Karamet Watan owed something to the influence of the popular movements that spread across the Arab world after the fall of President Zine el-Abidine Ben Ali in Tunisia. The crackdown followed the regional trend toward repression of dissent as the Arab Spring turned to ashes elsewhere in the Arab world.

Political turmoil in Kuwait has led to an increasing sense of disenchantment with the parliament among economic elites and others. Much of this stems from unfavorable comparisons between Kuwait and other Gulf states: Kuwait suffers from more corruption, less efficiency in its government, and less economic diversification than its fellow Gulf Cooperation Council (GCC) states. Much of this is blamed on the parliament, and with some reason. The Kuwaiti political system gives the parliament the ability to paralyze the government through the use of interpellations. Yet the parliament does not have the responsibility of actual rule. In a fully democratic parliamentary system, of course, the government is formed by a party in the parliament, or by a coalition of parties. Those parties then have a direct stake in the success of the government. In Kuwait the ruling family—rather than political parties—in effect appoints the government. Deputies who aggressively challenge the government, however, tend to win reelection, giving members of parliament a strong incentive to make a name for themselves by interpellating ministers. The result is a political system that often seems paralyzed and that does not serve as a particularly promising model of democratic development for the other Gulf monarchies.

Ruling Families and Opposition in the UAE

While the politics of Kuwait is raucous, freewheeling, and at least partially democratic, the politics of the UAE is subdued, opaque, and not at all democratic. While Kuwaitis are free to hold political meetings (*diwaniyyas*) on a wide variety of topics, with advance notice and coverage in the press, in the UAE the police actively intervene to prevent similar sorts of political gatherings. Most citizens work for the government in one way or another, and citizens who engage in conspicuous political activity—especially Islamists—can find themselves without a position, or with their work activity restricted. Increasingly, opposition results in long stints in prison.

Emirati politics have not always been quite as quiet as they have been in recent years. The 1938 *majlis* movement in Kuwait was matched by a reform movement—in the same year—in Dubai. In the 1950s and 1960s an Arab nationalist movement emerged in Dubai. Its criticisms focused on the autocratic rule of the Al Maktoum ruling family and its tendency to favor Persian merchants at the expense of Arabs (or so felt the Arab nationalists). In the second half of the 1970s, conflict between the leading ruling families of the UAE—the Al Nahyan of Abu Dhabi and the Al Maktoum of Dubai—over the shape of the federation opened up a space for political participation by Emirati citizens. The constitution adopted at independence in 1971 was a temporary constitution (the word *temporary* appeared in the title). In the mid-1970s, Shaikh Zayed of Abu Dhabi proposed a much stronger federation—one in which he and his family would play the dominant role—and he had a draft constitution written that strengthened the office of the president of the UAE (an office held by Zayed), strengthened the finances of the federation, weakened various powers held by the individual emirates (including the veto right held by Abu Dhabi and Dubai alone), and created a national parliament with powers similar to those of the Kuwaiti parliament.

The ruler of Dubai saw these proposals as a direct threat. A more powerful federation, especially one with a greater voice for Emirati citizens, would constrain Dubai's efforts to develop its economy. Since Dubai had far less oil than Abu Dhabi, the only way for the Al Maktoum to maintain their relatively privileged place in the federation was to find a different source of wealth, and they found this in the transformation of Dubai into a trading entrepôt and tourist destination. This required autonomy both from the UAE federal government and from Emirati citizens themselves, who have never been enthusiastic about Dubai's development model. For a period both in 1976 and 1979 the rulers of Abu Dhabi and Dubai faced off over the proposed constitution. In 1979 thousands of Emirati citizens came out onto the streets in support of Zayed and his draft constitution. No one demonstrated in favor of the status quo, but the ruler of Dubai nonetheless held his ground, and the proposals to strengthen the federation came to naught. In the end the only substantial change to the constitution to emerge from Zayed's efforts was a decision by the rulers to remove the word *temporary* from the title of the original constitution.

After the failure to revise the constitution in 1979, there were no further efforts to reform the federal system from within. The temporary federal arrangements of 1971 became permanent. The consequences of this were profound. Citizens lost their best chance to gain a real voice in how they were governed. And, in no small part as a direct consequence, Dubai preserved the necessary autonomy to pursue its own distinctive development model. In an economic sense, Dubai has achieved spectacular success—at least up to the economic crisis of 2009—but at the cost of an influx of foreigners into the UAE. This has long occasioned discontent among Emirati citizens, dating back even to the days before oil when Arab merchants in Dubai protested the ruler's favoring of Persian merchants. In the 1970s this was a central issue in the debate over changing the constitution; in the 1990s it was an issue in the FNC; and today Emirati intellectuals bemoan the "irreversible" tide of immigration and what they perceive to be the loss of their country's identity. Yet while individual Emiratis often express unhappiness about the state of their country and threats to their identity, there is little in the way of a formal opposition, apart from a Muslim Brotherhood group suppressed by the regime in 2012.

In the UAE the Arab Spring led to no street demonstrations, though over a hundred Emiratis signed a petition in March of 2011 demanding that the FNC be given real authority and that all citizens be allowed to vote. Later on, in 2012, additional signs of dissent emerged, albeit from a very low baseline. In the spring of 2012 the authorities initiated a series of arrests aimed at suppressing the Muslim Brotherhood in the UAE and launched a series of public attacks on the organization and those affiliated with it. Some Emiratis claimed that the group had the support of only a handful of Emirati nationals, though the group itself claimed 20,000 members. The Muslim Brotherhood is said to be particularly strong in the poorer northern emirate of Ras al-Khaimah, reflecting the increasing divergence in the privileges of Emirati citizens from the richer and poorer emirates, respectively. The vehemence of the regime's attacks on the organization suggested a deep unease among the rulers (Ulrichsen 2012).

What explains the failure of the UAE to be swept up in the Arab Spring in a more substantive way? Many observers point to oil, and it is true that the oil-rich Qatari regime was also spared the upheaval of the Arab Spring. The enormous improvement in the standard of living of Emirati citizens over the past two generations has no doubt damped down the sort of dissent that is generated by economic hard times. But Kuwait also has a great deal of oil, and that oil has not insulated its regime from pressures for greater political participation. One factor that does distinguish Kuwait from the UAE is the sheer number of foreigners in the UAE and their increasingly central economic role: While foreigners are a majority in Kuwait, in the UAE citizens have been reduced to a small, exceedingly privileged minority. Small minorities—especially those acutely aware that they are in fact privileged—can make revolutions only very carefully.

Over time, as the economy of the UAE diversifies, the economic role of expatriates will become more and more central to the economy. The issue of democratization, or an expansion of political participation, will eventually include the question of expatriates. In Kuwait, by contrast, expatriates do not generate foreign exchange and there is no question of allowing them to participate in the political process, which is limited to citizens and citizens alone. Emirati intellectuals—in sharp contrast to intellectuals and political figures in Kuwait—today openly discuss the link between democratization and expatriates, often with a great deal of concern. The concern grows in part from fear that the Emirati demographic structure, and lack of democracy, will in the future run afoul of international norms, and the UAE will be pressured to provide citizenship to expatriates. The consequences for Emirati citizens would be profound: Today they enjoy, if not political influence, a privileged claim on state resources (which is to say, on Abu Dhabi's oil wealth) in the form of state employment, free education, free health care, housing subsidies, and the like. A real democratic revolution would threaten all of this, and would threaten the Arab and Islamic identity of the country.

Identity and Politics: Citizens and Noncitizens

Kuwait

Before oil, to be a Kuwaiti was to be a resident of the town of Kuwait, or perhaps a member of one of the tribes settled in the immediate area. In the early years of oil and up to the 1980s, many bedouin in the desert hinterlands settled in the city's suburbs and gained Kuwaiti citizenship. This migration created one of the central cleavages of Kuwaiti politics—between the *hadhar,* those Kuwaitis whose families have long lived in Kuwait town, and the *bedu,* those Kuwaitis who descend from families who were until the past few decades pastoral nomads in the desert (Longva 2006). In the early years of oil the *hadhar* were better positioned than the *bedu* to exploit new commercial opportunities, and some *hadhar* families built great fortunes. Less-privileged *hadhar* families also had better access to education; a good education could quickly translate into a better job in the government bureaucracy. The result was a continuing class distinction that tends to echo (though never exactly) the distinction between *hadhar* and *bedu*. The *hadhar-bedu* divide also has a political component: Kuwait's Arab nationalists, who were the dominant opposition group in Kuwait from independence in 1961 to the 1980s, were almost exclusively drawn from the *hadhar,* and had difficulty winning elections in *bedu* districts. Today's liberal and nationalist candidates similarly are competitive in *hadhar* districts. Islamists, by contrast, emerged in *hadhar* areas but have had substantial success in winning votes in *bedu* districts.

The years before and after World War II also saw the migration of a sizable Persian Shi'i community to Kuwait, and many gained citizenship when citizenship was distributed before independence. These Persian Shi'a joined a smaller number of Arab Shi'a from Bahrain and what is now the Eastern Province of Saudi Arabia. All told, the Shi'a constitute perhaps 25 percent of the total citizen population of Kuwait, though there is some evidence the figure is lower (Louër 2008: 7). From independence up to the Iranian revolution of 1979 the Shi'i deputies in the National Assembly supported the ruling family, as they had in the *majlis* crisis of 1939. Shi'i support of the ruling family was bolstered by Arab nationalist hostility toward the Persian Shi'a. From 1979 forward, the Kuwaiti left moderated its attitude toward the Shi'a, and today it is the more strident of Kuwait's Sunni Islamists who have had poor relations with the Shi'i community.

The 1980s, after the Iranian revolution and in the context of the war between Iraq and Iran, saw a serious rise in tensions between Shi'a and Sunnis in Kuwait and the election of opposition Shi'i deputies to the

National Assembly. The most serious incident was the attempted assassination of the emir Jabir in 1985, likely by Shi'i militants from abroad. While Shi'i Iran was perceived as the greatest threat to Kuwait throughout the 1980s and had a divisive effect on Kuwaiti sectarian relations, the invasion in 1990 by the Sunni Arab regime in Iraq had the effect of bringing Kuwaitis together and reducing sectarian tensions, since both Shi'i and Sunni citizen communities in Kuwait virtually unanimously—and forcefully—rejected the Iraqi claim to Kuwait. Over the past two decades the ideological orientation of Shi'i deputies in the National Assembly has shifted; while the Shi'i delegation was dominated by opposition Islamists in the 1980s, in recent years the Shi'a have returned to their pre-1979 orientation as supportive of the ruling family.

While there is some societal discrimination against the Shi'a in Kuwait, they do not suffer anything like the persecution endured by the Shi'a of Saudi Arabia or Bahrain. Neither do the Kuwaiti Shi'a have any ambitions to remake the Kuwaiti political order, in contrast to the (relatively much larger) Shi'i communities of Iraq and Lebanon.

The United Arab Emirates

While Kuwait is essentially a single city with its suburbs, the UAE is composed of seven emirates. The emirate of Abu Dhabi, in its origins, governance, and ethos, was very much more an emirate of the tribal desert than that of a seaside city: The *bedu* predominated. Dubai, by contrast, was resolutely centered on its port, with a desert hinterland that received little attention from the rulers. The northern emirates had substantial tribal populations, but these were tribes of the mountains rather than the pastoral nomads of the Arabian deserts. The northernmost emirate, Ras al-Khaimah, has a substantial population of mountain-dwellers, the Shihuh, who traditionally spoke a dialect of Arabic distinct from that of other Arabs in the area (Heard-Bey 1982). With the exception of Ras al-Khaimah, the emirates of the UAE are distinguished also by the fact that the ruling families come from the largest tribe in the emirate, so that the emirates are—in their origins—more emanations of the dominant tribe than is Kuwait. The consequence of this is that Emirati society lacks the clear *hadhar-bedu* cleavage that runs through Kuwaiti society and instead is characterized by multiple regional or emirate-level cleavages. Naturalization by the rulers through the 1990s added a substantial number of Arabs from outside the borders of the UAE to the citizen population, many of them from Yemen, and these new citizens form a distinctive group within the Emirati citizen population.

UAE citizens, like those of Kuwait, are largely Arab and Sunni, with a substantial Shi'i minority, in the case of the UAE comprising about 15 percent of the total citizen population. Many Shi'a are of Persian descent and tend to live in cities on the coast, especially Dubai. Sectarian tensions in the UAE, as in Kuwait, are muted by regional standards, and there is little overt repression of the Shi'a. Indeed, the Shi'a of Dubai have built magnificent mosques in the town and have long benefited from the patronage of the rulers.

Noncitizen Residents

The most important identity cleavage in Gulf societies is that between citizens and resident noncitizens. The latter are often referred to as expatriates: that is, foreigners who have taken up long-term residence. In Kuwait, expatriates outnumber nationals by two to one; in the UAE the ratio is nine to one. Most expatriates come from Asian countries, especially India, Pakistan, and Bangladesh; others hail from Iran, the Philippines, Europe, North America, Africa, and, of course, other Arab countries.

In many cases, what distinguishes citizens from expatriates is not much more than the date of immigration: those who immigrated before the determination of citizenship became citizens; those who came afterward did not. It was not until just before independence that the governments set about formally distinguishing citizens from noncitizens. In Kuwait, only those whose families had lived in Kuwait since at least 1920 gained citizenship, but in practice many others also gained citizenship, and in the 1960s, 1970s, and 1980s the government handed out citizenship to many *bedu* who had settled in Kuwait. Similarly, the UAE citizenship law of 1971 gave citizenship by right to Arabs whose families had lived in the UAE since at least 1925. Others could gain citizenship by naturalization, and the UAE ruling families naturalized a very large number of Omanis, Yemenis, and others in the decades leading up to the 1990s. In Dubai, where the ruler tended to favor the Persian merchant community, many Persians and other non-Arabs gained citizenship.

Despite the variety of their origins, it is usually not difficult to distinguish citizens from expatriates. Citizens have a distinctive national dress and often wear it. For men it is a long robe (white in the summer) and the *ghutra* (scarf) and *agal* (cord) that make up the standard headgear of the Arab Gulf. National dress is somewhat less distinctive for women; younger Kuwaiti women, for example, tend to wear their hair in a bun on the top of their head, covered by a head scarf, resulting in an identifiable Kuwaiti style. Expatriates, even Arab expatriates, do not wear attire that could be confused with that of citizens, unless they are citizens of one of the neighboring Gulf monarchies.

Today in both countries noncitizen residents have virtually no prospect of gaining citizenship. The governments of these countries distribute vast amounts of oil wealth to citizens in the form of free education, free health care, jobs, subsidized housing, marriage payments, and so forth. Bountiful oil revenues, and not taxes, pay for these state services (though Dubai is beginning to become something of an exception). Noncitizens in the Gulf receive few of these benefits. Adding an additional citizen does not increase the total amount of oil revenue available but instead increases the number of citizens among whom a fixed sum of oil revenues must be divided. In "normal" economies, by contrast, immigrants, through their labor, typically increase the total size of the economy and pay their way by paying taxes.

Living conditions for expatriates vary according to nationality and income. Expatriates who earn a substantial salary, for example, are allowed to bring their families to the Gulf to live with them, while poorer foreigners must leave their families at home. Nationality also matters: for example, the author, a US citizen, was able to secure a Kuwaiti driver's license as a student, while a friend (also a student) was forced to sell his car that he had driven to Kuwait from Syria because, as a Syrian, he could not secure a Kuwaiti driver's license. The private sector also discriminates among various groups of foreigners. In Dubai especially, it is common to have separate pay scales for Westerners and South Asians, even when they do the same work, and this causes widespread resentment among South Asians and other non-Western expatriates. That said, in the UAE the gap between the experiences of a Western-educated citizen of India and an Indian citizen with no education will be substantially larger than that between a well-educated Indian and a well-educated US citizen.

In the UAE, and especially in Dubai, the rulers make determined efforts to attract foreign tourists, businesspeople, and investors. To do this the governments (again, especially Dubai's) have eased visa requirements, legalized alcohol, allowed foreigners to purchase real estate, and so forth. Kuwait has not taken similar steps, and the parliament has no desire to do so, given that its electorate is conservative and would gain few economic benefits from attracting foreigners to Kuwait. Overall, the effect of these differences is to make the UAE feel much more comfortable for foreigners than Kuwait. This is most pronounced for well-off foreigners, especially those from the West, but less-affluent expatriates from the Indian Subcontinent also tend to prefer the UAE to Kuwait. While there is a good deal of simmering unhappiness in both societies among less-privileged foreigners (along with an appreciation of the economic opportunities provided by both societies), in Kuwait this unhappiness is directed primarily at Kuwaitis, while in the UAE there are also complaints in the Asian community that Westerners receive preferential treatment in employment and salaries, and preferential treatment at restaurants, clubs, and other public places (Vora 2008).

Groups such as Human Rights Watch criticize the treatment of unskilled laborers in Kuwait and the UAE. To understand these criticisms, it is useful to compare immigration policies in the West with those in Kuwait and the UAE. Western countries typically limit the supply of foreign labor through immigration restrictions. Limited supply of immigrant labor ensures that the price of immigrant labor (that is, wages) rises toward the price of citizen labor. Moreover, immigrants—or their children—typically can gain citizenship, and this further reduces differences in wages between immigrant and citizen labor. Gulf countries, by contrast, allow a great deal of immigration (especially relative to their small populations), flooding the labor market and holding down wages. Restrictive naturalization policies maintain a very sharp distinction between citizen and expatriate labor. Wage scales in employment formally permit lower wages for expatriate labor. The result is a vast gap between the wealth of many citizens and the poverty of their servants: in Kuwait, wage rates for live-in household servants (exclusive of food, board, and other expenses) are around $150 monthly, and often less.

Many foreign laborers arrive in the Gulf already in debt and thus prone to exploitation. Employers are legally obligated to pay the costs of transportation and visas, but many do not. The trade in visas is particularly troublesome. Foreigners entering a Gulf state to work must legally have a visa sponsor: It is the sponsor who receives permission from the state bureaucracy to import workers. Some sponsors demand a payment from workers that is above and beyond the actual cost of the visa, effectively selling to the laborer the right to work in Kuwait or the UAE. The practice is illegal, but also common and brazenly exploitative.

Workers in construction, janitorial services, and the like are often housed in large labor camps in the outskirts of the major cities. These laborers are typically in debt from the moment they arrive in the country and often find that the job they were promised is not the one they are given. On top of everything else, employers often fail to pay their employees in a timely fashion. The consequence is labor unrest of the sort that occasionally occurs in Dubai and that led to riots in Kuwait in 2008. The end result is predictable: some effort is often made to meet the demands of the workers, but many are nonetheless deported.

Political Economy

Kuwait and the UAE are examples of what political scientists call rentier states—countries that depend on the sale of natural resources to fund their governments and underpin their economies. Because the oil wealth is owned by the government, it is the government that receives the natural resource income. But Kuwait and the UAE stand out from the general run of rentier states: While most rentier states—think Iran or Venezuela—annually receive a sum of rent that amounts to at most a few hundred US dollars per citizen, the annual per citizen rent income in Kuwait and the

UAE is measured in the tens of thousands of US dollars. This makes them a truly exceptional sort of rentier: only a few other states are as rich, among them Qatar and Brunei, but not Saudi Arabia, Oman, or Bahrain.

How do the regimes spend all of this money? The ruling families keep a hefty amount for themselves, except in Kuwait, where parliamentary oversight sharply limits the ruling family's access to the state's oil wealth. In years when the price of oil is high, these countries save vast amounts of oil income in investments abroad—Abu Dhabi's investment fund is worth hundreds of billions. The governments have also constructed elaborate welfare states to distribute some of the oil riches to citizens. Some items go far beyond what we find in Western welfare states: In Kuwait, the government gives most male citizens a loan of around $250,000 to build or buy a house. In both Kuwait and the UAE, newly married citizens receive a grant, students receive stipends when attending university (in addition to free tuition), and the state even covers the cost of a basic funeral.

The main way that the governments put cash in the pockets of citizens, however, is through jobs in the state or in state-owned enterprises. Around 90 percent of citizens who work as employees in Kuwait and the UAE work for the public sector, either directly for the government or for a state-owned enterprise of some sort. Kuwait and the UAE do not need all of the citizen employees they hire, but this is the main way that the regimes give citizens their share of the oil revenue. While there is a great deal of featherbedding in the government, these citizens are not wholly unproductive as a group: They do much of the business of running the state and providing public services such as education and health. They are also largely responsible for running the oil companies. In the end, however, the logic behind state employment is largely distributive.

Noncitizens also work in government but are paid substantially less than citizens are for the same work. This results not from informal discrimination but rather from the explicit creation of different pay scales for foreigners and citizens. The logic behind this is clear: expatriates' pay scales are set by the market (more or less) while citizens' pay scales are set by the political need to distribute oil revenues.

Alongside the massive public sectors in Kuwait and the UAE we also find very substantial private sectors with workforces composed almost wholly of noncitizens. Capitalists prefer to hire foreigners because they cost less than citizens, work harder, and are easier to fire. Capitalists, who are by and large citizens, generally have a jaundiced view of the quality of citizen labor as a whole: at least in economic terms, they often regard citizens as unproductive and inefficient clock-punchers. This is a result of the work culture among citizens that has developed in many parts of the state bureaucracy—though there are Kuwaiti and Emirati citizens who take their positions seriously and work hard. The average less-skilled citizen does not forget that, without the benefit of government jobs, he or she would be competing on the open labor market with foreigners from poor countries like Egypt or Bangladesh who are willing to work for wages that are very modest by Kuwaiti or Emirati standards.

Dubai's Boom

In the recent boom years of globalization, the UAE—and especially Dubai—succeeded in its efforts to partially diversify its economy away from oil. The government of Dubai created an attractive business environment by building developed-world infrastructure, levying few taxes, permitting the importation of cheap foreign labor, and creating a regulatory and policy climate favorable to business. Dubai is among the most globalized economies anywhere: First and foremost it is an entrepôt, a vast trading port where merchants from far and wide come to trade. Its economy also relies on tourism and its increasing status as a regional business center. The government of Dubai—and the ruling family—profited from Dubai's growth largely through the development and sale of real estate. In Dubai, the ruler owns undeveloped land as well as land reclaimed from the sea (such as the Palm Islands that have been built off Dubai's shoreline and whose unique shapes are easily visible on Google Earth).

The economic crisis that emerged in late 2008 struck Dubai particularly hard. The government of Dubai, and its related companies, borrowed heavily to support Dubai's rapid growth and to finance the real estate developments that lie at the heart of the government's—and the ruling family's—wealth. When the Dubai real estate market crashed, Dubai's government, which was deeply involved in real estate, ran out of money: Dubai's finances looked a lot like those of an overextended real estate developer in a downturn. Dubai did not go broke, but only because it was saved by a bailout by the emirate of Abu Dhabi, still flush with oil wealth. One consequence of the crash thus was to change the balance of power within the UAE (even more) in the direction of Abu Dhabi.

While the economic crisis hit Dubai hard, the underlying entrepôt economy survived and even prospered. The airport continued to move up in international rankings and in 2017 was the third busiest in the world. Tourists continued to visit. The real estate market, not surprisingly, has lagged behind, but it is clear that there is more to Dubai's economy than real estate speculation.

The economic boom in Dubai came at a substantial cost to citizens. They increasingly feel marginalized in their own society: marginalized economically by the construction of a thriving private sector that relies very little on their labor; marginalized demographically by the flood of foreigners, many of whom are putting down roots in the UAE; and marginalized politically by their lack of voice in their own government. While many UAE citizens enjoy the fact that their country (or at least Dubai) is now famous around the world, many wonder about the costs of this: Ibtisam al-Kitbi, a professor at the leading UAE university, points out that "[Emiratis have] been put in a situation they didn't choose. Nobody asked them, 'What do you want? Is it really, this is what you want?'" (CBS News, *60 Minutes* 2007). Thus it was not surprising that some Emirati citizens, at least initially, welcomed the economic crisis out of the hope that it would reduce the number and economic prominence of foreigners in their country.

Kuwait's Economic Paralysis

Kuwait's economy remains resolutely dependent on oil. It is not that the private sector is small in Kuwait, but instead that the Kuwaiti private sector is oriented toward providing services to citizens rather than generating foreign exchange. The Kuwaiti business sector is unhappy with this situation and often blames it on the parliament. There is a certain logic to this: The parliament represents Kuwaiti citizens, and Kuwaiti citizens by and large work for the Kuwaiti state. They do not work in the private sector, and their government jobs do not depend on taxes levied on the private sector. They thus have little stake in the growth of the private sector, and much to lose from the sort of growth seen in Dubai (Herb 2009). Thus the Kuwaiti parliament has little desire to legalize alcohol so as to attract foreign tourists. The parliament also has little desire to sell state land along Kuwait's shoreline to private entrepreneurs so that they can build developments that would attract foreign tourists. (In Dubai, by contrast, the ruler controls land and is happy to sell it to the private sector.) In response to the global economic crisis, in 2009 the government proposed to bail out private sector firms in Kuwait. One prominent member of parliament opposed the plan on the grounds that investment companies "do not pay taxes on their income and do not participate in any way worth mentioning in . . . creating jobs for Kuwaitis" (*al-Qabas* 2009: 16). What the parliament does care about is distributing oil wealth to citizens, and much of what the parliament does—in economic policy at least—revolves around this. Members of parliament frequently call for increases in public sector wages, state assumption of citizens' consumer debts, no-interest loans, and outright grants to citizens from state oil revenues.

After Oil?

Is all of this spending on citizens, in Kuwait especially but also in the UAE, sustainable in the long run? The UAE has vast reserves of oil, amounting to perhaps 7 percent of the world total. It also has vast sums saved abroad, amounting to several hundred thousand US dollars for each citizen. These investments generate income. There might be a day when the UAE runs out of oil money as well as money from its investments abroad, but that day is a long way off. Kuwait has less money invested abroad, in part because it drew down its reserves to pay the costs of the 1990 Iraqi invasion. It also spends somewhat more on its citizens, and its in-ground oil reserves are likely smaller than those of the UAE. Thus there will come a time, someday in the future, when Kuwaiti citizens will need to find productive jobs in the private sector.

Religion and Politics

The regimes in the UAE and Kuwait have no qualms about promoting and subsidizing religion—and specifically Sunni Islam. In both Kuwait and the UAE, most Sunni mosques are funded by the government, and their imams (prayer leaders) are state employees. Shi'i mosques typically do not receive government support. Religion is taught in the public schools, and despite Kuwait's large Shi'i minority the curriculum is entirely Sunni.

In Kuwait and the UAE, as in the Arab world generally, Islamism is a potent political ideology with a substantial following among citizens. Islamists are far more prominent in Kuwait than in the UAE because politics in general in Kuwait are conducted in a far freer atmosphere. The regime in the UAE is very hostile toward Islamists, especially those affiliated with the Muslim Brotherhood. Before the Arab Spring prominent Islamists were arrested, barred from teaching at university, and otherwise harassed by the government. Following the Arab Spring the regime cracked down with a vengeance on the Muslim Brotherhood. The regime arrested several dozen members of the organization in a 2012 crackdown and convicted many of them in a trial that did not meet international standards for fairness. Some of those associated with the Muslim Brotherhood lost their citizenship, and there were credible allegations of serious mistreatment, and torture, in Emirati prisons. The UAE's hostility to the Muslim Brotherhood carried over into its foreign policy: the association of the Qatari regime with the Muslim Brotherhood played an important role in motivating the blockade that was imposed on it by its neighbors, including the UAE.

Gulf Islamists come in two main forms. The Muslim Brothers are a well-organized political force with ties to the international movement that originated in Egypt in the 1920s. The Salafis, by contrast, are inspired by Wahhabi Islam, which is centered in Saudi Arabia. In the Kuwaiti parliament the Sunni Islamists (the Muslim Brothers, the Salafis, and unaffiliated Islamists) form the largest single bloc, though they constitute less than a majority. The bloc lacks discipline, however, and rarely acts as a cohesive group. Sunni Islamist groups first entered the Kuwaiti parliament in force in 1981 and moved over to the opposition from 1985 onward. Islamists have had a good deal of electoral success in outlying bedouin electoral districts, and this has contributed substantially to the government's loss of majority support in the National Assembly. That said, Kuwaiti Islamists, both Sunnis and Shi'a, support the existing political order under the 1962 constitution. Kuwait and the UAE have experienced very little Islamist political violence over the past decades, especially in comparison to other Arab countries.

Civil Society

Kuwait has a vibrant civil society. In the UAE, by contrast, civil society is noticeably less active, especially with regard to anything related to politics. The most distinctive aspect of Kuwaiti civil society is the *diwaniyya,* which refers both to a physical place and to a type of meeting. The place is a large meeting room built next to, or in, Kuwaiti houses, usually with an entrance separate from the entrance to the private living quarters. Kuwaiti men hold gatherings—usually weekly—in their *diwaniyyas*: these gatherings are usually social, but often take on a political nature. Some visitors are regulars, friends of the family, political allies, business associates, and so forth. Others visit occasionally, and these can include prominent visitors from abroad: at one *diwaniyya* that I attended, the head of the largest Bahraini Islamist party made an appearance and was greeted by several prominent Kuwaiti political figures. At times the *diwaniyyas* of prominent politicians are used to host political meetings or even rallies, as for example when a member of parliament wants to drum up support for an interpellation of a minister. The times and dates of these meetings are announced in the newspapers and on the internet. The right to hold such meetings, and the right to hold weekly *diwaniyyas,* is one that is cherished by Kuwaitis.

Traditionally, *diwaniyyas* have been an exclusively male phenomenon and by and large remain so today. The increasing prominence of women in political life, along with their right to vote, has made female attendance at some political events more common. Some Islamist candidates for parliamentary seats have held political gatherings specifically for women.

Alongside the *diwaniyyas* we find many formal civil society organizations in Kuwait. Some of these are associated with the government, given the general expectation that the government rather than private donations will fund sports clubs and the like. Politically oriented organizations, however, generally keep their distance from government funding. Several political organizations exist for the explicit purpose of competing in elections: these are nascent parties. Other organizations advocate a wide variety of causes: the Kuwait Transparency Society is concerned with corruption, the Chamber of Commerce is a powerful advocate for business interests, and so forth. The universities have elected student governments. Each Kuwaiti neighborhood (or district) has a cooperative movement that runs its supermarket and shopping area, which is usually found at the center of the district. The boards of these cooperative societies are elected and can serve as stepping-stones for citizens interested in running for parliamentary seats.

Kinship organizations also form an important part of civil society in Kuwait. We see this clearly in the tendency of Kuwaitis to vote for members of their tribe or family in elections. These kinship organizations can employ very modern technologies in building a common identity, constructing a common history, and maintaining communication among members. The larger tribes and families, for example, have their own websites.

The Kuwaiti press is both relatively free and extremely active, with the country supporting over half a dozen Arabic-language daily newspapers. The press reports extensively on Kuwaiti politics, though criticizing the emir is prohibited. The press, however, will freely criticize other members of the ruling family, and especially ministers who have run afoul of parliament. Personal lives of political leaders, and indeed of most others, are usually off-limits. Overall, the contrast with the press in the rest of the Gulf—and especially in the UAE—is sharp: the Kuwaiti press is interesting to read and provides excellent coverage of politics in the country, while the press in the UAE focuses on business news and politics in other countries.

Civil society in Kuwait—and in the Gulf generally—differs from that in other parts of the developing world in that it receives little funding from abroad, and little from the West especially. The consequence of this is that the agendas of civil society groups in the Gulf are driven by local concerns. Nonetheless, some international nongovernmental organizations (NGOs) have branches in the Gulf. For example, Kuwait has a particularly active branch of Transparency International, an international NGO that focuses on fighting corruption. Numerous Kuwaiti businesses sponsor the organization.

Many of the same sorts of civil society groups found in Kuwait are also found in the UAE. Chambers of commerce are particularly active, as are sports clubs and professional organizations. Political organizations, however, are much less active. There are no equivalents to the blocs that operate in the Kuwaiti parliament, or to the groups that compete in Kuwaiti elections. While UAE citizens hold gatherings at their homes that somewhat resemble Kuwaiti *diwaniyyas,* the government does not allow these to become public political events.

Gender and Politics

Three models of women's place in society compete in Kuwait and the UAE. The first is the recent memory of gender relations in the era before oil, in which the social roles of women were sharply delineated from those of men. The second is the Western model, usually associated with "liberals" in the Gulf. The economic, political, and cultural power of the West makes it a model, for better or for worse, in most spheres of life. The third is the Islamist reaction to the Western model, a reaction that claims to preserve the older traditions but that in many ways is an innovation. Thus some Islamist deputies in the Kuwaiti parliament assert that women should not be allowed to serve in cabinet posts and in other senior positions. Some Islamist women counter this by arguing that Islam gives women many more rights than conservative male Islamists recognize.

The sharp divergence between liberal and Islamist views on family and women (along with differences on religion and other cultural issues) contributes to one of the central political cleavages in Kuwaiti and Emirati society. In Kuwait, where politics are more open, important political battles have been fought over the right of women to vote, gender segregation in universities, the holding of concerts with a mixed audience, the legal framework governing the employment of women, and other issues. In the Gulf those arguing for a more liberal society suffer from the perceived foreign origins of liberalism, allowing the conservative side in the culture wars to make a claim to cultural authenticity. This cultural divide often has a class component: urban, well-off, and well-educated families tend to be more liberal than the poorer, less-educated *bedu* families, though there are of course many exceptions.

Kuwaiti women often vote for conservative Islamist candidates for the National Assembly. We can see this most clearly in the 2006 election returns. Before 2006 women could not vote, but in that year the parliament passed a law giving women political rights. Many deputies voted against the law, however. In the subsequent elections, also held in 2006, many of these same deputies ran for reelection. Men and women voted separately, and the election returns distinguished between male and female votes. An examination of the returns suggests that women did not show any particular inclination to vote against the male deputies who had opposed giving women their political rights.

Oil wealth has had some notably positive effects on the status of women in Kuwait and the UAE. Oil has funded an enormous expansion of educational opportunities for women and has created opportunities for employment in the state. Both Kuwait and the UAE offer free public education up to college, and enrollment rates for girls are comparable to those for boys. Literacy rates are very high for young adult women. At the university level, women far outpace men: over 80 percent of citizens who graduate from the main Emirati university are female. This is because men have alternate job opportunities in the military; teenage girls are better students given that they have fewer distractions; and men, to some degree, are more likely to study abroad.

In Kuwait the citizen labor force is around 40 percent female, a comparatively high figure by world standards. In the UAE the figure is smaller but has grown rapidly in the past decade. The explanation for this is straightforward. Kuwait and the UAE have offered citizens jobs in the public sector as a way of distributing oil revenues. Citizen employees do not have to work very hard in most of these jobs, and these positions come with generous retirement benefits. Kuwaitis widely consider the work environment in public sector jobs to be appropriate for women, unlike some private sector jobs. Imported and inexpensive household labor relieves women of some of their traditional childcare and other household duties. In short, there are strong financial incentives for citizen households to have women in the workforce and few cultural obstacles to female public sector employment.

Citizen women often complain about biases against women in marriage and citizenship law. When male citizens marry foreign women, their wives can eventually receive citizenship and their children are automatically citizens, whether Kuwaiti or Emirati. When Kuwaiti or Emirati citizen women marry foreign men, by contrast, their husbands and children typically cannot become citizens. If a Kuwaiti woman marries an Egyptian man, for example, this poses a very serious problem for her children, who have a great deal of difficulty in claiming most of the manifold benefits of Kuwaiti citizenship.

Women have made some tangible gains in recent years in Kuwaiti and Emirati politics. The first female Emirati joined the Council of Ministers in 2004 as minister of economy; she is a member of the ruling family of Sharjah. In 2008 the first woman was appointed as a judge in the UAE, making the UAE the second country in the Gulf, after Bahrain, to have a woman serving in the judiciary. Women have the right to vote in both Kuwait and the UAE and, though elections do not mean much in the UAE, women are at least equal to men in this regard. Kuwait's first female minister took her post in 2005: she was Shi'a and a professor of political science. Women competed in elections in 2006 and 2008, though none succeeded in winning a seat. That changed in 2009, when four women won seats, with one woman coming in first in her district. But in the February 2012 elections women were again shut out of the Assembly, and only a few won seats in subsequent elections.

The Impact of International Politics

The small, oil-rich Gulf states are both wealthy and weak. Their oil is a rich prize that they cannot easily defend. They need protection from occasionally avaricious neighbors, as the Iraqi invasion of Kuwait in

1990 showed. The United States has for a number of decades provided this protection. Kuwait hosts several large US military installations, and the Dubai port of Jebel Ali is widely said to be the foreign port most visited by US naval vessels. The United States also has major bases in Qatar and Bahrain. The United States, for its part, wants to ensure that Gulf oil remains in friendly hands. While the citizens of Kuwait and the UAE share many of the grievances of other Arabs toward the United States and the West in general, especially over the Arab-Israeli issue, this is tempered by recognition of the need for US protection. The searing experience of the Iraqi invasion of Kuwait taught the Gulf Arabs the limits of Arab solidarity, and tensions with Iran provide a reminder of the dangers of the neighborhood. As a result, Kuwaiti and Emirati public opinion quietly supports the US military presence in the Gulf and close ties to Washington. In Kuwait, especially, the close alliance with the United States is accepted virtually across the political spectrum.

The relationship between the Shi'i communities and the regimes in Kuwait and the UAE (and their majority Sunni Arab populations generally) is affected by developments in Iran and elsewhere in the region. The revolution of 1979 made monarchs in the Gulf worry about the loyalty of their Shi'i populations. Developments in Iraq and Lebanon in the past few decades have further heightened regional tensions between Shi'a and Sunnis. The widespread demonstrations by Shi'a against the Sunni ruling family in Bahrain, followed by the Saudi-assisted crushing of protests, have further exacerbated tensions. That said, the Shi'i citizens of Kuwait, the UAE, Bahrain, and Saudi Arabia are not—as some Sunni Arabs allege—tools of the Iranian regime; the Shi'i communities of Kuwait and the UAE on the whole have demonstrated a strong loyalty to their respective countries over the past decades. The sectarian problem in the Gulf monarchies is not that the Shi'a are an Iranian fifth column, but instead that tensions between the GCC monarchies and Iran will provide an excuse for state repression of Shi'a in the GCC and a corresponding alienation of Shi'i communities from their states. So far, this has not been as much a problem in Kuwait and the UAE as in Saudi Arabia and Bahrain.

The condition of foreign workers in Kuwait and especially the UAE has led major international human rights groups to pressure the regimes to do better in their treatment of foreign labor. The position of foreigners in the Gulf states is anomalous by world standards: no other countries have such a high percentage of foreign residents. While vast differences in wealth are found in many developing countries, in those countries most poor people are at least citizens; this is not the case in the Gulf.

Western powers have generally taken a hands-off approach toward domestic politics in the UAE and (to a somewhat lesser degree) in Kuwait. This is, of course, in no small part because the regimes cooperate with the United States, and their oil is important enough to outweigh Western concerns about democracy. The United States did, however, press for the extension of voting rights to Kuwaiti women, and the decision of the Al Sabah to keep open Kuwait's parliament certainly owes something to fear of the US reaction should the family close it. In the UAE, Western pressure has been even less noticeable: the UAE is among the least democratic regimes in the world, and Western powers take little notice. In part this is because the UAE, in comparison to the rest of the Gulf, has created a relatively liberal social environment and is hostile to Islamists. Some Emiratis nonetheless worry that, someday in the future, the international community will exert pressure on the UAE not only to democratize but also to give foreigners the right to vote. In a country in which citizens are only 11 percent of the population (and this percentage is falling), democracy does not mean a great deal if it includes only citizens.

The UAE in Regional Politics

In recent years the UAE has sought to play a much more active role in the region. Much of this has occurred in partnership with the United States and with Saudi Arabia, but the UAE has not always played the role of a junior partner. Two areas where we can see a more assertive Emirati foreign policy in the region are the blockade against Qatar and the military intervention in southern Yemen. Both have had important domestic political consequences in the targeted countries.

During the Arab Spring and after, Qatar pursued an aggressive foreign policy. Qatar's satellite television station, Al-Jazeera, acted as a cheerleader for Arab Spring protests. Much of Qatar's copious diplomatic activity in the region supported Islamist actors of various stripes, and especially the Muslim Brotherhood. Al-Jazeera provided a platform for Muslim Brotherhood figures, and Qatar sent aid to Mohammad Morsi's Muslim Brotherhood regime in Egypt. All of this provided something of a model for later Emirati foreign policy activism. Much of it also deeply angered the effective rulers of both Abu Dhabi (crown prince Mohammad bin Zayed) and of Saudi Arabia (crown prince Mohammad bin Salman). They saw the Arab Spring as a mortal threat to their rule and were deeply frightened by the fall of Husni Mubarak's regime in Egypt and the rise of Morsi. They supported Abdel Fattah al-Sisi during and after his coup against the Muslim Brotherhood regime.

These concerns with Qatar led the UAE, with Saudi Arabia and Bahrain, to withdraw their ambassadors from Qatar in 2014. Not long thereafter the two sides worked out an agreement, diplomatic relations resumed, and Qatar followed a much more subdued foreign policy under a new emir. In 2017, however, the conflict broke out again, in a more serious form. The trigger might have been a large payment made by Qatar to several groups associated with Iran and the Iraqi Shi'a in exchange for the release of several members of the Qatari ruling family who had been taken hostage in Iraq. The change in administrations in Washington, however, also likely had a role. The Obama administration had tried to dampen down conflict between its allies in the Gulf. The new Donald Trump administration—or, specifically, President Trump and his son-in-law Jared Kushner—took sides with the UAE and Saudi Arabia against Qatar. This opened a space for the crown princes of Saudi Arabia and Abu Dhabi to impose a blockade on Qatar. They were joined in this by Egypt and Bahrain, forming the anti-Qatar quartet. Saudi Arabia—the only country with a land border with Qatar—closed the border, while the other members of the quartet cut air routes, ended commercial ties, and demanded that their citizens return home from Qatar, while expelling Qataris.

A year after the crown princes imposed the blockade it appears that they failed to achieve their political objectives. The Qatari emir refused to give in to the quartet's demands on the grounds that it would be a surrender of Qatari sovereignty, and his stance earned him a surge in popularity at home. After a few months, Qatar won over Trump and Kushner. This might be because it became clear that siding with the quartet did not serve US interests, or it might be because Qatar negotiated to invest millions in Newsmax, owned by one of Trump's closer friends and confidants, and because Brookfield Asset Management—a network of companies in which the Qatari sovereign wealth fund has a major stake—rescued the Kushner family's disastrous investment in a midtown Manhattan office building. In any case, Trump no longer tweets against Qatar, and while he has not turned against the UAE and Saudi Arabia, the US approach is now much more balanced.

The Qatar blockade is by no means the UAE's only foreign policy entanglement. In 2015 the UAE intervened in Yemen with Saudi Arabia, and today the UAE's Yemeni allies control much of southern Yemen and the UAE has a major military presence in the country. The UAE and Saudi Arabia intervened in Yemen to reverse the gains of the Shi'i Houthi movement, which they saw as an arm of efforts by Iran to extend its influence in the region. The degree of Iranian sponsorship of the Houthis was much exaggerated, and the intervention by Saudi Arabia and the UAE has produced only a partial reversal of Houthi territorial gains in Yemen, and at a very high cost. Much of the cost, of course, has been borne by Yemenis, including Yemeni civilians, but UAE forces have also suffered battle deaths.

Note

1. In the terminology used by political scientists, this was a shift from block voting to a single nontransferable vote, or SNTV.

16

Palestine

Nathan J. Brown

Palestinians have been striving to create their own state for over a century. They have many trappings of success—a seat at the United Nations, a strong national identity, a string of international statements and resolutions supporting the idea, and many state-like structures (e.g., police, a school system, and law courts). These accomplishments were each hard won. But to speak of "Palestine" as a state like Mexico or Canada obscures how incomplete and fractured these efforts are. In fact, even as Palestine gets increasing symbolic recognition as a state, the prospects for the emergence of a sovereign Palestinian state seems to be receding. Palestine now lacks not only full international standing but also internal unity—Palestinians are deeply divided between two political systems, one based in Ramallah (on the West Bank) and another in Gaza, unable to work effectively together despite many pledges to do so (see Figures 16.1 and 16.2). Who are Palestinians? How are they governed? Why is establishing a Palestinian state so hard? These are the key questions this chapter seeks to answer.

Historical Background and Contemporary Political Structure

"Palestine" historically has been the term often used to refer to the strip of land along the eastern shore of the Mediterranean Sea, south of Lebanon and north of the Sinai desert. Prior to World War I, most areas of the Arab world, including the geographical area called Palestine, were governed by the Ottoman Empire. When the empire was dismantled after its defeat in the war, Great Britain sought and won a mandate

Figure 16.1 Map of the West Bank

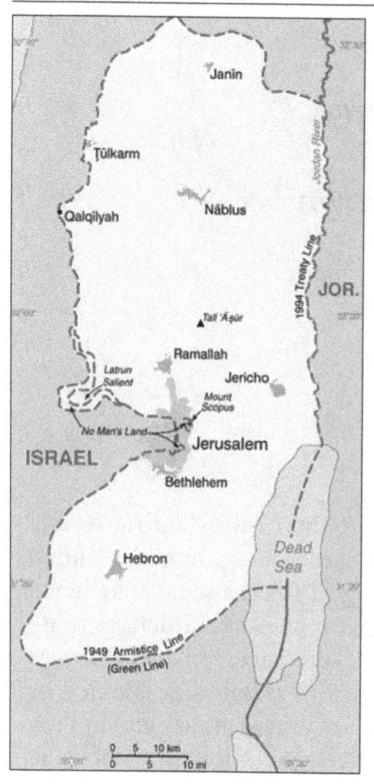

Figure 16.2 Map of the Gaza Strip

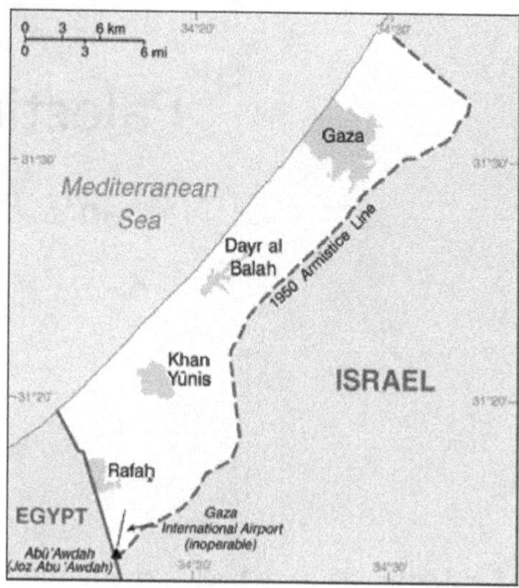

for Palestine from the newly created League of Nations. That mandate allowed Britain to govern the territory but imposed on it two obligations that operated very much in tension: it was to foster the development of the territory for self-government but also promote the development of "a Jewish national home." These terms were defined very vaguely. But if the first required that inhabitants move toward governing themselves, the second required that the territory be open to Jewish immigration—something the majority of the existing inhabitants opposed. While there was a substantial Jewish minority in the country, a large majority was Arab. The Arab Palestinian population pressed for democratic structures and independence. (Gradually the term "Palestinian" has come to refer only to the Arab population of the area, especially after the creation of the State of Israel in 1948 led to the emergence of a new "Israeli" national identity that included all the Jews.)

After facing revolts against its policies—first by the Arab population in 1936 and then by the Jewish population after World War II—Britain turned the Palestine problem back to the United Nations (the successor to the League of Nations). The UN recommended partition of the territory into an Arab state and a Jewish state, but it was powerless to implement its decision when the Arab population of the territory rejected it as unfair to the majority. Fighting broke out as the British withdrew. The Jewish leadership proclaimed a state of Israel in May 1948; two months later Arab leaders attempted to declare their own state of Palestine.

The effort in 1948 to create a state of Palestine for the Arab inhabitants was unsuccessful. It was defeated on the battlefield, even when the surrounding Arab states (chiefly Egypt and Jordan but also Syria, Lebanon, and Iraq) entered on the Palestinian side. When the fighting ended, the new State of Israel controlled most of the territory that the British had abandoned, leaving only a narrow strip in the southwest around the city of Gaza and the western bank of the Jordan River under Arab control.

The parts of Palestine under Arab control—less than one-quarter of the territory of Mandatory Palestine—were neither part of a state for Palestinians nor even under Palestinian control. Gaza was occupied by neighboring Egyptian forces at the end of the fighting, the West Bank by Jordan. Jordan annexed the West Bank rather than creating a new Arab state of Palestine out of the remnants under its control. Palestinians in the West Bank became Jordanian citizens. Egypt administered Gaza, allowing a modest amount of Palestinian self-government, but kept most critical questions under its control. But while Egypt wished to maintain security in Gaza, it had no wish to annex it, leaving the crowded territory's status in limbo.

Some of the Arab population who had lived in areas forming the new State of Israel fled; others were forcibly expelled, leading to a large refugee problem as well. Some remained in Israel, becoming Arab citizens of the new Jewish state. Others spread out to Israel's neighbors and then throughout the Arab world (and even farther).

Thus, after 1948 the Arab inhabitants of Palestine were divided. They lived under Jordanian, Israeli, or Egyptian rule but had no state or organization to represent their own interests. Some slow efforts were made in the 1950s to create new Palestinian political parties and movements, but these were monitored carefully by all concerned governments. The new movements often emerged among Palestinian communities outside Palestine (especially Cairo and Kuwait), where Palestinians had more freedom. Some began to launch guerrilla raids on Israeli targets in order to provoke a military confrontation between Israel and its Arab neighbors, successfully creating tension but also earning some international notoriety when they intentionally harmed Israeli civilians.

Timeline: What Is Palestine and Who Ruled It?

Until 1917: Geographical area of Palestine is part of the Ottoman Empire

1917–1922: Great Britain occupies Palestine during World War I

1922–1948: Great Britain governs Palestine with a mandate from the League of Nations

After 1948:

Israel

1948–present: Israel controls over three-quarters of the territory of the Palestine Mandate

West Bank

1950: Jordan annexes West Bank, administering it until 1967

1967–1994: Israel controls West Bank, administers Palestinian population, and establishes settlements in the region

1994–2007: Palestinian Authority administers towns and cities; Israel controls its settlements and most other land

2007–present: Palestinian Authority splits, with president controlling West Bank

Gaza

1948–1967: Egypt administers Gaza, allows it limited self-rule

1967–1994: Israel controls Gaza, administers Palestinian population, and establishes some settlements in the region

1994–2007: Palestinian Authority governs, although Israel retains its settlements and military installations until 2005, when it withdraws completely

2007–2014: Palestinian Authority splits, with prime minister and cabinet controlling Gaza under Hamas leadership

2014–present: Hamas cabinet resigns to pave the way for reunification with the West Bank, but reconciliation not fully implemented

Israeli counter-raids proved extremely harsh. The most prominent Palestinian movement, Fatah, emerged in this period, led by an engineer named Yasser Arafat.

In 1964 the Arab League created a new body to represent Palestinians, the Palestine Liberation Organization (PLO). But the PLO at first was more a creation of the Arab states than of the Palestinians themselves.

In 1967 a new round of Arab-Israeli fighting ended with Israel in control of the West Bank and Gaza. With their Arab allies defeated, Palestinians now felt much more on their own. Under Arafat's leadership, Fatah managed to seize control of the PLO and make it a more viable body for representing Palestinian interests. The PLO eventually received recognition by the Arab world as the "sole, legitimate representative of the Palestinian people." But the PLO controlled no territory. Israel did not recognize the PLO, nor did the PLO recognize Israel. The PLO sought to establish its state in all of the territory of the former British mandate, most of which was now Israel. Israel rejected the PLO because of its goals and its methods (Palestinian groups belonging to the PLO targeted Israeli civilians with violence). On a fundamental level, Israel did not recognize Palestinians as a distinct people with a right to a state. Indeed the Israeli government allowed and encouraged its own citizens to settle in the West Bank and Gaza. The PLO was left trying to represent all Palestinians while having its headquarters in different Arab countries rather than in the territory that it wanted for a state.

In 1987 Palestinians in the West Bank and Gaza launched an intifada (uprising) against Israeli rule. The intifada gradually petered out in the early 1990s, but it led some Israeli leaders to conclude that it would be better to negotiate with the Palestinians than to rule them indefinitely. Meanwhile some on the Palestinian side concluded that their only viable option was to accept Israel's existence but to negotiate with it to create a Palestinian state only in the West Bank and Gaza. In 1988 the PLO declared independence for a state called Palestine and in the process all but explicitly accepted the partition of historically Palestinian territory between the new state and Israel. Its leadership also met US demands that it renounce terrorism. The PLO declaration of independence came in Algeria, since the PLO could not meet in Palestine—demonstrating that much had to be done to make the paper declaration a reality. While it could not be implemented in practice, the new initiative did eventually make it possible to negotiate with Israel.

In 1993 those negotiations led to limited fruition. The Israeli government and the PLO came to an agreement in Oslo, Norway, to recognize each other. They then came to a series of agreements—collectively known as the Oslo Accords—that allowed Palestinians in the West Bank and Gaza to govern themselves for a transitional five-year period. During that period, Israel and the PLO were supposed to negotiate a permanent agreement—but almost all the details of that permanent settlement were left inchoate. In a sense, the two sides simply agreed to try to agree. They have failed to do so in a quarter century, however, leaving the supposedly interim arrangements, noxious to Palestinians, in place indefinitely.

The Oslo Accords were very controversial on both sides. Israelis saw that the accords were likely to lead to some kind of Palestinian state and to significant withdrawals from the West Bank and Gaza—a price many were not willing to pay. Some Palestinians felt that the PLO had played its only card—recognition of Israel—and would likely be left with only the right to handle municipal affairs in a few cities rather than the right to build a real state. Some rejected the idea of a peace agreement altogether. A Palestinian offshoot of the Muslim Brotherhood, Hamas, led the Palestinian opposition to the Oslo Accords.

Beginning in 1993 and 1994, the interim parts of the Oslo Accords allowed the Palestinians to set up a body they called the Palestinian National Authority (PNA) to administer Palestinian towns and cities in the West Bank and Gaza. They used this as an opportunity to create the basis of a state—founding ministries, building a parliament, writing laws, and creating security forces. In 1996, Palestinians in the West Bank and Gaza elected Yasser Arafat as their president as well as a parliament dominated by his Fatah party.

While this effort was occurring, little progress was made on a final agreement between Israel and the PLO. Only in 2000 were there serious negotiations, and those did not result in an agreement. While Israel had pledged to widen the areas under Palestinian control in the meantime, it unilaterally froze its withdrawals, meaning that even the interim measures negotiated in Oslo were not fully implemented. Palestinians increasingly despaired that they would receive a state through a negotiated peace process and saw the emerging PNA as a corrupt body ruling a shrunken territory—an entity designed to mask rather than end Israeli occupation. They also saw Israeli settlers continuing to move into the West Bank and Gaza, leading growing numbers to believe that Israel would never withdraw. Some Palestinian groups rejected the entire process and continued to attack Israeli targets. Israel imposed obstacles to Palestinian travel inside and between the West Bank and Gaza, and these seemed to grow far more severe even as peace was supposedly being negotiated. While international eyes focused on the hope of negotiations, Palestinians began to feel that there was no prospect of a genuine settlement.

In 2000 a second Palestinian intifada against Israeli rule was launched. The intifada and the harsh Israeli countermeasures took a severe toll on the PNA. Israel regarded PNA leaders—especially Arafat himself—as responsible for the violence directed against Israeli civilians. Israel sent its forces to surround the Palestinian president, holding him prisoner in his own office. Various Palestinian groups escalated their attacks in response to Israeli measures. Israel began construction of a barrier—a formidable wall in populated areas and a sophisticated fence in the rest of the territory—that protected many of its citizens in the West Bank and made it difficult for would-be attackers to reach Israeli targets. Israel withdrew from the Gaza Strip in 2005 but maintained close control over entry and exit from the territory.

The intifada gradually subsided, and Palestinians tried to rebuild their political institutions. President Arafat died in 2004; his deputy, Mahmoud Abbas, won elections that were immediately held to select his successor. Abbas had advocated returning to negotiations with Israel and had strong international backing. Arafat's death and the peaceful accession to power of a figure more acceptable to the United States and Israel seemed to be an opportunity to revive the PNA. The parliament that had been elected in 1996 was still sitting—because it had been intended to last only for a three-year period while peace was being negotiated, no second round of elections was ever held. So, the new president called for parliamentary elections as a way of renewing Palestinian institutions. Because he wanted to build a strong consensus among all Palestinians, he coaxed Hamas—which had boycotted previous elections—into participating. He anticipated that his Fatah party would win but that Hamas would become a loyal opposition within the PNA rather than a rejectionist group standing outside of it.

Yet Hamas won a significant electoral victory in January 2006—aided by Fatah's reputation for corruption, squabbling, and inability to deliver peace, as well as by an election system that rewarded the tactically more agile and disciplined Hamas. Hamas also enjoyed a reputation for being far more public-spirited and less corrupt than Fatah. Palestinians were certainly aware of Hamas's hard-line positions (though in the campaign Hamas emphasized its reform credentials rather than its rejection of a negotiated settlement with Israel), but since there seemed to be no viable diplomacy occurring, even many Palestinians who wished to negotiate a settlement with Israel voted for Hamas. Caught by surprise by the size of its victory, the Islamic movement realized that it would not be accepted internationally if it formed the PNA government by itself. It tried to form a coalition government with other parties (including Fatah) but was unable to persuade them to join. In March 2006, Hamas found itself forced to accept power and form a cabinet by itself. It was met immediately by a cutoff of funds (the PNA depended on Europe for some funding and on Israel for collecting its taxes), strikes by Fatah-led unions, and attempts by hostile Palestinian forces to keep it from governing. Since Fatah still controlled the presidency, the security services, and most top administrative positions, Hamas held only some levers of power.

In the summer of 2006, after Palestinians captured an Israeli soldier and held him hostage, Israel retaliated by arresting many Hamas members of parliament and even some ministers. It seemed that Hamas would not be able to govern. Hamas itself only vaguely hinted at softening its hard-line positions. To find a way out of the impasse, Hamas and Fatah briefly came to an agreement and jointly formed a cabinet, but Palestinian infighting did not cease, and the US and European funders of the PNA viewed the Fatah-Hamas government with suspicion. The agreement soon fell apart, and a brief civil war between Hamas and Fatah in 2007 left Hamas in control of Gaza but ousted from power in the West Bank. Palestinians now had two governments, but they still had not achieved their first state.

After the split, both the Hamas-led government in Gaza and the Abbas-led government in Ramallah rejected each other's legitimacy. While they went through the motions of attempting to reunify, both sides preferred to dig themselves in rather than make concessions to the other. They arrested each other's supporters and tried to show that they could rule their respective areas. In Gaza, Hamas had to do so under an extremely strict blockade imposed by Israel and enforced by Egypt as well; only some food and medicine could be reliably transported (though a vast array of goods was smuggled into Gaza through underground tunnels connected to Egypt). In December 2008, after the breakdown of an informal cease-fire between Israel and Hamas, Israel launched an invasion of Gaza that caused further economic devastation. But Hamas continued to solidify its hold on power, controlling the government and regulating the tunnel economy. On the West Bank, a respected international economist headed an effort to build a clean and efficient government; he was given extensive international support.

One possible way out of the division was new elections—and indeed, both the presidency and the parliament were supposed to have been subject to new elections in 2010. Yet elections became the subject of dispute rather than a way to resolve differences: after Hamas seized control of Gaza, Abbas issued a new election law by decree that effectively barred Hamas from running, and each side arrested the other's supporters, making campaigning impossible.

Palestinian public opinion grew increasingly critical of both Fatah and Hamas for refusing to bury their differences. The Palestinian leadership based in Ramallah became increasingly isolated from the population it sought to lead. With no elections on the horizon and the PNA reduced to what its critics always denounced it for being—a set of municipal administrations masquerading indefinitely as the kernel of a state—the PNA began to atrophy. Since it paid a large number of salaries, administered schools, oversaw courts, and controlled Palestinian finances, few Palestinians had any alternatives to offer, making the PNA part of the Palestinian landscape but not a strong political actor.

For their part, Hamas's leaders had little more to offer. Indeed, bottled up and besieged in Gaza, Hamas found itself in an increasingly untenable position. With no desire to turn itself into a tiny, besieged ministate forever, Hamas insisted it was still "resisting" Israel. But any attacks launched from Gaza led to harsh Israeli countermeasures—escalating to intense warfare between Gaza and Israel in 2008 and 2014. These rounds left little changed on the ground except for considerable destruction.

Pressured by Palestinian public opinion, Fatah and Hamas sometimes agreed to vague formulas for reconciliation. In 2014 the Hamas cabinet resigned to pave the way for reunification between the two territories, and some steps were taken in 2017. But Gaza remained under unofficial but effective Hamas control, and the numerous agreements for Palestinian reconciliation were never fully implemented.

Government and Opposition

Most Arab political systems have strong governments and weak and divided oppositions. Before the upheavals of 2011, the least authoritarian Arab regimes had some limited democratic mechanisms—like multiparty elections and parliaments—but none allowed political power to change hands as the result of elections. While some Arab systems allowed some opposition elements to operate, elections resembled more a cat-and-mouse game between government and opposition than robust democratic politics. In a few countries (most notably Tunisia and Egypt), the situation for political opposition became much more open for a period after 2011, but the rules of democratic politics were still not well established.

By these standards, Palestine has been more open for a while, in that political opposition has existed since the beginning of the PNA. But if politics is competitive at times, it is not well institutionalized. Rules of the political game are either unclear or routinely broken. In fact, since 2006 it has not even been clear which party is in government and which one is in opposition. So, while Palestine has a more open political system than most others in the region, it also has fragile, weak, and decaying institutions.

The PLO still claims to represent all Palestinians everywhere, not merely those in the West Bank and Gaza governed by the PNA. While most Palestinians continue to respect the PLO as a symbol, in reality it has become little more than a shell. To the extent that it survives, the PLO is dominated by the Fatah party—they both have the same aging leader (Mahmoud Abbas). Its main body is the Palestinian National Council, which consists of leading Palestinians throughout the world, but this only meets sporadically (its last meeting was in 1999). The real work of the PLO is carried out by its Central Committee and its Executive Committee—bodies dominated by Fatah but that also include other parties and independents.

The creation of the PNA in the West Bank and Gaza marginalized the PLO in Palestinian politics. Most leading Palestinian political figures left the PLO to join the PNA, taking most Palestinian finances with them, and the PLO was allowed to decay. The PNA acknowledges the PLO as its overseer, and the PLO remains important as a symbol of national unity. But even in that regard its usefulness has been limited by the rise of Hamas—which has not joined the PLO and refuses to do so until it is offered a significant share of power in the body.

This has left the PNA, since 1994, as the organization that administers the West Bank and Gaza. In some areas, the PNA is allowed to go beyond administration, to control police and security, but there is a steady tug-of-war with Israel on that issue, even in areas that are supposed to be under full PNA control (like West Bank cities). In other areas where according to the Oslo Accords the PNA is supposed to be able to operate (such as governing Palestinians in outlying West Bank villages), Israel allows it no effective presence.

The PNA takes on a host of governmental functions: it oversees schools, parts of the health care system, courts of law, and business licensing, and it carries out some foreign relations. It has no military and does not issue its own currency (the Israeli shekel is used). It cannot control who exits or enters its territory—indeed, it has no defined borders. It is not a recognized state but merely an administrative body, so it leaves most diplomatic relations to the PLO, which claims to represent the state of Palestine until that state is given territorial reality.

Since 2000 many of the PNA-controlled governmental functions have decayed under the combined pressures of the second intifada, Israeli restrictions, and the rivalry between Hamas and Fatah. Generally, the health and education systems have continued to function, but other governmental services work badly if at all.

For its first eight years (from 1994 to 2002), the PNA seemed to be emerging as a state that resembled other Arab political systems of the time, with all their authoritarian features. There was a single dominant party, Fatah. It governed in a heavy-handed manner. Dissent was often tolerated (much more, in fact, than in most Arab states), but the government could sometimes be very rough with critics. There were some democratic practices, but they were not allowed to threaten Fatah rule—for instance, local elections were not held for a long time because the PNA's leaders feared the opposition was too popular. Hamas, the largest opposition group, was sometimes tolerated, but when it launched attacks on Israel, PNA leaders sometimes cracked down hard, arresting and even torturing Hamas members.

When the second intifada erupted in 2000, the PNA began to decay. Various Palestinian groups competed with each other for their ability to "resist" Israel by launching attacks, and the PNA's ability to suppress the opposition (including Hamas) collapsed.

In 2002 a group of Palestinian reformers, supported by international donors in Europe and the United States, were able to use the weakness of the PNA to impose a series of changes on Palestinian politics. They forced President Arafat to approve a constitution he had long resisted and to accept a law creating an independent judiciary. They also made him turn over revenue to the treasury rather than control a portion himself with no accountability, as he had done earlier. For Palestinian reformers, the plan was to rebuild the PNA on a solid and professional basis. Other supporters of reform (like the United States) saw the effort not simply as about better governance but also as a way to undermine Arafat personally; the Americans and Israelis both wished to see him weakened or replaced. The combined result was the dismantling of much of the remaining ability of the PNA president to dominate Palestinian politics as an authoritarian leader.

The reformed system received its most severe test in 2006, when the opposition won the parliamentary election. For the first time in Arab history, a governing party had lost power through democratic means. This presented a difficult situation. First, the defeated party, Fatah, still controlled the presidency, since Abbas had won it a year earlier, and much of the governmental machinery was staffed by Fatah loyalists. Second, Palestinian political institutions were fragile and untested. Third, Hamas was rejected internationally because it had targeted civilians and rejected the negotiation process with Israel.

Under this harsh domestic and international pressure, Palestinian democracy simply failed the test. After a year and a half, the PNA split into two halves, with Hamas controlling in Gaza and Abbas controlling the West Bank. In neither territory is dissent fully tolerated. In Gaza, Fatah activists are harassed and arrested, and pro-Fatah newspapers are periodically barred; in the West Bank, Hamas supporters are fired from government jobs, its activists are arrested, and pro-Hamas newspapers are forbidden from entering. Rather than leading to a democratic transition, the 2006 elections led to a political breakdown.

If the PLO, representing Palestinians throughout the world, has become a shell, and the PNA is split and decaying, are there any sound structures left in Palestinian political life? Not really, though some continue to try to operate under difficult conditions. The political party system is very lively, but in some respects, this is a problem—the parties (like Hamas and Fatah) are strong at the expense of the government. The parties often have their own militias and treat government office as a way of furthering party rather than national goals.

Palestinian party life is also complicated by the fact that the parties aim not simply to win elections and government authority but also to achieve all sorts of other goals—including national liberation and provision of services. In fact, most do not call themselves "parties" but instead "movements." Hamas, whose full name is the "Islamic Resistance Movement," has a military wing and remains in part an underground organization. Fatah, whose full name is the "Movement of Palestinian Liberation," also has militias associated with it. Hamas has managed to retain some coherence even as its leaders often disagree; Fatah, by contrast, seems to be decaying, with its leaders sometimes more concerned with outmaneuvering each other than with achieving party goals. Other, smaller parties are similarly split among electoral, propaganda, social, and military activity.

Political Economy

The Middle East has witnessed a struggle over how much the state should control the economy. Palestine is not a state, but it still seems that politics drives economics. The mainstay of Palestine's economy in the early twentieth century was farming, though there was some limited manufacturing, long-distance trade, and nomadic activity as well. Economic development led to some migration to the cities, and the 1948 war left most Palestinians in the West Bank and Gaza in towns, cities, and camps. This had real effects on Palestinian society, parts of which became dependent on foreign assistance for basic services. The old Palestinian leadership of the early twentieth century—consisting of prominent landowning families—declined in the new environment, and new groups, grounded in fields like medicine and business, began to become more prominent.

But the Palestinian economy never experienced the ambitious state-led development projects launched by many Arab states in the 1950s and 1960s. Gaza remained tied to Egypt as a ward rather than the focus of development efforts. Having annexed the West Bank, the Jordanian government concentrated most of its attention on the East Bank instead.

Israel's occupation of the West Bank and Gaza in 1967 radically changed the Palestinian economy. Israel eliminated economic barriers among itself, the West Bank, and Gaza, meaning that residents of those areas now could work in Israel and trade freely. Palestinians paid taxes at the Israeli rate, largely switched over to using Israeli currency, and saw Israel integrate the Palestinian electrical grid and telephone network with its own. Israel was a far larger and more prosperous society, and it developed rapidly in the ensuing decades. Large numbers of Palestinians found work in Israel; some even worked in settlements that Israel built for its own citizens on the land it was now occupying in the West Bank and Gaza. Most goods for Palestinian markets came through Israeli ports, and Palestinians found that Israel was the best customer for some of their products.

The increasingly close linkages with Israel led to an increase in living standards for many Palestinians—accompanied by politically distasteful effects. First, they had no control over economic policy. Second, while the arrangement generated jobs, the lower economic and educational levels of Palestinian areas ensured that most employment for Palestinians was unskilled and poorly paid relative to that for Israelis. Third, while Israel applied the same tax system to the West Bank and Gaza that it did to its own territories, it used the revenues not to finance economic development in those territories but rather to underwrite its own costs. From a Palestinian standpoint, this meant that residents of the West Bank and Gaza were financing the cost of their own occupation. Finally, the health of the Palestinian economy depended on access to Israeli markets—which could be closed off for political or security reasons with devastating effect.

When Israel and the PLO negotiated the Oslo Accords, the Palestinian leadership first wished to detach the economies of the West Bank and Gaza from Israel's and reorient them toward the Arab world. But they soon realized that, as attractive as this might have been on nationalist grounds, it was problematic economically. This point was driven home when, toward the beginning of the negotiations, Israel constructed a fence around Gaza in order to allow it to restrict the traffic of people and goods in and out of the small territory. Such a closure would be a mixed blessing for Israelis—they would lose a source of cheap labor (but one that could be replaced by allowing Asian and African workers in) and cheap agricultural produce (which hurt Israeli consumers but satisfied Israeli farmers). But if the closure had mixed effects for Israel, it was catastrophic for Palestinians, who were thrown out of work and deprived of both basic goods and a market for their products.

Accordingly, when negotiating the economic arrangements of the Oslo Accords, Palestinian leaders felt forced to continue the close linkage between the Israeli and Palestinian economies. The arrangements required the PNA to continue to set its tax rates at Israeli levels. Some of these taxes were even collected by Israel; since goods destined for Palestinian markets had to come through Israeli ports, Israel would collect the tax and then deliver it to the PNA (after deducting an administrative fee). This provided the PNA with an immediate and easy stream of revenue—but also one that Israel could cut off at will. The PNA even agreed to set the price of gasoline, which was heavily taxed by Israel, at the Israeli price, to prevent Israelis from crossing over into PNA areas in search of cheaper fuel.

There were some exceptions to the close linkages between the two economies, but even these created problems. For instance, the PNA was allowed to import some commodities (such as cement) exempt from some taxes. But this system—proposed by Israel to allow the PNA some of the supplies it would need for economic development—opened the doors for tremendous corruption. First, PNA leaders could dole out the right to import these cheap commodities to their friends, who often reaped large profits; second, Palestinians could sell the cheap commodities back to Israel on the black market, deepening the corruption. In sum, the economic arrangements generated by the Oslo process left the Palestinian economy heavily dependent on Israel and created opportunities for corruption that would come back to haunt the PNA.

The Oslo period also saw the beginning of a tremendous international assistance program to the PNA. At first, assistance simply went to pay the normal PNA budget, but as the tax system was established, the international assistance program turned to long-term development projects. While development projects and priorities were negotiated with the PNA, the Palestinian entity was so new and inexperienced that it had a difficult time assessing its own needs without international help. The result was a system in which donors dominated development efforts and the PNA struggled to keep abreast of what the assistance program was doing. The PNA gradually earned a reputation for corruption, inefficiency, and heavy-handedness, meaning that some donors preferred to bypass it and work directly with nongovernmental organizations (NGOs), frustrating PNA officials even more.

The Oslo period, even when it seemed to be working well, still saw episodic flashes of Israeli-Palestinian violence, which in turn had serious effects on the Palestinian economy. Israel would generally respond to any attack from Palestinian areas with a "closure"—not only preventing movement in and out of the West Bank and Gaza but often movement within them as well. With goods and workers sometimes unable to move, the Palestinian economy was hostage to the political climate between Israel and the PNA.

The second intifada led to severe closures and a rapid deterioration in the Palestinian economy. Israel eventually began construction of a wall in the West Bank to separate its territory as well as large blocs of its West Bank settlements from Palestinian-populated areas. In addition, Israel stopped transferring revenues to the PNA for long periods, charging that the PNA was responsible for violence against Israel. Some of the international sponsors of the Oslo process stepped in with emergency assistance to Palestinians; they also kept the PNA supplied with enough funds to prevent its collapse. Israel dropped initial objections to this assistance program, realizing that humanitarian disaster and political collapse in Palestinian areas did not serve its interest. Eventually Israel resumed transfer of the revenue.

The election of Hamas in 2006 threw even these makeshift arrangements into doubt. The international supporters of the peace process were face to face with the reality that the government they were assisting was now partly controlled by Hamas. The initial response was drastic: Israel cut off tax transfers again, and this time the international community provided only limited funds to those parts of the PNA that were not under Hamas control. The result threatened political collapse and humanitarian disaster. Europe, therefore, built a slightly less strict mechanism by which it would make payments to Palestinian civil servants directly without going through the Hamas-controlled Ministry of Finance.

In 2007, when the PNA split into two halves, international assistance fully resumed to the Ramallah government. The willingness of that government to prevent attacks on Israel led Israeli authorities to lighten some of their restrictions on movement and access for Palestinians. The result was a sustained economic recovery—but one that was dependent on a favorable political environment.

The Gaza government, controlled by Hamas, was not so lucky. Some of its employees were paid by the Ramallah government (because those in power in Ramallah wished to maintain a toehold in Gaza), and others were paid with Hamas's limited funds. But the economic closure on Gaza was extremely severe, leading not to starvation (basic supplies and international relief efforts were allowed to continue) but to massive poverty, unemployment, and malnutrition. Hamas pressed hard to open the border between Gaza and Egypt (it was less interested in opening the border with Israel, since it wanted to reverse the close linkage between the Palestinian and Israeli economies), but the effort was largely unsuccessful. As time went on, it became clear that the economic closure was not going to bring Hamas down, that smuggling through tunnels on the Gaza-Egypt border was actually taxed by Hamas (strengthening the movement), and that the Israeli blockade generated negative international publicity. Israel thus relaxed the restrictions slightly.

The 2011 Egyptian revolution diminished Egypt's already weak impulse to prevent smuggling. As a result, Gaza enjoyed a limited reversal of its economic misfortune. But the election of a friendly Muslim Brotherhood leader as Egypt's president did not lead to a complete opening of the Egyptian border, disappointing Hamas. In 2013 the new military rulers of Egypt shut down the tunnel traffic as completely as they could. Facing their own insurgency in the Sinai Peninsula—the Egyptian territory adjacent to Gaza—Egypt's rulers put enormous pressure on Hamas to control movement across the border. The result strangled Gaza's economy even further. While basic goods are allowed in, the unemployment rate in Gaza is over 40 percent.

Civil Society

In the mandate period, the main structures of Palestinian society were centered on family and neighborhood, town, or village, but there were also some formal associations. Chambers of commerce for businessmen formed early. Various members of the elite began to form other organizations, such as charitable societies and women's clubs, though these did not reach deeply into the society.

After 1948 Palestinians in the West Bank and Gaza found themselves living under authoritarian governments that viewed independent organizations with some suspicion. Jordan was more liberal than Egypt, tolerating political parties and allowing more in the way of social and charitable organizations. The Muslim Brotherhood, for instance, was repressed in Egypt but allowed to operate as a charitable society in Jordan. Outside the West Bank and Gaza, Palestinian communities in places as diverse as Cairo and Kuwait also tried to organize community institutions and to use them to help Palestinians internationally.

When Israel occupied the West Bank and Gaza in 1967, those areas became more isolated from the rest of the Arab world. Accordingly, residents there made some effort to establish their own organizations, such as universities and newspapers. Israel kept a close watch on organized activity. Such efforts were sometimes viewed just as suspiciously by Palestinians outside the territories, and the PLO often discouraged them. The PLO was worried that if a Palestinian leadership arose in the West Bank and Gaza, it would negotiate a settlement with Israel that cut out the PLO and Palestinians on the outside. For instance, when a group of Palestinians tried to establish a university in the West Bank, it took them years to convince both the Israelis and the PLO to drop any objections.

Only the Muslim Brotherhood had an easier time—at least at first. The leadership of the Brotherhood stayed away from political activity at the time, arguing that Palestinians had to become more religious before they could worry about confronting Israel—a stance that made Israel look to the Brotherhood with some tolerance. The Brotherhood never accepted the leadership of the PLO, regarding it as too secular and friendly to radical ideas (such as Marxism). Instead the Brotherhood focused on religious education and social work.

The situation for Palestinian civil society began to change in the 1980s, for two reasons. First, Palestinian leaders on the outside began to change their attitude toward organizations in the West Bank and Gaza. Each political party based in the diaspora began to fear that the others would organize the population in the territories and thus competed to form loyal unions, organizations, and youth clubs. Sometimes they competed directly for control of the same organization, most often in elections for student associations. Second, Arab states began to give much more assistance to Palestinians through a fund overseen jointly by Jordan and the PLO. Since government institutions in the West Bank and Gaza were under Israeli control, Arab states preferred to give funds directly to private groups.

When the first intifada erupted in 1987, therefore, it found a network of groups and organizations with which to mobilize the population. Meanwhile the Muslim Brotherhood dropped its reservations about politics and metamorphosed into Hamas, a movement that enthusiastically joined the intifada. Israel tried to shut down some of these organizations, but many of them survived relatively intact until the ebbing of the intifada in the early 1990s.

Ironically, the Oslo peace process forced these new NGOs to adjust more than the intifada had. The influx of international assistance, the shift in donors from the Arab world to the West, the creation of the PNA, and the change in focus from resisting occupation to building a new political system rewarded some NGOs and penalized or passed over others. NGOs that could professionalize their operations, meeting the organizational and reporting requirements of Western donors, did well—particularly if they could satisfy the interests of those donors (some donors focused on service provision, others favored human rights and governance, and still others sought to build people-to-people contact with Israel). Such NGOs often built impressive operations but lost touch with their grassroots constituency. They also sometimes chafed at the PNA, which they felt was trying to control them. In some ways, the most effective critics of the PNA during this period came from this professionalized NGO sector.

The grassroots organizations built during the preceding periods did not disappear, but they often struggled for funds and discovered that the creation of the PNA did not make things easier for them. Some were associated with political movements and parties, including Fatah, the governing party. A large number were Islamic in coloration—sometimes gravitating politically toward Hamas and sometimes uninterested in politics—and these were largely passed over by international donors.

With the collapse of the peace process in 2000, donors shifted their attention once again to emergency relief and provision of services. NGOs involved in the health sector were favored in such an environment. Others, devoted to fields such as human rights, struggled to decide whether their primary target should be the PNA or Israel.

With Hamas's electoral victory, many professionalized NGOs were caught in a dilemma. Continued funding from the West depended on assurances that they had no connection with Hamas—and while most did not, some resented the political restrictions on aid. In 2007 when the PNA split, most of these NGOs swung behind the Ramallah-based PNA and against the Gaza-based PNA dominated by Hamas. In fact, the cabinet of the Ramallah-based PNA was drawn partly from NGO leaders—thus they had gone from being the opposition to the PNA during the Oslo period to dominating half of the government.

Religion and Politics

In most Arab states pre-2011 (and many still today), Islam was relevant to politics in two ways. First, the state dominated an official religious establishment that controlled mosques, religious education, and those areas of law (like marriage and divorce) governed by religion. Second, large Islamist social movements and sometimes political parties often formed the most effective political opposition. Freer elections often resulted in Islamists performing very well, as Tunisia and Egypt showed in 2011. Though Palestine is not an established state, the relationship between religion and politics looks very familiar in Arab terms.

The structures of the official religious establishment were largely set up during the British mandate and continue to this day. An institution known as the Waqf (also the Arabic term for "endowment") administers mosques and religious properties. A set of religious courts, headed by a chief judge, rules in matters of "personal status"—marriage, divorce, and inheritance. Students are required to study "Islamic education" in schools (with Christian students excused and given separate instruction in their religion). After the end of the British mandate in 1948, responsibility for this official apparatus was taken over by Egypt in Gaza and by Jordan in the West Bank. When Israel took over these territories in 1967, it tended to leave the situation alone. In the West Bank, it actually allowed Jordan to continue running the religious establishment. With the formation of the PNA in 1994, there was a brief rivalry between Jordan and the PNA over control of these institutions, but the PNA generally won out.

Just as the PNA resembles other pre-2011 Arab states in its management of religion, it has its own religious opposition in the form of Hamas as well as some smaller movements—but here, as with all matters connected with Hamas, there are significant complications. First, the religious opposition does not fully accept the legitimacy of the PNA. Second, this same religious opposition controls part of the PNA (in Gaza).

Hamas was born out of the Palestinian offshoot of the Muslim Brotherhood, originally founded in Egypt. For a long time, the Brotherhood in Palestine avoided political activity, so a younger group of leaders formed Hamas in the 1980s to "resist" the Israeli occupation through attacks on Israeli targets. That proved so popular among the Brotherhood membership that Hamas soon came to absorb much of the Brotherhood. Initially Israel tolerated the Hamas leadership, calculating that it would avoid politics as did the older generation. When Israel realized that a new, radical organization was emerging, it moved to suppress the movement, though without much success. Hamas became an active participant in the first intifada—but it never joined the PLO.

Hamas presented itself as acting in accordance with religious teachings and used religious symbols and rhetoric; it also drew support from more religious segments of the Palestinian population. But the core of its program was as much political as religious. Hamas supported the use of Islamic law, for instance, but generally de-emphasized this part of its program in order to stress resistance to Israel.

When PLO leaders negotiated the Oslo Accords, Hamas criticized them for compromising on Palestinian land. Hamas's position rejected any permanent agreement with the Jewish state. Still, Hamas recognized that the Oslo Accords had strong international backing and that resisting them would be difficult. Moreover, it realized that the creation of the PNA would allow for Palestinian elections. Members debated about whether to run in the elections and finally decided to boycott them, arguing that the PNA would not be allowed real self-governance and that Hamas did not want to lend legitimacy to the peace process. As a result, Hamas remained outside the PNA.

While many Palestinians regarded Hamas as a legitimate (if extreme) political actor, the PNA leadership was inclined to treat it as an illegitimate opposition. For instance, realizing that Hamas might be popular in some areas, the PNA repeatedly postponed local elections in cities and towns in order to deny Hamas the opportunity to gain a foothold. Hamas was totally shunned by much of the international community. During periods when Palestinian public opinion seemed supportive of the peace process, Hamas tended to scale back its activities or reorient itself toward its Muslim Brotherhood roots by emphasizing education and social work. When there were problems, it would often lash out with violent attacks, increasingly against civilian targets.

When the second intifada erupted in 2000, Hamas was able to move its model of "resistance" to the center of Palestinian politics. As the PNA leadership grew increasingly impotent and corrupt, Hamas's popularity grew. When local elections were finally held, beginning in 2004, Hamas ran and did well. In 2005 the PNA leadership decided to coax Hamas into running for parliament, hoping that such participation would help tame the movement and bring it inside the system. When parliamentary elections were held in 2006, this initiative backfired when Hamas won a majority, supported by Palestinians who viewed Fatah as corrupt and ineffective.

Thus the Islamic opposition was no longer in opposition. But the older PNA leadership and the international community were unwilling to accept a Hamas government, leading ultimately to the 2007 split in which Hamas assumed total control of the PNA in Gaza but lost it in the West Bank. If the electoral victory of Islamist movements in Egypt and Tunisia in 2011 gave Hamas leaders the sense that they were part of a strong regional trend, the fall of the Egyptian Brotherhood in 2013 left Hamas isolated. It then had to present itself as a Palestinian movement, downplaying its Brotherhood ties, to maintain relations with the new Egyptian regime.

Identity and Politics

While Palestine has had difficulty establishing itself as a state, Palestinian national identity has taken deep hold of Palestinian politics. This was not an automatic or easy achievement. Palestinians speak Arabic and most are Muslim, so they feel deep links with the Arab and broader Muslim world—yet they tend to insist that within these larger entities there is still a distinct Palestinian people. Family and place of origin still divide Palestinians, and many do not forget these other identities when they think about politics—the various PNA cabinets, for instance, have been carefully constituted to make certain that each major area within Palestine feels represented. But these local ties, though real, tend to receive far less public attention. Even the division between the West Bank and Gaza is rarely discussed in public.

Strong identities often are the result of government educational and language policies designed to inculcate loyalty to the nation. But the precise opposite may be the case for Palestinians—their insistence on their distinct Palestinian identity is a direct result of Palestine's political weakness. Palestinians seem to feel that in the absence of strong institutions or a recognized state to support them, an insistence on Palestinian identity is all that holds them together. Recognition of any alternative political loyalties risks splintering an already vulnerable population.

Still, there has been a subtle evolution in Palestinian identity. Over the course of the twentieth century, the Arab element in Palestinian identity, while it remained strong, showed some signs of mild decline. In the past generation the religious element in Palestinian identity has risen significantly. The most obvious testimony to the increase in religious identity is the rise of Hamas, but there are other signs of increased religiosity in public as well (for instance, dress has become more conservative, and public consumption of alcohol—allowed by law but forbidden by the Islamic religion—has greatly declined). Of course, not all Palestinians are Muslims—there is a substantial Christian minority. But this Christian population has gradually decreased, for several reasons. Christians tended to concentrate in urban areas and have higher levels of education; this often leads to lower birth rates. Better education has also provided them with more employment opportunities abroad, leading to higher emigration. As a shrinking minority, Christians find that their declining share of the population snowballs—as some Christians have left, those remaining find fewer of their co-religionists. In a society in which personal ties are often formed along family and religious lines, this makes some consider emigration themselves.

Gender and Politics

In a society striving for statehood, Palestinians have witnessed tremendous political changes, and some of these have strongly affected gender roles.

While many fairly conservative strictures on dress and comportment related to gender apply broadly, there are actually wide variations in prevailing practices and expectations. This is not only because of diversity within Palestinian society but also because of the cosmopolitan nature of some segments of the population. So many Palestinians have spent time in other societies and been influenced by them that some areas (most notably the Jerusalem and Ramallah areas) tolerate a wide variety of gender roles.

The founding of the PNA and the attempt to build a Palestinian state occasioned a series of debates about gender. First, it opened up greater possibilities for women playing a role in public life. Previous generations of leaders from armed political movements had largely excluded women, but the new focus on institution-building, constructing civil society, and writing laws opened new fields that were friendlier to women. There were no objections to granting women the vote, and a quota was introduced for women's representation in parliament without much controversy. Women also entered the judiciary—a field that is closed to women in some Arab countries.

Second, the new PNA had to tackle important tasks that had a strong bearing on gender relations. It developed a personal status code to govern marriage, divorce, and inheritance—setting off discussions about what are appropriate rights and obligations for men and women within the family. The PNA also developed the first Palestinian school curriculum (earlier schools had followed the Egyptian and Jordanian curricula), leading to arguments about how women should be portrayed and how gender issues should be discussed in schools.

The rise of Hamas and of religiosity more generally has also greatly impacted gender roles. Hamas is not hostile to some public role for women, and it produced female candidates for its parliamentary slate without hesitation. But it is even more strongly dominated by men than are the other already strikingly male political parties. A growing trend toward social conservatism has led to more social pressure on women to wear head coverings in public. While Hamas has not formally required any change in women's dress during its tenure in power, the increased popularity of Hamas has made some women feel less comfortable uncovered. When it gained full control of Gaza, Hamas formed squads that encouraged women (and undoubtedly intimidated them as well) to dress conservatively and avoid socializing in public with men.

The Impact of International Politics

Perhaps no political system in the Arab world shows the sharp impact of international politics more than Palestine. The international political system helped create the political situation in which Palestinians now find themselves. International politics help sustain that difficult situation by failing to recognize Palestinian statehood. It, therefore, should come as no surprise that many Palestinians feel a deep sense of historical injustice.

The impact of international politics has produced ambitions for change as well—indeed, many Palestinians place their hopes for redress in what they often term "international legitimacy." By this they mean that international norms and laws support their struggle for self-determination. The biggest successes of the Palestinian national movement have been connected with the international realm—the acceptance of a separate and distinct Palestinian national identity within the Arab world, and an international acceptance of the principle of Palestinian statehood. In November 2012 the UN General Assembly accorded Palestine the status of nonmember observer state, another victory in the international realm.

But the outside world is not looked to only for legitimacy. Various outside actors are very much players in Palestinian domestic politics. Iran, Syria, Qatar, and other Arab states have given varying amounts of support to Hamas; the European Union has bankrolled Abbas's government in Ramallah; Israel helped to undermine Arafat; and the United States has not hesitated to designate specific individuals as either absolutely necessary or completely unacceptable when it comes to its interactions with Palestinian officials.

In 2011 some youthful Palestinian activists attempted to bring in international factors in a new way: They worked to emulate Egyptian and Tunisian youth by generating a new movement that would press for political change. They generated some interest in Palestinian society and even helped pressure Fatah and Hamas leaders to agree to "end the division," as their slogan demanded. But the movement fizzled over time. Palestinians still talk about the possibility of renewing what they call "popular resistance," meaning a movement based on mass action rather than small armed groups, but they have not had the energy, organization, or focus realized recently by their counterparts in some other Arab societies.

The contradictory effects of international politics go even deeper. They help explain, on the one hand, why the PNA—a nonstate entity that cannot control its own territory or its own borders—cannot establish financial independence. But if international conditions create Palestinian dependence, they also explain, on the other hand, how the PNA—and Palestinians more generally—has become a recipient of an enormous amount of international financial assistance. This may be the greatest irony of Palestinian politics: the Palestinian national movement has been based on a desperate quest to make Palestinians independent actors, but the movement to realize that goal has been dependent on the Palestinian relationship with Israel and global support.

17
Saudi Arabia

Gwenn Okruhlik

Saudi Arabia is complicated. Although it is home to Mecca, the spiritual center of the diverse international Muslim community, the state has historically privileged one particular interpretation of the faith in its own home. Though it depends overwhelmingly on foreign labor to staff the economy, the country suffers from high local male unemployment and it limits the full economic participation of half its population, women. Though an economic powerhouse buttressed by oil revenues and sovereign wealth funds, the country has significant poverty among its citizens. Saudi Arabia is called many things: reformist and authoritarian, backward and modern, spiritually and materially inspired. This is an exciting time to study Saudi Arabia, amid demands for political reform, tensions over sociocultural change, and the dramatic, if erratic, actions of the crown prince, who assumed functional power in 2015 when his father became king.

Historical Background and Contemporary Political Structure

Saudi Arabia has a long, rich history given its place at the crossroads of ancient Nabatean civilizations, desert caravans, hajj (religious pilgrimage), maritime trade, and more recently the global political economy. It also received financial assistance from the United States, United Kingdom, and Ottoman Empire. The current rulers, the Al Saud family, trace their political origins to 1744 C.E. and the village of Al-Dir'iyyah, where the local authority, Mohammad ibn Saud, granted safe haven to a religious reformer named Mohammad ibn Abd al-Wahhab. He had been expelled from his hometown in a nearby oasis after criticizing the lax behavior of fellow townspeople. Al-Wahhab's strict interpretation of sharia, or Islamic law, and his efforts to rid Islam of innovation unsettled members of the village. He fled to Al-Dir'iyyah, where he and ibn Saud forged a pact through which the political authority of the Al Saud and the religious leadership of al-Wahhab were made mutually supportive. Political domination by the Al Saud family and the call for religious renewal were propagated together.

Historians speak of three states of the Al Saud. The first was from 1744 to 1818, when they battled the Ottomans and Egyptians for control of the Hijaz, on the west coast. This ultimately led to the destruction of Al-Dir'iyyah and the collapse of that period of rule. The second state lasted from 1824 until 1891. During this time, they battled mightily with a contending family, the al-Rashid, until eventually Abd al-Rahman Al Saud fled into neighboring Kuwait to take refuge.

The contemporary state began in 1902, with the decades-long conquests of Abd al-Rahman's son, Abdulaziz, across the peninsula. He created a military force called the Ikhwan (the Brethren) to battle his contenders for power in Arabia. They conquered rulers in region after region. Most significantly, these included the Ashraf, the rulers of the Hijaz in the west. The Ashraf claimed descent from the Hashimite clan of the Prophet Muhammad. The Al Saud, together with the Ikhwan, took the eastern coast from the Ottomans in 1912. And in the Najd, or the center of Arabia, they again battled the formidable al-Rashid family for authority. By 1929, Abdulaziz, feeling threatened by the very forces on which he had once depended, crushed the Ikhwan at the Battle of Sibila. The current state was formally declared in 1932. King Abdulaziz ruled until his death in 1953. He bequeathed power to his sons, who maintained a firm grip on rule until recently, when real power shifted to one of his grandsons.

Who Rules?

Authority in Saudi Arabia remains very much "all in the family" (Herb 1999). The monarchy has passed from Abdulaziz to six of his thirty-seven sons: Saud (1953–1964), Faisal (1964–1975), Khaled (1975–1982), Fahd (1982–2005), Abdullah (2005–2015), and Salman (January 2015–present). What this means in practical terms is that Saudi Arabia has long been ruled by older men, all brothers. The current King Salman is frail at eighty-three years old. Real power is exercised through his son, Crown Prince Mohammad bin Salman, a very young thirty-three years old. He is commonly known as MbS.

How have the Al Saud ruled for so long? They have perpetuated their rule through a skillful combination of distribution, penetration, and an ever-increasing dose of outright coercion, with a legitimating dollop of ideology. It is a blend of carrots and sticks, with religious underpinnings. At the end of the day, governance in Saudi Arabia is neither representative nor accountable. It does not protect basic civil and political rights for citizens, much less for foreign residents. The Saudi state prohibits free speech and the right to assemble. There are no unions or legal political parties, and public protest has historically been rare. Uttering public criticism, striking, joining political organizations, and spreading antigovernment ideas all are crimes. The regime grows ever more repressive today. Media outlets and publishing houses are strictly watched. Websites and blogs are censored. It is a criminal act to insult the king on Twitter or Facebook. Such coercive techniques are supplemented by distributive schemes made possible by oil revenues, even as MbS talks about moving beyond oil dependency. The Al Saud penetrate society through business deals in every economic sector, marriages into other families, control of all key political positions, and the jailing—if not worse—of any critical voice.

The recent transition in power to the next generation occurred in a period of rapid, dramatic jostling for royal position. King Salman appointed Mohammad bin Nayef as crown prince and interior minister. MbS was made deputy crown prince and defense minister. Two months after his father's accession, MbS launched a devastating war in Yemen. He then disrupted his allies in the Gulf Cooperation Council and began to remove domestic challengers to his power. By summer 2017 Crown Prince Mohammad bin Nayef was under house arrest and wearing an ankle bracelet so that MbS could exercise power and be next in line to the throne. In late 2017 MbS fired Miteb bin Abdullah, head of the National Guard, a tribal force designed to protect the ruling family and oil fields, and fired Navy Commander Prince Abdullah bin Sultan. He sought also to remove any privileges that tribes had attained through the National Guard.

Having secured his position from rivals, MbS jailed prominent Islamists in September, and in November 2017 eleven princes, several ministers, and hundreds of elite business executives were brazenly rounded up and sequestered in the Ritz-Carlton Hotel in Riyadh. Some were tortured or killed; others were released after paying extortion money. Throughout 2018, he continued to arrest women's rights activists and journalists.

In an awkward but parallel fashion, MbS also offered carrots. He hinted that the prohibition on women driving and the necessity of a male guardian would be relaxed; he championed "a return to moderate Islam" that thrived in the country before 1979; an entirely new $500 billion futuristic city was announced; he granted citizenship to a robot named Sofia and allowed new venues for social entertainment. He immediately began a rebranding and goodwill tour in the country, region, and abroad to bolster his image as a modernizing reformer. By early 2018 an ad-free, ninety-seven-page glossy magazine titled the *New Kingdom* was available for $13.99 in Walmart stores across the United States. Headlines trumpeted, "The most influential Arab leader transforming the world at 32"; "Improving the lives of his people and hopes for peace"; and "Our closest Middle East ally destroying terrorism."

The gruesome torture, murder, and dismemberment of journalist Jamal Khashoggi in October 2018 paint another picture: Is MbS an enlightened reformist or a draconian dictator; a bold, decisive ruler or a ruthless, impulsive despot? Indeed, when the government of Turkey released the gruesome tapes (Khashoggi's fingers were reportedly cut off while he was alive) the international community recoiled in horror. The anonymous Tweeter "Mujtahid" posted damning accusations of corruption at the highest levels of the ruling family. He reported that the killers brought MbS Khashoggi's fingers "so that he may quench his thirst [for revenge] by obtaining the part of his body with which he wrote" his criticisms (Mujtahid 2018).

Supporting Institutions

Saudi kings used to consult with leading merchant families, tribes, other branches of the Al Saud family, and religious authorities—largely descendants of al Wahhab. MbS consolidated power without consulting the usual institutions of rule—the Family Council, the Transitional Ruling Council, the Allegiance Commission, or historically important tribes and leading private families. He is a one-man show, yet he skillfully wraps himself in the language of reform, youth, feminism, nationalism, and anticorruption in order to mask his consolidation of power. In the midst of his anticorruption crackdown, he bought a yacht for $550 million and a French chateau for $300 million.

Leaders have long ruled in an awkward and unequal symbiosis with religious authorities (the ulama), who have been marginalized and made subservient. The ulama are still players when it serves the purposes of the ruler, but they are largely limited to moral, religious, and social questions, far from the corridors of power. Historically, the ruling family depended on them to justify policy decisions during major crises. The religious authorities include the Council of Senior Scholars, which issues fatawa (religious opinions); many affiliated bureaucracies; and the morality patrols (the *ha'ya*), which enforce codes of conduct in the public realm.

The judicial system is formally based on sharia or religious law. Any supplementary civil or commercial codes theoretically cannot contradict or supersede sharia. The Supreme Judicial Council is composed of senior jurists. The king acts as the highest court of appeal in the country. Over the years, the state has diminished the role of the judiciary with increasing oversight, greater reliance on royal decrees about legal questions, and the creation of a "shadow judiciary" that is based on state edicts (Alaoudh and Brown 2018). In summer 2017, MbS brought all criminal affairs under his direct control by setting up the Office of the Public Prosecutor, who is appointed by the king. His "anticorruption purge" showed little concern for transparency or due process.

The Council of Ministers, or cabinet, was first appointed by the king in 1953; it grew tremendously during the oil boom. Today it consists of the heads of twenty-three ministries and seven ministers of state that oversee the daily administration of the country. The king and crown prince preside over the cabinet, and princes hold most key posts. The cabinet's advice is nonbinding.

In the early 1990s, rancorous opposition arose to the Gulf War and the stationing of US troops in Saudi Arabia. In response to this dissent, King Fahd established a long-promised consultative assembly, the Majlis al-Shura, in 1992. The membership of the assembly now numbers 150 people, of which 20 percent are women. All are appointed by the king. Their role is strictly advisory rather than legislative, and the king can reject their advice. In 2005 there were limited elections to fill half of the seats on newly created municipal councils throughout the country. Islamists participated and won many seats. The other seats were later appointed by the king. The councilmen were unaware of the scope of their authority. Women could neither run nor vote in the elections. In December 2015 women were allowed to vote and to run for municipal office. Twenty-one women were elected. The positions remain devoid of authority.

MbS has chosen to ignore or diminish all these usual supporting institutions of consensus and consultation. There is no independent judiciary, no *majlis* with any power, no family council, and no empowered municipal councils. Religious authority has been diminished. MbS rules alone, albeit with the entire security apparatus at his service. He also seeks advice from a handful of confidants, some of whom were fired in the December 2018 reshuffle meant to contain the fallout from Khashoggi's death, and from foreign consultants such as Booz Allen and McKinsey & Co. (though an executive was detained in the 2017 crackdown). With MbS one step away from absolute power, the fear of many Saudis is captured with the phrase, "May God help us" (Bsheer 2018).

Identity and Politics: Diversity and Exclusion

While the local population is overwhelmingly Arab and Sunni Muslim, there are significant variations within it. There are followers of all four schools of Sunni Islamic law as well as the tradition of orthodox Wahhabism. The largest Shi'i community is in the Eastern Province; there are others in Mecca and Medina. The southern region of Najran is Ismaili, and there are Sufi communities throughout the country. Foreign workers bring a wide array of identities and religious beliefs.

There are also ethnic distinctions among the local population. The economy of the Eastern Province for centuries has been related to merchant activities and, more recently, to the oil industry. Families from Iran, Bahrain, and India migrated to this area for work reasons. Thus, Shi'i religious affiliation is prominent there. The western region is noted for a multiplicity of ethnic identities, for two reasons: its long history as the center of commerce from the port of Jeddah and the fact that it is the site of the annual hajj, or religious pilgrimage. Families that came to perform religious rituals often stayed and established thriving businesses. Some of the most prominent ones are originally from Persia, Indonesia, India, as well as other Arab states. In addition, there is a notable Hadrami community in the west, originally derived from Yemen's Hadramawt region. Saudi Arabia—and especially its central region, the Najd—is also home to many local tribes. It was less common for foreign families to settle in the heartland than in the coastal regions, and as a result the Najd remained insulated from migration flows for a longer period of time.

When does religious or ethnic identity become salient and, sometimes, politicized? People, Saudi Arabian or otherwise, carry multiple identities within them at all times. An ethnic, tribal, or religious identity may rise or fall depending on the particular context. A key problem in Saudi Arabia is that there are diverse religious practices but only one was empowered over the decades. Wahhabis were long rewarded with institutional and bureaucratic positions of authority—while other sects were largely excluded. The consequence was that although private religious beliefs were diverse, public discourse was dominated by an orthodox and austere interpretation of Islam sanctioned by the state.

Shi'i communities comprise about 15 percent of the population. They have protested their second-class status for decades. In the spring of 2009, protests occurred throughout the Eastern Province. These followed the arrest and intimidation of Shi'a who were praying at the Prophet's tomb in Medina. The incident tapped into a reservoir of resentment about their discrimination. Shaikh Kalbani, who was then the imam at the Great Mosque in Mecca, called the Shi'a "heretics." From 2011 into 2013 Shi'a demanded their full religious, social, political, and economic rights as citizens of Saudi Arabia. A prominent Shi'i cleric, Shaikh Nimr al-Nimr, was executed in January 2016, and more than fifty-one Shi'a were killed by authorities in backlash protests. Further, in 2017 a historic Shi'i neighborhood, called al-Musawara, was demolished under the banner of "redevelopment." More than sixty bulldozers flattened the neighborhood. It was the hometown of al-Nimr. The exclusionary structure of governance fails to represent the diverse population and fuels the politicization and activism of some Saudis. Were Saudis' diverse demographics incorporated into governance, those identities might become less politicized.

By virtue of oil, Saudi Arabia is integrated into the global capitalist economy. The oil-driven economy has been far larger than the indigenous population could support, necessitating the importation of a foreign labor force to run the day-to-day economy—from construction laborers to clerks to service workers to accountants. About 12.2 million residents of Saudi Arabia, or 37 percent of the total population, are foreign workers and their families. Most expatriate labor is from Bangladesh, Egypt, India, Pakistan, the Philippines, and Sudan.

The distinctions between citizen and foreigner are evident in everything from dress and living quarters to occupations and class. The state manages the flow of foreigners within its borders through an extensive system of oversight and sponsorship. Each worker must be "sponsored" by a local citizen or company and surrender his or her passport to the sponsor (*kafil*). Most workers, particularly from the developing world, are closely monitored. Thus far, their ethnic and religious identities have not been highly politicized. There have been worker strikes demanding better pay and conditions, but not to the extent seen in neighboring Dubai. The system is rife with abuse and leaves workers at the mercy of their sponsors, with no protection (Okruhlik 2010). In 2017 there was talk of allowing "self-sponsorship," but this would have required payment of a 20 percent self-employment tax, something few workers could afford. Human rights organizations have reported on the use of social media by employers to "sell" migrant domestic workers to other sponsors. Such online trading has been called "slavery 2.0" (ALQST 2018; Observers 2018).

Citizenship is tightly regulated in the country and is granted through parentage (passing through the father), not place of birth. Naturalized citizenship is extremely hard to obtain and rarely achieved. Applicants must be Muslims fluent in Arabic with a decade of residency who possess advanced degrees in sought-after technical fields.

Civil Society: Fluid and Creative but Manipulated and Intimidated

Collective action is against the law. Moreover, the potential for collective action is further inhibited by an extraordinary social concern with discretion and privacy. Behavior in the public realm (any place outside the home) has always been regulated by well-defined codes of conformity in dress, behavior, and decorum (Okruhlik 2018). This leads to a series of perplexing questions: When the mere act of meeting together to discuss potentially controversial issues is against the law, what then constitutes civic activism or civil society? How do you create a public space where constraints are overwhelming and lines are dangerous to cross? How and where are Saudis pushing the boundaries?

Because the home is a private place into which the state rarely imposes itself, civic activism happens within this space. Historically, the *majlis* (private gathering in one's home) was the only available venue for friends and colleagues to build networks and to voice opinions on politics, society, and economics. Replete with food, coffee, and lively conversation, the weekly *majalis* remain vital. They vary from the relatively structured to the informal. "Study groups" also meet in the privacy of Saudi homes and prove to be a dynamic mechanism through which agendas are articulated and ideologies made coherent.

The public social space in which people can interact legally increased significantly recently. Ubiquitous now are cafés, coffeehouses, salons, and resthouses (*istiraha*). At municipal levels, people meet together to improve neighborhoods and call attention to problems that authorities do not address adequately. There are a host of philanthropic organizations dedicated to charity, the environment, technology training, and welfare. An extensive network of chambers of commerce has long existed to serve private businesspeople. They are active and important sources of economic criticism but they are partially funded by the state.

MbS has further expanded the public space by investing in the leisure and entertainment sectors. Commercial cinemas are allowed, women can drive and attend events at sports stadiums, a futuristic "entertainment city" is planned, music concerts are allowed, tourist visas are allowed to attend specific events like Formula One auto races, more relaxed clothing can be worn on some restricted beaches, and yoga is permissible. The first ever Comic-Con and NASCAR (National Association for Stock Car Auto Racing) events were convened, wrestling matches have been held, and the fun flick *Baraka wa Baraka* was screened. It is available on Netflix and provides a glimpse into the complexities of these new dynamics.

Civic activism exists in the arts, literature, comedy, and film. Creative renderings make powerful statements in the abstract statements that cannot otherwise be published. This is particularly important under extreme authoritarian conditions where there are no outlets otherwise. People are freer to express critical opinions about politics and society when the characters are, at least superficially, fictional—and the locale a composite. Theater, clothing design, and dance are experiencing a rebirth. Live stand-up comedy is thriving. This is significant because laughter in the public realm was once grounds for confrontation with the morality patrols. Now, there are thriving comedy venues that host comedic pioneers as well as newcomers, and even a female comedian. Like other artists, comedians traipse a fine line, trying to push the boundaries of criticism and trying to remain safe from both state security and the morality patrols, even though the latter lost their authority to arrest.

Still, there are limits. The 2012 film *Wadjda,* by Saudi female director Haifaa al-Mansour, was filmed entirely in Saudi Arabia with Saudi actors. It tells the story of a ten-year-old girl living in Riyadh and her constant attempts to circumvent the many constraints on her lifestyle—from the clothing she wears to the bike she wants to ride to the music to which she listens. It was feted internationally even as it could not be shown in Saudi Arabia.

The state routinely bans books, but they somehow are slipped quietly into the marketplace and circulated privately. It controls the print and broadcast media. It appoints and removes editors. Still, writers and editors try to push the boundaries on the range of issues they address. Topics once taboo have now become the subject of intense debate, including crime, drugs, the alienation and boredom of youth, poverty, spousal abuse, and women's rights. A popular television comedy series called *Tash ma Tash* (No Big Deal) aired during Ramadan from 1992 to 2011. It offered satirical comedy about corruption, inequality, bureaucratic incompetence, and religion. An episode about a Saudi woman with four husbands enraged social conservatives. Eventually a fatwa was issued against the series, and under threats, the creators fled with their families. In 2018 a new Ramadan show called *Al-Asoof* (Winds of Change) was set in a Riyadh neighborhood in a more "open" time, between 1970 and 1975, the period just before the public rise of Islamism. One episode was about a woman who left a baby born out of wedlock outside a mosque, hoping to find him care. Outraged critics said it promoted adultery, but the show remained on air as it is consistent with MbS's disdain for Islamists. It implicitly blames Islamists for the current situation even as it ignores the complicity of authoritarianism. Always off limits, still, is any direct criticism of the ruling family.

Hard as it tried, the ruling family was long unable to control Twitter, YouTube, and Facebook. Social media has been the site of much sociopolitical activism. Saudis use Twitter as "a substitute for banned civil society organizations" (Aldohan 2016). *Alatayer* (On the Fly) is a YouTube channel that publicizes and makes fun of corruption, princely land grabs ("It's All Mine Now!"), and the way a big businessman can flout the law while small, struggling businessmen are held to the letter of the law. *La Yekthar* (Zip It) was an early pioneer YouTube comedy that posted videos about the $15 million it costs to repair toilet seats in a public park, or ridiculous traffic jams, or unemployment. Feras Bugnah and two of his colleagues were jailed in 2011 after they posted a brief, powerful video on YouTube called "We Are Being Cheated," which documents poverty in the al-Jaradeya neighborhood. Mohammad Maki's miniseries *Takki* follows young men in Jeddah as they try to make films and encounter difficulties with women. Many episodes address the shrinking middle class in Saudi Arabia and the dearth of affordable housing. Hisham Fageeh created a wildly popular fifteen-part YouTube series. His 2013 music video "No Woman, No Drive" was an international hit. The 2016 video "*Hwages*" (Concerns or Obsessions) features skateboarding women who advocate for their rights.

New media have created new dynamics in civic activism. To Eman al-Nafjan, a Saudi feminist, this is welcome: "No good has come of our defensive, hide-the-dirty-laundry approach. We just come off looking more closed and isolated" (in Faruqui 2010). Cyberspace enables Saudis to build communities of social activists without violating political prohibitions on unauthorized assembly, speech, or gender-mingling. The old methodology of presenting signed petitions to the king that request changes are passé; social media are far more effective. A blogger argues, "Asking the youth to use petitions instead of social media is like asking them to use carrier pigeons instead of mobile phones" (in Khalaf 2012).

While critics on social media may have escaped the retribution of the state before, this is hardly true today. Surveillance and the range of punishable offenses are both more draconian. An observer writes, "Suspects brought in by the secret service are confronted with years of tweets and Facebook posts that have been carefully documented. Emails are read, telephone calls are listened to" (Koelbl 2018). She quotes Loujain al-Hathloul, "All that we dare to do in Saudi Arabia, whether as a group or alone, is always connected with great personal risk." Al-Hathloul is again in jail for her leadership in the women's rights movement. Al-Omran reports that "activists are scared to communicate with each other . . . they already have their suitcases ready" (2018). In 2018 the imam of the Great Mosque in Mecca, Shaikh Saleh bin Humaid, warned believers against wasting their time on social media, saying, "Believers will be answerable to God for what their eyes saw, what their ears heard and what their hands did." This echoed his predecessor Shaikh Abdul

Latif Abdul Aziz al Shaikh, who lashed out against new media in 2012, charging that it was nothing more than a tool to promote lies.

Is there civil society? Yes, but it is under siege. It also looks unlike what we expect. Civil society is often defined elsewhere in terms of voluntary associations, business organizations, labor unions, and other entities located between the household and the state. In Saudi Arabia, it is more ambiguous but no less important. It is more fluid and less formal and incorporates social capital, more akin to civic activism. In 1989 I interviewed a woman who specialized in teaching computing skills to young girls as an effective way to promote achievement under conditions of gender segregation. She relayed many instances of women working quietly as individuals to advance women's rights. I asked if they ever got together to work jointly. She replied, "Of course not. We are more effective working alone. Organization is the surest way to get squashed [by the government]." Years later, in 2017, she was jailed under MbS for organizing women for rights—at seventy years of age.

The Saudi state often tries to mimic or co-opt civic activism by funding and creating duplicate associations with similar names that it can control and channel. The Human Rights First Society is a nonrecognized organization that monitors human rights abuse. Its founder, Ibrahim al-Mugateib, applied for a license in 2002 but received no reply from the government. In 2004 the similarly named National Society for Human Rights was established by royal decree. Another government-recognized body is the Human Rights Commission, whose head holds the rank of state minister. Neither of these two bodies directly addresses democracy, expression, assembly, or minorities.

In a similar vein, when Saudi feminists began to assert themselves by making their bruises from domestic violence visible in public, when they drove, and when they argued with morality patrols that there was no basis for their harassment (using quranic verses that affirm their rights), their voices were heard and resonated throughout the country. Suddenly, the state appointed loyalist women, who were accomplished but supportive of the status quo, into the Majlis al-Shura, the ministries, and into a state-sponsored assembly called the National Dialogue Forum—all nonthreatening venues. When journalists, engineers, and lawyers wanted to organize into professional networks, the state sponsored them. The Saudi Council of Engineers operates under the supervision of the Ministry of Commerce and Investment. Lawyers are regulated by the Ministry of Justice, and the home page of the Saudi Bar Association proudly proclaims its contribution to Vision 2030. The Saudi Journalists Association was formed in 2003 with government approval. Even its director said that the main responsibility of the press was to maintain national security (in Campagna 2006). Across professions, all associations are strictly monitored, paid for by the government, and unlikely to step out of line (Montagu 2015).

With the Arab uprisings in 2011, there was an explosion of graffiti on buildings. It became clear to the government that serious and effective criticism was being expressed and disseminated in this fashion. The state then stepped up its own interest in artistic creativity. As it had done in other venues, the state sought to replicate and channel what it could not control. When youth covered public buildings and freeway infrastructure in Jeddah with intricate graffiti, the state erected blank, official graffiti walls on which people could legally express themselves and protest on permissible space. When hip-hop began as protest through lyrics, dance, and musicality, the state began to sponsor hip-hop festivals. Similar dynamics have unfolded recently in the visual arts. Massive state funding of visual arts exists under the patronage of MbS. Major players include Edge of Arabia, the MiSK Art Institute, and Ithra. Very talented artists and their art are used as tools of cultural diplomacy and the rebranding of MbS to tell his narrative about the modernizing ruling family, the backwards society, and extremist Islam. Is co-opted art politically relevant or a political release valve? Today, art in all its forms is fertile, fluid, and creative but also manipulated and intimidated.

Political Economy: The Aches of Abundance

Saudi Arabia's pre-oil economy was based on date farming, merchant trade, and revenues accrued from hosting the hajj. Abdulaziz also received British arms and financial supplements. With the discovery of substantial oil reserves in 1938, he began to receive royalty payments from foreign oil companies. As the state renegotiated its relationship with foreign companies, acquiring all shares from 1973 to 1980, it grew wealthy. At times, Saudi Arabia reaps windfall wealth, yet it is also vulnerable to fluctuations in global demand and associated price gyrations. Its economy endures the frenzy of booms and the devastation of busts.

The extent and speed of the oil-driven transformation of Saudi Arabia are mind-boggling. In a few short years, families went from subsistence to affluence, from tiny rural villages to sprawling urban centers. Today, 84 percent of the population lives in urban areas. Since oil revenues flow directly to state coffers rather than corporations or individual entrepreneurs, the state mushroomed exponentially during the boom period. It is called a rentier state. The state's distributive function became critical. It became provider and patron—the source of contracts, jobs in the public sector, and land grants. A cradle-to-grave welfare system was built that provided health care, education, investment incentives, land grants for housing, subsidized food and energy, easy loans, and even stipends for achieving good grades. Citizens who were well situated at the beginning of the boom reaped the rewards of oil as monopolies and agencies were given to favored families. Such patron-client relationships became embedded, and much of the economy was feudal in character, with families "owning" an activity through a dynamic called rent-seeking.

While the prosperity of all citizens increased due to oil rents, there were marked discrepancies in the way it was distributed (Okruhlik 1999). As mentioned earlier, there is worrisome poverty among citizens. Like impoverished people everywhere, poor Saudi Arabians suffer from chronic joblessness, substandard accommodations, raw sewage, crime, and no electricity. Rural poverty is also a significant problem. The official estimate is that the poverty rate is 12.5 percent. Unofficial estimates are that the rate of poverty is closer to 25 percent. Sixty percent of citizens cannot afford to own their own home—this, in an oil-rich country. The *bidoon,* residents without any citizenship in any country, especially fall through the cracks. Poverty was a taboo subject for many years; its alleviation is now noted as a national goal.

Saudi Arabia remains heavily oil dependent. It is the world's leading producer and exporter. It is home to about 18 to 20 percent of the world's proven reserves, second to only Venezuela, and has some of the world's lowest production costs. Oil accounts for about 90 percent of the country's exports, 87 percent of government budget revenues, and 42 percent of gross domestic product. Yet the price per barrel of oil gyrates: 2018 boasted the highest price in four years ($75 in October) followed by an immediate 30 percent drop ($50.42 in November), the worst plunge since the financial crisis of 2008. For perspective, this contrasts to $110 per barrel oil in 2012 and $10 per barrel oil in 1998. Higher revenues allow the government to post budget surpluses, pay down public debt, increase distributive subsidies, and implement internal security measures.

Abundant oil revenues do not mean that Saudi planners have no worries. Saudi Arabia's population skyrocketed from 6 million in 1970 to 32.6 million in 2018, of which 63 percent are citizens. Population growth adds demands on spending. The Saudi state's (very expensive) pursuit of internal and external security complicates the demands for expenditures on education, employment, housing, and health care. In addition, a bulge in the numbers of younger citizens puts stress on an infrastructure that is already hard-pressed to keep pace with the growing population. Sixty percent of the population is under the age of thirty years.

For decades, the three-pronged mantra of state planners has been privatization, diversification, and Saudization. They have done all right on the first goal. The private sector now accounts for about 40 percent of gross domestic product (GDP) compared with around 20 percent twenty years ago, though the nonoil private sector is much smaller. They are progressing on the second goal, even if the diversified economy remains oil-driven. In Saudi Arabia, diversification means "moving downstream" to petrochemical products. Going downstream is a way to avoid the wild economic fluctuations associated with dependence on the simple export of crude oil. The state also hopes to turn the country into an industrial giant. The crux of this vision had been a $30 billion investment program to build six "economic cities" to diversify the economy, promote development, and create jobs for Saudi Arabian youth. Things have yet to pan out as hoped; King Abdullah Economic City could not entice tenants.

The third goal—Saudization—remains elusive. Considerable dependence on expatriate workers corresponds with a high rate of unemployment among Saudi Arabian males. Expatriates hold at least 88 percent of the jobs in the private sector. In 2011 the state introduced a new nationalization program called *niqatat*. It combines incentives for hiring locals with penalties for hiring a disproportionate percentage of foreigners, yet the resulting expatriate exodus of 800,000 workers has failed to create jobs for Saudis. There is apparently still Saudi resistance to taking the types of jobs being made available. There are even reports that the number of foreign worker visas is still increasing. The pay differential is that significant for business owners. Unemployment among Saudis is notoriously difficult to pin down. A 2018 official estimate is 12.9 percent unemployment; it is twice that for younger Saudis. The number of unemployed male college graduates is a particular concern. In 2018, 56 percent of unemployed Saudis had a college degree. What is clear is that after decades of state effort to Saudize the workforce, unemployment remains persistently high, and highest among the younger generation.

Women meanwhile remain subject to codes of conduct that inhibit their participation in many economic activities regardless of official pronouncements. Saudi Arabia ranks 138th out of 144 countries in the 2017 Global Gender Gap Report. Though estimates vary widely, unemployment is about 33 percent among women, several times the rate for men. The good news is that women used to be concentrated primarily in the fields of education and health; now they are also in information technology, physics, biology, math, and statistics.

In 2016 the age-old triad of privatization, diversification, and Saudization morphed into Vision 2030, an effort to move away from oil dependency and a welfare state and toward a diversified economy with booming tourism, entertainment, and high-tech hubs. The plan is also intended to reduce government spending, slash public wages, and cut subsidies. It includes mild extractive measures. For example, residential electricity rates were doubled and an across-the-board value-added tax (VAT) of 5 percent was imposed. The government did reduce the budget deficit in 2017.

Three major endeavors were heralded by MbS: NEOM, the Red Sea Luxury Resorts, and Al Qidiya Entertainment City. NEOM, or Neo-Mustaqbal/New Future, is a planned $500 billion futuristic city on the Red Sea in northwest Saudi Arabia by the Sinai Peninsula. YouTube videos highlight the centrality to the city of high technology, artificial intelligence, drones, clean energy, robots, free online education, high-speed internet, and virtual and augmented reality. It promises a lifestyle not available in today's Saudi Arabia. Moreover, it is intended to be a truly capitalist city, planned by financial institutions as a for-profit initiative and funded by global investors via stock purchases (Saif 2017).

Plans for NEOM stalled, however, when foreign investors got jitters after the fiasco at the Ritz-Carlton and the murder of Khashoggi. At the same time, many investors pulled out of the Futures Investment Initiative, also known as "Davos in the Desert," in late October 2018. Promises of foreign partnerships have plummeted, and in the meantime, some wealthy Saudi citizens have moved their assets out of the country.

The proposed $20 million Red Sea Luxury Resorts are to be constructed on fifty pristine islands and their surrounding barrier reefs, which are home to complex marine life. What remains to be seen is if hotels, airports, marinas, spas, and boutiques can be constructed to meet "the highest standards of ecological best practices and the highest standards of conservation of natural resources"—as promised in marketing material. That same material notes that the project will be managed within a "semi-autonomous regulatory framework" conceived by a "private committee on par with international standards." This might signal an effort to find a way around constraints on dress, driving, alcohol, and gender-mingling for wealthy visitors.

The third major developmental project is called Al Qidiya Entertainment City, which will be located to the southwest of Riyadh and represents an investment of at least $8 billion. A total of $64 billion will be dedicated to entertainment overall. The new city is dedicated to entertainment, education, indoor ski slopes, adventure, sports, culture, and excitement and will be replete with high-end accommodations and shopping. There will be an autodrome, wildlife experiences, "camping" in deserts and caves, and multiple virtual reality experiences. Using three-dimensional technology, children can experience the thrill of sports, walk on water, be an astronaut, or pretend to work in any job they want. Within the city will be a Six Flags franchise-branded theme park. Imagine a fun-filled, high-technology Disneyland that stretches from Los Angeles to San Diego.

Even with these development plans in place, foreign direct investment (FDI) plummeted to $1.4 billion in 2017 from $7.5 billion in 2016 (and $12.2 billion in 2012). This predates the 2018 exodus of elite local capital and the hesitation of foreign capital investment. The Saudi Arabian stock market is the largest in the Arab world and in some senses is top-performing, but it lacks that hard-to-measure attribute called "investor trust." Investors say that it is not business-friendly, transparent, or predictable. In late 2018, the state was propping up its stock market by buying stocks via its sovereign public investment fund.

The biggest announcement of late 2017 was the high-profile initial public offering (IPO) sale of 5 percent of Saudi Aramco (the Arabian-American Oil Company, said to be valued at $100 billion). This would have been the world's largest initial IPO ever. Though intended to fund the grandiose Vision 2030 development schemes, the $2 trillion valuation of Aramco was met immediately with international skepticism. More importantly, any public sale of stocks would expose the procedures, accounting, and books of Aramco to international standards of transparency—something the state is keen to avoid. In August 2018 this initial offering was "indefinitely postponed," putting a crimp on the effort to shrink the welfare state and move beyond oil.

Religion and Politics: Sustenance and Transformation

Islam is used by the ruling family to justify and legitimate the status quo. Islam is used by critics to challenge the status quo and to offer alternatives. From above and from below, Islam is a vital component of politics. There are many secularists in Saudi Arabia, to be sure. Many Saudis, however, are socially conservative, religiously devout, and politically liberal. The question is, will the broad diversity of beliefs ever be represented in governance? At heart, this is a political question.

From Above: The Political Economy of Guardianship

Islam is embedded in the structure of the state. The Quran and the Sunna of the Prophet are still said to be the constitution of the country, as stated in Article 1 of the 1992 Basic Law. A previous king, Fahd, changed his title from the regal "Your Majesty" to the more humble "Servant of the Holy Mosques of Mecca and Medina," in order to emphasize the centrality of Islam in governance and to wrap himself ever more tightly in its mantle. This move came just after the Iranian Revolution in 1979 and the takeover of the Great Mosque by Sunni rebels that same year.

The Saudi state has special obligations that it must fulfill as guardian of the holy cities. These include performing *dawa* (financial and moral outreach) and serving as host for the hajj. Saudi Arabia is praised and reviled for its management, or mismanagement, of the hajj. About 2.3 million Muslims from every corner of the world converge in the holy cities each year. It is meant to be a deeply spiritual experience; it is also a spectacle to behold. Efficient administration of the sheer mass and movement of people who perform five days of rituals is daunting. The state oversees the technical and logistical aspects of religious rituals, including transportation, accommodation, medicine, food, water, and communications technology. In the end, the ruling family is keen to tie its legitimacy to the efficient and safe performance of religious duties. It aligns everything, no matter how big (the expansion of the mosques) or how small (a bottle of water), with the generosity of the king. The state thus endeavors to assert the king's moral leadership in the Islamic world.

Islam is a double-edged sword for governing officials. While it is manipulated to grant them legitimacy, it also leaves them vulnerable to criticism when their behavior deviates from the "straight path." They have destroyed countless historic sites that date to the earliest days of the Prophet Muhammad in order to make way for expansion, luxury hotels, and parking decks connected to hajj logistics. Gone forever are the home of Muhammad and his wife, Khadija; the mosque of Abu Bakr, the first caliph; and tombs in Medina of close relatives of the Prophet. For many observers, these sites belong to the international community of believers, not to a particular sect. People bemoan the loss of the spiritual meaning of hajj and the introduction of class distinctions into what was intended to be an experience that highlighted the equality of all believers before God. The state's management of hajj has also been questioned as it relates to homogenization of ritual, the fairness of access for Shi'a, using the hajj to generate nonoil revenue in the form of "religious tourism," and responsibility for tragic deaths that occur during hajj due to tent fires, stampedes, or crowds.

Tragedies happen frequently: tent fires killed 343 and injured 1,500 in 1997; 251 were killed and 244 injured during a stampede in 2004; 346 were killed and 289 injured in a stampede in 2006. In 2015, a crane being used in the massive expansion of a mosque came tumbling down into the east side of the mosque. At least 111 hajjis died and 394 were injured. Their families were generously compensated. That same year, a stampede in the dense crowd occurred. Estimates vary, but about 2,400 people were killed. Government reports suggest that the carnage was due to the extreme heat, confusion, or the inexperience of pilgrims, but many unofficial reports and videos demonstrate that two pathways were actually closed off in order to allow the passage of dignitaries on a royal visit. Other reports specifically point to panic caused by the private convoy of MbS as he made his way to the site.

To determine the number of hajjis who can participate from each country, Saudi Arabia uses a quota system that is a percentage of the number of Muslims in each country. This system has been politicized. Qatar alleges that Saudi Arabia created hurdles to the participation of Qataris in hajj in 2018. Only 60–70 Qataris performed hajj, down from 12,000 the previous year. Saudi Arabia also barred about 3 million Palestinians living in Israel, Jordan, East Jerusalem, and Lebanon from performing their religious obligation. Most years, there is contentious fighting between Saudi Arabia and Iran over if and how many Iranians (who are Shi'a) will get to perform hajj. In contrast, 1,500 relatives of Yemeni and Sudanese soldiers who were killed in Yemen fighting against the Houthis (whom the Saudis allege are backed by Iran) have been invited to take part in hajj in 2019 under the sponsorship of the Saudi government.

Just as the hajj is used to bolster its international reputation, so too does the ruling family utilize Islam to consolidate its power domestically. For example, a group of Sunni shaikhs called "The Enlightened Shaikhs" has been encouraged to articulate support for MbS's "reform agenda." This includes Adil al-Kalbani, Mohammad al-Issa, and Abdullah al-Mutlaq. While their opinions are welcomed by many—they question the niqab (face cover) and abaya (cloak), support human rights, attend *baloot* (card game) tournaments, allow women to drive, allow cinema, and permit music—they speak only when their opinions align with the agenda of MbS. Were they to address class equality, social justice, and political participation, their voices would be taken more seriously.

In 2010 King Abdullah issued a royal decree that made the state-appointed Council of Senior Scholars the only body with authority to issue a fatwa. Previously, anybody could issue a fatwa. Whether or not it carried any weight among the populace depended on its reasoning and credibility. Believers could decide for themselves. Alaoudh (2018) demonstrates that in 2017 alone the council issued more than eight fatawa that warned against disobeying the ruler and that preached obedience to him. This is indicative of the ruling family's discouragement of independent reasoning.

From Below: Resonance and Challenges

Just as Islam is used by the ruling family to bolster the prevailing order, so too is it used to challenge that order. The cultural symbols and language of Islam resonate across genders, regions, ethnicities, sects, and classes. Citizens and activists thus have legitimated their concerns through the language and symbols of religion, even though, at heart, the problems they reference are political, economic, and social. Islamists have been more coherent, powerful, and organized than other social forces in Saudi Arabia, including those based on nationalism, liberalism, regional identity, or business activity. To date, the Islamists are the only movement(s) to cut across multiple cleavages (Okruhlik 2002, 2004).

After 1979 the ruling family instituted ever-tighter controls over social and political life. The Al Saud sought to bolster their own legitimacy by appropriating the power of Islam. They funded religious educational institutions throughout the country, even during the oil bust of the mid-1980s when other projects were scaled back. There were new restrictions on women's mobility, dress, and employment. The morality patrols were granted more leeway in their oversight of behavior in the public realm. An expanded Islamic education system fostered a new generation of shaikhs, professors, and students. During the 1980s an Islamic resurgence swept the country. What began as small, closed circles grew gradually into large, loose underground groups. All of this cultivated a fertile field for dissent, which politicized Islamism would soon effectively tap.

These developments culminated in the rise of an Islamist opposition movement during the Gulf War of 1990–1991. Festering anger suddenly exploded with the stationing of US troops in the country. Opposition groups organized domestically and abroad, most under the rubric of Islamism. A new generation of imams voiced strident political opinions in sermons, calling for the removal of US troops and the overthrow of the ruling family. When Friday sermons became an occasion for political criticism, there was resonance among believers. The alternative religious authorities decried waste and imprudence in government expenditures and highlighted the absence of a capable military despite massive expenditures on weaponry.

During this period, several petitions were presented to King Fahd that demanded structural reforms in the kingdom. The most influential were from dissident Sunni scholars, or the *sahwa,* the awakening shaikhs. The 1992 petition, known as the "memorandum of advice," was particularly important. Its tone was straightforward; its charges were specific. It criticized almost every aspect of domestic and foreign policy. It deplored bribery, favoritism, monopolies, the feebleness of the courts, and violations of human dignity. The *sahwa* were especially powerful at this time, but their leaders were imprisoned for several years and the movement was repressed (Menoret 2016).

From 2002 onward, there were loose and ambiguous working relationships forged among activists of different political orientations (Lacroix 2011). One such coalition of *sahwa* and human rights activists organized a new group called the Saudi Association for Civil and Political Rights (ACPRA) in 2009. It circulated an initiative in 2012 that called for an end to authoritarianism and for the implementation of constitutional governance. Its many founders, including Abdullah al-Hamid and Fahad al-Qatani, were sentenced to prison in March 2013 for forming a human rights organization. Their total combined sentences are 200 years. The organization was dissolved. Just beforehand, in 2011, during the Arab uprisings, the *sahwa* had promoted the petition "Towards a State of Rights and Institutions" in which they argued for elections.

In 2017 and 2018 some of the most influential and articulate Islamist leaders were arrested. Salman Alaoudh was detained in September 2017 just before the Ritz-Carlton charade, and remains so. Alaoudh had advocated for the 2011 petition. Days before his arrest, he tweeted his 14 million followers, "May God harmonize between their hearts for the good of their people," a way of welcoming possible Qatari–Saudi Arabian talks to move beyond the blockade. His son, Abdullah, said, "They target the moderate Islamists and keep the extremists close" (in Fahim 2018). Aidh al Qarni and Ali Alomari were also arrested. Safar Al Hawali was detained in July 2018 with three of his sons. These are older men, some of whom have health problems. They differ widely in their viewpoints; none are radical jihadis. A Saudi Arabian confided, "When you repress them, they go underground. But they will arise and you never know in what form."

Some observers champion MbS and his inclusion of Shi'a as he shifts away from Wahhabi exclusionary orthodoxy, but others wonder whether it is simply cosmetic. The appointments of two Shi'a to the ineffectual Majlis al-Shura mean little in comparison to his other actions. Wanting it both ways, MbS advocates a return to "pre-1979 moderate Islam," even as he jails moderate Islamists, stokes sectarianism with Iran, emboldens a crude populist nationalism, demolishes a Shi'i neighborhood, executes a Shi'i leader, and attempts to rewrite the historical narrative on the complicity of his family in the empowerment of the religious right after 1979. Abdullah Alaoudh is correct when he argues that "strangling moderate independent Islamic discourse may succeed in silencing democratic voices within Islam in Saudi Arabia, but it will also create a vacuum for the less moderate discourse that the state has shown it tolerates" (2018).

Government and Opposition: Dangerous Times

Opposition is creative, courageous, and multipronged to persist in the face of overwhelming odds. There is no doubt that this is necessary, especially now. Not all challengers seek to overthrow the ruling family. Some do. But many, if not most, agitate for serious structural and cultural reforms that guarantee the accountability of governance and the protection of rights within a monarchical framework. Even if the Al Saud remained as powerful players, they would not be above the rule of law.

Strategies of Protest

Historically, protest has come from many sources and taken many forms. Always, the *majlis* in private homes has been an important arena in which to converse, sift through contesting opinions, and articulate needs. In the 1950s Saudi workers at Aramco engaged in labor strikes to protest their deplorable living conditions. Nationalist movements found articulate leaders in the new technocratic cadre during the oil boom. There were even calls for reform from within the ruling family in the 1960s and 1970s from a group known as the Free Princes. (Its leader, Prince Talal bin Abdulaziz, died in December 2018, from a hunger strike he began after MbS arrested three of his sons.) Throughout the 1980s, strident political criticism was voiced often in conversations in the home, mosque, and market—but only in code words. No member of the ruling family was called by name, as that would result in retribution. In 1993, a demonstration protesting the imprisonment of dissident *sahwa* shaikhs took place in Buraydah, in the heartland of the ruling family's support.

There have also been several violent strikes against the government and related targets. In 2016 four police officers were killed in an attack on the Prophet's Mosque in Medina, and in early 2017 two ISIS members were killed in Riyadh and forty-six alleged militants belonging to a terrorist cell in Jeddah were arrested. In October 2017 there was an armed attack at Al Salam Palace. There have been car bombs at security headquarters in Riyadh and a petrochemical site in Yanbu, hostage-taking at an oil company compound in Al-Khobar, and frequent shootouts between security forces and militants. There are also repeated sophisticated cyberattacks on Aramco, its oil fields, and petrochemical facilities. In August 2018 a cyberattack on a petrochemical company was not designed to simply destroy data or shut down a plant; it was meant to sabotage operations and trigger an explosion.

A common misperception is that Saudi Arabia was immune to the waves of protests in the region in 2011–2012 known as the Arab Spring. The reality is that there were protests, including street demonstrations in Jeddah after devastating floods killed between 120 and 500 people in January 2011. Such demonstrations were followed by numerous labor strikes by both foreign and citizen workers; the declaration of the Umma Islamic Party and subsequent arrest of its founders; regular protests in front of the Ministry of the Interior by families who demanded that their sons, fathers, and brothers be released from jail; women driving; a hunger strike in support of political prisoners; a demonstration for women's rights; intense political debate on social media; student strikes in Abha; and multiple petitions with thousands of signatories that called for elections, an independent judiciary, and freedom of expression and assembly.

Perhaps most telling, there was a much-publicized call for a Day of Rage on March 11, 2011. Over 34,000 people signed a Facebook page in support of a massive uprising in Saudi Arabia to call for constitutional governance and basic human rights. The uprising itself did not come to pass, for reasons detailed in the next section. Still, there were many "silent protests" in front of the ministries in Riyadh in which a few men stood silently for hours each day to demand livable wages. Given the intensive political culture of privacy, it is clear how brave these protesters were to break the barrier of anonymity even at all costs.

In the Eastern Province, protest has been sustained by a Shi'i population that wants to be accepted as full citizens of Saudi Arabia. In 2012, when pictures were posted that showed Shaikh al-Nimr crumpled and bleeding in the backseat of a police car, thousands of people took to the streets in protest. He was later executed. Funerals became sites of protest. Israa al-Ghomgham was arrested in December 2015 for having incited protest, participated in protests in Qatif, chanted slogans hostile to the regime, filmed protests and posted them on social media, and attempted to inflame public opinion. She faces a possible death penalty. The state asserts that the Shi'i protesters are nothing more than Iranian-backed puppets doing the dirty work of Iranian theocrats. This allows it to respond with a heavy hand.

Today there is very little organized or open opposition in Saudi Arabia. MbS will brook no criticism whatsoever. Prisons are full of writers, bureaucrats, preachers, men, women, Shi'a and Sunni, journalists and activists. Charges often may not even exist, and when they do may be broad and ambiguous, such as "breaking allegiance with the ruler" or "participating in protests." Under such circumstances, it is no surprise that people go underground or silent to stay alive.

State Strategies to Blunt Protest and Opposition

The Saudi state uses numerous tactics to blunt opposition or calls for political reform. It co-opts, channels, stifles, and mostly, coerces dissenters. During the uprisings of 2011–2012, the state announced wide-ranging distributive schemes that eventually totaled $130 billion and included new jobs, salary raises, housing, and the like (Okruhlik 2015). In 2018 King Salman announced $13 billion in distributive handouts, including an increase in student stipends, bonuses for serving in Yemen, housing allowances, and salary increases for public sector employees. Why did the Day of Rage, so wildly popular on social media, fail to materialize in the streets on March 11, 2011? Here state strategy was to respond not with distribution but instead with a triad of political, religious, and coercive power to scare citizens. The state infiltrated the Day of Rage Facebook group and website and spread disinformation about who was really behind the organization. Potential protesters grew distrustful of each other. A fatwa argued that the duty of a citizen is merely to give advice to the king, which he is not obliged to follow. A circular was distributed to local imams telling them to limit their sermons to a show of loyalty to the Al Saud. There were also military tanks on every street corner, sirens screaming, antiriot police at the ready, and helicopters hovering in the skies over Riyadh on the appointed day. The state thoroughly and systematically intimidated its citizens.

The state continues to be brutal, as shown by new laws, new government bodies, new charges, and new tactics of repression. Effective in 2016, the state Law on Associations and Foundations enshrines the authority of the Ministry of Social Affairs to both license and unilaterally dissolve any organization. Rather than easing restrictions on civil society, the law enforces strict control by the government. This effectively mutes civil society. An overhaul of the security apparatus in summer 2017 usurped much power from the Ministry of Interior. It created the Office of Public Prosecution that "will function directly under the King's auspices whilst enjoying full independence" (Saudi Press Agency 2017). The new Presidency of State Security, under the direct authority of the royal court, handles all state security matters. The Anti-Cyber Crime Law is used to punish anyone who criticizes government actions. Article 6 states that crimes include "the production of anything that violates public order, religious values, morals, the inviolability of private life, or preparation, transmission or storage of it through the Internet or a computer" (Saudi Presidency of State Security 2017). It is a crime to tweet concern over the humanitarian crises created by the Saudi–United Arab Emirates (UAE) war in Yemen. Domestic dissent has been conflated with terrorism. Peaceful human rights defenders are labeled as "terrorists." A new Counter Terrorism Law introduced specific penalties, including the death penalty. In the wake of the blockade of Qatar by the UAE and Saudi Arabia, a criminal and very serious charge is that of acting as a foreign intelligence agent. Citizens are charged with being spies and accused of treason, and the foreign party is Qatar. In September 2018 hundreds of social media users, religious scholars, and judges were arrested and accused of acting in the interests of foreign parties.

As noted earlier, the family home was a sacrosanct unit rarely violated by the state; for example, individuals wanted for interrogation would be summoned to a government building. Now, homes are ransacked, parents are arrested in front of their children, and spouses are taken away by state authorities in the middle of the night (Lacroix 2017). This is a violation of a long-standing norm.

When advocates of meaningful and peaceful political reform put forward potential leadership, those individuals are arrested, jailed, or intimidated. The Saudi state has closed not only the ACPRA but also the Adala Centre for Human Rights, Monitor for Human Rights in Saudi Arabia, and the Union for Human Rights. Ironically, Saudi Arabia chaired the United Nations Council on Human Rights in 2015 and continued to serve as a member even as Khashoggi was murdered. Its membership is now being scrutinized.

Four men remain in prison for "protest-related charges" that they allegedly committed when they were children. Prominent blogger Raif Badawi is still serving his ten-year sentence. Dozens of Shi'i men are at risk of execution, some accused of spying for Iran. When newspaper editors or talk-show hosts step over the permissible boundary of criticism, they are simply removed from their posts. In 2011, in the midst of the pro-democracy Arab uprisings, the Saudi Press and Publications Law was amended to make it even more restrictive. In 2018 editor Saleh al Shehi was sentenced to five years in prison for criticizing the royal court.

Overall, the state uses two broad strategies to blunt protest. The first is to divert political and religious energy outward to foreign arenas like Iraq, Syria, Afghanistan, Yemen, Chechnya, and especially Iran, rather than focusing on internal issues. In the case of Iran, the point is to equate legitimate domestic dissent with the meddling of a foreign bogeyman. A corollary to this strategy is the purposeful deflection of debate away from political issues to social issues. There is intense debate in Saudi Arabia about gender, globalization, the economy, and how to reform religion. When minor reform on such issues does occur, however, the irony is that the "reform" is designed to consolidate the centrality of the Al Saud rather than broaden meaningful participation (Okruhlik 2005). Many outside observers conflate social opening with political liberalization, though they are fundamentally different. The distribution of political power and the protection of rights remain off-limits.

Gender and Politics

As shown in Chapter 8, the construction of gender roles in the Middle East is complex, reflecting culture, cultural resistance, and other factors. The situation is especially complicated in Saudi Arabia, where an exclusionary religious orthodoxy and state power were fused in a rigidly patriarchal nexus. Religious law, social tradition, and political authoritarianism converged to place enormous import on outlawing situations that may lead to sex outside of marriage. In Arabic the value is articulated as *sad bab al-dhara'i'* (literally, "the blocking of the means"). It is used in legal rulings, one of which states, "The Pure Law forbids those acts that lead to forbidden acts and considers those means to be forbidden also" (Ibn Baz cited in al-Musnad 1996: 310). This is a slippery slope and is the foundation upon which extensive constraints on the behavior of women have been legalized, justified, and codified (Okruhlik 2009). This is why unrelated men and women cannot easily mix.

Covering and segregation can be tedious but are not necessarily the most consequential issues in Saudi Arabian women's lives. They are the most visible, for sure, and are highlighted often in the Western press. But the single biggest constraint on the lives of women is the legal requirement that they always be accompanied, or their behavior approved, by a *mahram* (guardian). A *mahram* is a husband or, in cases where the woman is unmarried or widowed, an uncle, brother, father, or son—someone whom the woman cannot marry. He must grant permission for her to travel, study abroad, seek employment, have medical surgery, get married or divorced, or request her children's school files. Indeed, he can even constrain her daily movements about town. A seventy-year-old widow cried to me regarding her son, "I bore him between my legs. And now, I cannot shop for groceries without his permission!" The idea of guardianship—that somehow a woman is not capable of rational decisionmaking—is the nucleus around which much nonsense revolves.

Under the confines of this system, Saudi women were not allowed to drive. MbS may have lifted the ban on driving in summer 2018 as a part of his modernization program and projected himself as a feminist, but that title belongs to women who have long fought and sacrificed. In November 1990, forty-seven women protested severe constraints on their mobility by kicking their foreign drivers out of their cars and driving themselves through the streets of Riyadh. They paid dearly for their defiance. In an extraordinarily private society, their pictures were posted. They were publicly called "prostitutes" and they lost their passports and jobs. Manal al-Sharif defied the ban in 2011 and drove her car. She proudly posted the video on YouTube and was promptly detained for a week. The following month, forty women in Riyadh with international driver's licenses participated in a "women2drive" campaign. Many women now opt for services like Uber or Careem.

Before the formal lifting of the driving ban, MbS carefully did two things. In September 2017 he received a formal fatwa from the Council of Senior Scholars, the highest religious body, which endorsed his decision to allow women to drive. The council posted on its Twitter account, "Regarding women driving vehicles, the religious ruling in this regard is permissibility." Though the ruling family has constrained the religious authorities, it still uses them when it serves their purposes. On May 15, just before the ban was lifted, MbS began arresting the very women who had fought so hard for this right. Many still remain incarcerated. Saudi feminist, Hala al-Dosari, observes, "Mohammed bin Salman wants to be the arbiter. He wants to decide the reforms and when they happen" (in Sly 2018). MbS will promote a soft state feminism, but make no mistake—the very idea of collective mobilization and organization strikes fear in him.

At this writing, at least nine women remain detained without charge. In a letter that one of the detainees, Nouf Abdelaziz, had given to a friend "just in case I am arrested," she writes, "I am not a provoker, not a vandalizer, not a terrorist, a criminal or a traitor. . . . I have never been anything but a good citizen who loves her country and wishes for it nothing but the best" (Abdelaziz 2018). In late November 2018 there were tragic reports that the women were being tortured. They suffered electric shock, whipping on their thighs, and forcible kissing and hugging. They were subject to waterboarding, electrocution, threats of rape, and being thrown into sewage. The women show physical signs of torture: uncontrolled shaking of their hands and red marks and scratches on their faces and necks. One woman tried repeatedly to commit suicide (Human Rights Watch 2018).

Despite these constraints on women in Saudi Arabia, there have been advancements, mostly in consumerism, employment, and education. Women carry an identity card in their own name. They can check into a hotel without the permission of a male. There are shopping malls, banks, and hotels that cater strictly to women. Premarital genetic counseling is now required. This is significant because negotiated first-cousin marriages are common. A woman can refuse the marriage if tests indicate a medical problem. Female students can now major in law or political science, subjects that were long off-limits. Physical education classes have been approved for girls' schools, though it is not clear that they are actually instituted. In 2011, the world's largest women's university opened outside Riyadh.

In contemporary Saudi Arabia, women challenge and protest continuing humiliations and constraints. When the morality patrols were excessive in their zeal, women doused them with pepper spray, beat them so hard as to require hospital care, and, once, even opened gunfire on them. Women protest that divorce can be decreed through (men) text-messaging three times, "I divorce thee." Women now speak out about issues that once were simply off-limits for public discussion: partner rape, domestic abuse, and divorce. They provide shelters for victims of domestic crimes. Importantly, increasing numbers of women speak out without anonymity. They agitate for women lawyers so that they can be fairly represented. Trained female scholars are privately rewriting the many legal codes that have ossified over time. Still, these are treacherous times. Under MbS, women are used as symbolic markers of reform, modernity, and openness at the same time that they are imprisoned and tortured. In the end, it is important to note that a legal decree or a royal pronouncement is not automatically implemented and made real in people's day-to-day lives. There is a vast gulf between legality and life as it is lived on the ground. This is especially true for women.

The Impact of International Politics

MbS wants Saudi Arabia to be a regional power broker commensurate in status with Israel, Turkey, and Iran. This is why his Saudi/UAE-led coalition initiated a devastating war in Yemen in March 2015 to defeat the Houthis with the military support of the United States, UK, and France. Saudi Arabia markets the war as a necessary effort to combat the effects of Iranian influence, but the reality is far more complex. More than 60,000 people have died in the violence. The catastrophe is MbS's signature policy initiative. After more than 18,000 airstrikes and a crippling blockade, 18 million Yemenis are at risk of malnutrition and disease and 85,000 young children have already starved to death (Riedel 2018). The use of cluster bombs has been documented. Routinely attacked are school buses, weddings, and fishing boats. International outcry over the killing of Khashoggi had another impact: it put the war in Yemen in the spotlight and thus increased pressure on Saudi Arabia to reconsider its policy.

At the same time, the relationship with the United States continues, more or less, business as usual (Conge and Okruhlik 2009). President Donald Trump, at this writing, remains a staunch ally of MbS. Trump perhaps emboldened MbS when he tweeted his support for the Ritz-Carlton arrests, saying, "I have great confidence in the Crown Prince of Saudi Arabia, they know exactly what they are doing. Some of those they are harshly treating have been 'milking' their country for years!" On Khashoggi, President Trump offered, "It could very well be that the crown prince had knowledge of this tragic event—maybe he did and maybe he didn't! We may never know all of the facts surrounding the murder of Mr. Jamal Khashoggi. In any case, our relationship is with the Kingdom of Saudi Arabia." Further, Trump claims that the Saudi-led war is necessary to combat Iranian influence and Islamic extremists even as the US Congress has acted to put the brakes on US support for the war in Yemen. In this light, Trump highlighted how the United States has $110 billion in arms sales to Saudi Arabia. Industry watchers say the figure is inflated because the deals are not signed and include agreements made by President Barack Obama. But in 2017, the United States did clear $18 billion in arms sales to Saudi Arabia.

On its eastern border, Saudi Arabia (along with the UAE, Bahrain, and Egypt) cut all diplomatic ties with their former Gulf Cooperation Council (GCC) ally, Qatar, and instituted an expansive trade and economic embargo against the country. They claimed, among thirteen charges, that Qatar supported Islamic extremism, sponsored terror, and propagated falsehoods on Al-Jazeera news, all of which affected their own domestic politics. Saudi Arabia even proposed digging a moat along its border with Qatar to turn Qatar into an island. MbS's plan has backfired thus far; he overreached and miscalculated Qatar's alternative options. Rather than being isolated, Qatar built bridges of trade with Iran, India, Turkey, Oman, and China, among others.

The GCC is severely fractured and dysfunctional. It was intended to provide a protective "Peninsular Shield" for its six sovereign members, but Oman, Kuwait, and Qatar often bristle at Saudi Arabia's hegemony in the organization.

OPEC, the Organization of Petroleum Exporting Countries, is in disarray. Shortly before its meeting in Vienna in December 2018, Trump tweeted "Thank you, Saudi Arabia" in gratitude for its pledge to increase production and thus decrease prices. At the meeting, Qatar withdrew its membership after fifty-seven years, a symbolic jab at its rival Saudi Arabia. Members agreed to a production cut despite the pressure from Trump. The cracks in OPEC are evident. Longtime members feel marginalized by the assertion of a Saudi-Russian axis.

In a significant shift in policy, MbS has repeatedly reached out to Israel to "normalize" relations, to develop economic relations, and to share intelligence. Trump recognized Jerusalem as the capital of Israel and moved the US embassy from Tel Aviv to Jerusalem. The effect in Saudi Arabia was that an ailing King Salman had to assert his position in summer 2018, saying that any peace agreement must address the final status of Jerusalem and recognize the right of return of Palestinian refugees. He has declared to the Palestinians, "We will not abandon you."

Saudi Arabia and Iran continue to jockey for influence. Nevertheless, the rhetoric of a "Shi'i crescent" likely holds more weight for political elite in the United States and Saudi Arabia than it does for ordinary people in the region. It is, in effect, a useful tool with which to crack down on domestic adversaries. Also worth watching is how Saudi Arabia funnels arms and money to the rebel forces in Syria. It pays the salaries of soldiers who defect from the Syrian military. If Trump does indeed withdraw US forces from Syria as he announced in December 2018, a vacuum will exist. Further afield, Saudi Arabia has edged closer to both Russia and China in energy cooperation and economic and military engagement, even combining portions of their sovereign wealth funds into one fund.

The question at this writing is the future of MbS. He may be relegated to reforming social and economic policies in order to rescue Saudi Arabia's foreign relations; he may be replaced by his father or contending branches of the family in a palace coup, or he may be on the throne for fifty years.

18
Syria

Fred H. Lawson

Once upon a time, Syria displayed greater political instability than any other country in the Middle East and North Africa. Military commanders carried out a series of coups d'état beginning in March 1949, which culminated in the seizure of power by a group of officers affiliated with the Socialist Arab Resurrection (Baath) Party in March 1963. Persistent rivalry between the radical wing of the Baath and the Syrian Communist Party on one side and proponents of private enterprise—including liberal Islamist activists—on the other led a group of comparatively pragmatic commanders headed by General Hafiz al-Asad to seize control of the government in November 1970. This event brought to a close the era of military coups but opened a dozen years of intense, at times violent, conflict between supporters of the new Baathi leadership and radical Islamists.

During the course of the struggle against the Islamist militants, the authorities suppressed liberal critics of the Baathi order and forged a robust alliance of party cadres, military and security forces, and commercial and industrial elites that stabilized the country until the end of the twentieth century. This ruling coalition survived the death of Hafiz al-Asad in June 2000 and enabled his son Bashar to succeed to the presidency. More important, the Baathi regime that coalesced during the 1990s proved resilient enough to absorb the impact of both the global recession of 2008 to 2009 and the large-scale popular uprising that erupted during 2011. No matter what territorial, economic, or cultural transformations might emerge from the eight years of brutal warfare that followed the outbreak of the uprising, Syria's underlying political structure prevailed with no more than marginal alterations.

Historical Background and Contemporary Political Structure

In March 1963 a group of military officers seized control of Syria and began to rule in the name of the Socialist Arab Resurrection (Baath) Party. The party's explicitly redistributive, populist platform, combined with the dynamics of military governance, set the course for Syria's subsequent political, economic, and social development. The military-party regime at first limited the extent of land reform and the sequestration of industrial and commercial enterprises, in an attempt to mollify the liberal nationalists who had led the country since independence (Lawson 1988). But the new regime was propelled in a more radical direction by industrial workers and farm laborers, who occupied private factories and battled large landholders in the northern and central provinces, and then demanded that state and party officials put the principles of Baathi socialism into practice. The radical wing of the party enacted a comprehensive program of property seizure and redistribution in 1965, which set the stage for a coup d'état by doctrinaire socialists in February 1966. This extremist phase of the Baathi era ended three years later, when military commanders headed by General Hafiz al-Asad ousted the radicals. The shift toward pragmatism was consolidated when al-Asad and his allies took control of the state in the November 1970 coup d'état known as the Corrective Movement.

Baath Party doctrine is most authoritatively codified in the statement called "Some Theoretical Propositions," which was drafted for the sixth National (pan-Arab) Congress that met in Damascus in October 1963. This manifesto codified the party's memorable slogan: "Unity, Freedom, Socialism." Steps to promote unity of purpose and action among the Arab states are accorded highest priority. The party's concept of freedom mirrors that of Jean-Jacques Rousseau: it emphasizes the collective good of the community as a whole and has little if any respect for individual liberties or representative government. The third objective, socialism, proved to be the most elastic of all. From 1963 to 1965, the term denoted a mixed program that entailed not only redistributing property and equalizing income but also providing government support for "nonexploitative" forms of private enterprise. From 1965 to 1969, more collectivist notions of state ownership and central planning prevailed. Beginning in 1969–1970, Baathi economic doctrine shifted once again to encourage the reinstatement of private ownership. The underlying flexibility of Baathi ideology has thus provided a touchstone for the various leaderships that have ruled in the party's name after 1963.

Shortly after taking power, the regime headed by Hafiz al-Asad convened a parliamentary body, the People's Assembly, and charged it with drafting a permanent constitution to replace the provisional ones issued in 1964 and 1969. Delegates were at first appointed by President al-Asad and his closest advisers so as to represent the Baath Party and four other political organizations whose platforms were compatible with that of the Baath: the Arab Socialist Union, the Socialist Unionists Movement, the Arab Socialists Movement, and the Syrian Communist Party. The five parties in 1971 formed the Progressive National Front. A few independent delegates were also included in the initial assembly, along with representatives of the workers' federation, the farm laborers' union, the women's association, and other Baath Party–affiliated popular front organizations. In 1973 the People's Assembly submitted a draft constitution for the president's approval, which was then ratified in a popular plebiscite.

The 1973 constitution confers primary authority on the presidency. The president of the republic must be nominated by the Baath Party, approved by the People's Assembly, and confirmed by a majority of voters in a national referendum. The president serves a seven-year term and is authorized to appoint one or more vice presidents, as well as the prime minister and other members of the Council of Ministers. The president is also empowered to dissolve the People's Assembly and assume its legislative functions, nominate judges for the high courts, and appoint provincial governors. The elected People's Assembly is accorded the right to veto or amend presidential decrees by a two-thirds vote, although this provision has remained dormant in practice. In fact, for the first two decades of its existence, the legislature acted as no more than a sounding board for policies under consideration by the Council of Ministers, and usually as a rubber stamp for initiatives put forward by the president and his senior advisers.

Government and Opposition

Elections for the People's Assembly in May 1990 signaled a subtle shift in the role of the legislature. The Progressive National Front won 168 of the 250 seats, yet the number of independent representatives rose to 82 from the previous total of 35. The independents included a prominent Islamic television commentator from Damascus, four religious notables from the northern provinces of Aleppo and Idlib, several tribal leaders—including the son of the leader of the 1925 rebellion against the French—and an assortment of wealthy merchants and successful entrepreneurs (Perthes 1992: 17). The new delegates set out to "use parliament as a forum to call for economic reform and liberalization, presenting themselves as the people who know how to run economic affairs, and probably—in the long run at least—claiming that private sector representatives should also share political responsibility" (Perthes 1992: 18). Eberhard

Kienle (1997: 199) reports that "on several occasions during its four-year term the [1990] Assembly even used its right to pass a vote of no confidence in individual ministers leading to their resignation."

During the late 1990s, however, the Progressive National Front reasserted control over the People's Assembly. The subordinate role of the legislature at the turn of the century is illustrated by the events that were triggered by the death of Hafiz al-Asad on June 10, 2000. The People's Assembly immediately amended the constitution to lower the age requirement for the presidency from forty to thirty-four, which happened to be the age of the deceased president's eldest surviving son, Bashar. The Regional (Syrian) Command of the Baath Party then announced that Bashar al-Asad had been elected secretary-general of the party, and Vice President 'Abd al-Halim Khaddam announced that Bashar had been designated commander in chief of the armed forces. On June 13, the People's Assembly nominated Bashar al-Asad as the sole candidate in an extraordinary presidential election held on July 10. He elicited the approval of 97.3 percent of voters.

President al-Asad announced in January 2011 that the Baath Party would give greater weight to district elections in the selection of delegates to the upcoming party congress. This small step in the direction of institutional reform was quickly overshadowed by events in Tunisia and Egypt. Small-scale popular protests erupted in Damascus in early February, followed by a larger demonstration outside the Ministry of Interior in mid-March initiated by a group of women who demanded to know the fate of imprisoned family members. Security personnel used force to break up the initial outbreaks of unrest, but state officials also announced plans to create jobs for an additional 10,000 university graduates each year in a bid to dampen popular discontent.

Comparatively peaceful demonstrations in the capital were soon eclipsed by a more severe outbreak of disorder in the southern city of Dir'a. The third week of May, schoolchildren scrawled the slogan "The people want the fall of the regime" on a wall, prompting police to arrest them and rough them up while they were in custody. Protesters responded by sacking the local Baath Party headquarters, and riot police backed by regular army troops shot into the crowd. The authorities in Damascus tried to defuse the situation by claiming that commanders on the spot had disobeyed orders when they used live ammunition; Prime Minister Naji' al-'Utri promised new investments in the south to reverse years of official neglect. Despite these concessions, disorder erupted in the coastal city of Latakia, where anti-regime protesters clashed with armed groups of government supporters, commonly known as "ghosts" (*shabbihah*).

On March 30, 2011, President al-Asad addressed the country by television. He admitted that the reform process he had originally envisaged had stalled out but blamed the Palestinian uprising of 2000, the US-led invasions of Afghanistan and Iraq, and the 2006 war between Israel and Hezbollah for causing the failure. The government then set up a committee to explore the lifting of the state of emergency that had been in force since 1963 and another commission to confer full citizenship rights on the descendants of 150,000 Kurds who had been excluded from the 1962 census. Minister of Agriculture ʻAdil Safar was appointed prime minister, despite widespread criticism of his efforts to deal with the drought that had gripped the countryside for the previous five years.

Army units moved back into Dirʻa at the end of April 2011. Early May saw the beginning of severe fighting in the central city of Homs between armed protesters and security forces, accompanied by heavy machine gun fire and artillery barrages. Skirmishing spread to Idlib province, and in mid-May the army swept into the crossroads town of Tal Kalakh, sending residents fleeing across the border into Lebanon. The military advanced on the strategically situated town of al-Rastan at the end of May, but residents repelled the assault with small arms and rocket-propelled grenades. When police fired on a funeral procession in the town of Jisr al-Shughur in early June, enraged protesters stormed the main police station and confiscated weapons. In the ensuing battle, 120 troops were killed and military and security personnel defected to the opposition. Further defections took place around the eastern city of Dair al-Zur, and Lieutenant Colonel Husain Harmush declared himself head of an opposition military formation called the Free Officers. On June 20 President al-Asad once again addressed the country, this time charging that conspiracies and vandals were behind the unrest. He remarked that the protesters were "germs" that would infect the body politic if they were not suppressed. Protesters in Dirʻa and Homs immediately raised banners that proclaimed, "The germs demand the fall of the regime."

In July 2011 Colonel Riyad Asʻad announced the formation of the Free Syrian Army (FSA), headquartered outside Antakya in Turkey. Another group of deserters set up the Khalid bin al-Walid Brigade around al-Rastan in September. A congress of anti-regime groups convened in the Turkish city of Antalya, which eventuated in the formation of the Syrian National Council (SNC). The first full meeting of the SNC took place in Istanbul in early October; Burhan Ghalioun, a Paris-based academic, was elected to head the SNC, whose other prominent figures included the civil rights activist Riyad Saif, the communist leader Riyad al-Turk, and the general supervisor of the Muslim Brothers, Mohammad Riyad al-Shaqfah. At the same time, an assortment of autonomous militias coalesced inside Syria. Most of these named themselves after famous personages and events in Islamic history, like the 'Ali bin Abu Talib Brigade outside Idlib, the 'Umar bin al-Khattab Brigade around Dair al-Zur, and the Mu'awiyya bin Abu Sufyan and 'Ubaidah bin al-Jarah Brigades in the suburbs of Damascus.

Units of the Khalid bin al-Walid Brigade attacked patrols and convoys around al-Rastan in late September, then seized the military intelligence compound in the town. State armed forces counterattacked and expelled the militia. After abandoning al-Rastan, the al-Faruq Battalion of the Khalid bin al-Walid Brigade took up positions in the working-class Baba 'Amru district of Homs. On October 27 the FSA for the first time claimed responsibility for an attack that killed nine government soldiers. Fighting escalated in November, as the armed forces bombarded and then occupied Baba 'Amru and afterwards launched a massive offensive against Dir'a. FSA units repelled an assault against the town of al-Zabadani outside Damascus in January 2012, while the Khalid bin al-Walid Brigade retook parts of al-Rastan. The resurgence of opposition forces accompanied sporadic bombings of security installations in Damascus and Aleppo, responsibility for which was later claimed by the Assistance Front for the People of Syria, a group that boasted close ties to al-Qaeda.

Government forces regained the initiative as February 2012 waned. Baba 'Amru was overrun after the al-Faruq Battalion carried out a "tactical withdrawal" from the district. FSA units withdrew from Idlib and Dair al-Zur and were driven out of the northwestern towns of Saraqib and al-Qusair. As the regime improved its position, President al-Asad accepted a United Nations–sponsored cease-fire plan, which stipulated that government troops would evacuate the cities by April 10. Colonel As'ad promised that the FSA would abide by the cease-fire, so long as the regular army withdrew from all urban areas and returned to barracks. The regime riposted that it had not agreed to send troops back to their barracks, and that some continuing military presence might be necessary to deal with diehards like the Assistance Front. The FSA rejected the government's clarification, yet an uneasy calm descended across the country on April 12–13. The cease-fire did not last long. State-run media reported on April 14 that a half dozen soldiers had been killed outside Idlib, and a day later shelling resumed at Homs. Large-scale fighting subsequently broke out around Idlib and Aleppo.

By late spring 2012, the armed uprising had settled into a stalemate, with neither the FSA nor the independent militias able to win control of government strongholds, and neither the regular army nor the *shabbihah* able to crush the opposition. When news came of a massacre of more than 100 men, women, and children in the al-Hulah district of Idlib province, merchants in central Damascus closed their shops in disgust. Signs of discontent in the heart of the capital reinvigorated the flagging FSA, which in early July launched coordinated attacks outside Damascus combined with raids on crossing posts along the borders with Turkey and Iraq. Intense fighting raged around Aleppo and A'zaz throughout August, and a large amount of territory north and northeast of Aleppo fell into the hands of the FSA, radical Islamist militias, and the armed wing of the Kurdish Democratic Union Party (PYD).

Meanwhile, state officials in June 2011 promulgated a revised political parties law that made it easier for new parties to challenge the Progressive National Front. In the local council elections of December 2011, several candidates from minor parties in the front changed their affiliation to the newly created National Unity List. Candidates sponsored by the National Unity List won seats in the People's Assembly in the parliamentary elections of April 2012. Nine other new political parties contested these elections as well. Paradoxically, since the practice of reserving seats for minor parties in the Progressive National Front had been abolished, the Baath Party came away with greater representation in the People's Assembly than ever before. Such initiatives were overshadowed by the July 2012 bombing of the National Security Directorate in Damascus, which killed the minister of defense, deputy defense minister, head of state security, and influential former defense minister.

Civil War

By the fall of 2012, radical Islamist forces had moved into the vanguard of the armed struggle against the regime. Islamist militants frequently clashed with FSA units, as well as with local militias like the Unity Brigade of Aleppo. Radical Islamists assaulted members of the country's ethnic and sectarian minority communities, destroying Shi'i mosques and mourning houses and looting Christian churches. They occasionally attacked Sunnis as well, on the grounds that their places of worship or pilgrimage were "too pretentious for Islamic traditions." In April 2013, the Islamic State of Iraq announced that it had merged with the Assistance Front to form the Islamic State in Iraq and the Levant (ISIL). A sizable number of Assistance Front fighters rejected the merger, precipitating fierce fighting between cadres of the two organizations.

ISIL pushed the Assistance Front and a local FSA brigade out of the central city of al-Raqqah in August 2013, then launched an offensive to capture the towns of al-Bab and Minbij on the main route from Aleppo to al-Raqqah. ISIL fighters also engaged in an intense contest with FSA units and armed tribespeople for control of the oil fields around Dair al-Zur. The fighting set off a kaleidoscopic shift in alignments that led a number of powerful Islamist formations, including the Unity Brigade and the Battalions of the Free of Syria, to form the Islamic Front. In response, the al-Faruq Battalions and several smaller forces set up the Syrian Revolutionaries Front. The two blocs carried out a string of assassinations against each other, the Assistance Front, and ISIL throughout the winter of 2013–2014.

ISIL launched a large-scale attack against the Assistance Front in Dair al-Zur in April 2014 and captured several strategically located towns near the border with Iraq. At the same time, ISIL battled Kurdish forces along the Turkish border. After the PYD's armed wing—the Popular Protection Units (YPG)—and the FSA's al-Raqqah Revolutionaries Brigade regained control of large parts of al-Raqqah province, ISIL retaliated by initiating a major offensive in central and northern Iraq that June. The campaign won control of the northern Iraqi city of Mosul, a victory that emboldened the ISIL leadership to proclaim that it had restored the rule of the Successor of the Prophet (the Caliphate). ISIL then rechristened itself the Islamic State.

Kurdish and FSA forces inflicted a major defeat on the Islamic State in February 2015 at the town of 'Ain al-'Arab, on the Turkish border north of al-Raqqah, and advanced toward the nearby towns of Tal Abyad and Tal Tamr. To meet this threat, the Islamic State pulled its cadres out of Aleppo and al-Bab, which enabled the Assistance Front and the Nur al-Din al-Zanqi Battalions to take up positions in the area. Tal Abyad nevertheless fell to the YPG and FSA in mid-June. In the wake of this battle, the YPG and FSA formed a broader coalition called the Army of Revolutionaries, which included several Christian and Turkmen militias, as well as tribal forces. The Army of Revolutionaries gained ground all across the northeast that summer. Meanwhile, the YPG tried repeatedly to push westward, toward the border town of Jarabulus; each attempt was blocked by the Turkish army.

While the Army of Revolutionaries gained territory in the northeast, the Battalions of the Free joined the Hawks of Syria to seize the northwestern city of Idlib, working together as the Army of Conquest. The new partnership, fighting alongside the Assistance Front, went on to seize the nearby towns of Jisr al-Shughur and Ariha and moved westward toward predominantly 'Alawi districts along the Mediterranean coast. Farther south, near the border with Jordan, fighters affiliated with the Assistance Front captured the town of Busra al-Sham and took control of the crucial crossing station at Nasib. These victories prompted Hezbollah to move into positions along the Golan frontier and then attack the militant Islamists in al-Qunaitirah and Dir'a.

In September 2015, Russian warplanes and military advisers deployed to an air base outside Latakia. Their arrival prompted radical Islamist formations made up of fighters from Chechnya, Dagestan, Ingushetia, Uzbekistan, and western China to march into the northwest. Russian commanders undertook an extensive bombing campaign against these militants and also targeted FSA units around Homs and Aleppo. The air strikes enabled the Islamic State to move back into districts east of Aleppo. In October, the YPG announced that it had joined a dozen militias in the northeast to form the Democratic Forces of Syria (DFS). The DFS attacked the Islamic State in al-Hasakah province, and with the aid of US advisers cut the routes linking al-Raqqah to northern Iraq. At the end of 2015, the DFS captured the October Dam on the Euphrates River, a major source of electrical power and a key crossing point on the highway from al-Raqqah to Minbij.

January 2016 saw contingents of the DFS move against the Assistance Front and the Islamic State from the town of ʻAfrin near the Turkish border. After Kurdish fighters captured a large air base northwest of Aleppo in early February, however, the Turkish army launched a massive artillery barrage to compel them to abandon the facility. Kurdish forces outside Aleppo subsequently came under attack from an FSA-affiliated Turkmen militia. That spring, a cluster of radical Islamist formations in the south formed the Khalid bin al-Walid Army, which aligned itself with the Islamic State.

At the end of May 2016, the DFS carried out a two-pronged offensive against the Islamic State. One battle group captured the Revolution Dam across the Euphrates River just north of al-Raqqah, while the other drove toward Minbij. The Islamic State reacted by pulling its cadres out of Aleppo and reinforcing its strongholds at al-Bab, Minbij, and al-Raqqah; the Assistance Front then moved back into districts around Aleppo. Syrian government troops two months later severed the Assistance Front's last supply lines in Aleppo, forcing it to seek help from the Battalions of the Free. The Battalions of the Free insisted that in return the Assistance Front renounce its ties to al-Qaeda; in doing so, the Assistance Front renamed itself the Conquest of the Levant Front and tried to prop up its deteriorating position in Aleppo by carrying out joint operations with the militant Turkistan Islamic Party and the Nur al-Din al-Zanqi Battalions.

Minbij fell to the DFS in late August 2016. The Kurdish-led alliance set up a military council to administer the town and prepared to push on toward Jarabulus and al-Bab. Before the preparations were completed, a collection of FSA units backed by the Turkish armed forces overran Jarabulus in an offensive called Euphrates Shield. Ankara then demanded that the DFS withdraw from all of the territory it had taken west of the Euphrates River, while the commander of the predominantly Turkmen Sultan Murat Brigade threatened to attack Minbij. Turkish troops at the same time launched artillery barrages against Kurdish positions around ʻAfrin.

By fall 2016, the Army of Conquest remained in control of extensive areas in Idlib province and encircled two predominantly Shiʻi towns, which it pledged not to obliterate so long as government troops refrained from destroying the Sunni towns of al-Zabadani and Madaya. Other militant Islamists carried out a series of operations in northern Hama province that targeted ʻAlawi, Shiʻi, and Christian villages. Thanks to infighting among opposition forces, the Syrian army, along with Hezbollah and a handful of pro-government militias sponsored by Iraq and Iran, captured territory north of Hama and regained control of Aleppo in a brutal battle that December. After it was driven out of Aleppo, the Conquest of the Levant Front changed its name to the Committee for the Liberation of the Levant (CLL) and reinforced its redoubt in Idlib (Heller 2016). The Islamic State remained active south and east of al-Raqqah and in January 2017 reoccupied the desert town of Palmyra and destroyed several of its ancient monuments. Turkey-backed forces meanwhile captured al-Bab from the Islamic State, driving a wedge between Kurdish fighters in ʻAfrin and their DFS comrades to the east. FSA units sponsored by Ankara then squared off against the DFS and its US advisers for control of Minbij.

Opposition strongholds around Aleppo, Hama, Homs, and Damascus fell to pro-government forces one after the other as the spring of 2017 went by. Such operations usually involved the encirclement and intense bombardment of isolated towns and villages by Syrian government artillery, warplanes, and helicopter gunships, which inflicted horrific casualties on armed defenders and trapped civilians alike. Government commanders after a while called on anti-regime fighters to agree to a local cease-fire, during which they could choose to be transported to areas still in the hands of anti-regime militias—most often in Idlib province. CLL and Islamic State militants did their best to disrupt these truces by carrying out car and suicide bombings throughout the country. That June and July the DFS, supported by US air strikes, drove the Islamic State out of al-Raqqah. As Islamic State remnants in the city were hunted down, the Syrian government issued a new banknote that for the first time displayed a portrait of Bashar al-Asad.

Pro-regime forces consolidated control over the borders with Jordan and Lebanon during the late summer of 2017 and expelled the Islamic State from the city of al-Salamiyyah in eastern Hama province. Early September saw Syrian government troops, Hezbollah, and the paramilitary Desert Hawks Brigade take charge of Dair al-Zur city and its adjacent oil fields; DFS commanders then announced plans to seize Islamic State–controlled territory in northern and western Dair al-Zur province and warned Syrian army commanders not to cross the Euphrates River. As the autumn began, Turkish troops and Turkey-backed FSA militias confronted both CLL militants in Idlib and DFS fighters in 'Afrin and Minbij. Meanwhile, pro-government forces faced an assortment of radical Islamist and FSA formations in the southwest; various Islamist militants in the countryside around Homs, Hama, and Aleppo; and Islamic State remnants and the DFS in the far northeast.

These battle lines remained unchanged during the first half of 2018. The Turkish armed forces and FSA formations aligned with Ankara expanded the areas of northern Idlib and Aleppo provinces under their control; DFS units took charge of extensive regions across the northeast; and the Syrian armed forces, Hezbollah, and pro-government militias consolidated their positions in central and southern Syria and Aleppo, as well as along the desert frontier with Jordan and Iraq. DFS commanders met resistance from the residents of Minbij when they tried to conscript young men to strengthen the town's defenses. Turkish and FSA forces stepped up their attacks on Kurdish positions around 'Afrin in February, prompting the YPG to forge an unprecedented alliance with pro-government militias; 'Afrin nevertheless succumbed to the Turkish-led offensive. Supported by Russian aircraft, the Syrian army and its allies advanced cautiously toward Idlib from the south.

Growing pressure on the Committee for the Liberation of the Levant encouraged the Battalions of the Free, the Hawks of Syria, and the Nur al-Din al-Zanqi Battalions to form the Patriotic Front for Liberation (also called the National Liberation Front) to challenge CLL dominance over the country's last opposition-held enclave. Tensions in Idlib province soared during the spring of 2018, when the Army of Islam arrived after being expelled from the Damascus suburbs. In July a new militant Islamist formation, the Guardians of the Religion Organization, took shape in the countryside around Idlib. By September 2018 some 60,000 combat-hardened opposition fighters—almost all of them radical Islamists—had congregated in Idlib province. Armed clashes between rival militant groupings erupted throughout winter 2018–2019, resulting in the collapse of a cease-fire sponsored by Turkey and Russia. The Syrian army resumed artillery strikes against Idlib in February 2019. At the same time, DFS units surrounded the remnants of the Islamic State outside the city of Al Bu Kamal on the Iraqi border and in a final furious battle killed or captured more than a thousand fighters.

As pro-regime forces regained control of the country, the Central Committee of the Baath Party in April 2017 reshuffled the composition of the Regional (Syrian) Command and set up a Monitoring Committee to coordinate the activities of the party's various components (al-Alou 2017). Four senior military commanders, including the president's brother Mahir, constituted a new "ideological branch" of the Baath. Greater emphasis was assigned to the long-dormant popular front organizations, especially the students' and farm laborers' unions. Particular attention was devoted to the future of Kurdish areas, and two Kurds from 'Amudah were named to the Central Committee. President al-Asad told the committee that the events of 2011–2018 were "a continuation of the struggle between secular forces, represented by the Baath Party, and political Islam, represented by the Muslim Brothers."

Civil Society

Signs of increased Syrian civic activism appeared in three different arenas during the early 1990s. First, elections to the governing councils of the chambers of commerce in the cities became more fiercely contested. Campaigning for the December 1992 elections to the Damascus council got under way two months before the vote was scheduled to be held, and the press devoted considerable attention to the candidates' platforms. Three years later, the campaign became even more animated (Kienle 1997: 200). One prominent investor published an open letter to the Damascus chamber's membership that called for the creation of a stock exchange, the implementation of a single exchange rate, and tax reductions for private companies, as well as the abolition of laws that prohibited private and foreign banks. Somewhat surprisingly, that candidate won a seat on the governing council of the Damascus chamber.

Second, Syria's workers' and farm laborers' federations expressed dissatisfaction with the regime's efforts to carry out market-oriented economic reforms. Grumbling among the rank-and-file of the farm laborers' union escalated in August 1992, after Prime Minister Mahmud al-Zu'bi announced that the government planned to increase support for export-oriented projects in the private agricultural sector (Lawson 1997: 10). For its December 1992 congress, the General Federation of Workers' Unions compiled a lengthy list of grievances concerning the adverse consequences of economic liberalization. A restive faction inside the federation even proposed to cut the organization's connections to the Baath Party, so that workers' demands could be voiced outside the usual channels. The proposal was later taken up by the People's Assembly (Kienle 1997: 202).

Third, nonviolent demonstrations occurred more frequently. A group of women gathered in front of the presidential palace in 1989 to demand an accounting of political prisoners. In February 1990 a larger crowd, made up of "as many as 100 women, from several Syrian cities and various political orientations, assembled in front of the Presidential Palace and asked to see [President] Asad." According to Human Rights Watch (1991: 505–506), "when officials denied their request, the women refused to disperse and some cried out in protest. Police then violently broke up the demonstration, and three women had to be taken to the hospital with injuries." During the 1990–1991 Gulf War, there were reports of demonstrations in support of Iraq in the eastern town of Al Bu Kamal.

In September 2000 ninety-nine prominent intellectuals, academics, and artists published an open letter to President al-Asad in a Beirut newspaper. The letter urged the new president to expand political liberties and release all political prisoners. Other reformers circulated a broadsheet that demanded a return to "constitutional legitimacy" and the rule of law, and newspapers started openly to criticize government economic policy. The internal security forces tolerated such activity during the winter of 2000–2001, but in mid-February 2001 abruptly enforced new restrictions on all forms of public expression and assembly. Nevertheless, a coalition of civil society activists issued a manifesto in April 2001 that advocated the pursuit of liberal democracy as a precondition for economic growth (Ghadbian 2001: 638). Spontaneous popular demonstrations broke out in the larger cities in July 2002 to protest Israeli actions in the West Bank. These pro-Palestinian demonstrations soon included banners and slogans critical of the Baathi regime in Damascus, prompting the authorities to organize strictly supervised countervailing rallies and marches.

Syrian civic activism reemerged in the wake of the US military offensive against Iraq in the spring of 2003. In May, 250 prominent dissidents signed a petition that called on President al-Asad to recommit the government to political reform, rescind the state of emergency, and curtail the activities of the security services. Human rights advocates organized a demonstration outside the People's Assembly in March 2004 (Ghadbian 2006: 167). The reform campaign culminated in a May 2005 public meeting of the Jamil al-Atasi Forum in Damascus, at which a letter from the Muslim Brothers was read. This show of solidarity between liberal and Islamist critics of the regime prompted the security forces to shut down the forum and arrest its leading members. Still, five civic associations joined the Muslim Brothers in issuing a manifesto that October, known as the Damascus Declaration, which called on the authorities to tolerate greater pluralism in public life. The document set the stage for the formation in Paris five months later of the National Salvation Front, led by former vice president 'Abd al-Halim Khaddam.

Leaders of the Damascus Declaration initiative joined the Muslim Brothers in setting up the Syrian National Council in the fall of 2011. Prominent civil rights activists who argued that internal pressure was more likely than criticisms voiced outside the country to produce real reform formed the rival National Coordinating Committee of the Forces for Democratic Change (NCCFDC). Successive attempts to broker an alliance between the two groupings failed. As the 2011–2012 uprising steadily transformed into civil war, the NCCFDC and other proponents of nonviolent action found themselves alienated from the opposition camp and subjected to harsh measures by the authorities.

During the first years of the uprising, local councils sprang up in areas that fell out of the government's control. In Minbij, for instance, residents elected a Revolutionary Council to supervise public services. Most of the council's members were educated professionals; the council "marginalized the religious establishment because of [its] collaboration with the regime and its refusal to take a clear stance in support of the revolution" (Munif 2017: 5–6). The Revolutionary Council coordinated the activities of some fifty neighborhood committees, which took on the duties of the police and set up a 600-member Council of the Trustees of the Revolution to decide policy. Resistance to the new order arose from prominent families that had enjoyed close ties to the Baathi regime. Some of these families set up armed formations whose commanders refused to recognize the council's authority. Friction between the council and these militias, some of which affiliated with the FSA, reignited long-running interfamily feuds (Munif 2017: 8). Such feuding enabled the Battalions of the Free to take over the town, followed by the Assistance Front and the Islamic State. Similar trends can be found in many other parts of the country (Khalaf, Ramadan, and Stolleis 2014; al-Tamimi 2017; Sosnowski 2018; Schwab 2018). Islamist militants created parallel institutions in districts that fell into their hands (Heller 2016).

Political Economy

Throughout the nominally socialist years of the 1960s and 1970s, Syria maintained commercial and financial relations with the Western industrial economies. More than 44 percent of the country's exports were shipped to destinations in Organization for Economic Cooperation and Development (OECD) countries in 1970; this figure rose to over 54 percent in 1975 and then to 67 percent in 1980 (Lawson 1992: 202). Furthermore, and despite the Baathi regime's expressed commitment to building up local industry, the Syrian economy steadily evolved into a supplier of raw materials to overseas markets. Syria's most important primary exports—cotton and petroleum—made up half the value of total exports in 1972; three years later, they accounted for 82 percent of the total (Lawson 1992: 191).

Increased primary-goods production accompanied a rise in foreign direct investment. In 1977 a subsidiary of Royal Dutch Shell was awarded a concession to explore for oil, and two US companies were granted rights to drill in the high plains around Dair al-Zur. As a result of such activities, foreign investment in Syria, which had totaled US$43 million in 1970, jumped to US$89 million in 1975, exploded to US$587 million five years later, and reached US$754 million in 1985.

Moreover, the state-run industrial and commercial enterprises set up during Syria's socialist era began to operate according to principles of profit and loss. In 1975, state officials chartered a parastatal construction and engineering enterprise, the Military Housing Establishment (Milihouse), to coordinate building projects in both the military and civilian sectors. Each subsidiary of this establishment was given its own management and a high degree of autonomy with regard to investment decisions, which enabled it to operate as a virtual private company. Other state-run companies followed Milihouse's lead in relying on market forces, a trend that prompted growing disaffection among public sector workers (Longuenesse 1985).

Further measures designed to boost private enterprise were undertaken as the 1980s went on. Joint-stock farming companies were authorized in 1986; the next spring, private trading companies were allowed to export a wide range of agricultural and manufactured goods. The proportion of total trade moving through private hands jumped from 10 percent in the early 1980s to over 30 percent in 1988. The trend toward economic liberalization crested in May 1991 with the promulgation of a new investment law that permitted projects that increased jobs, reduced imports, or augmented exports to bring machinery into the country on a duty-free basis.

Syria profited handsomely from the regime's decision to join the anti-Iraq coalition in the 1990–1991 Gulf War. A flood of loans and grants washed into the local economy from Kuwait and Saudi Arabia. Improved relations with the United States and United Kingdom opened the door to greater credit and economic assistance, while the rise in world oil prices led to a surge in government revenues. State officials earmarked some of these resources for public sector projects but also stepped up support for private enterprise. By the mid-1990s private capital had moved into areas that had previously been reserved for the public sector.

Friction between the public and private sectors resurfaced in the late 1990s. The sharp drop in oil revenues after 1997, combined with two years of severe drought, created intense competition for investment monies. State officials tried to make up for falling oil income by opening the door to increased trade with Iraq. Damascus negotiated a series of agreements with Baghdad that sent processed food, textiles, and consumer goods to Iraq in exchange for cash payments and oil shipments under the terms of the UN-administered oil-for-food program. This trade revived production at state-run manufacturing plants and provided new opportunities for some private companies as well.

During the fall of 2000, Iraqi oil started to move across Syria in substantial quantities. Nevertheless, per capita gross domestic product began to slide, while unemployment increased, particularly in state-run industry. Government officials once again looked to private companies and entrepreneurs for relief. The return of higher oil prices beginning in late 2001 enabled the authorities to raise wages in the public sector and upgrade state-owned plants, but US military operations in Iraq in the spring of 2003 disrupted the flow of oil and sharply reduced investments from the Arab Gulf states.

Developments during 2004–2005 heightened the importance of the private sector. On one hand, the government negotiated an economic partnership agreement with the European Union, which included provisions that accelerated the shift from a state-led to a market-driven economic order. On the other, the tenth Regional (Syrian) Congress of the Baath Party, which took place in Damascus in June 2005, adopted a resolution that called for the creation of a "social market economy" to supplant the existing "state socialist" system. Informed observers estimated that such a transformation would require the domestic economy to grow at a rate of 7 percent annually and obligate the private sector to generate more than 150,000 jobs each year, if an acceptable degree of social stability were to be maintained. Such projections appeared overly optimistic in light of the facts that private enterprise accounted for only about one-third of Syria's total capital formation and that no more than 10 percent of private companies employed more than five workers each.

Meanwhile, state officials encouraged public sector enterprises to form partnerships with private companies (Abboud and Lawson 2012). New public-private partnerships took shape in housing, electricity generation, water and sanitation, and construction. Even as such ventures injected dynamism into the cities, severe drought gripped the farmlands of the northeast. By the fall of 2009, extensive areas of al-Raqqah and al-Hasakah came to resemble dust bowls, and their residents migrated to the outskirts of Aleppo, Homs, and Damascus. Problems in rural areas were compounded when yellow rust struck the wheat fields of al-Hasakah in the summer of 2010 and destroyed half of the harvest.

As popular unrest escalated during early 2011, the government raised salaries for public sector workers and increased subsidies on heating fuel and cooking oil. The next summer, state officials announced plans to rejuvenate the public sector, and the Eleventh Five-Year Plan included substantial new investment for state-run manufacturing companies. A General Organization for Desert Management and Development was created to manage the country's expansive wastelands. Despite such initiatives, prices for food, sugar, and other staples skyrocketed. By the spring of 2012, there were reports that farmers who had fled to the cities were returning to the countryside to escape the violence.

Syria's domestic economic order fragmented as the uprising transformed into a civil war. Local militia commanders, both pro-government and anti-regime, took charge of the distribution of goods in most areas outside Damascus, central Homs, and the Mediterranean coast (Yazigi 2014). Supplying scarce food, cooking oil, fuel, and medicine to beleaguered civilians proved particularly lucrative and gave fighters a strong incentive to capture crossing points along the borders with Turkey and Lebanon. Rival formations sometimes worked out collaborative arrangements to share the income generated by the transit fees collected at these stations, as the Unity Brigade and the FSA's Northern Storm Brigade did at the Bab al-Salamah entry north of Aleppo (Abboud 2017). In many districts commanders imposed informal taxes to support their units' tactical operations and fund rudimentary public services. Brokers with connections to state officials and/or local fighters amassed sizable fortunes as the civil war persisted. Meanwhile, foreign investment in Syria plunged, with the notable exception of purchases of abandoned property by Iran-based development companies.

The Impact of International Politics

External influences have played only a marginal role in shaping the overall development of the Syrian economy. The trend toward economic liberalization that gained momentum in the 1980s accompanied a sharp drop in trade and investment on the part of the wealthy capitalist countries (Lawson 1992: 189). Conversely, the collapse of the Soviet Union, which had become Syria's primary trading partner during the late 1980s, had only a minor impact on the local economy: Syrian products quickly found other markets in the former communist countries of Eastern Europe and the Caucasus (Lawson 1994). Furthermore, foreign trade made up such a minor part of total economic activity that even major transformations in the global economic order left domestic producers and consumers alike largely unaffected. Consequently, Syria suffered less than one might have imagined from the financial and commercial disruptions that shook the world economy during the first decade of the twenty-first century.

More significant consequences can be traced to the continual state of war that engulfed Syria in the decades after 1948. Ongoing conflict with Israel, along with sporadic armed confrontations with Iraq and Turkey and the 1975–1990 civil war in Lebanon, dramatically raised the stakes of domestic politics. Defeat in the 1948 war with Israel inspired disaffected military commanders to overthrow the parliamentary order and inaugurate a single-party system. Equally important, political contestation came to be seen as a threat to national unity and thereby detrimental to the struggle against Zionism. Efforts by liberal parties and organizations to resist military rule could, therefore, be framed as seditious by military commanders, who justified authoritarian governance on the grounds that extraordinary measures were required to protect national security.

Furthermore, perpetual warfare put an inordinate share of the country's material resources in the hands of the military establishment. The size of the armed forces jumped from 80,000 troops in 1970 to 430,000 in the early 1990s (Perthes 2000: 152). Total troop strength reached a peak of 820,000 in 2000 (Cordesman 2006: 333). To support this expansion in personnel, military spending soared from approximately 10 percent of gross domestic product in the late 1970s to more than 20 percent in the late 1980s. Meanwhile, pivotal components of the "regime structure itself have been reorganized along quasi-military, hierarchical lines" (Perthes 2000: 154). Both the Baath Party and the party-affiliated popular organizations abandoned deliberative decisionmaking procedures in the 1960s and 1970s and started to act as transmission belts for directives issued from commanders at the top.

Successive Baath Party–led governments made use of external crises to maintain their hold on power. Political-economic challenges at home led the doctrinaire Baathi regime of Salah Jadid to mobilize the home front for war against Israel in 1966–1967, just as the pragmatic regime of Hafiz al-Asad responded to internal problems by intervening in the Lebanese civil war in 1975–1976 (Lawson 1996). In each case, military initiatives directed outside set the stage for policies that heightened state intervention in the local economy. More important, mobilizing the populace for external warfare accompanied tighter supervision of labor activists, Islamist militants, and other dissidents. In this way, the persistence of armed conflict with external adversaries played a central role in the maintenance of Baathi rule.

Foreign actors became entrenched in local affairs during the 2011–2018 civil war. Qatar, Saudi Arabia, and Turkey provided financial backing for early FSA units, while fighters from throughout the Middle East, North Africa, and the Caucasus flocked to join radical Islamist formations. On the pro-government side, Hezbollah cadres played a crucial role in combating the FSA and Islamist militants in the southern and central provinces; militias sponsored by Iraq and Iran guarded symbolically important monuments around Damascus and assisted government troops in recapturing Aleppo; and Russian warplanes and helicopter gunships provided the air support that enabled the Syrian armed forces to regain the upper hand after 2016. Hezbollah and Moscow both announced plans to remain present after the fighting stopped. Meanwhile, Iranian enterprises invested in infrastructure and manufacturing, and gained possession of properties earmarked for postwar commercial development.

Religion and Politics

Syria's branch of the Muslim Brothers originated in the late 1930s, when severe economic problems led well-to-do Sunnis in the cities to set up a variety of political and social associations. Some of these were benevolent societies, headed by religious scholars who had received formal training in Islamic law. During World War II, one of these societies moved from Aleppo to Damascus, where it merged with other Islamist groups and, at a 1944 congress, rechristened itself the Muslim Brothers. In the summer of 1946, the organization elected Mustafa al-Siba'i, a prominent scholar from Damascus, to be its first general supervisor.

In the beginning, the Syrian Muslim Brothers championed a platform that called on the government to nurture Islamic morals, reform the state bureaucracy by applying laws and regulations in an unbiased way, and strive for national independence. These objectives were disseminated through schools and periodicals sponsored by the organization. The first manifestos published by the Muslim Brothers offered no detailed plan of action but underscored the broad goals of combating popular ignorance, immorality, and deprivation, and establishing a fully independent Syria whose political and legal systems did not discriminate along sectarian lines as they did under the French.

After the 1948 war, the Muslim Brothers gained a larger following in the cities and towns, especially in Damascus, where candidates endorsed by the organization won a fifth of the parliamentary seats throughout the 1950s. Intense rivalry among radical parties led the Muslim Brothers to formulate a package of economic reforms in the mid-1950s that pointed in the direction of "Islamic socialism." Deeply suspicious of Egyptian-style Arab socialism, the Muslim Brothers actively supported Syria's 1961 secession from the UAR.

Following the 1963 coup d'état, the Muslim Brothers opposed the economic and social policies that were carried out by the Baath Party. These policies undercut large landowners, wealthy merchants, and private industrialists, but more important, they jeopardized the livelihoods of the shopkeepers and small-scale manufacturers who formed the organization's primary constituency. Religious figures connected to the Muslim Brothers mobilized repeated protests against the government, centered in Aleppo, Hama, and Homs. Following Syria's defeat in the 1967 war and the rise of the more pragmatic wing of the Baath, however, a split developed inside the organization. Militants based in Aleppo and Hama pressed for armed struggle against the regime; they were countered by the Damascus-centered followers of ʻIsam al-ʻAttar, who had replaced al-Sibaʻi as general supervisor in 1957. The moderate wing under al-ʻAttar saw a convergence of interest between the country's small-scale traders and manufacturers and the al-Asad leadership's commitment to private enterprise and willingness to solicit foreign investment.

The honeymoon between the al-Asad regime and the Damascus wing of the Muslim Brothers did not last long. When the authorities issued the overtly secular 1973 constitution, the Muslim Brothers orchestrated mass demonstrations, which forced the government to amend the document to stipulate that the head of state must be a Muslim. During the mid-1970s, northern militants gained the upper hand in the organization and instigated anti-regime violence as the Fighting Vanguard. This phase of the campaign against the Baath Party–dominated order is identified with the leadership of ʻAdnan Saʻd al-Din, a teacher from Hama who became general supervisor in a disputed election in 1971.

At first, the militants targeted high-ranking officials and armed forces commanders, particularly ones from the minority ʻAlawi community. But as the 1970s went by, the struggle expanded to include armed attacks on state facilities and symbols of Baathi rule, including local party offices, police stations, and military and security installations. The violence peaked with the June 1979 killing of eighty-three ʻAlawi cadets at the military academy in Aleppo; a cluster of mass demonstrations and boycotts in Aleppo, Hama, and Homs in March 1980; and an attempt on the life of President Hafiz al-Asad later that same year.

In the face of widespread violence, the authorities decreed in July 1980 that anyone connected with the Muslim Brothers would be sentenced to death. The regime then cracked down on the organization with its formidable armed forces and internal security services, in particular the elite military and intelligence units, whose ranks consisted almost exclusively of ʻAlawis. The Muslim Brothers regrouped in October 1980 under the banner of the Islamic Front in Syria. Mohammad al-Bayanuni, a respected member of the Sunni religious hierarchy in Aleppo, became the front's secretary-general, but its leading light remained ʻAdnan Saʻd al-Din. The chief ideologue of the Islamic Front was Saʻid Hawwa, a prolific religious scholar from Hama who, along with Saʻd al-Din, had been a leader of the northern militants.

Six years of violence culminated in a brutal confrontation between the Muslim Brothers and the Baathi regime in the Islamist stronghold of Hama. There, in February 1982, militants proclaimed an armed uprising and seized control of large parts of the city. It took elite military and security forces two weeks to crush the revolt, during which time they killed between 5,000 and 20,000 civilians and razed the central business district and historic grand mosque. The showdown dealt a devastating blow to the Muslim Brothers, whose post-Hama orientation is evident in the November 1980 manifesto of the Islamic Front in Syria. This document emphasizes the Syrian people's right to regain the basic political and civil liberties that they enjoyed during the constitutional period of the late 1940s and early 1950s. It calls for an independent judiciary, and for representative government based on the rule of law and mutual consultation between rulers and ruled. Islamic values and principles receive little emphasis.

During the early 1990s, contacts between the Muslim Brothers and the authorities took place, and in December 1995 the organization's general supervisor, 'Abd al-Fattah Abu Ghudah, returned to Damascus from Saudi Arabia. He pledged to refrain from overtly political activity and settled down to teach theology and Islamic law in Aleppo. Radical activists in London then elected 'Ali Sadr al-Din al-Bayanuni to the post of general supervisor. As the decade ended, prominent figures expressed increasingly accommodative sentiments. In August 1999 they issued a proclamation that called on the government to abandon autocratic rule and establish democracy, freedom, and political pluralism. Shortly after the election of Bashar al-Asad to the presidency, al-Bayanuni told reporters that the Brothers did not even have to be permitted to operate legally inside Syria; it would be enough to come up with some sort of "formula" that would allow the organization to "express its views" concerning public issues.

In May 2001, the Muslim Brothers published a Covenant of National Honor, which called for the creation in Syria of a "modern state," that is, "a state of rotation" in which "free and honest ballot boxes are the basis for the rotation of power between all the sons of the homeland." The document made no mention of consultation between the ruler and the ruled, or of instituting Islamic law. An April 2005 statement again demanded "free and fair elections" and the termination of the state of emergency. General Supervisor al-Bayanuni announced in January 2006 that the organization had joined the National Salvation Front (NSF) in a campaign to establish a liberal democratic system. The Muslim Brothers thus allied itself with the reformers who had issued the Damascus Declaration.

Radical Islamists upset with the London-based leadership for allying with the secular organizations that dominated the NSF revived the armed struggle in an effort to discredit al-Bayanuni and destabilize the regime. The security forces raided a house filled with weapons in May 2005, and a month later killed an alleged radical Islamist leader in a shoot-out in a suburb of Damascus. Armed clashes between Islamist militants and the security forces erupted in Hama that summer and outside Aleppo in December. Further raids on Islamist hideouts in the coastal mountains were reported during the spring of 2006.

In April 2009 the Muslim Brothers pulled out of the NSF. General Supervisor al-Bayanuni attributed the split to unrelenting criticism of the organization by secularists, along with disagreements over the appropriate way to respond to Israel's 2008 invasion of Gaza. That May an influential Islamist figure with ties to the regime was arrested on charges that he had held unauthorized discussions with Western diplomats. Further controversy occurred in June 2009 when the government promulgated a revised personal status law that mandated uniformity across religious communities regarding marriage, inheritance, and child custody.

Leaders of the Muslim Brothers at first ignored the popular protests of 2011–2012. Representatives of the organization took part in the initial meetings of the Syrian National Council but had no connections to the civil rights activists who led the uprising inside Syria. The turn from peaceful demonstrations to armed struggle accompanied a pronounced shift toward the use of sectarian rhetoric and symbols by anti-regime forces. By the winter of 2011–2012, the Muslim Brothers found itself challenged by more militant Islamists, most notably the Islamic Liberation Party. Senior figures of the Muslim Brothers met in Istanbul in March 2012 and drew up a revised covenant, which laid out a liberal platform that called for a political system based on the separation of executive, legislative, and judicial powers.

While the Muslim Brothers collaborated with liberal movements outside Syria under the auspices of the SNC, radical Islamist formations took charge of the struggle on the ground (Lund 2012). Most prominent was the Assistance Front for the People of Syria, which carried out car bombings in Damascus and Aleppo and had close links to the al-Qaeda–affiliated Islamic State of Iraq. More important was the Battalions of the Free of Syria, which emerged around Idlib at the end of 2011 and advocated replacing the Baathi regime with some kind of Islamic government. September 2011 saw the appearance of the Hawks of Syria in the Idlib countryside, which also championed an Islamic system of rule. As fighting raged around Aleppo during the summer of 2012, groups of foreign fighters appeared that had less clearly defined objectives, such as the Community of Believers Brigade, made up largely of Libyans, and the Dawn of Islam Movement, whose ranks included Chechens, Britons, and a variety of other expatriates.

Islamic notions of justice and community defense (jihad) permeated the uprising as the Battalions of the Free, the Unity Brigade, the Army of Islam, and the Assistance Front elbowed the Free Syrian Army aside and became more pronounced with the emergence of ISIL (Lister 2015). A handful of veterans of the Fighting Vanguard set up Muslim Brothers–affiliated units, which constituted the Committee of the Shields of the Revolution (Lefevre and El Yassir 2013). As the fighting dragged on, however, many fighters who had originally joined formations aligned with the FSA and Muslim Brothers switched to radical Islamist militias. The leadership of the Muslim Brothers kept its distance from the militants, although it provided some support for the Battalions of the Free in its early struggle against the Assistance Front and the Islamic State (Lund 2013: 20–21). Beginning in 2012–2013, the Muslim Brothers took steps to win adherents among younger activists inside Syria and made overtures to members of the country's heterodox ʻAlawi, Ismaʻili, and Shiʻi communities (Lefevre 2013).

Identity and Politics

Syria's mountainous coast, hardscrabble southern hill country, and far-flung northeastern plains have provided safe haven for a remarkable collection of ethnic and sectarian communities. The great majority of Syrians are Arabic-speaking Sunni Muslims. Yet ʻAlawi, Ismaʻili, Shiʻi, and Christian communities flourish in the isolated valleys adjacent to the Mediterranean Sea. Districts southeast of Damascus are settled predominantly by Druze, alongside smaller concentrations of Shiʻites and Circassians. Kurds, Turkmen, and Yazidis can be found in sizable numbers in the northeastern provinces. Kurds join Armenians, Greek Orthodox Christians, and Maronite Catholics in the heterogeneous northern metropolis of Aleppo. And a vibrant Shiʻi district sits alongside a cluster of ancient Christian neighborhoods inside the walls of the old city of Damascus.

Minority groups have long played a crucial role in Syrian politics. Armed resistance to the imposition of French rule immediately after World War I galvanized ʻAlawis in the west, Kurds in the north, and Druze in the south in defense of the nationalist leadership in Damascus (Provence 2005; Tejel 2009). After local resistance was crushed, the French administration organized the country along sectarian lines during the 1920s and set up autonomous ʻAlawi and Druze states as a way to weaken residual Arab nationalist sentiment. More important, French military commanders recruited heavily among the comparatively disadvantaged ʻAlawi, Ismaʻili, and Druze communities to staff the auxiliary regiments upon which French domination rested (Bou Nacklie 1993).

At independence in 1946, the doors to the military academy were thrown open to all citizens, and Sunnis achieved a predominant position in the armed forces in general and within the officer corps in particular. Persistent discrimination against ‘Alawis, Isma‘ilis, and Druze in society at large nevertheless nurtured feelings of alienation and resentment among cadets and officers alike, and minority soldiers ended up gravitating toward such radical movements as the Baath Party and the Syrian Social National Party (Drysdale 1979). It was officers from the social and geographical fringes of Syrian society who carried out the coups d'état of the late 1940s and early 1950s, and who later engineered the March 1963 revolution. And it is generally agreed that the doctrinaire socialist leadership that seized power in February 1966 was more markedly ‘Alawi in composition than any previous collection of politically active officers. In fact, one can construct a persuasive account of the recurrent rivalries inside the armed forces that shaped Syrian politics from 1949 to 1970 in almost exclusively sectarian terms (Van Dam 1996).

Beyond the confines of the barracks, however, sectarian mobilization tended to be heavily muted. Armenians and other Christians did their best to maintain the solidarity of their respective communities but made a point of refraining from any sort of communal political activity. This was partly out of fear of attracting the attention of the security forces, but even more due to an underlying worry that the most likely alternative to Baathi rule would be an avowedly Islamist order that would tightly restrict the economic and social opportunities they enjoyed in a relatively secularist system. In a similar fashion, the Kurds found themselves better treated and more fully assimilated in Syria than in any of the surrounding countries and only rarely protested the Baath Party's campaign to convince the populace to abandon "outdated" ethnic and sectarian identities (Tejel 2009: 63–64).

Growing economic difficulties in the countryside sparked a series of clashes in November 2000 between the settled Druze population of al-Suwaida province and Sunni tribespeople. The fighting engulfed Sunni villages in the area, whose inhabitants were rumored to be sympathetic to the tribes. Lightly armed security forces attempted to impose a curfew, but failed. It was only when armored vehicles and elite military units from the capital intervened that order was restored. Members of the Druze community then organized protests not only in the provincial capital but also in front of the interior ministry in Damascus. A further demonstration involved some 200 Druze students on the campus of Damascus University. Attacks on Druze farmers at the end of the month precipitated another burst of unrest in al-Suwaida, which prompted the provincial governor to release members of the Druze community who had been detained after the initial clashes.

Some three years later, the influence of Kurdish nationalists in Iraq emboldened the Kurds of northeastern Syria to engage in renewed activism. During a March 2004 football (soccer) match in the city of al-Qamishli, Kurdish fans taunted the supporters of the visiting Arab team by waving a Kurdish flag and chanting slogans in support of US president George W. Bush. Some of the Arab team's supporters reacted by shouting pro–Saddam Hussein slogans, then attacked the Kurds with makeshift weapons (Gauthier 2009). News of the clash sparked rioting in nearby towns, during the course of which hundreds of Kurds were arrested by the security forces. On the one-year anniversary of the incident, Kurdish activists staged a sit-in outside the High Court in Damascus and demanded an end to the long-running state of emergency. This protest was broken up by club-wielding cadres of the Baath Party–affiliated students' federation.

When Jalal Talebani of the Patriotic Union of Kurdistan was elected president of Iraq in April 2005, Kurds in Damascus took to the streets to celebrate. A leading Kurdish figure, Mohammad Ma'shuq al-Khaznawi, went so far as to tell Agence France-Presse that "either the [Syrian] regime must change or the regime must go. . . . The reason I and others can speak out is because the Americans are trying to get rid of dictators and help the oppressed" (June 2, 2005). Al-Khaznawi disappeared on May 10, prompting a further round of large-scale demonstrations in al-Qamishli. The security forces responded by arresting not only those suspected of instigating the protests but also the country's remaining civil rights activists.

Ethno-sectarian antagonism increased as a result of the flood of refugees from Iraq after 2003. The first wave consisted almost entirely of Sunni Arabs, including senior members of the Iraqi Baath Party (Fagen 2009: 14). Later arrivals came from Iraq's disadvantaged Shi'i community and tended to be poorer than the individuals and families who had come before. The Syrian authorities permitted the refugees to obtain medical care at public hospitals and send their children to public schools, leaving these institutions less able to accommodate the needs of Syrian citizens. Furthermore, the influx of Iraqis, particularly in and around Damascus, caused housing and staples prices to soar. The rising cost of living, combined with a notable jump in criminal activity, galvanized popular resentment and animosity against the new Iraqi residents (Fagen 2009: 19).

Intersectarian animosity escalated sharply as the 2011–2012 uprising turned into a civil war. Members of the 'Alawi community, wealthy and impoverished alike, tended to rally behind the regime, while clashes between 'Alawis and Sunnis in the coastal provinces and the countryside around Idlib became increasingly frequent and bloody. Mixed neighborhoods of Homs and adjacent villages scattered across the Ghab plain of Hama province splintered along sectarian lines (Nakkash 2013), disrupting economic and social relationships that had joined their inhabitants together for decades.

By the summer of 2012, the Kurdish population of northeastern Syria had been drawn into the conflict. The military wing of the Democratic Union Party, the Popular Protection Units, took charge of areas that fell out of government control from al-Qamishli in the east to ‘Afrin in the west; PYD activists set up autonomous local councils to administer these districts. Eleven rival Kurdish parties, including the Freedom Party, coalesced into the Kurdish National Council in an attempt to offset the growing influence of the PYD. At the same time, the Kurdish Union Party aligned with the NCCFDC; the Kurdish Future Movement, by contrast, initially worked with the Syrian National Council but broke away when it became clear that the SNC had no interest in considering Kurdish autonomy. The PYD set up the People's Council for Western Kurdistan in an attempt to unify these disparate parties, but it remained paralyzed by infighting. The Kurdistan Regional Government in northern Iraq also tried to reconcile the competing factions and managed to craft an agreement whereby their respective militias would be replaced by unarmed protection committees (*The National* [Abu Dhabi], July 15, 2012). Nevertheless, PYD activists in October 2012 criticized the "traitors" inside the Kurdish community who they alleged were cooperating with the FSA, and armed clashes took place between Kurdish fighters and FSA units in Aleppo and the strategically located town of Ras al-‘Ain on the Turkish border.

External threats from the FSA and ISIL enabled the PYD to assert control over the lands guarded by the YPG. The PYD in November 2013 created three large cantons out of this territory, each one of which was accorded an elected legislative body, an executive council, and a dense network of municipal and district councils (Lowe 2014; Khalaf 2016). Tension between the PYD and Kurdish National Council led to the creation of an overarching Supreme Kurdish Council, while friction between Kurdish and non-Kurdish residents prompted the PYD to set up a multicommunal organization, the Movement for a Democratic Society (TEV-DEM). In March 2016 the three cantonal legislatures ratified a joint federal arrangement loosely connected to the central administration in Damascus. Fighting erupted shortly thereafter between YPG cadres and the remaining Syrian government troops in al-Qamishli. Pockets of popular resistance to PYD dominance persisted as well, particularly in districts less threatened by Islamist militants, like the northern town of ‘Amudah.

Gender and Politics

Baathi socialism in principle champions the interests of women and promises to protect families from the injustices inherent in capitalist patriarchy. The party's commitment to women's rights was most clearly evident during the mid-1960s, when a network of vocational schools and childcare centers opened in the cities and towns. The General Union of Women was set up under party auspices in 1967 to deal with issues and sponsor programs of particular concern to Syria's female population.

Programs instituted in the heyday of Baathi socialism laid the foundation for a dramatic expansion in women's participation in the labor force. The total number of paid female workers reached 804,000 in 2001—more than triple the figure two decades earlier. Half of women working outside the home were employed by the state, either in the bureaucracy or in public sector enterprises. About one-third worked in agriculture and forestry. Private sector industry employed some 7 percent, with the remainder found in the hospitality industry, real estate and banking/finance, construction, and transportation/communication (Zaman 2006: 154, 70).

In the political arena, the number of women seated in the People's Assembly rose steadily throughout the 1980s and 1990s. The biggest increase was evident in the 1981–1985 assembly, which served at the height of the struggle between the Baathi regime and the radical Islamists. In the 2003–2007 assembly, a woman won one of the independent seats—the first time that a female candidate had succeeded in the polls without being sponsored by one of the parties in the Progressive National Front. That same session saw the first woman elected as a parliamentary officer, specifically to the post of secretary. Women have served as government ministers since 1976, when a female was appointed to the post of minister of culture. Fifteen years later, two women held ministerial office, as minister of culture and minister of higher education.

Legal obstacles to full equality between men and women nevertheless remain firmly in place. The current citizenship law recognizes the offspring of a Syrian man and a non-Syrian woman as a Syrian national, even if the child happens to be born outside the country. By contrast, children of Syrian women and non-Syrian men are not recognized as citizens, even if they are born on Syrian territory. Similarly, men enjoy the exclusive right to initiate divorce proceedings, and females are only authorized to inherit one-half of what males inherit.

Faced with barriers to equal treatment under the law, Syrian women started to look outside the political arena for inspiration and redress. One source of succor begun in the 1960s was the Qubaisi movement, whose leader, Munira Qubaisi, resided in a quiet neighborhood of Damascus (Omar 2013). "The Miss" attracted disciples from many of the country's wealthiest and most prestigious families, including several well-known Islamic scholars. All of the movement's preachers were unmarried females, although the Qubaisis did not discourage young women from marrying. The movement actively promoted elementary education, particularly for girls, and sponsored the establishment of a large number of primary schools. Each school followed the curriculum mandated by the state but supplemented the official program of study with lessons in religion and morality. The exact precepts of the movement were known only to initiates, although they were said to combine the sophist ideas of Ibn 'Arabi and al-Hallaj with modern nationalist thought. Perhaps indicative of the appeal of this potent mix of religious mysticism and social activism is the fact that a prominent figure in the order was Amirah Jibril, the sister of the longtime secretary-general of the Popular Front for the Liberation of Palestine General Command.

Gender politics played out in contradictory ways during the uprising and civil war that broke out in early 2011 (Human Rights Watch 2014). Female protesters and fighters, particularly in the Kurdish forces, played an active part in the drama. The 'Alawi actress Fadwa Sulaiman inspired the crowds at early rallies in Homs. Women kept vital public services functioning in devastated areas denuded of men. Yet the SNC proved unable to fill the 30 percent quota of female delegates that it mandated for itself. The Assistance Front broke up women's centers in the territories it controlled, whereas the Islamic State assigned tasks to female cadres. Finally, women made up a large proportion of the writers, journalists, and bloggers who passed news about the war to the outside world.

19
Turkey

Marcie J. Patton

By 5:00 p.m. on Sunday, June 24, 2018, a record-breaking turnout of 86.2 percent of eligible Turkish voters, which included those living abroad, had cast ballots for both presidential and parliamentary elections. It was unprecedented to hold these elections simultaneously. For President Recep Tayyip Erdoğan and the opposition, the stakes had never been higher. A victory in the presidential race would seal Erdoğan's grip on power until 2028 (assuming he'd be reelected in 2023 for a second term), and it would transform Turkey's parliamentary system into an imperial presidency tantamount to one-man executive rule. Yet the playing field was distinctly skewed due to extreme bias in media coverage (the government controlled at least 90 percent of the media outlets), as well as restrictions on freedom of assembly and association (the government had renewed a state of emergency for the seventh time since the failed 2016 coup). The opposition was further disadvantaged by sixteen years of incumbency by the Justice and Development Party (Adalet ve Kalkınma Partisi, AKP), and Erdoğan's unmatched popularity.

Once the votes were tabulated, Erdoğan bested five opposing candidates in the presidential race with a commanding 52.6 percent of the popular vote. His AKP fell short of a one-party parliamentary majority, but by combining its seats together with those of its postelection alliance partner the Nationalist Movement Party (Milliyetçi Hareket Partisi, MHP), the AKP was able to secure control of parliament. Ultimately, however, having a parliamentary majority was of diminished importance because a new constitution went into effect immediately that replaced Turkey's parliamentary system with an executive presidential system—one that significantly curtailed legislative powers. In a referendum called a year earlier, voters approved the revised constitution by a slim margin (51.4 percent). These elections were the first to be held since then.

Turkey faces a conundrum. In spite of the persistence of electoral democracy, for the past ten of his fifteen years in power Erdoğan has acted like an autocratic ruler. Will the new sultanic powers of the presidency embolden him to consolidate an authoritarian regime in Turkey? When the Arab Spring uprisings erupted in 2011, Turkey was hyped as a democratic model for the Middle East. So, how, when, and why did Turkey come to be regarded, as Steven A. Cook, senior fellow at the US Council on Foreign Relations, aptly phrased it, "a case study in democratic reversal"?

Historical Background and Contemporary Political Structure

Modern Turkey emerged out of the collapse of the Ottoman Empire after World War I and remarkably was never colonized by any Western power. The Allied Powers' intention was to dismember the empire; however, unexpectedly, a national independence movement surfaced and, after two grueling years of fighting, was victorious and declared a republic. Together with his followers, Mustafa Kemal—the charismatic leader of the liberation struggle who was later bestowed with the honorific surname Atatürk (Father of the Turks)—made Westernization the state's chief political project. As Atatürk told the nation in 1933, on the tenth anniversary of the Turkish republic, his aim was to lift Turkey to the level of the most prosperous and civilized countries of the world. To this end, Atatürk and his followers initiated a program of radical social and cultural change, modeling the new republic on nationalist, secularist, and progressive lines, similar to what they observed in Europe.

What was distinctive about Atatürk and his supporters (referred to as Kemalists) was their radical ambition to construct a state and mold a society utterly disconnected from the Ottoman past, and their belief that it was imperative for Turkey to catch up to the West in the shortest time possible. The Kemalists were in a hurry to stomp out religious reactionism and did not hesitate to use force to suppress religious opposition. They introduced secularizing reforms not only to copy the "progressive" West but also to undermine Islamic "backwardness." Kemalist secularism has been termed "radical" or "militant" because its purpose was to exert state control over religion by excluding religion from public life (but not extinguishing personal belief), as opposed to the separation of religion and state, which is the Anglo-American understanding.

The first secularizing reform to be introduced was the abolition of the caliphate (1924), which was the spiritual symbol of power in the Ottoman Empire. This was followed by the adoption of a secular educational system; assignment of control over mosques, imams, and religious affairs to a state body; and closure of Islamic brotherhoods (*tarikats*). In addition, the Kemalists replaced the Islamic calendar with the European one, changed the alphabet from Arabic to Latin script, and made the weekly day of rest Sunday instead of Friday. They strongly discouraged veiling and prohibited men from wearing the traditional male headgear, the fez. The legal system too was secularized, with the Swiss civil code replacing Ottoman family law, which had been based on sharia (Islamic law).

Atatürk was impatient to unify the citizenry, but not around a Muslim national identity. Consequently Turkish nationalism replaced Islam as the unifying bonding agent. The Kemalists sought to minimize differences and maximize similarities; they therefore considered every citizen inside Turkish borders to be a Turk. But because of their uncompromising view of the indivisibility of the Turkish territory and people, they refused to acknowledge the many ethnic minorities inside the country's borders. Regarding the country's largest minority group, the Kurds, Kemalist leaders banned the Kurdish language, dress, and names. They used military conscription in an effort to assimilate Kurdish youth, and when assimilation did not work, armed repression was applied. The price of Kemalism was the imposition on Turkish citizens of a monolithic, homogeneous national identity that excluded other identities.

Until 1945 democracy in Turkey had shallow roots. To restrict opposition to the Kemalist reforms, Atatürk constructed a system of one-party rule that remained in place even after his death in 1938. However, following World War II, pressures for democratization came from two directions: externally from the West, which considered Turkey a key ally in the unfolding Cold War, and internally from pressures to liberalize the economy and to allow multiparty competition. A group of politicians split off from the Republican People's Party (Cumhuriyet Halk Partisi, CHP), the party that Atatürk had founded, and formed the Democrat Party (Demokrat Partisi, DP), which ended the former's monopoly on power by winning a parliamentary majority in the 1950 election. The Democrat Party identified itself as the party of the common people and promised greater religious freedom and liberal economic policies.

Although the Democrat Party was careful to emphasize that it supported secularism and was credited with modernizing agricultural production and building up the country's industrial base, over time it became increasingly authoritarian and restrictive of political liberties. It also opened itself up to criticism by changing the call to prayer from Turkish back to Arabic and boasting about the number of new mosques built and religious schools opened. After a decade in power, the DP government was toppled by a military coup.

The military held a unique role in Turkey as guardian of the Kemalist reforms. Its pivotal position was a legacy of Atatürk, who relied on the officer corps as the main defender of the Kemalist project to construct a modern nation-state along secular, Western lines. Although the Turkish military in principle accepted the desirability of democracy and the legitimacy of civilian rule, its paramount mission was to maintain Kemalist ideals by preserving national unity and defending the country's territorial integrity.

In May 1960 the Turkish military accused the Democrat Party of deviating from Kemalist principles and seized power. Democratic civilian rule was restored the following year under the very liberal constitution of the second Turkish republic (1961–1980), which allowed the expression of diverse ideological views and spurred the growth of civil society. The two parties garnering the largest share of votes for the next two decades were the Justice Party (Adalet Partisi, AP), which stepped into the shoes of the banned Democrat Party, and the Republican People's Party. Elections were hotly contested, with anywhere from six to eight parties gaining seats in the bicameral parliament. However, the new freedoms also made possible the emergence of far-right and far-left militant groups, whose violent clashes with one another and with authorities played a role in growing social fractionalization. During the 1970s various steps were taken to check political terrorism, including a brief military "coup by memorandum" in 1971. Nevertheless, lawlessness and street killings escalated, and the economy began to stagnate. The ineffectiveness of short-lived, unruly coalition governments also contributed to the mounting political polarization and continued deterioration of the economy.

Claiming that the situation had spun out of control, the military intervened for a third time in September 1980. The generals blamed politicians for partisan squabbling and inaction and decried the "overly permissive" civil liberties and social rights granted by the 1961 constitution. They banned all political parties, suspended the constitution, dissolved trade unions, and closed down civil society organizations—in particular women's, student, and human rights associations. Their harshest measures were directed at leftists, who suffered extended imprisonment, abuse, and torture.

The coup leaders oversaw the drafting of a new constitution in 1982, which in stark contrast to the 1961 constitution moved the regime in an illiberal direction, subordinating civil society to the state by restricting free expression and associational activities. Individual rights and liberties were subject to annulment and suspension on a range of nebulous grounds (threats to public order, national interest, national security, or public health); voluntary associations and trade unions were banned from engaging in any kind of political activity; and the education system was placed under tight state control, with universities administered by the state-appointed Higher Education Council (YÖK). The new constitution created a bounded electoral democracy by making it easy to close political parties and ban politicians from politics.

The 1983 election marked the beginning of the third Turkish Republic and the resumption of parliamentary politics, which featured a unicameral legislature. The newly formed center-right Motherland Party (Anavatan Partisi, ANAP) won and managed to maintain a majority in government until 1993 in spite of its unwieldy amalgam of religious conservatives and neoliberal secularists. Turkish voters have typically supported center-right parties like ANAP; however, once the ban on political activities by pre-1980 political leaders was lifted in the late 1980s, the center-right divided into two parties and the center-left into three. Turkey entered into a period of unstable coalition governments that lasted until the AKP's sensational win in 2002.

In the 1990s frustration with the failure of centrist parties on both the right and the left to deal effectively with economic and social problems translated into high levels of voter volatility. Turkey was caught in a double bind. On the one hand (until the 2018 elections) only parties that mustered 10 percent of the national vote could be seated in the National Assembly. The effect of this high electoral threshold was to deny representation to small parties (especially Kurdish parties). On the other hand, because Turkish parties are overwhelmingly personality-based, party leaders refused to either merge with other parties sharing similar views or to form cross-party alliances. The result was increasing ideological fragmentation of the party system as an ever-greater number of parties competed for office, making parliamentary majorities all but impossible to realize.

However, the unexpected happened on November 3, 2002. Not one of the five incumbent political parties garnered enough votes to enter parliament, whereas a newly formed party with Islamist origins—the AKP—received 34.3 percent of the vote, capturing 363 of the 550 seats. The adamantly secularist CHP was the only other party to enter parliament, with 19.4 percent of the vote and 178 seats. The AKP's landslide victory gave Turkey its first single-party government in over a decade and, for the first time since the 1954 election, a two-party parliament.

Subsequently, electoral competition entered a new phase in Turkey. Only three parties passed the 10 percent threshold in the 2007 and 2011 elections: the AKP, CHP, and MHP. The same three parties won seats in the 2015 and 2018 elections. They were joined in June 2015 by the Kurdish nationalist Democratic People's Party (Demokratik Halk Partisi, DEHAP) and in 2018 by the pro-minority Peoples' Democratic Party (Halk Demokratik Partisi, HDP), and the Good Party (Iyi Partisi), formed by defectors from the MHP. Table 19.1 displays the results of

Table 19.1 General Election Results in Turkey, 2002–2018

	Percentage of Popular Vote						Number of Parliamentary Seats[b]					
Party[a]	2002	2007	2011	06/2015	11/2015	2018	2002	2007	2011	06/2015	11/2015	2018
Justice and Development Party (AKP)	34.27	46.6	49.8	40.87	49.49	42.56	363	341	327	258	317	295
Republican People's Party (CHP)	19.39	20.9	26.0	24.95	25.31	22.65	178	112[c]	135	132	134	146
Nationalist Movement Party (MHP)	8.34	14.3	13.0	16.29	11.90	11.1	—	71	53	80	40	49
People's Democracy Party (HDP)	—	—	—	13.12	10.76	11.7	—	—	—	80	59	67
Independent candidates	6.22	5.2	6.6	—	—	—	9	26[d]	35[d]	0	0	0
Good Party (IYI)	—	—	—	—	—	9.96	0	0	0	0	0	43
Felicity Party (SP)	2.48	2.3	1.3	2.06	0.68	1.34	0	0	0	0	0	0
Patriotic Party (VP)	—	—	—	0.35	0.25	0.23	0	0	0	0	0	0
Free Cause Party (HUDA PAR)	—	—	—	—	—	0.31	0	0	0	0	0	0

Sources: Turkiye Buyuk Millet Meclisi Bakanligi (TBMM), "3 Kasım 2002 Tarihli Milletvekili Genel Seçim Sonuçları Seçim Sistemi: Ülke Barajlı d'Hondt (%10)," www.tbmm.gov.tr; Turkiye Buyuk Millet Meclisi Bakanligi (TBMM), "22 Temmuz 2007 Tarihli Milletvekili Genel Seçim Sonuçları Seçim Sistemi: Ülke Barajlı d'Hondt (%10)," www.tbmm.gov.tr; "2011 Genel Seçim Sonuçları," www.haberler.com; "7 Haziran 2015 Genel Seçim Sonuçları," www.haberler.com; "1 Kasım 2015 Genel Seçim Sonuçları," www.haberler.com; "2018 Seçim Sonuçları," www.haberler.com.

Notes: a. Because a multitude of parties have come and gone in Turkey, only the parties that were listed on the ballot for the 2018 parliamentary elections are shown.

b. The total number of parliamentary seats was 550 in the 2002, 2007, 2011, and 2015 elections. In 2018 the number was raised to 600.

c. In 2007 the Democratic Left Party (DSP) formed an electoral alliance with the CHP. The thirteen seats that it won are included in the seat total of the CHP. Also in 2007 a CHP deputy resigned from the party and joined Independents.

d. The threshold system requires a party to win 10 percent of the national vote to obtain a seat in parliament. This is the highest electoral threshold in the world. As a result of the high threshold, Kurdish candidates have often run as Independents. Although the Kurdish Democratic People's Party (DEHAP) won only 6.2 percent of the vote in 2002, eight of its members secured seats as Independents. After DEHAP was banned, a new Kurdish party, the Democratic Society Party (DTP), formed, which obtained twenty-one of twenty-five seats won by Independents in 2007. The Kurdish DTP was soon banned, and its successor, the Peace and Democracy Party (BDP), picked up the thirty-five Independent seats in 2011. After doing well in Kurdish areas in the 2014 local elections, the BDP decided to broaden its appeal by merging with the newly formed HDP in running candidates at the national level. As the table shows, the HDP has passed the threshold in every national election since it was formed.

parliamentary elections in Turkey from 2002 to 2018. Table 19.2 classifies the ideological stance of the political parties that ran in the 2018 elections.

The AKP is a party with clear Islamic roots, but it has pragmatically positioned itself on the center-right and is best described as a populist party. When it first came to power in 2002 it straddled a broad coalition that included many liberal voters who looked favorably on the party's pro-democratic reform agenda, pro–European Union (EU) stance, and pro–free market orientation. The AKP was also embraced by traditional religious voters who resented the secularist restrictions on religious freedom, as well as by poorly educated, low-income voters living in urban shantytowns and rural areas who suffered from a dearth of social services and welfare programs in their communities. While liberals have since deserted the AKP over its growing autocratic tendencies, the party's continuing popularity is best explained by its record of success on bread-and-butter issues, its hard-line nationalist stance on issues deemed to pose security threats (such as Kurdish nationalism), and the appeal of Erdoğan's personal piety.

Kemal Kılıçdaroğlu leads the CHP, the party founded by Atatürk and the main opposition party to the AKP. It claims to be a left-of-center, social democratic party, although until Kılıçdaroğlu became party chairman in 2010 it was known for dogmatically upholding Kemalist secularism and Turkish nationalism. Under Kılıçdaroğlu's leadership the party has undergone a makeover. The "new CHP" has opted for a more conventional social-democratic, populist platform that promises to focus

Table 19.2 Ideological Distribution of Political Parties in Turkey, 2018

Name	Orientation
Patriotic Party (VP)	Far-left, ultranationalist
People's Democracy Party (HDP)	Left, pro-Kurdish and minority rights
Independent Turkey Party (BTP)[a]	Center-left, Kemalist, nationalist
Republican People's Party (CHP)	Center-left, Kemalist, social democratic
Justice and Development Party (AKP)	Center-right, Islamist, nationalist
Democratic Party (DP)[a]	Center-right, Kemalist
Good Party (IYI)	Center-right, nationalist
Felicity Party (SP)	Far-right, Islamist
Nationalist Movement Party (MHP)	Far-right, ultranationalist
Grand Unity Party (BBP)[a]	Far-right, Islamist, ultranationalist
Free Cause Party (HUDA PAR)	Far-right, Sunni Islamist

Notes: These eleven parties were eligible to participate in the 2018 general elections.

a. These three parties chose not to field candidates. The BTP chose to boycott the election, whereas BBP candidates ran on the AKP's list, and DP candidates appeared on the CHP list but supported the IYI party's candidate for president.

on fixing the economy by lowering unemployment and transforming Turkey into a high-tech hub. Its core voter base is composed of Western-oriented, secular, urban, middle-class professionals, as well as members of the minority Alevi community. Regionally its strongest support comes from towns along the Aegean coast and Turkey's third-largest city, Izmir.

The ultranationalist MHP was founded in 1969. Led by Devlet Bahçeli since 1997, it emphasizes a homogeneous Turkish national identity. It views Kurdish nationalism solely through the lens of terrorism and opposes any form of Kurdish autonomy. It is against Turkey's open-door policy for Syrian refugees. And it takes a hard line on the Cyprus issue. Turkey invaded Cyprus in 1974 and the island has remained divided since then. Turkish membership in the EU would be conditional on recognition of Cyprus (i.e., the southern half of the island), which was admitted to the EU in 2004. The MHP vehemently defends the independence of the Turkish Republic of North Cyprus and holds the view that the whole of Cyprus belongs to Turkey. The MHP draws votes from pious, conservative nationalists living in rural areas and small towns, putting it in competition with the AKP. Disgruntled AKP voters generally swing to the MHP, which is what happened in the 2018 parliamentary elections. The AKP's loss was the MHP's gain. The Anatolian and the Black Sea regions tend to divide their support between the MHP and the AKP.

The IYI party, which broke away from the MHP in 2017, tends to be more secularist, less Islamically oriented, and more pro-Western than the MHP. Its fate is uncertain as after the 2018 elections its leader, Meral Akşener, a former interior minister from the MHP, stepped down as party leader. The MHP subsequently invited the party's newly elected members of parliament to consider rejoining the MHP.

The pro-Kurdish HDP has tried to differentiate itself from its pro-Kurdish predecessors by seeking to broaden support beyond its ethnic base (located mainly in southeastern Turkey) to include those who back representation and rights for minorities and desire safeguards on democratic freedoms. Although the party calls for a peaceful and democratic resolution to the Kurdish question and is the second-largest opposition party in Turkey, many leading members of the party are in jail, accused of ties to the banned PKK (Kurdistan Workers' Party). Indeed the HDP's leader, Selahattin Demirtaş, ran in the 2018 presidential elections from jail.

Following President Erdoğan's victory in the June 24, 2018, election, a presidential system went into effect ending ninety-five years of parliamentary rule. As in any presidential system, the president serves as both head of state and head of government, chooses a cabinet of ministers, and appoints senior civil servants. There is no prime minister. In Turkey, the president is also empowered to appoint an unspecified number of vice presidents.

The parliament has been expanded from 550 to 600 seats and is to be elected every five years (instead of four) in general elections held in tandem with presidential elections. The president's term of office is likewise five years, with a two-term limit. Although Erdoğan has already served one term, the new changes reset the clock, affording him the possibility of continuing on as president until 2028. Lawmakers will not be permitted to serve in the cabinet, which means that a parliamentarian would have to resign his or her seat if appointed to the cabinet.

What makes the Turkish executive presidency so controversial is that it removes the checks and balances that are customarily found in presidential systems that, as a rule, are based on the separation and sharing of powers among the executive, legislative, and judicial branches of government. In Turkey's new system, the president may issue decrees and dissolve parliament without its approval and call for a state of emergency or new elections at will. The president also controls the appointments of more than half of the judges to the nation's highest court. Critics point out that the ability of parliament to make the executive accountable is significantly curtailed, and the independence of the judiciary is likely to be significantly undermined. Power has not been so hypercentralized in the hands of one person since Atatürk founded the republic.

Some of these changes formalize what were informal practices, thus it can be said that the new executive powers essentially ratify Erdoğan's consolidation of power. It is also the case that what once were the key strongholds safeguarding the Kemalist formulation of secularism—the military, the judiciary, and the universities—now are under the thumb of the new president, who has free rein to appoint the top officers of the Turkish Armed Forces (TAF), university chancellors, as well as judges and prosecutors—without being subject to parliamentary approval.

There are potential limits on the president's exercise of power. For example, parliament can overturn a presidential decree, or refuse to approve the budget proposed by the president. However, these blockages require a simple majority (301 votes), which the opposition did not obtain in the 2018 election.

Religion and Politics

The rise of political Islam in Turkey is a consequence of its forced marginalization during the one-party period. Kemalist statebuilders implemented projects and reforms to reduce the influence of Islam in the everyday lives of people. Yet despite their efforts to modernize religiocultural traditions, an Islamic identity was never extinguished among the population at large.

The shift from one-party to multiparty politics in 1946 opened the door to the emergence of political Islam. In the 1950s rapid urbanization, the mechanization of agriculture, and rural-to-urban migration produced dramatic transformations in the economy and in social interactions, generating constituencies for a politicized Islam. The electoral success of the Democrat Party in 1950, 1954, and 1957 derived in part from its skillful use of religion to attract conservative, religious voters (e.g., restoring the call to prayer to Arabic from Turkish).

Necmettin Erbakan formed the first overtly pro-religion political party, the National Order Party (Milli Nizam Partisi, MNP) in 1969. After it was closed in the 1971 military intervention, he resurrected it as the National Salvation Party (Milli Selamet Partisi, MSP) in time for the 1973 elections. Erbakan founded a political ideology, the National View (Milli Görüş, MG), that emphasized strengthening Islamic morals, a greater role for the state in the economy, and closer ties with Muslim countries. His ideas found support among small-town shopkeepers, traders, and craftspeople suffering from social and economic dislocation caused by skyrocketing prices and shortages of fuel and goods when the Turkish economy contracted in the 1970s. The MG's anti-imperialist, anti-Western stance was also popular among marginalized urban and rural populations. While branded an Islamic fundamentalist because of his inflammatory rhetoric, Erbakan eschewed radical Islam and was willing to work within the existing political system. The MSP participated as a junior partner in three coalition governments with secular parties during the violence-racked seventies, a period that saw pitched street battles between armed socialist militants and ultra-right nationalists.

After the 1980 coup, a confluence of three factors gave fresh momentum to the rise of political Islam: the state's Turkish-Islamic synthesis strategy, the effects of the liberal economic policies of Prime Minister Turgut Özal, and the exceptional organizing skills of Islamist parties. The (then) pro-secular military was alarmed by the Islamic Revolution under way in neighboring Iran and, fearing its spread, sought to check the emergence of radical Islamist groups. At the same time, due to its strong anticommunist beliefs, the military felt it was necessary to curb the appeal of leftist ideologies. The military leaders turned to what they called the Turkish-Islamic Synthesis to engineer an alternative ideological basis for national identity. The new ideology was a blend of Turkish nationalism and conservative Sunni Islam that was disseminated through the introduction of compulsory religious education in public schools and by increasing the number of mosques and imams (prayer leaders). However, this had the unintentional outcome of reviving interest in religion and creating an opening for Islam in the public sphere.

The neoliberal economic reforms introduced during Prime Minister Turgut Özal's tenure in the mid-1980s contributed to strengthening the undercurrent of political Islam stimulated by the Turkish-Islamic Synthesis. The reforms gave rise to a new class of culturally conservative entrepreneurs and capitalists in the provincial towns of central Anatolia (e.g., Kayseri, Denizli, and Gaziantep). This Anatolian bourgeoisie favored the liberal economic policies but also wanted greater religious freedom. Özal himself adopted a more tolerant approach to religion, leading to the expansion of quranic schools and the establishment of private universities funded by religious endowments, as well as the acquisition of media outlets, newspaper chains, and publishing houses by a nouveau riche class of Islamist businessmen.

Özal's economic opening had also given rise to high unemployment and an influx of migrants from rural areas to urban shantytowns. The Welfare Party (Refah Partisi, RP) emerged on the heels of these developments in the early 1990s. Uprooted, poor, and pious, this underclass was an important source of voters for the RP. It became the most influential representative of political Islam until it was banned in 1997, yet its success stemmed not from religious dogma but rather from its extraordinary effectiveness at grassroots organizing and providing welfare services at the local level. RP volunteers, especially women, canvassed neighborhoods and formed face-to-face relationships with residents to whom they distributed free food and coal, helped with medical care, and aided in finding jobs. Donations to the party's coffers came from religiously conservative businessmen who had profited from the open economy. Both constituencies, although far apart economically, shared a common interest in religious practices and wanted the state to loosen constraints on the expression of religion in public life.

In the 1995 general election the Islamist Welfare Party won the largest bloc of seats in parliament. After more than a year of negotiations, the RP formed a coalition government with the center-right True Path Party (Doğru Yol Partisi, DYP), and soon thereafter the RP's party leader, Erbakan (formerly head of the MSP) became prime minister. Upon taking office Erbakan abandoned his wild campaign promises to withdraw from the North Atlantic Treaty Organization (NATO), to eliminate bank interest charges, and to form an Islamic Common Market. Still, the RP's populist allure and Erbakan's provocative religious rhetoric frightened Kemalists. Rather than directly intervening in the political process, on February 28, 1997, the military high command—in what was dubbed the country's first "postmodern" coup—engineered Erbakan's downfall by pressuring him to adopt a number of policy directives aimed at clamping down on pro-Islamic activities and institutions.

After he failed to do so, he was forced to step down. Not long afterward, the Constitutional Court banned the Welfare Party for violating the secular principles underpinning the republic.

The February 28th process, as this episode with Erbakan is known in Turkey, led to a rethinking among political Islamists about the risks of overtly pushing an Islamic agenda. Two camps formed. The traditionalists who sided with Erbakan refused to alter their approach, whereas a younger group of modernists and reformists wanted to discard the RP's anti-West positions. The Virtue Party (Fazilet Partisi, FP), which replaced the Welfare Party, reflected this new line of reasoning although it encompassed both groups. When as expected the FP was also closed, the movement split. The older generation led by Erbakan founded the Felicity Party (Saadet Partisi, SP) and adhered to the classical MG views (i.e., opposition to the West). A trio of reformists, Recep Tayyip Erdoğan (the former Welfare Party mayor of Istanbul), Bülent Arınç, and Abdullah Gül (both formerly RP members of parliament), cofounded the AKP in 2001. All three had Islamic roots—having belonged to the MG movement—but appeared to abandon ideology for political pragmatism in emphasizing support for Western political values (like democracy and respect for human rights), and backing Turkey's pursuit of EU membership. The AKP rapidly became a major political force, whereas the SP slipped into near electoral oblivion.

The turnabout in the fortunes of political Islam had much to do with the strategy of strategic moderation adopted by the AKP. Erdoğan and his followers believed that the Welfare Party had overplayed its hand with the secularist establishment and that a more conciliatory approach would give them a shot at gaining power. The transformation of the AKP was also influenced by the potential benefits of a pro-West posture, especially with respect to Europe's strong support for individual rights and liberties. While many have debated whether the AKP leadership was influenced more by political calculation or by religious conviction, there is no doubt that they recognized that guaranteeing freedom of religion could lead to lifting restrictions on expression of an Islamic identity in public spaces.

The AKP has benefited from the support of a number of religious forces and organizations, the most important of which was the Gülen movement, an Islamic social movement inspired by the teachings of Fethullah Gülen, a US-based Turkish cleric who has lived in Pennsylvania since 1999. Gülen and his followers are vocally opposed to political Islam, arguing that religion is about personal piety rather than political ideology. Operating as a secret Islamist sect since the 1970s, the Gülen movement (known in Turkey as the Hizmet movement) founded a network of private high schools globally and built up a chain of for-profit college prep courses in Turkey that churned out well-educated followers who sought jobs in the Turkish police, judiciary, media, state bureaucracy, private business, and even the military. The AKP, which lacked its own cadre of personnel to fill key state positions, benefited from the professional training of Gülenist graduates. Erdoğan and Gülen's shared objective was to crush the so-called deep state, the term for a nebulous web of Kemalist military and national security officers and government agencies that operated sub-rosa using illegal methods, like targeted assassination, to defend the political order from Communists, Islamists, and Kurdish nationalists.

This alliance of mutual ambition made it possible from 2008 to 2011 for Erdoğan to purge high-ranking Kemalist military officers and generals through a combination of arrests, dismissals, two sets of show trials called Ergenekon and Sledgehammer that were based on fabricated evidence, and promotion of officers who were either members of or sympathetic to the Gülen movement. At first the Gülenists and the AKP seemed to be natural allies against the Kemalist establishment: both were Islamists, nationalists, and pro-business, and they teamed up in the military trials. However, with the military weakened, a power struggle erupted between the two starting in 2012.

What began as a tiff over Erdoğan's efforts to initiate a peace process with the PKK (the Gülenists opposed it because of their Turkish nationalist views) turned into a tit-for-tat as Erdoğan moved to close down the Gülen prep schools, a major source of income for the movement. Gülenist police and prosecutors hit back in late 2013 and arrested four cabinet ministers on charges of money laundering, bribery, and fraud. This "mother of all corruption scandals" also implicated Erdoğan and his family. Fiercely defending his inner circle and claiming that the evidence was doctored, Erdoğan retaliated by going to war. In his opening volley he accused the Gülen movement of establishing a state within a state in concert with media outlets and began referring to Gülen and his followers as terrorists. His next salvo was to purge suspected Gülenists from the police and judiciary (along with the officials involved in the corruption investigation). Two months before a failed coup attempt in July 2016, the movement was officially designated the Fethullahist Terrorist Organization (Fethullahçı Terör Örgütü, FETO). In the wake of the coup Erdoğan identified Gülen and his followers as the coup-plotters, but the subsequent purges reached far beyond the military. Gülen himself has denied any involvement.

From the time Erdoğan and Gülen began their collaboration, Gülen has presented his faith-based movement as apolitical, differentiating it from the AKP's status as a political party and hence an explicitly political actor. The distinction can be debated as Gülen and Erdoğan were close political allies up to 2013, and Gülen supported the AKP's political agenda. Nevertheless victory at the ballot box gave legitimacy to AKP rule and allowed it to set the political agenda.

During its first term in office, fearing a Kemalist backlash, the AKP only gradually inserted Islam into the public sphere. Most notable was its failed attempt to criminalize adultery in 2004. However, following its overwhelming victory in the July 2007 elections, an Islamist outlook became more discernible when the AKP attempted to lift the ban on the wearing of Islamic head scarves in universities. Although the move was couched as an individual rights issue (i.e., head-scarfed women ought to have the right to an education), one that could be viewed as in alignment with previous human rights and democratic reforms initiated by the ruling party to meet EU accession criteria, it alarmed and angered the secular establishment. With its third electoral win in 2011, by an even larger vote count—and having weakened the military with Gülenist support—the AKP was emboldened to introduce measures that critics decried as intended to Islamicize society. Some examples of the AKP's injection of religion into public life since 2011 include placing restrictions on alcohol sales; a ban on teaching the theory of evolution in school; crusades against abortions, adultery, and kissing in public; and most notably, Erdoğan's pledge that "we [the AKP government] intend to raise a generation of pious youth."

Government and Opposition

The AKP's victory in the 2002 election has been called a political earthquake. For some, the AKP's electoral landslide was a step toward normalizing democracy, in that it seemed likely that the party most distant from the unelected Kemalist state institutions would insist that decisions concerning public life be made by a democratically elected majority government. For others it represented the gravest threat that Kemalist secularism had ever encountered. Similarly, the 2018 elections have been widely interpreted as a watershed moment in Turkey. Voters decisively reelected President Erdoğan to a second term with vastly expanded executive powers and gave the AKP and its nationalist ally the MHP a majority in parliament. Erdoğan's supporters believe that the new powers are necessary to enable the president to manage the country's many challenges (the economy, internal security, foreign policy), but his critics have insisted that he is seeking to cement a system of one-man authoritarian rule. By 2018 the accrual of conflicts between the government and opposition, stretching across sixteen years of AKP rule, had reached the point that Erdoğan's detractors feared his continuation in power posed a significant danger to Turkish democracy.

During the AKP's first term, CHP parliamentarians became increasingly uneasy over the mounting frequency in displays of public religiosity in dress and social mores, the increasing economic power of a religiously minded business class, and the AKP's pursuit of policies that appeared to promote the Islamization of society. The CHP claimed that the AKP had a hidden agenda to impose a religious lifestyle on society, but it lacked the votes in parliament to block legislation that might lead in that direction. This mission therefore fell to the Turkish Armed Forces (TAF) and to the Constitutional Court, which proceeded to check the AKP by dubious methods, starting with the 2007 presidential election.

The first major challenge to the AKP arose over presidential politics. The government and opposition collided in April 2007 when secularist President Ahmet Sezer's term was expiring. At that time, and since 1923, the president was indirectly chosen by parliament, which both nominated and voted on the candidates. A candidate required a two-thirds majority in the first two rounds of voting (for later rounds only a simple majority was needed). The AKP nominated its foreign minister, Abdullah Gül, whose wife wore a head scarf. That the president would be an individual with Islamist roots, and that the First Lady would wear a head scarf, was an abomination to Kemalists.

The military was the first to react, by means of a midnight posting on its website that warned it might be compelled to step in if the AKP did not withdraw Gül's name. The CHP, knowing that it couldn't block Gül's candidacy from making it to the third round of balloting, decided to boycott the first round, making a spurious argument that without a two-thirds quorum present in parliament any vote would be invalid. The CHP took its case to the Constitutional Court, which ruled in favor of the CHP, and annulled the voting. But the military's so-called e-coup and the politicized ruling by the Constitutional Court backfired.

In a surprise move, the AKP called for early elections that July, and voters returned it to power with a stunning 46.7 percent of the vote (although with fewer seats than 2002 because both the CHP and MHP cleared the electoral threshold). The election results strengthened the AKP's electoral mandate and were interpreted as a sharp rebuke to the CHP, which lost over 100 seats, as well as to the military, which had overplayed its hand. Several months later Gül made history when the parliament elected him as the country's first Islamist president by a simple majority in a third round of voting. However, this was much more than a symbolic victory, because it gave the AKP control of both the legislative and executive branches.

Later that summer the AKP claimed to have uncovered a deep-state conspiracy implicating a clandestine network called Ergenekon, which supposedly had schemed to overthrow the AKP government. The investigation, which lasted over five years, corkscrewed into another alleged conspiracy, Operation Sledgehammer, a purported plot to stir up sufficient chaos to justify a military coup against the AKP. Arrests and indictments led to the trials of hundreds of military officers (active and retired), as well as opposition politicians, academicians, and journalists.

At first the arrests were praised by pro-democratic voices for exposing threats to democracy and bringing the military under civilian control. However, as cases made their way through the courts, it became increasingly apparent not only that evidence had been fabricated and often planted, but also that those targeted were rivals, critics, or opponents of the Gülen movement. Most of the investigations were conducted by Gülenist cadres in the police and judiciary, and Gülen-affiliated media outlets kept public attention riveted on the unfolding conspiracies. The trials and convictions sounded the death knell for military tutelage in Turkey.

Although the AKP had captured the presidency (at least for the next seven years) and enjoyed a comfortable majority in parliament, it continuously faced challenges from the Kemalist judges in the high courts. As mentioned earlier, during its second term the AKP tried to rescind the university head-scarf ban. The chief public prosecutor of the Court of Appeals warned the AKP that such an attempt would have serious consequences, underscoring that it would harm the principle of secularity. When the AKP went forward with the reform, the CHP appealed to the higher court to overturn the new head-scarf law, and the chief prosecutor applied to the Constitutional Court to close the AKP for its anti-secular activities, and to ban seventy-one politicians, including Prime Minister Erdoğan and President Gül, from politics for five years. The opposition CHP defended the closure indictment, whereas EU politicians expressed their concern that the lawsuit was contrary to democratic principles. However, the strategy of ousting the AKP through a "judicial coup" failed when the Constitutional Court voted by a narrow margin not to close down the party, and only went so far as to fine the AKP for "being a center of anti-secular activities."

In a referendum held on September 12, 2010, a date that was symbolically chosen because it was the thirtieth anniversary of the 1980 military coup, voters endorsed modifications to the 1982 constitution that reduced the power of the military and judiciary. One change called for direct popular election of the president, which thereby increased the likelihood that the AKP would control the presidency into the near future. A second change strengthened the power of parliament and the president over the appointment and promotion of prosecutors, judges, and members of the highest courts. In lobbying for a "yes" vote in the referendum, the AKP argued that the judicial reforms would make the judiciary accountable to the elected branches of government. The AKP's opponents, who urged a "no" vote, argued that the changes would undermine the independence of the judiciary and enable the government to pack the court with AKP-friendly justices. With a 58 percent "yes" vote, Prime Minister Erdoğan hailed the passage of the amendments as a "turning point" for Turkish democracy, whereas the CHP opposition called the outcome a civilian coup d'état.

Thus during the AKP's second term in office it managed to survive the threat of party closure, assert unprecedented civilian control over the military, and take measures to rein in the independence of the judiciary. From the perspective of the democratically elected AKP government, those two unelected institutions interfered with the party's voter mandate. To its Kemalist opponents, by defanging these institutional actors, the AKP was undermining critical checks on the government's abuse of power.

The media acts as an additional check on the abuse of power through keeping the public informed, and as a watchdog in ensuring the government's accountability to the people. In Turkey the media has never been fully free from political or economic pressure, but in 2002 the AKP promised to pursue a democratic agenda that included recognition of media freedoms. Yet after the 2007 elections Turkey began to regress on issues of press freedom. The Ergenekon arrests and indictments that began in 2008 scooped up journalists critical of the anti-secularist moves against the military and judiciary. Many more journalists who reported on the views and activities of the banned PKK or other outlawed Kurdish groups were added to the jails, charged with aiding terrorism or being members of a terrorist organization. Within three years Turkey held (and continues to hold) the world record for number of journalists imprisoned, and by 2012 Kurdish journalists made up 70 percent of the jailed journalists. Erdoğan himself led the anti-press campaign, filing defamation and libel lawsuits (carrying large fines) against his journalist critics, withdrawing individuals' press cards, and ordering passports to be canceled. Journalists (print and broadcast) faced intimidation and were faced with having to choose between self-censorship and being fired.

The government has silenced Turkey's independent domestic media outlets by taking over or closing (often levying exorbitant tax evasion fines) private media conglomerates, broadcast stations, newspapers, and publishing houses critical of government policies. Yet another way to control the critical media is to ban or block sites like YouTube, Facebook, and Twitter as well as to trace and arrest people for expressing dissenting views in their social media posts. After the AKP-Gülenist alliance started to unravel in 2011, the government acted to crush the Gülenist-controlled media outlets, which had become openly critical of Erdoğan. Following the 2016 coup, thousands of journalists lost their jobs over alleged Gülenist ties or sympathies. For three consecutive years (2016–2018) Turkey has been the world's largest jailer of professional journalists according to the Committee to Protect Journalists, which began issuing reports in 2016.

Lastly there is the question of whether Turkey holds free and fair elections. During the 2018 election campaign only a limited number of independent opposition news sources (including websites) were able to function. Opposition parties railed against the "media embargo," a reference to the unequal allocation of airtime and saturation of the airwaves with pro-government media coverage. Freedom of assembly was impeded by the state of emergency that was often applied to ban "political" rallies, whereas state funds financed AKP rallies. One of the presidential candidates even had to campaign from his prison cell. Without a doubt, the playing field was not level, and the Turkish opposition lacked both the means and opportunity to participate in a fair contest.

Civil Society

In April 2018 Amnesty International surveyed and summarized the state of Turkey's civil society since the July 2016 failed coup in "Weathering the Storm: Defending Human Rights in Turkey's Climate of Fear." The report details the government's actions since the failed coup to stifle the country's once vibrant civil society. The government crackdown has methodically and punitively targeted human rights activists and civil society organization (CSO) members. Punitive measures against CSO members consist of threats, intimidation, detainment, and imprisonment. For example, Osman Kavala, Turkey's most prominent philanthropist and civil society leader known for his Kurdish peace and reconciliation efforts, was jailed in early November 2017 on the preposterous claim of involvement in the coup attempt.

Under the state of emergency that was renewed seven times from July 2016 to June 2018, over 1,300 nongovernmental organizations (NGOs) were shut down, including ones that provided services to battered women and refugee children. Besides outright closure, other means of repression employed by the state include censorship of CSO materials, criticism of CSOs in state media, phone surveillance, and financial repression through excessive auditing and/or fines. More hidden but also prevalent have been government endeavors at co-optation through offers of support and funding to ideologically like-minded CSOs that serve the purpose of spreading the state's ideas to society just as suppression of NGOs with incompatible objectives blocks alternative ideas from being articulated. Thus in Turkey the space for independent civil society has been shrinking, while the CSOs left standing (or newly formed) support state power.

This turn of events contrasts markedly with the AKP's early years in office, when the AKP government listened to and consulted widely with CSOs in making decisions. But as its confidence grew and its hold on power became more secure, the government began to consult exclusively with government-oriented Islamic NGOs (GONGOs). In return for significant amounts of state funding, these "friends with the state" were expected to promote the state's conservative agenda.

Friction between the government and CSOs that worked on politically sensitive issues like human rights monitoring and minority rights mounted after the Gezi Park protests that broke out spontaneously in June 2013. At first a small group of environmentalists occupied a park in central Istanbul upon learning of a government plan to pave over the green space and build a shopping mall. What started as a peaceful sit-in over uprooted trees turned alarmingly violent once riot police entered the park to forcibly evict the protesters. Word of these developments spread rapidly on social media, though the breaking story was not covered by the mainstream news outlets. Shocked by the police brutality and apparent media blackout, people flocked to Taksim Square, the area adjacent to the park. There they confronted the police, who shot rubber bullets, canisters of tear gas, and water cannons into the crowd and sprayed pepper spray directly into protesters' eyes, exacerbating public outrage. A wave of anti-government demonstrations quickly engulfed the country. Erdoğan's response was uncompromising and demeaning. He defended the tactics of the riot police and ridiculed protesters, calling them looters, bums, and extremists. After eighteen days the police regained control of the park and Taksim Square. The opening for civic activism produced by the Gezi protests lasted only briefly. Post-Gezi, the government began to crack down on civil society.

Concern for Turkey's shriveling civic space rose to new heights after the 2016 failed coup. Compared to the amount of associational activity in the late 1990s and early 2000s, civic space in Turkey is significantly diminished. Under the cloak of a state of emergency that was renewed for a seventh time just prior to the June 2018 elections, trumped-up coup-related charges and unsubstantiated accusations have been used to silence journalists, academics, human rights defenders, and other civil society actors. More than 169,000 civil servants, soldiers, teachers, and others working for the government have been dismissed or suspended from their jobs. There are so many citizens incarcerated that the Ministry of Justice announced plans in September 2018 to add more than 200 prisons to the existing 384 over the next five years. Despite this pessimistic picture, civic organizing independent of the state has not disappeared. Rather it is being channeled into less formal, less institutionalized forms of association. For example, locally based, ad hoc groups have been organizing environmental protests that have attracted activists from across the country. Thus, although government-dependent, clientelistic CSOs are transforming the makeup of civil society, it would be a mistake to underestimate the prospects for mobilizing civic dissent in Turkey.

Political Economy

At the time the republic was established, the Turkish economy was overwhelmingly agriculture-based and the majority of the population lived in rural areas. A shortage of entrepreneurs, skilled labor, and capital hampered the republican elite's aspiration to achieve industrial self-sufficiency. The Great Depression dramatically disrupted economic life and led the state to assume responsibility for developing the national economy by adopting an economic policy known as etatism (*devletcilik*) in which the state directly intervened in the economy by establishing state-owned enterprises to stimulate rapid industrial development. From the 1930s until 1980, the state pursued import substitution industrialization (ISI), a development strategy that employs protectionist trade policies to insulate domestic producers from foreign competition in order to promote the formation and expansion of a homegrown capitalist class. During the ISI years Turkey achieved rapid industrialization, economic growth, and a substantial improvement in living standards, but the shortcomings of the ISI model became apparent as technology and costly capital goods still needed to be imported. This led to a reliance on foreign borrowing that increased further under the impact of the twin oil shocks of 1973 and 1979. The result was that at the end of the decade Turkey owed a mountain of debt it could not repay.

The 1980 coup precipitated the abandonment of ISI. Turkey worked closely with the International Monetary Fund (IMF) and World Bank to reschedule its debt and transition to a growth strategy that favored export-oriented manufacturing. Neoliberal economic reforms—trade and financial liberalization, privatization, and deregulation—were introduced with the aim of integrating the Turkish economy into global markets. Economic liberalization created a more competitive economy and the overall growth rate soared, but the effects of economic adjustment were not felt evenly.

The new economy featured flexible work and subcontracting jobs that paid lower wages and had fewer worker protections. The number of people working in agriculture tumbled with the dismantling of agricultural subsidies and price supports, triggering a flood of rural migrants into *gecekondu* neighborhoods (shanty towns) on the outskirts of Turkey's largest cities. During the 1980s and 1990s the urban poor were the most important constituency for the Islamist political parties that won votes by providing services and support to *gecekondu* communities. The benefits of neoliberal economic policies introduced in 1980 have been lopsided, such that over three decades later income inequality in Turkey is exceedingly high. The top 1 percent controlled 55 percent of wealth in 2017; 22.4 percent of households lived below the poverty line; and one in five people fifteen to twenty-four years old was unemployed.

On the flipside, economic liberalization gave rise to an Islamic bourgeoisie that together with the urban poor were critical to bringing the AKP to power in 2002. Both have remained the AKP's core constituencies. During the 1980s a new class of entrepreneurs who combined capitalism with piety set up family-owned small and medium-sized enterprises in towns and cities across central Anatolia. Especially after the AKP came to power, the rise of these socially conservative, market-embracing, export-oriented business elites presented a challenge to the dominance of the Istanbul-based secular business elites who were represented by the Turkish Industry and Business Association (TUSIAD). The Anatolian Tigers formed their own Islamic business group, the Independent Industrialists' and Businessmen's Association (MUSIAD).

From a political economy perspective, the two major reasons for the AKP's continuing electoral successes have been its provision of welfare and social services to the poor and its creation of a patronage network to distribute rents and resources to Islamic businessmen. Through a web of clientelist ties the AKP has awarded lucrative infrastructure contracts for tunnels, bridges, and airports and steered billions of dollars of privatized state assets to Erdoğan's family, friends, and cronies. The AKP government also, both nationally and in AKP-controlled municipalities, confiscates and rezones state and private lands, after which it dispenses construction permits to government-linked developers for urban gentrification schemes. Starting in its first term the AKP rolled out a series of popular social policies, like free medical services for the poor, and cash transfers to the poor, single women, and the disabled. To reduce the cost burden of these social expenditures, the government drew on the Islamic ethical obligation of *zakat* (the duty of a Muslim to give charitable donations) to pressure Islamic businesses to contribute to religiously motivated charitable associations or to make philanthropic gifts to local municipalities in return for preferential business treatment. Thus regime cronies and clients pay for most of the social assistance services that AKP-run municipalities provide.

The AKP is able to maintain the loyalty of both constituencies through intersecting dependencies. Very simply, to do business with the government, Islamic businessmen must make donations to Islamic charities, which are the main funding mechanism for state assistance to the urban poor. The AKP has built a loyal state-dependent business class and fostered an impoverished but loyal underclass that is dependent on state aid for survival.

One month before the June 2018 elections, the Turkish lira suddenly plummeted, losing 20 percent of its value. At issue was Erdoğan's management of the economy and his strong opposition to raising interest rates. The problem was twofold. First, markets were spooked by the probability that should Erdoğan win the presidential election, he would use his newly enhanced executive powers to exercise direct control over the Central Bank. Indeed, shortly after the election he appointed his inexperienced son-in-law Berak Albayrak as treasury and finance minister, and through executive decree he granted himself the right to appoint the governor of the Central Bank, thus undermining its autonomy. Second, the markets were rattled that, contrary to economic orthodoxy, Erdoğan holds the belief that raising interest rates would raise inflation, which would curb economic growth.

Consequently, postelection the Turkish currency continued to depreciate, leading to rising consumer prices (inflation) and decreased consumer purchasing, making it nearly impossible for Turkish corporations to service their dollar-denominated debt (loans), 80 percent of which is owed to domestic banks. This put banks at risk of default, which would trigger a mass consumer panic. The ultimate cause of the financial crisis in 2018 is that unrestrained borrowing of foreign capital has been the main driver of economic growth under AKP rule. However, Erdoğan is opposed to raising interest rates to put an end to cheap credit (because that would curb economic growth) as well as to an IMF bailout (which would do the same). Despite the economic meltdown, Erdoğan has managed to deflect criticism by blaming outsiders (the Jewish lobby, the West, and US president Donald Trump) for the crisis, and since he controls the domestic media, he controls the narrative consumed by the Turkish public. In September 2018 Albayrak announced a new economic program that would reduce government spending (e.g., on mega-showcase projects) and sharply raise interest rates, but investors remain wary of the government's verbal commitment to monetary and fiscal discipline.

Identity and Politics

Since the republic's founding, the Kemalist establishment has regarded Turkey's minorities with profound mistrust and suspicion and thus adopted a restrictive definition of who is a minority. All three of Turkey's official minorities are non-Muslim: Greek (Rum) Orthodox Christians (2,000), Jews (16,000), and Armenian Orthodox Christians (90,000). These non-Muslim groups were guaranteed minority status under the terms of the Treaty of Lausanne (1923), whereas the country's two largest minority groups, ethnic Kurds and Alevi Muslims, have been granted no special recognition despite the fact that Kurds make up close to 20 percent of the population and Alevis around 25 percent (20 percent of Kurds are Alevi, the rest are Sunni Muslim). The state does not recognize a multitude of other ethnic, linguistic, and religious minorities. Some examples are Roma (Gypsies), Laz from the Black Sea region, Chaldean Christians, Syriac Orthodox Christians, Yezidis, Nestorians, Arabs, Pontic Greeks, Circassians, and Bosniaks.

Turkey's minorities have long been perceived by the state as a potential threat to national unity. In its first two terms the AKP pursued a pro-EU reform agenda that liberals and Kurds strongly supported. Yet issues of cultural incompatibility raised by EU member states helped fuel a nationalist backlash in Turkey that brought identity politics to the fore. Non-Muslim minorities quickly became the victims of hate crimes. Churches were defaced, synagogues bombed, Christian missionaries attacked, and a Catholic priest murdered. Virulent expressions of Turkish nationalism that defamed and vilified Armenians, Christians, and Jews appeared in television series, best-selling books, and box office blockbusters. As the EU reform process slowed, the AKP lost the pro-EU voting blocs. Consequently, the party sought to consolidate the electoral support of traditional religious voters and attract conservative nationalist voters. Since the 2011 elections, the AKP's strategy to ally with the far right by embracing anti-West ultranationalism has polarized the country, miring it in a crisis of identity politics.

Erdoğan's interpretation of Turkish identity has two strands that have a bearing on Turkey's minorities. First, he has a sectarianized Sunni conception of Turkish nationhood that excludes Alevi citizens. Second, he embraces those Kurds who prioritize their Sunni Muslim identity while suppressing those who would advance a Kurdish ethnic identity.

The Alevis, an offshoot of Shi'i Islam, are the country's largest religious minority. Politically they always backed secular political parties to immunize themselves from religious persecution. They consider the AKP a pro-Sunni party rather than an Islamist party. Prime Minister Erdoğan initiated an "Alevi Opening" in 2007 to improve relations with the Alevi community. Outreach steps included symbolic gestures of national reconciliation, like attendance at Alevi iftar breakfasts (to break the fast during Ramadan), speeches about unity, and sponsorship of an Alevi workshop series. In 2011 Erdoğan went further and issued an apology on behalf of the Turkish state for a 1937 massacre in the predominantly Alevi region of Dersim. Nonetheless, moves toward more meaningful change were not forthcoming: no compensation accompanied the apology; Alevi complaints that the compulsory religion courses introduced in schools privilege Sunni theology have gone ignored; and the government refuses to elevate Alevi *cemevis* (houses of worship) to the status of mosques that would qualify them to receive massive state subsidies.

Subsequent challenges faced by Alevis have been the impacts of the sectarianized civil war in Syria and the aborted 2016 coup. Islamic State in Iraq and Syria (ISIS) fighters consider Alevis apostates because they are not Sunni and have launched attacks on Alevi villages and cultural centers in Turkey. The Syrian refugees and opposition fighters who crossed the border into Turkey were mainly Sunni Arabs. This has exacerbated sectarian tensions inside Turkey, especially when Erdoğan falsely likened Syrian Alawites, the sect of Bashar al-Asad and his regime, to Turkish Alevis. This implied that Turkish Alevis supported al-Asad's authoritarian regime when in fact they are strong defenders of secular, democratic rule in Turkey. Lastly, since the coup, Alevi citizens have been arrested for purported ties to FETÖ; the Alevi television station was closed; and individuals have had threatening graffiti painted on their homes.

In the early years of the republic, ethnic diversity was regarded as a danger to the unity of the state, and Kurds, the largest non-Turkish ethnic group, constituted the greatest threat. Their ethnic identity was suppressed such that the use of the Kurdish language, dress, and names was outlawed, and they were decreed to be Turks. Any Kurd who accepted assimilation could hold important and high-level positions in the economy, military, and government, but harsh repression met those who resisted. Oppression in the wake of the 1980 coup played a key role in strengthening Kurdish identity and the formation of the Kurdistan Workers' Party (PKK), which launched a guerrilla offensive against the Turkish state in 1984 with the aim of establishing an independent Kurdish state. In 1999 the PKK's leader Abdullah Öcalan was captured and given a death sentence that was later commuted to life in solitary confinement. Despite his isolation Öcalan remained the uncontested leader of the PKK and has piloted a paradigm shift from the PKK's original hierarchical Marxist-Leninist political vision to the horizontalist notion of a democratic confederal system comprised of autonomous, self-organized communities.

The EU reform process spearheaded by the AKP in its first term granted Kurds the right to broadcast in Kurdish and take private Kurdish language courses. But as soon as the AKP began to sour on the EU, and dragged its feet on implementing these measures, PKK attacks recommenced. Between 2009 and 2012 the government held on-and-off secret peace talks first with the PKK in Oslo, and later with PKK leader Öcalan on Imrali Island where he is imprisoned. These meetings culminated in a cease-fire lasting from 2013 until the AKP suffered a major setback in the June 2015 elections when it lost its parliamentary majority.

Ultranationalist voters in the June 2015 elections punished the AKP for embarking on a peace process with the Kurds, resulting in a gain of seats for the MHP. The AKP lost the support of the majority of Kurdish voters, including religious Kurds, whose votes went to the Kurdish HDP, enabling the party to overcome the 10 percent threshold. However, afterwards Erdoğan balked at forming a coalition government with the CHP, which had come in second. In so doing, Erdoğan forced new elections to be called for in November. Between July and November he unleashed an all-out effort to win back ultranationalist voters through a two-pronged strategy: resuming military operations against the PKK and undermining the HDP by accusing it of supporting PKK terrorism. In the November election the HDP lost twenty-one of the eighty seats it had won in June, although it still made it over the 10 percent threshold. However, since the 2016 coup attempt, 55 out of 59 HDP deputies have been stripped of their parliamentary immunity, over 10,000 members of the party have experienced arrest, 9 HDP deputies await trial on terrorism charges, and the government has dismissed 89 out of 104 elected Kurdish mayors and replaced them with Interior Ministry appointed trustees. Eighty of those mayors are under arrest.

The results of the 2018 elections may be interpreted from two angles. In one optic Erdoğan's win and the AKP-MHP ultranationalist alliance does not bode well for resolving the Kurdish question so long as the alliance holds. Looking from another optic, continued Kurdish political representation (the HDP secured sixty-seven seats in parliament) and the popularity of the HDP's presidential candidate Selahattin Demirtaş, who came in third despite his having to contest the race from prison, will make Kurdish identity politics difficult to ignore.

Gender and Politics

Women's emancipation was a strategic component of Atatürk's intention to Westernize the country; however, women were viewed as vehicles of rather than partners in modernization. To this day gender inequality remains remarkably high. According to the World Economic Forum's

"Global Gender Gap Index," Turkey was one of the worst performers in 2017, ranking 131st overall out of 144 countries. Only 32.2 percent of women participated in the labor force, held back by barriers that include patriarchal attitudes, low levels of educational attainment, and migration. Men out-earned women by more than twofold.

In terms of political empowerment of women, Turkey has had one female prime minister, Tansu Çiller (1993–1995). While this was symbolically significant, it did not help rectify women's unequal access to positions of political power. One encouraging development is that women who wear the head scarf gained the right to be seated in parliament in 2015. Yet although the number of women in parliament jumped from 24 in 2002 to 103 in the expanded 600-seat parliament elected in 2018, women continue to be placed at the bottom of party lists, reducing their prospects of making it into parliament. Fifty-three AKP women deputies joined the 2018 parliament, representing 17.9 percent of the party's 295 lawmakers. The best performer in terms of gender equality was the pro-Kurdish HDP. Twenty-five of its sixty-seven deputies (37 percent) are female. Women also fare poorly at the cabinet level: only two of the sixteen ministers appointed by Erdoğan are women, and one is minister of the family. The president appoints governors to the eighty-one provinces, but women only run three. Women are also underrepresented in local politics, composing 3 percent of mayors, 10.7 percent of municipal council members, and 4.8 percent of provincial council members.

In the AKP's first years, spurred by the prospect of EU membership, the government worked with women's groups to draft bills to grant women equal rights and protections under the law. However, police, prosecutors, and judges have failed to enforce the law, and the AKP no longer works with these groups. The perception that women's rights are backsliding and that discrimination and violence against women are on the rise is confirmed in the UN's Global Database on Violence Against Women. According to its 2015 report, four out of ten Turkish women were subjected to physical abuse. The Turkish women's activist platform "We Will Stop Femicide" reported that, in 2017, 409 women were murdered and 387 children sexually abused.

President Erdoğan's patriarchal rhetoric and promotion of religious beliefs in all areas of life have contributed to normalizing gender violence. The president has said that equality between men and women is against human nature, working women are half persons, childless women are deficient, birth control is treason, abortion is murder, family planning is not for Muslims, and women should have at least four children. The AKP is not alone in being criticized for being misogynistic. CHP leader Kılıçdaroğlu has also made statements that appeared to justify wife beating. When men leading the government or senior politicians make such declarations, it filters down to the rest of society. The problem is deeply cultural.

Turkey's laws do not explicitly discriminate against individuals on the basis of sexual orientation or gender identity, and same-sex activity is legal. However, the LGBT community suffers from hate crimes, discrimination, and harassment in employment, housing, and health care. Symbolic of this lack of tolerance is the fate of the LGBT Pride Parade that was held in Istanbul for thirteen years but has been banned by AKP authorities four years in a row (2015–2018).

The Impact of International Politics

Atatürk's motto "Peace at home, peace in the world" translated into an isolationist foreign policy stance until World War II. Wedged between the competing interests of the Allied and Axis Powers, and being militarily weak, Turkey remained neutral through the war. But just as an Allied victory seemed imminent, Turkey chose to ally with the United States and Europe. Shortly thereafter it was quickly granted membership in NATO and subsequently applied to join the European Economic Community (the EU's predecessor). Fear of the spread of communism kept Turkey close to its Western partners during the Cold War. Greek objections to Turkey's EU bid (related to the status of Cyprus) in the late 1980s led Turkey to negotiate instead for a Customs Union with the EU in 1995, which led to full economic integration with the EU.

The AKP government made EU membership its top policy priority in its first term. It pushed through a series of impressive democratic reforms that included strengthening human rights, individual freedoms, and civilian controls over the military, as well as granting cultural rights to Kurds. These efforts paved the way to opening EU accession negotiations in 2005. Domestically the reforms worked to the advantage of the AKP. It could successfully represent itself to the liberal voting bloc as a paragon of support for individual freedom and minority rights, and to Europeans and the West as an exemplar of the compatibility of Islam and democracy.

The AKP's landslide victory in 2007 subsequently diminished the party's need to rely on the EU for legitimacy at home and abroad. Relations began to sour when several EU states wavered in their support for Turkish membership and suggested a "privileged partnership" instead. As additional stumbling blocks on the road to accession emerged, notably Turkey's refusal to recognize Greek Cyprus, the talks ground to a standstill. Turkey gained important leverage in its relations with the EU, however, through a deal on the migrant crisis signed in March 2016.

Turkey is an important transit point as well as a final destination for migrants from Syria, Afghanistan, Iran, Iraq, southwest Asia, and even Africa. Forcible displacement caused by the Syrian civil war that started in 2011 was a key catalyst for the flood of migrants into Europe. By 2016 Europe was desperate to stem the influx and signed a controversial "one-in, one-out" agreement with Turkey. The EU pledged 6 billion euros in cash to help subsidize the 3.6 million Syrian refugees that Turkey hosted and offered a conditional promise of visa-free travel for Turkish citizens to Europe. Turkey agreed that all undocumented migrants arriving in Greece from Turkey would be returned, and that for each Syrian sent back, a Syrian already in Turkey would be resettled in the EU. Two years into the agreement, the EU had delivered only half of the stipulated amount, and visa-free travel had not been implemented, even though aggressive Turkish interdiction had brought about a 97 percent drop in the number of migrants that reached Greece via Turkey. Although Erdoğan will likely press the EU to uphold its end of the deal, prospects for meaningful progress in membership talks are remote. The AKP's coalition partner, the MHP, holds strong ultranationalist views and has voiced skepticism about Turkey's EU bid, making it highly probable that Ankara will continue to adopt undemocratic policies that diverge from rather than converge with the accession criteria.

Separate from the European theater, Turkey's foreign affairs from 2002 to 2010 were guided by an idealistic "zero problems with neighbors" policy that aimed to improve relations with Middle East neighbors and establish Turkey as the dominant power in the region. In this period Turkey promoted business and trade relations with Iran and Arab states, attempted to mediate conflicts in the region (like the nuclear crisis between the United States and Iran), and brokered talks between Syria and Israel, and Hamas and Fatah. Erdoğan made frequent references to the glories of the Islamic past and Ottoman rule, championing a neo-Ottoman vision that imagined a revival of the Ottoman Empire under his leadership through the application of soft-power tactics. Turkey's Western alliance partners held up its successful marriage of Islam, democracy, and neoliberalism as a model for other Muslim countries in the region. However, the Arab Spring caused Turkey to lose footing, and its influence in the region diminished.

When the first revolutionary wave of demonstrations swept across the Arab world, Turkey quickly endorsed regime change in Egypt and Tunisia and embraced the Muslim Brotherhood–affiliated Islamist parties that came to power in democratic elections. Although Syria had been a major pillar of Turkey's zero problems foreign policy, the brutality of Bashar al-Asad's crackdown on peaceful civilian protests led

Turkey to sever its ties to the regime and openly back the Free Syrian Army rebels and the Muslim Brotherhood–dominated opposition Syrian National Council. Erdoğan's increasingly Sunni-sectarian policies at home were mirrored in his foreign policy. When General Abdel Fattah al-Sisi toppled Mohammad Morsi's Muslim Brotherhood in a military coup in 2013, Turkey's relations with Egypt became severely strained.

Early in Syria's civil war Turkey allowed thousands of jihadist fighters, many of whom joined ISIS, to cross its border into Syria. Turkey's relations with ISIS ranged from passive cooperation to collaboration based on a mixture of motives that included a desire to see al-Asad and his Alawite regime defeated, uneasiness with the growing influence of Iran's Shi'ite leaders in Damascus and Baghdad, and support for ISIS attacks on the YPG (Syrian Kurdish People's Protection Units) in northern Syria and its ally the Kurdish PKK in northern Iraq. Turkey's top national security concern domestically and regionally has been and remains the Kurdish issue.

Renewal of fighting between the Turkish army and the PKK in Turkey's southeast following the breakdown of the Kurdish peace process in 2015 coincided with the outbreak of ISIS attacks inside Turkey. Turkey then joined the US-led coalition to defeat ISIS and in 2016 sent troops into Syria. However, the two allies were at cross-purposes. The United States viewed the YPG in Syria and the PKK in northern Iraq as valuable partners in routing ISIS, whereas Turkey considered any YPG or PKK territorial gains an alarming security threat. During the civil war years, Syrian Kurds carved out a territorial enclave, Rojava, located in Syria's north. The Syrian Democratic Union Party (PYD), the political wing of the YPG, has had a self-governing arrangement with Damascus. In January 2018 Ankara launched a military operation to roll back the YPG's territorial gains west of the Euphrates River, which risked direct confrontation with US forces. In order to placate Turkey, the United States compelled the YPG to withdraw to the east of the Euphrates, but Turkey has made it clear that it aims to control those Kurdish-held territories as well.

Friction with the United States has played out in other areas as well. Turkish authorities have repeatedly criticized the United States for its refusal to extradite Fethullah Gülen, who they allege orchestrated the aborted 2016 coup. Relations with the United States continued downhill during 2018. Ankara refused to implement US sanctions on Iran by cutting its imports of Iranian oil, and over US objections it signed a deal with Russia to purchase a long-range missile defense system. The Trump administration retaliated by imposing a battery of financial sanctions and tariffs on Turkish products that caused the Turkish lira to drop to a record low.

Turkey's foreign relations are drifting rather than heading in a particular direction. Headlines from various online news sources capture this ambiguity through repeated references to Turkey's frenemies: "Turkey and the US: The Best of Frenemies?" "Turkey-Russia, New Frenemies?" "Turkey and Iran, Frenemies For Ever?" and "Friends, Foes, Frenemies? Unpacking the Future of EU-Turkey Relations." Inconsistencies and contradictions in Ankara's foreign policy under President Erdoğan, especially since the new executive presidency began, have made it increasingly difficult to answer these questions.

PART 3
Conclusion

20

Trends and Prospects

Michele Penner Angrist

This text has covered a lot of ground. The introductory chapter presented an overview of the states of the Middle East and provided crucial historical context for contemporary political dynamics in the region. Part 1 described seven key elements that animate politics and society in the Middle East: government and opposition, the domestic impact of international politics, political economy, civil society, religion, identity, and gender. The case study chapters of Part 2 illustrated the ways in which each of these seven elements is present with respect to twelve states of the region: Algeria, Egypt, Iran, Iraq, Israel, Jordan, Kuwait and the United Arab Emirates, Palestine, Saudi Arabia, Syria, and Turkey. This concluding chapter reflects on this material and offers some thoughts as to what the future likely holds for the region.

The closing pages of Chapter 1 highlighted a series of key problems, dilemmas, and issues in Middle Eastern politics. The first concerned the deterioration of basic political order in parts of the region in the aftermath of the Arab Spring protests. To different degrees in different cases, the recipe for the breakdown of order has included domestic social divides, weak states, polarization among political elites, and the intervention of outside actors. The countries most affected have been Libya, Yemen, and Syria. The toll on citizens, communities, and infrastructure has been immense. Ultimately it may be that some of these territories are not governable in their current geopolitical borders. While the international system is conservative in that it resists the redrawing of borders, a new set of arrangements may be necessary for the restoration of order.

The second key issue is regime type. While the vast majority of political communities in the region were authoritarian for most of the postindependence period, the uprisings of the Arab Spring felled autocrats who once had seemed invulnerable, while demonstrating on the world stage the depths of citizens' grievances with the status quo. Despite the hopes of many that the Arab Spring would usher in more democratic politics in more places, as Chapter 2 showed, the region still features more than its fair share of authoritarian politics. Indeed, Freedom House scores for political and civil liberties were *worse* in 2017 than in 2010, and only Tunisia managed to join Israel, Turkey, Lebanon, and Iraq on a journey toward a state of affairs wherein repeated, honest, competitive elections to determine who rules are the sole currency of politics.

The path is fraught with difficult obstacles and challenges, and countries can (and likely will) alternate between making forward progress and backtracking. Increasingly authoritarian behavior by Turkey's President Erdoğan raises profound questions about the prospects for democratic politics in that country, which once was a lodestar for the region's democratic potential. Tunisia faces economic and security challenges in its path to institutionalizing democratic governance. Lebanon and Iraq must overcome deep religious and sectarian divides, the presence or legacy of armed militias, and nontransparent, corrupt governance. Israel's status as a democracy confronts serious questions about equality between its Jewish and Arab citizens, and its deepening, de facto annexation of the West Bank and Gaza Strip.

The region's remaining autocrats faced a new political landscape in the wake of the Arab uprisings. For a time they were on the defensive, seeking new tactics for retaining the reins of power to add to their traditional toolbox (i.e., rigging elections, directing patronage to key clients, arresting opponents, banning political parties, and using brute force against rivals when all else fails). Stoking the fires of Shi'ite-Sunni hatred has been one key example. Yet the post–Arab Spring terrain now is not wholly discouraging for autocrats. Almost a decade out from the start of the Arab Spring, what has transpired in the countries most affected may give political activists pause regarding challenging the political status quo. From the violent repression of protesters in Bahrain, to the fragmentation and deterioration of the security environment in Yemen and Libya, to the emergence of a new, more repressive iteration of authoritarian rule in al-Sisi's Egypt, to the horrific civil war in Syria—the Arab Spring has ushered in multiple worrisome scenarios that in the long term might be a disincentive to the emergence of new mass protests.

The third issue flagged in the introduction is identity—how citizens and leaders alike connect issues of faith, sect, language, lineage, and place to their political actions. Since the 1970s Islam has been an important—if not the dominant—element of political discourse in the Middle East. Oppositions first, and then governments in reaction, appropriated the language and symbols of the faith in order to frame their respective arguments and mobilize their respective supporters. Chapter 7 demonstrated that the rise of politicized Islam as a major vector of politics in the Middle East was probably not inevitable, nor is it necessarily a permanent fixture of politics in the region. That chapter teaches us that how citizens identify themselves in politically consequential ways is not a constant but rather a variable that must be explained through careful analysis. In the 1950s and 1960s, politics in much of the Middle East was quite secular in nature in the heyday of Arab nationalism as articulated by Gamal Abdel Nasser and others. Pan-Arab unity, its proponents declared, would strengthen Arab states and deliver prosperity, dignity, and victory in the conflict with Israel. It was not until Arab nationalism was deemed to have failed in all of these respects (the evidence was in by the conclusion of the 1967 Six Day War) that a kind of collective regional soul-searching produced powerful Islamist leaders who argued convincingly to their followers that "Islam is the solution."

Until peoples and societies in the Middle East determine that bringing the values and laws of Islam into the public sphere is *not* the solution—or not the only solution, anyway—Islamism will continue to be a powerful dynamic in the region. As of yet, there is little evidence that large groups of political actors have reached such a conclusion. To the contrary, the success of regional Islamist movements either in obtaining some of their political objectives (e.g., Hezbollah forcing an Israeli withdrawal from southern Lebanon and Turkey's Justice and Development Party winning six consecutive parliamentary elections) or in assisting large numbers of citizens in the challenges they face in their daily lives (e.g., the charitable activities of groups such as Hezbollah and Hamas) no doubt sends the message that Islam still has quite a prominent role to play in politics. The victories of Egypt's Muslim Brotherhood and Tunisia's En-Nahda parties in elections in 2011 underscored the appeal and mobilizational capacity of Islamist political parties. And, between 2014 and 2017, ISIS's caliphate-building project in Iraq and Syria attracted thousands of committed foreign fighters.

Whether manifestations of political Islamism are peaceful or violent also depends on context. While from the late 1970s through the 1990s domestic Islamists and their government opponents both resorted to the use of force in places like Algeria, Egypt, and Syria, by the late 1990s oppositional Islamists had largely laid down their arms. As Chapter 6 noted, in the period prior to the Arab Spring the vast majority of oppositional Islamist movements eschewed violence, sought coalitions with other actors across the political spectrum, and confined themselves to working toward gradual change within their respective political institutional environments. The chaos and the repression that came in the wake of the Arab Spring changed these dynamics, however. Repression of Egypt's Muslim Brotherhood seemed to drive home the hopelessness of Islamists' making progress by working nonviolently within the system, while political breakdown and chaos in Syria, Libya, and Yemen opened the door for more extremist actors—in particular al-Qaeda and ISIS—to make a play for heightened political influence. Political Islam will continue to be a key ingredient in regional politics going forward.

Increasingly, divides between Shi'ites and Sunnis have become as polarized as those between Islamists and non-Islamists. Saudi Arabia has led the charge in stoking sectarian tensions in the wake of the Arab Spring. Shi'ite-Sunni strife poisons politics in many countries, including Lebanon, Syria, Iraq, Bahrain, Saudi Arabia, and Yemen. At the same time it helps to animate intraregional competition between Iran and Saudi Arabia. When leaders construct those of other sects as enemies or heretics, a politics where conflict is solved at the ballot box is much harder to achieve—and political violence is that much more likely.

The fourth challenge facing states of the Middle East is that of generating prosperity that is broadly shared by their citizens. While casual observers often are under the impression that the region is a rich one, it is in fact bifurcated between those states that are rich as a result of oil and natural gas, and those that aren't. In the latter category are countries like Egypt, Syria, and Jordan, which to varying degrees pursued state-led development schemes in the 1950s, 1960s, and 1970s that failed to yield diversified, productive, self-sustaining economies. The solution that the major international financial institutions have tended to offer countries in this situation is privatization and structural adjustment. Yet as Chapter 4 detailed, a political logic underpins deep state involvement in domestic economies, and authoritarian incumbents were reluctant to reform the political-economic status quo in substantial ways. Less state involvement in the economy means fewer opportunities to reward supporters or appease key constituencies with material perquisites. For this reason, economic liberalization and the prosperity it is supposed to generate generally have not proceeded in thoroughgoing fashion in the countries of the Middle East. Nor did these regimes invest sufficiently in education, infrastructure, communication, and technology in order to build and harness their human resources in productive ways.

Thus as the first decade of the twenty-first century drew to a close, economies across the region were facing ticking time bombs to the extent that, demographically, large portions of many Middle Eastern populations are under the age of twenty-five. This generation needs to be educated and employed if regimes are to avoid the political instability that can unfold when large numbers of young, unemployed citizens with profound material and political grievances conclude that they have little to lose from confronting their rulers. Tunisia's Mohammad Bouazizi symbolized this Achilles heel for dictators, and the political statement he made with his self-immolation attempt catalyzed a wave of instability that spread regionwide in 2010–2012. Three of the four presidents whose terms in office were ended by the Arab Spring—Tunisia's Ben Ali, Egypt's Mubarak, and Yemen's Ali Abdullah Salih—came from poorer Arab dictatorships with low per capita gross domestic products (GDPs) and comparatively little in the way of oil and natural gas wealth. Syria—where President Bashar al-Asad was still fighting for his political life at the time of this writing—also fits this profile.

This is not to say that the Arab uprisings and their aftermaths were solely a function of poor economic performance. Libya has significant hydrocarbon reserves and its per capita GDP is more than double that of Tunisia and Syria, yet President Muammar Qaddafi still proved politically vulnerable. Algeria's per capita GDP was one-third less than Tunisia's, yet President Abdelaziz Bouteflika remained in power. The Jordanian and Moroccan monarchs preside over economies with worrisomely low per capita GDPs, yet they survived as well. Clearly, many noneconomic factors bore on the question of whether regimes withstood the Arab Spring. Still, economic grievances loomed large among the motivations of protesters. And the region can expect new upheavals in the future if economic horizons do not brighten for its denizens.

In the richer Middle Eastern countries, oil and gas wealth does not exempt rulers from anxiety regarding their balance sheets. Those countries that possess significant such wealth relative to the size of their populations struggle with volatile world market prices for their commodity, for example. They also grapple with the question "What happens after oil?" and the imperative of economic diversification. From Dubai's odyssey in becoming a cosmopolitan regional trade and financial entrepôt, to Saudi Arabia's new "economic cities," to the sovereign wealth funds that Gulf governments utilize to ensure a steady revenue stream into state coffers for decades to come—these trends seem sure to remain a central reality in the oil-rich states, given growing global awareness of, consternation regarding, and activism around the link between the burning of fossil fuels and global climate change.

A fifth pivotal issue for Middle Eastern leaders and peoples is how to relate to the West, and particularly the United States. As Chapter 1 chronicled, the region has struggled with the superior economic, military, and political power of the West for centuries now—as the Ottoman Empire declined, as European imperialism became a reality, as the United Kingdom helped create the physical and political space into which Israel was born, and as, in the post–World War II era (and in a more pronounced way in the post–Cold War era), US policies shaped global political and economic institutions. The fact of Western power is problematic for governments and peoples in the Middle East for myriad reasons. To name just a few: US policies in the region (support for Israel, sanctions on and then war in Iraq, etc.) generate substantial popular political hostility; the economic dependence of poorer states that rely on international financial institutions (dominated by the United States) for debt relief engenders resentment; and many in the region have a deep concern about the spread of Western culture and values on the wings of globalization.

Yet at the same time, many Middle Eastern governments are in a position that requires productive diplomatic relations with the United States—whether because US power helps guarantee their security (in the case of Saudi Arabia and the smaller Gulf states), because access to US markets is a cornerstone of economic policy (as in Jordan), because of the levels of bilateral aid the United States provides (as in Egypt), or because US pressure on Israel will be critical to the creation of a Palestinian state if such an eventuality is to happen in the foreseeable future (many in the Arab world hope it will). And while many in the region dislike US foreign policy and aspects of what they perceive as American culture (materialism, individualism, etc.), many also admire the dynamic political, economic, and educational institutions that operate in the West. Thus, for both peoples and governments in the Middle East, forces of both attraction and repulsion condition a complicated relationship with the West.

The final dynamic highlighted in the introductory chapter is the impact of the earlier elements—the supply (or lack thereof) of political order, struggles over the right to participate in politics, economic realities, identity politics, and the region's relationship with the West—on struggles over gender norms. In terms of the region's penchant for authoritarian politics, while dictators have the power to simply decree (as many have) that women be placed in parliament, the cabinet, and the like, authoritarian political arenas do not grant women (or men) the political space and freedom to organize as they wish, for whatever types of policy changes they favor. Economic conditions in the region constrain women's opportunities to join the workforce: in wealthier societies, it is harder to make the argument that women "need" to work; in societies undergoing economic crises or painful reforms that produce unemployment, as Chapter 8 noted, often it is women who are asked to leave the workforce first, to preserve scarce jobs for male workers. Meanwhile, the rise and popularity of politicized Islam tend to bring expectations that women will veil and that they will play a complementary role to men (in the household primarily, as wife and mother). Many Middle Eastern women are supportive of such norms. For those who have a different vision, however, the strength of those norms is a significant political constraint. Finally, the legacy of Western powers justifying their interventions in the region in terms of gender rights, combined with regional hostility toward contemporary Western policy and presence, means that those activists who choose to push for the sorts of rights and equalities women have struggled for in the West run the risk of being portrayed by their compatriots as "siding with the enemy." All of these realities will continue to shape the context in which women in the Middle East operate politically.

References

Abboud, Samer N. 2017. "Social Change, Network Formation and Syria's War Economies." *Middle East Policy* 24 (1): 92–107.

Abboud, Samer N., and Fred H. Lawson. 2012. "Antinomies of Economic Governance in Contemporary Syria." In Abbas Kadhim, ed., *Governance in the Middle East and North Africa* (London: Routledge), pp. 330–341.

al-Abd al-Hadi, Mubarak, Ibrahim al-Sa'idi, and Tariq al-'Aydan. 2009. "Al-Hall al-'aql Kalifatan Su'ud al-Muhammad al-Mansa" [The least costly solution is for al-Muhammad to take the stand]. *Al-Qabas,* March 5, p. 1.

'Abd al-Jabbar, Faleh. 1994. "Why the Intifada Failed." In Fran Hazelton, ed., *Iraq Since the Gulf War* (London: Zed), pp. 97–117.

Abdelaziz, Nouf. 2018. "Saudi Arabia: Unrelenting Crackdown on Activists." Human Rights Watch. June 20. https://www.hrw.org/news/2018/06/20/saudi-arabia-unrelenting-crackdown-activists.

Abrahamian, Ervand. 1980. "The Guerrilla Movement in Iran, 1963–1977." *MERIP Reports* (March–April 1980): 3–15.

———. 1999. *Tortured Confessions: Prisons and Public Recantations in Modern Iran.* Berkeley: University of California Press.

———. 2008. *A History of Modern Iran.* Cambridge: Cambridge University Press.

———. 2013. *The Coup: 1953, the CIA, and the Roots of Modern U.S.-Iranian Relations.* New York: The New Press.

Abu-Lughod, Lila. 2002. "Do Muslim Women Really Need Saving? Anthropological Reflections on Cultural Relativism and Its Others." *American Anthropologist* 104 (3): 783–790.

Abu Odeh, Adnan. 1999. *Jordanians, Palestinians, and the Hashimite Kingdom in the Middle East Peace Process.* Washington, DC: US Institute of Peace.

Aghrout, Ahmed. 2008. "Policy Reforms in Algeria: Genuine Change or Adjustments?" In Yahia H. Zoubir and Haizam Amirah-Fernàndez, eds., *North Africa: Politics, Region, and the Limits of Transformation* (London: Routledge), pp. 31–52.

Ahmed, Leila. 1992. *Women and Gender in Islam: Historical Roots of a Modern Debate.* New Haven: Yale University Press.

Alaoudh, Abdullah. 2018. "State Sponsored Fatwas in Saudi Arabia." *Sada* (Carnegie Endowment for International Peace), April 3. https://carnegieendowment.org/sada/75971.

Alaoudh, Abdullah, and Nathan Brown. 2018. "The Saudi Regime Is Reshaping the Country's Legal Sector in Profound Ways." *Diwan,* January 18. https://carnegie-mec.org/diwan/75155.

Albloshi, Hamad H., and Michael Herb. 2018. "Karamet Watan: An Unsuccessful Nonviolent Movement." *The Middle East Journal* 72 (3): 408–430.

Aldohan, Majid. 2016. "How Saudis Express Their Problems." Raseef22, January 9. www.raseef22.com.

Al-Ali, Nadje. 2005. "Reconstructing Gender: Iraqi Women Between Dictatorship, Wars, Sanctions, and Occupation." *Third World Quarterly* 26 (4–5): 739–758.

Al-Ali, Nadje, and Nicola Pratt. 2009. *What Kind of Liberation?* Berkeley: University of California Press.

Allahoum, Ramy. 2018. "Tunisia's President Vows to Give Women Equal Inheritance Rights." Al-Jazeera, August 13. https://www.aljazeera.com/news/2018/08/tunisia-president -vows-give-women-equal-inheritance-rights-180813172138132.html.

Almond, Gabriel A., and Sydney Verba. 1963. *The Civic Culture: Political Attitudes and Democracy in Five Nations.* Princeton: Princeton University Press.

Alnasrawi, Abbas. 2001. "Iraq: Economic Sanctions and Consequences, 1990–2000." *Third World Quarterly* 22 (2): 205–218.

al-Alou, Sokrat. 2017. *The Arab Socialist Baath Party: Preparing for the Post-War Era.* Beirut: Arab Reform Initiative. https://docplayer.net/56234811-The-arab-socialist-baath-party-preparing-for-the-post-war-era.html.

ALQST. 2017, 2018. *Human Rights in Saudi Arabia.* London.

Alvaredo, Facundo, Lydia Assouad, and Thomas Piketty. 2017. "Measuring Inequality in the Middle East 1990–2016: The World's Most Unequal Region?" World Inequality Database. World Working Paper 2017/15. https://wid.world/document/alvaredoassouad piketty-middleeast-widworldwp201715.

Amawi, Abla. 2000. "Gender and Citizenship in Jordan." In Joseph Suad, ed., *Gender and Citizenship in the Middle East* (Syracuse: Syracuse University Press), pp. 158–184.

al-Amiry, Kholoud Ramzi. 2012. "The Prime Minister Who Plays with Fire." *Sada* (Carnegie Endowment for International Peace), April 19. http://www.carnegieendowment.org/sada/47909.

Amnesty International. 2018. "Saudi Arabia: Reports of Torture and Sexual Harassment of Detained Activists." November 20. https://www.amnesty.org/en/latest/news/2018/11/saudi-arabia-reports-of-torture-and-sexual-harassment-of-detained-activists.

Anderson, Benedict R. 1991. *Imagined Communities: Reflections on the Origin and Spread of Nationalism.* New York: Verso.

Anderson, Lisa. 1995. "Democracy in the Arab World: A Critique of the Political Culture Approach." In Rex Brynen, Baghat Korany, and Paul Noble, eds., *Political Liberalization and Democratization in the Arab World,* vol. 1, *Theoretical Perspectives* (Boulder: Lynne Rienner), pp. 77–92.

———. 2001. "Arab Democracy: Dismal Prospects." *World Policy Journal* 18 (3): 53–60.

Anscombe, Frederick F. 1997. *The Ottoman Gulf: The Creation of Kuwait, Saudi Arabia, and Qatar.* New York: Columbia University Press.

Arab-Barometer. 2016. *Public Opinion Survey Conducted in Algeria, Egypt, Jordan, Lebanon, Morocco, Palestine, Tunisia, 2016.* Ann Arbor, MI: Inter-university Consortium for Political and Social Research.

Arat, Yeşim. 1989. *The Patriarchal Paradox: Women Politicians in Turkey.* Rutherford: Fairleigh Dickinson University Press.

———. 2005. *Rethinking Islam and Liberal Democracy: Islamist Women in Turkish Politics.* Albany: State University of New York Press.

Arjomand, Said Amir. 1988. *The Turban for the Crown.* New York: Oxford University Press.

Badawi, Tamer. 2018. "Iran's Economic Leverage in Iraq." *Sada* (Carnegie Endowment for International Peace), May 23. http://carnegieendowment.org/sada/76436.

Bahar, Dany. 2016. "Five Years After the Social Protest in Israel, What Has Changed?" *Markaz,* August 1. https://www.brookings.edu/blog/markaz/2016/08/01/five-years-after-the-social-protests-in-israel-what-has-changed.

Bajoghli, Narges, and Arang Keshavarzian. 2017. "Iran and the Arab Spring." In Mark L. Haas and David W. Lesch, eds., *The Arab Spring: The Hope and Reality of the Uprisings,* 2nd ed. (Boulder: Westview Press), pp. 174–193.

Baram, Amatzia. 1981. "The June Elections to the National Assembly in Iraq: An Experiment in Controlled Democracy." *Orient* 22: 391–412.

———. 1997. "Neo-Tribalism in Iraq: Saddam Hussein's Tribal Policies, 1991–1996." *International Journal of Middle East Studies* 29 (1): 1–31.

Barnett, Michael N. 1992. *Confronting the Costs of War: Military Power, State, and Society in Egypt and Israel.* Princeton: Princeton University Press.

Batatu, Hanna. 1978. *The Old Social Classes and the Revolutionary Movements of Iraq.* Princeton: Princeton University Press.

Bates, Robert. 1983. "Modernization, Ethnic Competition, and the Rationality of Politics in Contemporary Africa." In D. Rothchild and V. A. Olunsorola, eds., *State Versus Ethnic Claims: African Policy Dilemmas* (Boulder: Westview), pp. 152–171.

Bayat, Asef. 2007. *Making Islam Democratic: Social Movements and the Post-Islamist Turn.* Stanford: Stanford University Press.

———. 2018. "The Fire That Fueled the Iran Protests." *The Atlantic,* January 27.

Bellin, Eva. 2004. "The Robustness of Authoritarianism in the Middle East." *Comparative Politics* 36 (2): 139–157.

Bellingreri, Marta. 2018. "Challenges and Hopes: The Women Standing for Iraq." New Arab, May 11. https://www.alaraby.co.uk/english/indepth/2018/5/11/challenges-and-hope-for-female-parliamentary-candidates-in-iraq.

Benhabib, Seyla. 1992. "Models of Public Space: Hannah Arendt, the Liberal Tradition, and Jürgen Habermas." In Craig Calhoun, ed., *Habermas and the Public Sphere* (Cambridge: MIT Press), pp. 73–98.

Berglas, Eitan. 1983. "Defense and the Economy: The Israeli Experience." Discussion Paper no. 83.01. Jerusalem: Maurice Falk Institute for Economic Research in Israel.

Bill, James A. 1988. *The Eagle and the Lion: The Tragedy of American-Iranian Relations.* New Haven: Yale University Press.

Blumi, Isa. 2018. *Destroying Arabia: What Chaos in Arabia Tells Us About the World.* Berkeley and Los Angeles: University of California Press.

Bou Nacklie, Nacklie E. 1993. "Les Troupes Speciales: Religious and Ethnic Recruitment, 1916–1946." *International Journal of Middle East Studies* 25 (November): 646–660.

Brand, Laurie A. 1992. "Economic and Political Liberalization in a Rentier Economy: The Case of the Hashimite Kingdom of Jordan." In Iliya Harik and Denis J. Sullivan, eds., *Privatization and Liberalization in the Middle East* (Bloomington: Indiana University Press), pp. 167–188.

———. 1995. "'In the Beginning Was the State . . .': The Quest for Civil Society in Jordan." In Augustus Richard Norton, ed., *Civil Society in the Middle East,* vol. 1 (Leiden: Brill), pp. 148–185.

———. 1998. *Women, the State, and Political Liberalization: Middle Eastern and North African Experiences.* New York: Columbia University Press.

Brookshaw, Dominic Parviz, and Seena B. Fazel, eds. 2008. *The Baha'is of Iran: Socio-Historical Studies.* London: Routledge.

Brown, Nathan. 2002. *Constitutions in a Nonconstitutional World: Arab Basic Laws and the Prospects for Accountable Governance.* Albany: SUNY Press.

Brumberg, Daniel. 2002. "The Trap of Liberalized Autocracy." *Journal of Democracy* 13 (4): 56–68.

Brynen, Rex. 1992. "Economic Crisis and Post-Rentier Democratization in the Arab World." *Canadian Journal of Political Science* 25 (1): 69–97.

Bsheer, Rosie. 2018. "How Mohammed bin Salman Has Transformed Saudi Arabia." *The Nation*, May 21.

Campagna, Joel. 2006. "Saudi Arabia Report: Princes, Clerics, and Censors." Committee to Protect Journalists, May 9. https://cpj.org/reports/2006/05/saudi-06.php.

Carver, Terrell. 1998. "A Political Theory of Gender: Perspectives on the 'Universal' Subject." In Vicky Randall and Georgina Waylen, eds., *Gender, Politics, and the State* (New York: Routledge), pp. 18–28.

CBS News, *60 Minutes.* 2007. "A Visit to Dubai Inc.: Steve Kroft Reports on a Success Story in the Middle East." Transcript of segment broadcast October 14, 2007, updated July 30, 2008. http://www.cbsnews.com/stories/2007/10/12/60minutes/printable3361753.shtml.

Central Bureau of Statistics (Israel). 1976–1989, 2011, 2017, 2018. *Statistical Abstract of Israel.* http://www1.cbs.gov.il/reader/shnatonenew_site.htm.

———. 2016. *Social Survey.* http://www.cbs.gov.il/reader/?MIval=cw_usr_view_SHTML&ID=576.

Charrad, Mounira, and Amina Zarrugh. 2014. "Equal or Complementary? Women in the New Tunisian Constitution After the Arab Spring." *Journal of North African Studies* 19 (2): 230–243.

Chaudhry, Kiren Aziz. 1991. "On the Way to the Market: Economic Liberalization and the Iraqi Invasion of Kuwait." *Middle East Report* 170: 14–23.

Chazan, Naomi. 2011. *Women in Public Life.* Jewish Virtual Library. http://jewishvirtuallibrary.org/jsource/Society_&_Culture/Women_in_public_life.html.

Chehabi, Houchang E. 1991. "Religion and Politics in Iran: How Theocratic Is the Islamic Republic?" *Daedalus* 120 (Summer): 48–70.

———. 1997. "Ardabil Becomes a Province: Center-Periphery Relations in Iran." *International Journal of Middle East Studies* 29 (2): 235–253.

Chowdhury, Najma. 1994. "Gender Issues and Politics in a Patriarchy." In Barbara J. Nelson and Najma Chowdhury, eds., *Women and Politics Worldwide* (New Haven: Yale University Press).

Clark, Janine A. 2004. *Islam, Charity, and Activism: Middle-Class Networks and Social Welfare in Egypt, Jordan, and Yemen.* Bloomington: Indiana University Press.

Clayton, Amanda. 2016. "Comparative Regional Patterns in Electoral Gender Quota Adoption: A Social Network Approach." KFG Working Paper Series No. 71, The Transformative Power of Europe, Freie Universität Berlin.

Coalition Provisional Authority (Iraq). 2004. "Full Text of Zarqawi Letter." Press release, February 12. https://2001-2009.state.gov/p/nea/rls/31694.htm.

Cohen, Asher. 2004. "Changes in the Orthodox Camp and Their Influence on the Deepening Religious-Secular Schism at the Outset of the Twenty-First Century." In Alan Dowty, ed., *Critical Issues in Israeli Society* (Westport: Praeger), pp. 71–94.

Cole, Juan R. I., and Moojan Momen. 1986. "Mafia, Mob, and Shiism in Iraq: The Rebellion of Ottoman Karbala, 1824–1843." *Past and Present,* no. 112 (August): 112–143.

Conge, Patrick, and Gwenn Okruhlik. 2009. "The Power of Narrative: Saudi Arabia, the US, and the Search for Security." *British Journal of Middle Eastern Studies* 36 (3): 357–371.

Coppedge, Michael, and Wolfgang Reinicke. 1991. "Measuring Polyarchy." In Alex Inkeles, ed., *On Measuring Democracy: Its Consequences and Concomitants.* New Brunswick, NJ: Transaction, pp. 47–68.

Cordesman, Anthony H. 2006. *Arab-Israeli Military Forces in an Era of Asymmetric Wars.* Westport: Praeger Security International.

Crystal, Jill. 1995. *Oil and Politics in the Gulf.* Cambridge: Cambridge University Press.

Dahl, Robert A., ed. 1966. *Political Oppositions in Western Democracies.* New Haven: Yale University Press.

———. 1971. *Polyarchy, Participation, and Observation.* New Haven: Yale University Press.

Darbouche, Hakim, and Yahia H. Zoubir. 2008. "The Algerian Crisis in European and US Foreign Policies: A Hindsight Analysis." *Journal of North African Studies* 14 (1): 33–55.

Davidson, Christopher M. 2007. "The Emirates of Abu Dhabi and Dubai: Contrasting Roles in the International System." *Asian Affairs* 38 (1): 33–48.

———. 2008. *Dubai: The Vulnerability of Success.* New York: Columbia University Press.

Davis, Eric. 2005. *Memories of State: Politics, History, and Collective Memory in Modern Iraq.* Berkeley: University of California Press.

Dawisha, Adeed. 2009. *Iraq: A Political History from Independence to Occupation.* Princeton: Princeton University Press.

de Silva de Alwis, Rangita, Anware Mnasri, and Estee Ward. 2017. "Women and the Making of the Tunisian Constitution." *Berkeley Journal of International Law* 35 (1): 90–149.

Dessi, Andrea. 2012. "Algeria: Cosmetic Change or Actual Reform?" *Actuelles de l'IFRI,* July 9. https://www.ifri.org/fr/publications/editoriaux/actualite-mom/algeria-cosmetic-change-or-actual-reform.
Dowty, Alan. 2001. *The Jewish State: A Century Later.* Berkeley: University of California Press.
Dris-Aït-Hamadouche, Louisa. 2008. "The 2007 Legislative Elections in Algeria." *Mediterranean Politics* 13 (1): 87–94.
Drysdale, Alasdair. 1979. "Ethnicity in the Syrian Officer Corps: A Conceptualisation." *Civilisations* 29: 359–373.
Dziadosz, Alexander. 2011. "Could Suez Be Egypt's Sidi Bouzid?" Reuters, January 27.
Earl of Cromer. 1908. *Modern Egypt.* Vol. 2. New York: Macmillan.
Economist Intelligence Unit. 2016. *Democracy Index 2016.* http://eiu.com.
Ehsani, Kaveh. 1995. "Islam, Modernity, and National Identity." *Middle East Insight* 11 (5): 48–53.
———. 2009. "Survival Through Dispossession: Privatization of Public Goods in the Islamic Republic." *Middle East Report,* no. 250 (Spring): 26–33.
Ehsani, Kaveh, Arang Keshavarzian, and Norma Claire Moruzzi. 2009. "Tehran, June 2009." *Middle East Report Online,* June 28. http://www.merip.org/mero/mero062809.html.
Eickelman, Dale. 2002. *The Middle East and Central Asia: An Anthropological Approach.* 4th ed. Upper Saddle River, NJ: Prentice Hall.
Esman, Milton J., and Itamar Rabinovich, eds. 1988. *Ethnicity, Pluralism, and the State in the Middle East.* Ithaca: Cornell University Press.
European Union. 2008. "The Euro-Mediterranean Partnership." http://ec.europa.eu/external_relations/euromed/index_en.htm.
Fagen, Patricia Weiss. 2009. "Iraqi Refugees: Seeking Stability in Syria and Jordan." Occasional Paper no. 1. Washington, DC: Georgetown University, School of Foreign Service in Qatar, Center for International and Regional Studies.
Fahim, Kareem. 2018. "Saudi Arabia's Once-Powerful Conservatives Silenced by Reforms and Repression." *Washington Post,* June 5.
Farhi, Farideh. 2004. "The Antinomies of Iran's War Generation." In Lawrence G. Potter and Gary G. Sick, eds., *Iran, Iraq, and the Legacies of War* (New York: Palgrave Macmillan), pp. 101–120.
Faruqui, Fahad. 2010. "Saudi Youth Are Struggling with Their Identities." *The Guardian,* June 25.
Fathi, Schirin H. 1994. *Jordan: An Invented Nation? Tribe-State Dynamics and the Formation of National Identity.* Hamburg: Deutsches Orient-Institut.
Freedom House. 2017. "Freedom in the World: Israel." http://www.freedomhouse.org/country/israel.
Friedman, Thomas L. 1990. *From Beirut to Jerusalem.* New York: Anchor.
Gallup Polls. 2018. "Americans Staunchly in Israel's Corner." March 13. https://news.gallup.com/poll/229199/americans-remain-%20staunchlyisraelcorner.aspx?g_source.
Gasiorowski, Mark, and Malcolm Byrne, eds. 2004. *Mohammed Mossadeq and the 1953 Coup in Iran.* Syracuse: Syracuse University Press.
Gause, F. Gregory, III. 1993. *Oil Monarchies: Domestic and Security Challenges in the Arab Gulf States.* New York: Council on Foreign Relations.
Gauthier, Julie. 2009. "The 2004 Events in Al-Qamishli: Has the Kurdish Question Erupted in Syria?" In Fred H. Lawson, ed., *Demystifying Syria* (London: Saqi), pp. 105–119.
Gellner, Ernest, and Charles A. Micaud. 1972. *Arabs and Berbers: From Tribe to Nation in North Africa.* Lexington, MA: Lexington Books.
Gelvin, James. 2008. *The Modern Middle East: A History.* New York: Oxford University Press.
Gerber, Haim. 1987. *The Social Origins of the Modern Middle East.* Boulder: Lynne Rienner.
Gerschenkron, Alexander. 1962. *Economic Backwardness in Historical Perspective: A Book of Essays.* Cambridge: Belknap.
Ghadbian, Najib. 2001. "The New Asad: Dynamics of Continuity and Change in Syria." *Middle East Journal* 55 (4): 624–641.

———. 2006. *Al-Dawlah al-Asadiyyah al-Thaniyyah*. Jiddah: Dar al-Rayya.
Ghaffari, Sonia. 2009. "Baluchistan's Rising Militancy." *Middle East Report,* no. 250 (Spring): 40–43.
Gitelman, Zvi. 2004. "The 'Russian Revolution' in Israel." In Alan Dowty, ed., *Critical Issues in Israeli Society* (Westport: Praeger), pp. 95–108.
Golan, Esther. 1977. "Political Culture in Israel: A Case Study." Master's thesis, University of Haifa (in Hebrew).
Gole, Nilufer. 1996. *The Forbidden Modern: Civilization and Veiling*. Ann Arbor: University of Michigan Press.
Gordon, Neve. 2008. *Israel's Occupation*. Berkeley: University of California Press.
Habibi, Nader. 2014. "Can Rouhani Revitalize Iran's Oil and Gas Industry?" *Middle East Brief* no. 80. Waltham, MA: Crown Center for Middle East Studies, Brandeis University.
al-Haj, Majid. 2004. "The Status of Palestinians in Israel: A Double Periphery in an Ethno-National State." In Alan Dowty, ed., *Critical Issues in Israeli Society* (Westport: Praeger), pp. 109–126.
Halliday, Fred. 2005. *The Middle East in International Relations: Power, Politics, and Ideology*. Cambridge: Cambridge University Press.
Harrigan, Jane R., and Hamed El-Said. 2009. *Aid and Power in the Arab World: World Bank and IMF Policy-Based Lending in the Middle East and North Africa*. New York: Palgrave Macmillan.
Harris, Kevan. 2017. *A Social Revolution: Politics and the Welfare State*. Berkeley: University of California Press.
Hashim, Ahmed S. 2003. "Saddam Husayn and Civil-Military Relations in Iraq." *Middle East Journal* 57 (1): 9–41.
———. 2006. *Insurgency and Counter-Insurgency in Iraq*. London: Hurst.
Heard-Bey, Frauke. 1982. *From Trucial States to United Arab Emirates: A Society in Transition*. London: Longman.
Heller, Sam. 2016. *Keeping the Lights on in Rebel Idlib*. New York: The Century Foundation.
Henry, Clement M., and Robert Springborg. 2001. *Globalization and the Politics of Development in the Middle East*. Cambridge: Cambridge University Press.
Herb, Michael. 1999. *All in the Family: Absolutism, Revolution, and Democracy in the Middle Eastern Monarchies*. Albany: SUNY Press.
———. 2009. "'A Nation of Bureaucrats': Political Participation and Economic Diversification in Kuwait and the United Arab Emirates." *International Journal of Middle East Studies* 41 (3): 375–395.
Heydemann, Steven. 2007. "Upgrading Authoritarianism in the Arab World." Saban Center Analysis Paper no. 13. Washington, DC: Brookings Institution.
Hinnebusch, Raymond. 1979. *Party and Peasant in Syria: Rural Politics and Social Change Under the Ba'th*. Cairo: American University in Cairo.
———. 2003. *The International Politics of the Middle East*. Manchester: Manchester University Press.
Hobbs, Joseph J. 2009. *World Regional Geography*. 6th ed. Belmont, CA: Brooks/Cole.
Hoodfar, Homa. 2009. "Activism Under the Radar: Volunteer Women Health Workers in Iran." *Middle East Report,* no. 250 (Spring): 56–60.
Hoodfar, Homa, and Shadi Sadr. 2009. "Can Women Act As Agents of a Democratization of Theocracy in Iran?" United Nations Research Institute for Social Development and the Heinrich Böll Foundation, Geneva, Switzerland. October. http://www.unrisd.org/unrisd/website/document.nsf/8b18431d756b708580256b6400399775/2e975aca2a81aa54c12576580028735c/$FILE/WebIran.pdf.
Hoodfar, Homa, and Mona Tajali. 2011. *Electoral Politics: Making Quotas Work for Women*. London: Women Living Under Muslim Laws. http://www.wluml.org/resource/electoral-politics-making-quotas-work-women.
Hooglund, Eric. 2009. "Thirty Years of Islamic Revolution in Rural Iran." *Middle East Report,* no. 250 (Spring): 34–39.
Horne, Alistair. 2006. *A Savage War of Peace: Algeria 1954–1962*. 2nd ed. New York: New York Review Books Classics.

Human Rights Watch. 1991. *World Report 1990*. New York.
———. 2014. "'We Are Still Here': Women on the Front Lines in Syria's Conflict." July 2. https://www.hrw.org/report/2014/07/02/we-are-still-here/women-front-lines-syrias-conflict.
———. 2018. "Saudi Arabia: Detained Women Reported Tortured." November 20. https://www.hrw.org/news/2018/11/20/saudi-arabia-detained-women-reported-tortured.
Husry, Khaldun S. 1974. "The Assyrian Affair of 1933." *International Journal of Middle East Studies* 5 (2–3): 161–176, 344–360.
Hyde, Susan D. 2011. *The Pseudo-Democrat's Dilemma: Why Election Observation Became an International Norm*. Ithaca: Cornell University Press.
ILO (International Labor Office). 2017a. "Labor Force Participation Rate, Female (% of Female Population Ages 15–64) (Modeled ILO Estimate)." Data file. https://data.worldbank.org/indicator/SL.TLF.ACTI.FE.ZS.
———. 2017b. "Labor Force Participation Rate, Male (% of Male Population Ages 15–64) (Modeled ILO Estimate)." Data file. https://data.worldbank.org/indicator/SL.TLF.ACTI.MA.ZS.
———. 2017c. "Unemployment, Female (% of Female Labor Force) (Modeled ILO Estimate)." Data file. https://data.worldbank.org/indicator/SL.UEM.TOTL.FE.ZS.
———. 2018. *World Employment and Social Outlook: Trends for Women 2018—Global Snapshot.* Geneva.
IMF (International Monetary Fund). 2003. *World Economic Outlook.* Washington, DC.
———. 2018. "Israel: Selected Issues." IMF Country Report No. 18/112, April 13. http://www.imf.org/external/ns/search.aspx?NewQuery=Growth+in+Israel+2018&submit=.
Inglehart, Ronald, and Pippa Norris. 2003. *Rising Tide: Gender Equality and Cultural Change.* Cambridge, MA: Cambridge University Press.
Institute for National Security Studies. 2018. *National Security Index: Public Opinion Survey 2017–2018.* http://www.inss.org.il/wp-content/uploads/2018/01/Survey-2017-2018.pdf.
International Institute for Democracy and Electoral Assistance (International IDEA). 2018. *Gender Quotas Database*. https://www.idea.int/data-tools/data/gender-quotas.
IPU (Inter-Parliamentary Union). 2018. "Women in National Parliaments." Data table. November 1. http://archive.ipu.org/wmn-e/classif.htm.
Ismael, Jacqueline S. 1980. "Social Policy and Social Change: The Case of Iraq." *Arab Studies Quarterly* 2: 235–248.
Ismael, Jacqueline S., and Shereen T. Ismael. 2008. "Living Through War, Sanctions and Occupation: The Voices of Iraqi Women." *International Journal of Contemporary Iraqi Studies* 2 (3): 409–420.
Issawi, Charles. 1982. *An Economic History of the Middle East.* New York: Columbia University Press.
al-Istrabadi, Feisal Amin Rasoul. 2009. "A Constitution Without Constitutionalism: Reflections on Iraq's Failed Constitutional Process." *Texas Law Review* 87: 1627–1655.
Jacoby, Tim, and Nassima Neggaz. 2018. "Sectarianism in Iraq: The Role of the Coalition Provisional Authority." *Critical Studies on Terrorism* 11 (3): 478–500.
Jalabi, Raya. 2017. "Yazidis Caught in 'Political Football' Between Baghdad, Iraqi Kurds." Reuters, December 10.
al-Jawaheri, Yasmin Husein. 2008. *Women in Iraq.* London: Tauris.
Joseph, Suad. 1991. "Elite Strategies for State Building: Women, Family, Religion, and the State in Iraq and Lebanon." In Deniz Kandiyoti, ed., *Women, Islam, and the State* (Philadelphia: Temple University Press), pp. 176–200.
Kandiyoti, Deniz. 1991. "Islam and Patriarchy: A Comparative Perspective." In Nikkie R. Keddie and Beth Baron, eds., *Women in Middle Eastern History: Shifting Boundaries in Sex and Gender* (New Haven: Yale University Press), pp. 23–42.
Karam, Souhail. 2011. "Moroccans Protest Polls, Violence in the Capital." Reuters, October 23. http://www.reuters.com/article/2011/10/23/us-morocco-protests-idUS-TRE79M3ZU20111023.
Karawan, Ibrahim A. 1994. "Sadat and the Egyptian-Israeli Peace Revisited." *International Journal of Middle East Studies* 26 (2): 249–266.

Karl, Terry Lynn. 1997. *The Paradox of Plenty: Oil Booms and Petro-States.* Berkeley: University of California Press.

Karpat, Kemal. 1988. "The Ottoman Ethnic and Confessional Legacy in the Middle East." In Milton J. Esman and Itamar Rabinovich, eds., *Ethnicity, Pluralism, and the State in the Middle East* (Ithaca: Cornell University Press).

Kashani-Sabet, Firoozeh. 1999. *Frontier Fictions: Shaping the Iranian Nation, 1804–1946.* Princeton: Princeton University Press.

Kazemipur, Abdolmohammad, and Ali Rezaei. 2003. "Religious Life Under Theocracy: The Case of Iran." *Journal of the Scientific Study of Religion* 42 (September): 347–361.

Kerr, Malcolm H. 1971. *The Arab Cold War.* London: Oxford University Press.

Kerr, Malcolm H., and El Sayed Yassin, eds. 1982. *Rich and Poor States in the Middle East: Egypt and the New Arab Order.* Boulder: Westview.

Keshavarzian, Arang. 2005. "Contestation Without Democracy: Elite Fragmentation in Iran." In Marsha Pripstein Posusney and Michele Penner Angrist, eds., *Authoritarianism in the Middle East: Regimes and Resistance* (Boulder: Lynne Rienner), pp. 63–88.

———. 2007. *Bazaar and State in Iran: The Politics of the Tehran Marketplace.* Cambridge: Cambridge University Press.

Keshavarzian, Arang, and Naghmeh Sohrabi. 2017. "Lessons Learned (and Ignored): Iran's 2017 Election in Context." *Middle East Report Online*, May 26.

al-Khafaji, Isam. 1994. "State Terror and the Degradation of Politics." In Fran Hazelton, ed., *Iraq Since the Gulf War* (London: Zed), pp. 20–31.

———. 2000. "War as a Vehicle for the Rise and Demise of a State-Controlled Society: The Case of Ba'thist Iraq." In Steven Heydemann, ed., *War, Institutions, and Social Change in the Middle East* (Berkeley: University of California Press), pp. 258–291.

Khalaf, Rana. 2016. *Governing Rojava: Layers of Legitimacy in Syria.* London: Royal Institute of International Affairs. https://www.chathamhouse.org/publication/governing-rojava-layers-legitimacy-syria.

Khalaf, Rana, Oula Ramadan, and Friederike Stolleis. 2014. *Activism in Difficult Times: Civil Society Groups in Syria, 2011–2014.* Beirut: Friedrich Ebert Stiftung. https://badael.org/wp-content/uploads/2015/01/Activism-in-Difficult-Times.-Civil-Society-Groups-in-Syria-2011-2014.pdf.

Khalaf, Roula. 2012. "Saudi Whispers Turn into Online Roar." *Financial Times,* March 23.

Khalfan, Mohammed. 1997. "The Practicality of Having the Federal National Council of the United Arab Emirates Become an Elective Body." PhD diss., University of La Verne.

Khalidi, Rashid. 1997. *Palestinian Identity: The Construction of Modern National Consciousness.* New York: Columbia University Press.

al-Khalil, Samir. 1989. *Republic of Fear.* Berkeley: University of California Press.

Khosravi, Shahram. 2017. *Precarious Lives: Waiting and Hope in Iran.* Philadelphia: University of Pennsylvania Press.

Kian-Thiébaut, Azadeh. 2002. "Women and the Making of Civil Society in Post-Islamist Iran." In Eric Hooglund, ed., *Twenty Years of Islamic Revolution* (Syracuse: Syracuse University Press), pp. 56–73.

Kienle, Eberhard. 1990. *Ba'th Versus Ba'th: The Conflict Between Syria and Iraq.* London: Tauris.

———. 1997. "Authoritarianism Liberalised: Syria and the Arab East After the Cold War." In William Hale and Eberhard Kienle, eds., *After the Cold War: Security and Democracy in Africa and Asia* (London: Tauris), pp. 194–226.

Kimmerling, Baruch. 1993. "Yes, Returning to the Family." *Politika* 48 (March): 40–45.

Kimmerling, Baruch, and Joel S. Migdal. 1993. *Palestinians: The Making of a People.* New York: Free Press.

Kirkpatrick, David. 2012. "Jordan Protesters Dream of Shift to King's Brother." *New York Times,* November 21. http://www.nytimes.com/2012/11/22/world/middleeast/jordan-protesters-dream-of-shift-to-prince-hamzah.html?pagewanted=all&_r=0.

Koelbl, Susanne. 2018. "Exploring the New Saudi Arabia from the Inside." *Spiegel,* July 25. http://www.spiegel.de/international/world/the-new-saudi-arabia-a-revolution-from-above-a-1217678.html.

KOF Swiss Economic Institute. 2018. "Index of Globalization." https://www.kof.ethz.ch/en/forecasts-and-indicators/indicators/kof-globalisation-index.html.

Kuran, Timur. 2004. "The Economic Ascent of the Middle East's Religious Minorities: The Role of Islamic Legal Pluralism." *Journal of Legal Studies* 33 (June): 475–515.

Kurzman, Charles. 2004. *The Unthinkable Revolution*. Cambridge: Harvard University Press.

———. 2008. "A Feminist Generation in Iran?" *Iranian Studies* 41 (June): 297–321.

Labdaoui, Abdellah. 2003. "Universality, Modernity, and Identity: The Case of Morocco." In Roel Meijer, ed., *Cosmopolitanism, Identity and Authenticity in the Middle East* (London: RoutledgeCurzon), pp. 145–158.

Lacroix, Stephane. 2011. *Awakening Islam: The Politics of Religious Dissent in Contemporary Saudi Arabia*. George Holoch, trans. Cambridge: Harvard University Press.

———. 2017. "Saudi Arabia Finally Let Women Drive. Don't Mistake It for Democratic Reform." *Washington Post*, Monkey Cage, October 5. https://www.washingtonpost.com/news/monkey-cage/wp/2017/10/05/saudi-arabia-finally-let-women-drive-dont-mistake-it-for-democratic-reform.

Lawson, Fred H. 1988. "Political-Economic Trends in Ba'thi Syria: A Reinterpretation." *Orient* 29: 590–603.

———. 1992. "Economic Liberalization in Syria and Iraq During the 1980s: The Limits of Externalist Explanations." *New Political Science* 11: 185–205.

———. 1994. "Domestic Transformation and Foreign Steadfastness in Contemporary Syria." *Middle East Journal* 48 (1): 47–64.

———. 1996. *Why Syria Goes to War*. Ithaca: Cornell University Press.

———. 1997. "Private Capital and the State in Contemporary Syria." *Middle East Report*, no. 203 (Spring): 8–13, 30.

———. 2006. *Constructing International Relations in the Arab World*. Stanford: Stanford University Press.

Layne, Linda. 1994. *Home and Homeland: The Dialogics of Tribal and National Identities in Jordan*. Princeton: Princeton University Press.

Lefevre, Raphael. 2013. "The Muslim Brotherhood Prepares for a Comeback in Syria." Washington, DC: Carnegie Endowment for International Peace.

Lefevre, Raphael, and Ali El Yassir. 2013. "Militias for the Syrian Muslim Brotherhood?" *Sada* (Carnegie Endowment for International Peace), October 29. http://carnegieendowment.org/sada/53452.

Lehman-Wilzig, Sam. 1986. "Conflict as Communication: Public Protest in Israel, 1950–1982." In Stuart A. Cohen and Eliezer Don-Yehiya, eds., *Conflict and Consensus in Jewish Public Life* (Ramat Gan: Bar-Ilan University Press), pp. 128–145.

Leopold, Till A., Vesselina Ratcheva, and Saadia Zahidi. 2017. *The Global Gender Gap Report 2017*. World Economic Forum. http://www3.weforum.org/docs/WEF_GGGR_2017.pdf.

Lerner, Gerda. 1986. *The Creation of Patriarchy*. New York: Oxford University Press.

Levy, Shlomit, Hana Levinsohn, and Elihu Katz. 1993. *Beliefs, Observances, and Social Interaction Among Israeli Jews*. Jerusalem: Guttman Israel Institute of Applied Social Research.

Lewis, Bernard. 1998. *The Multiple Identities of the Middle East*. New York: Random House.

Lijphart, Arend. 1984. *Democracies: Patterns of Majoritarian and Consensus Government in Twenty-One Countries*. New Haven: Yale University Press.

———. 1994. "Democracies: Forms, Performance, and Constitutional Engineering." *European Journal of Political Research* 25 (January): 1–17.

Lister, Charles R. 2015. *The Syrian Jihad*. London: Hurst.

Livani, Talajeh. 2007. "Middle East and North Africa: Gender Overview." Washington, DC: World Bank.

Longuenesse, Elisabeth. 1985. "The Syrian Working Class Today." *MERIP Reports*, no. 134 (July–August): 17–24.

Longva, Anh Nga. 2006. "Nationalism in Pre-Modern Guise: The Discourse on Hadhar and Badu in Kuwait." *International Journal of Middle East Studies* 38 (2): 171–187.

Looney, Robert E. 2008. "Reconstruction and Peacebuilding Under Extreme Adversity: The Problem of Pervasive Corruption in Iraq." *International Peacekeeping* 14 (3): 424–440.

Louër, Laurence. 2008. *Transnational Shia Politics: Religious and Political Networks in the Gulf*. London: Hurst.

Lowe, Robert. 2014. "The Emergence of Western Kurdistan and the Future of Syria." In David Romano and Mehmet Gurses, eds., *Conflict, Democratization, and the Kurds in the Middle East*. New York: Palgrave Macmillan.

Lucas, Russell. 2004. "Monarchical Authoritarianism: Survival and Political Liberalization in a Middle Eastern Regime Type." *International Journal of Middle East Studies* 36 (1): 103–119.

Lund, Aron. 2012. *Syrian Jihadism*. UI Brief no. 13, September 14. Stockholm: Swedish Institute of International Affairs.

———. 2013. *Struggling to Adapt: The Muslim Brotherhood in a New Syria*. Washington, DC: Carnegie Endowment for International Peace.

Lust, Ellen. 2011. "Morocco Elections Aren't a Model for the Arab Spring as West Claims." *Christian Science Monitor*, November 28. http://www.csmonitor.com/Commentary/Opinion/2011/1128/Morocco-elections-aren-t-a-model-for-the-Arab-Spring-as-West-claims.

Lust-Okar, Ellen. 2004. "Divided They Rule: The Management and Manipulation of Political Opposition." *Comparative Politics* 36 (2): 159–180.

———. 2006. "Elections Under Authoritarianism: Preliminary Lessons from Jordan." *Democratization* 13 (3): 456–471.

Lynch, Marc. 1999. *State Interests and Public Spheres: The International Politics of Jordan's Identity*. New York: Columbia University Press.

———. 2016. *The New Arab Wars: Uprisings and Anarchy in the Middle East*. New York: Public Affairs.

Macintyre, Donald. 2003. "Exiled Cleric Returns Home to Call for Free Islamic State." *Independent* (London), May 11, p. 18.

al-Madfai, Madiha Rashid. 1993. *Jordan, the United States, and the Middle East Peace Process, 1974–1991*. New York: Cambridge University Press.

Makdisi, Ussama. 2000. *The Culture of Sectarianism: Community, History, and Violence in Nineteenth-Century Ottoman Lebanon*. Berkeley: University of California Press.

Mamouri, Ali. 2018a. "Religious Disputes Escalate over Upcoming Iraqi Elections." Al-Monitor, April 22. https://www.al-monitor.com/pulse/originals/2018/04/ira.html.

———. 2018b. "Will Iraq's Sunnis Get Own Political-Religious Authority?" Al-Monitor, February 23. https://www.al-monitor.com/pulse/originals/2018/02/iraq-sunni-marja-kubaisi-humim.html.

Marr, Phebe. 2004. *The Modern History of Iraq*. 2nd ed. Boulder: Westview.

———. 2007. "Iraq's New Political Map." Special Report no. 179. Washington, DC: US Institute of Peace.

Marshall, M. G., and G. C. Elzinga-Marshall. 2017. "Global Report 2017: Conflict, Governance, and State Fragility." Center for Systemic Peace. www.systemicpeace.org/vlibrary/GlobalReport2017.pdf.

Martinez, Luiz. 2000. *The Algerian Civil War: 1990–1998*. New York: Columbia University Press.

Massad, Joseph A. 2001. *Colonial Effects: The Making of National Identity in Jordan*. New York: Columbia University Press.

McDougall, J. 2017. *A History of Algeria*. Cambridge: Cambridge University Press.

McDowall, David. 2004. *A Modern History of the Kurds*. London: Tauris.

Mearsheimer, John J., and Stephen M. Walt. 2007. *The Israel Lobby and U.S. Foreign Policy*. New York: Farrar, Straus and Giroux.

Medani, Khalid Mustafa. 2004. "State Building in Reverse: The Neo-Liberal 'Reconstruction' of Iraq." *Middle East Report*, no. 232: 28–35.

Menoret, Pascal. 2016. "Repression and Protest in Saudi Arabia." *Middle East Brief*, no. 101. Waltham, MA: Crown Center for Middle East Studies, Brandeis University.

Milani, Mohsen M. 1994. *The Making of Iran's Islamic Revolution*. Boulder: Westview.

Moaddel, Mansoor, and Taghi Azadarmaki. 2002. "The Worldviews of Islamic Publics: The Case of Egypt, Iran, and Jordan." *Comparative Sociology* 1 (3–4): 299–319.

Moghadam, Valentine M. 2003. *Modernizing Women: Gender and Social Change in the Middle East*. Boulder: Lynne Rienner.

Mohammed, Abeer. 2012. "Alarm as Shia Paramilitaries Enter Politics." Institute for War and Peace Reporting, January 17. www.iwpr.net/global-voices/alarm-shia-paramilitaries-enter-politics.

Montagu, Caroline. 2015. "Civil Society in Saudi Arabia: The Power and Challenges of Associations." Chatham House, March 31. https://www.chathamhouse.org/publication/civil-society-saudi-arabia-power-and-challenges-association.

Moore, Pete, and Bassel F. Salloukh. 2007. "Struggles Under Authoritarianism: Regimes, States, and Professional Associations in the Arab World." *International Journal of Middle East Studies* 39 (1): 53–76.

Morrow, Johnathan. 2005. "Iraq's Constitutional Process II: An Opportunity Lost." United States Institute of Peace, Special Report no. 155. https://www.usip.org/sites/default/files/sr155.pdf.

Mortimer, Robert. 2004. "Bouteflika and the Challenge of Political Stability." In Ahmed Aghrout, ed., *Algeria in Transition: Reforms and Development Prospects* (London: Routledge), pp. 185–199.

Moruzzi, Norma Claire, and Fatemeh Sadeghi. 2006. "Out of the Frying Pan, into the Flame: Young Iranian Women Today." *Middle East Report*, no. 241 (Winter): 22–28.

Mottahedeh, Roy P. 1985. *The Mantle of the Prophet: Religion and Politics in Iran*. New York: Pantheon.

Muasher, Marwan. 2008. *The Arab Center: The Promise of Moderation*. New Haven: Yale University Press.

Mufti, Malik. 1999. "Elite Bargains and the Onset of Political Liberalization in Jordan." *Comparative Political Studies* 32 (1): 100–129.

Mujtahid. 2018. "Interview with Mujtahid—Part One." Mideast Wire. https://mideastwire.com/page/articleFree.php?id=68286.

Mundy, J. 2015. *Imaginative Geographies of Algerian Violence*. Stanford: Stanford University Press.

Munif, Yasser. 2017. *Participatory Democracy and Micropolitics in Manbij*. New York: Century Foundation.

Murphy, Caryle. 2008. "Saudi Women Reunite to Remember Driving Protest." NPR, December 16. https://www.npr.org/templates/story/story.php?storyId=97541372.

al-Musnad, Muhammad bin Abdul Aziz, comp. 1996. *Islamic Fatawa Regarding Women*. Jamal al-Din Zaraboro, trans. Saudi Arabia: Darussalam.

Myers, Steven Lee. 2011. "The Hot-Money Cowboys of Baghdad." *New York Times Magazine*, May 18.

Nakkash, Aziz. 2013. *The Alawite Dilemma in Homs*. Beirut: Friedrich Ebert Stiftung.

Nasr, Vali. 2006. *The Shia Revival: How Conflicts Within Islam Will Shape the Future*. New York: Norton.

National Geographic Society. 2008. *Atlas of the Middle East*. 2nd ed. Washington, DC.

Neurink, Judit. 2017. "Iraqi Christians Return After IS amid Safety Concerns." Centre for Religious Pluralism in the Middle East, December 28. http://www.crpme.gr/iran-iraq-and-the-gulf/iraq/7282-iraqi-christians-return-after-is-amid-safety-concerns.

Novikov, Evgenii. 2004. "Baathist Origins of the Zarqawi Letter." *Terrorism Monitor* 2 (6).

Observers. 2018. "In Saudi Arabia, Domestic Workers Are Auctioned Online." France Médias Monde, March 15. https://observers.france24.com/en/20180315-saudi-arabia-domestic-workers-are-auctioned-online.

OECD (Organization for Economic Cooperation and Development). 2018. "Poverty Rate (indicator)." http://doi.org/10.1787/0fe1315d-en.

Ofer, Gur. 1986. "Public Spending on Civilian Services." In Yoram Ben-Porath, ed., *The Israeli Economy: Maturing Through Crises* (Cambridge: Harvard University Press), pp. 192–208.

Okruhlik, Gwenn. 1999. "Rentier Wealth, Unruly Law, and the Rise of Opposition: The Political Economy of Oil States." *Comparative Politics* 31 (3): 295–315.

———. 2002. "Networks of Dissent: Islamism and Reform in Saudi Arabia." *Current History* 101 (651): 22–28.

———. 2004. "Making Conversation Permissible: Islamism in Saudi Arabia." In Quintan Wiktorowicz, ed., *Islamic Activism: A Social Movement Theory Approach* (Bloomington: Indiana University Press), pp. 354–384.

———. 2005. "The Irony of Islah (Reform)." *Washington Quarterly* 28 (4): 153–170.

———. 2009. "State Power, Religious Privilege, and the Myths About Political Reform." In Mohammed Ayoob and Hasan Koselbalaban, eds., *Religion and Politics in Saudi Arabia: Wahhabism and the State* (Boulder: Lynne Rienner), pp. 91–107.

———. 2010. "Dependence, Disdain and Distance: State, Labor and Citizenship in the Arab Gulf States." In Jean-Francois Seznec and Mimi Kirk, eds., *Industrialization in the Arab Gulf: A Socioeconomic Revolution* (New York: Routledge with the CCAS Georgetown University), pp. 125–142.

———. 2015. "Re-Thinking the Politics of Distributive States: Lessons from the Arab Uprisings." In Kjetil Selvik and Bjorn Utvik, eds., *Oil States in the New Middle East* (London: Routledge), pp. 18–38.

———. 2018. "Authoritarianism, Gender and Socio-Politics: Saudi Arabia." In Janine Clark and Francesco Cavatorta, eds., *Doing Political Science Research in the Middle East and North Africa* (New York: Oxford University Press), pp. 46–61.

Omar, Sara. 2013. "Al-Qubaysiyyat: Negotiating Female Religious Authority in Damascus." *Muslim World* 103 (2): 347–362.

al-Omran, Ahmed. 2018. "Crackdown on Activists Highlights Saudi Paradox." *Financial Times,* May 29.

Organski, A. F. K. 1990. *The $36 Billion Bargain: Strategy and Politics in U.S. Assistance to Israel.* New York: Columbia University Press.

Osanloo, Arzoo. 2009. *The Politics of Women's Rights in Iran*. Princeton: Princeton University Press.

Paidar, Parvin. 1995. *Women and the Political Process in Twentieth-Century Iran.* Cambridge: Cambridge University Press.

Palestine Center for Survey and Policy Research. 2017. "Palestinian-Israeli Pulse: A Joint Poll." August 1. http://www.pcpsr.org/sites/default/files/Summary_%20English_Joint%20PAL-ISR%20Poll%203_2017_0_clean.pdf.

Parker, Christopher, and Pete W. Moore. 2007. "The War Economy of Iraq." *Middle East Report,* no. 243: 6–15.

Parra, Francisco. 2004. *Oil Politics: A Modern History of Petroleum.* London: Tauris.

Perthes, Volker. 1992. "Syria's Parliamentary Elections." *Middle East Report,* no. 174 (January–February): 15–18, 35.

———. 2000. "*Si Vis Stabilitatem, Para Bellum:* State Building, National Security, and War Preparation in Syria." In Steven Heydemann, ed., *War, Institutions, and Social Change in the Middle East* (Berkeley: University of California Press), pp. 149–173.

Peters, Anne, and Pete Moore. 2009. "Beyond Boom and Bust: External Rents, Durable Authoritarianism, and Institutional Adaptation in the Hashemite Kingdom of Jordan." *Studies in Comparative International Development* 44 (2): 256–285.

Posner, Daniel N. 2005. *Institutions and Ethnic Politics in Africa.* New York: Cambridge University Press.

Posusney, Marsha Pripstein. 1997. *Labor and the State in Egypt: Workers, Unions, and Economic Restructuring.* New York: Columbia University Press.

———. 2002. "Multiparty Elections in the Arab World: Institutional Engineering and Oppositional Strategies." *Studies in Comparative International Development* 36 (4): 34–62.

Powell, G. Bingham. 1982. *Contemporary Democracies: Participation, Stability, and Violence.* Cambridge: Harvard University Press.

Provence, Michael. 2005. *The Great Syrian Revolt and the Rise of Arab Nationalism.* Austin: University of Texas Press.

Przeworski, Adam, Michael Alvarez, José Antônio Cheibub, and Fernando Limongi. 1996. "What Makes Democracies Endure?" *Journal of Democracy* 7 (1): 39–55.

———. 2000. *Democracy and Development: Political Regimes and Economic Well-Being in the World, 1950–1990.* Cambridge, UK: Cambridge University Press.

al-Qabas. 2009. "Ajwa al-Tabayun al-Mustamira Hawla Mashru'al-Hukuma Da'm al-Sharikat al-Istithmariya" [Continuing crosswinds around the government plan to support investment companies]. February 10.

Quamar, Muddassir M. 2016. "Municipal Elections in Saudi Arabia, 2015." *Contemporary Review of the Middle East* 3 (4): 433–444.
Ramazani, R. K. 1986. *Revolutionary Iran: Challenge and Response in the Middle East*. Baltimore: Johns Hopkins University Press.
Rassam, Amal. 1992. "Political Ideology and Women in Iraq." In Joseph D. Jabbra and Nancy W. Jabbra, eds., *Women and Development in the Middle East and North Africa* (Leiden: Brill).
Richards, Alan, and John Waterbury. 1990, 2008. *A Political Economy of the Middle East: State, Class, and Economic Development*. Boulder: Westview.
Ricks, Thomas E. 2007. *Fiasco: The American Military Adventure in Iraq*. New York: Penguin.
Riedel, Bruce. 2018. "Saudi Crown Prince on Goodwill Tour as Royal Family Frets." Al-Monitor, November 26. https://www.al-monitor.com/pulse/originals/2018/11/saudi-arabia-mbs-khashoggi-killing-yemen-reputation.html.
Rivlin, Paul. 2009. *Arab Economies in the Twenty-First Century*. Cambridge: Cambridge University Press.
Roberts, Hugh. 2003. *The Battlefield: Algeria, 1988–2002*. London: Verso.
Robinson, Glenn. 1998. "Defensive Democratization in Jordan." *International Journal of Middle East Studies* 30 (3): 387–410.
Rodgers, Gerry, and Janine Rodgers. 1989. *Precarious Jobs in Labour Market Regulation: The Growth of Atypical Employment in Western Europe*. Geneva: ILO.
Rodrik, Dani. 1997. *Has Globalization Gone Too Far?* Washington, DC: Institute for International Economics.
———. 1999. "Where Did All the Growth Go? External Shocks, Social Conflict, and Growth Collapses." *Journal of Economic Growth* 4 (4): 385–412.
Ross, Michael E. 2001. "Does Oil Hinder Democracy?" *World Politics* 53 (3): 325–361.
———. 2008. "Oil, Islam, and Women." *American Political Science Review* 102 (1): 107–123.
Roy, Olivier. 1994. *The Failure of Political Islam*. Cambridge: Harvard University Press.
Roy, Sara. 2007. *Failing Peace: Gaza and the Palestinian-Israeli Conflict*. London: Pluto.
Rubin, Barry. 1981. *The Arab States and the Palestine Conflict*. Syracuse: Syracuse University Press.
Rubinstein, Alvin Z. 1977. *Red Star on the Nile: The Soviet-Egyptian Influence Relationship Since the June War*. Princeton: Princeton University Press.
Rustow, Dankwart. 1967. A World of Nations: Problems of Political Modernization. Washington, DC: Brookings Institution.
Ryan, Curtis R. 1998. "Elections and Parliamentary Democratization in Jordan." *Democratization* 5 (4): 194–214.
———. 2002. *Jordan in Transition: From Hussein to Abdullah*. Boulder: Lynne Rienner.
———. 2008. "Islamist Political Activism in Jordan: Moderation, Militancy, and Democracy." *Middle East Review of International Affairs* 12 (2): 1–13.
———. 2009. *Inter-Arab Alliances: Regime Security and Jordanian Foreign Policy*. Gainesville: University of Florida Press.
———2018. *Jordan and the Arab Uprisings: Regime Survival and Politics Beyond the State*. New York: Columbia University Press.
Ryan, Curtis R., and Jillian Schwedler. 2004. "Return to Democratization or New Hybrid Regime? The 2003 Elections in Jordan." *Middle East Policy* 11 (2): 138–151.
Sacks, Harvey. 1992. *Lectures on Conversation*. Oxford: Blackwell.
Sadeghi, Fatemeh. 2009. "Foot Soldiers in the Islamic Republic's 'Culture of Modesty.'" *Middle East Report*, no. 250 (Spring): 50–55.
Sadowski, Yahya. 1993. "The New Orientalism and the Democracy Debate." *Middle East Report*, no. 183 (July–August): 14–21, 40.
Saif, Salem. 2017. "Blade Runner in the Gulf." *Jacobin Magazine*, November 2. http://www.jacobinmag.com/2017/11/gulf-states-oil-capital-ecological-disaster.
Saktanber, Ayşe. 2002. *Living Islam: Women, Religion, and the Politicization of Culture in Turkey*. London: Tauris.
Salehi-Isfahni, Djavad. 2001. "The Gender Gap in Education in Iran: Evidence for the Role of Household Characteristics." In Djavad Salehi-Isfahani, ed., *Labor and Human Capital in the Middle East* (Reading: Ithaca Press), pp. 235–255.

———. 2008. "Iran's Economy: Short-Term Performance and Long-Term Potential." Brookings Institution, May 23. https://www.brookings.edu/on-the-record/irans-economy-short-term-performance-and-long-term-potential.

———. 2015. "Will Rouhani Complete the Reform of Subsidies?" Tyranny of Numbers, September 9. http://djavadsalehi.com/2015/09/09/will-rouhani-complete-the-reform-of-subsidies.

Salloum, Saad. 2016. "Iraq's Caucasus Tribes Demand Formal Recognition." *Iraq Business News,* December 14. http://www.iraq-businessnews.com/2016/12/14/iraqs-caucasus-tribes-demand-formal-recognition.

Sanasarian, Eliz. 2000. *Religious Minorities in Iran.* Cambridge: Cambridge University Press.

Sandler, Shmuel, and Aaron Kampinsky. 2009. "Israel's Religious Parties." In Robert O. Freedman, ed., *Contemporary Israel* (Boulder: Westview), pp. 77–96.

Saudi Presidency of State Security. 2017. "22 People Arrested for 'Incitement' and Violating Saudi Anti-Cyber Crime Law." *Arab News*, October 5. http://www.arabnews.com/node/1172601/saudi-arabia.

Saudi Press Agency. 2017. "Saudi Arabia: Revamped Prosecution Office Now Directly Under King." Al Bawaba, June 18. https://www.albawaba.com/business/saudi-arabia-revamped-prosecution-office-now-directly-under-king-987680.

Schedler, Andreas. 2002. "The Menu of Manipulation." *Journal of Democracy* 13 (2): 36–50.

Schirazi, Asghar. 1998. *The Constitution of Iran: Politics and the State in the Islamic Republic.* John O'Kane, trans. London: Tauris.

Schmitter, Philippe C. 1978. "The Impact and Meaning of 'Non-Competitive, Non-Free and Insignificant' Elections in Authoritarian Portugal, 1933–74." In Guy Hermet, Richard Rose, and Alain Rouquie, eds., *Elections Without Choice* (New York: Wiley), pp. 145–168.

Schwab, Regine. 2018. "Insurgent Courts in Civil Wars: The Three Pathways of (Trans)Formation in Today's Syria (2012–2017)." *Small Wars and Insurgencies* 29 (4): 801–826.

Schwedler, Jillian. 2006. *Faith in Moderation: Islamist Parties in Jordan and Yemen.* Cambridge: Cambridge University Press.

Seale, Patrick. 1987. *The Struggle for Syria.* New Haven: Yale University Press.

Shahrokni, Nazanin. 2009. "All the President's Women." *Middle East Report,* no. 253 (Winter): 2–6.

Shambayati, Hootan. 1994. "The Rentier State, Interest Groups, and the Paradox of Autonomy: State and Business in Turkey and Iran." *Comparative Politics* 26 (April): 307–331.

Sharkansky, Ira. 2004. "A Critical Look at Israel's Economic and Social Gaps." In Alan Dowty, ed., *Critical Issues in Israeli Society* (Westport: Praeger), pp. 129–150.

Sikkuy. 2009. "The Equality Index of Jewish and Arab Citizens in Israel." http://www.sikkuy.org.il.

Sly, Liz. 2018. "Change Is Coming for the Women of Saudi Arabia. But for How Long?" *Sydney Morning Herald*, June 19.

Smooha, Sammy. 1978. *Israel: Pluralism and Conflict.* Berkeley: University of California Press.

Sonbol, Amira El-Azhary. 2003. *Women of Jordan: Islam, Labor, and the Law.* Syracuse: Syracuse University Press.

Sosnowski, Marika. 2018. "Violence and Order: The February 2016 Ceasefire and the Development of Rebel Governance Institutions in Southern Syria." *Civil Wars* (forthcoming).

Spivak, Gayatri Chakravorty. 1988. "Can the Subaltern Speak?" In Cary Nelson and Lawrence Grossberg, eds., *Marxism and the Interpretation of Culture* (Urbana: University of Illinois Press), pp. 271–313.

Susser, Asher. 2008. "Jordan: Preserving Domestic Order in a Setting of Regional Turmoil." *Middle East Brief*, no. 27. Waltham, MA: Brandeis University, Crown Center for Middle East Studies.

Swirsky, B., and M. P. Safir, eds. 1991. *Calling the Equality Bluff: Women in Israel.* New York: Pergamon.

al-Tamimi, Aymenn Jawad. 2017. "Hay'at Tahrir and Civil Society in Jabal al-Summaq." Syria Comment, March 4. www.syriacomment.com.

Taylor, Charles Lewis, and David A. Jodice. 1983. *World Handbook of Political and Social Indicators.* 3rd ed. New Haven: Yale University Press.

Tejel, Jordi. 2009. *Syria's Kurds.* London: Routledge.

Tezcür, Güneş Murat. 2008. "Intra-Elite Struggles in Iranian Elections." In Ellen Lust-Okar and S. Zerhouni, eds., *Political Participation in the Middle East* (Boulder: Lynne Rienner), pp. 51–74.

Tezcür, Güneş Murat, Taghi Azadarmaki, and Mehri Bahar. 2006. "Religious Participation Among Muslims: Iranian Exceptionalism." *Critique* 15 (Fall): 217–232.

Tilly, Charles. 2007. "Grudging Consent." *The American Interest* (September/October): 17–23.

Tlemçani, Rachid. 2008. "Algeria Under Bouteflika: Civil Strife and National Reconciliation." Carnegie Paper no. 7. Washington, DC: Carnegie Endowment for International Peace.

Trading Economics. 2018. "Israel Foreign Direct Investment." www.tradingeconomics.com/israel/foreign-direct-investment.

Tripp, Aili Mari, and Alice Kang. 2008. "The Global Impact of Quotas: On the Fast Track to Increased Female Legislative Representation." *Comparative Political Studies* 41 (3): 338–361.

Tripp, Charles. 2000, 2007. *A History of Iraq.* Cambridge: Cambridge University Press.

Ulrichsen, Kristian Coates. 2012. "The UAE: Holding Back the Tide." openDemocracy, August 5. http://www.opendemocracy.net/kristian-coates-ulrichsen/uae-holding-back-tide.

UNDP (United Nations Development Programme). 2004. *The Arab Human Development Report: Towards Freedom in the Arab World.* New York.

———. 2016. *Human Development Report: Human Development for Everyone.* http://hdr.undp.org/sites/default/files/2016_human_development_report.pdf.

———. 2017. "Human Development Report: Gender Inequality Index (GII)." http://hdr.undp.org/en/content/gender-inequality-index-gii.

———. 2018. Human Development data (1990–2017). "Gender Inequality Index (GII)." http://hdr.undp.org/en/composite/GII.

UNDP (United Nations Development Programme) and Plan and Budget Organization of the Islamic Republic. 1999. *Human Development Report of the Islamic Republic of Iran.* New York.

UNESCO (United Nations Educational, Scientific, and Cultural Organization). 2017a. "Government Expenditure on Education, Total (% of Government Expenditure) 1970–2017." Data file. https://data.worldbank.org/indicator/SE.XPD.TOTL.GB.ZS.

———. 2017b. "Literacy Rate, Adult Female (% of Females Ages 15 and Above) 1970–2017." Data file. https://data.worldbank.org/indicator/SE.ADT.LITR.FE.ZS?view=chart.

———. 2017c. "School Enrollment, Primary and Secondary (Gross), Gender Parity Index (GPI) 1970–2017. Data file. https://data.worldbank.org/indicator/SE.ENR.PRSC.FM.ZS?view=chart.

———. 2017d. "School Enrollment, Tertiary (Gross), Gender Parity Index (GPI) 1970–2017." Data file. https://data.worldbank.org/indicator/SE.ENR.TERT.FM.ZS.

Unified Democracy Scores. 2014. unified-democracy-scores.org.

Valenzuela, J. Samuel. 1990. "Democratic Consolidation in Post-Transitional Settings: Notion, Process, and Facilitating Conditions." Kellogg Institute Working Paper no. 150. University of Notre Dame.

Van Dam, Nikolaos. 1996. *The Struggle for Power in Syria.* London: Tauris.

Vanhanen, T. 1991. *The Process of Democratization: A Comparative Study of 147 States, 1980–88.* New York: Crane Russak.

V-Dem Institute. 2017. "Democracy at Dusk: V-Dem Annual Report 2017." www.v-dem.net.

Visser, Reidar. 2005. *Basra: The Failed Gulf State.* Berlin: Lit Verlag.

———. 2008. "The Western Imposition of Sectarianism on Iraqi Politics." *Arab Studies Journal* 15 (2): 83–99.

Vitalis, Robert. 2007. *America's Kingdom: Mythmaking on the Saudi Oil Frontier.* Stanford: Stanford University Press.

Vitalis, Robert, and Steven Heydemann. 2000. "War, Keynesianism, and Colonialism: Explaining State-Market Relations in the Postwar Middle East." In Steven Heydemann, ed., *War, Institutions, and Social Change in the Middle East* (Berkeley: University of California Press), pp. 100–148.

Vora, Neha. 2008. "Producing Diasporas and Globalization: Indian Middle-Class Migrants in Dubai." *Anthropological Quarterly* 81 (2): 377–406.
Waldner, David. 1999. *State Building and Late Development.* Ithaca: Cornell University Press.
Waleed, Khalid. 2012. "Clashes Spread Between Iraqi Shia Groups." Institute for War and Peace Reporting, April 19. http://www.wiwpr.net.
Waterbury, John. 1993. *Exposed to Innumerable Delusions: Public Enterprise and State Power in Egypt, India, Mexico, and Turkey.* Cambridge: Cambridge University Press.
White, Jenny. 2002. *Islamist Mobilization in Turkey: A Study in Vernacular Politics.* Seattle: University of Washington Press.
Wickham, Carrie Rosefsky. 2002. *Mobilizing Islam: Religion, Activism, and Political Change in Egypt.* New York: Columbia University Press.
Wiktorowicz, Quintan. 2000a. "Civil Society as Social Control: State Power in Jordan." *Comparative Politics* 33 (1): 43–62.
———. 2000b. *The Management of Islamic Activism: Salafis, the Muslim Brotherhood, and State Power in Jordan.* Albany: SUNY Press.
———. 2002. "The Political Limits to Nongovernmental Organizations in Jordan." *World Development* 30 (1): 77–93.
Wiley, Joyce N. 1992. *The Islamic Movement of Iraqi Shi'as.* Boulder: Lynne Rienner.
Willis, Michael J. 2008. "The Politics of Berber (Amazigh) Identity." In Yahia H. Zoubir and Haizam Amirah-Fernàndez, eds., *North Africa: Politics, Region, and the Limits of Transformation* (London: Routledge), pp. 227–242.
Wilson, Mary. 1987. *King Abdullah, Britain, and the Making of Jordan.* New York: Cambridge University Press.
Wittes, Tamara Cofman. 2008. *Freedom's Unsteady March: America's Role in Building Arab Democracy.* Washington, DC: Brookings Institution.
World Bank. 2008. *World Development Indicators.* Washington, DC.
———. 2018. World Bank Data Catalog. "World Development Indicators and Global Financial Development." http://data.worldbank.org/data-catalog.
Wright, Lawrence. 2006. *The Looming Tower: Al-Qaeda and the Road to 9/11.* New York: Vintage.
Yazigi, Jihad. 2014. "Syria's War Economy." European Council on Foreign Relations Policy Brief. https://www.ecfr.eu/page/-/ECFR97_SYRIA_BRIEF_AW.pdf.
Yildiz, Kerim. 2007. *The Kurds in Iraq.* London: Pluto.
Younis, Nussaibah. 2011. "Set Up to Fail: Consociational Political Structures in Post-War Iraq, 2003–2010." *Contemporary Arab Affairs* 4 (1): 1–18.
Zaman, Constantin. 2006. "A Review of Syrian Economy." Institutional and Sector Modernization Facility (ISMF). http://www.ismf-eusy.org.
Zoubir, Yahia H. 1995. "Stalled Democratization of an Authoritarian Regime: The Case of Algeria." *Democratization* 2 (2): 109–139.
———. 1999. "State and Civil Society in Algeria." In Yahia H. Zoubir, ed., *North Africa in Transition: State, Society, and the Limits of Transformation* (Gainesville: University Press of Florida), pp. 29–42.
———. 2002. "Algeria and U.S. Interests: Containing Radical Islamism and Promoting Democracy." *Middle East Policy* 9 (1): 64–81.
———. 2003. "The Rise of Civil Society in Arab States." In D. Lesch, ed., *History in Dispute: The Middle East Since 1945* (Detroit: St. James Press), pp. 81–85.
———. 2009. "The United States and Maghreb-Sahel Security." *International Affairs* 85 (5): 977–995.
———. 2018. "Algeria and the Sahelian Quandary: The Limits of Containment Security Policy." In D. Ghanem-Yazbeck, ed., *The Sahel: Europe's African Borders.* Euromesco Joint Policy Study 8 (Barcelona: European Institute of the Meditteranean), pp. 70–95.
Zoubir, Yahia H., and Ahmed Aghrout. 2012. "Algeria's Path to Reform: Authentic Change?" *Middle East Policy* 19 (2): 65–83.

The Contributors

Michele Penner Angrist is professor of political science and dean of studies at Union College. She is author of *Party Building in the Modern Middle East* and coeditor of *Authoritarianism in the Middle East: Regimes and Resistance.*

Nathan J. Brown is professor of political science and international affairs at George Washington University and nonresident senior associate at the Carnegie Endowment for International Peace. His most recent book is *Arguing Islam After the Revival of Arab Politics.*

Sheila Carapico is professor of political science and international studies at the University of Richmond. She is author of *Civil Society in Yemen: The Political Economy of Activism in Modern Arabia* and *Political Aid and Arab Activism: Democracy Promotion, Justice, and Representation* and curator of "Arabia Incognita: Dispatches from Yemen and the Gulf," a Middle East Report and Information Project (MERIP) compilation.

Alan Dowty is professor emeritus of political science at the University of Notre Dame. He was previously chair of International Relations at the Hebrew University in Jerusalem and holder of the chair in Israel Studies at the University of Calgary. In 2017 he was awarded the Lifetime Achievement Award in Israel Studies by the Association for Israel Studies and the Israel Institute. Among his published works are *The Jewish State: A Century Later* and *Israel/Palestine.*

F. Gregory Gause III is professor of international affairs and John H. Lindsey '44 Chair at the Bush School of Government and Public Service, Texas A&M University. He also serves as head of the school's Department of International Affairs. His most recent book is *The International Relations of the Persian Gulf.*

Mona El-Ghobashy is clinical assistant professor in liberal studies at New York University. Her research on Egypt's politics has appeared in *Middle East Report, International Journal of Middle East Studies, Boston Review,* and *American Behavioral Scientist.*

Michael Herb is professor and chair of political science at Georgia State University, where his research focuses on Gulf politics. He is author of *The Wages of Oil: Parliaments and Economic Development in Kuwait and the UAE.*

Danielle Higgins is a PhD candidate in comparative politics and an instructor at American University. She also conducts research and writes on spatial inequality and local governance in Middle East and North Africa for TADAMUN: The Cairo Urban Solidarity Initiative.

Arang Keshavarzian is associate professor of Middle Eastern and Islamic studies at New York University and a member of the editorial committee of *Middle East Report.* He is author of *Bazaar and State in Iran: The Politics of the Tehran Marketplace.*

Fred H. Lawson is visiting professor of national security affairs at the Naval Postgraduate School. He is author of *Global Security Watch—Syria* and *Constructing International Relations in the Arab World*, and has been Fulbright lecturer in international relations at the University of Aleppo and Fulbright lecturer in political science at Aden University.

Pete W. Moore is the M. A. Hanna Associate Professor of Politics at Case Western Reserve University and serves on the editorial board of the *Middle East Report.* He is author of *Doing Business in the Middle East: Politics and Economic Crisis in Jordan and Kuwait* and coauthor of *Beyond the Arab Spring: Authoritarianism and Democratization in the Arab World.*

Gwenn Okruhlik specializes in the politics of the Arabian Peninsula, with a focus on Saudi Arabia, where she has had two Fulbrights. She is founder of the Association for Gulf and Arabian Peninsula Studies and has worked throughout the Gulf. Her work has appeared in *Comparative Poli-*

tics, Middle East Journal, Middle East Policy, and *Middle East Report,* as well as numerous edited volumes.

David Siddhartha Patel is a research fellow at the Crown Center for Middle East Studies at Brandeis University. His recent research has focused on religious authority and social order in Iraq, identity, and the emergence of the state system in the Middle East.

Marcie J. Patton is professor of politics at Fairfield University. She specializes in Turkish politics. Her work has appeared in *Middle East Journal, Mediterranean Politics, Middle East Report,* and *Comparative Studies of South Asia, Africa and the Middle East,* as well as edited volumes.

Curtis R. Ryan is professor of political science at Appalachian State University in North Carolina. He has served as a Fulbright scholar and guest researcher at the Center for Strategic Studies, University of Jordan, and was twice named a Peace Scholar by the United States Institute of Peace. He is author of *Jordan in Transition: From Hussein to Abdullah*; *Inter-Arab Alliances: Regime Security and Jordanian Foreign Policy*; and, most recently, *Jordan and the Arab Uprisings: Regime Survival and Politics Beyond the State.*

Jillian Schwedler is professor of political science at the City University of New York, Hunter College and the Graduate Center. She has conducted research in Jordan, Yemen, and Egypt and has traveled extensively throughout the Middle East with support from the National Science Foundation, the United States Institute of Peace, the Fulbright Scholars Program, and the Social Science Research Council. She is author of the award-winning *Faith in Moderation: Islamist Parties in Jordan and Yemen* and, most recently, coeditor of *Policing and Prisons in the Middle East.*

Diane Singerman is associate professor in the Department of Government, School of Public Affairs at American University. She has been the codirector of TADAMUN: The Cairo Urban Solidarity Initiative since 2011. She is editor of *Cairo Contested: Governance, Urban Space, and Global Modernity* and coeditor of *Cairo Cosmopolitan: Politics, Culture, and Urban Space in the New Globalized Middle East.*

Joshua Stacher is associate professor of political science at Kent State University. He has served on the editorial committee of Middle East Report and Information Project (MERIP) and is a member of the Middle East Studies Association's Committee on Academic Freedom. Stacher is the author of *Adaptable Autocrats: Regime Power in Egypt and Syria.*

Yahia H. Zoubir is professor of international relations and international management and director of research in geopolitics at KEDGE Business School, France. He is the editor of *The Politics of Algeria: Domestic Issues and International Relations* and coeditor of *North African Politics: Change and Continuity*.

Index

About the Book

The rise and decline of ISIS in Iraq and Syria. Deepening authoritarianism in Turkey. The return to military-led rule in Egypt. The impact of Crown Prince Mohammad bin Salman in Saudi Arabia. Heightened sectarian tensions throughout the region. These are among the many current topics covered in the third edition of the acclaimed *Politics and Society in the Contemporary Middle East*.

With the Arab Spring uprisings now viewed with the perspective of time, this new edition also provides an accessible analysis of the longer-term political currents, changes, and dynamics set in motion by those dramatic events. Offering insightful analyses and a wealth of accessible information, it encourages comparative, critical thinking by students at all levels.

Michele Penner Angrist is professor of political science and dean of studies at Union College.